SCARLET TO GREEN

A HISTORY OF INTELLIGENCE IN THE CANADIAN ARMY
1903–1963

MAJOR S.R. ELLIOT
C.D., B. COMM., PSC, C.INT.C. (RETD)

CANADIAN MILITARY INTELLIGENCE ASSOCIATION
ASSOCIATION CANADIENNE DU RENSEIGNEMENT MILITAIRE
2018

 FriesenPress

Suite 300 - 990 Fort St
Victoria, BC, V8V 3K2
Canada

www.friesenpress.com

Copyright © 2018 by Canadian Military Intelligence Association - Association canadienne du renseignement militaire
First Edition Editorial: T.C. Fairley & Associates, Toronto

First Edition Maps: Majs R.C. Dale and K.N. Lord

All rights reserved. No part of this book may be reproduced in any form or by any means, electronic or mechanical, including photocopying, recording or any information storage or retrieval system, without permission in writing from the Canadian Military Intelligence Association.

Photo on front cover: Lieut. Robert Sherrill, Intelligence Officer with the Algonquin Regiment, oversees use of stereoscopes by Pte. Francis Crawford and Pte. William Korpen to analyse air reconnaissance photos, 22 Nov 1943. (G. Barry Gilroy/Canada. Dept. of National Defence/Library and Archives Canada, PA-142629)

Photo on book bind: Lieut. C. Tweedale, Corps of Guides, in full dress uniform during an annual inspection, circa 1913. (City of Vancouver Archives, Mil P225)

Address all inquires to:

CMIA-ACRM
PO Box 70068
Place Bell PO,
160 Elgin Street, Ottawa, ON.
K2P 2M3

Library and Archives Canada Cataloguing in Publication

Elliot, S. R. (Stuart Robert), 1922-2015, author
      Scarlet to green : a history of intelligence in the Canadian Army, 1903-1963 / Major S.R. Elliot, C.D., B. Comm., psc, C.Int.C. (retd).

Reprint. Originally published: 1981.
Includes bibliographical references and indexes.
Issued in print and electronic formats.
ISBN 978-1-77511-360-7 (hardcover).--ISBN 978-1-77511-361-4 (softcover).--ISBN 978-1-77511-362-1 (ebook)

      1. Military intelligence--Canada--History--20th century.
I. Canadian Military Intelligence Association, issuing body II. Title.

UB251.C3E44 2018   355.3'4320971   C2017-906156-9
                                            C2017-906157-7

CONTENTS

Maps and Illustrations \ v

Foreword \ x

Preface \ xiii

Author's Note \ xvi

Introduction \ xvii

1. In the Beginning \ 1

2. War – and Peace \ 23
   The Canadian Expeditionary Force (C.E.F.); Counter-Intelligence; Canada – Control of Information; Canada – Aliens, Espionage, and Subversion; 1919–1929

3. To War Again: Canada 1929–39 \ 61
   I(b): Pre–1939; War Clouds Gather

4. Build-up in Britain – Canadian Military Headquarters \ 81
   Censorship; Invasion Planning; Peace Again

5. Battlefield Intelligence – the Beginnings \ 113

6. Field Security and Counter-Intelligence in Britain 1939–45 \ 129

7. Dieppe \ 153

8. The Other Side of the Hill: I(a) in Italy \ 170
   Sicily; Italy – BAYTOWN to Ortona; Ortona to Rome; The Gothic Line to the Po

9. Agents and Refugees: I(b) in Italy \ 208

10. To Know the Enemy: I(a) in North-West Europe \ 240
    OVERLORD to Falaise; The Channel Coast; The Winter "Lull"; VERITABLE and the Rhine; The Rhine to the Elbe

11. Liberation and Occupation: I(b) in North-West Europe \ 301
    F.S. Details – Germany; C.I. in the Canadian Army Occupation Force (C.A.O.F.)

12. Field Press Censorship \ 346

13. Subsidiary Operations \ 352
    Greenland ("X" Force); Iceland ("Z" Force); Spitsbergen; Hong Kong; Newfoundland ("W" Force); Kiska; Canadian Army Pacific Force (C.A.P.F.); Special Wireless Unit – Australia

14. Off the Beaten Track \ 370
    Clandestine Operations: *S.O.E. – France; Italy and the Mediterranean; Far East*
    Escape and Evasion: *Mediterranean Theatre*
    Psychological Warfare: *Overt Psychological Warfare*

15. Organization and Training: Ottawa 1939–45 \ 408
    Japanese Language Training

16. Strategic and Operational Intelligence in Canada 1939–46 \ 431
    M.I.2

17. Security and Counter-Intelligence in Canada \ 451
    M.I.3(a) – Security of Personnel; M.I.3(c) – Security of Personnel: Aliens; M.I.3(b) – Security of Information; Press Censorship; Telegraph and Postal Censorship; Security – Commands and Districts

18. Prisoners of War \ 479

19. Peace and Reconstruction \ 499
    Intelligence Units

20. Peacekeeping \ 517
    Korea; Cyprus

21. The Reserves \ 539
    The Canadian Military Intelligence Association (C.M.I.A.)

L'Envoi \ 549

Afterword \ 554

Annexes: Personnel and Organization \ 556
    Annex 1: Senior Intelligence Appointment, Army Headquarters 1903–1964
    Annex 2: Censorship Organization, 1939
    Annex 3: Intelligence Organization, Canadian Military Headquarters, 1940–1946.
    Annex 4: Organization of Intelligence, Canadian Army Overseas
    Annex 5: A.H.Q. Intelligence Organization, 1939–1946
    Annex 6: Honours and Awards Intelligence-Employed Officers and Men, 1939–1945
    Annex 7: Casualties, 1939–1945
    Annex 8: Canadian Intelligence Corps Trophies and Prizes
    Annex 9: List of First Edition Personnel Annexes

Notes \ 573

Index \ 599
    Part I: General Index
    Part II: Canadian Intelligence and Intelligence-Associated Units
    Part III: Canadian Formations, Units and Corps
    Part IV: British Commonwealth, United States, and other Allied Forces
    Part V: Former Enemy Forces

Abbreviations \ 637

About the Author \ 643

MAPS AND ILLUSTRATIONS

MAPS

1. Pigeon Hill – June 1866 \ 3
2. North-West Rebellion – 1885 \ 8
3. Western Front – 1915–1918 \ 24
4. Britain – 1939–1945 \ 94
5. Dieppe \ 154
6. Sicily \ 171
7. BAYTOWN to the Winter Line \ 175
8. Liri Valley \ 185
9. Adriatic Coast \ 197
10. Normandy \ 242
11. Caen to Falaise \ 250
12. Falaise to the Scheldt \ 261
13. Crossing of the Rhine \ 274
14. Holland \ 282
15. Rhine to the Elbe \ 293
16. Greenland–Iceland–Spitsbergen \ 354
17. Hong Kong \ 356
18. Kiska \ 364
19. Clandestine Operations – Europe \ 372
20. Clandestine Operations – Far East \ 381
21. Canada – Commands and Military Districts 1939–45 \ 441
22. Korea \ 518
23. Cyprus \ 533

ILLUSTRATIONS

Capt. Donald Lorne MacDougall and Trooper John R. Mathewson, The Royal Guides, Montreal, Quebec, 1866 / 2

Capt. J. French, French's Scouts, 1885 / 5

Dominion Land Surveyor's Intelligence Corps, 1885 / 5

Lt.-Col. Victor Brereton Rivers, R.C.A., the first Intelligence Staff Officer / 10

Lt.-Col. William C. Denny, (Bvt. Maj., A.S.C.), the first Director General of Military Intelligence, April 1903–January 1905 / 13

Corps of Guides officer, Lieut. C. Tweedale at an Annual Inspection 16 May 1914 and on horseback, circa 1918 / 15

Corps of Guides on horseback, date and location unknown / 16

Officers of the Corps of Guides after a reconnaissance ride, Niagara-on-the-Lake, 1905 / 16

No. 11 Detachment, Corps of Guides, on strike duty at Nanaimo, B.C., 1913–1914 / 21

Searching P.W. after Arleux, April 1917 / 28

Interrogating a prisoner, Hill 70, August 1917 / 28

Receiving prisoners at the Canadian Corps P.W. Cage after Arras, August 1918 / 30

Capt. C.W. Erlebach, Corps of Guides, interrogating a German P.W. near Canal du Nord, September 1918 / 30

Brig.-Gen. C.H. Mitchell, C.B., C.M.G., D.S.O., Corps of Guides, when he was a Capt. on the Cavalry Field Officers Course, Stanley Barracks, Toronto, January 1911 / 34

Detailed map of no-man's-land in front of 11th Canadian Infantry Brigade, produced by the Intelligence Section, West Flanders region, Belgium, possibly 1916 / 36

Air photo of trench systems taken by a R.F.C. reconnaissance aircraft, 16 May 1918 / 39

Sgt. E.N. Jungbluth, Field Security/ C.I. in Bapaume 1918 / 44

Christmas card, Season's Greetings from Militia and Air Force Intelligence Section, Ottawa, 1937 / 67

Maj. John Page, "Father of the Corps" / 91

Canadian officer questioning a German prisoner near the Hitler Line, Liri Valley, 24 May 1944 / 192

Interrogation of a German soldier caught entering San Leonardo di Ortona, Italy, in civilian clothes, 13 December 1943 / 220

A man accused of collaboration is brought before Maj. W.M. Harrison, in Bagnacavallo, Italy, to plead his case / 234

Map showing known enemy dispositions in France, 4 June 1944 / 241

Officers of Canadian Air Liaison Sections in England, February 1944 / 245

Maj. Odlum, with the aid of a stereoscope, studies photos taken by air reconnaissance flight over enemy territory / 245

Capt. G.B. Shellon, Intelligence Officer of the 10th Canadian Infantry Brigade, talking with armed Dutch civilians near the Belgium–Netherlands border, 16 October 1944 / 264

Air photo mosaic of Schouen Island, 12 September 1944 / 267

Lt.-Col. P.E.R. Wright, O.B.E., G.S.O.1 (Int) H.Q. First Canadian Army from 21 June 1943 until the end of the war / 280

Air photo mosaic of Kessel, Reichswald, February 1945 / 287

Four members of the No. 3 Field Security Section, C.Int.C., sharing a glass of wine with a French couple, Thaon, France, 20 June 1944 / 302

No. 16 Field Security Section, England, May 1944 / 306

Maj. C.R. Rafe Douthwaite, M.B.E., Field Security Officer / 315

Field Security vehicle entering The Hague, 8 May 1945 / 321

Esterwegen Internment Camp, June 1945 / 333

Movement control on the Aurich road, 26–27 August 1945 / 338

No. 1 Field Press Censor Unit / 348

Brig. L.F. Page and Capt. R.T. Bonnell, Intelligence Officer / 353

Maj. Gustave "Guy" D.A. Biéler, D.S.O., M.B.E.; photo of his French identity card issued by the British Special Operations Executive / 373

Amplifier van of No. 2 Unit, 21 Army Group, gives news broadcast in a Caen suburb, July 1944 / 396

Propaganda leaflets, North-West Europe / 399

First Intelligence Officers' Course, Royal Military College, Kingston, 1940 / 412

Students on the first Field Security Course, 1941, conducting a field exercise / 415

Col. W.W. "Jock" Murray, O.B.E., M.C. and Bar, Director of Military Intelligence, 4 July 1942–16 February 1946 / 417

D.M.I. Staff, Ottawa, July 1945 / 418

M.I.1 Section, 13 December 1944 / 433

German espionage equipment, 1944 / 445

Lt.-Col. Edward Drake (C.Int.C.), M.I.2, July 1945 / 449

Lt.-Col. Eric Acland, O.B.E., E.D., Deputy Director of Military Intelligence (Security), circa 1945 / 452

Grand Ligne P.W. Camp, Quebec, 1943 / 485

P.W. Camp, Sherbrooke, Quebec, November 1945 / 485

German P.W. using the library at internment Camp 42, Sherbrooke, Quebec, 18 June 1944 / 492

Staff at the Canadian School of Military Intelligence, Petawawa, Ontario, summer 1949 / 512

Brigade Intelligence Section on night duty during an exercise at a Militia Summer Camp Concentration, Petawawa, 1954 / 512

Lt.-Gen. G.G. Simonds, C.B., C.B.E., D.S.O., C.D., Chief of the General Staff, inspecting a C.Int.C. Guard of Honour, during the official opening ceremony of C.S. of M.I. Camp Borden, July 1953 / 513

Students at C.S. of M.I., Borden, conducting a practical exercise as part of the Photo Reading Instructors Course, October 1955 / 513

An unidentified C.Int.C. corporal servicing an underwing camera on a Cessna L-19 Bird Dog, circa 1964 / 515

No. 1 Canadian Field Security Section, Soest, West Germany, summer 1957 / 515

Trace of probable enemy dispositions issued by 1 Commonwealth Division, Korea, 1 October 1951 / 525

Operations (B) Platoon, Nicosia Zone, Cyprus, April 1965 / 535

Lieut. K.E. Edmonds beside Whirlwind helicopter, Kokkina, Cyprus, 6 October, 1964; air reconnaissance photo taken over the Nicosia Zone by Operations (B) on 20 September 1964 / 536

Militia Summer Concentration parade, 25 June 1967 / 540

No. 4 Intelligence Training Company with trophies won during Summer Camp 1958 / 543

No. 5 Intelligence Training Company with trophies won during Summer Camp 1967 / 544

Gen. H.D.G. "Harry" Crerar, C.H., C.B., D.S.O., C.D., P.C., Honorary Colonel Commandant of the C.Int.C., 1949–1964; message from Gen. Crerar to all members of the C.Int.C., 20 August, 1963 / 545

Major (retd) S.R. Elliot, C.D. / 643

FOREWORD

By Dr. David A. Charters
Professor of Military History (retd) and Senior Fellow, The Gregg Centre for the Study of War and Society, University of New Brunswick, Fredericton

When the first edition of *Scarlet to Green* was published in 1981 the academic study of intelligence, which has consumed much of my career, was in its infancy. The Ultra secret had been revealed barely seven years earlier, and the first volume of the official history of British intelligence in the Second World War had preceded Major Robert Elliot's tome by only a couple of years. There were no academic associations for the study of intelligence and no journals dedicated to it. It was, at that time, as noted intelligence historian Christopher Andrew later described it, the "missing dimension" of modern historical studies. So much has changed in the ensuing thirty-seven years that the earlier period is scarcely recognizable, even to those of us who were embarking on the field at the time. And it is for these reasons that *Scarlet to Green* stands out. It was a pioneering work in an almost neglected field.

Pioneering historians are not necessarily forgotten, but their place in the pantheon tends to fade with the passage of time and the accumulation of newer work. Thus, it is important to occasionally remind ourselves of their signal accomplishments, and this book is no exception. Indeed, one could easily say that in Major Elliot's case this reminder is long overdue. I met him only once and briefly at that, so cannot claim to have known him or presume to speak for him. But I am sure he would agree that this occasion – marking the 75th Anniversary of the activation of the Canadian Intelligence Corps and the moment of its contemporary reactivation – is a most appropriate moment to reissue his book. I am not going to attempt to summarize what is in the volume; that is readily apparent from the table of contents. Rather I intend to reflect on what his project represented, from the perspective of an intelligence historian.

First, one cannot fail to be amazed at the scale of the task Major Elliot set for himself. He initially conceived a 200-page history suitable for soldiers and civilians, a popular history that would lay the foundation for a much more ambitious project. The latter would trace Canadian military intelligence history from the time of Wellington's 'Guides', through the two world wars, to the place of intelligence in the modern Canadian Army on the eve of Integration/Unification: a span of almost 150 years! It would cover organization, training, command and administration, personnel changes, intelligence support to operations (expeditionary and domestic), communications, liaison duties, field security and counter-intelligence, prisoner of war interrogation, and more.

Commencing work in 1963, by 1971 he had written a 1,200-page manuscript, hardly surprising given the scope of the project. He, of course, recognized that a book that size was unmanageable and would have to be down-sized, as it was. Even so, the result was a massive tome: 769 pages, more than 400 of which were devoted to the Second World War. That part alone would have been a daunting task for an academic historian, but he saw the whole through to completion.

Second, what is equally impressive is that Major Elliot did this by himself. Of course, he received input from others, but he did the research, the writing, and the inevitable re-writing. His accomplishment is all the more impressive when one realizes that in writing the official history of British intelligence Harry Hinsley had the assistance of an assigned team of three historians, not to mention the benefit of his own experience at the very heart of the intelligence struggle, as a cryptanalyst at Bletchley Park. And unlike Hinsley et al, Major Elliot was not a professionally trained academic historian.

Third, Major Elliot's work is notable for his extensive use of original document sources, particularly for the chapters on World War Two. While this was partly out of necessity, since little had been written in published sources, Major Elliot did not scrimp on his efforts to mine the documentary record. He meticulously cited war diaries, intelligence summaries, message traffic, training materials, counter-intelligence reports, meeting minutes, private correspondence, and interviews with participants in the events. That revision of the historical record has since given us a clearer picture of events such as the Dieppe Raid and the campaigns in Italy and North-West Europe cannot be held against Major Elliot. This is the natural result of the historical process. He was working with the sources available at the time and within the commonly held historical understanding of his era. Indeed, given the paucity of original-source-based historical writing on Canadian intelligence in general and on military intelligence in particular, it is fair to conclude that when *Scarlet to Green* was published Major Elliot was 'ahead of the curve' and fully deserving of his status as a pioneer in research on Canadian intelligence.

Finally, the sheer size of Major Elliot's volume is due in large measure to his intention to tell the military intelligence story at both the level of higher command and "down in the weeds". This also allowed him to tell it 'warts and all'. He drew attention to the 'growing pains' during the early years of World War Two: the initial lack of trained personnel, and the problems of retaining them once they had been trained; disputes over control of intelligence tasks and their associated units; gaps in language skills; security breaches; intelligence sharing problems; inconclusive or inaccurate reporting; and lack of timely dissemination of information. All of these issues will be familiar to today's military intelligence professionals and to scholars of the subject. At the same time, in every theatre of combat there were numerous examples of initiative, improvisation, and adaptation 'on the fly', which are hallmarks of the Canadian way of war. Out of necessity they also were features of Canadian military intelligence during and after the war.

Scarlet to Green was a remarkable work of research and writing for its time. Since its publication the study of intelligence, including that of Canada, has matured dramatically. There are now university courses, academic books and journals, associations, and regular conferences dedicated to intelligence studies. But Major Elliot's work has not been superseded by any study equal in scope and depth. It stands as a tribute to the founders and practitioners of the military intelligence craft in its first sixty years in the Canadian Army, and remains a major contribution to the study of intelligence in Canada.

PREFACE

By Captain (N) (retd) Andrea L. Siew
President
Canadian Military Intelligence Association

Major S.R. Elliot's book *Scarlet to Green: A History of Intelligence in the Canadian Army 1903–1963*, is a tribute to the first sixty years of the Canadian Army intelligence tradecraft. Originally published in 1981, just one year before the establishment of the Canadian Forces Intelligence Branch, this book is also a major contribution to the study of military intelligence in Canada. The Canadian Military Intelligence Association (CMIA) is therefore pleased to publish a second edition of *Scarlet to Green* as a fitting commemoration of two important milestones in the history of Canadian military intelligence in 2017: the 35th anniversary of the Intelligence Branch and the 75th anniversary of the recently reactivated Canadian Intelligence Corps of the Canadian Army.

On behalf of the CMIA, I would like to extend our sincere gratitude to Major S.R. Elliot's wife, Shirley Elliot, as well as his daughter and son, Lyn Elliot Sherwood and Stuart Elliot respectively, for kindly agreeing to permit the CMIA to republish *Scarlet to Green* and for generously transferring copyright of the book to the Association. Their support will ensure that *Scarlet to Green* will remain in print and accessible to current and future generations of military intelligence professionals who otherwise may not have had the opportunity to acquaint themselves with the rich history and heritage of the military intelligence function in Canada that was so diligently and comprehensively recorded by the late Major S.R. Elliot.

I would also like to acknowledge all members of the original CMIA, and its later manifestation, the Canadian Intelligence and Security Association (CISA), who made the original publication of *Scarlet to Green* in 1981 possible through their generous donations and support. This was a huge undertaking for what was then a relatively small Association – spanning 18 years of effort beginning in 1963 to publication in 1981.

The idea of republishing *Scarlet to Green* to commemorate the 35th anniversary of the Intelligence Branch and 75th anniversary of the Canadian Intelligence Corps would not have been possible without the outstanding support, dedication and leadership of Captain (N) (retd) D. Martins. Captain (N) (retd) Martins first proposed the idea to the CMIA Board of Directors (BoD) in November 2016 and since then, he researched, organized, coordinated and executed this CMIA project.

I would also like to acknowledge and thank a number of individuals who helped Captain (N) (retd) Martins with republishing the second edition of *Scarlet to Green*.

Former Honorary Lieutenant-Colonel H.A. Skaarup generously supported and provided advice on many aspects of this project, including providing suggestions for new photos, reviewing new footnotes and captions, and proofreading chapters and rebuilt maps. His three-volume history, *Out of Darkness–Light*, which, among other things, chronicles the evolution of CMIA's support to the writing of *Scarlet to Green*, also provided important historical context that helped shape efforts to republish the second edition.

A number of the photos in the original edition of *Scarlet to Green* were found at the Canadian Forces School of Military Intelligence (CFSMI) in Kingston. I would like to thank Lieutenant-Colonel P. Ratté, the former Commandant of CFSMI and Commander of the Intelligence Branch's Home Station, and his staff, particularly Sergeant D. Couture, for facilitating the many visits to the school that made locating these photos possible. Other individuals who helped acquire or offered new photos for inclusion in the second edition include Master Warrant Officer J. Moreno, Clive Law, Pipe-Sergeant (retd) T.J. Stewart, Captain C.J.P. Anderson, Captain B.L. Carter, and Jacqueline Biéler. Master Warrant Officer (retd) C.A. Beattie also provided assistance with the scanning of the many photos found at CFSMI.

The maps, line diagrams and the Canadian Intelligence Corps crest in the first edition were reproduced by *Siteline Productions, Inc.* I would like to thank Former Honorary Lieutenant-Colonel D.A. Rubin, a former President of CMIA, who contacted *Siteline Productions, Inc.* about this project and for the company's very generous offer to donate graphic design work for the second edition on a pro bono basis.

I must also acknowledge the many CMIA members who proofread the 21 chapters to ensure that the manuscript for the second edition was reproduced and accurately formatted, including Colonel (retd) R.H. Smallwood, Master Warrant Officer (retd) C.A. Beattie, Major (retd) L. Lander, Warrant Officer L. McFadden-Davies, Lieutenant-Colonel (retd) G.W. Jensen, Lieutenant-Colonel (retd) M. Beauvais, Brigadier-General (retd) J.S. Cox, Major (retd) A. Barnes, Lieutenant-Colonel L.J. LeBlanc, Major (retd) G.P. Ohlke, Lieutenant-Colonel M. Mahood, Sergeant P. Paradis, Second Lieutenant M.C. Whitlaw, Major S.J. Andrusiak, Lieutenant-Colonel (retd) S.F. Beharriell, Major P.A. Dawes, Lieutenant (N) J.L. Dziadyk, Captain (retd) M. Bourdon, Lieutenant-Commander L. Scott, Captain L. Aubin, Captain D.M. Sargent, Major (retd) J.L. Malainey, Chief Petty Officer 2nd Class W.E. Marriott, Petty Officer 2nd Class G.M. Lewis, Master Warrant Officer (retd) R.L.A. Gill, Warrant Officer K.W. Bogle, Major S.E. McNeill and Captain (retd) S.W.D. Swan.

I would also like to extend a special thank you to Elisa Funnell and Jilly Funnell for their support throughout this project. In addition to proofreading a dozen chapters and locating a number of photos at Library of Archives Canada, Elisa ensured that Captain (N) (retd) D. Martins was available and provided her support to ensure he could complete this CMIA project. Jilly Funnell reviewed all 21 chapters to help weed out errors and idiosyncrasies that were introduced as part of the initial digital scan of the original book.

I would also like to note George Holdron's kind donation of a copy of *Scarlet to Green* – which has become a rare-book, collector's item – to the CMIA Board of Directors.

The second edition of *Scarlet to Green* respects the integrity of the first edition as originally written, including the use of British spelling for some words and gender-specific language, and retaining the original capitalization scheme and rank abbreviations; the few alterations to the original edition are clearly identified in editorial footnotes or endnotes. In this context, I would like to thank Dr. Steve Harris, Director of History and Heritage at the Department of National Defence, for reviewing chapter 10 and suggesting a minor alteration to the narrative regarding Canadian operations in the Dutch Scheldt. New notes in parenthesis have also been added to the text to assist the reader in locating places on a particular map or to highlight additional information in a specified annex; these added parenthetical notes are in italics. Additionally, to reduce the overall size of the book, and the time required to republish the second edition, 16 of the original 24 annexes have not been included; a list of the titles of these omitted annexes, which chronicle the names of personnel who served with various intelligence units during the period covered in the book, is provided in annex 9 as a reference for readers. Lastly, over forty new photos with accompanying captions have been added either to supplement or replace photos in the original edition which were not located.

In closing, the republication of *Scarlet to Green* will ensure that this record of a significant period in our military intelligence history will not be forgotten. However, *Scarlet to Green* is only the beginning of our great story. In keeping with its mandate to preserve and promote the traditions, heritage and *esprit de corps* of the Canadian military intelligence community, CMIA will continue to sponsor efforts to document and record our history for the benefit of future generations of intelligence professionals.

AUTHOR'S NOTE

This history of Intelligence in the Canadian Army does not reflect Department of National Defence or Canadian Armed Forces official opinion or policy. The selection of material, the inferences drawn therefrom, and the views and conclusions expressed are my own.

It is impossible to thank everyone who has helped with this book over the last 18 years. But special mention must be made of the staffs of the Public Archives Record Centre, National Defence Headquarters Document Control, and the Canadian Forces Records Centre. In the Canadian Intelligence and Security Association, special thanks are due to Col. Cyril Meredith-Jones, who devoted many frustrating hours to reviewing and editing the manuscript. I owe him a great deal. Contributors include A.V.M. Kenneth Guthrie, Brig.-Gen. C.S. McKee, Cols. Graham Blyth, Bob Raymont, and Peter Wright; Lt.-Cols. J.M. Catto, J.W.G. Macdougall, Eric Acland, Dave Wiens, D'Arcy Kingsmill, John Page, and Ray Labrosse; Majs. Eddie Corbeil, Bill Cooper, Cec Jones, and Bob Wodehouse; Capts. Phil Bachand, Ernie Jungbluth, and Ken Young; and Lt. D. Somerville. Finally, I would like to thank, most warmly and sincerely, Dolly Friend and Eleanor LeCavalier, who typed it all, some of it several times. Most especially, I owe much to my wife, without whose support the work would not have gone on.

S.R.E.
London, England
April 1980

INTRODUCTION

There is this saying in the Intelligence Community: "Intelligence is the second oldest of the world's professions. It is only slightly more respectable than the oldest one and, like it, suffers from the activities of enthusiastic amateurs." And, truly, Intelligence has existed from the earliest times. In the Bible (Genesis xlii: 9) Joseph, Governor of Egypt, pretended to accuse his brothers of espionage: "To see the nakedness of the land ye are come." In Numbers xiii: 2-19, Moses sent a leader from each of the 12 tribes of Israel to spy out the land of Canaan – a Strategic Intelligence mission to:

> . . . see the land, what it is; and the people that dwelleth therein, whether they be strong or weak, few or many; and what the land is . . . good or bad; and what cities they be . . . tents or in strong holds; and what the land is . . . fat or lean, whether there be wood therein or not.

They succeeded, but misinterpretation of their findings started the Israelites on a 40-year tour of the Sinai. This is an example not only of Strategic Intelligence but also of how a lack of confidence in the Intelligence agency can lead to avoidable difficulties and wasted effort.

Many misconceptions exist about Military Intelligence. One senior British civil servant allegedly doubted its very existence, saying: "Military Intelligence? Why, the terms are mutually contradictory!" Most people firmly believe that Intelligence simply means spies. The reminiscences of former secret agents tend to reinforce this misconception, mainly because they seldom mention the higher organization of their craft, or explain how and where the material they obtained at such risk was used.

The professional Intelligence Officer may, and perhaps should, have personal characteristics that set him apart. He often has a streak of scepticism – which may be mistaken for cynicism – because he has learned that things are seldom what they seem. He tries to couple this scepticism with an ability to identify any object that stands apart, even slightly, from the normal. His most frequent question is "Why?" followed closely by "When?" "Where?" and "How Many?" A good Intelligence Officer (I.O.) must not only be observant, he must know his subject, have an infinite capacity for taking pains, the patience to hunt for the one small item that completes the picture, the wit to recognize it, and the intellectual honesty and maturity to admit what he does not know or when he has been wrong.

Information that something has, or has not, taken place is of value only when it has been placed in its proper context. This procedure called the "Intelligence process", is a tedious, continuing, and often difficult task. It involves collecting all possible items of relevant information from all possible sources, placing them in their proper relationship to other data, and ensuring that they can easily be found and compared. This process concludes with an assessment of the reliability of the source and of the accuracy of his information. From it, the I.O.'s considered judgement is prepared in the most usable form and distributed in sufficient time that his commander may take appropriate action. Military Intelligence, therefore, is evaluated information that is prepared for a military commander by his Intelligence staff.

Intelligence is required in every phase of war, by every commander at every level of command. Governments also need it in times of peace. Obviously, the more senior the level, the broader and deeper will be the scope, nature, and detail of the Intelligence required. The Intelligence process continues as long as the commander's need exists. This same process is common to each of the many Intelligence functions and applies at every level in the system. Differences between Intelligence functions are merely differences of method, not principle.

A commander needs to know all he can about his enemy; he also has to prevent his enemy from knowing much about him. Until the Canadian Army ceased to exist as a separate entity at Integration, the two functions were known respectively as Intelligence (a) and Intelligence (b). Each had some of the attributes of the other. Acquiring and processing information about an enemy in the field – called, variously, I(a), Battle Intelligence, Combat Intelligence, or Operational Intelligence – took place only during wartime. During peacetime, there was a requirement to know what a potential enemy was capable of doing. This function, called Strategic Intelligence, was performed by a senior subdivision of I(a) at Army Headquarters (A.H.Q.) in Ottawa. Ideally, close contact should have been maintained with government departments and with industry to ensure that the picture was as complete as possible. The finished product was presented to senior commanders and, after co-ordination with other departments, to national political leaders. The agency also maintained data to brief the senior commander and staff of any Canadian force being sent abroad. As their operation proceeded, information was sent to Ottawa so that data at A.H.Q. could be revised and updated.

Without information, there can be no Intelligence. During wartime, information comes from all troops in contact with the enemy. It is obtained through their personal observations, from observation posts, from reports of hostile fire and other enemy activities, and particularly from patrols, which must be carefully controlled and coordinated by the Operations staffs so as to ensure optimum coverage at minimum cost in effort and lives. Before the First World War, units sent out to collect information were called "Scout" or "Guide" units. Later they were called reconnaissance ("recce") units. Although in the British Army the senior Scout officer was often responsible for field Intelligence, this was never the case in Canada. In the same way, the recce unit was a vital part of the information-gathering system, but it was never an integral part of the I(a) organization. There were, however, specialist agencies.

The first of these was responsible for air photograph interpretation. The aerial camera, today augmented with airborne radar, infrared, and television, offered a new and valuable means of collecting information. The unit responsible obtained photographs and data from the Air Force elements trained to gather them, read them, and notified the Intelligence staff of what had, or had not, been found. The Intelligence staff tried to ensure that its demands on these units were realistic, that current demands were met, and that future ones were anticipated.

Another agency monitored enemy radio transmissions and determined the nature and location of his headquarters, or, if enemy security was very bad, of his activity and even his plans. There is no black magic in this: military signals follow a pattern that trained men can interpret. Codes and ciphers are more difficult, but, given time, skill, and equipment, they were broken. There is, however, some danger in relying too heavily on radio monitoring, for deceptive messages, devised to provide false patterns, can mislead the analysts.

Linguists were used as translators, interpreters, and interrogators, to gain information from captured enemy documents, radio broadcasts, prisoners of war, and internees. These specialists were often the Canadian descendants of enemy nationals; occasionally they were actual enemy nationals whose political affiliations were in opposition to the enemy regime; and sometimes they were Canadians expert in languages. The primary criterion for their employment was linguistic skill.

The Technical Intelligence specialist might only have had sufficient linguistic knowledge to enable him to read the markings on equipment, but he had wide technical knowledge to enable him to assess the capabilities of any captured item. His greatest problem, which he shared with the translator, was to get to the enemy equipment or documents before some souvenir-hunter removed the more interesting parts.

Lastly, there were informants, generally unofficial. They existed in wartime as they do in peacetime. In peacetime they could be travellers, journalists, or businessmen. In wartime, most were involuntary refugees who might have seen something of the enemy's activities as they passed through the lines or fled before an advancing column. Some were deliberately sent through the lines on short-duration missions. High-level agents, who had to be specially planted and left to do their work, were used by both sides, but not by the Canadian Army. The problem that agents at all levels shared was the difficulty of communicating with their control. To be useful, information had to be sent back quickly.

In the Canadian Army, I(b), the other main branch, was more recent. Intelligence (b) officers and men operated during the First World War, but their function ceased in 1919. In Canada, the social unrest of the Depression and the Army's standing commitment of "aid to the civil power" led to the establishment of an Intelligence early-warning watch over possible civil disorder that could involve the Army. Then, responsibility for counter-intelligence in Canada lay with the Royal Canadian Mounted Police (R.C.M.P.). During the Second World War, Intelligence was obliged to take over this work within the Army because the R.C.M.P. did not itself have sufficient resources.

Intelligence (b) had two major subdivisions: Security, and Counter-Intelligence, also called counter-espionage. The senior I(b) officer in the field directed both functions. The double aim of I(b) was to frustrate the espionage attempts of the enemy I(a), and to protect our own forces against subversion and sabotage. In the Second World War, preventive – security – measures were used to deny enemy agents access to friendly secrets or to areas where those secrets could be learned. These measures were enforced by the unit commanders, using unit security personnel. Formation commanders with larger security responsibilities used Field Security (F.S.) men. Counter-Intelligence used detective measures in police-type investigations. Regulations were devised to make it difficult for an agent to operate. These imposed controls on access to military areas, on residence, assembly, movement, employment, on press and communications, and on the segregation and identification of individuals. There were two main categories of suspects. One was the confirmed supporter of the enemy; the other, any individual who, through political, social, or moral weaknesses, could be vulnerable to politically directed blackmail.

Field Security did most of the routine tasks in training units in security and in enforcing regulations, but were not engaged in I(b) detective work until they were actually in operations. Other I(b) units included interrogation centres and their staffs, special radio sections (mainly for direction-finding (DF) duties), and special technical units.

In the past, one branch of I(b) – Censorship – was given its own subdivision, I(c). To be effective, it had to be applied to the civilian population as well as to the military. It tried to ensure that information about our activities was not sent through the normal communication channels. It provided information to I(a) and to I(b); from I(b) it was given information on how the enemy worked and on what information had to be protected. Censorship staffs frequently reported suspicious leaks of information that revealed weaknesses in our own security organization, employment, or training. Occasionally they identified an individual who threatened the war effort. Often, they pin-pointed situations where poor morale made a unit less effective as a fighting force. While Censorship was not part of the original field organization, it was imposed early within units, and eventually was added to the organization, with special liaison officers operating within the Intelligence staff. Intelligence staffs provided advice, guidance, and assistance, and retired or seconded service officers often held Censorship posts in Canada. But the greater part of the Censorship story lies outside the scope of this book.

Finally, there was Intelligence (x) – Administration. This small element connected Intelligence units and their personnel with the administration of their senior command, and was located at the highest field headquarters. It controlled training, reinforcements, replacements, and much of the financial responsibility.

Psychological Warfare and Special Operations, though closely linked to Intelligence, were actually Operations functions. Psychological Warfare obtained from I(a) a knowledge of the tactical situation and of the geographical, social, psychological, and military characteristics of the enemy target. In return, it provided I(b) with expert opinion on enemy propaganda, and about possible weaknesses that enemy propaganda could exploit. Special Operations, responsible for sabotage, espionage, and subversion in the occupied territories, required detailed knowledge of enemy activities. In action, they often forced the enemy to disperse his forces to guard possible targets. The collection of information was often quite incidental to their main duties, but what information they did obtain was shared.

Intelligence must not undertake operations on its own. If a combat operation is needed in order to get information, it must be planned and conducted by the Operations, not the Intelligence, staffs. The risk is that Intelligence would soon find itself approaching its problems with less than clear objectivity. More time would be spent in preparing for the operation than in analysing the information already at hand. It is important to remember that Intelligence is an investigative and research agency only, not an executive or operational function.

Scarlet to Green attempts to tell the story of Intelligence in the Canadian Army between 1903 and 1963. It shows how its organization developed and then declined, what it did, and, as far as possible, who did it. It is partly a military history, partly a study of one aspect of Canadian national and international decision-making, and partly a tribute or memorial to those Canadians who performed its functions.

1.
IN THE BEGINNING

The British Army of the 19th century, which included such colonial militias as the Canadian, owed much of its organization and procedures to principles laid down by the Duke of Wellington. In India, and in his Peninsular campaigns, Wellington had been his own intelligence officer, and he created an intelligence organization based on the scout or guide. Guide units were composed of irregular, light horsemen, recruited in the country and employed solely to collect information, either by observing, or by conversation with the inhabitants. The Guides were under the control of a "Captain of Guides", an officer on Wellington's staff whose "services . . . are most essential, there being no map of the country and no person capable of giving information of a topographical nature".[1] On June 2nd, 1809, Wellington wrote to Marshall Beresford, his liaison officer with the Portuguese: "I am endeavouring to form a corps of Guides. . . . We have got some Officers, but we shall want . . . men of good character, who can speak either English or French, to make Sergeants or Corporals."[2] Most of the officers were Portuguese students from the University of Coimbra. They were chosen for: ". . . intelligence, some honesty and a knowledge of the Spanish or Portuguese languages and English or French".[3]

Wellington's Guides disappeared at the end of the Napoleonic Wars. But in 1846, after the British East India Company's victory over the Sikhs at Sobraon had opened for it the Punjab and the North-West Frontier, Sir Henry Lawrence, who was then agent to the Governor General, proposed the formation of a local corps to keep the area under surveillance. Part of this 4,100-man force was to be: "1 Troop of Guides, 100 men and 2 Companies of 200 . . . half of them always employed in making themselves acquainted with localities and with the highways and byways of the frontier." Later he proposed that a European officer be attached to these Guides to direct their movements, to record the information they brought in, and to train them; in other words, to perform the specific duties of an intelligence officer. The Guides were formed on December 14th, 1846, recruited from every warlike tribe on the Frontier. They were the first unit to wear khaki uniforms; and, in 1878, they also became the first to wear the Sam Browne belt, named after their one-armed commander, who invented it. They participated in the Indian Mutiny, in every campaign on the North-West Frontier of India, and in both world wars. In 1920, the Guides were split into separate infantry and cavalry (reconnaissance) components and, after the Partition of 1947,[4] were absorbed into the new armies of India and Pakistan.

Thowmas Davidson was promoted to acting lieutenant. Cornet Robertson retired and was replaced by William Cunningham. On July 1st, 1868, the establishment was two officers and 47 men; two officers and 31 men were on strength, and they paraded two and 22 for the annual inspection. Ramsay resigned on November 29th, 1868, and Davidson took over the unit. He and Cunningham resigned on August 13th, 1869, probably when the unit disbanded.[11]

In 1884, Louis Riel returned to the Canadian Northwest from the United States. By mid-March 1885, there were reports of unrest. The Minister of Militia and Defence, the Honourable A.P. Caron, ordered his General Officer Commanding (G.O.C.), Maj.-Gen. Frederick Middleton, to go at once to restore law and order. Middleton left Ottawa on March 23rd, arriving in Winnipeg on the 27th. There he learned that Riel's forces had attacked a mixed body of Mounted Police and Prince Albert volunteers at Duck Lake on March 26th, and that blood had been shed. Quick counter-action was essential.[12] Middleton raised a field force from local Militia units and asked Ottawa for further reinforcements.[13] Among them were scout units.

The Minister himself authorized one such unit of three officers and 30 men from the Dominion Land Survey, then holding a conference in Ottawa. Its commander was Capt. J.S. Dennis, whose father, Lt.-Col. J.S. Dennis, was the Surveyor-General. Militia Orders called the unit the "Intelligence Corps"[14] – the first such identification in the British Empire. It was also known as "Dennis's Scouts", "Surveyor's Scouts", "Intelligence Mounted Corps", "Land Surveyor's Scouts", and "The Dominion Land Surveyor's Intelligence Corps".

Another unit was formed at Winnipeg by Maj. Charles A. Boulton, an ex-Regular, who had been Lt.-Col. Dennis's assistant during the first Riel Rebellion in 1869. It had five officers and 108 men, was organized into the "Russell" and "Birtle" Companies, commanded by Capts. J.A. Johnson and Meopham Gardiner respectively, and was variously known as "Boulton's Scouts, "Boulton's Mounted Infantry", and "The Mounted Corps". At Qu'Appelle, an ex-Inspector of the North West Mounted Police (N.W.M.P.), Capt. John French, raised a troop of two officers and 30 men called "French's Scouts".[15] Capt. George W.R. White, with Lieut. F.L. Oslee, commanded 50 men, known either as "White's Scouts" or "The Moose Mountain Scouts", who were employed south and east of Qu'Appelle.[16]

There were three scout units in Alberta. Maj. S.B. Steele, Inspector, N.W.M.P., with Capt. Oswald and Lieut. Coryell, formed "Steele's Scouts" with 50 Mounted Police and 60 civilians. Maj. Hatton, with two ex-police sergeants – Dunn and Lauder – formed the 60-man "Alberta Mounted Rifles" or "Scout Cavalry". Finally, Maj. Stewart, a local rancher, formed a 150-man force known as the "Rocky Mountain Rangers". This force was stationed at Fort Macleod and Lethbridge, from which it patrolled the reservations and ranch country along the Alberta border.[17]

Capt. J. French, French's Scouts, 1885. (Library and Archives Canada, C-018942)

Dominion Land Surveyor's Intelligence Corps, 1885. (Library and Archives Canada, C-007865)

On April 6th, 1885, French's and Boulton's Scouts led Gen. Middleton's 850-man force out of Fort Qu'Appelle up the Touchwood Trail. On April 16th, the column reached Clarke's Crossing on the South Saskatchewan River. Here Middleton split his force, putting a detachment on the west bank covered by French's Scouts and about 20 of Boulton's, while keeping the remaining 60 of Boulton's as the advance guard of his main body. The two columns then moved down-river, arriving at Fish Creek on April 23rd. Here the Scouts located a body of rebels and, on the 24th, the Battle of Fish Creek was fought. Middleton's force lost 10 killed and 40 wounded, including eight Scouts – Capt. M. Gardiner, Sgt. Alex Stewart, and Troopers F.H. Thompson, Charles King, D'Arcy Baker (mortally), V. Bruce, J. Langford, and H. Perrin, all of Boulton's. [18]

The advance was resumed on May 7th with 28 of French's and 65 of Boulton's Scouts in the lead. Dennis's Scouts, who had been deployed as pickets between Swift Current Creek and Long Lake, rejoined the column on May 10th, as the force deployed against the rebel positions in Batoche. During the subsequent attacks, the Scouts were in the line, on the right flank, fighting as infantry. When the action was over, on May 12th, the government forces had lost five killed and 25 wounded, among whom Scouts were tragically prominent. Of the five killed, three were Scout officers: Capt. French, whose command passed to his second-in-command, Lieut. Brittlebank; Capt. E.L. Brown of Boulton's; and Lieut. E.A.W. Kippen of Dennis's. The wounded included Lieut. J.F. Gordon and Privates Hay, Allen, Cook, and Wheeler, all of Dennis's.[19]

The Rebel resistance was broken, although Riel himself remained at large. The contemporary press reported his capture in these words:

> ... since the capture of Batoche, General Middleton has had scouts constantly scouring the country ... for the purpose of apprehending Riel.
>
> On Friday, May 15th, three of these scouts encountered four men sauntering along a trail about a mile and a half from Batoche, one of whom was Riel. A Scout, recognizing him, approached, saying: "I am surprised to see you here". Riel replied: "I was coming to give myself up. My wife and family are across the river." Other scouts were then seen approaching. Riel, becoming afraid of being shot, begged his captor to take him to General Middleton's Camp.[20]

The three Scouts were Bob Armstrong, William Diehl, and Tom Hourie, all of Boulton's.[21]

In the meantime, Lt.-Col. Otter moved north from Swift Current with a force of about 550 men. He had 75 police, of whom 50 were mounted. These he placed under the command of Lt.-Col. Herchmer, N.W.M.P. He also had five Boulton's Scouts whom he placed under the command of Lieut. J.W. Spears of the Infantry School Corps. They seem not to have been used in their proper role with that unit. One of Inspector Herchmer's men, Charlie Ross, spent a good deal of his time in the enemy lines, both at Battleford and at the later Battle of Cut Knife Hill. He was specially commended for his services.

After he had relieved Battleford on April 24th, Col. Otter decided to make a reconnaissance in force against Chief Poundmaker, whose reservation lay nearby. His Scouts found the band, but lost one of their number, Baptist Lafontaine, in the process. On May 2nd, an engagement took place at Cut Knife Hill which cost Otter's force eight killed and 14 wounded, among them some police Scouts whose names appear not to have been recorded. Otter withdrew to Battleford, but his Scouts stayed on Poundmaker's heels until, after hearing of Riel's surrender, the Chief decided further conflict was useless.[22]

The Alberta Field Force, commanded by Maj.-Gen. T.B. Strange, a retired British Army officer, left Calgary for Edmonton on April 20th, led by Steele's Scouts. On May 1st, they crossed the North Saskatchewan River at Edmonton and halted to regroup, train, unload stores, and build boats. A world of fractious horseflesh and cursing, struggling men is apparent in a laconic statement in the general's report concerning "partially broken horses, unused to fire." On May 6th, he moved down-river to attack Chief Big Bear and his band, covered by 25 Mounted Police and 110 Scouts.[23]

At Fort Saskatchewan, Inspector A.H. Griesbach, N.W.M.P., was appointed Major of Militia and directed to take a mixed party of Scouts and Alberta Mounted Rifles to check Salois, about 50 miles to the southeast. He found nothing, returned to Fort Saskatchewan, and sent his troops forward to rejoin Gen. Strange, then at Victoria, six days march eastward.

The Scouts deployed well forward of the main party. At Frog Lake, they heard that a large band of Indians, under Chief Big Bear, was at Fort Pitt, but when they reached the fort's smoking remains on the 25th, they found no one. On May 26th, Gen. Strange sent some of his Scouts to the northeast and others along the south side of the river, all to try and locate the main Indian force. On May 27th, the Scouts located the rebel positions at Frenchman's Butte, about three miles down-river from Fort Pitt. The area was heavily wooded, and Maj. Steele, ordered to work around the enemy's right flank, was unable to determine the exact line of the defence. Apparently, the Indians had sent a force to parallel the Scouts, and this tactic gave the impression that their strength was larger than it was. In any case, after suffering a few casualties, among whom was Pte. J. McRae of the N.W.M.P., Gen. Strange withdrew to Fort Pitt, the Scouts covering his withdrawal.[24]

Meanwhile, Middleton and Otter had joined forces at Battleford on May 24th. Both columns resumed the advance and met the Alberta Field Force about six miles downstream from Fort Pitt on May 31st. The pursuit of Big Bear was continued with columns sent northward. Steele's Scouts, 60 Boulton's, 20 Brittlebank's, and 40 Dennis's formed the main thrust. They caught up with the Indian rearguard at Loon Lake, and the resulting skirmish cost the Scouts Squadron Sgt.-Maj. W. Fury seriously wounded, and Scouts Fisk and William R. West wounded.[25] The band disintegrated under pursuit, and the Chief surrendered to Sgt. Smart, N.W.M.P., on July 2nd.

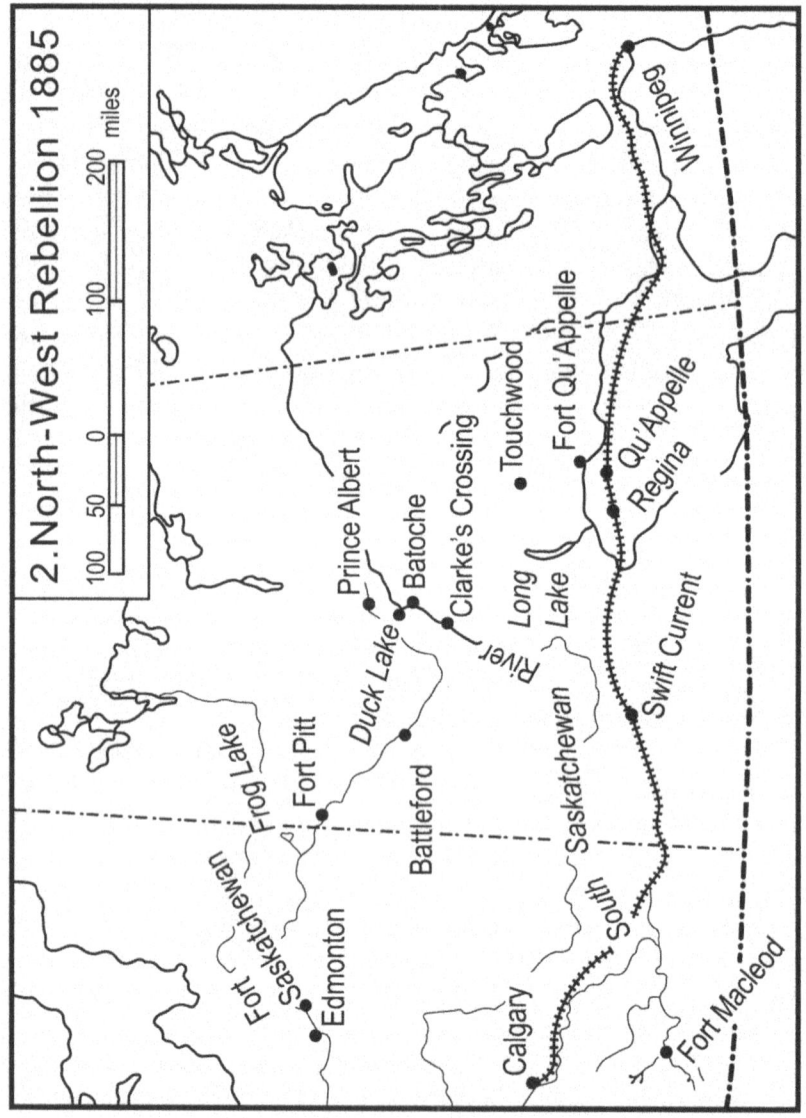

During this campaign, the Scout units performed a light cavalry function as well as their more normal role of long-range patrol reconnaissance, locating and reporting on parties of Indians. They may have been undisciplined, untrained, and unused to war, but they were tough, self-reliant outdoorsmen who were much less costly to raise and maintain than regular cavalry would have been. The units were all disbanded by September 18th, 1885, and, with two exceptions, vanished from the Canadian Militia scene. Boulton's Scouts have been perpetuated in the Fort Garry Horse, and the Moose Mountain Scouts in the North Saskatchewan Regiment.

Many Canadians served in the contingents which were officially raised for the South African (Boer) War. Others served in the small irregular forces raised in the colony itself. Some of these men were already resident in South Africa, others enlisted from Canada; still others served their time with the regular contingents, took their discharge in South Africa and then joined these irregular forces. The unit most open to Canadians was a corps variously known as "Howard's Scouts", "Ross's Scouts", or the "Canadian Scouts". Maj. William Hamilton Merritt of the Governor General's Body Guard was second-in-command of "Brabant's Horse". Charlie Ross, N.W.M.P., was a lieutenant in "Robert's Light Horse". "Kitchener's Horse", "Bethune's Mounted Infantry", and "Rimington's Guides", to name but three, are all known to have had Canadians in their ranks.

There was one unit, however, that was wholly Canadian: "500 rough riders from the Canadian North West . . . under Inspector S.B. Steele, 'an ideal scout and leader of scouts' . . . fighters and not only intelligence men".[26] It was raised by Lord Strathcona at no cost to the Canadian government and is now better known as Lord Strathcona's Horse (Royal Canadians), of the Regular Establishment.

The British Army in South Africa fielded a large intelligence organization. There was a Director of Military Intelligence, graded as Assistant-Adjutant-General, an A.A.G. (Topography), four Deputy-Assistant Quartermaster-Generals (Intelligence), and two Press Censors, all at Force H.Q.; a Press Censor and a Baggage and Intelligence Officer on the Railway Staff; and a Field Intelligence Staff of 15 D.A.Q.M.G.s (Intelligence), 13 staff captains, a staff lieutenant, seven staff intelligence officers, four officers employed on Provost duties (perhaps the forerunners of Field Security), 24 intelligence officers, most of whom were, or had been, members of irregular mounted units, and the necessary clerical staff.[27*] In April 1900, a Canadian lieutenant, A. Clyde Caldwell, who had been invalided to Cape Town from Paardeberg, was attached to the mapping staff of this Intelligence Department. When the officer in charge was posted, Caldwell was given his position and held it until November, 1900.

This system of intelligence staffs commended itself to the then General Officer Commanding Canadian Militia, Maj.-Gen. R.H. O'Grady Haly, C.B., D.S.O., who was attached from the British War Office. In his annual report to the Minister on December 31st, 1900, he said:

> Heretofore no organized system of Intelligence work appears to have existed in the Militia Department . . . this very important matter should at once be placed upon a sound practical basis. I have recommended that an Intelligence Staff Officer should be added to the department of the Quarter-Master General.[28]

---

*   Critical comments as to the role of this element may be found in Byron Farwell, *The Anglo-Boer War* (Fitzhenry and Whiteside, Toronto, 1976) pp. 42, 297–8.

Lt.-Col. Victor Brereton Rivers, R.C.A., the first Intelligence Staff Officer. A member of the "Old Eighteen", the first class of cadets that entered R.M.C. in 1876, Lt.-Col. Rivers is a young Lieut. in this photo, which was possibly taken sometime shortly after his graduation. (Photo courtesy of Royal Military College of Canada Museum)

His recommendation was accepted and, on February 6th, 1901, the first Intelligence Staff Officer (I.S.O.) was appointed. He was Lt.-Col. Victor Brereton Rivers, R.C.A., a career soldier and veteran of the battles of Fish Creek and Batoche. His work during the next two years culminated in the authority which created the Corps of Guides in the Canadian Army, General Order 61 of April 1st, 1903.

The Order directed that, at each of the 12 Military Districts across Canada, there would be a District Intelligence Officer (D.I.O.) whose duties included command of the Corps of Guides in his District. He was "to have special qualifications which will be defined by the General Officer Commanding". Each Military District was to be divided into sub-districts, each under a Sub-District Intelligence Officer (S.D.I.O.). These sub-districts were to "conform as far as possible to regimental areas; in Ontario and Quebec following county divisions and in other parts of Canada other areas which will be defined". Each sub-district was to be further subdivided into Guide Areas "for each of which a specially qualified man or men with good local knowledge will be appointed", as circumstances permitted. When it was formed into a regiment, the whole organization was to be called the Corps of Guides.

Its head was to be a Director General of Military Intelligence who, under the control of the G.O.C., was charged with "the collection of information on the military resources of Canada, the British Empire, and foreign countries". In addition, he was to prepare maps of Canada of a suitable scale for the use of an army in the field, and handbooks of military information for every portion of the country. Also, he was to command the Corps of Guides, and supervise and arrange for their instruction and duties. Finally, he was responsible for instruction in reconnaissance and military surveying.

The Directorate was to be divided into two Branches, Information and Mapping, each under an Assistant Intelligence Staff Officer (A.I.S.O.). The Information Branch would operate a library of books "of information under various headings", and provide information on Canada. It was to obtain from the provincial governments reports on agriculture, the census, trade and commerce, surveys, and public works, and, from the Dominion government, reports on public works, the post office, railways and canals, surveys, marine, and agriculture. The railway companies were to be asked for details of coal supplies, bridges, junctions, stations, tunnels, location of repair materials, water supply, ramps for unloading horses and cattle, embankments "and other necessary information". Telegraph and telephone companies were to provide the locations of all their offices, to advise when new ones were opened, and to report the numbers of their operators.

A sub-section of the Information Branch, the "Foreign Information Branch", was to form a library, keep a scrapbook, and gather information on foreign armies, militia, military engineering, agriculture, public works, railroads and canals, trade and commerce, census and "other reports from which information might be drawn". It was to prepare a report with maps, suitable for an army in the field, to "cover States or parts of a State, and will be fuller in detail when the ground reported on is at or near the Frontier . . . foreign troops, their headquarters, strength, arms, etc." The primary target country was not mentioned, but memories of the Fenian raids and other examples of American expansionism were fresh in Canadian minds. The Information Branch also had to run "Section C of the Mapping Branch", which apparently administered that branch.

In his place, the A.I.S.O. of the Mapping Branch was responsible for surveying, drafting, and reproducing maps, preparing "skeleton" (outline) maps for field use, and for collecting maps from the appropriate governments (provincial, municipal and Dominion) as well as those published by civilian firms. The Branch corrected published maps. It had to watch all official surveys, attaching an officer to the survey party if necessary. It collected the detailed reports prepared by the Guides on the military geography of their respective regions, in accordance with their Corps instructions. No mention was made of any responsibility for storage or issue of finished maps but Section C may have had this additional task.

The Corps instructions in this respect required the Guides to be "intelligent men and capable of active work with a knowledge of the topographical features of the country . . . roads, the country between the roads, side paths, names of farmers, etc. . . . when possible should be in possession of a horse". The S.D.I.O. would be supplied with a sketch map which he was required to fill with military information "from his own observation or collected from the Guides in his sub-district". He was also "called upon to reply to . . . questions bearing on information necessary for military purposes". The D.I.O.s were to collect the reports and sketch maps and forward them to Section C at Army H.Q.

The duties of this organization differ quite markedly from those of later Army intelligence directorates. The foreign intelligence interest obviously remained, although its more geographical studies have disappeared and the studies of foreign armed forces have become much more sophisticated. The library became a separate, and highly regarded, organization. Given the situation that pertained in 1903, the major functions were highly relevant. Until that time, there had been no stock-taking of Canadian national resources. Army officers, conditioned by their experiences in the Northwest and in South Africa, were very much the product of their age. They were well aware of the difficulties of waging war in areas where resources, transportation, and other facilities were little known, undeveloped, or, at best, limited. It must be remembered that major operational and strategic moves were still tied to the railway system. Tactical moves used the horse, either as part of the combat arm or as the main motive power for field logistic support. Facilities governing the use of these transport facilities, separately or in concert, were vital objects of attention to military planners.

The first Director General of Military Intelligence was Brevet Major William A.C. Denny, Royal Army Service Corps, *psc.*[*] He was a veteran of South Africa, where he had been successively a Railway Staff Officer, Provost Marshal, Supply and Transport Officer, Brigade Major, and Intelligence Officer. He had seen

---

[*] psc. – passed Staff College. As a Service Corps officer, Denny would not normally have had either the course or such an appointment. There were very few such qualifications in the Canadian Militia of the day.

Lt.-Col. William C. Denny, (Bvt. Maj., A.S.C.), the first Director General of Military Intelligence, April 1903–January 1905. (Photo collection Canadian Forces School of Military Intelligence, Kingston/Canada. Dept. of National Defence)

action at the Relief of Ladysmith, Colenso, Spion Kop, Vaal Kranz, Tugela Heights, Laing's Nek, Transvaal, and the Orange River Colony, and had been mentioned in dispatches three times. When he took up his appointment, he was given the rank of lieutenant-colonel in the Canadian Militia. His pay and allowances came to $3,000 a year.

His staff consisted of Lt.-Col. Rivers as I.S.O., responsible for the detailed supervision of the Directorate and paid $1,800 a year; two A.I.S.O.s, A.C. Caldwell and W.B. Anderson, responsible respectively for the Information and Mapping Branches and paid $1,500 each; four staff lieutenants (only three were appointed), H.L. Bodwell, W.E. Stephenson and L.C. Van Tuyl, paid $900 each; a clerk, S/Sgt. H.D.G. Johnson, Corps of Military Staff Clerks, who was paid $800, and two N.C.O.s, at $720 each. One of these N.C.O.s was a qualified draftsman, the other a "qualified N.C.O., accustomed to Intelligence work". The prospects of getting good Imperial N.C.O.s were admittedly poor; British ration and quarters allowances were inadequate in Ottawa.[29]

In the Districts, all officers and men were Militia. C.H. Mitchell of Toronto, for example, was a prominent consulting engineer. The Militia Act of 1904 limited the Permanent Force strength to 2,000; this was increased to 5,000 in 1906, but the actual strength, as late as 1913, was only 3,000 all ranks. The Army could not, therefore, staff an organization like the Guides on the Regular Establishment. Such part-time duty carried the pay of rank in the Active Militia, service counted towards the Long Service Medal, and postage costs, paper, pens, ink, and other stationery were furnished if the I.O. cared to submit a claim for them to Militia Headquarters.

That first summer was a busy one. Col. Denny instructed at London, Niagara-on-the-Lake, Trois-Rivières, Sussex, and Aldershot. The two latter camps added a new Intelligence Officer appointment to their staffs and filled the positions with Capts. W.E. Earle and H.S. Tremaine, respectively.[30] In the autumn of 1903, all Militia Arms and Services heads had to set an examination to be taken by men with no previous service when applying for a commission. The Guides examination, which was the first to be published officially, included field sketching, reconnaissance reports, use of survey instruments, military organization, and knowledge of provincial and municipal survey systems. There was a written test, a practical field test, and equitation. For the practical portion candidates were required to:

> sketch and report at a scale of 3 inches to one mile a road report of three miles of road, without instruments, 1000 yards on either side, distances to be estimated by eye, shape of ground . . . indicated by form lines. . . . two hours to complete.[31]

Daily pay and allowances were now $5.00 for lieutenant-colonels, $4.00 for majors, and $3.00 for captains and lieutenants. An officer joining the Corps had to pay a $5.00 subscription, captains paid $10 when appointed, majors $15, and lieutenant-colonels $20. In addition, each promotion called for a $5 donation to the common fund.[32]

The first Dress Regulations were published in May, 1904. The Guides were the junior mounted unit and were dressed accordingly: a white, standard-pattern helmet, khaki tunic with lancer front and scarlet collar and cuffs, khaki trousers with a 1 3/4-inch scarlet stripe, black boots, box spurs, cavalry pattern sword, and greatcoat. The khaki and scarlet in the uniform were the same as those worn by the Guides of India. Their badges were "In silver or white metal, 'The true and magnetic North points' entwined in a scroll inscribed: 'Guides, Canada'. Below, a scroll bearing the motto *'Virtute et Labore*'*, the whole enclosed within a wreath of maple leaves surmounted by the Tudor Crown".[33] These regulations were later amended to include a gilded helmet spike, a gilded curb chain chin strap to replace the original leather, and a cross belt with pouch and badge for field dress; a blue patrol uniform; a cap with a removable khaki cover so that

---

*   VIRTUTE ET LABORE – "By Valour and Exertion": the motto of Earl Dundonald, McClintock of Drumcar, and others.

Corps of Guides officer, Lieut. C. Tweedale, in full uniform, at an Annual Inspection, 16 May 1914; on right, Tweedale on horseback, circa 1918. (Vancouver City Archives, Mil P199 and CVA 99-153)

it could be worn with service dress, and a winter fur wedge hat; a summer uniform of "khaki tartan" with a scarlet stripe on the "pantaloons"; brown leather gauntlets, boots and gaiters, and a long khaki cape. Officers later wore the scarlet-staff-band on their caps. In 1917, a green band replaced the scarlet on the D.I.O.'s cap; green gorget patches and a regimental gorget button were added to his tunic; and the coloured shoulder straps, cape, scarlet stripe on the pantaloons, and removable cap cover all disappeared.[34]

Militia officers from other arms were invited to attend courses in military sketching and reconnaissance; of the 18 who came in 1904, three later became Guides. The first exclusively Guides camp was held at Niagara-on-the-Lake, June 14th to 25th, 1904. Eleven officers, seven men, and six horses were on parade, possibly the entire District strength. Their rations cost $5, forage for the horses $2.45, and baggage transport $6.20; the total pay and allowances was $305.07.[35]

The Militia Council, which had been established by the Militia Act of 1904, first met on November 28th of that year and read into the record the terms of reference of the staff branches at Army H.Q. The Chief of the General Staff

Corps of Guides on horseback, date and location unknown, but possibly at Niagara-on-the-Lake. (Photo courtesy of MilArt photo archives. Original photo part of Lawrence Hurt Sitwell collection/Library and Archives Canada)

Officers of the Corps of Guides having refreshments after a reconnaissance ride, Niagara-on-the-Lake, 1905. (Lawrence Hurt Sitwell/Library and Archives Canada, PA-111891)

(C.G.S.) was shown as responsible for Intelligence. His "Director of Training and Intelligence" was the officer specifically responsible for "the task of collection, compilation, and distribution of intelligence, including topographical information and mapping, issue of maps for war and for military attachés" (of which there were none).[36]

On November 29th, the Council changed the command structure of the Military Districts (M.D.s).[37] On December 6th, 1904, reflecting these changes, General Order No. 12 authorized peacetime establishments for the Guides totalling three lieutenant-colonels, 13 majors, 40 captains, 60 lieutenants, one R.S.M., 26 chief guides and 52 guides. The other rank wartime establishment was to be increased to 100 chief guides, and to 400 guides. The lieutenant-colonel vacancies were not to be filled until the new command structure was fully operative. In the meantime, the eastern Districts were given an increase of one Chief Staff Officer to whom the D.I.O. reported. The Director at Ottawa exercised administrative control of the Corps through the D.I.O., who was answerable to his G.O.C. for the efficiency of the Guides in his Command. This duality continued to apply until the disappearance of the geographical Command system in Canada in 1965.

At Militia Headquarters, Col. Denny, who had been on leave for most of the last half of 1904, relinquished his appointment on January 15th, 1905, and he was not replaced. On May 1st, 1906, Mapping and Survey became a separate Directorate of Survey. Lt.-Col. Rivers was officially transferred to the branch of the Master General of Ordnance, where he had been working for over a year. Maj. Caldwell and Capt. Anderson qualified for permanent commissions in the Royal Canadian Engineers (R.C.E.) and left the Guides. Anderson became the first Assistant Director of Survey and Caldwell became the first Assistant Director of Military Intelligence (A.D.M.I.) on July 1st, 1905. These officers headed their respective branches, since no full Directors were appointed. The staff lieutenants were left with Survey, but they were used occasionally on jobs within the A.D.M.I.[38]

The Intelligence Branch obviously suffered greatly from these changes, and it was apparent that the intelligence requirement that had been considered to exist when the Directorate was formed was now not looked on as having the same importance. However, considering the desperate need for maps during this period, it was clear that the General Staff had arranged its priorities correctly.

A mapping program, involving the Royal Military College, had been in operation since 1895. By 1900, some 1,700 square miles of the Eastern Townships of Quebec had been mapped. In 1901, Capt. J.L.H. Bogart and Lieut. Caldwell took cadets to three points in western Ontario. In 1902, Capt. Bogart and Lieut. W.B. Anderson went out with 12 cadets and a sergeant. The map that resulted was "valuable from an Intelligence point of view, provided that it is reduced to a convenient scale and that means exist for issuing it at once, when needed, in sufficient quantities".[39] In 1903, the head of the Mapping Department of the War Office visited Canada and discussed the exchange of British tradesmen to assist in the program. In 1904, 2,000 square miles were mapped, and the survey section did 600 miles of level and 600 miles of transit lines in the area between London and Niagara-on-the-Lake. With some help from the Guides, manoeuvre (sketch) maps were prepared for the areas around the camps at Sussex, New Brunswick, and Kentville, Nova Scotia. Because Canada still did not have a topographical survey or triangulation against which the Department could check its work, these Departmental maps were the "only maps of Canada which record the physical features . . . essential for military purposes".

In November 1907, the C.G.S. reported that the maps of the Niagara area that his department had made, and which had been lithographed in England, included, in considerable detail, some areas of the adjacent United States. It was agreed that no great harm would accrue if these were made available to the general public.[40]

The years before the outbreak of the First World War involved the Corps in little more than the minutiae of peacetime soldiering. In 1905, the A.D.M.I. saw no reason why Guides should spend "more time than necessary . . . on parade movements, a knowledge of drill being of minor importance in a corps intended for intelligence duties in time of war". In 1906, "a number of foreign newspapers and professional magazines as well as British Service papers and magazines had been examined". Over the winter of 1907–8, the Corps carried on a survey to "ascertain the manufacturing capability of Canada in respect to those articles which would be required for the use and upkeep of an army in the field, not only for . . . the Dominion but . . . to acquaint . . . the Imperial authority with the natural resources upon which the Empire might reckon in the event of a great war". In 1909, Maj. Caldwell vacated the post of A.D.M.I. to become Command Engineer in Toronto. His official replacement was Capt. L.H. Sitwell of the Guides, but there were long periods when the appointment was vacant. It was filled on one occasion by Capt. Charles J. Bruce Hay of the Queen's Own Corps of Guides (Lumsden's), Indian Army, who was then on exchange at Militia H.Q. (He had to be given an extra $18.31 per month to bring his pay up to Canadian levels).[41]

In 1911, a further reorganization changed the eastern Military Districts to "Divisional Areas". Nine Detachments of Guides were authorized, six in the three new Divisional Areas, three in the western M.D.s. There was to be a Divisional Intelligence Officer and a Detachment Commander in each Area. The Detachment Commander was to be the senior Guides officer in the divisional area (if the D.I.O. was senior, he would also command the Detachment). The total establishment was to be six lieutenant-colonels, 16 majors, 32 captains, 64 lieutenants, one R.S.M. (H.D.G. Johnson, who had been appointed May 5th, 1905), 28 chief guides and 56 guides, a total of 203 all ranks. This was later raised to 118 officers and 381 other ranks, but training was restricted to 302 all ranks. New regulations governed the relationship between staff and units; others detailed the conditions of officers' reconnaissance rides. (The officer could take 75 pounds of kit including bedding, his groom 50 pounds, the cook 300 pounds including his shelter and kettles, and two days' rations of hay and oats; the complete outfit was to be carried in a wagon obtainable through normal Canadian Army Service Corps channels at Command.)[42]

In 1912, a mounted Guides company in No. 2 Divisional Area (Central Ontario) and detachments in No. 1 (Western Ontario) and No. 5 (Quebec) Areas, were authorized. The Inspector General, Col. (T/Maj.-Gen.) W.D. Otter, C.V.O., C.B. – who had been appointed honorary colonel of the Corps on March 7th, 1911 – said in his 1912 annual report:

> This Corps . . . has made material progress during the last year, its training being . . . more advanced . . . and upon stricter lines. Its officers . . . with very few exceptions are most enthusiastically responding to the requirements.
> The selection of officers for this service entails the most careful scrutiny . . . as in no other branch does "dead wood" so materially mar efficiency as in the Corps.
> Hitherto in the eyes of many . . . it has been looked upon as a comfortable refuge for such as desired rank . . . without . . . sacrifices.[43]

Obviously not all Guides officers had been paragons of military virtue, but they were probably no worse than those of other corps.

The new Guide Companies had a major or captain as officer commanding, two, later three, subalterns, three sergeants, three corporals, 21, later 24, guides, four grooms, a transport driver, a cook, a transport wagon, and 36 horses. Each man was armed with a Ross rifle and a pistol. In 1913, each company was given flags, a heliograph, a signalling lamp, and six compasses. The newly-formed Canadian Signal Corps assigned one officer and six men to each Guide company to operate the signalling equipment.[44] One of the personalities in the Guides of that time was Lt.-Col. A.J. Van Nostrand, D.I.O. No. 2 Divisional Area, who was the only Guides officer officially on the Coronation Contingent of 1911. In 1911 and 1912, three subalterns, C. Sifton, J.W. Sifton, and W.B. Sifton, from Toronto and Kingston, were granted permission to compete as a team representing the Canadian Militia at the International and the Richmond Horse Shows at London, England, as well as at The Hague and in other continental shows. The president of the International wrote to the C.G.S. on July 26th, 1912, saying that the Siftons "represented your Army splendidly and are a great credit to your country".[45]

The official authorization merely confirmed an existing situation. The Guides prided themselves on their horsemanship and most officers rode. In 1912, the Guides offered a challenge cup. It was clear that, although the task given each rider was demanding, it was not allowed to take precedence over care for the horse. The first race was held at Petawawa, Ontario, on August 31st, 1912,

3. Western Front 1915-1918

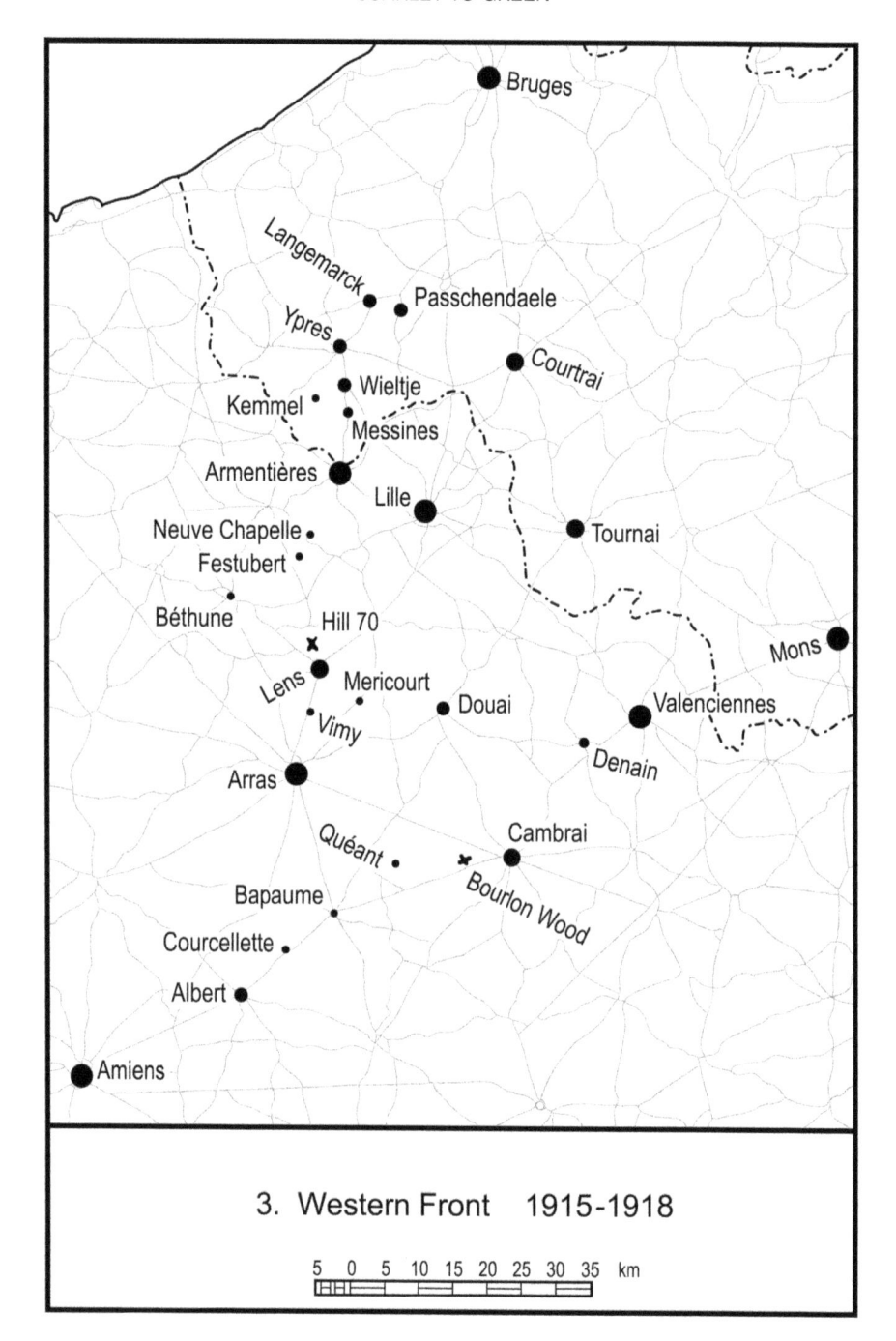

pleasure several times to visit Valcartier and also to be present at what is perhaps no longer a secret, the embarkation of Canadian troops . . ." The Prime Minister was reported to have said on the same occasion: "You . . . may be assured that the expeditionary force which has just embarked . . ." It was claimed later that these statements were intended as deception. But the fact that they were made during the operation itself suggests that they were, in fact, errors of judgement.

On September 29th, the War Office, which always enciphered its important cables, asked for details of personnel, horses, and material in each transport. On October 2nd, the Minister for Militia advised that the list was so long that it would be sent in clear. The War Office immediately replied: "On no account must the details . . . be cabled in clear." Sam Hughes answered: "Your telegram . . . received too late." When the War Office again demanded that all such information be enciphered, the C.G.S. cabled: "Embarkation return in clear unlikely to do harm because names of transport and strength of contingent had already been published. This return is very inaccurate but if I can obtain corrected figures I will cable them." The Germans apparently misread the destination of the force, for a letter from Grand Admiral von Tirpitz, dated October 8th, stated that 20,000 Canadians were then in Le Havre. To guard against accidents, the Royal Navy sent the battleship *Majestic* and the battle cruiser *Prince Royal* to meet the convoy. Not even Rear-Admiral R.E. Wemyss, the escort commander, was told that they were on their way.[1]

The Canadians initially found little information on which to base a training program for their intelligence elements. The British were fighting the First Battle of Ypres and were too preoccupied to pass on their experience. The Canadians therefore followed their own initiative. Intelligence was a part of Operations on the divisional staff; First Division added a G.S.O.3 and an interpreter to be responsible for intelligence organization and functions. An intelligence officer and an interpreter were appointed to each brigade. These variations from the British structure proved to be most advantageous. Later, in 1915, infantry battalions were also given an extra officer to look after intelligence, but no fixed unit personnel establishment was ever slavishly followed.

Between the 11th and 15th of February, 1915, First Division, under General Alderson, crossed to France and went into reserve. While in reserve, and after it had moved into the line with the British Second Army between Neuve Chapelle and Armentières, its intelligence organization was attached to, and received instruction from, its British counterparts. It was thus able to learn techniques before being required to perform its duties. Units in the line reported to Brigade, and this, in turn, to Division. These reports very soon became a routine, daily, typewritten report and, about mid-March, an Intelligence Summary was produced in First Canadian Division. Sir Arthur Currie claimed that this "was about the first instance of the issue of a regular, daily Intelligence Summary from a Division in the British Army at that time".[2] Its information

Searching P.W. after Arleux, April 1917; sandbags for documents and personal papers. (Canada. Dept. of National Defence/Library and Archives Canada, PA-001210)

"Tactical squeeze", probably in reserve trenches, Hill 70, August 1917. The carnival atmosphere obvious here is rarely conducive to a profitable interrogation. (Canada. Dept. of National Defence/Library and Archives Canada, PA-001743)

contained all known enemy information, including translations from enemy documents. The "outside" organization of the Corps H.Q. Section consisted of a small pool of observers, who manned the occasional Corps observation posts, and passed information directly to the Division concerned.

As 1915 ended, the Canadians replaced the casual daylight trench raids of the early days of the war with organized night raids. Raiders would quietly cut the enemy wire, pounce on the trench behind it, kill or capture all enemy soldiers who could be reached, pick up all the documents they could find, destroy any installations, and then withdraw as quickly as possible. These raids gained information "concerning the enemy's trenches, dispositions and *moral* [morale], and the confidence and steadiness of his troops [were] greatly undermined".[7] In 1916, this night technique was replaced by the large formal daylight raid.

In late 1915, and in 1916, both sides turned to the medieval practice of mining, or sapping. A tunnel was driven under a trench, explosives were planted and detonated, and a force was sent in to occupy the resultant crater. In watching for enemy mining, Intelligence concentrated on reports from prisoners and on the external and visible signs – shoring material being brought up, material from excavations being removed. The miners in the tunnels listened carefully for any indication that the enemy was himself at work. Success was not at all one sided. A British attack near St. Eloi on April 3rd, 1916, launched to support a blown mine, failed when "careless conversation on a British field telephone, loose talk in neighbouring towns and villages, and telltale subterranean noises" were detected by the enemy, who withdrew before the explosion.[8]

The German attacks on Mount Sorrel, in June 1916, enjoyed some initial success due, in part at least, to an Allied Intelligence failure. Some weeks before the assault, air reconnaissance had spotted the practice trenches used to train the German troops. There was unusual activity by the German heavy mortars, artillery, kite balloons, and aircraft, which normally would have indicated preparations for an attack. However, the fact that the enemy did not move forward the usual large body of infantry reinforcements, combined with the bad weather that made air observation difficult, misled the Canadians as to the actual time and place of the assault. When the battle began, the intense German fire hampered both Artillery and Intelligence; their forward observers became casualties and their telephone lines were destroyed.

The Battle of Courcellette, which began on September 15th, 1916, gives an excellent example of co-operation between Intelligence (a) and (b). The Operations Branch of the Canadian Corps wanted detailed information on the strongly fortified ruins of a sugar factory beside the Bapaume road, which covered the approach to the town, the Second Division's objective. Canadian Corps Intelligence asked Intelligence at Fifth Army to find refugees from Courcellette. Two N.C.O.s (one a Canadian, Sgt. Jungbluth) were sent out. Within two days they found several people, including a former night watchman at the

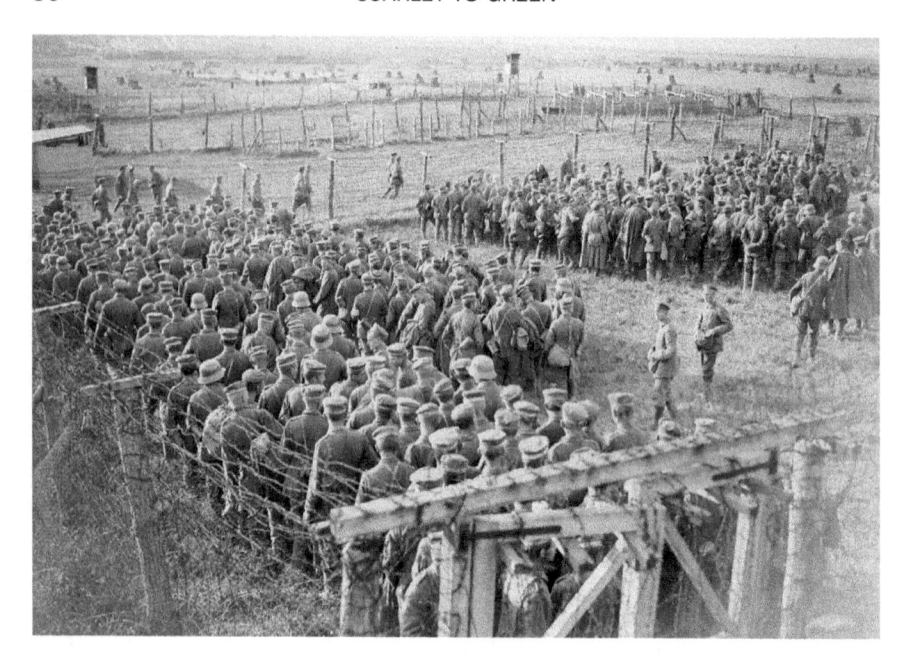

Reception and grouping, German P.W. in Corps Cage after Arras, August 1918. (Canada. Dept. of National Defence/Library and Archives Canada, PA-003035)

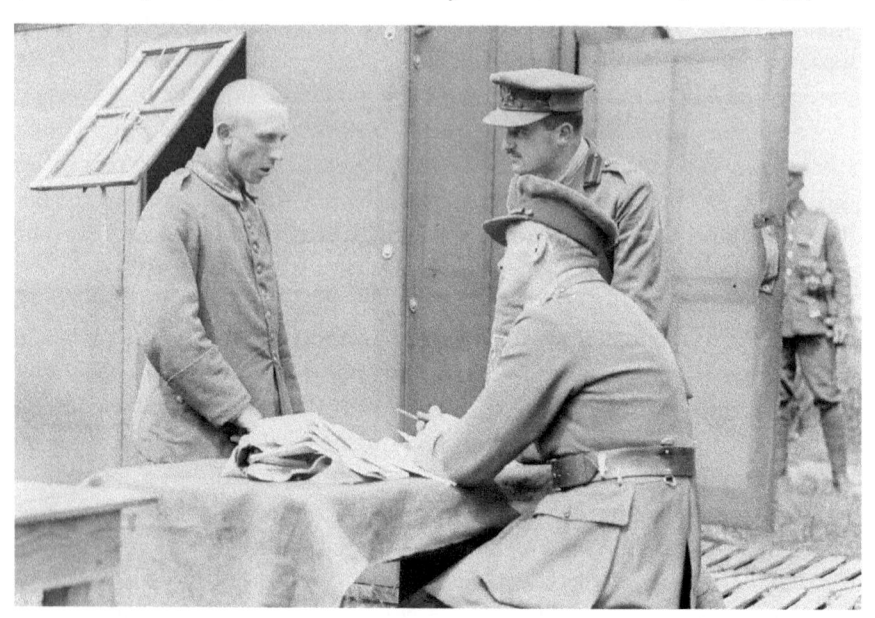

Capt. C.W. Erlebach, Corps of Guides, interrogating a German P.W. near Canal du Nord, September 1918. The Intelligence Staff Officer with him is unidentified. (Canada. Dept. of National Defence/Library and Archives Canada, PA-002433)

sugar factory who knew all about the buildings and even had picture postcards of the factory and the village.[9] The information was passed on at once. Zero hour was 0620; Fourth Brigade was on its objectives by 0700, and its 21st Battalion took 145 prisoners out of the factory. The Division needed two more days to consolidate its occupation of Courcellette but, without the information, the initial attack would have been much more costly.

Planning for the 1917 spring offensive gave the Canadians the task of capturing Vimy Ridge in order to form a strong defensive flank for Third Army. The attack was carefully prepared. Every enemy position was meticulously located and its activity recorded. All intelligence staffs were closely integrated under Lt.-Col. J.L.R. Parsons, C. of G., and close contact with all arms and staffs was established. A full-scale replica, based on air photos, was made of the battle area, kept up-to-date, and used by the troops to rehearse their roles. The only information about the attack that was kept secret was its timing.

In October, after the summer battles of Hill 70 and Lens, Third Division planned an attack against Mericourt. Its preparations were aided by the capture at Hill 70 of a large-scale map of the enemy defences. Prisoners were carefully interrogated and all other sources of information were intensively exploited. The Divisional Intelligence staff prepared a detailed model on a scale of 1:50, with all the contours and natural features of the area, the state of repair of the village buildings, the trenches, and the wire. It was too detailed, and was finished only just in time. The operation, however, was cancelled at the last minute and the information was never put to the test.[10]

The Canadian Corps was transferred to Second British Army on October 12th, 1917. Third Division was ordered to take Bellevue Spur, one of the approaches to Passchendaele Ridge. The G.S.O.2 (Int), Canadian Corps H.Q., went immediately to II ANZAC Corps to obtain records of the enemy defences and organization. The divisional intelligence staffs made a reconnaissance of the battle area, and obtained maps and Intelligence Summaries from the Australian divisions in the line. Detailed logs and files were prepared and passed to the units on October 17th. As soon as they were available, air photos and mosaics were reproduced and issued, in some cases right down to infantry companies and artillery batteries. One officer and six observers from each brigade of Third Division went forward to Wieltje and, on the 18th, the G.S.O.2 (Int), Third Division, was attached to H.Q. New Zealand Division where he could receive reports direct from his observers.

A report on the assault preparations, however, written shortly afterwards, contained a number of criticisms which showed that, although much had been done, many lessons were still to be learned. The existing system that required maps to be supplied to the divisions from Army was too slow. Corps was better able to assess their needs. To enable it to supply these, Corps asked for a light truck ("box car" was the term then used) and a small lithographic press for printing maps and overlays. Air photos were valuable, but conditions could preclude coverage as frequently as was desirable. Prisoner-of-war Cages were too far back and, in many cases, the traffic and muddy roads caused excessive delays in obtaining prisoners for interrogation. And a common complaint was repeated: the troops were keeping documents as personal souvenirs.[11]

The great German offensive of March 1918 was halted on the Marne in late July. Foch, by then Commander-in-Chief, issued a formal order for an offensive in the Amiens area. The Canadians were to form part of this attack. To do so, they had to move south from First Army to their new area without revealing their movements. Radio silence was imposed. Strict instructions, beginning with the words "KEEP YOUR MOUTH SHUT", cautioned troops against revealing anything more than name or rank if captured. Obvious preparations for a local attack in their former sector continued, while reconnaissance of their new front was restricted and carefully concealed. The Canadian Mounted Rifles and the 27th Battalion, together with all the Corps wireless and hospitals, were placed in the north, near Kemmel, where they ostentatiously set up and transmitted a flow of false radio traffic. The enemy located these units, but apparently did not draw the desired conclusion that an attack was scheduled for the area they occupied. The German High Command foresaw the probability of an attack on August 4th, but considered that either the British Third or Fourth Army sectors were more likely to be the new Canadian location.[12]

The actual move of the Corps on July 30th took place under cover of intense security. Even the senior administrative officer was not told of it until the 29th. Fourth Army ordered all movement in both front and rear areas to take place at night, while false deployments were made in daylight to the accompaniment of much radio traffic, noise, dust, and bustle. Rumour and fictitious orders "moved" the troops to Ypres. Col. Nicholson, critical of the need for such a tight security screen, cites a Canadian brigade commander who protested the delay in planning caused by the security measures and who suggested that officers who could not keep a secret were unfit to command.[13] His protest was naive; officers often talk "shop" injudiciously, and they often possess valuable information. The danger from compromise was so great that protection was mandatory. Of course, security was not the sole or even the major reason for the success of this battle. Bad weather prevented German reconnaissance aircraft from flying over the Canadian rear areas; heavy aircraft were flown over the lines to cover the noise of the assembling Allied tanks; an early morning mist blanketed the battle area; there was no lengthy pre-assault bombardment. But security played an important role in making Amiens "the finest operation of the War."

Documents captured during the battle brought home to Intelligence the fact that the earlier assessments of German capabilities were too high. German battalions were under-strength, and desperate measures had had to be introduced to keep adequate forces in the field. The spring defeat had shaken their belief in

German invincibility. There were many reports of a breakdown in morale. But German troops in the line still fought on, although seldom as bitterly as before.

The Canadians returned to First Army and to the battles that ended the summer, the Scarpe, the Drocourt-Quéant line, Canal du Nord, Bourlon Wood, and Cambrai. At the Canal du Nord, Canadian patrols reported an important tactical feature as being unoccupied. Unfortunately, the map reference was given incorrectly and reconnaissance parties sent to follow up the report suffered casualties.[14] On October 1st, the battle before Cambrai was bitter as the enemy put in his last available reserves. As far as Intelligence was concerned, the subsequent advance through Valenciennes to Mons was uneventful. By November 3rd, the enemy had withdrawn behind the Aurelle River, the border between France and Belgium, and indications were received that he intended to make a stand there.

By the end of 1918, the Intelligence organization had become an efficient and successful system. Its chief architect was a Corps of Guides officer, Lt.-Col. Charles Hamilton Mitchell. In 1914, as a major, he was a G.S.O.3 on the staff of H.Q. First Division. When the Canadian Corps was formed in August 1915, Col. Mitchell was sent to its H.Q. as G.S.O.2 (Int), the senior Intelligence appointment in the C.E.F. He therefore became involved from the very beginning in establishing a Corps Intelligence organization. He had no Canadian precedent to guide him, although he could call on his experience in First Division and on the considerable help he received from his British counterparts.

In September 1916, Col. Mitchell was asked to head the Intelligence Branch of H.Q. Second Army. When its G.O.C., General Plumer, went to Italy in charge of the British division sent to bolster the Italian defences after Caporetto, he took Lt.-Col. Mitchell with him. It is interesting to note that the historian Cruttwell states that "Plumer . . . was the most uniformly successful of all the British army commanders. He chose his staff admirably."[15] Col. Mitchell made a hurried trip to the War Office to collect information and equipment to take with him. He then had to find interpreters for each of the nine different languages and dialects spoken in the Austrian Army. Col. Mitchell was promoted Brig.-Gen. in October 1918 and returned to the Canadian forces in June 1919. His decorations included the C.B., the C.M.G., the D.S.O., seven Mentioned-in-Despatches, Officer of the Legion of Honour (France), Officer of the Order of Leopold (Belgium), Croix de Guerre (Belgium, Italy), and Officer of the Order of the Crown of Italy.[16]

Col. Mitchell's replacement was Lt.-Col. J.L.R. Parsons, also C. of G. Building on Mitchell's foundations, Lt.-Col. Parsons and his successors improved the procedures and made sure that they were implemented throughout the C.E.F. At the same time, we must emphasize that, although these procedures were generally applied, local commanders and their staffs often made modifications.

Brig.-Gen. C.H. Mitchell, C.B., C.M.G., D.S.O., Corps of Guides, when he was a Capt. on the Cavalry Field Officers Course, Stanley Barracks, Toronto, January 1911. (Lawrence Hurt Sitwell/Library and Archives Canada, PA-111942)

By January 1918, infantry battalions had an establishment of one I.O., one scout officer, a minimum of eight observers, eight battalion scouts (there were to be others in the companies), eight snipers, and one photo reader draftsman. The I.O. was responsible for all aspects of intelligence within the battalion, for liaison with Artillery, training and employment of observers, and the compiling of the battalion Intelligence Summary, based on reports from observation posts, the scout officer, patrols and sentries, and on reports of hostile bombing, mortaring and shelling. He distributed the information received from higher H.Q. The photo reader/draftsman received a two-week course, normally given at Divisional H.Q. by an expert loaned from Corps. Initially he had no stereoscope and was expected to achieve stereovision – the three-dimensional result essential to the full use of air photos – with the naked eye.[17] This is possible, but it is difficult and takes much practice. Eventually the Baird stereoscope was issued, but rarely below Divisional H.Q. Perhaps because it was rare for the battalion to get more than a set of individual prints, these instruments were not generally issued.

Early in the war a system of trench logs was devised to systematize the reporting of information. Each unit, using the map squares covering the enemy positions opposite its location, recorded in the log every activity that could be observed. These were passed on initially to relieving units, but experience demonstrated it was better for them to be controlled centrally at Division. Units then passed information back to Division, which added its own information and returned its confirmed identifications. Divisions also passed all major new enemy positions to Corps, which verified them and allocated a "target number," and then sent them back to Division. In this way common identification was possible. From time to time Corps also issued its own map summarizing the confirmed targets. Subsequently both log and map were issued together to ensure that all units would use similar maps with common references. A divisional intelligence file was devised in order to co-ordinate information at that level and to offer a complete résumé of enemy defences and dispositions. It contained a copy of the corps log; corps log map; map of enemy dispositions; map of no-man's-land; and map of enemy wire and trench mortar positions; together with specialist maps, as required, of the local area, i.e., town water systems, etc.[18] The procedure was fully operational by the time of Passchendaele, where it proved to be of much value.

Each Brigade H.Q. had one Staff Captain (Intelligence), 12 observers, one air photo clerk, two draftsmen, and one clerk. The Staff Captain generally worked directly for the G.O.C., advising the Brigade Major (B.M.) of his activities. In a few cases he worked directly for the B.M., receiving the G.O.C.'s instructions second-hand, and passing his information through the B.M. Under his direction, the observers were responsible for reconnoitring the enemy front, support, reserve, and rear defence areas. Brigade Observation Posts (O.P.s) were set up as required. Scouts and observers were drawn from units in the Brigade and, when opportunity permitted, they were trained with men from the battalions on Brigade-run courses. Towards the end of the war, two Brigade observers were also employed at Division to obtain unit identifications from prisoners. German-speaking staff were earnestly sought and, when a sufficient number had been found, were given a short course, generally lasting two weeks, on German Army organization, uniforms, documents, and similar aids to identification. The air photo clerk was responsible for reading photos, distributing prints to the battalions and maintaining a complete file at Brigade. The two draftsmen were responsible for marking and updating the maps used by the Commander and Brigade staff. In addition, they had to obtain, store, issue, and account for the maps used by the Brigade. Intelligence maps included a general map of enemy defences on the Brigade front; an enemy disposition map of the area opposite the Brigade sector; wire maps, showing the location, number of belts, and type of both enemy and Allied wire, together with information on no-man's-land; and an artillery brigade zone map, which included artillery O.P.s, and locations and fields of vision of all O.P.s. The Staff Captain maintained close liaison with all supporting arms and units and passed reports of activities within his Brigade sector to the units and to Division.[19]

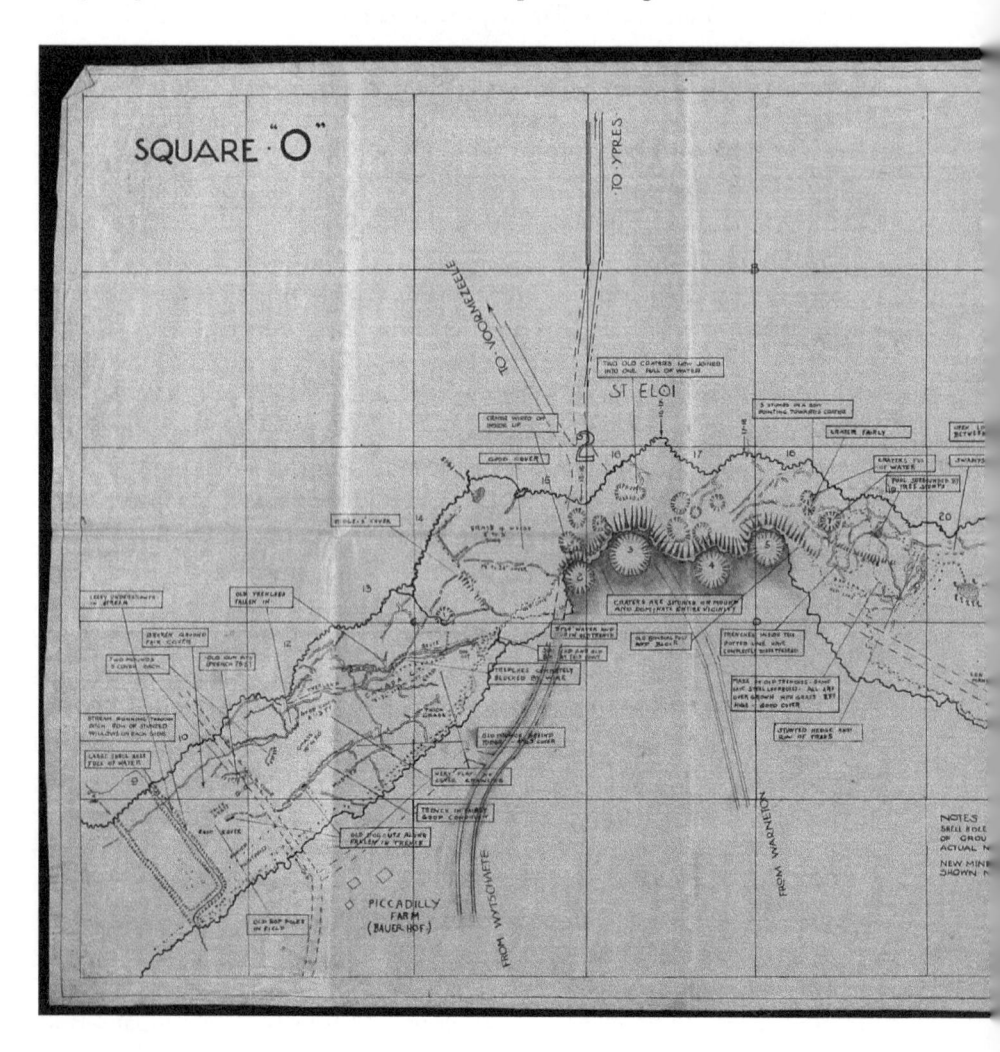

Divisional H.Q. had a G.S.O.2, one G.S.O.3, one attached I.O., three draftsmen, one air photo clerk, and two clerks. The G.S.O.2 supervised all intelligence policy and duties within the Division. He was responsible for liaison between the supporting arms and the infantry, down to battalion level. At the brigade level, the detailed work was done by the Staff Captain (Intelligence). His counterpart in artillery was the Divisional Reconnaissance Officer on the staff of the Commander, Royal Artillery, at Divisional H.Q. Intelligence was responsible for giving him all available information on possible targets. The G.S.O.3 was responsible for O.P.s, and for supervision of the brigade and battalion intelligence sections. The attached I.O. was an expert on the German Army, specially trained by the British. He examined prisoners and captured documents, and he maintained the log, air photo, map, and Intelligence Summary files.

Corps provided maps in four scales: 1:100,000; 1:40,000; 1:20,000 and 1:10,000. One map, kept for a week at a time, was used to record hostile shelling; a different colour was used for each calibre of gun; concentrations of fire could indicate the areas the enemy intended to soften up, and information

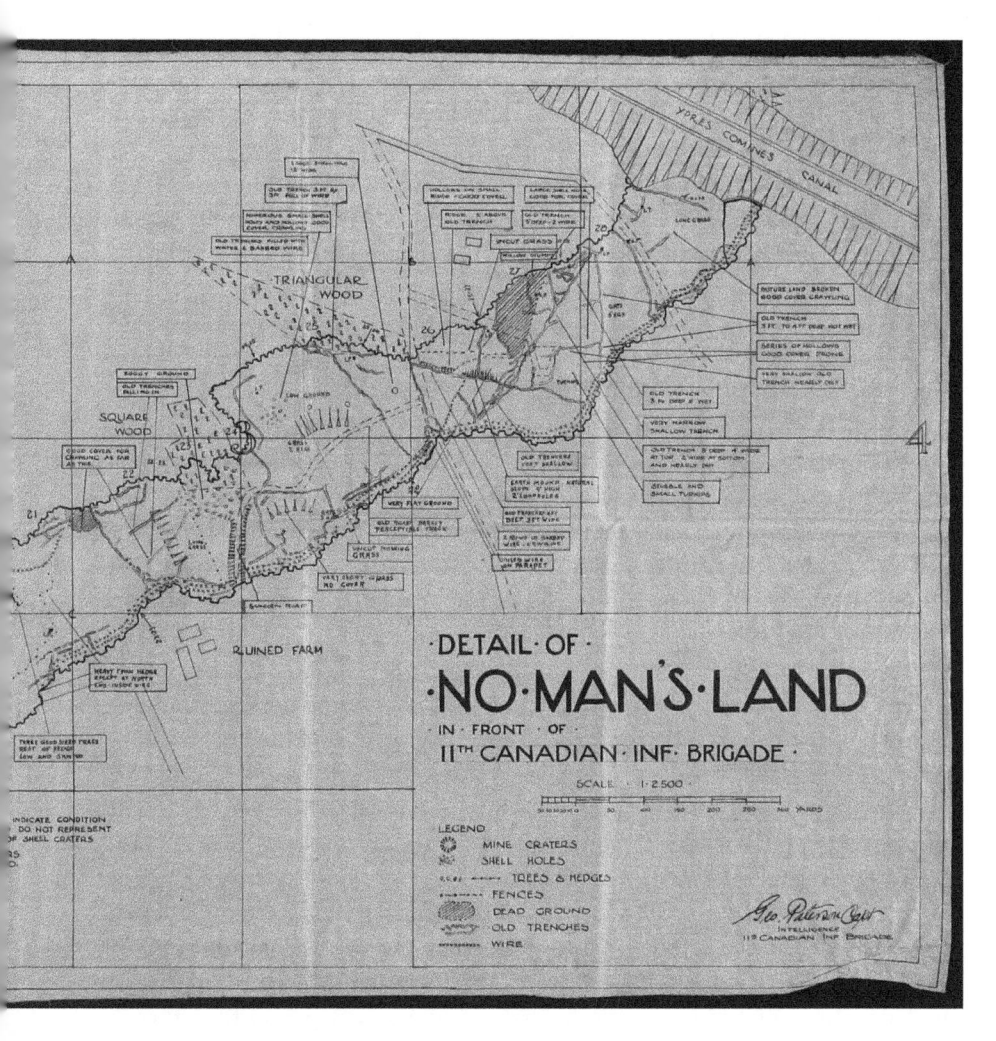

Detailed map of no-man's-land in front of 11th Canadian Infantry Brigade, produced by the Intelligence Section. Shows mine craters, shell holes, wire and trenches around St. Eloi and the Ypres Comines Canal in West Flanders region, Belgium, possibly 1916. (Library and Archives Canada, MIKAN 178369)

on the sources of that fire was passed to the counter-battery staffs for retaliation planning. A similar map was kept to show enemy mortar action. A third map covered enemy defence construction; it was dated and covered with tracing paper to enable comparisons to be made as the work progressed. So that harassing gunfire could be planned, another map, compiled from air photos and observer reports, showed enemy routes and centres of activity. A map of enemy dispositions, mainly compiled from prisoner interrogations at Corps, enabled an assessment to be made of enemy strength, the location of his strong points, and the time it would take him to move his reserves. A map of no-man's-land was maintained, showing the wire in front of each line, including gaps, types, and the number of belts, and the location of enemy advanced, listening, or observation posts. Finally, another map showed the raid activity of both sides; it enabled the Operations staff to ensure that Canadian raids did not either develop a dangerous, routine pattern or ignore any vulnerable part of the enemy line. It also helped Intelligence identify any stereotyping of the enemy raid activity and any undue interest he might show in some sector of friendly positions. Divisional Summaries were passed to the two flanking formations as well as to units that could be affected within the Division.[20]

The whole purpose of this complex series of maps and files was to ensure that every scrap of information about the enemy was recorded and placed in context. Armies operate according to patterns which, with experience, become familiar, understandable, and, within limits, predictable. Any deviation from a routine generally indicates that some change in activity is being prepared. The problem is to determine what that change is likely to be and where and how it is likely to occur. The relatively static nature of the First World War meant that changes generally took place slowly; therefore care could be taken to build up the large picture from the many small pieces of information gathered. Most of this information was shallow, derived from visual observation or, at best, from artillery range-finding techniques based on simple listening devices, on flash-spotting, and on shell-burst analysis. Deeper coverage depended on facilities that existed only at Corps and above, such as aerial reconnaissance and agents.

One of the most profitable sources of information was the interrogation of prisoners. Units would ask a few quick questions to clarify immediate uncertainties, and then send the prisoner back to Division where the attached I.O. might try to get a little more detail for use within the Divisional sector. He could then be sent back to Corps for still further interrogation if such action seemed warranted. In active operations, when prisoners were captured in hundreds, the Corps staff of I.O.s was augmented. They would separate the officers, N.C.O.s, and machine-gunners into groups, select those who appeared to be the most intelligent, and send them for interrogation. The remainder would be formed into small squads and sent to the rear. All their belongings were put into sandbags, tagged to show the man's name and the date and place of his capture.

Air photo of trench systems (place unknown) taken by a R.F.C. reconnaissance aircraft, 16 May 1918. (E.N. Jungbluth photo collection/Canadian Forces School of Military Intelligence, Kingston/Canada. Dept. of National Defence)

German soldiers had an almost universal habit of keeping personal diaries filled with details of places they had visited, of friends in other regiments, of where, when, and how long they had stayed in rest billets. Letters often gave valuable information about their units. N.C.O.s often carried battalion orders and, on at least one occasion, a man carried an order stating that his regiment was to be relieved by another at a stated time and by a specific route. Collecting and checking these papers was obviously vitally important, and this accounts for the disapproval of the actions of souvenir-hunters. When time permitted, the documents were screened at Corps, then translated and forwarded to Army. Those of less immediate interest were forwarded directly to Army where there was a larger interpreter staff. When anything interesting was found, the prisoner was called before the I.O. for questioning.[21]

Prisoners generally remained in a state of shock for some time after their capture. It was then that they could be questioned profitably. On at least one occasion, when information was needed quickly, an interrogation was actually carried out by telephone so that the prisoner could be questioned before his shock had worn off. He usually became much more conscious of the value of silence after he had been given food and a cigarette. The intelligence staffs were annoyed by "unofficial" interrogations, mainly because they "spoilt" the prisoner for later questioning.

Some P.W. were "difficult", and, in order to get them to talk, "pigeons" were sometimes put into their Cages. These were usually other captured soldiers who had a grudge against the German Army or, on occasion, our own Allied interpreters. The "pigeon", who had to know German dialects and army routine perfectly, would get the prisoner talking. The conversation would be picked up by a microphone linked to a receiver at which a clerk sat to record it. Officer behaviour varied greatly. Some were arrogant and refused to talk to N.C.O.s. These were usually put into a room with other officers so that their conversations could also be picked up by microphone. Late in 1918, German prisoners gave information willingly, but I.O.s still had to be on guard against a "deserter" primed with false information. The Germans, of course, were aware of these leakages, and towards the end of the war tried to counter them by warnings that the Allies were especially brutal to prisoners falling into their hands.[22]

Aircraft, and particularly kite balloons, were the major source of visual and photographic information. The slow, vulnerable, two-seater aircraft used for artillery spotting, visual reconnaissance, and aerial photography, were formed in groups of R.A.F. squadrons. Initially two squadrons formed a wing, which was allotted to an army. On January 30th, 1916, the R.F.C. strength in the field was doubled. The wings were then grouped in pairs to form a brigade, with one wing in support of a corps and the other of an army. By mid-1916, a kite-balloon section and an aircraft replacement park had been added to the original two wings. By 1918, R.F.C. H.Q. had a wing of its own, and each corps had its reconnaissance /artillery observation squadron. The Army wings were made up of fighter (scout) squadrons, day and night-bombing squadrons, a kite-balloon wing, and an aircraft park.[23]

In January 1917, Branch Intelligence Sections were formed in the Corps squadrons to act as a link between Corps and the pilots and observers. The Section was responsible for interpreting the air photos, and for collating all items of information brought back by the crews. It comprised one I.O. (British), two draftsmen from the Engineer Field Survey Company, a clerk, and an orderly. The I.O. lived at the airfield and was linked by telephone to Corps H.Q.[24]

During the summer of 1915, the Canadians discovered that the pipelines and water channels which ran from their lines to the enemy could act as carriers for the electrical impulses emitted by the field telephones then in use. A simple amplifier made it possible for an enemy to listen to conversations. Until this time there had been no apparent need to use ciphers, guarded conversation, or speech-privacy equipment. The unexpected discovery prompted the British to introduce such things as twisted cable, code names, and position calls for units and signal offices, and, in addition, led to the establishment of listening posts that were of obvious value to Intelligence. The first listening sets, a British adaptation of a French invention, came into use after February, 1916.[25] By that summer:

> it had been found [by] our spark stations that the Germans were sending a large part of their traffic in clear or . . . a very simple figure code which could easily be deciphered. On August 15th an Interception Station was erected near the Advance Corps Headquarters at Demuin . . . in operation until August 21st . . . an average of thirty messages per day were taken. All German priority messages were sent by wire direct to Intelligence "E" Fourth Army. Ordinary traffic was . . . forwarded by despatch rider three times a day. This station also proved of value to the Canadian Corps Staff since copies of all messages received were immediately delivered to them. The interception activities of the Canadian Corps were not . . . a duplication of the . . . Army Intelligence Corps. The number of [Army interception] stations . . . was limited and [it was] therefore impossible for them to intercept all the traffic going through in clear. In addition much of the information would have been valueless unless delivered to the Corps staff as soon as received.[26]

The Canadian Corps also had Topographical Sections and Intelligence Observation Sections whose main role was flash-spotting and accurate siting of battery positions. Although their titles would suggest an Intelligence connection, the units were actually Artillery. They worked closely with the intelligence staffs, and information was regularly exchanged between the Counter-Battery Officer and the Intelligence Branch. In early 1918, the two were combined, renamed the Canadian Corps Survey Section, given a drafting staff (one officer and 26 men) and relocated at Corps H.Q. When they were made responsible for the reproduction and distribution of maps throughout the Corps, they relieved the Intelligence Branch of one of its roles. Five men in the Section worked with the Branch I.O. to interpret topographical information provided by air photos.[27]

Although the systems were not as sophisticated as they are today, they exploited the same major specialized information-gathering agencies that the Canadian Army was to develop much further in the Second World War. The principles that were developed between 1914 and 1919 have remained relatively unchanged. In 1939, however, the techniques and the organizations using them were improved almost beyond the imagination of C.E.F. I(a) staffs.

COUNTER-INTELLIGENCE

The story of Counter-Intelligence (C.I.) within the Canadian Corps during the First World War is far less well documented than that of I(a). The C.I. element of the three divisions of Intelligence at the War Office was small (one source says about 14 men), but it was very efficient. It broke the German espionage network in the United Kingdom so thoroughly, by arresting all but one of its members within 24 hours of the outbreak of war, that subsequent attempts to rebuild the operation were largely unsuccessful.[28] But C.I. was not sure that it had eliminated all enemy agents when the First Canadian Contingent arrived overseas. There were suspicions that subversive elements, enlisted in Canada, had come to Britain in the C.E.F. A small number of aliens who had enrolled, but who had not been identified, were indeed removed by the Divisional Intelligence staff, assisted by the C.I. staff of the War Office and the Canadian Military Police.

In 1914, Capt. (Bvt.-Maj.) W.M. St. G. Kirke, R.G.A. (later General, K.C.B., C.M.G., D.S.O.), a G.S.O.3 in Operations and Intelligence at the War Office, was ordered to raise an Intelligence Section in the British Army. Applicants had to have a knowledge of French or German, be able to drive a motorcycle or car, or to remain on a horse for "a reasonable length of time". Their early duties in 1914 included acting as interpreters for the cavalry, organizing civilian work parties, obtaining food for the retreating infantry, blowing up bridges with the Engineers, occasionally interrogating a prisoner or translating claims for damages from French or Flemish peasants. When the front stabilized, the Section, now called Intelligence (b), was given the task of patrolling the rear areas to watch for suspects and possible enemy agents recruited among the French or Belgian civilian population or disguised as British soldiers.

On September 4th, 1915, Second Army asked II and V Corps for six men who would form, at Army H.Q., the nucleus of a "corps of Intelligence police within the army", similar to the Section formed by Capt. Kirke. They were to be junior N.C.O.s or private soldiers, able to speak French fluently, of good character, reliable and energetic, with experience of life in the ranks, service of at least three months in France, and experience of the conditions in the trenches and the immediate rear areas. It was suggested that men from the Canadian division would be more likely to be of use than those from other units.[29]

The N.C.O.s and men were grouped into detachments commanded by an officer and attached to the corps and armies. When on duty in the forward areas, they wore a dark blue armband, or brassard, with the letters "I.P." (Intelligence Police) on it in light green. In 1918, the letters became "I.C.", for Intelligence Corps. All I.P. carried a special *laisser passer*, valid for 12 months and countersigned monthly by the officer in charge. Later they were given documents authorizing them to examine the papers and effects of soldiers, civilians, prisoners, and Allied and enemy dead, and to "take necessary action as instructed". They usually wore the badges of the Engineers, sometimes Army Service Corps, occasionally General Staff; but in 1918, when the Royal Fusiliers took over their administration, they changed to the badges of that regiment. They could circulate freely at all hours, day or night, could ask for assistance or transport, and were not to be interfered with in the course of their duties. With them were French Intelligence and Scotland Yard members.

Because the I.P. were controlled by Army H.Q. rather than by Corps or Division, they tended to stay in one area long enough to become very familiar with it. Strangers to the area could be readily identified and had to give a valid reason for their presence "or it was just too bad". Larger towns, like Amiens, had a permanent staff which built up a large index of the regular inhabitants. When a visiting statesman was shown this particular index, then totalling some 20,000 cards, he is said to have misunderstood its purpose and to have asked in horror "Good Lord, were they all shot?"

If an attack was planned, the I.P. advanced to the forward area, placed themselves at strategic points on main roads or near villages, and entered towns as soon as the attacking units had taken them. Before September 1917, there were few civilians left in these towns, but as the war went on, and especially after the crossing of the Canal du Nord, I.P. had their hands increasingly full of suspects. They also checked trains, ammunition dumps, and airfields and watched for booby-traps and poisoned wells. During the German push of March 1918, the I.P. had to work in reverse, evacuating civilians to Amiens, trying to move them on side routes to keep the main roads clear for military traffic and, at the same time, keep them away from Allied dispositions.

Enemy agents had a great deal of difficulty getting messages back to their controls. Radio was not yet compact enough to be practical; carrier pigeons, though used, were an obvious target for suspicion. Messages therefore had to be physically carried through the lines, and ingenious tricks of concealment had to be devised. Messages were carried in glass eyes, wooden legs, cigars, cigarettes, or pipes. One Belgian agent had a special pipe which could be lit without burning the message hidden in it, but which, if turned a certain way, would ignite the paper. Chemically impregnated soft collars, socks, or shoelaces were carried in luggage; when these articles were soaked in water they provided invisible inks. Vials of inks were also found in talcum powder tins, hollow soap cakes, ointment, patent medicines, and toothpaste. Many codes were of the dictionary or stencil type that required a prearranged key before they could be deciphered. Code messages were passed in dots and dashes embroidered on Belgian lace, in pincushions having pins set in a certain order, in microscopic writing under stamps, or by placing the stamps on an envelope in specific positions. They were hidden in sheet music and newspaper advertisements which were then sent on through neutrals, and in toy balloons. There were also "silent transmitters", Belgian windmills whose sails would be set and moved to order, fields plowed in odd patterns, or washing hung to preset patterns on a line.

Until August 1918, the Canadian Corps had been assigned I.P. by the army to which it was attached. During that summer, all the Canadian soldiers on these duties in the different British armies were recalled to form a new Intelligence (b) or Counter-Espionage Section on the Canadian Corps H.Q. establishment.[30] The Section, about 20 men and a captain, came under the D.A.A.G. at Corps for administration, and under Intelligence for duty. It contained the best-trained men, some of whom spoke six or seven languages or

A member of the Canadian Corps Cyclist Battalion, Sgt. E.N. Jungbluth, on left, shown in Bapaume 1918, was assigned to Field Security/ C.I. where he put his fluency in German and French to good use, earning him the Distinguished Conduct Medal and Belgium's Croix de Guerre. The W.O.I on right from 2 Canadian Division Cyclist Company is unidentified. (Hal Skaarup/E.N. Jungbluth photo collection, Canadian Forces School of Military Intelligence, Kingston)

dialects fluently. These keen and well-disciplined men soon made a reputation for themselves. During the advance around Denain and in the Valenciennes sector, they identified over two hundred suspects, and arrested many of them and turned them over to the French.

In Belgium, through which the Canadians passed en route to Germany after the Armistice, C.I. was left mostly to the British I.P. However, during the period when it operated with the Army of Occupation on the Rhine, the Canadian Counter-Espionage Section kept a close watch on German suspects; in general, it found little of concern.[31]

Canadian participation in other theatres of war was not extensive and required little or no intelligence input; but, just before the Armistice, two battalions of 16th Brigade were assigned to form the Canadian Siberian Expeditionary Force (C.S.E.F.). The Brigade I.O. was Maj. J.F. Adams, 14 Cdn. Bn. All tactical and situation maps and intelligence summaries were provided by the British, who also sent a weekly report to Ottawa on activities on all the Russian fronts. The maps supplied by the War Office were of the Russian pattern, measured in versts.* They lacked grids, and Intelligence had to apply unofficial ones before

---

* A verst is 3,500 feet; the maps were copies of the Russian 1 inch to 10, 25, and 40 verst scale issues which would have provided the unusual equivalents of 1:35,000, 1:87,500, and 1:170,000.

they could be used. Interpreters for Japanese, Chinese, Italian, French, Czech, and Russian were employed, but many were liaison rather than intelligence officers. There was little combat activity in the theatre and thus little intelligence work to be done. There were many reports of espionage, which was to be expected given the confused political situation, but no mention is made of Canadian involvement in C.I., which seems to have been the responsibility of Force H.Q. The C.S.E.F. was withdrawn in 1919.

CANADA – CONTROL OF INFORMATION

Official planning for the measures that would have to be adopted in the event of war had started in 1908. Maj.-Gen. Sir William Otter had recommended then that an Interdepartmental Committee be formed to discuss matters of mutual interest to Marine and Fisheries and Militia and Defence, including specifically naval and hydrographical intelligence. The Committee was formed in 1910, the year the Department of the Naval Service was created, and enlarged in 1912. Its discussions remained at the theoretical level until the British Overseas Defence Committee sent a strong recommendation that a Canadian "War Book" should be drawn up to show the steps that would have to be taken by each government department.

An Interdepartmental Committee met in January 1914 to deal with this request. Its members were the Secretary of State for External Affairs, the Governor General's Secretary, the Deputy Minister of Militia and Defence, the Chief Commissioner of Dominion Police (representing the Minister of Justice), the Deputy Minister of the Naval Service, the Commissioner of Customs, the Deputy Postmaster-General, and the Deputy Minister of Railways and Canals. The War Book that resulted from their deliberations contained provisions for actions to be taken in what was called the "Precautionary Stage", i.e., the period when relations with any foreign power had become so strained as to cause fears of a surprise attack.

Among the measures included were control of all, and closure of some, radio stations, and the enforcement of censorship on radio and cable messages. Order-in-Council P.C. 1836, issued May 20th, 1914, vested authority for control of radio stations in the Minister of the Naval Service.

On July 29th, the Secretary of State for the Colonies advised the members of the Committee that he had ordered the imposition of the Precautionary Stage. On August 2nd, Order-in-Council P.C. 2029 authorized the Minister of Militia and Defence to take possession of any cable company and to control all transmissions. At 2300 that night, the Minister despatched a telegram ordering the Officers Commanding 5th Division, Quebec, 6th Division, Halifax, and Military District No. 11, Victoria, to establish censorship control of overseas cable and radio telegraph stations. Officers were appointed to assume this function and, by August 6th, censorship staffs were installed at the five cable and eight radio stations (four on each coast) that were allowed to remain open for commercial traffic. The other 17 coastal radio stations were all closed by September 17th.

One of the first to be closed was the Newcastle, New Brunswick, station. Powerful enough to reach England, it was British-owned, but managed by an American and operated by Germans. With the exception of those working the Great Lakes, all of the 92 Canadian private radio stations were ordered to cease operations at once. The British ambassador advised Washington that two powerful stations controlled by the German government were in direct communication between the U.S. and Germany. As a result of his representations, the United States Navy Department assumed control of all American radio stations on August 8th.[32]

Control of land telephone and telegraph lines was instituted by Order-in-Council P.C. 2409 issued on September 20th, 1914. Authority was given to the Minister of Justice in January 1915, and transferred 11 months later to the Secretary of State for External Affairs.

Press Censorship came under the control of the Minister of Militia and Defence. On August 5th, 1914, the Minister, Col. Sam Hughes, appealed to the press "proprietors and their staffs alike to exercise wise reticence upon matters affecting military operations". He explained the reasons for his request and then listed the items he specifically wished to protect, "the assembling of regiments, the purchase of remounts, stores and supplies, the erecting of fortifications, etc." The story of the embarkation of the C.E.F., already narrated, shows how carelessly this control had been exercised, even at the top governmental level.

An officer was appointed and named Deputy Chief Censor, to be directly responsible for Press Censorship at Militia H.Q.; he was Lt.-Col. C.F. Hamilton, C. of G., a former war correspondent in South Africa. On August 12th, he privately reinforced the Minister's advisory note. On August 17th, he sent to all the editors of daily and weekly newspapers in Canada a third and official warning, entitled "Memorandum on the Duties of the Press in War". On November 6th, Order-in-Council P.C. 2821 provided more detailed control. Publications containing material useful to an enemy or "bearing directly or indirectly on the present war and not in accord with the facts or influencing the people of Canada or any section of them against the British cause or in favour of the enemy", were forbidden to use the mails. Under this prohibition, any person found with a copy of an offending document was just as liable to a fine as the person who had produced it.

These requests and orders did not always prevent breaches of press security. More than once the Chief Censor of the Empire at the War Office complained that stories which the British press had been refused permission to print had been published in Canada. When the incidents were investigated, the Canadian Censor discovered that, in almost every case, the story had previously appeared in some American paper. The neutral United States, of course, had no censorship.[33]

If the British practice had been followed, censorship should have been a part of Intelligence rather than the separate establishment that had been set up. In fact, there appears to have been little direct connection between the Censor and the A.D.M.I. Undoubtedly there was consultation, but the disparity in rank alone would suggest that the A.D.M.I. functioned as a consultant to the Censor rather than the other way around. In 1918, the title of "Deputy Chief Censor" was changed to "Director of Cable Censorship", and the press and cable functions were combined under Col. E.J. Chambers, C. of G., and transferred from the Militia Department to the Office of the Secretary of State.[34]

The other branch of Censorship – Postal – was the responsibility of the Deputy Postmaster-General (Chief Mail Censor), not the Militia Department. However, close links were maintained between the two departments. Postal Censorship had three aims: to prevent military information from reaching the enemy; to check the dissemination of information prejudicial to the Allies; and to acquire information for our own use. It was necessary to interfere as little as possible with the pursuit of legitimate private interests carried by the mails. But when Britain discovered that censorship could be used as a weapon of economic warfare, Canada followed her lead by stopping all commercial correspondence that could benefit the enemy. The new regulations were first applied only to correspondence with enemy nationals, but were later extended to include all mail to and from aliens.[35]

Military censorship was a unit responsibility. Officers censored their men's mail, franked it with the Unit Censorship Stamp, and forwarded it through Service channels into the civilian mail stream. The system in the field seems to have been planned and operated under British direction; Canadians played little part in its control.

CANADA – ALIENS, ESPIONAGE, AND SUBVERSION

Before the First World War, Canadian officials were concerned that a major internal threat to security might come from people living in Canada whose birth and background lay outside the boundaries of the British Empire. It seemed reasonable to believe that some non-British subjects would retain an overriding feeling of sympathy or loyalty to the country where they or their parents had been born. With the outbreak of war, measures to combat the threat they could offer had to be drawn up and implemented without delay.

In England, aliens had been the peacetime responsibility of the Home Office; when war broke out their supervision was transferred to the War Office. Canada followed the British pattern. On August 3rd, 1914, Britain advised Canada to allow German army reservists, except those suspected of espionage, to leave for home, but to detain all navy reservists. On August 7th, London asked Canada to detain all of them as prisoners of war, "in order to have the means of ensuring the proper treatment of British officers and men". Officers Commanding Districts and Divisions were asked to seek police co-operation in order to arrest German officers and reservists and to keep Austrians under surveillance.

The Department of Immigration rejected a suggestion that it prevent all aliens from leaving the country, because it felt that maintaining good relations with the United States, where most of them would go, was more important than the danger that some reservists might avoid arrest. In any case, Immigration was not geared to prevent – or to check – outward movement. On August 15th, the R.N.W.M.P. and the Dominion Police were empowered to arrest "all officers, soldiers or reservists of the two Powers who were attempting to leave Canada to assist their countries, and all subjects of these Powers who, while remaining in Canada, engaged in subversion, espionage or sabotage". Any person arrested could be freed or, more accurately, paroled, if he simply signed an undertaking that he would refrain from hostile acts and report regularly to the police.

Until the end of October 1914, all responsibility for interning aliens rested with the District Officers Commanding (D.O.C.s) each of whom had to make his own arrangements for housing and guarding them. Because this threw an additional load on H.Q., already overworked by the pressures of mobilization and reinforcement, a separate aliens organization was set up under Maj.-Gen. Sir William Otter. Registrars were appointed and aliens were ordered to report directly to them. The military, assisted by the police, were to provide such compulsion as might be necessary. On February 27th, 1915, the new organization was transferred from Militia to the Department of Justice. In the few months during which Militia had been responsible, it had established 15 internment camps, five of which remained in use until the end of the war.[36]

It is difficult to decide how much of a threat espionage posed to Canada. But, given the premise that a well-placed agent could obtain useful detail on Canadian troop movements, military production, and national morale, he could have transmitted it through a well-financed German Secret Service organization in New York. At the beginning of the war this apparatus was headed by Capts. Karl Boy-Ed, German Naval Attaché, and Franz von Papen, Military Attaché. A third officer, Capt. Franz von Rintelen, joined them in the United States in April 1915.[37] They communicated with local agents through the German consular service, through business firms, and by direct contact. The agents, who were not known to each other, sent their information to New York, and it was transmitted to Germany by radio. Because the United States was neutral, the organization could function freely, provided it did not directly violate the neutrality laws. In practice, these laws were not really enforced until after May 14th, 1915, when President Wilson directed the Secret Service to investigate violations. In August 1915, von Rintelen was decoyed out of the United States, arrested by the British, returned to New York in April 1917, and convicted, largely on evidence that came from the files of his colleague, Capt. von Papen. He was sentenced to four years in a U.S. jail. Despite setbacks, the German organization enjoyed considerable success until 1917, when the U.S. entered the war and ended its activities.[38]

German propaganda campaigns were certainly successful. German newspapers and news copy were widely distributed and often reprinted. In 1914 and 1915, many rumours of impending invasion were circulated in Canada in the hope of creating so much fear among civilians that political pressures would hold the army in Canada. Raids were "threatened" through Maine and Vermont; Germans "were drilling" in Michigan; 8,000–9,000 Germans "were marching" from Chicago and Buffalo – the number later grew to 80,000; raids against Halifax and Saint John, and others against Port Arthur, Fort William, and Winnipeg were rumoured. The populace in B.C. was especially worried by reports that German cruisers were preparing to support an invasion. Nothing came of any of these rumours and they failed in their aim of diverting troops from the C.E.F. But the Fenian raids were still a green memory in eastern Canada. District commanders, therefore, were warned "to take reasonable precautions without attracting too much attention".[39]

Sabotage was a more serious threat. To counter it, a protective service was organized under Lt.-Col. Percy Sherwood, Chief Commissioner of the Dominion Police, composed of telegraph operators, customs and immigration officers, and local police. This service reported to District H.Q.s, which had men available to support the police when needed. Military guards were used to protect public property; special police and watchmen guarded private concerns. Despite these precautions, a number of serious incidents did occur:

1914

August 8	an attempt to blow up the Montreal Light, Heat & Power works;
12	grain elevator burnt at Saint John;
16	attempted sabotage of a radio station at Sault Ste. Marie;
24	attempted bombing of the canal at Cornwall;

1915

February 12	a German reservist, Werner Horn, blew up the centre span of the C.P.R. bridge at Vanceboro, Maine (it was repaired in six hours and Horn was caught);

April 29 two separate bridges damaged by fire in Vancouver;

June 17 separate attempts to derail trains in Manitoba;

June 21 a sentry at the Windsor armouries found a suitcase containing a clock fuse and 26 sticks of dynamite;

June a bomb partially wrecked the Peabody Overall plant, Walkerville. (The German agent responsible was caught and sentenced to life imprisonment.)

Other abortive attempts included arson against crops, and bombs in the Welland Canal and the St. Clair Tunnel.[40]

In 1918, the move of the 16th Brigade to Russia involved both censorship and subversion. The war was nearly over. Some editors were less co-operative than they had been in its earlier stages. Others, who had been conscientious in obeying press restrictions, now protested that, as a consequence, they were being "scooped". In addition, a highly vocal minority of citizens protested "the iniquity of sending Canadian troops to suppress the Russian working class effort to break the chains of Tsarist tyranny and oppression". Within the Army, so-called Bolshevik sentiments did not immediately become apparent. There was some opposition to intervention, but it was not easy to separate simple war-weariness from ideologically motivated protest. For instance, two platoons of Russian-born troops, sent back from Britain to form part of the C.S.E.F., were considered to be suspect. The men were checked, a number were released from the Service, and the remainder were distributed to other units. After considerable discussion, Militia H.Q. decided that, subversive tendencies apart, it was unreasonable to expect men who had left Russia because they disapproved of the Tsarist regime to fight to maintain it in power.[41]

Most of the problems mentioned were resolved by forces other than the military. But the Department of Militia and Defence had to maintain a watching brief on every situation likely to lead to a request for direct military action or for military support to another agency.

At Militia H.Q., the promised Director of Training and Intelligence was never appointed. The A.D.M.I., Capt. (Bvt.-Maj.) F.E. Davis, was responsible for the "exchange of information with the Intelligence Director at the War Office, the Headquarters of the C.E.F. in France and England, Dominion Police, Censorship Staff, Naval Service, other Dominions, R.N.W.M.P., British Naval and Military Attachés and D.I.O.s". In 1918, he also "established close liaison with the Intelligence Department of the United States". In the Districts in 1916, G.S. 55, which had authorized one D.I.O. per Military District, was reconfirmed. In 1917, their duties included liaison with the local civil authorities.[42]

Many from the Corps of Guides enlisted early in the war, but some Districts were fortunate in being able to secure and to retain a Guides officer. Others suffered through a succession of temporary incumbents who were merely waiting for more permanent appointments elsewhere. Some D.O.C.s tried to appoint a full-time "Secret Service officer" to aid in the investigation and handling of German and Austrian reservists, but the R.N.W.M.P. rejected the request, saying that they themselves had the situation in hand. A few Districts hired private detectives; Halifax paid them $15 (interpreters $35) per month. The firm most used, the U.S.-owned Thiel Detective Service Company of Canada Ltd., with its head office in Montreal and branches in Toronto and Vancouver, was employed almost continuously until August 1916, but only rarely thereafter.[43]

The range of activities the Army Intelligence organization had to deal with in Canada was surprisingly wide and extensive. A few of the more interesting cases will serve to show its nature. On January 21st, 1915, Lt.-Col. G.E. Burns, D.I.O. 4 Division, Montreal, advised Militia H.Q. that he had heard that asbestos shipments to the United States had increased at an abnormal rate and that they were being reshipped through neutral nations to Germany. He asked Customs and Excise to give him data he could use to assess the validity of the reports. His next report stated that 160 tons of Thetford Mines asbestos had been re-consigned to a German firm. Three months later he was able to name the consignee as a certain firm in New York. The next day the Cable Censor in North Sydney (Cable Censorship was a Militia responsibility) sent M.D. 4 and the police an intercept of a message between a Montreal firm and a firm in Barcelona known to be a German contact. The message described a deal in which asbestos had been sent to a Hamburg-controlled company in Rotterdam. On May 22nd, Burns reported that the Montreal firm had been organized by a broker in Philadelphia and was mostly financed by German money. The acting A.D.M.I. (Capt. Davis) and the C.G.S., feeling that the case was now properly a police matter, ordered Col. Burns to transfer the enquiry to them.

On September 16th, the Secretary of State for the Colonies advised Militia H.Q. that a company in New York, having the same name as the one reported by Col. Burns, was indeed suspected of shipping, to Sweden, asbestos "of the best class . . . largely used in the building of submarine boats . . . electrical [parts]. . . . These people have received propositions from Germany asking for offers to be shipped through Holland." A further report said that the president of the Montreal firm (also identified by Burns) had visited a German firm in London (now operated by the Public Trustee) and had then visited Denmark. The Secretary of State linked the two firms together through the Montreal president "who was believed to have many European contacts, to be a fluent linguist, and to have, we believe, decidedly pro-German ideas". Further enquiries made in May 1916, revealed additional evidence that the Montreal firm, knowing that asbestos shipments to Greece were officially prohibited, had nevertheless offered to act as buyer for the Greek government.

Although shipments of long-fibre asbestos had been banned in March 1915, short-fibre asbestos could still be legally exported to the U.S. until June 1916. On June 29th, despite the suspicious nature of the transactions, and probably because insufficient evidence was available to support a legal action, the authorities decided that the alleged links between German industry and the firms in Montreal and New York had not been established and that the enquiry should be closed.[44] The tightening of controls that had taken place was thought to be adequate to prevent future abuses. Though he had been withdrawn from the case before it was concluded, Burns had obviously done a great deal of work and may have provided much of the incentive for these controls. One must wonder, however, if an organization more aware of economic warfare might have taken the investigation further.

Occasionally the D.I.O. seemed to have a police function. In December 1916, for example, someone stole the overhead copper trolley wire from the electric railway running along Portage Avenue to the government rifle range at St. Charles, Winnipeg. "Despite a searching investigation by the D.I.O. [whose name, unfortunately, has not come down to us] and the police of St. Charles, the culprit has not been apprehended." The Militia Department replaced the wire at a cost of $1,179.71.[45] To this day the case has remained unsolved, and one must feel a certain reluctant admiration for a thief who contrived to steal two miles of overhead wire and got away with it.

During the first years of the war, civil unrest in Canada was low-key, localized, and, for the most part, directed against aliens or pro-German sympathizers. D.I.O.s and their staffs watched such activities carefully, and became the eyes of the Department in its role as an agency supporting the civil power. In 1917, there was official concern that there might be a massive hostile reaction to the Military Service Act which introduced conscription; as it turned out, there were few demonstrations.

The emergence of radicalism within the labour movement caused increasing concern, however. In July 1917, first reports were received of Industrial Workers of the World (I.W.W.) activity. D.I.O.s were ordered to watch this and to report anything of interest. It soon became obvious that the main centres of I.W.W. activity were Vancouver, Fernie, the Crow's Nest Pass, Winnipeg, Sault Ste. Marie, Cobalt, Windsor, London, and Guelph. In August 1918, increasing numbers of I.W.W. were reported to be coming to Canada because they were being driven out of the United States. Some business firms asked for protection, and close co-operation was established between the R.C.M.P., the Dominion Police, and the Army. The Censor banned, among others, the I.W.W. newspaper *The Labour Defender*. On September 27th, the government banned the I.W.W. and 12 other organizations on the grounds that they were revolutionary or Bolshevik in character. In December, C.S.E.F. troops in Vancouver broke up an

I.W.W. meeting called to protest participation in Siberia. The D.I.O. in M.D. 11 had to ask for more surveillance staff to watch for signs of further trouble.

On January 18th, 1919, D.O.C.s were ordered to increase the guards posted at armouries, and in some cases to remove the ammunition from them. On the West Coast, there was considerable agitation in favour of a new union of all workers, to be called the "One Big Union". The D.I.O. M.D. 11, Maj. A.E. Jukes, watched it closely and had his N.C.O.s attend public meetings in plain clothes. Union agitators exploited the grievances of the more than 400 unemployed aliens in the lumber industry. Longshoremen objected to loading munitions for Siberia. Arms reportedly were stolen from cargoes. Veterans complained of breaches of faith by the B.C. government in civil service and other provincial appointments, and the Trades and Labour Council Union tried to form them into a Soldiers and Sailors Labour Club. Subversive literature began to circulate at Edmonton, Calgary, and Winnipeg, as well as in Vancouver. Some returning members of the C.S.E.F. had brought Bolshevik propaganda home with them, and Customs and Immigration, and the D.I.O., were ordered to seize it on entry.

A general strike was threatened on the West Coast. As it could be successful only if the returned soldiers agreed to co-operate, agitators worked hard to win their support. There were fears – discounted by Maj. Jukes – that if a strike occurred, the B.C. regiments might be unreliable. The strike did begin in Vancouver on June 3rd, but the utility workers and telephone operators did not support it, and the veterans, most of whom belonged to the "Great War Veterans Association" (G.W.V.A.), actively opposed it. The strike was a failure, and, by July 3rd it was over. The One Big Union movement was to last until 1953, but never again was it to be a significant force on the West Coast.

1919–1929

The strength reductions and the reorganization which took place in the Canadian Army in 1919–20 significantly affected the Guides and Intelligence. On April 28th, 1920, the Adjutant-General (E.C. Ashton, C.M.G.) told the Militia Council:

> The Corps of Guides has . . . no role . . . in its present form in the War organization. . . . The Intelligence duties performed by the Corps . . . in . . . peace could be better performed by the Battalion and Brigade Intelligence Sections . . . based on what was actually found necessary in . . . war. . . . The War organization ensured that members of combatant units were trained to the need of close co-operation between the sources of "Intelligence" and the means of action. In concentration of Intelligence into one Corps there is a tendency to divorce Intelligence from action, which is fatal. The suggested reorganization . . . provides

each Military District with a Cyclist Company, with two companies for Military District No 2, which will have a liberal establishment of officers, who, in addition to the regimental duties, will carry out any special Intelligence work required by the G.O.C. . . . On mobilization . . . Companies would be combined into Cyclist Battalions.[46]

The decision to turn the Guides into Cyclists was understandable, given the circumstances. Cyclist units were a British development that dated from 1885. On November 7th, 1914, some 51 Yeomanry and 23 Territorial Force Cyclist Battalions were formed into an Army Cyclist Corps which, by late 1916, had grown to a strength of 14,624 men. In 1914, the Canadian Army had no Cyclists. Therefore, First Division, conforming to the British organization, formed a Cyclist Company as part of its divisional mounted troops. The Company was commanded by Maj. C.C. Child, with Capt. W.W. Everall as second-in-command, both Corps of Guides. Company H.Q. had a Company Sergeant Major, a Company Quartermaster Sergeant, an artificer, three signallers, and a batman. There were three platoons, each with a subaltern, one sergeant, two corporals, two lance corporals, 24 privates, and a batman. In May 1916, the Divisional Cyclist Companies were formed into a battalion on the Corps Troops establishment.[47]

Cyclists were originally intended to protect the main force from surprise, much as do the armoured car or reconnaissance regiments of today. They were mobile, and had a larger ratio of machine guns to rifles than an infantry battalion. But, as the report of the British manoeuvres of 1912 said, "numerous and good roads are a necessity for [their] effective employment". In France they dug trenches, carried material forward, acted as stretcher bearers, observers, runners, Lewis gun crews on anti-aircraft defence, traffic controllers, trench wardens, and prisoner-of-war escorts. In 1918, Gen. Currie strengthened his defences against the German offensive with extra machine-gunners from the Cyclists and the Canadian Light Horse. In August, at Amiens, the Cyclist Battalion covered the right flank of the cavalry. They formed part of Brig.-Gen. R. Brutinel's Automobile Machine Gun Brigade's thrust through the Hindenburg Line, and were active in the pursuit of the Germans around Mons. Parenthetically, of the first eight officers appointed to that Brigade in 1914, four were Corps of Guides; Maj. J.E. Browne, Capt. F.A. Wilkin, and Lieuts. G.A. Bradbrooke and J.W. Sifton, his principal administrative officer. Replacements for both of these units came from the Guides in Canada.[48]

The British disbanded them in 1922; in the Second World War only the Japanese Army used them tactically. They needed good roads, but in the Canada of 1920 these were rare, and even the best were unsuitable for bicycles for much of the year. The men were not interested in a vehicle that was becoming increasingly associated with small boys; they wanted the new cars. Most important, the use to which Cyclists had been put was markedly different from the Intelligence function that had been accepted as the prewar Guide function. It is probable that, given the pressure to reduce the forces that existed, the only way the Guides could be retained was to link them to a recognized wartime activity and try to retain as much of the intelligence role as possible by giving them the extra officers. But the decision to retain the Cyclist arm was technically impractical, and a better decision would have been to amalgamate the Guides with one of the light cavalry regiments. This would have required foresight; the concept of complete units equipped with armoured car reconnaissance vehicles was only just beginning to appear. The decision which was reached did provide a position for the Guides in the peacetime establishment; but the difficulties of their anomalous position would return to haunt A.D.M.I.s for ten years to come.

At Militia H.Q., Capt. F.E. Davis was promoted substantive Major (he had been Brevet and Temporary Lt.-Col.) and retired on December 31st, 1920. His replacement, Lt.-Col. H.H. Matthews, did not arrive until April, 1921. In the interval the Director of Military Operations and Intelligence (D.M.O.&I.), Maj. (Bvt. and T./Col.) J. Sutherland-Brown, acted as his own A.D.M.I. At Headquarters, Intelligence reverted to its prewar basis: military – to assist in the defence of the country and "to promote efficiency"; and domestic – to deal with sedition. Col. Sutherland-Brown took an active interest in his new tasks. In his Intelligence Circular Letter No. 21 (*sic.*, No. 1) of January 3rd, 1921, he pointed out that the domestic side now replaced the foreign in importance. A reorganization of Intelligence was due and he would co-ordinate it with assistance from his A.D.M.I., who would deal with the R.C.M.P., with special agents when appointed, and with the D.I.O.s through their respective G.O.C.s.

The D.I.O.s were to deal with Brigade and Regimental I.O.s and with a new group of Area I.O.s, who would be recruited from the Guides or Guides Reserve and who would be stationed in counties and locations bordering on the United States in Quebec, New Brunswick, and British Columbia. They were to reconnoitre and to map defensive positions, lateral communications, and routes to the frontiers. This was, in effect, a return to the prewar Guide function. In addition, they were to compile a lengthy list of information on United States transportation and military facilities. M.D. 11 was to collect what information it could about Asians in general and Japanese in particular. In conjunction with the R.C.M.P., all were to collect any domestic intelligence that had a bearing on aid to the civil power.

At the end of January 1921, M.D. 11 told the D.M.O.&I. that the Guides in Vancouver felt that the Army reorganization had removed them from Intelligence and that they would rather not serve as Cyclists. Col. Sutherland-Brown's reply reveals not only his own weakness in the field of intelligence, but also the trap the Army had dropped into in its desire to avoid having a specialist Intelligence Corps. It also conflicted with his Circular Letter No. 21 [1]:

> ... the experience of war has been that Intelligence duties must be performed by personnel belonging to the ... units and not by a special Intelligence Corps attached to those units. There has been in the past and will be in the future, Staff Officers ... and other officers, other ranks, and agents, employed on intelligence duty ... with the Armies in the Field; within the Hostile Territory ... [in] Neutral Powers. ... The troops, themselves, must collect Intelligence and transmit it to the proper sources [*sic*]; therefore the Corps of Guides as they formerly existed had no place on mobilization and outside of training several useful officers they served no useful purpose.

He expected to use the Cyclist companies as divisional troops for security and protection duties. "Because they train in peace for [these] duties they should be very useful as Area Intelligence Officers". I.O.s and other ranks were to be drawn from the most useful personnel available. Suitable Guides "should be made use of on Mobilization". He was trying to amend the peace establishments at brigade and regiments to provide for intelligence duties, but, if this was not possible, to require that a specially selected officer would be found to perform them.[49]

No one can deny that troops must collect and pass information. But there has to be someone at the receiving end trained to accept and process it – the "proper sources". Even in the units there is a small, trained section, headed by an officer, which co-ordinates the reports received from the troops. Too much importance was attached to the reconnaissance function of the Guides and not enough to the staff aspects of their role. Moreover, Col. Sutherland-Brown appeared to have accepted the requirement for senior I.O.s in a somewhat nebulous system, and acknowledged that the earlier organization had produced some, but he made no provision to ensure their early selection and training either with the conventional arms or on their own. His method further divorced the two functions – action and intelligence – a tendency which the A.G. had said the Army was doing its best to avoid. Finally, his desire to use the Cyclists for screen protection was a reversion to the old role of his light cavalry units and traditionally was not a function of the Guides.

But despite the weaknesses of his background and of his concept, which are now obvious, Col. Sutherland-Brown did a great deal to try to build an intelligence organization. On April 14th, 1921, he proposed to establish a District Intelligence Section which, on mobilization, could be split into a Command Section and a District Section. M.D.s 1, 3, 5, 7, 11, and 12 were to get a second officer, five N.C.O.s, and one man. The other M.D.s were to get two extra officers, ten N.C.O.s, and two men. He also listed the intelligence requirement for a brigade (one I.O., three N.C.O.s) and for each battalion of infantry, cavalry and artillery regiment, engineer group, signal battalion, and railway group. The infantry received an I.O., two sergeants and 10 men; all others an I.O. and two to four men. He also asked for Area Intelligence Officers for Nova Scotia, Prince Edward Island, the Eastern Townships, Ontario, and Saskatchewan, in addition to his earlier list. When the C.G.S. invited him to sound out the Districts, the answers he received showed no marked enthusiasm for the plan. This was understandable, for most of them just did not have the staff to implement it. In May 1921, there were 10 D.I.O.s, five of them Corps of Guides officers. In January, 1922, in order to avoid confusion with the navy's nomenclature, Halifax had to change its man's title to D.M.I.O. In M.D.s 1, 4, 6, 7, and 11, the position was not filled. M.D. 5 used a regimental officer on a part-time basis. In M.D. 13, Jennings, at his own suggestion, served without pay. Col. Sutherland-Brown's proposals clearly fell on arid ground.

Although the emphasis was placed on the domestic side, Intelligence (a) was not ignored. Its staff was small: D.M.O.&I., A.D.M.I., three military clerks, and a stenographer, who also worked for the G.S. Branch. But it managed to produce around ten intelligence summaries per month. The demand for quantity may, perhaps, have impaired their quality; although they contained "material of value for the general education of officers", they enjoyed only a limited circulation. When Districts were asked to comment on the use made of them, they were politely noncommittal.

In 1921, the War Office began to rebuild files that had been allowed to lapse during the war. The D.M.O.&I. was asked to collect, under 12 headings, a wide range of information on aspects of military geography. They included: topographical and geological features – climate and health – inhabitants – campgrounds. Under topography for instance, he was asked to give data on "mountain ranges, cultivation, forests, rivers, roads". The D.M.O.&I. referred the project to his D.I.O.s on December 6th, 1921, and suggested, probably paraphrasing the British request, that sources should be "officers on Intelligence duties, Intelligence reports, reports received from other Government Departments . . . ." On December 15th, the obviously unimpressed D.O.C., M.D. 5, bluntly asked the cost, and the time when it would have to be completed. His question drew a somewhat shamefaced admission that the paper was only a general guide, to be acted on if it fell in with circumstances, that there was no money, and that emphasis was still to be placed on Defence Scheme No. 1, which detailed the action to be taken in the event of an attack on Canada by the United States.[50]

In 1924, the War Office circulated details of a suggested system designed to standardize collation procedures throughout the Empire. Each country was to be given a "book" or shelf, divided into subject "volumes": I. Organization and strength of Army and Air Service; II. Technical details of war material used by the Army and Air Service; III. Tactics and military training; IV. Military Education; V. Strategy; VI. History; VII. Politics; VIII. Geography; IX. Material and economic resources of a country; and X. Navy. Each book was to be further subdivided into "chapters" and "paragraphs". Items relevant to more than one paragraph were to be copied and filed under each appropriate heading. An alphabetical index would list every item, by book, chapter, and paragraph.

In the Canadian version, some 75 countries were divided into four groups, in order of their military and political importance. Because the special stationery was not available in Canada, the Department had to use its own portfolios and folders. The initial requirement was:

Group	Books (countries)	Volumes (subjects)	Portfolios (chapters)	3-fold Folders (paragraphs)
1	16	160	1,776	16,080
2	26	260	2,886	26,130
3	12	120	1,332	12,060
4	21	210	2,331	21,050
Totals	75	750	8,325	75,320

By March 21st, 1922, the A.D.M.I. reported that he had prepared books for six Group 1 countries, namely, U.K., France, Germany, Japan, the U.S., and Canada, but that his coverage would be less extensive than the original plan called for. The data on the six countries were contained in only 18 portfolios, of 20 folders each. The others would be correspondingly reduced, and the whole study would be contained in 103 portfolios and 735 folders.

It was a simple system, capable of being as limited or as comprehensive as the staff available to operate it permitted. Canada introduced it at Defence H.Q. and, on a smaller scale, at the Districts. M.D. 10, in particular, made a serious and not unsuccessful attempt to operate it. Sources were local newspapers, foreign service journals and maps, reports on topographical subjects, natural or manufactured resources, and comments by travellers. The library grant made to each District was used to buy British and Canadian Service journals. All District General Staff officers were to take an interest in the collecting, filing, and transmitting of "matters of military interest". The D.M.O.&I. called for a monthly report which, among other things, was to include information on current events, provincial political questions, public opinion, highway construction, social problems, and any data on the adjacent areas of the United States that could be used to support planning for Defence Scheme No. 1.[51]

The A.D.M.I. also had charge of the Library, which had been set up under Intelligence auspices in the original 1903 terms of reference. In 1924, he was given the post of Chairman of the Editorial and Managing Committee of the *Canadian Defence Quarterly*, the forerunner of the *Canadian Army Journal*, with a circulation of about 4,000.[52] The Chairman was, in effect, not only the editor, but also the author of a great deal of its text. He was required to edit the reports of the annual inspections by the Inspector General and, in his spare time, do research and lecture. The Branch was also responsible for handling a map which was produced by the Department in 1925 showing the positions of the Allied armies on the Western Front on September 25th, 1918. In 1928, a charge of 50 cents was imposed, and by 1931 it was out of print. Requests, however, continued to come in until 1940, when its circulation was turned over to the Historical Branch.

Despite the attention paid to intelligence at the D.M.O.&I. level, the units across the country remained largely uninterested. In the 10 years following the war, only one intelligence course was held in Canada, by the D.M.I.O. at Winnipeg in 1925. It consisted of lectures on Japan, Russia, Cuba, the Near East, U.S./U.K. relations, the League of Nations, intelligence at battalion and divisional levels, intelligence methods and techniques, and the intelligence corps in general (obviously the wartime British version, for no corps existed in the Empire at that date). The course ended with a three-hour written examination, a staff ride, and practical work with the prismatic compass and plane table. Only three candidates applied. Their small number hardly justified the work that went into the preparation of the course.

Lt.-Col. Matthews was by no means in favour of a specialist corps. Col. Sutherland-Brown tried to have the 1925 Winnipeg course repeated, saying that it was necessary to give officers of the Permanent Force and Militia a knowledge of intelligence. Matthews agreed, but he was afraid that such courses might give the impression that "Intelligence duties in peace or war would necessarily require specialists . . . a danger which was to be carefully avoided". He thought that officers on the General Staff should be able to carry on both Operations and Intelligence training, for "there is really no fundamental difference between the work of Operations and the Intelligence Sections". His own field experience – he had been a Divisional Intelligence Staff Officer in 1917 – would have given his opinion much weight. He thought that the Training Branch should simply include intelligence subjects in the various general courses conducted throughout the year. He would prefer that officers whose examination results were good should be given special instruction in such subjects as map-reading and field-sketching, interpretation of air photos, army/air co-operation, military history, geography "and possibly other subjects". Unfortunately, the training staff needed was simply not available. Foreign languages, and the organization and tactics of potential enemies, were obviously not considered important enough to mention. The D.M.O.&I. stated in March 1926, rather plaintively, that "if a junior officer could be employed, the A.D.M.I. could then visit all District Headquarters once in two years to set up courses in "I" work for the P.F. and the N.P.A.M."[53] This lack of instruction was to have unfortunate effects on the training programs after 1939.

The Guides, who could have given this training, were virtually in a state of limbo. Only a few companies were formed, and training was limited. No training was authorized in 1920, and between 1922 and 1924 it was restricted to 50% of the establishment. In 1926, the company establishment was changed to one major, one captain, four lieutenants, one W.O.II, one company quartermaster sergeant, one sergeant (artificer), four sergeants, eight corporals, one driver, two cooks, six batmen, and 88 privates. Two horses, 117 bicycles, and one wagon made up the equipment table; the horses, wagon, and, at least in the early days, the bicycles, had to be hired for the camp period. The organization was much the same as it had been in wartime: an H.Q. of 10, and four platoons of 27, a total of 118 all ranks. Junior officer training included normal military subjects, plus instruction in such special-to-corps subjects as characteristics of Cyclists, platoon drill with cycles, Cyclists in reconnaissance, employment of Cyclists for protection, tactical action of Cyclists, map-reading and field-sketching, employment of Cyclists with corps or divisional troops, the role of the unit in war, and, almost as an afterthought, intelligence in peace and in war. Captains had to know these subjects and, in addition, become proficient in dismounted action and the employment of Cyclists in coast defence. Majors had to have a full knowledge of intelligence in peace and in war. N.C.O.s took a modified version of the subalterns' course.[54]

But the role, and the methods used to fill it, had lost their appeal. Recruiting declined. Few companies were really active; among the active were the two in Toronto, through which passed some 855 all ranks between 1912 and 1929.[55] Small units cost a great deal to administer for little apparent return. General Order 191, of December 1st, 1928, disbanded the Guides, effective March 31st, 1929.

Today the Corps of Guides is virtually forgotten, except for one memorial, a prize offered each year at the Royal Military College, Kingston. In January 1926, Col. A.C. Caldwell, then Director of Engineer Services, wrote to Colonel-Commandant C.F. Constantine, Royal Military College, to tell him that the Corps of Guides Association wished to donate an annual prize to the cadet of R.M.C. who achieved the highest mark in topography, reconnaissance, or other subjects the Corps considered particularly relevant to its own role. Col. Constantine was happy to accept the offer; the sum of $841.40 was duly invested, to provide a return to pay for the annual prize. The first year, map-reading and field-sketching were the two subjects to be tested. The first award was made in 1927, and the competition remained active until 1941. The prize itself took the form of some article of personal equipment, binoculars, a travel case, a watch, etc. No awards were made between 1941 and 1952, when a change in curriculum led to a change in the terms. Since the closest modern specialties are survey and field-sketching, these have become the subjects for competition. A cash award, rather than a purchased item, is now made.[56]*

---

* Second edition note: As of 2017, the Corps of Guides Prize continues to be awarded annually to the RMC cadet who obtains the highest marks in surveying and terrain analysis.

3.
TO WAR AGAIN: CANADA 1929–39

The decade before the Second World War was a trying one for the Canadian Army. The "War to end war" had been fought; until nearly the end of the decade, no other war appeared to threaten. Government expenditure programs put the Defence Department well down the priority list. The fight against subversion was an R.C.M.P. responsibility. But the increasing risk of civil unrest in protest against economic conditions, which could lead to direct Army support for the forces of law and order, meant that more attention had to be paid to the circumstances, real and potential, which could give rise to that unrest.

Accurate and timely information had to be supplied to the Chief of the General Staff, but financial limitations made it impossible to maintain sufficient staff to do this adequately. The principal staff officer to the C.G.S. for much of this period was the Director of Military Operations and Intelligence (D.M.O.&I.). He combined the knowledge of what was likely to happen and of the forces available to deal with it. His senior intelligence officer was the A.D.M.I., but that appointment was not always filled.

General A.G.L. McNaughton became C.G.S. on December 31st, 1928. On January 18th, 1929, he wrote to his Minister:

> Most of the incoming [Intelligence] information stops in the Department and ... I do not think that we as a country are getting all the benefit out of it that we should. I think much of it would be of use to ... External Affairs and possibly to the Commercial Intelligence Section of ... Trade and Commerce. I would like to have your authority to discuss the matter with Dr. Skelton and Mr. O'Hara with a view to seeing in what way we could make our information of use to them.[1]

Apparently, no exchange was ever made with Trade and Commerce. But Gen. McNaughton's letter instituted the regular exchange of information and the close working relationship between External Affairs and the Defence Department that still exist. Previously the British Foreign Office would send intelligence to the Governor General, who would pass it to the Prime Minister or to External Affairs. In its turn, External would pass selected items to Defence.

The earliest recorded intelligence exchange with a foreign agency took place privately in October 1927, when a collection of United States newspaper editorial comments on the St. Lawrence Seaway negotiations was made available to the War Office. This unofficial channel was expanded between 1928 and 1930 by the receipt of British material. The exact dates when the links with the British Attachés abroad began are not clear, but they probably grew out of personal contacts between Canadian officers and the War Office.[2] Some senior officers, including, in later years Col. Crerar and Col. Stuart, maintained close contacts with friends in the British Army, many of whom occupied senior posts. Much of the information derived from these individuals was incorporated into the A.D.M.I.'s assessments.[3] Unfortunately, Dr. Skelton had such a deep and lively suspicion of British intentions that he was often reluctant to accept reports from such sources. As a result, Defence found it difficult to have its point of view accepted or even fairly evaluated.

By the end of 1933, the A.D.M.I. had become officially responsible for direct liaison with Intelligence at the War Office, with the British Military Attachés at Washington and Tokyo, and with the British Intelligence officers at Singapore, Hong Kong, and Shanghai. During the mid-1930s, the British Foreign Office sent External Affairs a periodic summary of reports from its diplomatic posts. After 1935, the A.D.M.I. would frequently expand some item of special interest to Canada, such as reports on foreign industrial development. He would pass the reworked product through the D.M.O.&I. to the C.G.S. and to External Affairs. But despite strenuous efforts, the Prime Minister, Mr. King, could never be persuaded to read these items.[4]

In 1935, the A.D.M.&A.F.I., S/L K.M. Guthrie, R.C.A.F., attempted to modernize an intelligence structure whose operating methods had remained mostly unchanged since the early 1920s. His General Staff Memorandum reflected his attempts to return to basic principles. It was necessary to have a clear appreciation of the type and scope of intelligence that was now needed. Canada's principal links were with the Empire and the League of Nations, and so the intelligence services did not need to cover the whole world. One central organization was required, equipped with facilities to ensure maximum collection with minimal duplication, and with the capacity to collate and quickly disseminate the results of its studies. More effort was needed.

Army H.Q. would exploit external sources. The Districts would cover the United States and Japan and report their findings to A.H.Q. Ottawa would then add its own material and send it all back to Districts as periodic Intelligence Summaries. District I.O.s were to use as guides the British *Manual of Military Intelligence in the Field, 1930* and the *Guide to the Collection and Collation of Air Intelligence, 1930*. They were to follow the Book System, a description of which was appended to the Memorandum. They were to "take some initial time and trouble in the organization of an Intelligence service from means available within each District". Sources included the U.S. and Canadian press, reports from officers who had visited U.S. installations, the R.C.N., the R.C.M.P., and provincial and municipal police forces.[5] Many travellers and businessmen also freely gave information received from abroad. In practice, few of the Districts devoted much time to this activity. Their reports were relatively valueless, lack of training in their duties apart, for not only were they being asked to provide information that only A.H.Q. was equipped to evaluate, but they were given no direction concerning the actual intelligence requirement they were attempting to meet.

The official external source material available to Canada was all British: a Special Monthly Secret Intelligence Summary; a monthly Confidential Intelligence Summary; a Weekly Secret Intelligence Summary from India; periodic Secret Summaries from Hong Kong, Singapore, and the Air Ministry; liaison reports from Australia, New Zealand, and South Africa; and reports from British Attachés. Professor James Eayrs has criticized the Department for relying "too exclusively upon Imperial sources and too little upon its own". The explanation, he feels, is to be found largely in the Prime Minister's refusal to appoint Canadian Military Attachés.[6]

Mr. King's idiosyncrasies and their effects on external policies have been extensively discussed elsewhere. The government departments involved in external relations had no option but to make the best of the situation as it was. But this created a fundamental weakness at the very top. No direction seems to have been given which would have assigned national priorities on information-gathering to support Canadian foreign and military policy. Canada's main interests now lay in Europe. Asian material was interesting, but still irrelevant, and handling it took valuable time. Fortunately, after 1935, the situation corrected itself and attention became more closely focused on Italy and Germany. In the same context, the requirements imposed on Districts before 1935 were maintained far too long. There was no need to collect information to support planning for Defence Schemes Nos. 1 and 2, which were based on the possibility of a war involving the U.S. Further, if D.I.O.s had to collect information, they should not have been required to process it themselves but to pass it immediately to Ottawa. The Book System was a valid *collation* tool, but it was not appropriate for use at the District level where emphasis should have been placed on directed *collection*. The two reference texts, which dealt with conditions on the battlefield, were quite irrelevant to the strategic requirement but were appropriate to a training mission had one been assigned. One gets the impression that the A.D.M.I. was trying to force the C.G.S. to make a decision concerning intelligence requirements which he could then use as a guide.

Even if the requirements listed in the Memorandum had been assigned, the A.D.M.I.'s Branch could hardly have carried them out. The government did not believe a threat to Canada existed. It therefore would not have supported action to collect information on such a threat. The Branch staff was inadequate to handle any large flow of material, and there was no money for more staff.

For most of this period, all Service activities were restricted by a requirement to spend money as sparingly as possible. On March 11th, 1929, Col. H.H. Matthews, then D.M.O.&I., told the C.G.S. that he had "a number of important questions . . . some . . . in hand and some . . . untouched or indefinitely postponed for lack of staff." His small Directorate had to compile the Department War Book and the Dominion War Book (procedures to be taken if war broke out); to write mobilization plans for the defence of Canada under Defence Schemes No. 1 (by then moribund) and No. 2 (plans for the protection and enforcement of Canadian neutrality in the event of war between the U.S. and Japan); to organize, man, and train the forces necessary to support these Schemes and to supervise District defence schemes; to plan industrial mobilization, censorship, and aid to the civil power; to handle codes and ciphers, in which it followed British practices; to watch developments in disarmament, the International Court of Justice, and the League of Nations; and to watch changes in British Army organization in order that Canadian establishments could conform. Granted, he had these responsibilities; with such a small staff he could do little in-depth work on many of them.

Col. Matthews claimed that "all the work of the Operations Section devolves on the D.M.O.&I. himself; the A.D.M.I. has more than enough to do to keep abreast of the duties of the Intelligence Section". Intelligence, in fact, provided much background material for the Defence Schemes, and later in the planning of censorship and aid to the civil power, in covering reports on disarmament, in liaison with the international agencies, and in handling the routine work of codes and ciphers. Because of the increasing load it carried, the Directorate was eventually given one extra G.S.O.1 and a first-class stenographer, but at that time it had a total strength of seven officers, 12 R.C.E. N.C.O.s, five stenographers, two typists, all of whom were Corps of Military Staff Clerks (C.M.S.C.), and 24 civilians. The Geographical Section had three officers, the 12 R.C.E., and 22 civilians. The Intelligence Section had only two officers, three stenographers (one of them shared with the G.S.O.1), and two civilian typists.[7]

The D.M.O.&I. controlled Intelligence funds. The importance the Department attached to Intelligence can be gauged from the paucity of its annual expense grant. In 1927 the total was $1,500. The Geographical Section spent $612 on bond paper; Districts were assigned $520, but spent only $205.23. When the D.M.O.&I asked Col. Parsons, G.S.O.2, M.D. 2, why he had not spent his particular allocation of $70, Parsons replied that the auditors had decided that, in order to save the Pay Office the work of handling a large number of small sums, no advances should be made from this fund! In fact, one of his staff had paid for items he needed out of his own pocket.[8] In the 1928–9 fiscal year, the Directorate spent $1,212.20, including the expenses of five trips by D.I.O.s to the United States and to sea with the R.C.N.; the Districts spent $725.54. By 1930, such items as the construction costs of a cupboard for the D.M.I.O., M.D. 10, were charged to the grant. (In 1929, the title of D.I.O. was changed to D.M.I.O. – District Military Intelligence Officer.) In 1931–2, the total – $250 – was shared among five Districts – 2, 6, 10, 11, and 13. The D.M.I.O. positions in the other Districts had been suspended on April 1st,

1930, and were not reinstated until November 1935. By 1935, of the $250 total, $100 went to N.D.H.Q. In 1935, when the grant was raised to $1,000, only $600 was spent. The five posts that were revived cost $658.80.[9]

On April 4th, 1932, the D.M.O.&I. directed the A.D.M.I., Lt.-Col. K. Stuart, to "examine the amalgamation of Military and Air Force Intelligence". This followed a proposal by the Director, Civil Government Air Operations (C.G.A.O.), R.C.A.F., who saw it as one possible way of reducing expenditures. Col. Stuart discussed it with his R.C.A.F counterpart, F/L C.C. Walker, whose duties, on paper at least, were very similar to his own. F/L Walker was required to hold and issue all training and other publications, to maintain liaison with the Air Ministry and British Air Attachés, to obtain, hold, and issue all air maps, and to collect, record, and disseminate general and Air Force intelligence, but he did no general intelligence. When the Director, C.G.A.O., told Walker that three of his tasks could be assigned to other offices (maps, for example, went to Operations), the proposed amalgamation was greatly simplified.

Col. Stuart recommended that the two offices be combined under an "Assistant Director of Military and Air Force Intelligence", who would be responsible for collecting, recording, and distributing both Military and Air Force intelligence and who would have a Staff Officer, Military and Air Force Intelligence, to work on material common to both Services. He stressed this latter point; the new office was not to have an Air Force "cell". He recommended that the Air Force files be integrated into the Army Book System by simply replacing the Air chapters of the Book with the contents of those files. And, as he pointed out, if later "it should become necessary to separate again . . . the Air files could be removed from the Book System". The general portions, however, could not be so separated, and Col. Stuart warned that this situation would have to be accepted because no practical alternative was available. Custody and distribution of secret documents would be handled by the Section for both Services. The R.C.A.F. were to supply a qualified typist/stenographer "junior to Quartermaster Sergeant". A simple reallocation of offices would solve the accommodation problem. Stuart recommended that the unification be undertaken on the grounds of economy and efficiency.[10]

The Minister approved the proposal on April 22nd, and the order promulgating his approval, No. 240, issued on May 20th, read as follows: "A combined Military and Air Force Intelligence Section will be formed under the direction of the Director of Military Operations and Intelligence, with effect April 22nd, 1932."

Economy was achieved; the R.C.A.F. "saved" three clerks, the Army one officer. That amalgamation was not extended to any of the Districts except Winnipeg, where, on March 19th, 1932, F/L K.M. Guthrie (the Air Staff Officer) replaced

Capt. F.F. Worthington as D.M.I.O. The position continued to be an Air Force perquisite until 1939. Ken Guthrie was admirably qualified to hold it. He had been actively connected with the Army, had flown in Army Co-operation exercises, and had become a "trooper" in a cavalry unit when he was "shot down". He passed Militia Staff and Army Staff College entrance examinations and, while he was attending the R.A.F. Staff College in England, spent some of his leave time with the Armoured Corps School. In Winnipeg, he maintained close links with the R.C.M.P. on security matters, and built himself an enviable reputation within the miniscule Intelligence Community. In June 1935, he was the obvious choice for the A.D.M.I. post in Ottawa, which had been vacant since December 1933.[11]

S/L Guthrie's appointment required the Army to concede as a principle that, regardless of whether the Staff Officer position was Grade II or Grade III, the Section should have both an Army and Air Force officer. This in turn produced another difficulty, because the junior Army officer appointed to assist Guthrie received staff pay to which the airman was not entitled. In late 1938, when the R.C.A.F. nominated S/L C.J. Duncan as his replacement, the C.G.S. protested that, if the post was to be considered as a permanent Air Force nomination, no military officer could have "the opportunity of holding the important appointment". He was willing to accept S/L Duncan or any other Air Force officer, and was happy to continue the combined Section. The Senior Air Force Officer, who believed that the appointment would be equally valuable to Air Force officers but who also saw great advantage in opening it up to officers from both Services, agreed that the combined Section should remain, and withdrew his nomination. Maj. J.F. Preston, M.C., R.C.A., replaced Guthrie; Duncan became his G.S.O.3, Staff Officer (Intelligence).[12]

By 1939, Maj. Preston's Section was handling many more secret and confidential documents and was producing a daily Press Summary. His only Air Force clerk had to spend much of his time "in liaison with the Canadian Building" (Air Force offices), and was not readily available to help with the Summary. On July 31st, he asked for an additional Air Force clerk. The R.C.A.F. studied his request and, in November, decided to reform its own Intelligence Section. The C.G.S. concurred, asking only that he be given two weeks to find a replacement for S/L Duncan. The Chief of the Air Staff directed his staff to implement the separation and to ensure that the sources available to the Army were also made available to the Air Force. Authority to make the change was granted, effective December 31st, 1939; the actual separation took place on January 6th, 1940.[13]

Christmas card, Season's Greetings from Militia and Air Force Intelligence Section, Ottawa, 1937. © Government of Canada, reproduced with the permission of Library and Archives Canada, 2017. Drawn by S/Sgt. Bert Goldie, a member of the Intelligence Section at N.D.H.Q. (Library and Archives Canada/Kenneth MacGregor Guthrie fonds, MIKAN 2962584)

I(B): PRE-1939

The "Great Depression" bore most heavily on the Prairies, although no part of Canada escaped the impact of mass unemployment and the social consequences which accompanied it. Many feared that the unemployed might riot. If they did so, the Army, which had as one of its roles aid to the civil power, could find itself in actual conflict with large numbers of the civilian population. Towards the end of the decade, the growing influence of extremist ideologies made the threat of mass demonstrations a very real danger. It was even possible to imagine that radical philosophies could seriously affect members of the armed forces. It would seem, however, that measures for controlling demonstrations were based more on reaction to a situation as it occurred than on conformity with a prearranged plan.

In July 1930, after a minor disturbance in Montreal, the District reported that foreigners had attempted to gain information about the Lewis and other machine guns held in one of the armouries. Protective measures were taken and the R.C.M.P. were advised, but nothing further came of the incident.[14] When the Carden-Lloyd armoured car was first made available for public trial in July 1931, many feared that its appearance would be looked on as an act of provocation by a civilian population already highly emotional over the issue of strike-breaking. All Districts were informed that the vehicle was merely a replacement for the horse, and that there was no question of it being used to aid the civil power. When the vehicle itself was found to be unsuitable, interest in it waned. On August 22, the *Toronto Star* printed its photograph; by August 30th, technical details were made available for general release.[15]

On August 15th, 1931, C.G.S., Gen. McNaughton, told all the D.O.C.s that it was their

> responsibility to keep National Defence Headquarters informed of any conditions in their respective Military Districts as may, from time to time, possibly lead to, or actually result in, threats of violence or violence, or rioting and breaches of the peace, and whether such disturbances or threats of same are likely to result in calls for aid to the Civil Power.[16]

This information was sent to H.Q. in monthly reports. They were useful to a headquarters which had to give advice to the government, and they formed a significant part of the work load of both Intelligence and Operations. Decisions arising out of the information contained in them were directly linked to plans for the deployment of Special Service Companies – units of the Non-Permanent Active Militia (N.P.A.M.) detailed to be called out under "Aid to the Civil Power" in the event of disorders resulting from strikes. These Companies had first been conceived in 1931, and a great deal of thought had gone into their development. Both the fact that they had been planned and the terms under which they were to be used were secret. All intelligence reports that had any bearing on their deployment were passed to the D.O.C.s to assist local contingency planning.[17]

In July 1931, both public and official opinion demanded that the Army be used against the Doukhobors of southern British Columbia, who had refused to be enumerated. The C.G.S., with support from the R.C.M.P., managed to resist these pressures and to convince the Minister of Justice not to ask for Army support. Two officers and 11 men, however, were called out at the Yorkton, Saskatchewan trial of Peter Veregin, the Freedomite leader. M.D. 12 forwarded a report from the R.C.M.P. which stated that their presence had prevented a serious outbreak of violence.[18]

Isolated Communist agitation took place. Troops were called out at Oshawa in April 1932. When this agitation came to a head at a Workers' Economic Conference held in Ottawa on August 2nd, 1932, H.Q. M.D. 3 kept in close touch with Defence Headquarters. In October, Communist prisoners, led by Tim Buck, rioted in Kingston Penitentiary; the R.C.H.A. was called out to quell the disturbance.[19] Troops were also called out at St. Catharines and at Stratford in 1933; though they were never used, the Permanent Force units in British Columbia remained on call until 1935.

In order to help counter the unemployment situation, the C.G.S. proposed in 1932 that relief camps should be set up to house able-bodied, single, homeless, out-of-work men. They were to be given food, clothing, shelter, and some pocket money in exchange for their labour. The Defence Department was the only federal department that had the organization and the personnel to operate them. The C.G.S.'s detailed proposal was approved and implemented on October 8th.[20] At once the radical elements claimed that the camps were really a disguised system of paramilitary training. By concentrating men who felt themselves especially aggrieved, the camps may have unintentionally made it easier for agitators to influence the unemployed. On the other hand, the kind of control that was exercised did deprive them of opportunities to create perhaps greater trouble in the cities. In British Columbia, there were 237 camps and nearly 20,000 men. They formed almost one-third of the total relief camp population of the entire country; they also seemed to have attracted rather more than one-third of all the troublemakers in Canada. Maj.-Gen. E.C. Ashton, D.O.C., M.D. 11, frequently expressed his concern over the reports of subversion, and of public reaction to incidents created by these agitators. At Army H.Q. the Intelligence Section was given two additional tasks: the preparation of a record of the numbers of single, homeless men on relief projects; and a clipping service of items about them appearing in the newspapers.[21]

In January 1936, a strike by relief workers in Dundurn, Saskatchewan, threatened to escalate into a "hunger march" on Saskatoon, which would form part of a national uprising. The D.O.C.s were asked to report events as they happened, but were warned that they were always to approach the local police first; the police could best deal with individual troublemakers. D.O.C.s had direct responsibility only for Departmental employees working on relief works property. Fortunately, the unrest was limited to major centres where it was controlled without Army intervention.[22]

By mid-1937, Army H.Q. noted a marked decline in incidents that could be attributed to Communist subversive activity. The possible exception was British

Columbia, where the Communists were supporting the Social Credit Party then being organized in the province. In general, however, since labour unrest was more directly connected with wage demands than with ideology, strikes were quickly settled.[23] In the slowly improving economic climate, extremism began to attract less public sympathy.

In a few cases the general unrest had an effect on the Armed Forces themselves. In March 1931, the A.D.M.I. warned Gen. McNaughton that Communist infiltration and subversion in the Army was expected to increase. The warning was based, in part at least, on a study of Communist Party propaganda containing clear indications that action against the Services would be increased. Gen. McNaughton directed recruiting officers to make sure that applicants for enlistment in both the Permanent Force and the N.P.A.M. were carefully and discreetly screened. The enquiries were presumably made by the recruiting staff, for, as we have seen, most of the Districts no longer had intelligence staffs. By mid-1931 the normal reply had to be, "Sorry, no vacancies", an answer more easily explained by lack of funds than by security needs.[24]

Later events proved the warnings to have been valid. On the West Coast, a soldier of the P.P.C.L.I. was accused of inciting His Majesty's Forces to mutiny by distributing subversive literature to his fellow soldiers. His trial revealed that he was a card-carrying member of the Communist Party; he was convicted and jailed. At about the same time – exact date is obscure – a Party worker in Winnipeg asked another member of the Patricia's to steal rifles. In the soldier's own words: "There was no responsible person [sic] or policeman in the neighbourhood, so I knocked him down and left him laying [sic] there." By July 1934, the Adjutant General reported that some 13 to 17 Communists had been identified in the Army. He asked that all new recruits be put under observation, and that reports be made about their habits, associates, and spare-time activities.[25] All information on subversion had to come from the R.C.M.P., for the Army had no agency that could handle the detailed work of surveillance.

The first mention of Canadians being recruited to serve in the Spanish Civil War appears on Army files in October 1936. Enlistments continued into 1937, and culminated in the formation of the Mackenzie-Papineau Battalion. Most of the recruits came from Quebec, Ontario, and Manitoba; only a few seemed to have connections with the N.P.A.M., which, in general, was scornful of these volunteers. "Mac-Pap" recruiting did attract the attention of some right-wing elements, and occasional clashes occurred. In October, thugs from a Fascist party in Montreal wrecked the office and printshop of a Communist firm supporting the Mac-Paps. The violence was short-lived, possibly because, by this time, recruiting for Spain in that city had become less openly conducted. In February 1937, Regina advised that five Militia men had obtained passports for Spain. The Adjutant General asked that their names be obtained and that Ottawa be advised of their movements. In the event, only one man actually left; a deserter from a B.C. Militia unit who found his way to Spain in June, 1938. When the Mackenzie-Papineau Battalion was finally demobilized in November of that year, there was renewed concern that some of its members might cause trouble on their return.[26]

The rise of Nazism in Germany was accompanied by a constantly increasing flow of propaganda. This caused many, in particular those with vivid memories of the last war, to become alarmed. As a result, beginning in March 1934 and continuing until 1945, Members of Parliament and D.O.C.s began to receive reports of espionage and subversion. All complaints made to a D.O.C. were forwarded to the Intelligence Section in Army H.Q., to be passed to the R.C.M.P. They were seldom founded on facts. For example, in May 1938 A.D.M.&A.F.I. received a report that a "beautiful foreign-speaking young lady" had been particularly pleasant and friendly to the writer and his military friends. The R.C.M.P. investigated and replied that "the young woman has a typical New York accent and came to Toronto with some other young ladies for the purpose of being in that city during the Canadian Corps Reunion."[27] Fanny Hill, perhaps; Mata Hari, no.

Other reports were more serious. On September 3rd, 1938, the German Consul at Winnipeg was reported to have held a Bund-type rally complete with swastika flags and Nazi songs. In May 1939, M.D. 7 reported that a map showing the contours and routes throughout the province of New Brunswick, ostensibly keyed to the pulp and paper industry, was being prepared and kept up-to-date by German nationals. The Master of a German ship which regularly visited Saint John was reported to be in contact with them and to be transmitting code messages as soon as he was outside the three-mile limit. In spite of these allegations, the Army files, which are admittedly incomplete, do not reveal the existence of any proven espionage rings until early 1938. The detection of espionage was the responsibility of the R.C.M.P.; the Army was advised of the results of an investigation only when it was directly involved.[28]

Towards the end of the decade, two Canadian Fascist parties were formed in Eastern Canada: the National Socialist Christian Party in Quebec, with about 5,200 members; and the Canadian Nationalist Party (C.N.P.), with 500 members in Toronto and an additional 2,000 in Ontario as a whole. The Fascist personalities were known, for in 1936 the C.N.R. had delivered three big boxes addressed to the Director of Intelligence, Ottawa. S/L Guthrie called in the R.C.M.P., and the cases were opened and found to be filled with dossiers on Canadian Fascists, and on non-Fascists who had relatives in Italy on whom pressure could be exerted. The documents were copied and replaced, and the C.N.R., advised that a mistake had been made, then delivered them to the Italian Embassy.

Although the two groups were reported to have merged in March 1938, they seem to have maintained separate entities throughout that year. They had contacts in some of the more moderate Italian, German, and Ukrainian ethnic groups, with various Front organizations, and with a C.N.P. branch in Winnipeg. Each had a uniformed branch, each was publicly anti-Jewish. Both groups campaigned strongly for increased membership during early 1938, and attempted to unite with similar groups that had been formed in the Maritimes and in British Columbia. The response these campaigns evoked was not significant and they were closed in late December, 1939.[29]

In December 1937, reports were received of a wave of Japanese propaganda, apparently emanating from agencies in New York and other eastern United States cities. Investigation showed that the vehicle being used was the Tokyo Rotary Club, which sent some 30,000 propaganda pamphlets to Rotary clubs around the world, inserting them into its general business correspondence. A number of M.D.s received copies, but their impact was negligible.

In late January 1938, M.D. 11 reported that Japanese were photographing the west coast and its harbours. The D.M.O.&I., Col. Harry Crerar, replied that it was quite legal to photograph the coastline and open harbours, but not fortresses, arsenals, dockyards, and other military installations. He invited the D.O.C., M.D. 11, to "take such steps as may be necessary to prevent unlawful acts of this nature". The D.O.C., in his turn, ordered his D.I.O. to maintain close liaison with the local police forces. In March 1939, attempts were made on the west coast to use both Army and Air Force to collect information on Japanese activities. Only those that were overt could have been reported, for there was only one Japanese interpreter in all three Services.[30]

WAR CLOUDS GATHER

The European crisis of 1936 gave clear warning that war was possible and that time to prepare for it was short. Ever since the end of the First World War, Canada's obligations had been discussed within the Department of National Defence and between officers of the Department and their opposite numbers abroad. These discussions, however, had been conducted without much sense of urgency or of direction. Planning for Defence Scheme No. 3 – to cover participation in a war outside Canada – had been started in 1927. The Scheme was approved by the Minister in 1932, then revised to reflect increased emphasis on the direct defence of Canada and on internal security, and finally approved on March 17th, 1937, and distributed to the Districts on January 22nd, 1938.

At the end of the First World War, the Otter Commission had proposed a field force of six infantry divisions and one cavalry division supported by the necessary ancillary troops. The 1932 plan called for the mobilization of a field force of two infantry divisions, a cavalry division, and corps, army, and lines-of-communication troops under the command of a Corps Headquarters. Base units were to be provided both in Canada and overseas. There was no detailed plan to expand this force, although a possible need to form four additional divisions with the necessary supporting troops was foreseen. At this period the Canadian Army had no formations larger than brigades. Certain units and individuals were nominated to fill vacancies in the order-of-battle and at Headquarters, and H.Q. tried to keep the lists up to date. Preliminary planning conferences called to deal with the technique of sending a force overseas did not ask for any Intelligence contribution about the nature of the possible enemy threat or the theatre in which it would be posed.[31]

On September 5th, 1936, a Joint Staff Committee Memorandum gave focus to the military and political aspects of planning for the higher direction of an expected war. It listed Canadian obligations to the League of Nations, and discussed the thinking that had formed the basis for the three Defence Schemes.[32] Approval was sought to set up Interdepartmental Planning agencies.

The C.G.S., Maj.-Gen. E.C. Ashton, finally received approval in detail to establish Sub-Committees and a Secretariat to support the work of the Defence Committee on March 14th, 1938 (Order-in-Council P.C. 531). A Sub-Committee to deal with Internal Security already existed; others were added to make plans for "Treatment of Aliens and Alien Property", "Censorship", and "Vulnerable Points". Since all four fields involved areas for which the D.M.O.&I. had responsibility, his Intelligence Staff was needed to prepare papers and to act as the Directorate's representative on some of the Sub-Committees.

The first of these Sub-Committees had to define a policy for dealing with aliens from what were now thought to be potentially enemy countries. It was still thought that natural and sometimes deep-seated loyalties to their former homelands might induce them, in some cases, to become involved in espionage and subversion against Canada. Internment and census statistics therefore had to be carefully re-examined. They showed that of the 8,579 persons interned by the Department in the First World War, 5,954 had been Austro-Hungarian, and 2,009 German; 3,138 of them had been military reservists. The census of 1931 showed a total of 529,139 aliens: 41,595 were males under the age of 20 and 303,381 were males over 20; 24,120 were German, Italian, or Japanese in origin, about two-thirds of whom had settled in Ontario and British Columbia. On September 16th, 1938, the Aliens Sub-Committee recommended that the whole problem should be handled by the Office of the Secretary of State, that arrests should be a police responsibility, and that a Director of Internment Camps should be appointed from the Army Retired List. Defence would select and train a staff to guard the internees during the first weeks of the war and would be responsible for housing and feeding them. Revised estimates from the Dominion Bureau of Statistics, coupled with the results of a new Sub-Committee study, then led to an assessment that only about 25% of the 9,713 German and 9,560 Italian aliens, but 100% of the 4,920 Japanese, would have to be interned. Roughly 2,000 men would be needed to guard approximately 9,800 internees.[33] Obviously, mobilization planning would have to make provision for this sizeable guard force.

Censorship planning was assigned to Lt.-Col. M.A. Pope, G.S.O.1, D.M.O.&I. He had little information to guide him: a British *Handbook for Use of Cable Censors, 1925*, which dealt only with low-grade cipher censorship, the minutes of the Signals Sub-Committee of the Defence Committee which, in 1921, had briefly discussed Cable Censorship, and the Minutes of an informal Censorship Planning Sub-Committee organized in November 1927. With the then D.M.O.&I. as Chairman, this Sub-Committee had held eight meetings between February 17th, 1928, and March 16th, 1933, and had recommended that Censorship should accept the broad principles and lines laid down during the 1914–18 war. The Secretary of State would control Press Censorship; Defence would be responsible for Cable; Transport would monitor Radio; Postal would be under the Postmaster-General. An Editing Committee had then been instructed to compile and edit new Canadian Censorship Regulations, using the British regulations as a guide. The Sub-Committee eventually produced a five-chapter paper, with 22 appendices, but its recommendations were never approved.[34]

On March 23rd, 1938, the D.M.O.&I. advised the C.G.S. that an Interdepartmental Committee on Censorship had been instituted by Order-in-Council, to "enquire into and report on a comprehensive scheme for the institution of censorship of all forms or means of communication in time of war or emergency". Its Chairman was the Minister of National Defence; its members were representatives of the Secretary of State, Transport, the Post Office, External Affairs, Trade and Commerce, and National Revenue. Two days later, in a paper outlining the organization of the Defence Department component, the D.M.O.&I. was made responsible for Censorship. He was given an establishment increment of a Chief Telegraph and Telephone Censor to deal with cable, telegraph, and telephone communications other than those used by the press, and an Information Section responsible for collecting, co-ordinating, and distributing the necessary information to all Canadian Censorship and other government departments as and when it was required. The system was expressly designed to ensure that a Service representative would explain to the Censorship organization what information the Services desired to protect, and possibly the reasons why they desired that protection.[35] At the beginning of the war, both Sections were part of the Directorate, but only the Information Section remained in it throughout the war *(see Annex 2 for line diagram, Censorship Organization)*.

This Interdepartmental Committee on Censorship met on March 30th, 1938, and again on April 20th. It decided not to impose censorship on mail or telephone communications within Canada, nor on mail, telephone, or telegraph services to the United States. Censorship was to be limited, at the beginning, to overseas cables, radio, some postal communications, and the press. On May 14th, it defined the aims of Censorship: the enemy was to be prevented from acquiring any information about Canada; all messages liable to damage civilian or military morale, to cause dissatisfaction, or to prejudice relations with allied or neutral powers, were to be stopped; enemy commercial traffic was to be cut. A new Editing Committee was set up to draft the Order-in-Council that would impose censorship. The Cabinet approved the Committee's first interim report on September 24th, 1938, and, on the 28th, Lt.-Col. Pope issued the first two chapters of a Censorship Handbook to M.D.s 2, 4, 6, and 11. It dealt with the general concepts as well as the detail of Cable Censorship operations. It included a warning that all radio telegraphy would cease when censorship was ordered, and it provided a list of registered telegraphic addresses. A revised draft was sent out on October 21st and a complete new edition on November 10th.[36]

Although the problems of the two Sub-Committees on Internal Security and Vulnerable Points tended in practice to overlap, their functions were fundamentally different. One dealt with the threat from espionage and the other with the threat from sabotage. Counter-espionage in Canada was handicapped by the lack of any legal protection of information. In 1921, Winston Churchill, then Secretary of State for the Colonies, asked Ottawa to consider introducing legislation similar to the British Official Secrets Act of 1911, as revised in 1920. His suggestion was discussed by Militia H.Q. on September 23rd, 1921, but, at that time, it was believed that the Criminal Code of Canada afforded sufficient basic protection. In 1922, 1936, and 1938, the appropriate Sections (85 and 86) were brought to the attention of anyone having access to sensitive material.[37]

The Sub-Committee "with respect to Civil Security and Counter-Espionage" held its first meeting on September 19th, 1938. Asst.-Commissioner King, R.C.M.P., Lt.-Cdr. Gow, Naval Intelligence, S/L Guthrie, A.D.M.&A.F.I., and Maj. C. Vokes, Secretary of the Naval, Army, and Air Force Supply Committee, were present. The Sub-Committee thought that its title was too all-embracing, and asked for clearer terms of reference and for a parent body to which it could report. The members proposed that they be made responsible for Vulnerable Points only. After discussion within the Departments involved, their recommendations were approved and counter-espionage was returned to the R.C.M.P.

The R.C.M.P. was seriously worried about the possibility that enemy agents would uncover sensitive information on equipment contracts for the Armed Forces. On December 2nd, 1938, Commissioner Wood asked if the Department of National Defence was currently taking, or was contemplating taking, any action to bar aliens from access to defence contracts. Industry was also concerned, but for a different reason. It feared that some aliens who were then employed in key jobs might be interned with the outbreak of war and that their loss would impair production until replacements could be trained.

The Judge-Advocate-General (J.A.G.) told D.M.O.&I. that, although no defence contract contained any specific bar, some contracts did have a clause banning communication "to unauthorized persons of any matters relating to the Contract which ought not to be so communicated". The J.A.G. thought that this provision could be useful and suggested that, after a security check had been made, a confirming pass be issued. Air Force contracts were similar in form, but plants working under them had to display posters containing extracts from the Official Secrets Act [sic] and use every effort to ensure that only British subjects were employed. The R.C.M.P. asked that the matter be submitted to the Aliens Sub-Committee and recommended that a clause be inserted in future contracts that would prohibit the employment of aliens on defence projects.[38]

The need to control access to classified information in armaments and other production contracts became a serious and continuing problem for Security staffs not only throughout the war but also in the postwar period. Low-level information did not cause much difficulty, for systems of screening and education could reduce the risk to an acceptable level. Very sensitive information, on the other hand, called for the complete range of measures to restrict access, sometimes to the extent of segregating management and production teams within an industry. It required that some work areas be isolated, that security clearances be obtained for individuals working on contracts, and that all correspondence, documentation, articles produced, and wastage be closely controlled. Even with these precautions, nagging doubts as to their efficacy would always be present.

Chapter III, Section 8, of Defence Scheme No. 3, required D.O.C.s to make lists of Vulnerable Points and to include them in their plans for local defence and internal security. A Vulnerable Point (V.P.) was defined as a target

> the destruction or damage of which would have an important adverse effect on either
> (a) Mobilization or military movements or military operations either within or beyond Canada.
> (b) The production, manufacture or movement of essential supplies of all kinds.[39]

Because some D.O.C.s had difficulty deciding what should or should not be included in their listings, a table of those V.P.s that had been considered vulnerable in 1917 was drawn up and sent to Districts on December 7th, 1937. District lists were then brought up-to-date and returned to D.M.O.&I., where they were consolidated and standardized. In late August 1938, a Master List was prepared and a copy sent to the R.C.M.P. As we have seen, in September 1938, the task of formulating the protection program became the responsibility of the Sub-Committee on Civil Security and Counter-Espionage; the recruiting of the guards themselves was handed to the Operations staffs. As a result,

Operations and Intelligence had to work so closely together in this field that the lines separating their responsibilities often disappeared.

The provision of guards for V.P.s faced the Department of Defence with a difficult dilemma. By definition, the V.P.s were vital to the Canadian defence effort. But they were so numerous! They included, among others, "railway bridges, tunnels, canal locks ... docks ... dams, power plants, telegraph and telephone exchanges, cable landing places ... munition plants". And they were not uniformly distributed across the country. M.D. 11, for instance, listed 151 V.P.s, including oil companies and coal mines; M.D. 2 had 70, including the Welland Canal and urban water supplies; M.D. 7 had 30; and so on. The Districts' estimates of the number of guards thought necessary to protect all the V.P.s was the equivalent of five cavalry regiments, plus detachments from four others; 19 complete infantry battalions, plus 24 detachments; 10 artillery batteries, plus four detachments; and one Field Company R.C.E., plus details from two others. This represented, in short, the fighting equivalent of about three divisions. Even though the units were calculated at only peacetime strength, to fill these demands would have removed most of the experienced men from the mobilization system.

Civil or "private" authorities would obviously have to assume some of the duties, and it was equally obvious that there would have to be a considerable reduction in the number of V.P.s. Agreement was not easily reached. The Department of Transport, for instance, stated that protection should be given only where the destruction of some facility could not be compensated for, at least temporarily, by diversions. The Canadian Pacific Railway (C.P.R.) accepted this view, but the C.N.R. asked for protection along the entire length of its main line. The John Inglis Company was manufacturing 12,000 Bren guns at its Toronto plant (5,000 for Britain), and the R.C.M.P. were asked to supply the modest number of one guard for the main gate and another for inside. The Commissioner demurred because he felt that this was properly an Army task. It was imperative that such differences of opinion between companies and between Army and R.C.M.P. be avoided.

Col. Pope asked the C.G.S. for guidance. He suggested firstly that the military assume responsibility for guarding only those V.P.s whose destruction would be clearly detrimental to the national interest. Secondly, he felt that troops should be sent only to places where their own particular skills could be used. He gave as an example the C.P.R. Angus Shops at Montreal, where "the danger in time of war would not be a massed attack by a gang of armed fenians [*sic*] but rather some act of sabotage by a disaffected employee who might blow up the power house or injure some essential machinery by surreptitious means, the only defence against which is a police trained in secret service work." The V.P.s he considered should be given military protection were: the St. Lawrence, Welland, and Sault Ste Marie Canals; a few railway V.P.s, the destruction of which would completely tie up trans-Canada communications, and Defence establishments. He thought that power plants, waterworks, telephone exchanges and the like should be the responsibility of the firms or municipalities concerned. He wished, however, to "encourage the R.C.M.P. to assume responsibility for guarding industrial establishments engaged in the production of munitions."[40]

On December 31st, 1938, Commissioner Wood, R.C.M.P., advised that he had obtained a British handbook on plant security. This required that contractors provide their own guards, that the police and military confine themselves to ensuring protection against attack from the outside, and that for official installations, special constabulary, often drawn from veterans' organizations, should be recruited. He suggested that Canada might well adopt similar arrangements. As a result, the Department informed Districts that the R.C.M.P. would inspect local V.P.s and make recommendations for their protection, including the suggestion that firms supply their own guards. This directive attracted unfavourable publicity and questions in the House. Nevertheless, on February 21st, 1939, the R.C.M.P. warned its Divisions that they would be responsible for counter-sabotage until plants were taken over by their own guard systems. Defence, in its turn, advised the D.O.C.s to co-ordinate their plans with the R.C.M.P.[41]

Commissioner Wood agreed with the policy of the Defence Department, but was not convinced that all the V.P.s had been identified or that the full implications of guarding them were understood. He wanted a survey to be made to check these V.P.s, and feared that the quickening pace of events in Europe might require him to act before the survey was completed. He suggested that the Department of Justice should reach immediate agreement with all the provinces regarding the key V.P.s. If the "proprietors of such Points" refused to act, their protection would then become a police matter. He also felt that disturbances might not be so serious as to require troops to be called out; and that, in any case, there would necessarily be a delay between the declaration of the emergency and the arrival of troops. Police protection would be required for both kinds of contingencies. He recommended that the R.C.M.P. provide protection for all V.P.s of national importance until D.N.D. was ready to take them over. Other V.P.s should be a provincial concern and, even if the R.C.M.P. were policing a province, the costs of protecting them should be borne by that province. He informed his Minister that to perform these tasks he would need additional men and that the veterans' organizations were prepared to help.[42]

On May 8th, all R.C.M.P. Divisions were told that a paper organization could be set up in which the Canadian Legion would be used to guard the V.P.s. Officers Commanding were to contact their local Legion Command to determine how many volunteers could be ready for duty; volunteers could be told that questions of salary, equipment, badges, etc., were being discussed. A new Sub-Committee, formed to consider the final division of responsibility for V.P.s, met on May 10th. It reviewed the arrangements already made. Private concerns – railways, for example – were to be responsible for their own protection; the provinces were responsible for their own measures to maintain law and order. Canadian Legion members were to be enlisted as Special Constables. As a guide, The King's Printer was to issue 500 copies of a booklet, *Notes on Industrial Security*, containing the text of the new Official Secrets Act that was being enacted by Parliament. Many firms, including Imperial Oil (Sarnia), had already initiated programs of their own.[43]

On July 13th, the Deputy Minister of National Defence sent the D.M.O.&I.'s latest review to Commissioner Wood. It called for an increase in the number of R.C.M.P. stationed in the "inland Military Districts". The number of Legion members available for duty was estimated to be 60,000; 2,500 of these would be needed immediately to serve for periods of 12 to 72 hours; the Militia would then take over until the veterans who were being recruited were ready to replace them. The Minister felt that, since the Legionnaires were going to be sworn in as Special Constables in the R.C.M.P., they should logically remain with that Force. On July 20th, the R.C.M.P. accepted the plan, but the necessary arrangements had not been completed when war broke out. The Militia took over the protective duties until the Special Constables became available, and were then withdrawn.[44]

In 1938, the higher control and direction of Intelligence was discussed at N.D.H.Q. On March 19th, Col. Crerar, then D.M.O.&I., suggested to the three Service Chiefs that a Joint Service (or Inter-Service or Joint Staff) Intelligence Section should be formed, to operate possibly as a Sub-Committee of the Joint Staff. He said, quoting Hong Kong as a precedent, "With the world situation as it is, Intelligence duties are becoming of increasing importance and it may be that greater efficiency might result from a merger [of the A.D.M.&A.F.I. and the R.C.N. Intelligence Sections]". He believed that, if this were done, unnecessary duplication of effort and of the resulting Summaries could be avoided. On the recommendation of the Navy, a committee, chaired by S/L Guthrie, was duly appointed to study the proposal.

On July 22nd, the Navy representatives advised the committee that, since they were part of the Royal Navy's, worldwide organization, their plans were already based on Intelligence controlled by a higher authority. They thought that Army and Air Force problems, being more local in nature, could be dealt with in other ways. They suggested, however, that a Central War Room ought to be set up to co-ordinate Operations and Intelligence supplied by the different agencies. The Air Force also held the view that each Service should control its own organization, but that a degree of collaboration was very desirable.

Col. Crerar, more or less disregarding their discouraging conclusions, sent his proposals to the Joint Staff Committee with a recommendation for favourable consideration. The Committee did not act on them.[45] As we have seen, the Air Force soon withdrew from the joint arrangement with the Army. From then on, as far as Intelligence was concerned, each of the three Services went its separate way. At a much later date, however, they did meet again and agreed to a joint Defence presentation. Their actions should not be judged too harshly; there are many advantages in specialization and they often outweigh the benefits that can be achieved by amalgamation.

The Canadian force to be sent abroad was intended to parallel in organization the British Army formations with which it would be working. Some considerable effort had been made within D.M.O.&I., therefore, to make sure that its organization conformed as far as was possible to British War Establishments. General Order No. 135 of September 1st, 1939, specified the Corps of the Active Militia that would be mobilized for active service (see Chapter 5). In the Divisions, there was some doubt as to who was actually going to supply the Intelligence component, because at that time Intelligence Sections were shown as separate serials or units in the Divisional organization. The confusion was not resolved until November, after discussions had taken place between Canadian Military Headquarters in London and the War Office.[46]

We must remember, however, that despite the known and agreed requirement for an Intelligence component, either as an Intelligence Corps or as a simple collection of individuals, no one, except for Air Liaison, had been selected for training, no courses had been set up, and there was no clear understanding of what Intelligence should be called on to do. Some idea of what it had done in the previous war could have been found in the copies of Hahn's *The Intelligence Service within the Canadian Corps, 1914–18* that were held by some of the military libraries, if anyone had cared to look for them. But no attempt had been made to keep abreast of current techniques, doctrine, or planning.

Perhaps some blame can be laid at the door of the A.D.M.&A.F.I. for not having stressed these three fields actively enough. S/L Guthrie had, indeed, arranged exercises at Camp Borden for the Army Co-operation Squadron Intelligence Liaison staffs. But he did not have the Army background to plan a Field Intelligence organization. And the Staff College training he had taken would not have given him the detailed knowledge he needed; the subject was not taught there in sufficient depth. It is also possible that, with all the new activities they were called on to direct, the N.D.H.Q. Intelligence staff simply did not have – or did not take – the time to press for the urgent development of Army Intelligence. As we shall see, an efficient Intelligence service takes a long time to develop. It is perhaps fortunate that the Canadian Army Overseas was not called to go into action as quickly this time as it had been in 1915.

4.
BUILD-UP IN BRITAIN – CANADIAN MILITARY HEADQUARTERS

The Intelligence Section at Canadian Military Headquarters (C.M.H.Q.) was probably the most important single link in the entire Intelligence chain during the Second World War. Located in London, where the highest Allied planning and control was centred, it was ideally situated to act as a listening post both for the Department in Ottawa and for the Canadian Army Overseas. In 1914–19, the senior command structure – Ministry of Overseas Military Forces of Canada in Britain – had been essentially administrative, and, as such, it had been given no formal Intelligence component. It therefore left no precedent on which C.M.H.Q. might draw for guidance in deciding its own structure and duties.

From the beginning, the C.M.H.Q. Intelligence Section *(see Annex 3 for line diagram)* gathered information on British plans and policies for Ottawa and for Canadian formations in Britain. It initially controlled the cipher protection of Army messages between Ottawa and London. It was the agency responsible for security liaison between Canada, the Canadian formations in England, and the Security agencies in Britain. It was directly involved in Censorship. Later it had charge of all aspects of recruiting for the Intelligence establishments it helped to form, and for the training and professional development of all Canadian Intelligence personnel. It was involved in handling Canadian and enemy prisoners of war and a host of other minor, but important, local tasks.

The Canadian Army mobilized on September 1st, 1939. Canada formally declared war on the 10th. On the 16th, Ottawa offered Britain a token force of one division. Its offer was accepted and, on September 26th, the Minister of National Defence authorized the formation of C.M.H.Q. Brig. H.D.G. Crerar was appointed Brigadier, General Staff (B.G.S.); Col. The Hon. P.J. Montague was made Assistant Adjutant and Quartermaster General; Lt.-Col. E.L.M. Burns, then at the Imperial Staff College, became G.S.O.1.

In addition to its administrative role, C.M.H.Q. was required to perform two functions that directly involved Intelligence:

> (d) To maintain close liaison with the War Office and with the G.O.C. Canadian Forces in the theatre of operations (or in the United Kingdom when separate command is specified). . . .
> (f) To furnish the High Commissioner for Canada with information on military questions. . . .[1]

On November 11th, C.M.H.Q. exchanged the first intelligence information with the War Office – details of the Intelligence Sections in First Canadian Division and its three Brigades – two officers, 16 other ranks.[2]

C.M.H.Q. had no staff to handle the many cipher messages from Ottawa. After discussing this with the Secretary of the High Commission, Mr. Lester Pearson, Col. Burns advised N.D.H.Q. that it was "urgent that a cipher officer be appointed". On December 11th, 1939, Capt. T.G. Birkett, a Canadian living in England, was appointed to that post, first as a civilian and then as an officer when he was commissioned on January 1st, 1940. His first cipher, a new standard War Office version, was introduced on December 12th to replace one which was considered to offer inadequate protection; first instructions, dealing with the proper handling of that cipher, appeared on December 14th. His operators were supplied by First Canadian Division, which landed in mid-December. These men were untrained, and it was not practical to train them on the job because of the volume of work and the acute shortage of replacement staff.[3] They were therefore sent on course on January 15th, 1940, and did not become fully available until February. First Division was understandably unhappy at losing its men, but C.M.H.Q.'s needs were greater, and trained men were too few in numbers to staff two H.Q.s. On May 25th, 1940, they were replaced with men of lower medical categories from the infantry depot and returned to H.Q. First Division.

The communications facilities soon proved inadequate. To overcome this difficulty, Maj. N.E. Rodger, G.S.O.3, arranged on February 28th, 1940, for Army messages to be passed by British Air Ministry radio. The G.S.O.1, who perhaps had a better idea of the political implications of such an arrangement, stopped it at once, but as there was no other practical solution, the link was reopened and the Air Ministry continued to allow Canadians to use its facilities until well into 1941. They were busy. In the week ending March 9th, the three-man C.M.H.Q. Section handled 106 messages, 13,178 words in all. The two operators had worked a total of 96 man hours, a decrease from the 56 hours each had worked in the preceding week.

By May 4th the volume had become too great. The Section asked for an extra machine and new teleprinter links, and began a succession of demands for more staff. In September 1940, it asked for four clerks, six operators (cipher), and five teleprinter operators to replace those which the Air Ministry was providing without cost. One additional officer (Lieut. Sloan) arrived in July; his appointment was not authorized until September. In October, Capt. Birkett introduced a system of numbering messages to save the time previously spent in searching through files for text. On March 7th, 1941, the Section again quoted figures to justify its demands for staff: in July 1940, there were 3,137 groups; in January 1941, the number had increased to 7,421. The 8,000 words per day they were then receiving were quite beyond their capabilities. Eventually, sufficient personnel were provided to operate three shifts a day, each with an officer – Capt. Birkett, Lieut. W.C. Innes, or Lieut. J.D.W. Halbert.

On June 23rd, 1941, Lt.-Col. H.A. Young, G.S.O.1 Staff Duties, recommended that the teleprinters be given to the C.M.H.Q. Signals Section, provided that Signals could guarantee that the enciphering and deciphering services would not be affected. His proposal would reduce the work of Intelligence by some 40%; the 69 all ranks of the cipher staff were examined to see if they were qualified to retain their pay and positions. Though the actual date is not clear, the function probably went to Signals in September 1941; but M.O.&I. was still being asked to find personnel for it as late as October.[4]

On December 16th, 1939, Brig. Crerar asked his G.S.O.1 for a list of Intelligence material received regularly by C.M.H.Q. "I consider that the time has now come when the flow of Intelligence to the centre should be properly organized. At present, we get little 'inside' information and that is usually stale." He warned that Col. Burns would probably have to visit the War Office daily, and said that he wanted to be able to keep the C.G.S. informed at least weekly. C.M.H.Q. routinely received the daily Summary given to the High Commissioner by the Dominions Office, the notes from the weekly meeting between the Director of Military Operations (War Office) and the B.G.S., a weekly Intelligence Commentary, weekly Intelligence Summaries on China and Japan, a daily Intelligence Signal, and a weekly report from the foreign-broadcast monitoring service of the B.B.C. At "irregular intervals", the War Office issued tactical and technical notes on the German Army which were sent both to Ottawa and to First Division.

In his reply, Col. Burns said: "Before setting up any system of forwarding Intelligence to N.D.H.Q., we should be clear as to the object. . . . This should be to give the Canadian military authorities and government an accurate picture of the *general* strategic situation and up-to-date information on all factors affecting it." This could only be done in the form of an Appreciation – a formal Staff assessment of the factors affecting that situation. N.D.H.Q. could not write it because its staff lacked full and up-to-date information; C.M.H.Q. could not do so for lack of staff. One could be prepared using the British Chiefs-of-Staff Appreciations, but Col. Burns doubted that the War Office would release these highly sensitive documents. He therefore suggested that C.M.H.Q., after consultation with the War Office, should produce a modified Appreciation, which would omit any highly secret matters but which would contain enough data and argument to justify the current war policy. Several Appreciations might be needed to cover the various possible theatres of war. They could be kept up-to-date by cabling amendments to explain changes in situation and the resulting alterations in policy or plans. The weekly Summaries and other routine material would continue to be sent to provide background. "If this work is to be adequately performed, a G.S.O.3 (Intelligence) is required for the routine [and continuous] checking of Intelligence."

Brig. Crerar was not convinced that C.M.H.Q. was competent to provide Appreciations. He thought that the most that could be expected was a weekly summary of important Army, Naval, and Air events, followed by whatever deductions C.M.H.Q. could logically draw from them. In his opinion, the weekly report of the British Chiefs of Staff, together with his own notes of the meetings and other items they received, would be adequate for Canadian needs. However, in a remarkable burst of generosity the British Chiefs-of-Staff Committee decided that, although they could not release their full reports to Canada, they would allow a Canadian representative to see them and to extract anything that Ottawa needed. Their decision was passed to the C.G.S. on January 29th.

In doing this, the War Office was making an enormous concession. The matter contained in the reports was often highly sensitive. Much of it reflected worldwide British interests that were of no concern to Canada. Indeed, the arrangement, running counter as it did to the cardinal Security principle of "need to know", indicated absolute confidence in an as yet unnamed Canadian officer. For his part, that officer would have to select from the material what was of interest to Canada and ignore the rest. And if, at some later date, he were asked for additional information, he would have to know where and how it had previously been discussed.

The first of these Appreciations was prepared by the G.S.O.1 on February 1st, 1940, in two copies, one for the code room and transmission to Ottawa, one for the High Commission. In April, the Officer Commanding R.C.A.F. in Britain, G/C G.V. Walsh, asked for a copy. By February 11th, 1943, some 45 copies were in circulation, of which 14 alone were for C.M.H.Q., "to meet the demands of senior officers". The list was pruned periodically, but circulation continued to grow.[5]

On January 3rd, 1940, following up his December proposal to Brig. Crerar, Col. Burns asked for "a G.S.O.3 . . . to study and summarize Intelligence . . . to supervise the collection of War Diaries pending the appointment of an Officer in . . . the Historical Section . . . and to compile the monthly Progress Reports on the Canadian units in the U.K."[6] Only the first of these tasks was strictly an Intelligence responsibility. The other two were, of course, very important and may have been included to provide greater justification for the position. The latter was long to remain an Intelligence Section function.

The new G.S.O.3, Maj. N.E. Rodger, R.C.E., arrived on February 9th, 1940. His duties went far beyond those listed in Col. Burns' request. In fact, he has since described his function as "a general dogsbody", and the following list underlines this. He was a most capable officer, but he neither had the Intelligence background and training that the job required, nor, and more significant from Col. Burns' point of view, was he staff-trained. Despite these shortcomings, his contribution was impressive.[7] He was in charge of Cipher and Cryptography and had to arrange courses for the cipher room staffs. On February 15th, he was to be found checking the Canadian War Establishment against the British, normally a Staff Duties job. In March, he was required to work out trade statistics for Scandinavia, a task for an analyst rather than the liaison officer he was supposed to be. He had, with M.I.5, to devise procedures for checking subversion within the Canadian Army. He was the Canadian liaison officer responsible for Censorship, a role which required him to maintain contacts with both the War Office and British Censorship authorities to ensure co-ordination in coverage and in methods of handling releases. He spent much time trying to develop a Press Censorship system that would reconcile the need for security with the need to get material into print quickly, a contradiction that was to continue throughout the war. He worked out a policy with the War Office for the clearance of personal mail. He was closely involved in the security arrangements that had to be made before the First Canadian Division went to France in June 1940. A ruling had to be given on the question of whether or not the "Canada" shoulder badges constituted a security hazard in operations. It was decided that, since the men also had "Canada" on their identity disks and their distinctive formation patches, one more identification did not matter.

When Second Division arrived in August, all the censorship problems and minor security breaches that always accompany new and inexperienced troops began again. The Division took very seriously the regulations laid down in the *British Field Service Pocket Book* for censoring the men's mail; they had to be told that different regulations were applied in Britain. In mid-August, the German air campaign against England accelerated, and Maj. Rodger became involved in censorship intended to deny the enemy information on the success or failure of his raids. The attacks were to be acknowledged, but no reference was to be made to their locations.

Major Rodger also dealt with Intelligence administration. In May 1940, he organized the transmission to Ottawa (M.I.2) of intercepted enemy radio traffic. He arranged for British training centres to provide Intelligence courses for Canadians – and then had to seek names for them from the units. In June, he arranged showings of a training film "Interrogation of Prisoners of War" to make troops aware of the conduct expected of them in case of capture by the enemy. The film was not the best, but it was the only one available.

He was responsible for the physical security of C.M.H.Q. On June 28th, it was decided that all cleaners at C.M.H.Q. would be screened, a precaution that may, indeed, have been necessary, for on the same day an order had to be issued that "officers were not to leave their revolvers lying around at night". Because careless talk was reported in the Beaver Club, the centre for Canadian other ranks in London, the first of many Security conferences on this subject was convened on July 1st, 1940. At C.M.H.Q., the Senior Intelligence Officer became responsible for air raid warning and for local firefighting (Passive Air Defence). While raids were in progress, the staff would leave the upper floors and no work would be done. Spotters were posted on the roof of the building to watch for incendiary bombs. Clerks who had been employed all night as fire-watchers were seldom bright and alert the following day.

He had charge of maps and historical records. And about July, someone discovered that he had not prepared the C.M.H.Q. War Diary for February, March, and April. The omission was hurriedly repaired. It was possibly due to a misunderstanding for, in February, the Historical Officer had taken over the collection of War Diaries. For all his tasks, he was allotted one assistant, a clerk-draftsman.

On February 13th, Capt. W.G. Abel, the new Public Relations Officer, was given the responsibility for obtaining from the B.B.C. its Daily Digest of Foreign Broadcasts, which had been one of Maj. Rodger's minor tasks. The material which appeared in the Digest was a useful source of information on enemy propaganda (Counter-Intelligence used it for tracing rumours and subversion), on activities within enemy and enemy-occupied countries (troop movements, order-of-battle, damage assessment, vulnerable points), on comments on Canadian activities (which could point to leaks in security), and on the reactions of neutral nations to events as they occurred. The Digest itself was, and still is, procured very simply by commercial purchase, and presumably Capt. Abel was chosen to handle it under his "liaison with the Press" function. Fortunately, the material itself was sent directly to Intelligence. In fact, at one of Maj. Rodger's first recorded meetings on February 20th, the G.S.O.1, Mr. Bryan Meredith of the B.B.C., Mr. Maynard of Canada House, and Maj. Rodger considered false statements concerning Canada and Canadian troops in German broadcasts.

To close the gap as perceived by Col. Burns, C.M.H.Q. asked for an additional G.S.O.1 or G.S.O.2 (and a clerk to serve him) to prepare "appreciations of the strategical situation and the Intelligence required to keep them up to date". The G.S.O.3 was ". . . handicapped in dealing with appreciations or other military papers of an elaborate kind". The new officer should have "Operations or Intelligence experience at N.D.H.Q. or at least Passed Staff College (*psc*), be a good writer and have experience in composing military papers". His appointment would then release the G.S.O.3 for Staff College. The need was genuine; at the end of April Mr. Lester B. Pearson unsuccessfully proposed a parallel link with the Chiefs-of-Staff Committee.

Col. Burns' proposal was rejected. The C.G.S. questioned:

> . . . the need for Intelligence Reports and Appreciations on the European situation being supplied to N.D.H.Q. by CANMILITARY [radio address for C.M.H.Q.] While some of the items included . . . are of interest, they are mostly duplications of daily reports received through External Affairs.

A number of reasons of varying importance can be adduced to explain Ottawa's decision. Ostensibly it was to prevent the creation of an "empire" such as existed at Argyle House in the First World War. Though the Intelligence requirement itself was small, it was lumped with others, and Ottawa was seriously trying to control expansion. But it must be remembered that the initiative had come from C.M.H.Q. The C.G.S. had not given any guidance as to what data should be sought nor, in fact, had he given any indication that he wanted any at all. It is possible that the then C.G.S. did not fully appreciate the degree to which Canada had become independent, and therefore saw no need for additional information to support the Canadian decision-making process, or for the staff to handle it. A more likely explanation is that no qualified officer was then available to perform the function that Col. Burns had outlined. A "chicken-and-egg" situation seems to have developed. The product coming from C.M.H.Q. had not convinced its recipient that it was worth receiving. And it was not very good; it takes practice and experience to produce professional material. At that time, also, Ottawa would not have been receptive even to first-class material. The demands of creating a military force virtually from scratch led staff officers to focus on the situation immediately before them, not on future events and on reasoned speculation concerning their possible effects. The fact, however, that no one was qualified for the job, and that apparently no one understood that it was an essential one which should almost automatically have been filled by a trained officer, reveal a significant weakness in pre-1939 Canadian defence planning.

Maj. Rodger was replaced in November 1940 by Maj. John Page, Toronto Scottish. One of John Page's first acts was to evaluate Intelligence and consider how to promote the idea that the Canadian Army should form its own Intelligence Corps. On November 18th, 1940, he began by asking the B.G.S. for authority for men on Intelligence duties to wear British Intelligence Corps flashes with their "Canada" badges. His request was refused. On November 19th, he discussed the formation of a Corps with Lt.-Col. R.R.M. Perceval, M.I.1 (Administration) at the War Office; this was the first time any such steps were actually taken.[8] But he did not immediately follow this up, partly because, on November 25th, he became involved in a difference of opinion with the B.G.S. VII Corps, who felt that the Deputy Provost Marshal, not Page, should control all Field Security Sections. He wired Ottawa on the 27th, asking for clarification of responsibilities, but N.D.H.Q. was not able to give a ruling. On December 16th, he prepared a short study of the whole question. At that date, about 60 all ranks were posted to Intelligence duties; he foresaw a future need for 200. Reinforcing his position with arguments presumably derived from his conversations with the War Office, he repeated his contention that Field Security (F.S.) formed no part of Provost, and suggested two possible solutions. The first was to form a Canadian Intelligence Corps along the lines of the recently formed British Corps. The second was to parallel the British system of an administrative Intelligence Staff Officer (I(x)) by appointing an officer to administer F.S. Sections. Either course would allow records to be centralized and enquiries to be followed up more easily. He proposed that officer establishments be set at 75% captains, 25% lieutenants. The I.O. I(b) at Corps would be a captain; the major at C.M.H.Q. would be the officer administering the F.S. Sections.[9] The only result was an interim decision that we will discuss later.

On January 25th, 1941, Ottawa replied, "doubtful whether the size of the Canadian Army warrants the formation of a special corps or the establishment of a special body". On February 4th, the A.A.G. (Organization) at C.M.H.Q. told Maj. Page that he thought it undesirable to limit F.S. personnel to any particular, distinctive uniform. He saw two alternatives: "to create a Canadian Intelligence Corps and post Field Security and Intelligence to Security units of that Corps or to continue them as extra-regimental establishments as at present". A Defence Council ruling, on February 2nd, 1941, gave F.S. officers authority to wear the Royal Arms, and N.C.O.s the Maple Leaf, as cap badges.[10] Little enthusiasm was shown for the insignia of the "Cross and Blackwell's Fusiliers", the name given to the General List badge which comprised The Royal Coat of Arms, also borne on the label of a well-known condiment that held an Appointment to Royalty. The N.C.O.s showed even less enthusiasm for the maple leaf badge, then normally worn only by recruits at a depot.

On July 14th, 1941, Maj. Robertson (I(a)), and Capts. Chamberlain (I(b)) and Catto (Cipher), all of I Corps, met with Maj. Page to discuss the establishment of a Canadian Section of an Intelligence Corps. This was to act as a Depot, i.e., a general military training, specialist training, and holding unit from which officers and men could be drawn to fill vacancies; it was also to provide a centralized administration. It was agreed that Staff Duties (the office responsible for establishments) would be asked to review the recommendations, which would then be discussed informally with the B.G.S. at C.M.H.Q. before a formal submission was made.[11]

The transfer of Cipher to Signals during the summer of 1941 prompted a review of the over-all control and administration of the whole Intelligence organization. On October 10th, Gen. McNaughton, Commander I Canadian Corps, stated that the act reduced the Intelligence function so greatly that re-forming Intelligence into a separate Corps would impose too great an administrative overhead. In his view, all that was needed was some central authority to select, train, and post Intelligence personnel. He believed that this could most easily be done by slightly augmenting the M.I. Branch at C.M.H.Q., and he was "definitely opposed to the formation of an Intelligence Corps".

Brig. Beament, Deputy Adjutant General, C.M.H.Q., pointed out to Corps that there was no central administration for Intelligence. If Cipher went to Signals and F.S. to the Provost, there was no one left to handle the remaining elements. He suggested that I Corps assume that responsibility. Brig. Guy Simonds, B.G.S. I Corps, was reluctant to do so. John Page prepared a further staff paper pointing out that supervision of Intelligence-employed personnel was not possible without an Intelligence Corps. He documented his case with a reasoned, logical study of the background, problems, and possible future trends of Intelligence.[12]

This led to another interim solution. Approval was granted on January 3rd, 1942, for the formation of an Intelligence and Field Security Reinforcement Pool within No. 1 Canadian General Reinforcement Unit (1 C.G.R.U.), with a strength of one officer, a Warrant Officer II, one N.C.O., and a clerk. Under the Officer Administering Canadian Intelligence Details Overseas (Maj. Page), this Pool was to be responsible for interviewing, selecting, and training suitable personnel. It was to hold 18% of the Intelligence field strength, a number then judged sufficient to provide an estimated three months' reinforcements. Only other ranks were to be trained by it; officers would continue to be sent to British Intelligence schools. An overseas training system was necessary because many reinforcements trained in Canada were too often "lost" to Intelligence by being returned to their parent regiments before they even reached Britain.[13]

The competition for good men was keen. A Canadian I.O. was expected to be of Staff College calibre, with a firm knowledge of tactics, staff duties, organization, and administration, and to be able to make quick decisions. He was to have a university education or equivalent, and be able to speak or read German or Japanese in addition to English and French. If he qualified in all respects except Service experience, he was sent for six months to a field unit. Other ranks had to be fluent linguists, but lower military and educational standards were accepted.

A campaign was launched to persuade Gen. McNaughton to change his mind. He did so on April 29th, 1942, but he insisted on adding one condition – that no man should be transferred against his will. A comprehensive submission was prepared and sent to Ottawa on May 22nd. It contained a detailed list of all the various Intelligence units in being or authorized, together with their functions and locations: Intelligence Sections at H.Q. First Canadian Army, I Canadian Corps; First, Second, and Third Infantry, and Fifth Armoured Divisions; No. 1 and No. 2 Canadian Special Wireless Sections Type B; seven Field Security Sections (Army, Nos. 1, 2, 3, 7, 11, 12); I(x) at C.M.H.Q.; and the Pool. There were no Air Photo, Censor, Interrogator, or Interpreter units. Ottawa's approval added the field units serving in Canada, or those approved but not yet formed, the Security Intelligence Sections at the Districts, and the date the Corps was created, October 29th, 1942.

The new Corps grouped all these units together, as well as all the personnel in Intelligence duties at various H.Q. who did not hold General Staff appointments. Members of the Corps were to be posted to a General List and transferred within the Corps as necessary.[14] This organization gave Intelligence a home, and had an obviously beneficial effect on morale. But, still more important, it enabled Intelligence to administer its personnel in a tidy, logical, and efficient way. The plan did not include the senior staff officers, most of whom served throughout the war without ever becoming members of the Corps. This was a deliberate decision. It was thought that the anonymity of senior overseas staff would enhance security. Those overseas also feared that officers in D.M.I. Ottawa would block any plan that did not provide vacancies for themselves. The logical solution would have been to create an over-all common Intelligence Establishment, but this was not done. Nor, incidentally, did the plan include the junior I.O.s in the brigades and battalions. The failure to do so was a grave planning error that was to have serious adverse effects on the postwar status of the Corps.

About the middle of June 1942, a submission attempted to upgrade the G.S.O.2 position to G.S.O.1 (lieutenant-colonel), to retitle it "Director of Military Operations and Intelligence (D.M.O.&I.)", and to add a new captain vacancy. It enumerated the several duties, and the changes in their scope and nature since 1940 are obvious. The G.S.O.2 was responsible for organizing and administering all Intelligence personnel overseas; formulating policy on Intelligence, Security, and Censorship, and Internal and Military Security (counter-subversion and counter-sabotage); dealing with reports of suspicious incidents, enemy aliens, internments, and discharges; clearing all civilians in the Canadian Army Overseas; clearing articles for publication; and liaison with the military advisors to Censorship. The G.S.O.3 was responsible for liaison with Royal Navy, War Office, and R.A.F. Intelligence; preparing appreciations for N.D.H.Q.; Intelligence Circular Letters; all Intelligence publications; translations; statements of enemy order-of-battle; and the Intelligence Map. He controlled all codes; all secret Canadian Army Overseas passes, permits and identity cards, i.e., those giving access to very sensitive establishments; and all matters relating to telegraph, telephone, and postal censorship. The new lieutenant in charge of administration (I(x)) was to handle all appointments, postings, transfers, attachments, and promotions of Intelligence personnel; keep records of Intelligence courses and attachments to the British; and conduct administrative liaison with the British Intelligence Corps. A G.S.O.3 (Operations) was needed to take over the distribution of maps, the local defence of all units under C.M.H.Q., and the preparation of "Location States" – periodic reports showing the exact locations of all Canadian units, including a map. An Historical Officer and a P.R.O. were also to report to the M.O.&I.[15] On June 25th, 1942, the Section gained Lieut. S.H.S. Hughes, who came in as M.I.(x). But, unfortunately, it also suffered a severe loss when John Page was sent to H.Q. First Canadian Army as G.S.O.2 (Int).

4. BUILD-UP IN BRITAIN – CANADIAN MILITARY HEADQUARTERS

Maj. John Page, "Father of the Corps", on right. Photo was taken in 1944 in the U.K, when he was a Lt.-Col. on staff at Supreme H.Q. Allied Expeditionary Force, serving Gen. Eisenhower (on left). (Photo courtesy of Pipe-Sergeant (retd) Tim Stewart, C.D., curator of the Toronto Scottish Regimental Museum Archives)

Maj. John Page's work at C.M.H.Q. was outstanding. He reinforced and enlarged the foundations of co-operation with the British that had been laid by General Burns. He did much to clarify the sometimes confused differences over administration and control between C.M.H.Q. and the senior field command. He was the man who, more than any other, put Intelligence on a firm administrative footing. If anyone can claim to be "Father of the Corps", it is John Page. He was transferred to give First Army the advantage of his knowledge, and to give him field experience. But the move was not an unqualified success; Page, a brilliant administrator, worked better as the leader of a small dynamic group than as a subordinate member of a larger team. And at that time, the senior command at H.Q. First Canadian Army seldom considered Intelligence important enough to include it in briefings, consultations, or planning. John Page found it too frustrating to work in such an environment.

Page's replacement, Maj. John D. Halbert, found himself immediately involved in administration. A conference was held in June 1942 to review the current state of training and to estimate future requirements. Halbert had to prepare the C.M.H.Q. position papers. One immediate result was that a full range of courses was activated at the Pool, then called the Intelligence Company, 1 C.G.R.U.

An even more significant conference was held in December 1942. Here, for the first time, officers from N.D.H.Q., C.M.H.Q., and the formations, were able to exchange ideas and experiences. The Chairman was the B.G.S., C.M.H.Q. Present were: Lt.-Col. The Lord Tweedsmuir, G.S.O.1 (Int), H.Q. First Army; Lt.-Col. Eric Acland, D.M.I. (Security), N.D.H.Q.; Majs. J.P. Page, J.D. Halbert, and A.M. Fordyce, G.S.O.3 (Int), H.Q. I Corps; Capts. J. Green, I.O. I(b), I Corps, J. Timmerman, G.S.O.3 I(a), First Army, B. Foreman, 3 Division F.S., J.M. Gray, First Army F.S., and S.H.S. Hughes, I(x), C.M.H.Q.; and R.L. Raymont, O.C. Training Company, and his assistant, J.C. Defries.

The meeting attempted to resolve some areas of friction which still persisted in spite of the agreement reached the previous April: that C.M.H.Q. would deal with War Office Censorship and Public Relations, and maintain central security records, while field problems would be handled by First Army. The agenda included organization, training, and reinforcements in Canada, Security (including Halifax), aliens and "vetting", and an explanation of the current status of the Intelligence Corps and the choice of a design for the new Corps badge. This latter was hotly debated; members felt strongly that it should have a Canadian, not a British, motif.[16] The same continuously recurring complaints were aired: pay anomalies; that good men were hard to find; that selection methods had not been adequate; and that recruiting must in future be more energetic. The criticisms were a little unjust. John Page had long found that units were unwilling to part with well-qualified officers, and the officers were reluctant to go to an organization which could offer little or no hope for promotion.

On May 8th, 1943, Halbert was replaced by Maj. Felix H. Walter, who was to remain at C.M.H.Q. until the end of the war. Felix Walter, too, had to learn his duties quickly; almost at once he had to solve one of the minor frictions mentioned above. On May 17th, Page's successor at H.Q. First Army tried to reopen negotiations on the agreed responsibilities of each H.Q. regarding individual postings. Maj. Walter rejected this, but was careful at the same time to warn his staff that any future moves of personnel must be first discussed with the H.Q. affected.

The first head of the Intelligence and Field Security Pool was Lieut. John Timmerman. He was followed in July 1942 by Capt. Robert L. Raymont. In November 1942, the Pool, then known as the Intelligence Company, moved from Cove, near Farnborough, to Barossa and Corunna Barracks, Aldershot. It had presented basic courses for brigade and battalion I.O.s as well as for F.S. (other ranks) and Unit Security Officers. In May 1943, a new Regimental Officers Intelligence Course and a Field Security Refresher Course were held. They were followed in August by the first German and French Language Refresher courses, and Photographer Clerks and I(b) Officers courses, all of which had been planned in the previous autumn. The course load placed an enormous burden on the staff, and help had to be obtained from wherever it could be found, usually from officers awaiting their field appointments at the unit.

When the Pool was established, there were many I(a) and some 20 F.S. vacancies in the formations. In addition, First Canadian Army, formed on April 6th, 1942, and II Canadian Corps, formed on January 14th, 1943, each required an Intelligence component. Despite the acknowledged need for more people, all unit establishments had been "frozen" until the demands imposed by the formation of First Army had been met. On November 10th, 1943, the increased establishment requested for the Pool in July 1942 was approved. It promoted the O.C. to major, and added an officer and sufficient staff to run both an administrative and a training wing. It also added two responsibilities: to be the clearing house for all C.Int.C. records and to administer the postings of C.Int.C. personnel.

Long before 1939, the question of aliens and the potential threat to Canadian security that they represented had been a source of worry to the Ottawa planning staffs. Some aliens had, in fact, been enrolled in the Army. But, from 1942 on, recruiting shortages began to be serious, and aliens did comprise a sizeable source of possible recruits. In April 1942, the authorities decided that Canadians of alien enemy stock, but born to naturalized parents, could be enrolled in the Canadian Army. A month later records revealed that some 505 aliens were then serving in Canadian units in Britain, some of them in sensitive duties. Of these, 261 had been cleared immediately, either because their duties gave them no access to classified information or because they were known to be loyal in spite of, or even possibly because of, their backgrounds. The other 244 cases were sent for investigation on the grounds that they presented a potential risk of espionage, sabotage, or subversion.

The presence of these men posed a serious dilemma. In spite of training, and the diligent efforts of the F.S. Sections, security standards were known to be still too low to guarantee that an agent could not cause mischief. The men therefore had to be supervised. But if the individual soldier was "clean", he had to be overtly recognized as such. Many discussions were held in an attempt to hammer out a policy that would combine maximum use of the talents of these men with the utmost protection of their, and Canada's, security. If men were singled out for special attention within a unit, their daily lives could be made unpleasant. The obvious alternative led to the suggestion that a special Pioneer (construction) unit be formed, where men could be sent for two or three months while they were being unobtrusively investigated, and where they could be watched by two F.S. N.C.O.s who would be assigned to the new unit permanently. The men could then either be returned to their units, or be dealt with in other ways if their reports were unfavourable.[17]

4. Britain 1939-1945

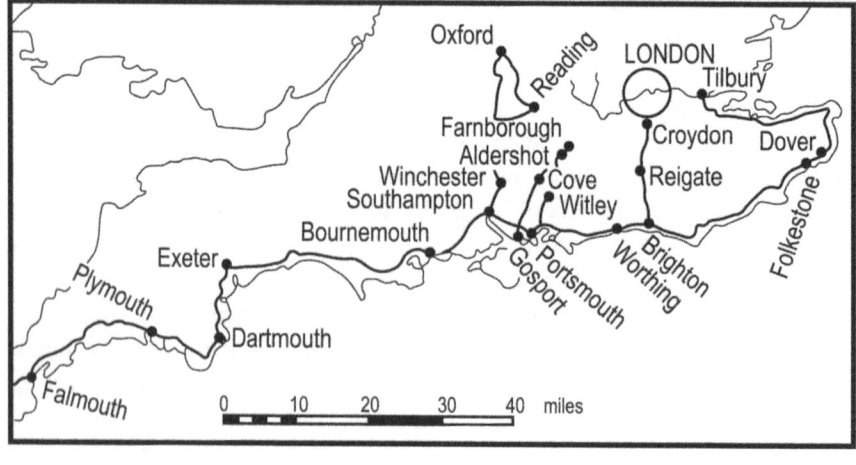

The B.G.S. First Army, Brig. Stein, was not convinced. He thought that segregation would identify the men even more clearly, that the F.S. N.C.O.s would quickly be identified, and that the tradesmen so removed would be lost to the Army. He suggested, instead, that the men ought to be returned, first to their Base Units and then to Canada, and that, in the meantime, F.S. should be advised. Maj. Halbert replied that the men had been concentrated principally so that they could be more easily supervised and kept away from classified material. Field Security clearly could not cover the whole Base Unit area as efficiently as it could one single unit. He pointed out that the men could be re-employed as soon as they were cleared. He admitted that there would inevitably be some loss of personal dignity, but felt this was not too high a price to pay for the protection of the Army. He also pointed out that evidence developed from many harrowing reports and trans-Atlantic messages tended to show that the clearance system operating in Canada was itself a long way from being perfect. The two F.S. N.C.O.s were J. Kelman and L.C. Brown; there is no evidence to show that they had been identified.[18]

No Romanian, Greek, Belgian, Czechoslovak, Polish, or French nationals were to be employed on radio duties until and unless they were cleared. No citizen with dual nationality was to be employed. Aliens could not be used as telephone operators, orderly room clerks, or in any post where they would have access to classified material. The investigations revealed 91: 15 Finns, 21 Hungarians, six Japanese, 10 Germans, 18 Italians, five Austrians, 12 Romanians, and four of "unknown" origin. In October 1942, No. 2 Pioneer Company was functioning with about 60 men; at least eight had already been returned to Canada. By November 16th, six more were sent home. M.I.3, the office in Ottawa responsible for Security of Personnel, pointed out that it was not possible to segregate all naturalized aliens, and that each case must be separately investigated. In January 1943, it was decided to cease withdrawing aliens already serving in the field, and to send alien arrivals from Canada straight to the Pioneer Company.[19]

First Army was told on February 12th, 1943, that, out of a total of 60 aliens who had been identified, 36 were actually sent to the Company. Four were cleared and posted, one was returned to Canada, one died; 30 were still under investigation, and preliminary reports indicated that 24 would probably be cleared. At a somewhat later period, when more F.S. N.C.O.s were available, an investigation could be handled and a report completed without taking a man away from his unit. Aliens were transferred to non-sensitive, non-field units which had no classified material, where the investigation could be handled by the O.C. in association with the appropriate Security authority. The preliminary screening before the men arrived in Britain reduced the burden on F.S. Later, N.D.H.Q. policy permitted such men to be used in certain named, non-sensitive units; still later the list of these units was modified to allow more flexibility. In November 1943, any alien whose signed Declaration of Intention to become a Canadian citizen had been accepted was permitted to serve in some categories of sensitive employment. Aliens of Japanese origin, however, remained excluded from this privilege, except where enlisted for special duties.[20]

C.M.H.Q. was the clearing house for all security-clearance cases initiated in Canada and investigated in Britain. A summary had to be sent to Ottawa so that the file could be completed. The procedure took time to organize and it was not until June 7th, 1941 that it began to work properly. In the same way, responsibility for security in Canadian military hospitals in Britain took months of discussions before it was eventually given to C.M.H.Q.

The Section at C.M.H.Q. handled a great number of minor problems. These were more numerous in the early years of the war, partly because the troops were inexperienced and unfamiliar with the needs of Security, partly because it takes time to build an experienced organization, and partly also because all members of the various agencies had to feel their way through the constantly evolving Security policies and procedures.[21] In May 1941, an N.C.O. of 1 R.C.H.A. forgot to turn in the Unit Censor Stamp when he went to hospital; it had to be recovered. A soldier married an alien and took her to live with him in a prohibited area; they moved. I Canadian Corps wanted German uniforms for training purposes; the Section obtained them from the War Office. Some members of the Hungarian Embassy in Canada, which had been closed, had engaged in activities inappropriate to their diplomatic position. Since they were scheduled to return to Europe on a ship carrying Canadian officers, they could be in a position to obtain useful information. C.M.H.Q. suggested that the officers be warned; the solution was accepted. Every Canadian officer was issued an Officer's Identity Card (A.F.B. 2606) with an attached record stub or counterfoil; no one had thought of what should be done with them if the officer died. The Officer-in-Charge, Records, considered both card and stub should be destroyed. But such action could not legally be taken without a Court of Enquiry; common sense took over, and that formality was dispensed with.

On June 21st, 1941, Maj. Page heard that the United States had a list of Soviet agents operating in Canada. He tracked the report to its source and successfully asked that it be sent via him to N.D.H.Q. After Finland had declared war on one of Canada's allies, Russia, Records asked Intelligence for information on the legal status of Finns in the Canadian Army. This same problem had not greatly worried the British. Their Military Operations 2(b) reported that there were no Finns in the British Army and no Free Finnish Forces comparable to those of the exile groups. A call to the Foreign Office, channelled through Canada House, elicited the following magnificent compromise: the Russians were not our official allies and the Finns could not, therefore, be official enemies.

One of C.M.H.Q.'s perennial tasks was the provision of linguists. In December 1939, a need for French-speaking liaison officers was easily met. In April

1940, the War Office asked for Norwegian interpreters as part of the Canadian contribution to the Norwegian Campaign. C.M.H.Q. quickly found in First Division a sufficient number of men skilled in all the Scandinavian languages. The Canadian force (2 Brigade) never reached Norway, but two interpreters, Ptes. G. Hansen and A. Johannson, of the Saskatoon Light Infantry, seconded to their unit's allied regiment, the King's Own Yorkshire Light Infantry, saw action near Dombass and returned safely after the withdrawal. As they said afterwards, they had no difficulty with Norwegian, but the Yorkshire version of English was another matter. Later the War Office asked for a sergeant and three privates who could speak Bulgarian; I Canadian Corps provided them.

On November 17th, 1941, the War Office asked for two Danish speaking and two Finnish speaking officers for part-time service on B.B.C. foreign language broadcasts. It took John Page a month, but he found suitable candidates. A similar request for Japanese linguists took nearly six months to fill. The enquiries continued, and their range widened until, by the end of the war, in addition to French and Norwegian interpreters, Canadians were providing translators in Austrian, Bulgarian, Danish, Dutch, Finnish, Greek, Icelandic, Italian, Japanese, Polish, Portuguese, Romanian, Russian, Serbo-Croat, Spanish, Turkish, and Ukrainian.

On January 14th, 1942, John Page reviewed the question of foreign attachments. The British were so eager to find fluent linguists that they were almost invariably willing to grant them commissions in their Intelligence Corps, as they did for certain other specialists loaned to them for Intelligence duties. The routine practice was to discharge men from the Canadian Army so that they might re-enlist with the British. Page, considering that our loan policy was shortsighted, suggested that our men be granted a Canadian General List commission and loaned for a stipulated period of about six months. His proposal was accepted only in part.[22]

The outbreak of war with Japan had little immediate effect on C.M.H.Q., but the Section did set up a large map on which to plot Japanese dispositions. The first report on Canadian prisoners was received from the British Military Attaché in Chungking in February 1942; it said that conditions were bad and that dysentery was prevalent, but it gave no information on casualties. John Page made clear to the War Office Canada's urgent desire to be given all available information.[23]

When the G.S.O.2 reported to Ottawa a War Office briefing to him on the defences of the Falkland Islands, he was directed to tell the War Office, tactfully, that Canada would not participate in any defence plan for that colony. (This matter had been under consideration in Ottawa since mid-January. A formal refusal was sent, via the British High Commissioner in Ottawa, on March 11th, 1942.) A Beirut company advised that it would no longer recognize commitments from its headquarters in France, only those from its branch office in Montreal; the information was passed to Ottawa. N.D.H.Q. reported that a search made in Canada for a special kind of quartz crystals may have been sabotaged; C.M.H.Q. passed the report to the appropriate British office. Mr. Richard Grew, a former Canadian Trade Commissioner in Oslo, had had contacts in that city with German commercial circles. When he returned to Canada through London, John Page questioned him thoroughly about what he had learned of conditions in Germany and passed the answers to all interested Intelligence parties.

Occasionally, some of the odd tasks and proposals had their amusing sides. In August 1942, Maj. Halbert received a strange letter: "I am an author ... attached program ... [is] one of my plays. ... I am ... highly educated ... graduated from the Church ... Rome University ... I speak Italian." The enquirer demanded "a senior paid Commission for the duration of hostilities in the Canadian Army for service in Canada". If a post was not immediately available, he was not interested. In a somewhat vitriolic reply, Halbert declined his generous offer.[24]

August 1942 marked the beginning of a closer link between the Intelligence training establishments in Kingston, Ontario and in the U.K. Maj. Charley Krug visited C.M.H.Q. and the British training school at Matlock. He examined all aspects of training, organization, channels of communication, censorship, First Army Intelligence organization, and the relationship between Canadian offices and the War Office. The program that he eventually developed at R.M.C. owed much to this visit.[25]

This heterogeneous mixture of activities unfolded against the grim background of the Dieppe Raid. Although C.M.H.Q. did not have any direct connection with that operation, it was well aware of the preparations that were being made and it watched events with interest and concern. After it was over, at the request both of First Army and of N.D.H.Q., the Section did its best to obtain information from the War Office (Joint Intelligence Committee) not only on what had happened, but also on German reactions to it. Information picked up from intercepted German radio communications was passed to Army and to Corps as soon as it was received. They were anxious to find out whether the Germans had shot prisoners and equally concerned that Canadians may have been guilty of similar crimes. M.I.12 (British Censorship, War Office) sent a great deal of information on the reaction of the Canadian troops to the Raid, as it showed up in their correspondence. In return, C.M.H.Q. checked the Secret List, a compilation of information on equipment whose characteristics could not be disclosed, in order to delete references to items that had fallen into enemy hands. The amended list was then passed to Censorship.

CENSORSHIP

During mobilization planning, the British had set up a cadre civilian censorship organization to work closely with Intelligence at the War Office. Because Canadians were guests of the country, they conformed closely to British press and postal regulations and, after a quite short period of mutual adjustment, both sides learned to work together amicably. The C.M.H.Q. Intelligence Section played an active part in this.

Press Censorship presented a challenge from the very beginning. In November 1939, even before the first contingent of First Canadian Division reached England, C.M.H.Q. had to decide how to handle news releases for the move. Both Col. Burns and the British D.D.M.I. worked out the correct procedure to be used and, on December 15th, instructed the press accordingly. The procedure was ignored by Mr. Churchill, then First Lord of the Admiralty, who released the story regardless. Fortunately, his timing was such that disclosure brought no danger to the convoy already en route. On December 20th, C.M.H.Q. issued its first Censorship order designed to prevent future leaks of this sort; and especially to protect the Second Contingent, due to leave Canada December 30th. The press received instructions for handling news of troop movements, and the troops themselves were ordered not to mention movements of ships, aircraft, and troops, or to discuss any details connected with them.

N.D.H.Q. was asked to tighten controls on information regarding movements of convoys and formations. One of the points at issue was the timing of releases. The press, bound by their deadlines, wanted releases to be made quickly. Censorship, understandably, wanted to protect the information against enemy Intelligence. The procedure agreed on between C.M.H.Q. and Major Leo Heaps, Military Advisor to the British Military Censorship, on February 16th, 1940, required the Censor to call C.M.H.Q., which had a stenographer ready to accept dictation over the telephone of any item which had been stopped (intercepted). It could then be examined carefully and a decision made regarding its disposition.

In March, the War Office pointed out that Canadian unit serial (identity) numbers, assigned for administrative convenience during mobilization, were similar to those allotted to British units. This was confusing, but what was really dangerous was the fact that these numbers were openly published in the Canada Gazette. The enemy was thus presented with a complete Canadian order-of-battle. N.D.H.Q. replied that the units would be re-numbered, but the decision was never implemented. It did alter arrangements to publish official posting orders. In April, the British Press Censor complained that his office was being flooded with photographs our soldiers wished to send home. He asked that they be clearly instructed that he was not the agency responsible for clearing private pictures. Maj. Rodger, then G.S.O.3, arranged for them to be cleared through War Office channels. A later Routine Order prohibited all photographs of key areas.[26]

When Second Division arrived in England, Censorship held the story, much to the annoyance of the press. The arrangements made earlier had broken down. Three things were badly needed: a carefully thought out policy of stops and releases; the appointment of a trained Public Relations Officer to act as supervisor and mentor (Capt. W.G. Abel, who had been appointed P.R.O., was still learning to live with Censorship); and lastly, and perhaps most important of all, mutual trust, backed up by stiff penalties for any correspondent who abused it.

Censorship decided that Canadian units would be identified only by broad territorial designations, e.g., eastern Canada, western Canada. The R.22e.R. for instance, was referred to as "an Infantry battalion from Eastern Canada". Such vagueness presented no problems for Canadians, but did tend to confuse the British, who were less familiar with Canadian geography. Also, in practice, its usefulness was often nullified by other careless disclosures. For example, in October 1941, the published pictures of the visit of the Minister of National Defence, Col. Ralston, to an "unnamed unit" showed the unmistakable flashes of the Calgary Regiment.

A formal policy amendment was announced in December 1941. The names of Divisional Commanders could be mentioned. Patches could remain, but no unit would be identified with its particular senior formation. Cavalry and infantry units could be identified, but units from such elements as the Royal Canadian Ordnance Corps were to continue to be referred to by the area of their recruitment. It took nearly two years, until July 1943, for these complicated refinements to be dropped in favour of the earlier, simpler, territorial designations for all units.

Order-of-battle was not the only subject requiring protection. In March 1942, for instance, the RAM Mark II tank, which was then on the "totally restricted" list, provoked an unnecessarily bitter dispute. Some of the pictures taken in England were intended for general release in Canada; others, showing more detail, were for military use only. It took much time and effort to persuade Canada that all of them had actually been censored before despatch, and that Directorate of Public Relations (D.P.R.) Canada had been properly advised of the use to be made of them. There were many unresolved questions, and communications between London and Ottawa were not always as clear as they should have been. Intelligence believed that the close link between Press Censorship and Public Relations that had been established from the beginning was at once logical, efficient, and satisfactory. It knew, however, that both would suffer from "growing pains" as the military establishment expanded. Press Censorship was to be a field function of Intelligence; it will be described in Chapter 12.

The Postal Censorship of the troops' private correspondence was applied slowly and after much discussion. On December 30th, 1939, Ottawa advised

C.M.H.Q. that complaints in some French-Canadian newspapers expressed the fear that letters not written in English would be stopped by the Censor. C.M.H.Q. assured N.D.H.Q. that Canadian soldiers' mail was not being censored by the War Office. It subsequently transpired that the complaints were not only false, but had been spread by a trouble-maker in the R.C.A.F. On January 5th, 1940, the British Chief Postal Censor raised the question of checking the Canadian troops' mail. He did not have sufficient staff to do it himself and suggested that, after they had taken a short course he offered to set up, Canadians might prefer to do their own. After a conference at the High Commission on January 9th, Mr. Vincent Massey reported to Ottawa that "experience of the last war shows indiscretions can be expected. Censorship in units in a war theatre would be possible". Gen. McNaughton, however, considered that it was not then necessary to censor mail, and the British were duly advised.[27]

On May 28th, 1940, units of First Canadian Division, bound for France, were ordered to enforce unit censorship as soon as the formation arrived at its concentration point in the Northampton area. They were issued envelopes marked "Free" to indicate that letters would not be censored after they left the unit office, unless mailed in civilian postboxes, a point stressed by their unit officers. When the move to Northampton was completed, and when the Division later moved to France, full Postal Censorship was imposed and maintained until July 13th.[28] Unit Censor Stamps, which were used to indicate that the unit had censored the letters, were not available from Canadian sources, and C.M.H.Q. had to obtain them, with some difficulty, from the British.

In July 1940, all British civilian mail, including airmail, was intercepted, but Canadian "Free" mail was allowed to leave the country unchecked. When British Field Censors (Home) realized that important information could readily be passed through this open channel, they asked for and were granted permission to censor an arbitrary 15% of this "Free" mail. Examples were found immediately of breaches of practically every Censorship regulation. In addition, the Censors found offences against Post Office regulations, demands for large quantities of cigarettes, clothing, and food for resale, and evidence of administrative irregularities "including payment of Dependents' Allowance to an unmarried woman using the name of an existing wife". In August 1940, the British, rather than clog the wheels of justice with trivia, ruled that only serious breaches of security would be stopped. Minor ones would be excised and forgotten.[29]

In late September 1940, soldiers were reported to be evading the Censors by sending letters by hand to Ireland, which had no censorship. Such evasions were probably prompted by a desire for privacy; but the risk that an agent might make use of this channel could not be ignored. A Routine Order duly closed the loophole.[30] The Canadian Forestry Corps had units stationed in prohibited areas near Inverness, Scotland. C.M.H.Q. allowed the local civilian authority to censor their mail. Air Ministry wanted to know if mail from Canadian addresses to Canadians serving in the R.A.F. should be censored. They were told that a spot censorship was being applied in Canada, and that only correspondence arriving in Britain by bomber mail needed to be censored.

By 1941, whenever a breach of Security regulations was noticed in a Postal Censorship intercept, it was routine to inform C.M.H.Q. in writing. The information would then be passed through F.S. channels to the units, with instructions to use the same channels to report the disciplinary action that had been taken. A card file was maintained to facilitate the identification of repeated offenders. Yet, despite these controls, Censorship protection was still not as complete as it needed to be. Maj. Page, who was then G.S.O.2, M.O.&I., drew up three alternative proposals for improving it: to impose unit censorship; to attach Canadians to British Censorship units; or, to create Canadian Censorship units. He warned that soldiers were using the civilian mail, and that, since there were no Canadian Base Censorship facilities, the men's mail was being badly censored, and the officers' not at all. He preferred his second alternative. On July 28th, C.M.H.Q. decided instead to authorize the civilian agency to apply selective censorship. Of each daily batch of 16 50-lb. bags, three would be checked; intercepts would be passed to C.M.H.Q. for disciplinary action.

On August 25, 1941, M.I.12 picked up its initial three bags, sorted them according to the Unit Censor Stamps, or, if unstamped, into one general pile, censored the contents, resorted the letters by destinations, and sent them on. The report submitted on the 29th said that 25 Censors dealt with 2,500 items (one bag) in one day. They discovered four serious leaks; the minor items were merely excised and not reported. Continuous security education was clearly needed. On December 2nd, 1941, C.M.H.Q. decided to transfer the actual examination to the Canadian Base Post Office at Manchester.

By January 1942, Censorship problems began to fall into recognizable patterns. Fluctuations in volume handled, conflicts with Ottawa, training of new Censors, and the results of inexperience by new "users", all had routine solutions – usually after time-consuming exchanges of views. Occasionally, a 100% censorship was imposed on correspondence from individual units in order to meet specific control demands or to check their morale. The information collected was often useful in identifying the causes of poor morale and in pointing the way towards restoring the unit's efficiency. Poor security existed on both sides of the Atlantic. At certain periods, particularly around Christmas, telegrams of good wishes to Canadians in Britain were found to contain more names of units and formations than was normal. The Canadian Telegraph Censor was to forward these censored messages through the Canadian Records office in London.

INVASION PLANNING

The Censorship story, important though it is, has led us a long way from the narrative of the main day-to-day tasks of the C.M.H.Q. Section.[31] Security was always a major preoccupation, but staffing, recruiting, administration, and meeting emergencies probably occupied more hours in its daily routine. The build-up for the Invasion, and the arrangements to handle information during the build-up and after the actual landing, had to be thought out, discussed, and implemented.

During 1943 and the early months of 1944, C.M.H.Q. was not directly involved in the mechanics of preparation for the landings in Italy and North-West Europe, but it was the agency where the details of many of the actions taken to support the operations were co-ordinated. In early 1943, a new code word, BIGOT, was assigned as a warning that the contents of the document bearing it could be seen only by a very few persons. Even knowledge of the existence of the word was severely restricted. The word itself had no particular significance; it was selected from a long list kept by Intelligence for security uses. At C.M.H.Q. the security of BIGOT and the control of the list of persons permitted access to BIGOT material were to absorb a lot of D.M.O.&I.'s time and energy.

During the planning phase of First Division's move to Italy, C.M.H.Q. obtained copies, in English and in French, of the pamphlets on Italy prepared by the British Political Intelligence Directorate and of a War Office publication entitled "Notes on the Italian Army". It drafted a Routine Order to protect information on Escape and Evasion. As soon as action became imminent, it discovered, of course, all the things it could have done better, or which it had entirely overlooked. To repair some omissions, it set up refresher courses at the British Intelligence School, now located at Cambridge, and obtained permission to hold reinforcement levels at 100% of the field force totals. Because this decision automatically doubled the strength, arrangements were made to recruit additional I.O.s with Air Photo skills and to train them with the 21 Army Group Photo Pool. D.M.O.&I. set up at C.M.H.Q. an Information Room to display location maps and situation reports on the Italian campaign. And, when the campaign itself began, Maj. Walter approached D.M.I. (War Office) to reinforce arrangements already made for obtaining information for his maps, and for N.D.H.Q. and the Cabinet in Ottawa, on the actions and dispositions of Canadian troops and support bases in the Mediterranean.

Then followed the standard mixture of minor, yet very important, problems that Intelligence always has to solve in periods of preparation for action. Because the Canadian Army in Italy recruited locally, arrangements had to be made to ensure that clearance procedures were adequate. The Field Security Sections and Central Records had to be warned. In March 1944, many Canadians asked Security for permission to send private cable messages to the Mediterranean.

C.M.H.Q. found that the War Office did not object to British messages sent to the area, and saw no reason why Canadians should not do the same, so long as they used the official channels.

Planning and preparations for the Invasion followed hard on the heels of the Italian operation. As far as Intelligence was concerned, some of the problems had direct connections with earlier ones which had already been met and resolved. The fact that Felix Walter remained at his post at C.M.H.Q. and was available to provide knowledge, advice, and guidance made a great deal of difference to the success of First Army's planning. For example, that Army liked the handy pocket guide to Italy that C.M.H.Q. had obtained for the troops, and asked for a similar one for North-West Europe. In December 1943, the Political Intelligence Division (P.I.D.) agreed to produce a booklet geared to Canadian, rather than British or American, readers and to forward a first draft for comment to C.M.H.Q. by January 21st, 1944. A second amended text followed, and a final version was readied in time for the Invasion. A companion Canadian "Guide to Belgium and Luxembourg" was compiled and completed in May 1944; Felix Walter himself translated its text into French.

Steps were also taken to ensure that all useful information would be exchanged between Canadians and others working on the many aspects of Invasion preparations. For instance, in the first week of January 1944, the Allies were still concerned lest Germany use poison gas. The D.M.O.&I. therefore arranged with the British Deputy Assistant Director of Medical Services (Chemical Warfare) to maintain close links with Medical Intelligence.

The Intelligence Section obtained and circulated to all formations and to N.D.H.Q., a British Technical Intelligence Section pamphlet that showed the insignia and rank badges of Russian units serving in the German Army. It also obtained copies of the French and Soviet regulations governing their awards for the Military Secretary's Branch, which was responsible for recommending Canadians for foreign decorations.

Security protection was essential for those agencies directly involved in preparations for the Invasion. In February 1944, No. 30 Canadian Air (Survey) Liaison Section, R.C.E., was "buttoned up", to prepare maps of the Continent. Guarantees of reliability were provided on all Canadians in the British Technical Intelligence Sections. In April, the Postal Tracing Section, which forwarded mail to individual soldiers, needed information on future unit locations. Because this was highly sensitive, classified, operational information, the Section itself had to be made highly secure. A Routine Order was prepared which gave cover addresses; the Section operated within that protection. Additional orders provided for the censoring of mail in languages other than English and French and for the recall of Intelligence publications not needed for the coming operation. D.M.O.&I. was asked to prepare special maps showing the areas to be closed to visitors – the whole of south England, from the Wash to Land's End. The

G.S.O.3 I(b) arranged with First Army for unit censorship to be imposed on all troops landing in the Invasion and on the immediate follow-up forces. A Security Board meeting on April 21st recommended that all Officers' Service Books be recalled before the landing; its advice was acted on. In May, Security arrangements were made for assistance to Movement Control, for emergency security clearances for both Canadian and British personnel, and for Security checks on all professional entertainment groups visiting camps, barracks, and other military premises. In June, N.D.H.Q. issued an order that Intelligence badges be worn. Felix Walter, now called the A.D.M.I., felt obliged to argue that the order should not be enforced while troops were in action. His response must have caused Ottawa to wonder when it remembered how urgently and for how long it had been pressed to yield on this point.

Even at this late stage a good many of the Intelligence training and establishment difficulties had still not been solved. Visits were arranged to the Intelligence Training Directorate at European Theatre of Operations U.S. Army (E.T.O.U.S.A.) and to the U.S. Counter-Intelligence Corps (U.S.C.I.C) training centre at Lick. The Free French Security Officer was asked for, and agreed to supply, current French Security documents for use in Canadian Field Security training. Canadian "Town Majors", who were being trained for Occupation duties, were given a short course in security. In June 1944, the training courses at the British Intelligence Centre had to be filled by men needed to satisfy last-minute British requirements and C.M.H.Q. was warned that Canadians might have to be placed on a quota.

Many of the decisions were now urgent and should not have been left until the last minute. The Staff, for example, was not convinced that armoured divisions, whose tactical doctrine did not require them to capture and hold "real estate", needed F.S. Sections. But these divisions were not continuously in action, and, even when they were, their support and rest areas had to be protected. Intelligence had to check with Supreme H.Q. Allied Expeditionary Force and 21 Army Group to confirm this stand. A similar planning deficiency occurred in the case of Interpreters. As late as May 1944, the A.D.M.I. was asked to supply French-English interpreters for 21 Army Group; as a result, a Canadian Interpreters Pool (French language) was formed.

At the same time as he was completing these preparations, many of them highly important and urgent, the A.D.M.I. also had to continue his routine and sometimes trivial administrative duties. In late December 1943, the Section was asked to prepare a map showing Prime Minister King's itinerary during his visit to Britain. It had to arrange for the disposal of abandoned regimental pets, a task which Intelligence inherited probably because authority could find no one else to deal with it. Procedures had to be set up with the War Office for receiving information on Far Eastern operations. The G.S.O.3 I(a) was asked to secure a supply of operational maps for the Officer-in-Charge Canadian Section, G.H.Q.

1 Echelon, 21 Army Group, who claimed he had no other source for them. In February 1944, new Security regulations were drawn up and issued to Canadian Reinforcement Units. Medical Intelligence was asked to advise Intelligence when psychopaths, who could present a security hazard, were being returned to Canada. And, almost as a spare time task, the G.S.O.2 was detailed to chair meetings of the Priorities Sub-Committee of the Demobilization Committee.

In the last few months before the Invasion began, the Intelligence staff found itself involved in a new responsibility – the handling of prisoners of war, both enemy and Allied. We will return to this problem in more detail in later chapters, but chronology requires that we at least mention it here. From the earliest days of the war, many enemy prisoners had been sent to Canada. Initially, their control and re-education along democratic lines had not been an Intelligence responsibility. The situation was now changing, and this re-education task was handed over to Intelligence. In April 1944, it received and shipped to N.D.H.Q. the first batch of War Office information-sheets for use in prisoner-of-war handling. Maj. Paul Lieven, M.C., and Maj. N. Ignatieff, R.C.E. (representing the War Office), discussed Soviet P.W. held in Canadian camps with the Soviet Military Attaché. As far as the Canadian Army was concerned, this was the beginning of the return to the Soviet Union of Russian nationals who had fought with the Germans. Interrogators had to be trained; they were sent to the London District P.W. Cage, where the first prisoners captured in Europe would be held, rather than to the Intelligence Course at Cambridge. The theory, eventually proved to be wrong, was that on-the-job training would be more valuable. Similarly, though Escape and Evasion were well within the Intelligence sphere, the prospect of recovering not just an isolated individual or two, but whole prison camps of Canadians, posed new and difficult challenges.

Rules had to be drawn up, on the one hand, for dealing with Canadian P.W. suspected of collaboration with the enemy, and, on the other hand, for recognizing those who had distinguished themselves by their loyalty during their captivity. Censorship had already arranged to pass information obtained in mail from these men. An Intelligence officer was assigned to the London District Transit Camp, through which returned prisoners would pass. He was to obtain this sort of conduct-information and also assist in identifying Germans involved in atrocities against P.W. Three additional officers were assigned to debrief returning Canadians: Capts. Surbeck and J. Certain de Beaujeu, and Lieut. W.I. Binkley. In their first week, they interviewed 85 men; in the following five weeks, their average was 57 a week. They missed a good many others who were repatriated before interviews could be arranged.

The Director of History decided to turn over to the A.D.M.I. the material he was collecting, arguing that he was being overwhelmed by the amount of documentation the field units were sending him. Temporary staff, borrowed from other units, was brought in, but did not prove to be satisfactory. One new captain was added, but only after the main work had been completed. At this time, Felix Walter was promoted to Lt.-Col., and the G.S.O.3 I(b) became a major.

When operations began in France on June 6th, 1944, a new office was set up in the Information Room, new maps were mounted on the walls, and arrangements were made to have information plotted. An Intelligence Liaison Service was formed to link H.Q. First Canadian Army, the information centres at the War Office, H.Q. 21 Army Group, H.Q. E.T.O.U.S.A., and C.M.H.Q. On June 16th, arrangements were also made to receive Operations as well as Intelligence reports.

As the summer slipped by and the action moved farther away, the A.D.M.I. seemed almost to have been left on the edge of things. His problems, now mainly routine, included such trifles as disputes over areas of responsibility. No. 13 F.S. Section, for instance, argued with the Provost in London, and both had to be reminded that breaches of security belonged to F.S. while crime was a Provost matter.

Occasionally, the A.D.M.I. was assigned special and unusual tasks. One of these involved him in the question of looting. During the occupation, Germans had made off with a large number of art treasures. The Vaucher Commission was set up to trace these so that they could eventually be restored to their rightful owners. It built up a card index of the names of German officers and men who had been involved in their original removal and of all available information that would help to identify, find, and question them. Some of these individuals were believed to be in P.W. Camps in Canada; their cards were passed through C.M.H.Q. to Canada for action.

In early September 1944, conflicts between the training syllabi in Canada and at the C.G.R.U. were resolved. The Directorate of Education was asked to provide elementary and advanced German courses at the Education Company, C.G.R.U. The British, who by this time were beginning to concentrate on the Far East, were offered vacancies at the Canadian War Intelligence Course. Information Control Units, a part of Psychological Warfare, 21 Army Group, were being formed with Canadian personnel. They had to be trained, but there were no appropriate Canadian courses. Arrangements had to be made with S.H.A.E.F. to fill vacancies at its facility at Cobham. They were not completed until February 1945.

The A.D.M.I. visited Italy for two weeks in October 1944. He took with him a sheaf of small matters which he had been unable to settle by correspondence alone. His trip was not long enough, and the number of problems too great, to allow him to deal with all of them, but both sides at least had a chance to discuss their differences at length. Not long after his return, Lt.-Col. Walter became involved in discussions on the security precautions covering the move of I Canadian Corps from Italy to North-West Europe.

A difficult administrative problem that was having increasingly adverse effects on morale in the Corps was examined. Intelligence linguists did not draw trades pay. Many of them had what was called an "inherent skill", meaning that the language they spoke was not a learned language but their mother tongue. The Army considered that, since no special training was involved, compensation was not called for. As a result, the linguist found himself at a disadvantage compared, for example, with a cook, a driver, or a storeman. Following a discussion, held on January 3rd, 1945, with the Army Trades Committee Overseas, Col. Walter was asked to prepare a submission to cover all linguists. He did a great deal of research, then drew up and forwarded to Ottawa a proposed Trades Test. D.M.I. did not give it support, and N.D.H.Q. rejected it.

The problems passed to the A.D.M.I. were mostly minor, but all were time-consuming. The Historical Section was circulating, for training purposes, reports it had collected from the Front. A.D.M.I. had to examine and clear them. In order to streamline control procedures and to eliminate duplication of records, the Central Registry handed over to the Section the registration of War Office Accountable Documents (documents that had limited, controlled circulation). The task of physically examining these documents at periodic intervals has remained an Intelligence responsibility ever since. 1 C.G.R.U. was asked to cease giving motorcycle training to Intelligence reinforcements; the superiority of the jeep was finally recognized. Plans were prepared for the employment of F.S. Sections during the occupation of Germany. N.D.H.Q. wanted an Intelligence Section to be readied for the Pacific and C.M.H.Q. had to find suitable personnel. New Routine Orders on security of information and of correspondence had to be prepared and issued.

The C.M.H.Q. Intelligence Section had been established, in part, to link the Intelligence organization in the European Theatre with N.D.H.Q. By the end of the war in Europe, it was sending the following items back to Ottawa: its own summary of events in all theatres, sent directly to the C.G.S.; General Appreciations (No. 134, for example, dealt with the Balkan area); Intelligence Summaries from H.Q. First Canadian Army, I and II Corps; a Western Europe Situation Report; a Mediterranean Situation Report; and Far East Summaries (the first Burma Theatre reports were sent on August 25th, 1944). The Section also provided material for internal distribution within C.M.H.Q. and the Intelligence Company. It handled the Army "Intsum", the 21 Army Group Censorship Report, and the Field Censors "Home" (British) reports. It prepared the periodic list of locations of Canadian units. Issue No. 33, amendment No. 6, of this Location Statement was distributed to the offices at the end of April. It issued maps (the requirement then was 175). It did translations; in April 1945 alone, 14 were prepared, four for the Military Secretary, six for the Canadian Army Operational Research Group, three for Internal Security and one for Censorship. Its Security commitments included: reports on Counter-Intelligence,

Security investigations of men selected for special duties or for the Special Wireless Sections, and a review of applications for employment at C.M.H.Q., and for permission to marry aliens. It controlled the issuing of all passes and all Canadian Identity Cards (M.F.M. 182).

PEACE AGAIN

With the German surrender on May 8th, the tempo and pressures slackened noticeably. The Section considered that the continuing war with Japan was an N.D.H.Q. responsibility, and that its own role was to deal with the problems of reorganizing Intelligence for the Canadian Army Occupation Force (C.A.O.F.), to reconcile this reorganization with current demobilization policies, and to evaluate their effects on the manpower resources. On May 18th, in order to facilitate administration and to avoid confusion, the title of A.D.M.I. was changed to D.M.I.; a few days later it was changed to D.D.M.I.

The C.A.O.F. duties were chiefly carried out by the Field Security Sections, augmented by German-speaking personnel from the Special Wireless Sections and from other Intelligence units as they became available. One of the major tasks was "War Crimes". Some P.W., many still in enemy hands, were suspected of dishonourable conduct during captivity; each case had to be investigated. The Sections were handicapped because they were restricted to specific areas; they did not have the flexibility to follow up leads which could involve searches over the whole of Germany. On May 2nd, a representative from the War Office was the principal speaker at a briefing at Canada House on this delicate matter.

On the 12th, at another meeting, measures were drawn up to co-ordinate information received. Reports of crimes against Canadian soldiers were collected and sent to the High Commissioner; they were also sent to S.H.A.E.F., where Lt.-Col. John Page administered the War Crimes Section, with Lt.-Col. B.J.S. Macdonald (Essex Scottish) as a Court of Enquiry, and several Canadian C.Int.C. and C.Pro.C. N.C.O.s as investigators. The Allied survey of war crimes in Italy was obtained and passed to the D.C.G.S. (C.M.H.Q.). A brief recommending that a special unit be established to collect information on crimes against British and Dominion troops was accepted. Another report on the handling of prisoners overrun by the Russians and repatriated through Odessa was sent to D.N.D. and to interested parties in London. In late July, the prosecution of offenders was discussed with M.I.5; investigations continued until well into 1946.

Most of the men in the Canadian Army Overseas wanted only to return to Canada and to civilian life. The authorities therefore had good reason to be concerned about their morale. F.S. was asked to watch for situations that could have an adverse effect, and to report directly every two weeks on units controlled by C.M.H.Q. and by H.Q. Canadian Reinforcement Units. The first report was received on June 22nd. Special reports were ordered on the rioting that took place at Aldershot during the weekend of July 1st; it was believed to have started as a result of poor morale.

When hostilities ended, security precautions no longer needed were quickly cancelled and duties were rearranged. The D.D.M.I. offered Photo-Interpreters to the Education Service as mathematics instructors. On June 1st, Intelligence officers were assigned to assist the Chief Historical Officer in preparing special reports and interviews on German Army activities. H.Q. Counter-Intelligence wrote its final report on June 14th, 1945, and the H.Q. First Canadian Army Intelligence Report followed on September 14th. In July, arrangements were made to catalogue and ship to Canada a collection of seven and one-half tons of German military documents from Delmenhorst that had been located by Field Security and offered as a prize of war to Gen. Crerar. This "Crerar Collection", as it is now known, is at R.M.C. Officers and men who had worked with the Special Operations Executive in France prior to D-Day were considered ineligible for the 1939–45 Star. D.D.M.I. prepared a submission on July 20th to rectify this. Censorship was cancelled when hostilities with Japan ceased, and the G.S.O.2 Censorship vacated his post on September 7th. The Information Room at C.M.H.Q. was closed on September 14th. On that same day, Security arrangements that had been imposed in 1939–40 were officially relaxed. Maj. Bob Raymont closed the Intelligence Wing at 1 C.G.R.U. and came to the Section as G.S.O.2.

On October 12th, the D.C.G.S. authorized a special weekly Political Intelligence Report to be based on information received from the sector of Germany occupied by Canadian troops. It appeared on October 17th, and two weeks later, when the D.D.M.I. was asked to brief Lt.-Gen. M.A. Pope, the newly appointed head of the Canadian Military Mission to Berlin, he offered him copies of the new report.

Two minor, but interesting, activities are worth mentioning. Lieut. J.E.R. Wood, R.C.E., had made a collection of P.W. stories. He asked for and received permission to publish them in book form and agreed to give the proceeds to the Canadian Red Cross. The British Escape and Evasion authority (I.S.9) willingly allowed him to use the material in its files, and the D.D.M.I. himself translated the French narratives. The second incident involved two Canadian officers, Maj. C.J. Webster, then O.C. 3 Canadian Intelligence Pool, Canadian Army Occupation Force (C.A.O.F.), and Capt. M. Shulman, G.S.O.3, Special Interrogations, who were both asked to assist the Historical Section. They were sent to Haltwhistle, on Lake Windermere, where the camp for senior German officer P.W. was located, to interrogate Lt.-Gen. Heim and Oberst-Lieut. Schroeder, the former commanders of Boulogne and Calais respectively.

On December 5th, Lt.-Col. Walter was promoted acting-colonel. On the 14th he began a farewell tour of all the British Intelligence branches to say, on behalf of the C.G.S., goodbye and thanks for all the assistance given during the war. He was replaced by Lt.-Col. R.L. Raymont, M.B.E. Col. Walter hoped that, on his return, he would replace Col. Murray as D.M.I., but his hope was not to be realized. His association with radicals during his prewar academic life had made him unacceptable to Washington. He returned to civilian life and died in 1960. He did a magnificent job during a strenuous and difficult time. He carried a heavy responsibility for a wide spectrum of important negotiations and secrets, some of which, if revealed, would have brought death to many people. He was privy to complex problems that were closely connected with high-level political and military decisions. He could not discuss them with anyone else or even, in many instances, admit that he had knowledge of things that others discussed in his presence. He bore a weight of responsibility that was far heavier than would normally be entrusted to a man of his rank and position. It was little short of a tragedy that he was lost to Intelligence at the very time his experience and ability should have been used to build the postwar Corps.

By January 3rd, planning for the departure of the Intelligence staff was almost complete. Captain Shulman had gone to the Historical Section on December 28th. The small detachments of Japanese interpreters moving to and from the Far East still required administrative support, and the nature of their duties while they were abroad had to be defined and controlled. Arrangements to remuster the Intelligence personnel stationed in Germany were completed by January 25th. An F.S. Section had to be assigned to, and given responsibility for, the Reinforcement Unit area. Returning P.W. still had to be interviewed; 175 were processed in January, and 244 more in February, many of them Canadians captured by the Japanese. War Crimes reports and investigations continued, particularly those dealing with misbehaviour by men in Japanese camps, and with the conduct of German P.W. in Canada. At the end of March, a Canadian officer was sent to Sylt, on behalf of the Canadian Ambassador, to investigate the disappearance of furniture from the Canadian Embassy in The Hague. And, of course, there was a good deal of internal housekeeping. C.M.H.Q. files had to be stripped and cleared; one and a half tons of maps had to be returned to Ottawa; all the multifarious loose ends that generally accompany the closing of an office had to be tied up.

C.M.H.Q. (M.I.) activities slowly and almost imperceptibly changed to the normal routine role of Canadian liaison with the War Office. Maj. R.W. (Dick) Hampton was the last remaining member of the wartime team. By September 1945, he was filling in the hours trying to discover how disciplinary action taken against Allied P.W. had been recorded by Allied Camp administrative officials. He left his appointment on October 24th. On January 20th, 1946, C.M.H.Q.

moved out of its wartime premises on the third floor of the Sun Life building, near Trafalgar Square, into a small suite on the next floor.

In most respects the role of Intelligence at C.M.H.Q. was a difficult one. The Section was created without benefit of advance planning, and in the face of disinterest, if not actual opposition. Its function and responsibilities grew as the size of the Canadian force overseas increased. And, to carry out its functions, it had to remain outside that force. Serving, in effect, three masters, it had to ensure that it met the requirements of all without becoming too rigidly tied to one. Its primary mission was to collect and disseminate information on the course of the war, and to ensure that information on Canadian activities was properly protected. It had the scantiest resources of its own. Yet it had to obtain men, equipment, and material for C.M.H.Q. itself and for First Army. It had to rely for men and supplies on agencies it did not control. Not infrequently, its task was made unnecessarily difficult by the actions of Canadian elements over which it had little or no authority and by troublesome cultural and technical disagreements between Canadians and other nationals. Often its role was simply one of rebuilding confidence and co-operation.

The tasks given to its staff required of them the highest qualities of patience, diplomacy, intelligence, and hard work. The Intelligence staff officers at C.M.H.Q. were privy to some of the most sensitive secrets that existed in London. Yet none was a professional; all of them had to learn their jobs as they went along. The account we have given of their activities is, in many ways, merely an introductory outline. In succeeding chapters, we will have to fill in the practical detail of the arrangements they made, the actions they took, and the support they provided to the forces in the field. Most of those who served in the Section at C.M.H.Q. were more than adequate; others were outstanding; and some showed brilliance. All of them have earned an honourable place in the story of Intelligence.

5.
BATTLEFIELD INTELLIGENCE – THE BEGINNINGS

The first Intelligence units to be called out under General Order 135 of September 1st, 1939, were a Corps H.Q. Section, Intelligence Corps, two Divisional H.Q. Intelligence Staffs, and Nos. 1, 2, and 3 Army Co-operation Squadron Intelligence Liaison Sections, Canadian Active Service Force (C.A.S.F.).[1] Canada did not have an "Intelligence Corps" then; the title was used because it appeared on the British organization tables on which the Canadian mobilization order was modelled. Some personnel had already been selected but, with the exception of the officers in the Air Liaison Sections, none had had any training or experience.

Intelligence Section establishments in 1939 called for two officers, one warrant officer, one sergeant, and eight men at Division; and one officer, one sergeant, and two corporals at Brigade. On October 29th, 1939, N.D.H.Q. sent a list of vacancies to all D.O.C.s, and asked that the openings be filled.[2] All appointees were untrained. Capt. J. Belleau and Mr. John Buchan (later Lord Tweedsmuir) were appointed to First Division at the end of November, just in time to accompany the first elements overseas. Buchan, who had been in the Cipher Section in A.D.M.&A.F.I. at N.D.H.Q., went on a British cipher course on January 1st; three of his men followed him two weeks later. On their return, P.S.M. A.W. Watson went to the cipher room at C.M.H.Q., while Buchan stayed to arrange courses for the brigade and battalion cipher men.[3] Additional courses were set up at the units. Capt. Alex M. Fordyce, 3 Canadian Infantry Brigade (C.I.B.), with three other ranks, attended the first Intelligence course given Canadians at the British training centre at Minley Manor.[4]

The Canadian Divisions deployed in England were to come under a Corps H.Q., and on February 15th, 1940, Lt.-Col. Burns, C.M.H.Q., told Ottawa that this H.Q. would need a 17-man Corps Section, Intelligence Corps, and that it would have to be provided from Canada. He could provide an eight-man Air Intelligence Liaison (A.I.L.) Section from his own resources. Canada was not yet able to assemble the Corps Section, and, as a result, most of that staff also had to be found in the U.K. In May 1940, someone at N.D.H.Q. discovered that no authority had been issued to form the Corps Section; G.O. 135 had not been fully implemented.[5]

During the spring of 1940, a revised battalion Intelligence Section of one I.O., eight Intelligence men, and eight scouts/observers/snipers was tried out during an exercise. This was a British idea that had been found useful in the

First World War. Some units adopted it later in Italy, but Sections of one officer and four men were more usual.[6]

These first steps were taken against the background of the collapse of France, and, ready or not, First Division was ordered to Calais. Gen. McNaughton, with a small party including the Divisional I.O., Lieut. E.D. Magnus, sailed in. H.M.S. *Verity* on May 23rd, 1940, amid a fog of war that drew the comment, "not much was known about the enemy".[7] Gen. McNaughton was himself compelled to derive most of the information he used from personal conversations and briefings arranged for him at Calais. On his return the next day, his information was combined with that available at the War Office and resulted in the decision to cancel the mission.

After the British withdrawal from Dunkirk, a second British expeditionary force was formed to establish a bridgehead in Brittany. First Canadian Division's role in this operation required it to deploy northeast of Brest. Brig. A.A. Smith's 1 Brigade was moved to that port on June 12th and 13th. The British had lost contact with the enemy, and there was no Intelligence organization active; once again the information was limited to what could be gleaned from casual contacts.[8]

When the Canadians were withdrawn, they went into G.H.Q. Reserve in the Oxford area, to be ready for use as a mobile counter-attack force in the event of a German invasion. On July 21st, VII Corps was formed to command British First Armoured Division, First Canadian Infantry Division, and a New Zealand Force of two infantry brigades. It was commanded by Gen. McNaughton, who set up his headquarters at Headley Court, near Leatherhead, Surrey. The VII Corps Intelligence Section organization table called for one G.S.O.2 (Int) (a Canadian, Maj. C.C. "Church" Mann), a G.S.O.3 (British, Capt. A.F. (Bos) Bosworth, who had served with the C.E.F. in 1917–18), an I.O. (British), a G.S.O.3 Air Liaison (Canadian), four clerks and a draftsman, one map clerk (Canadian), up to five orderlies (British), and two drivers (Canadian). The Cipher and the Field Security Officers were both Canadians (Capts. The Lord Tweedsmuir, and E.A. Chamberlain).[9] The Corps had no Signals Intelligence or Air Photo specialists of its own.

I Canadian Corps was formed, replacing VII Corps, on Christmas Day 1940. During that winter, Canadians replaced the British staff officers. The channel for information was straightforward. Intelligence from the War Office was passed to G.H.Q. Home Forces, General Staff (Intelligence). This agency was divided into two parts, responsible respectively for Intelligence (a) and (b). I(a) material was passed to Corps, which in turn sent it on to the Divisions. In 1941, however, the primary emphasis had to be put on building a cadre of trained manpower, a goal which, as we saw in the last chapter, was dependent on the establishment of an Intelligence School.

H.Q. First Canadian Army was formed under C.M.H.Q. Administrative Order No. 66, dated April 4th, 1942. It had an Intelligence Section with 13 I.O.s; two captains or lieutenants, one, W.O.I, two W.O.IIs and four sergeants for cipher duties; 10 batmen, and an attached R.A.F. Intelligence officer. In the Army there were Intelligence Sections at I Corps, at First, Second, and Third Infantry, and Fifth Armoured Divisions, and the two Air Intelligence Liaison Sections. At that time, the Corps establishment called for a G.S.O.2, a G.S.O.3, five I.O.s I(a), one I.O. I(b), and a captain/lieutenant working with the Special Wireless Section, Type B. The Corps Cipher Section had two captains, a W.O.II, three sergeants, and a corporal, and there were nine batmen. The Divisions each had a G.S.O.3, an I.O., and a Cipher section of an officer and eight men. The Brigade I.O.'s staff included two cipher N.C.O.s. *(See Annex 4 for line diagrams.)* All these establishments reflected the British 1931 Mobilization Plan.

The first officer assigned to the new H.Q. First Canadian Army Intelligence Section was Capt. Bosworth, from I Corps. He was followed shortly afterwards by Maj. The Lord Tweedsmuir, who had been Air Liaison Officer with 400 Squadron, R.C.A.F. At the beginning, the Section was ordered to maintain a collation file, content unspecified, and to set up an information table in the Intelligence Room to display the current reference materials. Regular receipts included: the G.H.Q. Home Forces Daily Intelligence Summary, War Office Weekly Intelligence Summary, C.M.H.Q. Intelligence Summary and its "Notes on Enemy Weapons", and G.H.Q. Home Forces Weekly Appreciation of German Air Force and Enemy Shipping Activities. Reference material included two series of "Notes on the German Army", a "Note on the German Air Force", a study on enemy minor tactics, and an "Armoured Fighting Vehicles Pocket Book". The room had a variety of maps: a "1:1 million" showing German order-of-battle in Europe, a "1:4 million" showing Japanese forces in Asia and the Pacific, and a "1:2 million" showing German order-of-battle in Libya, with Italian information added as it became available.[10] The Section was acting more as an information bureau than as a working Intelligence agency, but it did seem to have all the basic tools of its trade. In action, however, the Information Room would have had to be placed outside the Intelligence Office proper.

The oldest Intelligence units were the three Air Intelligence Liaison Sections. When war broke out, there were three Army Co-operation Squadrons: No. 110 at Malton, Ontario, No. 112 at Winnipeg, and No. 2 Corps Army Co-operation Squadron, initially with flights at Saint John and Halifax, but subsequently concentrated at Ottawa. At the request of the R.C.A.F., the A.I.L. Sections were to be co-located with them. On October 30th, H.Q. First Division detailed Lieuts. F. LeP. T. Clifford, R.C.A., and J.C. Bereau, Le Régiment de Québec, to be A.I.L. officers, with Capts. G.L. Kent, R.C.A., and C.H. Campbell, Ld.S.H. (R.C.), and Lieuts. C.A. Ballard and L.L. Wiswell as alternates. All had taken the A.I.L.O. training course. The men were: a gunner clerk, F.W.W. Needham,

R.C.A., two C.M.S.C. clerks, Cpl. H.O. Tresidder and Pte. D.M. Currigall, one R.C.E. draftsman, L/Cpl. J.S. Souter, and two R.C.A.S.C. drivers, Ptes. N. Robinson and W.R. Demery. Only Tresidder and Souter were Regulars. None of the men had had any training, and a course had to be arranged for them.[11] Capt. A.R. Roy, R.C.R., was given this task.

On December 30th, 1939, G.O.C. First Canadian Division asked that A.I.L. personnel be sent over to him to participate in exercises scheduled for the first six weeks of 1940. No. 2 Section at Ottawa was the only one ready, and, on January 11th, 1940, Capt. Clifford took it to England. No. 1 Section was formed on May 20th, 1940, during the preparations for departure overseas of its parent 112 Squadron, R.C.A.F. Its two officers spent the rest of May and the first week of June much hampered because neither the Army nor the R.C.A.F. was prepared to admit responsibility for it. They found only two men, Sapper C.C. McAllister and Pte. W. Eaton, and went overseas four short. The unit never did recruit up to strength, and was temporarily disbanded on December 26th, 1940.[12]

On September 11th, 1940, the Officer Commanding R.C.A.F in Britain advised that R.C.A.F. A.I.L. officers would be assigned to Corps H.Q. They were to: work closely with the formation Intelligence staffs; hold all information on enemy air forces that might be required by the Army; pass any relevant information to subordinate Army formations and to the Army Co-operation Squadrons; and act as a channel to G.H.Q. and the Air Ministry for any information acquired by the Army. Such information could include: the weight of air attack to be expected, types of enemy aircraft, enemy bombing and reconnaissance policy, tactics, enemy anti-aircraft defences, and methods and results of Allied attacks. These A.I.L.O.s came under the Air Staff Officer of their Regional (Air Force) Command for administration and discipline, and were not to be Air advisers to the G.O.C.[13] This arrangement paralleled the Army A.I.L.O. role and was untidy. Obviously, the two Services had not discussed the matter conclusively.

The Army officers in the Intelligence Liaison Sections with the Squadrons had at first to "sell" their own role, to outline the ways in which the Air Force supported the Army, and to give detailed instruction in the methods used for making that support effective. During the early period when the Air Force was on the defensive, their duties consisted mostly of artillery spotting over the ranges in southern England, and of exercises designed to teach the troops march discipline, use of roadside cover, and reaction to air attack.[14] Camouflage was checked by flying photographic sorties over the troops and submitting annotated photographs to the unit commander, a training technique familiar from prewar exercises at Camp Borden, Ontario. The first such mission in Britain was handled by No. 2 Section in March 1940, using the F 24 camera, which had a five-inch plate. The Section made mosaics and provided individual prints. In April, they experimented with two four-power Zeiss stereoscopes, and tried to speed up processing by using heated solutions, and streamline their dissemination procedures by pre-printing the titling data, such as map sheet, map references, number of the sortie, and altitude. They need not have been ashamed of their speed; on one occasion in May 1940, one mosaic of 25 prints was ready for despatch 51 minutes after the camera was out of the aircraft. Their photos from 2,000 feet gave a scale of 1:4,800, which was said to be of little value unless it could be supported by visual reports. During a later exercise in August, they complained that reports they had sent to H.Q. First Armoured Division had been delayed; since no one had assigned them a priority, their messages were held in an Advanced H.Q. until the lines were clear, by which time, of course, their information was out of date.

On August 15th, 1941, No. 2 Section was redesignated No. 1 Canadian Air Liaison Section. At the end of September, it was doing simulated gas spray attacks and dropping paper-bag bombs filled with ashes over the troops. In November, it flew photo reconnaissance sorties over the Thames estuary in a Lysander, while the Squadron flew top cover. By January 1942, the Section was reduced to one camera, and was unable to fill its commitments. In March, it received a Mobile Pigeon Loft, minus pigeons, which, it was assured, would follow. In August, Maj. Macdonald, then O.C., briefed the pilots supporting the Dieppe Raid. In October, the men fitted a C-33 radio set into an Armoured Command Vehicle. Called the C-44, it gave them good communications with both the aircraft, and Croydon, their base. On January 13th and 15th, 1943, they tried to rebroadcast on High Frequency the Tactical Reconnaissance reports transmitted on Very High Frequency from their aircraft. The V.H.F. air-to-ground was good, but the V.H.F.19 set linked with the artillery was unsatisfactory. Nevertheless, the principle was deemed to be sound, and development continued. It resulted in the Tactical Reconnaissance (Tac R) Broadcasts that later became such an important source of immediate information in North-West Europe.

By September 1943, the Sections had become ancillary Intelligence staffs to the Squadron and Wing Intelligence officers, and their links with Army Intelligence became tenuous. In October, they were reorganized and renamed by function. The one Type "A", located at Reconnaissance Wing H.Q., R.A.F., was Canadian; it had one G.S.O.2, one G.S.O.3, and eight men. The two Type "B" at the reconnaissance airfields (two officers, six men each) were also Canadian. Of the four Type "C" at the Reconnaissance Squadrons (one G.S.O.3, one man), three were Canadian. The Type "D" at Group Control was British. Three Type "E" (one G.S.O.2, two men) at Fighter Wing H.Q. included one Canadian. Two of the four Type "F" at the fighter airfields (two G.S.O.3s, six men) were Canadian. The two Type "G" at the Tank Buster Squadrons were British. Of the 14 officers, four were majors, 10 captains. The 37 men consisted of 14 clerks, 14 batmen /drivers, and nine motorcyclists.[15]

The separation of Intelligence and Air Reconnaissance was unsatisfactory. Successful efforts were made to reverse the trend, and, though formal authority was not given, H.Q. First Army followed 21 Army Group and Second British Army and placed Air Recce within Intelligence. Intelligence Directive No. 6 defined its responsibilities. By the end of the war, 13 sections had been formed, including one for service in Canada. New units were also briefly created; No. 1 Canadian Army Air Liaison Group, and an Air Liaison increment. The Sections themselves were moved to different Air Force units as their tasks changed.

Perhaps part of the reason for the weakening of the connection between the A.I.L. Sections and the Army lay in the fact that they were trying to do two tasks, and were doing one of them badly. In addition to briefing and de-briefing aircrew, they also read air photos. From about mid-January 1943, an organization dealing solely with air photo interpretation began to appear. This new unit was formed initially on an experimental basis and, because the British had not decided on their organization, was based on purely Canadian ideas. On October 24th, 1943, an experimental "No. I Canadian Air Photo Interpretation Section" was formed, using officers and men working in the field. It later became "No. 1 Canadian Army Air Photo Interpretation Section" (A.P.I.S.). This comprised an H.Q. and Corps and Divisional Detachments with 19 officers, and 46 rank and file. At Army, it had a strength of one G.S.O.3, four I.O.s (Photo Interpreter), four plotting clerks, and two general duty clerks. Its Corps unit consisted of two I.O.s and one clerk. In addition, an R.C.A.F. Mobile Field Processing Section (M.F.P.S.), with a Photo Officer and 14 men, was attached to the Army. The G.S.O.3 was an advisor to the G.S.O.1 (Int), supervised the Photo I.O.s, and edited and wrote reports. He also carried out liaison with the A.P.I.S. at G.H.Q., the Central Interpretation Unit (C.I.U.), 39 Wing, R.A.F., and Central Air Support (C.A.S.C.).[16] The I.O.s were responsible for First, Second, and Third Phase interpretation.

First Phase took place as soon as possible after the aircraft returned from its mission. The film was developed and printed by the Mobile Field Processing Unit (M.F.P.U.), which operated in a trailer at each squadron. Much of this phase had previously been done by the A.I.LO.s. An I.O. (Photo) from the Corps or Army A.P.I.S. was added to units assigned to Army Co-operation Squadrons to watch for signs of any abnormal activity and obvious new construction on the enemy side. The A.I.L. Sections were critical of what they described as the amateurishness of early A.P.I.S. drafts.

Second Phase interpretation involved a more careful scrutiny of the prints by the two I.O.s at formation H.Q. They were interested in any item that would assist Intelligence in evaluating enemy capabilities and, if possible, intentions. They looked for and studied numbers and types of defensive positions, guns, equipment, changes in dispositions, H.Q., indications of increased activity, reinforcements, construction, demolitions, and occupation of positions.

Third Phase interpretation not only tried to discover things missed at lower levels, but also had a primary strategic mission. It was interested in enemy rear areas, movement forward of logistic support such as engineer construction units, activity around rear road and railheads, identification of unusual hospital facilities, dumps, bases and depots, construction of airfields and roads, and general information on terrain and topography.

The M.F.P.S. reproduced, titled, and distributed the prints made from the negatives produced by the Mobile Processing Units at the Army Co-operation Squadrons. One of their major tasks was to devise a cataloguing and storage system that would allow the prints and negatives of previous sorties to be easily retrieved.[17]

Photo Intelligence was probably the most important source of combat information during the war. But, running it a close second on the battlefield, and much more important at the strategic level, was Wireless Intelligence ("Y")* which dealt with the interception and analysis of enemy radio transmissions. Its use in the Canadian field forces was first discussed at C.M.H.Q. in May 1940. At that time, it was believed that facilities would initially be provided by the British, and that Canadians would be trained to replace them. When the proposal was referred to Ottawa, N.D.H.Q. suggested, on July 31st, that C.M.H.Q. should consider mobilizing two Special Wireless Sections, a Type "B" and a Type "C". (The difference between the two types hinged on the nature of the interception required.) C.M.H.Q. thought these were G.H.Q. troops, and therefore a British responsibility. But Ottawa told C.M.H.Q. that the British would welcome a Canadian contribution in this field and, after further discussion, authority was given to mobilize No. 1 Section, Type B. Its establishment called for two captains or lieutenants, six corporals, and a batman. In April 1941, it was enlarged by the addition of another sergeant, eight corporals, and five drivers. In December 1942, a second amendment increased the officer establishment by one. It also required the N.C.O.s to be "linguists C", because an intercept clerk had to be able to handle clerical work at high speed in a foreign language, and do this while he was actually intercepting enemy transmissions. Afterwards, he had to make translated records of his interceptions.[18]

It was one thing to create the unit; it was quite another to find men to staff it. The embryonic Canadian prewar Wireless Intelligence organization had not been able to build up a cadre of experienced people. New personnel had to be recruited and since they would have to come mostly from the same ethnic group as the major enemy, their employment could present security difficulties, particularly in such a sensitive unit. Further, not all those who spoke fluent German had the temperament, motivation, education, or intelligence needed to work in "Y". And once they had been recruited, trained, and sent to a unit,

---

* "Y" was a usage pun for W.I. – Wireless Intelligence.

they often passed through a period of "let-down". They felt that they were not in action, nor really in a position where their skills were being utilized. The men complained that their Signals unit C.O. lacked interest and understanding of their role, that they did not receive trades pay, and that their general administration was poor.

Their dissatisfaction stemmed in large part from the broader question of who actually "owned" the Section. The Corps Signals Officer considered that the Section was part of his organization and that he, therefore, controlled what, when, and, to a large extent, how, they performed. In his view they were Signals personnel performing Intelligence duties, rather than Intelligence personnel attached to a Signals unit for administrative and operational convenience. During the First World War, all intercept personnel had been Signals. The British had now swung away from this concept. They made Signals responsible for receiving the enemy transmissions and for maintaining the Section in the field. The Wireless Intelligence Section was responsible for monitoring and recording the material, for forming the necessary deductions about enemy activities or intentions, and for reporting the results to the Intelligence Staff for which they worked. This monitoring only applied to communications at formation level and higher. It was thought that analysis, reporting, and reaction times for unit and sub-unit traffic were so long that the information would be useless. The decision to restrict coverage in this way proved later to be a most significant weakness in the system.

The British had a senior officer at the War Office responsible for all Intercept activities, and for adjudicating disputes between Signals and Intelligence. His basic working principle was that the whole purpose of "Y" was interception, direction-finding, and the production of intelligence drawn from enemy transmissions. It had no responsibility for friendly communications. The unit's mission, therefore, was intelligence. At all levels, from the British D.M.I. down, the function was under the direction of Intelligence. The senior Signals Officer of the formation concerned was responsible only for the discipline and well-being of the Signals personnel; he had nothing to do with Intelligence operations, training, or personnel. The Canadian organization had not kept pace with this concept.[19]

After much discussion with C.M.H.Q. and with British H.Q., and incorporating experience gained in SPARTAN, First Canadian Army issued an Intelligence Directive in June, 1943, which set Canadian "Y" policy for the rest of the war.[20] The control vested in the D.M.I. at the War Office was, as far as First Army was concerned, to be exercised by the G.S.O.1 (Int). He was assisted by a G.S.O.2, one G.S.O.3 to handle the technical and training aspects, and three I.O.s to deal with the collation and interpretation of information gathered by the Sections. At Corps, the G.S.O.2 (Int) exercised operational control of the attached section. At Army, the 1943 organization had an "A" Section of ten officers and 28 men, 22 of whom were tradesmen. They were responsible for supporting the Army Intelligence Staff, for providing information of value to the other sections, and for direction-finding. Strategic material which they obtained was passed back to G.H.Q. At Corps, the "B" Sections had three officers and 17 men, 15 of whom were tradesmen. They dealt with comparatively short-range interception and direction-finding of enemy radio links in the field.

The few linguists available were much in demand, not only in the Special Wireless Sections but also as interrogators, the men who obtained information from prisoners of war. An I.O. was expected to have some knowledge of the enemy language; but an interrogator had to have not only a very good knowledge of the language but also of the culture and background of the people he was dealing with. He had to be taught this background and also the techniques of getting a prisoner to talk. The first mention of interrogator training came when the War Office offered C.M.H.Q. vacancies on a one month course beginning May 18th, 1940. A course as short as this would have been little more than an introduction. The first interrogators (Lieuts. H.S. Coulter, J.A. McCordick, and V.R. Bowers) were sent directly from Canada, but they did not arrive until October 1940. Sections were not formed, however, until 1943. These, too, were experimental, like A.P.I.S., reflecting purely Canadian ideas.

H.Q. First Canadian Army's first exercise, TIGER, took place in late May 1942. Here I Corps used Wireless Intercept for the first time. A section from Third British Division, working with it and using the same material, far outclassed Canadian "Y" in speed, quantity, and clarity. Other aspects also showed alarming weaknesses. Information was not passed laterally to supporting formations. Security was generally poor, and at some H.Q. it was particularly bad. Officers were captured still carrying Operation Orders, order-of-battle summaries, and code books. A great deal of training was still needed.[21]

In June 1942, Lt.-Col. G.P. (Pat) Henderson, R.H.C., was appointed to H.Q. First Canadian Army as G.S.O.1 (Int). He was a former G.S.O.1 (Operations) and, as an arms officer who knew what the "consumer" required, he was in an excellent position to reinforce the generally accepted view that an Operations staff officer could deal effectively with intelligence. Unfortunately, on May 8th, only a month after the Section he was to head was formed, he was sent to work on the planning for Operation JUBILEE. He did not return until September 3rd.[22]

The Dieppe Raid in August 1942 will be discussed in Chapter 7. It brought a new sense of purpose to First Canadian Army, a new realization that Intelligence was indeed needed, and that Security routines had to be re-evaluated to meet the allegations that, at Dieppe, they had proved faulty. The lessons supposed to have been learned in TIGER did not seem to have penetrated very deeply. No major intelligence training was given at formation level, but unit I.O.s were given more instruction, and Intelligence staff officers began to be attached to the War Office.[23]

A first tangible intelligence result of Dieppe appeared on December 28th, when First Canadian Army issued Intelligence Directive No. 1, dealing with "Conduct after Capture". It described in broad outline the international law governing the treatment of prisoners, and reminded all ranks of their duty to escape, if they were unlucky enough to be captured, and of the code of conduct expected of them while they were in enemy hands. It authorized instruction in special aids in escape and evasion for selected officers and N.C.O.s so that they, in their turn, could pass on to the troops what they had learned. Intelligence was responsible for this.[24]

In November 1942, someone discovered that the First, Second, Third, and Fifth Division Intelligence Sections had never officially been placed on Active Service and that therefore there was no authority to pay for them. The accounts had been closed and there was an outstanding obligation of $186,000, of which $84,000 was a recurring cost. The error was remedied in September 1943 by absorbing the Sections into the H.Q. of their respective formations, an arrangement that should have applied from the beginning.[25]

The unit Sections now consisted of the I.O., a sergeant, three corporals, and 20 men. The I.O. was considered to be interchangeable with the Adjutant, whom he assisted. He also went on reconnaissance with his C.O., acted as guide when his unit moved, and was responsible for the unit observers, for liaison with nearby units, supervision of the snipers, issue of maps and air photos, and for the maintenance of battalion Intelligence records. The sergeant, aided by a corporal and six men, ran the unit Intelligence Office, maintained the situation map, observation logs, and Diary, and dealt with any P.W. One corporal and seven men were snipers, the other corporal and seven men were observers.

Fifth Armoured Division considered its problems to be unique. Perhaps basing its concepts on reports of the North African campaign in which armoured divisions had captured many P.W., it intended to augment its few officer linguists with N.C.O.s, and placed linguists at brigade, at support group, and at Armoured Car Regiment H.Q. It also asked for an additional Intelligence clerk at Division and at Brigade H.Q. But the solution was not to be found in merely increasing its linguists. It would have been far better to add more military police and arrange for them to evacuate the P.W., and to concentrate the linguists it did have.

Towards the end of 1942 the British offered Canada about 150 vacancies with First Army in North Africa to allow officers and men to gain battle experience. A number of Intelligence officers were selected: Maj. V.R. Bowers; Capts. W.E. Austin, Censorship; J.P.D. Bradley; C.R.R. Douthwaite, F.S.; E.G. Kuhlbach, I.O. Fourth Armoured Division; E.H. Kates and R.F. Wodehouse, Photo; and Lieuts. A.C. Kinnear, Photo; G.M.C. Sprung, Second Division, and P.N. Cotton.[26]

The largest of the many exercises designed to practice Canadian Army units, and one from which many valuable lessons were to be learned, was SPARTAN, held in southern England in March 1943. It was intended to simulate the role that First Canadian Army would play during the Invasion of France. Canadians were assumed to have landed in a bridgehead and were to break out through the defences. Gen. McNaughton had three corps under his command: Gen. Crerar's I Canadian Corps, with Second and Third Canadian Infantry Divisions; Gen. Sansom's II Canadian Corps, Fifth Canadian and Guards Armoured Divisions; and XII British Corps with 43rd and 53rd British Infantry Divisions. Nineteen R.A.F. and R.C.A.F. squadrons were in support. During the preparation period, Intelligence's greatest problem was to find enough staff to fill the vacancies. Lt.-Col. Pat Henderson already had most of his senior staff, but only one of them had Staff College, only three others had previous experience at an H.Q., and five were untrained. He had only 10 of his establishment of 20 I.O.s, six of them untrained. He could have taken the easy option and filled his own staff posts with trained officers. Instead he tried to spread their knowledge and experience throughout the sections at the lower formations as evenly as possible. He did weaken his system unnecessarily by splitting the staff into two teams in a "shift" system with himself on one and his G.S.O.2, Maj. Halbert, from C.M.H.Q., on the other. This meant there was no central authority to ensure that co-ordination was maintained. During the exercise the "shift" was replaced by a "watch" system, which gave better control and more continuity. The teams learned a great deal about the practical difficulties of passing information. Intelligence has never had its own signals network, and in this exercise messages had to be sent to the Signals centre, enciphered, transmitted with other traffic, deciphered at the other end, and then distributed. Intelligence messages tend to be lengthy because of the often inconclusive nature of their content, and even to this day the practical aspects of handling intelligence data have still not been satisfactorily solved.

It was necessary to define more clearly the nature and extent of the Intelligence function itself. Lt.-Col. Henderson also had a number of ancillary tasks. He had to draft a daily "Official Communique". Since most of its content was operational in nature, Pat Henderson justly argued that it should be handled by Operations. He was in charge of Map Codes, another time-consuming duty which, in his opinion, did not belong to Intelligence but was a residue of the old Cipher function. He recommended that they, too, be transferred to Operations, and that a specific policy for their use and issue be developed. He was the Deputy Director of Public Relations (D.D.P.R.), responsible for controlling the war correspondents (news to home), the I.O. Censorship (of copy) and the press (news to troops). He even had the often impossible task of taking correspondents around to places from which they could observe the action!

There were a number of serious weaknesses within the Intelligence system. Signals security on both sides was breached far too often. Lt.-Col. Henderson recommended a retraining period during which radio procedures would be strictly supervised, breaches corrected, and strong measures taken to raise performance to more satisfactory levels. He noticed that both sides tended to use "jargon codes" which were easily broken. He recommended a greater use of land line, and also that "Y" Sections be linked directly with their Intelligence "masters". He repeated the perennial suggestion that Signals should man and control all the radio sets.

An Amplifier Unit was provided in the Army organization to simulate battle noise. It was not used in SPARTAN. Pat Henderson thought it should have been used on a number of tasks, like civilian traffic control, crowd control, refugee handling, and psychological warfare. His suggestion led ultimately to the establishment of Psychological Warfare Amplifier Units which, on occasion, were used by Operations to broadcast battle noises. His Signals Intelligence was inadequate. It had three Type "B" Sections (Nos. 104, 108 British, and No. 1 Canadian), but it needed one to be a Type "A" (Army) Section (10 I.O.s and 28 men). He found shortcomings in his own office, which, in his view, could only be overcome by adding 14 officers and 13 men, including a G.S.O.2 understudy.

There were significant shortcomings in the Air Photo and Air Reconnaissance systems also. The Intelligence (a) Air Reconnaissance post that had been authorized had not yet been filled, partly because of staff shortages, but also because the Composite Group (Air Force) H.Q. had been co-located with Army H.Q., a lesson learned from Eighth Army, and this was thought to have eliminated the requirement. But unity had obviously not brought with it automatic co-operation. A.P.I.S. co-ordinated and controlled all requests for air reconnaissance and photography. Tactical reconnaissance requests came to Intelligence at Army, and were passed by radio-telephone to Corps and Division. This was not only time-consuming, but it led to frequent inaccuracies. Strategic reconnaissance reports were also co-ordinated by A.P.I.S. and passed to 140 Squadron. The response by the Air Force to demands made on it was poor, and A.P.I.S. had to split staff to form teams to work on those areas where coverage was weakest. At Corps, the A.P.I.S. I.O.s were used as spare I.O.s in the Intelligence Office, a great waste of specialists. SPARTAN also revealed that unacceptable delays had occurred in processing important sorties, and Capt. H.J. Basso attempted to overcome this by deploying air photo officers to the airfields to control them. This, in effect, duplicated the A.I.L. function, but it did provide enhanced control. The system, slightly modified, was called "Blue Train", and was used extensively and successfully in the North-West European campaign.

Control and direction of Security was not efficient. F.S. had failed to examine vacated enemy H.Q., perhaps partly because they had not been told where they were. Intelligence (c), which was responsible for watching enemy propaganda and its relationship to Canadian morale, as well as Censorship, had been underworked. Lt.-Col. Henderson proposed integrating both into the

D.D.P.R. organization, which was later done. In addition, there were many other weaknesses that indicated that Security training in the Canadian Army had not been as successful as I(b) would have liked.

In his summation, Col. Henderson asked that the whole Intelligence system be re-examined, in effect criticising the weakness of his own organization. He called for tighter central control, for an organization large enough to be divided into smaller groups without losing its flexibility, for improvements in dissemination of information, and for centralization of records. Because he thought he should control the Reconnaissance and Photographic elements, he wanted the Air Liaison Sections to be made responsible to him.[27] To show the Army Commander exactly what his organization needed, he prepared a detailed establishment table. For a Field Army of two Corps, made up mainly of Canadians and including the Field Security Sections, he stated he needed 89 officers and 64 men, and he was short of this total by 31 officers and 28 men.[28] His calculations actually understated his case, for he had neglected to multiply some establishments by the number of units to which they applied, he did not include all the men, and he made some mathematical errors. He should have listed 98 officers and 174 men, and really needed an additional 40 officers and 108 men. However, his lower figures gained him the support he was looking for, and the necessary steps were taken to remedy the weaknesses he had stressed in his careful review.

Unfortunately for him, Lt.-Col. Henderson did not enjoy the benefits that came from his recommendations. On June 17th, 1943, he was replaced by Lt.-Col. Peter Wright. Pat Henderson had had very trying problems to contend with. But, perhaps because of these, he saw very clearly where the weaknesses lay, and he did a great deal to build solid foundations for the structure that would eventually overcome them. His successor carried on that work and accelerated its pace. Only a month after Lt.-Col. Peter Wright took over, First Division departed for Sicily. There was little time left to make major changes.

Lt.-Col. Henderson, of course, was not the only newcomer to the profession. Unfortunately, the few senior Army officers who had gained intelligence experience frequently had to be used in posts where the planners thought that their knowledge and experience would be of more value to the Army as a whole. With the exception of such officers as Majs. George B. MacGillivray and J.W.G. Macdougall, who were good staff officers as well as good I.O.s, there were not many trained Intelligence staff officers available. Though he had had the War Staff Course at Camberley, had served at Dieppe, and had been a member of the Canadian Planning Staff for the Sicily operation, Lt.-Col. Peter Wright, on his own admission, had no detailed knowledge of intelligence. He had only one university year of German and one short familiarization course on the German Army. He, too, had to find his road by ceaseless enquiry and hard work, backed by a retentive memory, a logical mind, and the ability to inspire others by the force of his own personality and leadership ability.

This strong personality quickly gained him the support and guidance of British staffs and their specialists, without whose help, as he himself has said, his task would have been much more difficult. They gave First Army the benefit of their experience, they inspired in them a willingness to learn and to develop a Canadian environment, and they gave "Colonel Peter's Team" the capabilities they had developed in themselves. The fact that the Canadian Army generally conformed to British practice and organization meant that it usually was spared the need for evolving doctrine and establishing routines of its own without a pattern to draw on. The worst was now over, and First Army Intelligence could concentrate on recruiting and training. In these areas Col. Wright's efforts received unlimited support from two strong and dedicated men who held positions of great importance. Maj. (later Col.) Felix Walter, at C.M.H.Q., set out to find "self-starters", men of initiative who would be able to make a real contribution. And Maj. (later Lt.-Col.) Bob Raymont, at "Raymont's Academy", 1 C.G.R.U., Aldershot, gave these recruits the training they would need in their new roles. Field units cheerfully gave Intelligence some of their best men. Most important of all was a change of climate that came with the general realization that Intelligence was indispensable to an army, and that it needed support. Gens. McNaughton and Crerar, Brigs. Foulkes and Mann, and Col. G.E. Beament, all provided the understanding and help that played a significant part in the development of their revived component.

Exercises allowed Intelligence to sharpen its skills and improve its standing. Recruiters searched for "fluent German-speaking officers, aggressive, quick-witted, with experience in handling men". I.O.s could be accepted without the language requirement; F.S. officers had to have French or Italian; I.O.s Censorship had to have a spoken and written knowledge of French.[29] In November, Army gave formal authority to Felix Walter to allow him to select candidates for courses. Units were encouraged to bid for vacancies on the 5-weeks War Intelligence Course, and on a one-week course on the German Army (open to major unit and formation staff officers), or a longer course at battalion level. Staff officers were encouraged to attend Unit Security Officers courses. And, most important, an Other Rank Intelligence Duties Course was arranged at all levels of command.[30]

To ensure that adequate replacements would be available, planners had to calculate the volume of casualties that could be expected when the force went into action. The calculation was complicated by the fact that not all men required the same length of training, nor would they have the same potential exposure to danger. To take one example only, C.M.H.Q. considered it necessary to have a 100% pool of linguist replacements, simply because it took a great deal of time to train them. And, of course, planners had to keep within current establishment limits. As of April 30th, 1944, Intelligence had 96 officers and 381 men (about 150% more than John Page had originally estimated); of these, 47 officers and 200 men were considered to be linguists. The replacement requirement for all establishment positions was 81 officers and 363 men.* A pool of 100% was obviously not possible, particularly when the Army knew that it had already practically exhausted the visible supply of linguists. Fortunately, the wastage rates turned out to be much lower than had been anticipated. Replacements were held in various Increments and Pools created during 1944. All were used, but not always in the roles for which they had been trained.[31]

At this time a novel and little-known Intelligence unit was created. The U.S. Army had developed a new method of making models to brief troops before an operation. The Deputy Director of Survey agreed that Intelligence should recruit and control a similar Canadian unit. Lieut. D.W. Taylor, who was then at the Reinforcement Unit, and six men from No. 1 Canadian Engineer Reinforcement Unit, formed No. 1 Canadian Modelling Team.[32]

For Command purposes, on March 7th, 1944, First Canadian Army divided some of its Branches, including Intelligence, between Tactical and Main H.Q. Lt.-Col. Wright, Majs. Broughall and Macdougall, Capts. Depew, Robertson, and Wodehouse, and Lieuts. Fairley, Burrell, and Paulin went to Tactical H.Q. at Headley Court. Main H.Q. lived under canvas in the nearby woods. On March 27th, 1944, a meeting of all Intelligence staff officers and I.O.s was held at I Mess. It was followed by a dinner. Present were: Brig. E.T. Williams, D.S.O., General Staff, Intelligence, 21 Army Group; Brig. C.C. Mann, D.S.O.,

* The replacement rates were calculated on the following establishments:

		Officers	*Men*
a.	14 F.S. Sections at 1 officer, 11 men each	14	154
b.	11 F.S. Reserve Detachments: most had 6 men; four had 1 officer, 7 men	4	70
c.	Wireless Intelligence Sections: Type "A" at 10 and 26; 2 Type "B" at 3 and 18.	16	62
d.	Interrogation: H.Q. (3 and 10), 4 teams (2 and 5)	11	30
e.	1 Canadian A.P.I.S.	19	43
f.	2 Censor Sections at 2 and 4 each	4	8
g.	Attached personnel (Army: 15 and 8), two Corps at 3 officers; two Armoured Divisions at 1 officer each; Special increments (5 and 4)	28	12
h.	General Duty Company, C.M.H.Q.		2
	Totals:	96	381

a former Intelligence staff officer, then Chief of Staff, First Canadian Army; Brig. N.E. Rodger, now B.G.S. II Corps; and some 90 junior members of the "Community". Brig. Williams spoke on the need for teamwork and the importance of Intelligence in the difficult days to come. He pointed out how necessary and how hard it was to develop a feeling of unity within a profession that is dispersed not only by geography but also by the varied nature of its duties. Lt.-Col. Peter Wright's selection of this moment to mount an "occasion" did much to strengthen the team spirit of his people.

II Corps now began to prepare for action. It cleared out its classified waste, and organized lectures on Belgium, France, and, as part of the cover story, on Norway as well. On April 8th, 1944, unit censorship was imposed and accompanied by a firm warning that the authorities considered it a serious offence to use the civilian mail or to send messages by travellers. Private telephone calls were allowed, but their content was subject to restrictions and the caller's telephone number could not be given. Corps issued its first Intelligence Summary, covering the period 6th–10th April; another one followed on the 14th. From then on it tried to issue Summaries daily. The content was almost exclusively exercise material, but it was intended to perfect a working system and to train the Intelligence staff to think in terms of a "daily paper". By this time many staff changes had been completed. Maj. Broughall replaced George MacGillivray, who had unfortunately developed an ulcer; Capt. Ernie Offenheim became G.S.O.3; Lieuts. V.G. Ursaki, R.J. Pootmans, and Basil Robinson were the I.O.s; Capt. John M. Gray and Lieut. Jake Steen handled the I(b) duties.

On April 24th, 1944, Capt. T.C. Rogers, Lieut. R. Westway, and nine men took two trucks, a "penthouse" (canvas shelter), and a jeep, and set up a joint A.P.I.S./M.F.P.S. (R.A.F.) mess. On the 26th they were given three 160-pound tents and a "Canadian Hut" (a heavy, prefabricated structure designed to replace tents in more or less static areas), in which they could set up an Advanced Interpretation Centre, an organization that would be able to supervise the ordering and distributing of all the photo demands made on it. The actual distribution was to begin on May 4th. Meanwhile a detachment of four photo plotters, under at first Capt. E.H. Kates, and later Capt. Charles Taggart, was operating at No. 130 Airfield. For the benefit of staff officers at Army, A.P.I.S. Camp set up a photo exhibition designed to clarify the function of Air Reconnaissance and to explain the facilities it offered. On May 14th, the Chief of Staff, II Corps, visited H.Q. First Army to ensure that photographs for Operation AXEHEAD – the capture of Le Havre and Rouen – were available in sufficient time to permit planning to take place before the Invasion.[33]

Between October 29th, 1939, and May 14th, 1944, an immense amount of preparation had taken place in Britain. But now the training was completed, the material was assembled, and the men were as well prepared as they would ever be. They were ready and even eager to go.

6.
FIELD SECURITY AND COUNTER-INTELLIGENCE IN BRITAIN 1939–45

During the "Long Armistice" the Canadian Army had no direct responsibility for Field Security/Counter-Intelligence (F.S./C.I.). Consequently, when Militia H.Q. was asked to plan a Canadian I(b) organization, the natural thing to do was to follow the British lead. It did not really try to understand the principles involved or to enquire into current practices. Oddly, this was one area where First World War I(b) experience would have been valuable; the British had retained, almost unchanged, the system they had developed by the end of that war.

The British 1931 Mobilization Plan, as amended in 1936, included an Intelligence Corps with a C.I. component comprising a G.H.Q. Section of Field Security Police, Corps Sections, and Lines of Communication (L. of C.) Sections. Initially, no personnel were earmarked to fill these positions nor was an Intelligence Corps formed to command them. In 1938, the Corps of Military Police Depot at Mytchett began to train Regulars who were soon to retire. In 1939, because the supply of Regulars was too limited, it started training civilians also. The Military Police badges they wore were replaced after July 25th, 1940, when the British Intelligence Corps badge and insignia – "a rose flanked by laurel leaves, resting on a scroll inscribed 'Intelligence Corps', the whole surmounted by a crown" – were approved by the Secretary of State. By December 1940, when all F.S. responsibility was assumed by the Intelligence Corps, the Military Police Depot had trained 77 Field Security Police Sections.[1] The Canadian Army F.S. Sections were formed within the framework of the British experience.

Canadian Field Security was first mentioned by Col. E.L.M. Burns on February 1st, 1940. In a memorandum discussing the composition of the Third Contingent, he said that it should include "a Divisional Detachment of Field Security Police".[2] A planning conference on February 9th decided that, in addition to other Intelligence units, sections of F.S. Police were to be raised for certain formations, including First Canadian Division. On February 17th, the War Office suggested that one of the two officers then on course at Mytchett should take about 20 men from the Division to the depot. The officer could be used as an instructor and the men could join the standard course in March. When they had finished their course, the 20 men would make up a complete Section: one warrant officer, two staff sergeants or sergeants, 10 lance-corporals, and seven reinforcements.

The G.O.C. First Division approved the suggestion, asked C.M.H.Q. to seek formal authority for the Section, and advised that his Division would select suitable men.[3] The G.S.O.3 First Division, Capt. C.C. Mann, was named to supervise the group. On February 23rd, 1940, the first F.S. N.C.O., C.Q.M.S. E.A. Chamberlain of No. 1 Provost Company was selected. The Section was named No. 1 Field Security Section, Intelligence Corps. N.D.H.Q. approval was given on March 13th and Chamberlain was commissioned three days later. The first Field Security course students were Sgts. J. Green, J.R. Jean, K.E. Andrews; Cpls. E.G. Norman-Crosse, H. Martin, M. Littner; L/Cpl. L.M. Taschereau; and Ptes. A. Hutchison, G. L'Hereault, and T.H. Lines.[4]

On March 8th, 1940, a conference at C.M.H.Q. decided that a Corps of three divisions would include Divisional Field Security Sections and a Corps Section. The Corps Section had a strength of 15: a captain or lieutenant, one W.O.II, two staff sergeants or sergeants, four corporals, six lance-corporals, and a batman-driver; its transport was 16 motorcycles and a two-seater car. The Divisional Section had an officer, 10 rank and file, eight motorcycles, and three bicycles.[5]

On May 29th, No. 1 Section was brought up to full strength and equipment for service in France. Its members were: Lieut. E.A. Chamberlain, C.S.M. J. Green, S/Sgts. J.R. Jean and C.E. Williams, and Sgts. K.E. Andrews, W.A. Symes, R.F. Hedges, J.F.E. Howarth, A. Hutchison, G.L. L'Hereault, T.C. Mulvihill, A.A.B. Noble, F.G. Quinn, and W.L. Robinson. With the exception of the O.C., the C.S.M., and the two S/Sgts., the ranks were all acting, without pay, "while employed on F.S. duties". Hedges and Noble were paid as L/Cpls.[6] The practice of having men hold acting ranks, without pay, was to continue through the war.

On May 29th also, First Division advised C.M.H.Q. that a Field Security Police Section was needed for the Canadian Reserves Area at Aldershot and Bordon, where troops not being sent to France were being held. This, in effect, legitimized the *ad hoc* Lines of Communication (L. of C.) Section being set up by T.H. Lines, who had just returned from officer training. At the same time, Intelligence units were being mobilized for Second Division and a Canadian Corps H.Q. The files give the impression that the task of raising these small Intelligence units tended to "fall into the cracks" between the two headquarters on either side of the Atlantic. Correspondence received in April from N.D.H.Q. stated that the Corps Section and Second Division F.S. Section would be raised in Canada. In June 1940, authority was received to form the L. of C. Section, now renamed No. 2 and later VII Corps Section.[7] Actually, it worked with the existing No. 1 Section until July 21st and the formation of VII Corps at Headley Court near Leatherhead, Surrey.

On August 15th, VII Corps observed that there could be confusion if No. 1 Section in First Division and No. 1 L. of C. Section retained the same numbers.

C.M.H.Q. proposed to Ottawa that the L. of C. Section be renumbered 11 and that the Divisional Sections be numbered according to the Division they originally served. A new L. of C. Section (No. 12), formed in Canada on July 16th, was assigned to the Holding Unit area to be used as a reinforcement unit. Lieut. Lines' Section, which still called itself No. 2, became No. 11 on October 3rd.[8] Obviously, the F.S. organization was being created in reaction to the problems being faced by the respective H.Q., rather than within the framework of a carefully thought-out system.

On September 10th, Maj. C.C. Mann, now G.S.O.2 (Int), VII Corps, outlined the channels of communication his F.S. had to use. He vested control in his I.O. I(b), Capt. Chamberlain, who was to centralize all reports and reporting procedures. Corps General Staff Intelligence was to lay down policy and exercise control; the Field Security Officers (F.S.O.s) were to carry out this policy in their respective zones. A meeting held the next day was attended by the Staff, and by Lieuts. T.H. Lines, P.B. Miller of No. 2 Divisional Section, Green, who had replaced Chamberlain as O.C. of the Corps Section when Chamberlain was appointed I.O. I(b) at Corps, and H.N. Pickford of No. 12 (L. of C.) Section. It was agreed that all information on military personnel would be passed to "A" Branch (which was responsible for discipline and administration), and that information on civilians would be passed through the G.O.C. to G.H.Q. and then to the civil authorities. No. 12 Section would be subordinate to Corps. All F.S. personnel would be considered as being in one unit for promotions and appointments. And a number of minor administrative matters were settled. The decisions were passed to the Deputy Provost Marshal (D.P.M.) who concurred with them. Both the referral by the G.S.O.2 and the concurrence of the D.P.M. were mistakes.[9] F.S. had nothing to do with the D.P.M., who was responsible to the "A" Branch, not to the General Staff. The error, taking place as it did a year after the war had started, shows clearly how unfamiliar even an officer as experienced as "Church" Mann could be with the position of F.S., and how vague that position was.

On August 29th 1940, B Group Holding Unit asked for F.S. help. It pointed out that the Bordon reinforcement camp area had no F.S. Section and that, with so many men coming and going, individuals spreading disaffection would be difficult to identify and isolate. Five weeks later on October 2nd, C.M.H.Q. agreed with VII Corps that the L. of C. Section (No. 12) should be moved from Aldershot to Bordon; it would be attached to the Provost Company and controlled by A Group Holding Unit. It was then discovered that none of the men in it had been cleared; N.D.H.Q. was asked to deal with their clearances quickly. No. 12 Section personnel were not the only ones who had been missed. Another group of eight F.S., recruited to serve with "Z" Force (Iceland), had been shipped from Canada in late August before their documentation was complete. Fortunately, all had clear records. By late November the Provost

Company at Bordon administered all the Sections. This meant, in effect, that the latter had three masters. The G.S.O.2 (Int), C.M.H.Q., was responsible for general supervision of their role. The G.S.O.2 VII Corps was responsible for their detailed direction. And the O.C. Canadian Base Units, through the O.C. Provost Company, was responsible for their administration.[10]

Maj. John Page, G.S.O.2 (Int), C.M.H.Q., disliked this arrangement and, as we have already seen, took immediate steps to forestall the problems that it was bound to raise. He had found that there was no standard system of filing Security reports and considered that standardization would always be difficult because of the different reporting procedures laid down by Corps for military and civilian cases. The division of responsibility was, however, by far the most unsatisfactory part of the arrangement. On December 16th, 1940, Page wrote to VII Corps commenting favourably on the steps that had been taken to control seniority and promotion and to centralize records at Corps. And he firmly stated his opinion that Field Security formed no part of Provost. By that time the British F.S. itself had been completely divorced from Military Police.

In a proposal to Brig. Pope at C.M.H.Q., the D.A.G., at Page's urging, recommended that one officer be made responsible for F.S., and outlined the kind of establishments he thought suitable. He thought that units with the formations should be left under the control of VII Corps, that the Sections in the Canadian Base Units should be under C.M.H.Q., and that pooling and dissemination of intelligence should be kept in the hands of the G.S. Branch, C.M.H.Q. The D.A.G. made it clear that, in his view, the D.P.M. at C.M.H.Q. did not have the knowledge to deal with Intelligence; he recommended in addition that the G.S.O.2 (Int) at C.M.H.Q. should continue to handle all F.S. On December 21st, the D.P.M., Lt.-Col. C.H. Hill, chaired a meeting attended by Capt. The Lord Tweedsmuir, G.S.O.2 (Int), VII Corps, Capt. Chamberlain, and Maj. Page. They agreed that C.M.H.Q. should handle F.S. reinforcements, courses, and administrative problems; that the I.O. I(b) at Corps should have operational control over all units including the Base Units Section, No. 12; that both C.M.H.Q. and Corps H.Q. were to get extra clerical staff, and that a direct link between Corps and M.I.5 (Internal Security) would be sought.[11]

This meeting was discussed with Brig. Pope and, on December 31st, the B.G.S. in his turn told Corps, in precise terms, the role that F.S. was expected to play: "The defeat of the enemy's efforts to prejudice the defence of the Realm and the success of military operations. This object is achieved by contra-espionage and the neutralization of the activity of subversive elements and of so-called Fifth Column organizations, together with a positive action to preserve secrecy and security." As for method, Brig. Pope felt that the ". . . neutralization of subversive elements within [our] ranks will possibly prove to be its primary preoccupation. If this be so, then the identification, observation and even segregation of men disposed to spread 'Red' doctrines within the Canadian

Army will be of outstanding importance."[12] For the first time the F.S. task in the Canadian Army Overseas was exactly and officially laid down.

In his opinion, the need for control to be centralized under Corps was not immediately apparent, although he admitted that Corps had to control the Divisional Sections. He thought that C.M.H.Q. should be given control over Base Units and No. 12 Section, and have responsibility for co-ordinating their activities with those of the Corps Sections.

Corps was dissatisfied with these proposed changes, and a second round of negotiations began. It was decided that selection of men and control of matters of general security would be vested in the F.S.O. at Corps (Chamberlain). Co-ordinating control was to be established at C.M.H.Q., where the G.S.O. (Int) was in a better position to maintain records of suspects within the field force. The I.O. I(b) was to deal with recommendations for postings, promotions, and courses offered through C.M.H.Q., with collection and collation of information for C.M.H.Q. and with control of the central F.S. account. Page would deal with the administration of No. 12 Section, maintain the files and records compiled by Corps I(b), handle postings between Base Units and Corps, and make arrangements for courses demanded by Corps. All questions of Security policy would be settled by consultation and agreement between the Senior Officer, C.M.H.Q., and the Corps Commander. No. 12 Section was to act as a holding unit for F.S. personnel discharged from hospital. Corps H.Q., rather than C.M.H.Q., was to be the link between its Sections and M.I.5.[13]

This second allocation of responsibilities was a little better, but it still contained weak areas. The first of these involved the links with M.I.5. That extremely sensitive organization was understandably anxious to keep its contacts to a minimum, on the perfectly valid grounds that the fewer people it had to deal with, the fewer would be the opportunities for information to leak out. Accordingly, it continued to deal exclusively with Page's office in C.M.H.Q. Secondly, No. 12 Section was sufficiently busy with its own duties; it could not properly handle an additional "depot" burden, particularly as the men coming out of hospital were generally returned to the depot for reassignment to their original arm of Service rather than to Intelligence. No. 12 Section had to chase after them, a time-consuming and difficult task. When the Intelligence and Reinforcement Pool, which we have already mentioned, was formed on January 3rd, 1942, it took over a large share of the routine administrative load, and by the end of 1942 Intelligence people were assigned to the Pool as if it were a depot. Corps finally agreed, in mid-March 1941, that C.M.H.Q. should hold all files of completed cases. A month later C.M.H.Q. also became the official channel to the Censorship authorities. Because reports of violations had to be sent to most of the Sections each month, a central registry was necessary to ensure that persistent offenders could readily be identified. The revised system, once it was implemented, worked reasonably well for the remainder of the war.

In the closing months of 1943, it became increasingly evident that the Sections, most of which had been created following the formation of First Canadian Army in April 1942, did not have adequate linguistic skills. Many members tried seriously to improve by private study, but their unaided efforts were still inadequate. Accordingly, in February 1944, approval was sought to form small sub-units of a sergeant, two corporals, and three lance-corporals, to provide linguistic and other support to the regular Sections. Mobilization of these Reserve Detachments began in May 1944. No. 1 F.S.R.D., under Lieut. Ray Shelley, spoke Dutch; No. 2 spoke German; No. 3, French. No. 5 F.S.R.D., under Capt. Graham Blyth, and Nos. 6 and 7, laid no claim to linguistic ability. No. 8, formed in Italy, regarded itself solely as an extra staff. No. 4 F.S.R.D. was immediately attached to No. 3 Section and Third Canadian Infantry Division for the early stages of the Invasion. Nos. 9, 10, and 11 were formed for Italy. No. 12 was formed in May 1945 in Holland. Now that we can see things in perspective, it looks as though these Detachments were formed partly to absorb reinforcements which had been provided in case casualties were heavy, and partly in response to last-minute fears that the Sections would be unable to handle their commitments. As it turned out, the roles that most of the Sections were destined to play were far too big for their modest resources and these had to be augmented. It would have been preferable to form a larger central group from which personnel could have been detached as they were needed.

No. 1 Section had been told what was expected of it on its course in March 1940. But it barely had time to organize during April and May before it had to prepare for its move to France. On June 11th, the Section left Aldershot for Exeter and Falmouth. On the 12th, the troops loaded their transport into the vessel *Port of Montreal*, spent the night at a transit camp, and moved the next day to Plymouth, whence they sailed for France in the *Ville d'Algiers*. They landed in Brest harbour about 0900 on the 14th. That afternoon Chamberlain and one of the French-speaking N.C.O.s patrolled the town, contacting the French civil and military authorities and the British Command in the port area. But Gen. Brooke, who commanded the British forces in France, heard that day that the French were in no position to fight on, and issued orders that all units not fighting under French command be withdrawn. The Section re-embarked about 1800, this time reunited with their transport aboard the *Port of Montreal*. She sailed on the 15th, arriving in Falmouth about midnight, and the first field service tour of duty of a Canadian F.S. Section ended.

During the summer which followed, the Sections taught officers of other units to ride motorcycles, lectured on security, watched for suspicious lights (a counter-espionage task), chased rumours and "careless talk", and carried out directives issued by Ottawa with respect to the surveillance of German and Italian nationals. These directives did not extend to the details of disposal of these individuals, and guidance had to be sought from Col. M.A. Pope, then Col.

G.S. at C.M.H.Q. A more definitive terms-of-reference was not forthcoming until the end of the year.

Field Security was responsible for the neutralization of subversive elements within the Army. This was to be done through identification, observation, and even segregation, of all individuals within the Army whose actions were motivated by a desire to cause disaffection. In professional language, actions taken to protect people are grouped under an umbrella term, "Security of Personnel". Those taken to protect material and installations – counter-sabotage – come under the heading "Security of Materiel". Actions designed to protect friendly field activities are "Security of Operations and Plans". There are, inevitably, activities that cannot be conveniently grouped under a particular heading. We must also emphasize that the small F.S./C.I. units could not ever cover every possible source and channel of leakage or threat. Security always attempted to educate others to recognize the nature of the threat and the methods used by enemy agents. F.S. tried hard to make all members of the Armed Forces so aware, that the precautions they would take automatically would frustrate all but the most determined subversive. When measures failed, as did happen, enquiries would be set in train, not to seek a culprit to punish, but instead to try to find out what had happened, how serious the damage was, and what measures would be best suited to make certain that any future attempt of this kind would be unsuccessful.

The most important activity in the Security of Personnel category was what was familiarly called the "vetting" of individuals or, more formally, "Security Clearance Investigation". In Canada, the agency responsible was the R.C.M.P. But there were not enough police investigators to cover the Army, and permission was given to the Army Intelligence component to conduct its own enquiries. These investigations began in the Canadian Army Overseas even before they were introduced at home. Vetting involved a check on the man himself, on his associates, and on his spare-time activities. His political views were studied, his general behaviour observed, and his reaction to his military environment evaluated. At C.M.H.Q., Brig. Pope had been concerned about the possible presence of "Reds". Some were indeed uncovered. But the number of aliens of enemy national origin who had enlisted in the forces was far larger, and represented potentially a more serious threat. The estimate of this did not remain constant; the shortage of manpower, and political considerations forced changes in the regulations made to govern their status. The few men who could not be cleared had to be placed where they could do no harm. The majority were returned to take their place within the Service as soon as they were cleared of suspicion.

Security clearances were far from being the only problem. Poor morale could and did lead quickly to unrest, disaffection, and even desertion. A constant watch had to be kept on conditions that, by lowering morale, could make it easier for subversive influences to reduce the efficiency of a unit.[14] Every report received had to be investigated, including a few that had their amusing side. One of No. 1 Section's first enquiries, for instance, was thought to be a case of subversion leading to desertion. A Liverpool girl was alleged to be offering to "get soldiers back to Canada for $10". When she was checked at her address – the Purple Parrot pub – she could not be found. Experience would have identified her proposal as a prostitute's offer of briefer and more elemental transports.

No. 1 Section started 1941 at Croydon by investigating business relations between Canadian soldiers and the British public. No. 2 Section heard that a civilian in Guildford was destroying the troops' mail, and that local Communists were active. No. 12 Section interrogated a Roman Catholic priest who was alleged to be using the privacy of his confessional to spread disaffection. In April 1941, No. 1 Section reported that "there was reason to believe that an effort has been made to persuade French-Canadian soldiers to take no part in any action which might ensue between France and Britain." G. L'Hereault, of the Section, visited the Free French forces in London while he was on leave. He was shown around the French "district" and was told that there were indeed places where French-Canadian troops could obtain passports, identity cards, and civilian clothes. One of them, Le Cercle Français, in Old Compton Street, was identified and placed out of bounds.

No. 2 Section uncovered a case of revenge that involved the members of a Field Ambulance unit. One man in the unit was believed to have given a voluntary statement that caused another man to be charged with a crime. The victim's friends then severely beat up the squealer. When investigations into the assault proved abortive, the O.C. ordered extra drills for all members of the unit in the hope that the guilty parties would then confess. The Section quickly identified the culprits. Another enquiry produced a sergeant-major who was attempting to corner the gambling in his unit; he used pressure to ban all gambling except at times and places that he himself would authorize.

Many F.S. felt that lack of activity during the winter of 1940/41 would lead to a lowering of morale and an increase in desertions. In reality very little trouble occurred, but the risk remained. Men managed to disappear into the shadow world of London, while others availed themselves of an escape route to the Irish Republic. In June 1941, a Canadian soldier managed to return to Canada by signing on as a stoker on a merchant ship. When he was questioned, he said that he had merely asked around the docks area for a ship, and had been able to sign on without any questions being asked. The game was not without its hazards, however. One deserter was especially lucky, for the ship he had selected, and from which he was arrested, sank with all hands on the very voyage he had intended to take. In August, No. 1 Section reported that, while on leave, some Seaforth Highlanders of Canada had been offered money for current expenses, a safe and unquestioned journey to Eire, and a job when they arrived there on the understanding that, in the event of hostilities, they would immediately join the I.R.A. Eire, however, was not the only possible destination. In November 1941, when No. 1 Section checked a private soldier who had more money than seemed normal or reasonable, it discovered that the consul of one of the Latin American countries had been recruiting seamen, and providing enough papers and funds to attract volunteers from among Canadian troops. When closing these "bolt-holes", F.S. Sections always received excellent co-operation from the civilian police.

The Sections also watched for signs of possible friction between Canadians and troops of other nationalities. In July 1941, clashes between Canadian and Irish soldiers at a Croydon dance hall led to a recommendation by No. 1 Section that put the hall out of bounds. A similar problem, in the same area but at a lower intensity level, arose between Canadian and Czech troops. Military Police was the proper agency to deal with such conflicts and, after 1941, F.S. gradually became less involved.

The unit War Diaries occasionally indicate that there were Canadians suspected of associating with known Communists or Fascists, and that a man sometimes appeared to be contributing to disaffection even though his political leanings could not be firmly identified. In late November 1941, an alien was discovered to be expressing anti-British views, and attempting to persuade both civilians and servicemen not to co-operate with the authorities. No. 1 Section, encouraged by the local police, managed to get sufficient evidence for M.I.5 to take action against him. In another area, a woman was found putting up pro-Fascist posters. She turned out to be a former member of the British Union of Fascists whose husband had already been interned. In August 1943, No. 14 Section N.C.O.s overheard a man state, in the course of a single short evening, that Canadians had stolen slot machines in Crawley for their units, that they had held up cars on a road north of Caterham, that one unit was 80% "jail-birds" recruited from prisons, and that, thanks again to the Canadians, 85% of the women of Caterham had venereal disease. He was arrested and handed over to the local police. This list of canards is fairly representative of those F.S. had to handle. It is unusual only in that so many of them came in at one time and that the source was so clearly identified. The above catalogue of incidents is by no means exhaustive.

Investigations coming under the heading Security of Materiel tended to some degree to overflow into areas for which the Military Police, rather than F.S., were mainly responsible. Basically, Military Police act to detect theft, Security to protect key points against sabotage and to protect information on new or sensitive material, including weapons, knowledge of which would give an enemy an advantage. The division of authority required Security to recommend the measures to be taken to protect an installation. The officer in charge would decide whether he would follow the advice given and, if appropriate, would order guards to be mounted; they were often supplied from the Military Police. Some of the other functions seem to have been allotted in a fairly arbitrary way. One, for instance, was investigating the sale of cigarettes sent to Canadian soldiers in Britain by relatives, friends, and patriotic organizations at home. The trade was a lucrative one, for the cigarettes were gifts, no duty had been paid on them, and the rationed society of Britain offered a ready and eager market. Its connection with Security, however, seems remote, and no reasons have been found to explain why a task of this kind, which continued throughout the war, was not turned over to Provost. Its main value to F.S. came from the practical training it gave. In February 1941, for example, Cpl. Kirk of No. 2 Section was specially commended for his work in cracking a case of theft of cigarettes.

Credit must be given to No. 12 Section for making, in January 1941, the earliest recorded counter-sabotage recommendation. It discovered that the water supply for the Canadian concentration area at Bordon was not protected, and correctly pointed out that the installation was a prime target for sabotage; the local water authority took action at once. A number of suspected cases of sabotage were reported but few seem to have been conclusively proven.

In January 1944, No. 3 Section was given what was perhaps the most important Security of Materiel task ever handled by the Sections: to protect one of the secret items of Invasion equipment – the Duplex Drive, or D.D., tank, a Sherman tank fitted with flotation gear. While two Canadian armoured regiments were being re-trained to use it, a Security of Personnel incident occurred. An inadequately identified officer from a special D.D. training course was reported to have talked imprudently about the tanks. The course list of students was checked, and all were assembled for an identification parade. No. 3 Section worked its way through the personnel of the four units involved, but failed to locate the offender, quite possibly because his associates were protecting him. In the meantime, consignments of D.D. tanks had to be delivered from Chilwell and from Manchester; and the Section had to provide protective escorts. Sgt. Kazakoff drew the Manchester assignment; Cpl. Kapala went to Chilwell. On January 30th, 1944, each man made his trip by road, without maps and at night. When the 13 tanks arrived at 0530 on February 2nd, No. 17 Section had to find seven additional guards. At Studland Bay, where the tanks were to be tested in exercises, one became stranded and had to be watched (by Cpl. Shook) until it could be recovered. The escorts had to continue their protective role until the tanks were actually loaded on to their landing craft for the Invasion. Security for the D.D. tanks was successful; they came as a complete surprise to the Germans in Normandy.

Occasionally F.S. was asked to protect enemy equipment until it could be studied by I(a). In February 1941, No. 2 Section recovered from souvenir-hunters parts of the guns from a crushed Heinkel, and drawings of parts of the aircraft itself. In May 1941, No. 11 Section captured the crew of a German aircraft downed near Cobham. An error in the count led to a request to hunt for the "missing" man. A fruitless search was made the following day in the crash area, in the course of which one fool tried to drive through a roadblock. The shot fired at the car by the Home Guard sentry ricocheted off a roof brace and killed the driver. The F.S.O., Lieut. Bill Cooper, attended the inquest.

Security of Operations and Plans covered a very wide front indeed. It included counter-espionage, investigation of rumours, and all the security protection required for the operations themselves. From 1940 to 1944, these operations consisted mainly of exercises designed to train troops in battle techniques. In these, F.S. sections played varied and important roles. They acted as Security advisers and as "enemy intelligence", and sought out information about the "enemy" by checking his vacated H.Q. The only role they did not play, in practice, turned out to be the one that absorbed most of their time and energy when they went into action, namely, control of the civilian population.

Counter-espionage was not simply a matter of watching for persons who showed an excessive interest in army activities. It included investigation of all those situations that could make it easier for hostile persons to discover what they wanted to know. For example, in late 1940, it was learned that Canadian soldiers were leaving their paybooks with local merchants as security for purchases or loans. A paybook contained a full description of the owner and a record of his military service. For the shopkeeper it was excellent collateral, for he knew that the man needed it back. But it could also be a very convenient document for an enemy agent who wished to gain access to a Canadian installation, to obtain the order-of-battle information it contained, or to use as a model from which to make counterfeit copies for other agents.

Reports that soldiers were selling information were received throughout the war. In January 1941, No. 1 Section discovered a case, not of information but of equipment being sold; it turned the culprit over to the Provost. In August 1941, a gunner of 1 Field Regiment, R.C.H.A., noticed a man taking photographs of troops on an exercise; he arrested him and turned him over, through his unit, to Sgt. Dave MacAulay, No. 1 Section, who interrogated him and passed him to the civilian police. In April 1942, the same No. 1 Section heard that a man, known to be a successful black market operator, had a radio transmitter near Worthing. The police went to the location but found only signs that a powerful set had been there. In late 1942, one of the Sections received a report that a woman who was often seen in a bar frequented by officers seemed to know too much about the movements and locations of naval vessels. Her social status was such that the F.S.O. decided to investigate her himself. The next morning when they were dressing, he noticed a picture of an extremely senior naval officer on her vanity table. He questioned her; her reply, "Oh, that's my husband", explained why she knew so much about the Navy. She was warned to be more discreet in future.

Loose talk, in fact, did offer many opportunities for important information to find its way into the hands of persons whose business was to seek it. In March 1941, a private soldier was heard to say, fairly accurately, that Canadian troops were to be sent to Gibraltar. When he was questioned, he said that he had learned about the move when he overheard his own colonel talking to two other colonels. He was punished, not for eavesdropping, but for repeating what he had heard. In November 1941, an officer and 40 men of the Royal Regiment of Canada were sent to take a classified course of some sensitivity. When they returned, they found that the substance of their course was a matter of common knowledge. The officer suspected that the disclosure had come from within his own group, although he knew that all the members had been sworn to secrecy. No. 2 Section was alerted. It discovered that, even before the course started, its subject matter had been freely discussed in a Women's Voluntary Services canteen. Little more than a general reprimand could be inflicted. Canteens were always a special problem, if only because civilians working on a unit site were often allowed in them, and could overhear a good many conversations among soldiers. Most units tried, not always successfully, to restrict non-military access to them. Occasionally even some of the staff were suspected. No. 2 Section had a "lady-friend" who had managed to find a job in the Canadian Auxiliary Services, a formal, uniformed group that worked in canteens. This woman specialized in "trying to obtain detailed information and also Army revolvers and ammunition". The occasional announcement that an imposter had been caught, or that someone had been found wearing a uniform to which he was not entitled, was widely publicized to remind all soldiers of the risk of enemy agents. The security posters of the day ceaselessly pointed out the danger of careless talk. Their message was valid; the enemy did indeed have agents in Britain.

Rumours abounded in wartime; some were obviously nonsensical, but many others had a certain basis in fact. I(b) always had the fear that someone, somewhere, would unintentionally leak information he should have kept to himself. Whatever their origin, all rumours had to be checked, but only rarely was it possible to trace them back to their original sources. Any major army activity could start speculation which, more or less simultaneously, would appear in a number of different places. Tracing rumours was a frustrating and never-ending job. Even the poster program, which reminded those who knew something not to disclose that knowledge and those who knew nothing to keep quiet, had little effect on their flow. It took a long time for Security to limit the incidence of dangerous discussion.

The first recorded example of rumour-mongering occurred just before Christmas 1940. Canadian soldiers at Reading were reported to be telling all who cared to listen that they had been inspected by the Secretary of State for War, that they were en route to the Middle East, and that there had been a good deal of sabotage in Canada. Unfortunately, British Field Security learned that the soldiers also claimed they had never been given any security instruction. In June 1941, No. 1 Section heard stories of drunken troops announcing that they were "not interested in fighting for bloody England". No. 2 Section was told, on the one hand, that all Canadians were to be returned home and that liners were waiting in Scottish ports to transport them; and, on the other, that the exercises then in progress were actually preparation for an invasion. Rumour had it that the R.22e.R. was engaged in a sit-down strike (rumours of incidents involving French-Canadian units were common but rarely even remotely factual), and that Rudolf Hess was in custody in the divisional area. The Section did not manage to find the sources of any of these fabrications.

In August 1941, there were widespread rumours that Second Division would be moved; in this case, the source may have been the security breaches that were particularly common among officers. Yet, even though rumours did circulate about the September Spitzbergen expedition, its departure remained a secret.

In September 1943, a large First Canadian Army training program provoked a spate of rumours. No. 14 Section was told that "all the troop movements were a blind. . . . We plan to invade the Channel Islands on September 7th. . . . American Headquarters were at . . . Airborne troops and gliders were at . . . There is to be a curfew put on this area soon." This time the sources were identified and severely dealt with. When, in January 1944, Gen. Montgomery returned from Italy, his arrival was correctly interpreted as presaging the launching of the Invasion. No. 15 Section reported a widely held view that the Canadians were going to spearhead the Invasion; presumably, similar rumours were current in the British and American areas as well.

Security coverage of exercises and operations involved F.S. in both direct protection and security training. When a unit moved, papers and minor items of equipment would frequently be forgotten in the normal excitement and confusion. From January 1941 up to the end of the pre-Invasion period, F.S. continuously checked premises vacated by major units and formations to make sure that nothing of importance had been overlooked. The reason was obvious; men had to be trained to know that material allowed to fall into unfriendly hands could reveal secrets, and a physical check was the only way to reinforce that training.

But F.S. did more than mere building searches. In. February 1941, when No. 2 Section was working with a Divisional exercise, it noticed an unnecessary volume of vehicle activity around the H.Q., an act of carelessness that would be dangerous in action. This and many other similar errors were due primarily to a lack of experience that training would correct in time. In another exercise (DAVID) later that month, a No. 2 Section N.C.O. successfully infiltrated the British 38th Divisional area. He used his own motorcycle, bearing an obviously false 38th Division sign, was dressed differently from 38th Division riders, joined their convoys, drove through unit concentrations and, though he was stopped once, was not questioned. Two other N.C.O.s, driving a captured 38th Division car, even managed to pass false messages into the Divisional Despatch system. A fourth N.C.O., carrying a number of notes on 38th Division's activities, was captured and questioned, but not searched. As a result of these experiences, procedures for dealing with enemy infiltration were quickly tightened up.

Exercise BUMPER, held September 26th to October 3rd, 1941, to practice Canadians in their anti-invasion role, involved a major move of the forces in southern England to areas north and west of London. Nos. 1, 2, and 11 Sections were deployed. During the exercise, the Canadians found that enciphering messages was very time-consuming, so they sent them in the clear. The "enemy" intercepted them, ambushed a column, and captured a Brigade H.Q., including its men and its radio and cipher vehicles. The Brigade I.O., Lieut. Sorby, the men of his section, and the attached F.S. men, managed to burn all their documents. But the unfortunate corporal in charge of the cipher section "was under the impression that the authority of an officer was necessary before the records could be destroyed". He would have been right – in peacetime. Other errors, more in the F.S. field, were discovered: umpires and liaison officers left marked maps exposed; in one serious case, a briefcase containing the exercise details was left unattended in a pub; careless talk, neglecting to cover lights, laxity in using camouflage nets, use of civilian postboxes to mail letters, and inadequate facilities for prisoners were also noted. When one considers the inexperience of officers and men, the number of faults should not be thought excessive.

In a "Security Week", run by I Canadian Corps in December 1941, F.S. "agents" using false identification papers gained access to the Signals office of 3rd Brigade and came away with information on lines within the area. An "agent" failed to get information from one infantry battalion but, on his way out, left behind a "time bomb" and cut most of the telephone lines. A false despatch rider made away with a unit's outgoing mail. Another "agent" managed to steal a revolver and ammunition. Acting on information obtained by F.S., two detectives disguised as labourers succeeded in planting "time bombs" at the site of a secret project in the Southern Railway workshops. One "agent", whose identity card bore the portrait of a notorious prison escapee instead of its bearer, asked to see a unit Adjutant about a totally unfounded charge of unscreened lights. He asked for and was given the locations of all the companies in the unit. While the material was being compiled, the Adjutant said, "I suppose this fellow is all right?", and was assured by the R.S.M. that the "agent" was legitimate. The exercise showed that larger units were more careful than smaller ones, and that telephone security was still too lax, mainly because senior officers asked for – and received – information that should not have been passed by phone. The training was real: an officer, not F.S., was shot and killed when he failed to stop at a sentry's challenge.

By the second quarter of 1942, the Canadian Army Overseas switched from training for a purely counter-attack role to training for offense. In Exercise BEAVER III (April 22nd–24th), First Division played the role of a German invasion force to be counter-attacked by Second Division. In BEAVER IV (May 10th–13th), Second attacked Third Division while the Home Guard acted as a Fifth Column behind each one. In both exercises, breaches in security were minimal. A larger exercise, TIGER (May 19th–30th), conducted by British South Eastern Command, involved I Canadian Corps (and all the Sections). Other than the exploit of an "enemy" sergeant who penetrated the office of the G.O.C., Third Division, "shot" him, and almost got away, and the usual rash of lost mapboards, undestroyed documents, and so forth, the exercise was reasonably uneventful from a Security point of view. But one of the many rumours about the exercise was serious, for it "identified" I Canadian Corps as being on the Isle of Wight.

At that time, Second Division actually was on the Isle of Wight, preparing, under conditions of tight security, for the Dieppe Raid. As we shall see in a later chapter, breaches of security had indeed occurred, and this rumour, garbled as it was, might have been indicative of serious laxity. After Exercise KLONDIKE, which, had the weather co-operated, would have been the actual operation against Dieppe, No. 2 Section returned to Sussex, where it heard a good deal of loose talk about the operation itself, and the training exercises on the Isle of Wight. Cpl. Jezewski, of No. 2 Section, reported that one private soldier of the R.Regt.C. answered his warning about careless talk by retorting that "most of what he had said was already published in the newspapers". Capt. Campbell, O.C. No. 14 Section, commented that: "It is unreasonable to expect that troops will keep information of operations to themselves when the newspapers give out the facts." Rumours of moves and invasions were becoming so widespread that the Sections simply abandoned attempts to track them down.

On August 18th, 1942, the F.S.O. No. 2 Section, Lieut. MacMillan, his C.S.M., J.S. Milne, and Sgts. Corson, Pals, Chauvin, Kirk, Skippon and Feeny, together with Sgts. Holt, of No. 1 Section, and Hawkins, Jordan, Mymka, Bishop, and Hedges, of No. 11 Section, left for Exercise JUBILEE – the Dieppe Raid. On August 20th, MacMillan wrote: "A/Sgts. Skippon, Kirk, Mymka, Sgt. Jordan and F.S.O. returned from Exercise JUBILEE. Others are missing." His entry the next day read: "Section getting readjusted after Jubilee." On the 30th and 31st, the kits of the missing men were checked, packed, and turned over to the Quartermaster of H.Q. Second Division. The nine men were the first F.S. casualties caused by enemy action. The Raid also earned Sgt. Skippon the M.M., the first Intelligence decoration. The Landing Craft, Tank, he was in came under heavy fire, and some hydrogen cylinders aboard caught fire. He helped put them overboard. He then tended some wounded comrades. "His coolness and disregard for his personal safety saved numerous lives", according to the citation.*

According to No. 1 Section, the Raid had one valuable Security result: "... there has been a decided change in the general attitude towards careless talk. More people seem to appreciate that harm can be done." No. 14 felt that the "... Raid made both officers and O.R.s realize the importance of and take more interest in Security." In Second Division: "Security-mindedness has been instilled in the individual soldier and many occurrences have been drawn to our attention where troops ... say they would no longer tolerate breaches of Security on the part of their comrades." Yet, paradoxically, September saw a significant increase in breaches of telephone security as men told their friends of their activities.

A minor footnote to Dieppe appeared in a German Psychological Warfare broadcast from *Radio Deutschland, Bremen, Friesland und Calais*. Sgt. Pickup, No. 1 Section, heard a conversation between a German and an alleged French Canadian. It emphasized the cruelty of the British who were forcing French Canadians to fight for England, while Hitler "wouldn't dream of asking Sudeten Germans, for example, to fight for Germany". We do not know whether this particular broadcast ever reached the ears of Quebec units.

In December 1942, No. 1 Section began to prepare for the Italian Campaign, and was attached to the British Embarkation Establishment, the name given to the planning group assembled for that operation. No. 2 Section was sent to work with British Port Security Sections, followed by Nos. 7 and 11; they covered inward moves, and acted as a sort of Immigration control. Their duties involved counter-espionage and counter-sabotage rather than the counter-subversion and security which were the main preoccupations of a normal section.

Exercise SPARTAN occupied the whole of March 1943. All Sections took part, except No. 1, which was now working directly on its Division's impending move to the Mediterranean. No. 3 Section, and a detachment of No. 11 under C.S.M. Skippon, M.M., worked on "enemy H.Q." at Headington, Holton Park, and Wheatley, where they found "enemy" documents, and passed them to I(a). The Winnipeg Rifles gave No. 11 Section some "enemy" prisoners together with their truck-mounted gun. Fortunately, other units followed the laid-down procedures – Military Police to the P.W. Cage. In SPARTAN, security at the unit level had improved. There were still weak spots; inquisitive people who knew too much about Canadian movements were still to be found; the reports were passed to M.I.5.

After SPARTAN, the Sections returned to their regular areas and to the familiar routine of unit training and security lectures. All Section members, not

---

* Second edition note: E.K. Skippon is in the photo of No. 16 Field Security Section, May 1944, in Chapter 11.

merely the F.S.O. and the C.S.M., were sent, in turn, to any unit that requested security lecture services. Stories were being circulated that the Canadians were leaving. Some of the rumours actually identified First Division; few were specific, and their dissemination was too wide for the Sections to trace their sources. No. 14 Section attributed them to wives of First Division troops who had visited their men in Scotland. A woman in Robertsbridge, Sussex, caused a furore when she telephoned a Service Corps company to ask for a friend, because she had heard that there had been a move. No. 1 Section sent down an N.C.O. With the local police, he talked to the girl and discovered that her boyfriend had not contacted her for some time. She had been worried, and had spoken of the "move" simply because she was afraid that he had been transferred, and not because she had any knowledge of the unit's move. First Division did leave in June 1943. There were gaps in its security. No. 2 Section managed to have one woman arrested and fined £7 in a civilian court for making an injudicious comment about First Division. Many others, however, were equally indiscreet but were never prosecuted.

In preparation for its departure to the Mediterranean, Fifth Division, with its No. 7 Section, moved up to Norfolk in July for large-scale exercises. Exercise HARLEQUIN, in August, tested I Canadian Corps, Second and Fifth Divisions. Fourth Armoured Division replaced Fifth in September. There were no significant security breaches during any of these moves. At the end of HARLEQUIN, No. 2 Section was sent to Southampton on Port Security duty with the resident British Section. No. 3 Section moved to Portsmouth to cover Exercise PIRATE. On October 17th, its men were loaded on board a Landing Craft, Infantry: "Craft under way at approx 0700 hrs, in Build Up Force Convoy. Weather fine. All ranks enjoying the trip. As craft cleared the Needles, Isle of Wight, choppy weather encountered, and when in sight of Studland Bay, wind increased, necessitating . . . return to port. . . . Water breaking over decks, and troops ordered below and hatches battened down. Due to violent pitching of ship, an anxious and seasick time was spent. . . . Out of 97 [not including the crew] on board, nine were not sick." No. 3 did not then know that it was earmarked to be the Section that would accompany the Invasion force into North-West Europe.

The build-up of units and reinforcements in England towards the end of 1943 greatly increased the work load of the F.S. Sections stationed around the C.R.U.s. In September, No. 12 Section complained that it had to handle the security problems of a military population of 60,000 men, whereas all the Army Sections put together handled only about 20,000. Despite this disparity, only one extra section was added, presumably on the grounds that the reinforcements would soon be absorbed by the formations and then the pressure within the C.R.U.s would be relieved. In late December 1943, No. 13 Section was authorized, and assigned to London. Its principal duty was to watch for careless talk, subversion, and morale problems in those areas of London where Canadians gathered. It reported directly to the G.S.O.2 I(b) at C.M.H.Q.[15] It was created amid some doubt that the Canadian system of assigning sections permanently to specific formations was wise. The British used an Intelligence Pool, with units controlled centrally and sent where they were needed. No change was made, perhaps because of the considerable upheaval it would have caused, but it remained a lively subject of debate as long as the war lasted, and after.

In October, Fifth Canadian Armoured Division, I Canadian Corps H.Q. and Corps troops, and elements of Army troops left for the Mediterranean Theatre (TIMBERWOLF). Included were three F.S. Sections: No. 7 (Fifth Division), No. 11 (H.Q. I Corps), and No. 14 (First Canadian Army). No. 14 was later replaced by No. 16 Section, formed on October 23rd and commanded by Capt. Rafe Douthwaite, who had just returned from an attachment to No. 78 British F.S. Section in Sicily. Convoy movement to and through the Mediterranean was now much less hazardous, but all danger had not been eliminated. "Security regulations . . . prescribed restrictions . . . upon all means of communication by personnel . . . warned for embarkation . . . removal of identifying unit and formation badges and patches from uniforms . . . marking of baggage by non-revealing serial numbers and . . . avoidance of conversation with stevedores or other civilians at the ports." The instructions ended on an uncompromising note: "No units, formations or individuals will give farewell parties."[16]

Since the cover plan announced only that the force would move to Northern Ireland for joint exercises with American forces, No. 7 Section was not told of its real destination until it was actually at sea. No. 11 Section heard rumours of a move on October 2nd, was advised on the 13th to prepare for a permanent move, and received its orders on the 28th. No. 12 Section, covering the Farnborough area through which the force would pass, reported that no untoward interest was being displayed and that no rumours were circulating. When No. 14 arrived at 2 Canadian Base Reinforcement Depot, it found security so good that it was not even expected. No. 15 Section (II Corps), on the other hand, found evidence of a great deal of loose talk, some of which was terribly accurate. An R.C.A.S.C. private from I Corps said they were going to Sicily. A Polish soldier from Fifth Armoured Division told his girlfriend that they were going overseas and that she was seeing him for the last time. A member of Fifth Division R.C.A.S.C. told his girl that his unit was "ready . . . to move overseas next week". Another man from the same unit said that "all vehicles are ready to move in convoy to a training area and then overseas". Others stated that "their unit was going on a ten-day scheme to Wales and then overseas". Some men "had been issued with tropical kit . . . Thompson submachine guns . . . going to Italy". I Canadian Corps Signals was "going overseas". On October 18th, L/Cpl. Boyd, 7 Section, saw Ordnance unloading mosquito netting, fly swatters, and insect sprayers, at H.Q. Fifth Armoured Division, in a public thoroughfare in Brighton! Capt. Chown reported: "It is firmly believed that information is very injudiciously [*sic*] and unwittingly given to civilians by military personnel having knowledge of, or forecasting future operations."[17] A number of soldiers had to be punished. O.C. 5 Div. Transport Company sent two of his men to court-martial, as did the C.O. of R.C.C.S., I Corps, and I Canadian Provost Corps. Obviously, Security still had a great deal of educating to do before it could feel satisfied.

During the first five months of 1944, No. 3 Section, then at Otterbourne neat Winchester, had the most active role. Third Division was the lead Canadian division for the Invasion, and a great deal of special preparation had to be done. The most experienced F.S.O., Capt. Rafe Douthwaite, was assigned to its No. 3 Section; Capt. Drury took over No. 16. About the end of January, a series of brigade-level exercises began, culminating in May in FABIUS, a consecutively numbered, six-part exercise which was the Invasion rehearsal.

On February 12, 1944, Exercise SAVVY, a seaborne artillery experiment, was watched by H.M. The King, Gen. Montgomery, and other distinguished observers. Security for it was extra strict. March was relatively less busy for the Sections, probably because people were becoming more familiar with the problems they were trying to solve, and with the personalities engaged in them. Not that breaches did not occur. Exercise FRANK took place on March 10th, and drew a harsh criticism, by unnamed officers, of Security interference. The G.O.C. supported his F.S.O., and no more was heard of the incident. But, according to 2nd Armoured Brigade, a "bad breach by C.M.H.Q." did occur. No. 3 Section checked and found "it wasn't bad, it was criminal and someone should be issued with a nice new bowler hat. Reported matter to G.O.C. who is sending up a blistering letter and also reported it to I British Corps." Like many other security breaches, this one left no detailed record in the files, and is not now recalled by the Section members. The Section had probably over-reacted, perhaps through excessive fatigue.

The last few months before the Invasion began brought much stricter security precautions, imposed and controlled by M.I.5, and greater emphasis on training within the Sections. Much of this training took place on the job, and attempted to counter concern that the men were spending so much time on day-to-day routine tasks that their military skills would deteriorate. It included exercises in German, French, map-reading, weapons, and fieldcraft. Some of the instruction could be provided from the Sections' own resources. No. 3, for instance, had claimed, albeit in 1943, that it had 12 linguists competent in German, French, Russian, Italian, Hungarian, Dutch, Norwegian and Czech, in its 15-man establishment. Visiting instructors gave the Sections specialist, detailed training on such subjects as: French and German police forces, political party structures and political environments, legal, fiscal and public welfare systems; German organizations in France; anti-Semitism in France (useful in checking the reliability of a source); French youth movements; German documentation, including map symbols, for which courses were offered at the London District Interrogation Centre; German Intelligence organization, methods, uniforms, signs, etc; and police methods, usually by attachment to civilian police forces. They were also given lectures on subjects that the I(b) planners thought would help them to handle the special problems they would encounter during the actual Invasion, and in operations in and near the battlefield. The Section C.S.M. and clerk concentrated on last-minute administrative items that had to be settled before the unit moved out. Top priority was given to such vital tasks as waterproofing vehicles, and ensuring that equipment and weapons were in first-class order and boots and clothing in good repair.

As far as the Sections were concerned, the final build-up to the Invasion started in March 1944, when the War Office closed off the south and southeast coastal regions. The whole east coast had already been declared a Security area. First Army sent No. 17 Section to Third Division to conduct an independent survey of the state of its security arrangements. In April, all Sections were given their Unit Censorship Stamps, with instructions for their use and protection. In May, in addition to their own last-minute preparations, they reinforced the security clamp that had been established. No. 15 Section, in Counter-Int. Report No. 1, sent to H.Q. II Canadian Corps, stated that "careless talk and rumour appear to be negligible [sic], guards were alert and all ranks were reporting suspicious incidents to their Unit Security Officers." The months of training were bringing their rewards.

There was a little relatively harmless curiosity and speculation on the part of civilians who were seeing Canadians deployed in Kent for the first time. No. 2 Section, then in Dover, toured eastern Kent, checking bus stops and railway stations for people who were visiting the area without valid reasons. The F.S.O. 15 Section considered that the closing of the area would keep the "curious friends and camp followers out as well as keeping the troops mentally at ease". It may have done the former; it might even have done the latter; but it certainly reduced the risk of leakages through incautious conversations, rumours, and speculation.

Nos. 16 and 17 did routine Section tasks for FLIT, an exercise to practice First Canadian Army and H.Q. 84 Group – the Air element responsible for providing close support to the Canadians – in operating together in the field. They were issued "Canadian huts", to provide more permanent and suitable billets. Their erection required rather more men than the Sections could supply and they consequently were not used. Lieut. R.N. (Paddy) Bligh took eight men of No. 18 Section to Glasgow on Port Security duties. For all the other Sections it was merely, "Business as usual".

Just before D-Day, however, General Crerar received a report of a serious security breach in Third Division, then in marshalling areas in southern England.

He sent his G.S.O.2 I(b), Maj. Bud Macdougall, to interview Maj.-Gen. Keller, the Divisional Commander. Gen. Keller told Bud that a tank brigade commander, Brig. Wyman, was reported to have made statements in public which might be prejudicial to the security of the starting date of OVERLORD. Bud's investigation revealed that Brig. Wyman and some other officers, on the way home from a local pub, had been showing off their horsemanship on some cows, and talking loudly of what they would do to the Germans, with enough comment that a listener might be able to guess the date and place of the Invasion. What was not clear was whether anyone had actually heard them. After several days of investigation, the Army Commander finally considered that probably no real leakage had occurred. Disciplinary action was taken against the officers involved.

About the same time, men from the Sections were deployed to H.Q. Airborne Troops as follows: No. 2 – Cpl. Osipoff, L/Cpl. Croll; No. 4 – L/Cpl. Baraniecki; No. 15 – Sgt. Bendell, L/Cpl. Lake; No. 16 – Cpls. Bake and Weissman; No. 17 – Cpl. MacPherson, L/Cpl. Singer. Their task was "to throw a Counter-Intelligence ring around the spearhead of the Invasion forces (Airborne and Paratroops) prior to their take-off." Though exciting, their actual duties were uneventful, and they returned to their units on June 8th. D-Day came and went and, as one of the Sections put it, "here we remain dead static". The entry into France did not go as quickly as the planners had hoped, and the follow-up forces had to be kept waiting. Some units were warned for moves, some actually moved to the marshalling areas, but, except for No. 3 Section and No. 4 F.S.R.D., no move to France took place for F.S. until after the beginning of July.

By July 1st, 1944, the Sections were deployed as follows:[18]

Nos. 1, 7, 11, 14, and Nos. 8 and 11 F.S.R.D. – in Italy.
No. 3 and No. 4 F.S.R.D. – in France.
No. 2 – in Dover; it loaded on July 4th.
No. 4 – at Forest Row, Sussex; embarked July 22nd.
No. 15 – Folkestone; embarked July 2nd.
No. 16 – near Boxhill, Surrey; turned over spare vehicles and billets to No. 17; embarked July 23rd.
No. 17, Nos. 1, 2, 3, 5, 6 F.S.R.D. – Boxhill; embarked July 30th.
No. 18 – H.Q. No. 12 Lines of Communication Area, Farnborough; embarked July 10th.
No. 12 and No. 7 F.S.R.D. – Farnborough, Reinforcement Units area.
No. 13 – London.
No. 20 – Newark-on-Trent.
Nos. 9 and 10. F.S.R.D. – Farnborough; embarked for Italy July 16th.

In the last few weeks before they, too, went to Normandy, the Sections were not overly busy. They did, however, share with the civilian population of the southern counties the unpleasant experience of the "flying bombs" (V-1).

On June 15th, No. 15 Section reported that one was shot down about 750 yards from their billets. On July 16th, No. 16 Section reported a near miss (200 yards) on C.S.M. Skippon's quarters. It complained, but only mildly, that Boxhill seemed to be exactly in the direct flight path of the bombs, four or five of which could quite commonly be seen – and heard – overhead en route to London. No. 18 Section caught an imposter masquerading as a Security N.C.O. and turned him over to the British Security Control Organization. No. 18 had a little difficulty getting its area of responsibility precisely defined. H.Q. 21 Army Group thought it should confine itself to Canadian units only and not cover, as in effect it did, the Lines of Communication and all the units in that area. Eventually it handed over to No. 7 F.S.R.D., which then came under command of No. 2 Canadian Base Reinforcement Group. Maj. J.W.G. Macdougall, who had managed to get over to Normandy and back, visited the units to tell them what was being done and what they could expect in France. The men's morale, which was already quite satisfactory, improved noticeably after he had spoken, simply because they now had a better understanding of what they could expect. Shortly after the Invasion got under way, restrictions were lifted, men were given short leaves, wives and girlfriends were allowed to visit, and units held social evenings where "Contributions from parcels from home helped ease the entertainment situation."

Nos. 12 and 13 Sections remained in Britain until 1946; No. 20 went to Holland in January 1945. As the campaign in Europe developed, and as Germany became increasingly less able to exploit any breaches of security, the work of the Sections became more and more a matter of security education. Their task was still twofold. They had to forestall the possibility of breaches occurring in the operational areas to which many of the men would be going. And they continued to investigate reports of poor morale and security offences in the troops remaining in Britain. Capt. King McShane's No. 20 Section's report for November gives examples of the ordinary soldier's reactions to events and their effect on his morale. The troops had strong feelings on the conscription issue which was then at its height. They believed that Home Defence personnel "should be sent overseas immediately. Col. Ralston's stand has been applauded by the troops while the actions of Gen. McNaughton has [sic] tended to lower his prestige with the overseas soldiers". Capt. McShane also reported "considerable confusion as regards to the special 30-days leave to Canada". Some wives apparently had heard that leave could be applied for after a man had spent two years overseas. The men were angry because of the small number who were actually permitted to return. The motives behind the scheme were good; its administration was poor.

No. 12 Section took over No. 20's duties and, with No. 13, covered troop movements through London, checked the reliability of employees in canteens and hostels where Canadians gathered, and dealt with the perennial problems of receipt and recovery of classified correspondence discovered in briefcases and parcels that careless personnel, generally officers, left behind as they passed through. Both Sections were involved in interviewing Canadian prisoners of war who had missed the screening network on the Continent. Their last few months of service were increasingly routine, reflecting the run-down of the Canadian Army overseas machine.

Security in Britain in the build-up period before the Invasion went through a succession of phases. In the early days, there were many spy scares, with the usual accompaniments of mysterious strangers, flashing lights, and suspicious movements. It was also recognized that Canadian troops could be the authors of their own misfortune by carelessly revealing secrets that they should protect. Merely to acknowledge this had little practical usefulness; protection had to be provided, and unit Security Officers were given the training responsibility for this. The experienced F.S. staff knew how to identify the risks and pinpoint the remedies. Occasionally they were able to persuade senior officers to listen and to authorize proposals for remedial action. Some units were co-operative; but higher authority had to be asked to use its influence against others who were less so. There was some resentment against "snoopers", who were engaged in the campaign against careless talk. But these investigators detected many examples of laxity which a few court-martials greatly helped to curb. The big breakthrough for Security came with Dieppe. There is no evidence to prove that the Germans were warned of the operation sufficiently in advance for the Dieppe garrison to be ready for the landing. One source states that a German agent did report the Canadian concentration, but his report was ignored.[19] Nevertheless, the troops, particularly those in Second Division, believed strongly that the prevalence of loose talk had played a significant part in the failure. After that, security became much more vital to them. The lessons they had learned did not, however, seem nearly so compelling to the new waves of reinforcements that flowed into Britain just before the Invasion, and the tempo of security training had to be increased. Fortunately, the climate of opinion was now more receptive to the importance of security instruction. Intensive training continued, and the newcomers soon conformed. For as the need for security declined in Britain, it grew in importance in the operational theatres where they were going.

The Sections and Reserve Detachments that made up the F.S. component were small, close-knit, independent units whose character usually reflected that of the officer who commanded them. They had their casualties: Sgt. H.L. Hornberger (No. 1), Sgt. R.O.H. Fuller (No. 11), and Pte. J.W. Place (No. 2) were killed in motorcycle accidents; C.S.M. J.S. Milne, Sgt. W. Corson, and Sgt. J. Holt were killed at Dieppe; J.H. Bishop was wounded and captured; L. Chauvin, L.K. Pals, and R.F. Hedges were captured. Others were to be lost before the war was over. The Sections were plagued with equipment difficulties. The Harley-Davidson motorcycle was not well suited; it was heavy and tended to burn out its clutch at low speeds. The Norton was ideal, but the Coventry factory had been bombed and spares were not available. The Security units also had their moments of triumph; words of praise from C.O.s whose security problems they had resolved; successful exercise "infiltrations"; clandestine operations and activities that revealed weaknesses in the Security system which could then be remedied. Their reward will be only this: the knowledge that they did a difficult job well, with companions who knew what that meant, and superiors who were able and ready to provide wise advice and guidance.

7.
DIEPPE

Raids on Occupied Europe were part of the agreed Allied strategy. Combined Operations Headquarters (C.O.H.Q.), which was responsible for selecting the targets and for drawing up the operational plans, conceived the idea of an attack on Dieppe in April 1942. The operation was intended to examine the problems involved in capturing a major port, to test new techniques and materiel in an actual assault, and to study methods of controlling an invasion fleet. An outline plan was approved on April 25th. On April 30th, Gen. Montgomery asked Lt.-Gen. McNaughton for Second Canadian Infantry Division. The operation was code-named RUTTER, and the Security cover for it was to be a combined operations training exercise involving Second, First, and Third Canadian Infantry Divisions successively.

About May 13th, the proposal was approved by the Chiefs of Staff Committee as a basis for detailed planning. Second Division moved to the Isle of Wight on May 18th–20th. Exercises were conducted, and the detailed plan was issued on June 20th. On June 27th, Maj.-Gen. Roberts, G.O.C. Second Division, explained it to his officers. The troops embarked on July 2nd–3rd and were told of their mission only after they had been sealed in their ships. The operation was cancelled on the 8th because of bad weather; the troops returned to their camps.

Between July 10th and 14th, the operation was revived by C.O.H.Q. in its original form. Some changes in detail were made, in part for security reasons, and the final Combined Plan was issued on July 31st. The exercises and demonstrations were continued as Security cover.

The Outline Plan which was approved on April 25th read as follows:[1]

1. Intelligence reports indicate that DIEPPE is not heavily defended and that the beaches in the vicinity are suitable for landing infantry, and A.F.V.s, [Armoured Fighting Vehicles] at some. It is also reported that there are 40 invasion barges in the harbour.

2. It is therefore proposed to carry out a raid with the following objectives:
    a. destroying enemy defences in the vicinity of DIEPPE,
    b. destroying the aerodrome installations at ST. AUBIN,
    c. destroying R.D.F. [Radio Direction Finding = Radar] stations, power stations, dock and rail facilities and petrol dumps in the vicinity,
    d. removing invasion barges for our own use,
    e. removal of secret documents from the Divisional Headquarters at ARQUES,
    f. to capture prisoners.

5. Dieppe

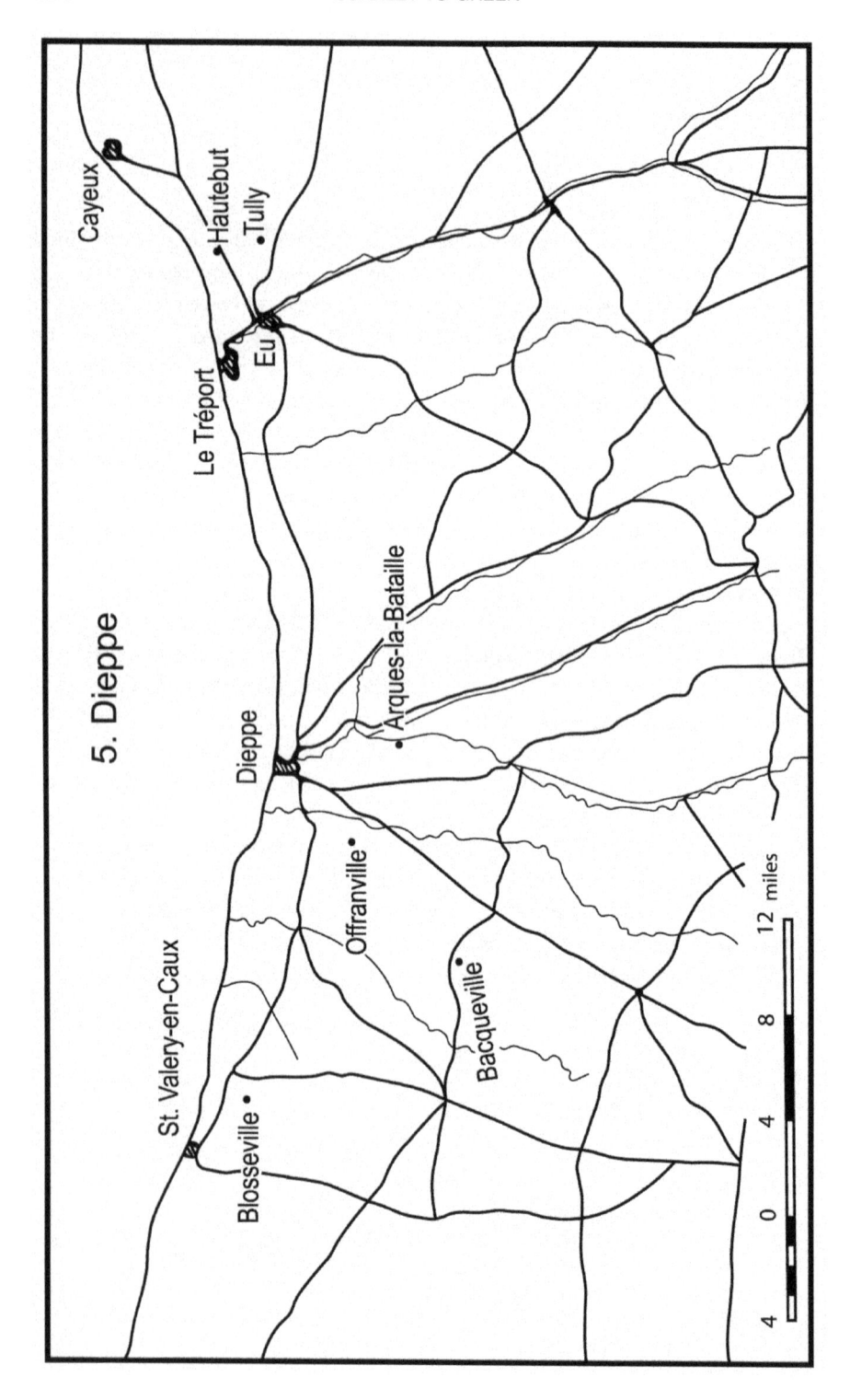

The planners were told that information available to C.O.H.Q. indicated that the exits from the beaches at Pourville were not favourable for tank operations. The information was forwarded to Second Division and was repeated later in an Appreciation signed by its G.S.O.1, Lt.-Col. C.C. Mann.

The "sources of information" available to C.O.H.Q. represented the full range of all that were available to the Allies. The most important single one was Air Photo. Its coverage of the target was complete, frequent, and current. Unfortunately, most of the photographs were "verticals", which cannot clearly show any object hidden by the roofs of buildings, or in holes in cliffs. The Allied Photographic Intelligence Centre at Danesfield Hall, Medmenham, Buckinghamshire – the agency responsible for interpreting air photos covering enemy activity – provided excellent service. To help its research, the Centre included information from tourist photographs collected through a national appeal. And it constructed a 10-foot x 6-foot scale relief model of Dieppe and its surrounding areas, in which it included as much detail as possible from the photographs.

Before Second Division arrived in the Isle of Wight, the place and purpose of its training were kept secret. Security was continuously stressed but the strict measures imposed were evaded by men who sent letters and post cards as they passed through Portsmouth and who made telephone calls from the island after arrival. Security can be forgiven for its sour comments about "wives and other female encumbrances" who joined their men on the island. Security responsibility was shared and well-co-ordinated between the Naval staff on H.M.S. *Tormentor II*, the Permanent Security Staff on the Isle of Wight, and the Divisional staffs. Force Headquarters had been split into two parts, one for training and the other for RUTTER. Field Security personnel were permanently on duty with the RUTTER section. One Divisional study group selected for its beachhead the exact area where the landing was planned to take place; the breach was not thought to be serious. But Security did observe that anyone could easily infer that a Canadian force was involved from the code names chosen.[2] The detailed plan issued by C.O.H.Q. on June 20th had a section on Intelligence,[3] with enemy information corrected up to June 19th, and a trace, based on information from the Central Intelligence Unit at Medmenham, corrected to June 14th.

The area was known to be held by *302 Infantry Division*, with its H.Q. at Arques-la-Bataille. One regiment, with its H.Q. at Dieppe, had three battalions at Blosseville, Bacqueville, and Offranville. *13 and 14 Gun Companies* were also in the Dieppe area. A second regiment was located at Eu; the third was at Cayeux, with its three battalions at Tully, Hautebut, and St. Valery-sur-Somme. The Engineer battalion was also in the Dieppe area. The document then detailed the known defences:

DEFENCES

(a.) *The Town* . . . held by one infantry battalion. Three 4-gun troops are sited right, left and centre, behind the town. Possibly they are three troops making up a battery of field gun/howitzers.

(b.) *Flak*
- (i.) A mixed flak battery defends the ports. The three heavy troops are arranged round the harbour, right, left and centre; one at least is sited for firing at sea targets.
- (ii.) The eight light sections are arranged as required, some being for aerodrome defence.

(c.) *Flank Defences*
- (i.) There is no infantry on either side of the town. There is one troop of coastal artillery to the East, and one to the West, each being some three miles away from the town defences.
- (ii.) The troop at Varengeville, being of six guns, is probably a troop of coastal artillery equipped with 15.5 cm (6") French guns.
- (iii.) Each troop has two light flak guns for local defence and two light machine guns sited to guard the nearest beach exits.

(d.) *Machine Guns*
- (i.) The layout of machine guns indicates the probable dispositions of the infantry. It is probable that one reinforced rifle company holds the town east of the river Arques, another the town west of the river Arques and another the area round the mouth of the river Scie.
- (ii.) This distributes the observed pillboxes in the proportion of 12:18:11, total 31 [sic]; there are in all 48 machine guns in the battalion.

(e.) *Strong Points*
- (i.) The most interesting feature of the defence is the development of strong points inland and the rudimentary all around defence of the port itself.
- (ii.) The West Company has constructed strong points up to two miles inland to cover the valley of the Scie.
- (iii.) The Central Company may be responsible for the central inland position, probably Battalion H.Q. and reserves are here. . . .
- (iv.) The East Company has made a strong point at Neuville.
- (v.) All three positions could be used to fire inwards in case of infiltration from the harbour.

STRENGTH OF RESISTANCE

Up to 3 hours: One battalion in Dieppe area, supported by some 500 divisional and regimental troops. Personnel of Anti-Aircraft and Coastal Defence Batteries. Total: 1500 (Approximately)

RATE OF REINFORCEMENT

(a.) *Within 3–8 hours.*
One battalion from the south; one battalion from the west; two companies from along the coast; Divisional troops from direction Arques = 2,500

(b.) *After 8 hours.*

Two battalions and regimental troops from Rouen; one battalion from direction Arques = 2,400

(c.) *After 15 hours.*
Armoured forces from direction Paris.
NOTE: The Plan envisages that re-embarkation will be completed in 12 hours.

EQUIPMENT
Troops in Dieppe area are not mobile. They will have the normal equipment of a German Infantry Division but may be slightly short of mortars and anti-tank equipment.

Despite its apparent wealth of information, the document is remarkable for its many omissions. First of all, the listing of the Division and its major infantry units is incomplete. Possibly the recipients were assumed to have enough knowledge of German organization to fill in the missing units themselves. Exact identifications of the German units were probably not available, but the order-of-battle given should have indicated the gaps in the knowledge of them. Secondly, no effort seems to have been made to estimate the areas of responsibility of the German units (they were not shown on the maps, either). This would, of course, have had to be based on supposition, but the known information on concentrations of observed activity should have been used as a basis for a tentative assessment of those areas. Thirdly, no attempt was made to locate in detail the infantry positions within the town of Dieppe; in fact, the summary did not attach an Intelligence map enlargement of the town at all. This would have helped locate, or at least suggest, the possible whereabouts of the machine guns of the battalion. Finally, Terrence Robertson, in his book *The Shame and the Glory*, justly criticizes Intelligence for having seriously underestimated the numbers of guns. A detailed assessment of their calibre could hardly be made from the aerial photographs. But the known characteristics of certain guns, together with a knowledge of the order-of-battle and the equipment in use, should have enabled C.O.H.Q. certainly, and Second Division possibly, to make a more detailed evaluation of the number of, and threat posed by, the weapons deployed.

The document also gave a detailed list of tasks to be performed by Intelligence.[4] This was to be amended only slightly in the actual operation; to save space, those changes are shown in the extract from the original text, within square brackets.

1. OBJECT
   a. To provide battle Intelligence.
   b. To secure Intelligence material, including P.W. . . .
   c. To deny information to the enemy. [deleted]

2. PERSONNEL
   In addition to 2 Canadian Division personnel, the following special personnel are available:
   a. 12 German speaking Other Ranks.
   b. 5 Officers and 3 Other Ranks provided by Special Operations Executive. [French Commando Group]
   c. 1 R.D.F. expert provided by R.A.F.
   d. 1 representative of Ministry of Economic Warfare.
   e. Four liaison officers.
   f. Detachment of the G.H.Q. Reconnaissance Regiment.

The plan provided for the transmission of information. The techniques to be used in handling P.W. were dealt with at length.

P.W.
(a.) *Disposal and Custody*
   (i.) A divisional Collecting Post will be established by the Divisional Intelligence Officer (Captain Insinger) [Capt. E.D. Magnus, 2 N.C.O.s. to aid] in the vicinity of White beach [manned by 3 Provost].
   (ii.) Units will send back P.W. under unit escort to Divisional Collecting Post, via Brigade; Walking wounded should be used as escorts.

(b.) *Interrogation*
   Interrogation will be confined to the following points:
   (i.) Information of immediate tactical value. For this purpose attached Interrogation Officers will accompany forward companies [Camerons, I.T. Burr; R. Regt., F. Morgan – GREEN, BLUE beaches].
   (ii.) Identifications, which will be reported immediately to H.M.S. *Fernie*.

(c.) *Embarkation*
   Captain Insinger will inform . . . numbers . . . and times.

DOCUMENTS
a. All documents will be labelled and packed in sandbags . . . sent to H.M.S. *Fernie* by Intelligence Officer's launch.
b. P.W. will be searched at P.W. Cage, their documents removed, labelled and despatched . . . .
c. If all P.W. cannot be searched, their hands will be bound to prevent destruction of their documents.
d. P.W. will be left in possession of all badges, marks of identification, decorations, etc., until they are searched at P.W. Collecting Post. [P.W. will be searched for arms, tagged to show unit making capture, time, and location]

ENEMY WEAPONS
   Enemy weapons are urgently required in large numbers for Intelligence and training purposes. Every effort will be made, by every soldier, to collect enemy weapons, which will be carried back to the Administrative Dump on the beach.

The tasks were allotted:

SEARCH OF H.Q.
Field Security personnel will be attached to the following units to assist in the searching of H.Q.
Camerons of Canada – 3; Royal Hamilton Light Infantry – 2; Essex Scottish – 2.

Five Field Security personnel under Officer Commanding 2 Canadian Field Security Section will be under command 4 Canadian Infantry Brigade to assist in cleaning up town.

GERMAN SPEAKING PERSONNEL
Twelve German speakers [Sudeten Germans] will accompany the Force. They will be allotted as follows:

Royal Regiment of Canada	– 2	} Interrogation of P.W. Fifth Column activity
Essex Scottish	– 2	
Royal Hamilton Light Infantry	– 2	Search of H.Q.
South Saskatchewan Regiment	– 2	} Assistance in use of enemy weapons
Camerons of Canada	– 2	
6 Canadian Infantry Brigade H.Q.	– 2	For duty at Divisional Collecting Post.

SPECIAL TASKS
a. [Nine man] S.O.E. party will occupy Town Hall and carry out a special mission. [Release Resistance men, remove documents]
b. M.E.W. representative will search the town for material required by M.E.W. [with Fusiliers Mont-Royal]
c. R.D.F. expert will search R.D.F. station after capture.

Gen. Roberts' briefing on the 27th did not mention the actual objective, and officers were warned that the other ranks were not to be told until they were on board ship. They embarked on the 2nd and 3rd and were then briefed. The cancellation of the raid on the 8th and the return of the Division to its home area in Sussex were accepted by many as indications that no further interest would be taken in RUTTER. Censorship, however, intercepted and deleted a number of references to the projected raid.

On July 11th, the RUTTER Force Commanders met at C.O.H.Q. to conduct a post-mortem and to plan for the next operation.[5] In answer to a question, Air Vice-Marshal Leigh Mallory, the Chief of Combined Operations, said that it was essential that demands for intelligence should be co-ordinated by C.O.H.Q. so that all Force Commanders would be given the same data. Operational intelligence on the movements of enemy forces should, however, be sent directly to the Force Commanders by their own Service Intelligence organizations. Rear Admiral H.T. Baillie Grohman, who believed that the intelligence provided by C.O.H.Q. had been inadequate, stated categorically that it was essential for a commander to have a permanent Intelligence Staff Officer. The meeting finally agreed that one or more Intelligence officers from C.O.H.Q. would be detailed to act as Liaison Officers with the Force Commanders and would be connected with the plan from its earliest stages.

Security felt that the troops should be embarked only at the last possible moment and should not be briefed without the approval of the Chief of Combined Operations. The cover plan should provide for the training to continue after the forces had been assembled. The H.Q. were not sufficiently secure. The identifying badges of the British Airborne Division and the Special Service Brigade should have been removed before the formations moved to the assembly area. Finally, a Security conference should have been held.

The Security problems of re-mounting an operation for which the cover could justifiably be regarded as "blown" were simply and logically "solved" by Capt. Hughes-Hallett of C.O.H.Q. Through the usual channels, G.H.Q. Home Forces issued a letter asking the Canadians to produce a detailed paper covering the experience gained in their recent training on the Isle of Wight so that existing Combined Operations pamphlets could be revised. This gave an excuse for concentrating planning staffs at C.O.H.Q. and Combined Forces H.Q., Portsmouth. It also gave an excuse to call in anyone with a specialized knowledge of the area or target installations. G.H.Q. Home Forces then asked 14th Canadian Army Tank Battalion (the Calgary Regiment) to prepare for and stage a demonstration of an opposed landing. The real purpose was to make sure that tanks were waterproofed, that Signals received their special equipment, and that all sets were on the correct frequency. The demonstration was to include the setting-up of signal communications with a co-operating infantry force, although no infantry were actually to be used. By including the problem of evacuating casualties from a tank unit, the specially prepared stretcher-bearing vehicles were also able to concentrate. C.O.H.Q. asked Second Division to return all equipment and engineer stores used in the exercise. A special dump was established where they could be collected and easily reloaded on to landing craft. The infantry were to continue training with full equipment and to make a number of moves by road. This would be the cover for the final move to the ports.

At a conference held on July 16th, Force Commanders were told that models, mosaics, and other special intelligence would be collected, that the Senior I.O. at C.O.H.Q. was to supply the necessary photographs, and that these would be made up into convenient packages and sent on board the various assault ships before the troops were loaded. A few changes were made in the composition of the special parties. The parent organizations were to be warned the day before the operation and the specialists were to be confined on board their ships. Lt.-Col. Henderson (First Army) was given charge of press control. The 25 correspondents (11 British and foreign, 9 Canadian, and 5 special reporters from the Navy) were assigned to a number of ships. Their presence and their duties raised fresh problems of transportation, security, equipment, and arrangements for obtaining information and getting it to their agencies.

The brigadiers were briefed on August 1st. The battalion commanders were given a broad outline on the 4th. The Detailed Plan for Operation JUBILEE (the new name for RUTTER) was issued, in part, on the 8th, and completed in the next few days by the addition of its appendices. The battalion commanders were given their detailed briefing on August 10th, the company commanders on the 14th, the F.S. (still called "police" in First Army's report) on the 15th, and the troops on the 18th, on board ship or immediately prior to their embarkation.

The Intelligence Plan was very similar to the RUTTER plan.[6] Seven men of No. 10 Inter-Allied Commando were to select up to 12 French nationals for evacuation, establish liaison with the population, and distribute propaganda leaflets and posters. The Ministry of Economic Warfare specialist was to work on his own. The Special Intelligence Officer also had a mission of his own, and was to be assisted by four men from 8 Canadian Reconnaissance Regiment (14 Hussars). The R.D.F. expert, Flt/Sgt. J. Nissenthall, R.A.F., accompanied by Sgt. R. Hawkins of No. 11 Field Security Section and an S.O.E. man, Callaghan, was to land on GREEN beach (Pourville–Caude–Coté) with the South Saskatchewan Regiment. The three men had two objectives: La Maison Blanche, and the R.D.F. station at Caude-Coté. The exact location of La Maison Blanche in Pourville was not known; it was believed to be a white house [*sic*] used as an officers' mess; it was to be searched for papers. The R.D.F. station was to be entered and searched for details and parts of the apparatus. The Flt/Sgt. was to be carefully protected by the other two men, and Sgt. Hawkins was to kill either or both if there was any risk of them falling into enemy hands. They were to withdraw to the P.W. Cage through 6 Brigade H.Q.

The (British) Special Intelligence Officers' party was split into two detachments. The first (one S.I.O. and one F.S. N.C.O.) was to move with the Camerons to St. Aubin aerodrome to search for papers, pamphlets, code books, signal papers, and equipment. The men would then move to Arques-la-Bataille to search the *110th Division's* H.Q. for secret files, order-of-battle, and information code books. The H.Q. was possibly in the Chateau and /or an L-shaped building nearby, but a terse note pointed out: "Div H.Q. may have moved." They also were to withdraw through 6 Brigade.

The second detachment (one S.I.O. and one F.S. N.C.O.) was to move with the Royal Regiment of Canada, also to search for papers. It had five targets listed in order of priority: 1) a barracks at Les Glycines Holiday Camp at Puits (Puys), precise location unknown (infantry were to attack the camp); 2) Coast Guard houses on the cliff tops between Puits and Dieppe manned by German marines; 3) Engineer Battalion H.Q. in the Boys' School at Neuville-les-Dieppe;

4) Kommandantur H.Q. in the Hotel les Vieux Puits on the Dieppe road, "likely to be an Administrative H.Q. Important papers are likely to be found here"; 5) the prison on the Quai de la Somme, next to the Pollet church, to look for prison records and to capture military P.W. Withdrawal was to be via 4 Brigade to the P.W. Cage.

The remainder of the reinforced Field Security Section was divided into five parties, each of two F.S. N.C.O.s and one S.O.E. man. Each separate search was timed for one half hour, including travel time. The routes, timings, and destinations were given in detail.

No. 1: [with each of its three men on a different ship!] 1) The Wireless station, to pick up its schedule (Funkplan), 3 letter codes, instruction pamphlets; 2) To search three hotels suspected of being sub-H.Q. or billets: Grand, Bellevue and Etrangers, all on Boulevard de Verdun; 3) Gare Maritime, on Quai Henri Quatre, for military passes, R.T.O. papers, movement control tables; 4) Return to P.W. Cage through 4 Brigade H.Q. A second task began at Zero plus 4 hr 30: to search 1) the Port Office for naval and military papers; 2) The Post Office for Field Post numbers, military address lists, correspondence, rubber stamps, pads, etc. Withdrawal as before.

No. 2: [also attached to 6 Brigade, but at least in the same ship] 1) To search six hotels: Metropole, Rhin, Aguado and Regina, all on Boulevard de Verdun, and Grand Cerf and Rocher de Cancale, on rue de la Moriniere [Morxiniere]; 2) At Zero plus 6 hours, barracks in rue Gambetta and German H.Q.

No. 3: [attached to 4 Brigade] 1) To search Hotel Moderne, on rue Vauquelin and Hotel des Arcades, Quai Duquesne, supposed H.Q. and billets; 2) Custom House, Quai Duquesne. At Zero plus 3 hours 30 minutes; 3) Gare Principale, Quai Clemenceau, for passes and R.T.O. material; 4) Hotel Terminus; 5) Hospital, rue des Hospices, for military papers.

No. 4: [attached to 6 Brigade, working closely with the R.H.L.I. and Sgt. Hickson's party of R.C.E.] 1) Post Office and Telephone Exchange, rue Victor-Hugo for Field Post Number lists, address lists, rubber stamps and pads, list of phone numbers. At Zero plus 2 hrs 30, Sgt. Hickson's party would blow up the Post Office; 2) Hotel Normandie, rue Claude Groulard, possible billets; 3) Palais de Justice, Justice de Paix, Sous-Prefecture, for identifications and police records.

No. 5: [attached to 4 Brigade] 1) Starting at Zero plus 2 hrs, to search Artillery Regimental H.Q., believed to be in Hotel Select, Place de la Barre, for technical information, maps, charts, text-books; 2) Other Artillery Regimental H.Q., 21 rue de la Barre. The order stated that these were important targets that must be found and searched; 3) To search houses in rue Doublet and near avenue Boucher de Perthes.

C.O.H.Q. issued the "Enemy" Annex on August 10th.[7] It identified *110th Infantry Division*, which was alleged to have relieved the *302nd*. Its three infantry regiments, the *252nd, 254th*, and *255th*, were said to be deployed along the coast from St. Valery-en-Caux to St. Valery-sur-Somme. The *332nd Division* held the area west from St. Valery-en-Caux to the estuary of the Seine; the *321st Division* held the area to the east from Boulogne to the Somme. The *10th Panzer Division* in Amiens and Albert (just east of Amiens) was available to support Dieppe; tanks were reported at Abbeville, 36 miles from Dieppe. Dieppe itself was garrisoned by one battalion of infantry and ancillary troops. A number of buildings facing the sea, notably the hotels, were occupied. Another battalion was eight to 10 miles west of Dieppe with its headquarters at Blosseville. The third battalion was unlocated, but it was considered to be in reserve with its headquarters at Bacqueville. Its regimental identification was not known. The regiment east of Dieppe was believed to have one battalion in the Le Tréport–Eu area. The other two were unlocated, but one was believed to be near Dieppe on the east side of the Arques.

The line of the coast was held by a system of "posts", each with about 30 men and four machine guns, probably sited fairly close together to keep the whole beach under fire. Machine gun casemates had been built along the coast, especially at the beaches. Not all were continuously occupied; some were "known" to be dummies. In Dieppe itself, machine gun posts were located at many of the street junctions, sited to enfilade the main roads and to cover open places. Six positions were particularly important: one at a road junction; a casemate on the Boulevard Maréchal Foch; one on the barracks roof in the rue Gambetta, about a mile from the shore; a pillbox covering the southern approach to the town; a casemate on the north edge facing east and north; and, finally: "It has not been possible to deny or confirm the existence of machine gun posts in the low cliffs to the east of the entrance to the harbour."

Heavy anti-aircraft guns were located on the cliffs about one half mile east and west of Dieppe, with a third battery southwest of the town. There were light, mobile anti-aircraft guns near the radar station at Caude-Coté for use on an "as required" basis. Nine known battery positions were identified: two under construction; four unoccupied; a six-gun battery southwest of Varengeville; a four-gun battery on the southwest outskirts of Dieppe; and a second four-gun battery south of Puits. The divisional artillery, which consisted normally of 48 guns and 12 anti-tank guns, was not usually permanently sited. The guns at Varengeville were probably wheeled, the battery southwest of Dieppe was probably field artillery. All of them could probably be brought into action at short notice at strategic points.[8] The likely locations of the other 34 guns and of the anti-tank guns were not identified.

The document repeated its earlier assessment of the likelihood that defence was all-round, with strong points inland. Troops were warned that the wire on the beach might be electrified; nothing definite was known about the Dieppe wire, but the wire at Boulogne was certainly electrified. Some detail about obstacles was given. All roads off the RED and WHITE beaches were blocked by masonry or concrete blocks 3–4 feet thick and 5–6 feet high. The roadblock on the Quai du Hable was 5–6 feet thick and had a 9-foot gap that could be closed. The one in the rue Syngogne had a 5-foot gap. The roadblocks in Puits were probably wire. There was no evidence that the Germans had planted mines either on the beaches or inland.

The strength estimate showed: west of the river, one battalion in Dieppe, supported by some 500 divisional or regimental troops; east of the river, a company with artillery and engineer troops, perhaps 1,700 in all. *10th Panzer Division*, if still in Abbeville, could be in Dieppe within 3 hours. By Zero plus 5 hours, an additional three companies of infantry, plus divisional troops, a total of about 850, and a *Mechanized Reconnaissance Unit* of 12 heavy and 36 light armoured cars and 130 motorcyclists could be in Dieppe. The caves in the cliffs overlooking the east side of the harbour were reportedly being used as storage for 2,300 torpedoes. The harbour had four trawlers, each armed with two 4-inch guns, and 10 E-boats capable of mounting the torpedoes. A note at the end of the paper stated: "This information is changing all the time, therefore cannot be considered as firm." The only map given merely showed the general order-of-battle, but not dispositions. Just before the force sailed, detailed oblique photographs of the harbour and the east cliff arrived. These showed gun positions at the edge of the cliffs – in Col. Wright's recollection "the most menacing defences which had appeared, and by that time it was too late".

H.M.S. *Calpe* was the H.Q. ship for the force. In her Operations Room, Lt.-Col. G.P. Henderson manned the "A" wave set, while Maj. P.E.R. Wright operated the Motorola inter-ship set and kept the Intelligence Log. Maj. R.C. Unwin, G.S.O.2 (Int), First Army was in H.M.S. *Fernie*. Shortly after the landing, the Germans attempted to confuse by broadcasting in English on Canadian frequencies. But the very English accent used was readily identified as bogus.

The story of the landings has been told elsewhere. Casualties were heavy as the landing craft reached the shore. Some units were unable to land at all, others landed and were unable to advance. Capt. Insinger was killed when his L.C.T. was blown up, and Capt. Morgan was killed shortly after he came ashore. The only advance inland was made by the South Saskatchewan Regiment and the Camerons of Canada in the western sector. The South Saskatchewans reached the radar station, but could not enter because of the heavy defensive fire. The Camerons were not able to reach their objectives, but the F.S. detachment collected documents from buildings as they passed through the outskirts of Pourville. Sgt. W. Corson, the N.C.O. in charge, was killed on the way back. In the operation as a whole, three F.S. men were killed (C.S.M. Milne, and

Sgts. Holt and Corson) and five captured, one of whom (Sgt. Jack Bishop) was wounded. Intelligence casualties totalled ten; three officers and seven other ranks returned. Thirty-seven prisoners were brought back, eight of them taken by the Army. S.O.E. brought back some individuals of interest to them.

Following the Raid, a post-mortem was held by the Intelligence Branch using information derived from prisoners and other sources. H.Q. First Canadian Army issued a summary of the findings on September 22nd. The presence of *110th Division* could not be confirmed, and presumably *302nd* had never been withdrawn. The latter's order-of-battle was listed, and the sub-units located. The defences had been found to be sited in an anti-raid, not an anti-invasion, role, with firepower concentrated to cover landing beaches. A sketch of enemy weapon locations on the main beaches showed "how completely the beach is covered by enfilade fire from the west headland". The details of defences on the east headland were not known, but the enemy was clearly able to cover not only the sea approaches to the harbour and the main beaches but also the greater part of the main beach, in enfilade. Light machine guns on the promenade were sited to fire out to sea only, not to sweep the beaches. The infantry sections were instructed to fire only at landing craft, the supporting arms were to defend the town. "It is of particular interest that on both east and west headlands some weapons were sited in artificial caves. On the east headland, it is reported that some of these weapons came out to fire and were then pulled back into the caves. Fire from positions such as these is extremely difficult to locate and it must be realized that their existence could not have been established prior to the operations by air photographs."

The Official Historian has stated that: "Our own Intelligence ... was on the whole excellent."[9] The gaps in photo coverage do not entirely support this. And its British Commander, Earl Mountbatten, said in September 1973 that C.O.H.Q. greatly underestimated the concentration of troops around the port itself. This possibly could have been rectified if the known positions had received a more careful assessment in the light of known German tactical doctrine. And this would also have enabled a more realistic appreciation to be made of the defences of the beaches themselves, in terms of the numbers of automatic weapons deployed. Granted, German concealment techniques made it difficult to locate anti-tank and machine gun positions. But the mis-identification of *110th Division* for the *302nd* was of academic interest when it came to actual contact with the defences on the beaches. It might perhaps have made a difference in the total casualties, particularly as the *110th* was regarded as a "high calibre formation". Failure to pick up the move of its Divisional Headquarters, though also a lapse, had no effect on the results.

Each Brigade H.Q. was allowed to take ashore two copies of the complete Operation Order, one in each H.Q. craft. This was so that, if either of the Headquarters ships became a casualty, the other Brigadier would become the

Military Force Commander; he would then have the fullest information. One copy of this Order was captured on the beach. In some units, other ranks were allowed to carry their paybooks ashore with them. Unlike the British book, the Canadian paybook contained all the details of the man's unit, training, and record of service. Officers' personal papers and identity cards were supposed to have been collected by the senior military officer in each ship and handed to the captain of the vessel. This had not been done. Identity cards and private letters were found in discarded battle-dress jackets. The German interrogators must have been delighted at the laxity that made nonsense of all the "name, rank, and number" training the troops had been given.

In its report on the Raid, H.Q. First Army identified a number of breaches of security that had arisen from careless talk. They were, however, hard to investigate, for Commanding Officers either were reluctant to assist or else were willing to shield persons implicated in or suspected of such lapses. The general attitude was simply: "The operation is now over, why rake up the past."

Censorship examined 8,455 letters written by participants and by non-participants in the Raid. Many of the latter had thought it was just another training exercise and their first intimation that it was "for real" came with the radio reports. The principal conclusions drawn were that security had been inadequate, and that the troops believed they had been expected.[10] The Censor was convinced that the enemy had made special plans and had brought in extra reinforcements. The official statement quoted a variety of comments that supported this view and even suggested that a Fifth Column in England was busy funnelling information back to the Continent.

The morale of the troops remained high. They felt a pride in their achievement as well as regret at the loss of friends. They were now taking a more realistic view of the nature of the war that the Canadian Army was being trained to fight. They now knew that what they had been taught was indeed valuable, and that the leadership given by their officers was of high quality.

First Canadian Army Intelligence now prepared a number of recommendations: the Prisoner of War Interrogation Service (British) should be forbidden to interfere in Canadian interrogations; captured documents should be sent to the Cages; souvenir-hunters should be educated; Operation Orders either should not be taken on board assault ships or should be destroyed en route; orders should be issued piecemeal so that no complete order would be in one person's hands; there should be more instruction in conduct after capture. No solution was offered regarding changes in the policy on paybooks and their contents.

The intelligence that was supplied to Second Canadian Division through Combined Operations H.Q. had been "proved accurate in so far as it was possible to confirm it". But Intelligence recommended that "for future occasions where a unit or formation of the Canadian Army is involved in a similar operation . . . a senior Intelligence Officer of H.Q. First Canadian Army should be appointed to act as direct liaison between the Planning Staff and G.H.Q. Intelligence ... not ... to insert an extra link in the chain ... but rather to ensure that best use is made of the direct and constant liaison that is maintained between this Headquarters and G.H.Q. Intelligence."

Col. Henderson pointed out that it was useless to prepare a comprehensive Security Plan for an operation if one could not investigate afterwards to see if the plan had worked and, if necessary, make recommendations to improve it. He was practically certain that there had been no leakage of information. But at the same time, he was convinced that this fact should not be used as an excuse for allowing opportunities for leakage to occur in the future. This was the reason why investigations into alleged breaches of censorship and security were being conducted. He felt that all possible lessons should be learned now, and that examples of actual breaches involving Canadian troops would be far more valuable to us than mere reports of incidents involving other forces. He recommended that, during the planning stage, an Intelligence (b) officer be attached to co-ordinate the execution of the Cover Plan with the Operational Plan. His duty would be to detect and to remedy inconsistencies between the two plans, to initiate and to circulate counter rumours, to advise on security, and to notify the Planning Staff of any leakages that were discovered.

For some time after the Raid, a good deal of attention was paid to the reactions in Germany. The official German communique stressed as a "fact" that the Raid was the opening of the "Second Front" and produced a number of "corroborative" details. It said that the captured Operation Order called for the capture of Arques-la-Bataille, commented on the ability of the port of Dieppe to support an invasion, and "identified" a reserve force of "six or seven large transport ships also fully laden with tanks, and three freighters". This was in addition to groups of landing barges, transport ships, and light naval forces up to cruiser size which, it claimed, had been detected between Dieppe and Portsmouth. Farther north, another strong group, "no doubt the bulk of the landing forces, was held in 25 transport ships, on whose decks troops could be seen standing closely packed together." The order against looting was interpreted as another manifestation of the intention to remain, and "the high standard of individual decency displayed by the German occupation forces was given as a reason not to indulge in such behaviour" – a gratuitous propaganda theme. The communique commented on the evacuation of Frenchmen, the treatment of prisoners of war and the reason for the withdrawal "in order to meet all eventualities". It praised the efficiency of the High Command: "Reserves called out and sent on the march ... within the shortest distance reached the area of Dieppe at the appointed time but no longer found an opportunity for intervention."

In point of fact, Germany's propaganda services had been taken by surprise. Four and a half hours after the first German radio broadcast, the

German-controlled Radio Calais had made no mention of the Raid, other than to allude to "night target practice on the French coast". By that time, the Raid was over. The High Command made an early attempt to silence the Propaganda Ministry: "No comment will be forthcoming from political circles upon a matter which is obviously a military affair." Political comment was, however, extensive and varied. There was some initial uncertainty as to whether to describe the Raid as negligible, as on a small scale, or as an attempted invasion. By the evening of the 19th it was being described as a "second Dunkirk". The German Home Service called it an abortive invasion, undertaken by Churchill at the behest of Stalin, who was alleged to have given the British and United States governments an ultimatum with a time limit of 12 days from July 22nd "in view of the collapse of the (Russian) southern front". Churchill, "in the face of all the warnings of his military experts, had ordered an immediate large-scale landing on the French coast."

The two "black" propaganda "English Stations" broadcasting from Germany took different lines. The "New British Broadcasting Station", although anxious to prove that a Second Front had been attempted, admitted that there were people "high up ... who say frankly that this is no Second Front". It went on to say that others had a theory that this was an ordinary commando raid in which tanks had been used in order to give Allied leaders some idea of the difficulties that must be faced when a real invasion takes place. "Supporters of this full dress rehearsal admit that this try-out is likely to prove expensive, but they know that the knowledge thus gained by our [Allied] High Command would be worth paying a high price in losses for." The next day, August 20th, the themes were enlarged upon and became somewhat contradictory. In almost consecutive sentences the broadcasts declared that the expedition showed signs of hasty preparation and that "responsible British headquarters had prepared the expedition for a long time". The conclusion was that the coast was impregnable, that losses did not justify the results gained, and, in short: "In the light of long term strategy it is of singularly little importance whether the raid succeeded or failed, as operations of this kind are not destined to have any effect on the course of the war."

Allied monitors maintained a watch on the German broadcasts for the rest of the month. A summary of their findings was added to the report. The broadcasts merely became more and more stereotyped, and kept repeating the themes that had been developed in the first two days: the impregnability of the German defences, the attitude of the French (favourable to the German cause), the disappointment of Stalin at the failure, and a comparison with Gallipoli.

So Dieppe ended. German documents and persons, not then available, have since confirmed that there was no prior leakage of information. The state of readiness was the result of a careful appreciation by the German authorities, whose extensive air reconnaissance over British ports and beaches had observed the concentration of landing craft. Bad weather had limited that reconnaissance to coverage up to the end of July, at which date it had observed that the number of vessels had increased since the June deployments. Agents' reports had been received, but they could not be confirmed and were not believed. On August 15th, a change in Allied wireless procedures made interception more difficult. Allied air operations did not appear to be unusual. The German appreciation of the strategic situation, including the periods when moon and tides were right for invasion, had selected the following dates: July 27th to August 2nd; August 10th to 19th; August 25th to September 1st. The location of the possible target was linked to the known range of the British aircraft and landing craft then in service. The *15th Army* would have been remiss indeed if it had not taken precautions. When dealing with a professional enemy, it is always wise to do him the honour of assuming that he will react to a military situation in a professional military manner. The German Commander responsible for Dieppe was no exception.

8.
THE OTHER SIDE OF THE HILL: I(A) IN ITALY

SICILY [1]

First Canadian Infantry Division had no specialist Intelligence facilities under its direct control. The Intelligence staff received very extensive material obtained by Eighth Army Special Wireless, Air Photo, and Interrogation facilities, but its day-to-day tactical material was only what its own units could provide. The Divisional Intelligence staff consisted of a G.S.O.3, an I.O., a warrant officer, one sergeant, and eight men. Each brigade had an officer and three N.C.O.s. Each battalion had an I.O. and a variable number of men.

The material given the Division prior to its departure to join XXX British Corps in the Mediterranean was provided by the senior Allied Intelligence agencies. These had gathered a great deal of accurate background topographical information on the Italian peninsula and islands. However, because no direct contact had been made with the enemy in Italy itself, new order-of-battle information was limited to the data obtained from special wireless and some P.W. interrogation. Data on enemy fixed defences was collected through aerial photography.

The initial Planning Intelligence Summary (Intsum) stated that Sicily was garrisoned by about six low-grade, static, Italian coastal divisions, backed by three mobile divisions. The eastern sector – Eighth Army's objective – was held by the Italian *VI Corps*, under General Agostino Cinti; his H.Q. was at Piazza Armerina. Its subordinate *4th (Livorno)* and *54th (Napoli) Divisions* were located at Caltagirone, and between Vizzini and Syracuse respectively. The *206th* and *213th Coastal Divisions*, some independent coastal units, six airfield defence units, and five mobile groups were located inland. Each airfield defence unit comprised at least one infantry company, with one or more machine gun platoons and as many as two batteries of howitzers. The mobile groups were based on an armoured company equipped with light tanks. This data was not quite correct. The senior Italian command in Sicily was *Sixth Army*; Cinti commanded *XVI Corps*; there was an additional field division; and the *206th Coastal* actually manned the coast from Punta Braccetto to Masseria Palma.[2]

A special German headquarters under Colonel Bogislaw von Bonin co-ordinated defence planning. He formed a three-regiment *Kommando*, later renamed *15th Panzer Grenadier (Pz.Gr.) Division*, comprising the *104th*, *115th*, and *129th Pz.Gr Regiments*. Allied Intelligence expected the Germans to reinforce the island garrison with up to eight mobile divisions, two of which could be German. In mid-May 1943, the *Hermann Göring Panzer Division*, re-formed after its destruction in Tunisia, was sent to Sicily. It was not identified before the assault, but its existence was suspected. *15th Pz.Gr. Division*, less one regiment, was deployed to cover Palermo; *Hermann Göring*, plus *15 Division's 115th Pz.Gr. Regiment*, was in the Catania–Gerbini area. A third German division (*90th Pz.Gr. Division*), was being organized to defend Sardinia, and drew many reinforcements that otherwise might have bolstered the Sicily garrison.

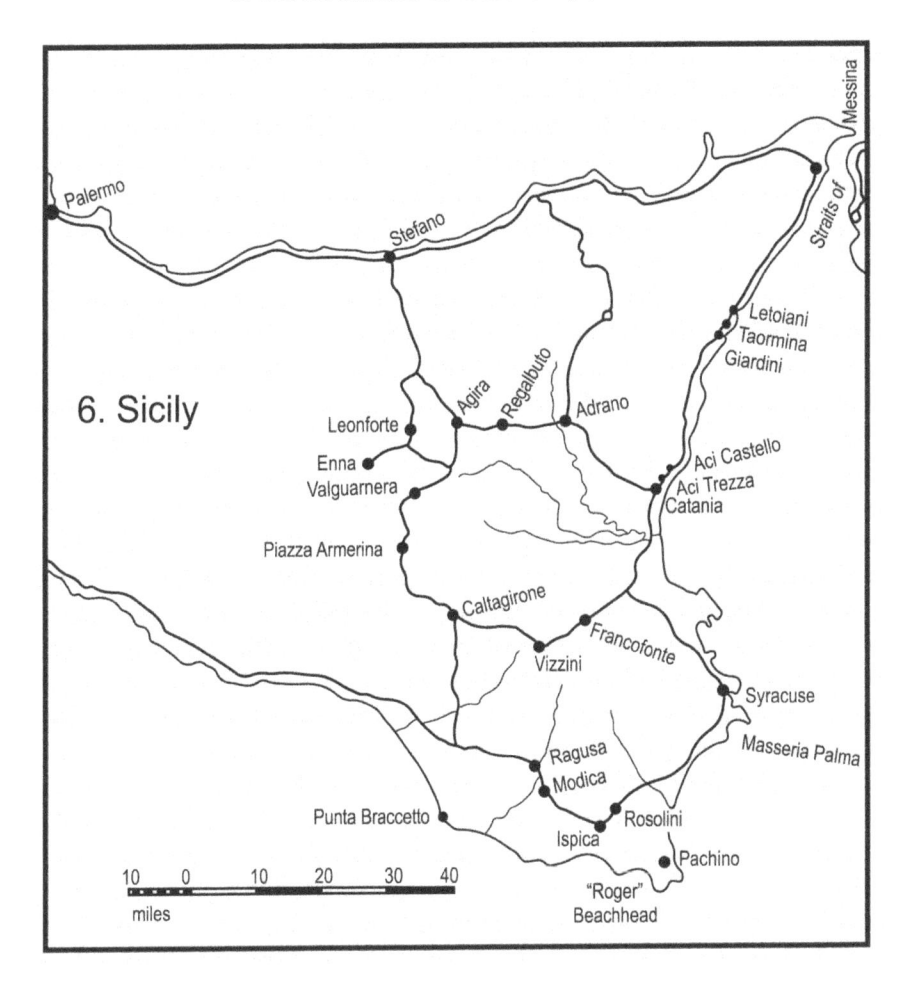

On May 3rd, First Division's Planning Intsum, written from British material, evaluated the situation. After describing the roads, it identified "*54 (Napoli) Division* in the southeast as a first line division without previous battle experience". On the coast was "*206 Coastal Division* with headquarters at Pachino".[3] (Wrong: that H.Q. was at Modica; *517th Airfield Defence Unit* was at Pachino.) "The relationship of the various units in the organization of the particular district and the part they play in the defence scheme is not known and can only be

This caused unnecessary casualties. During his interrogations of German prisoners, Spike Sprung discovered this error and passed it on to the Commander for correction. After the fall of Regalbuto on August 3rd and Adrano on August 7th, the Canadians were withdrawn into reserve and placed under XIII Corps for the landing in southern Italy.[8]

ITALY – BAYTOWN TO ORTONA

The decision to invade Italy, reached at the "Trident" Conference at Washington in May 1943, had a double purpose: to knock Italy out of the war, and to contain in Italy a maximum number of German forces. Initially, the limit of the Allied advance was to be the major port of Naples. Until late July, the main Allied thrust was intended to take place from about Reggio to Gioia, some 35 miles up the coast, with a supplementary assault against Crotone. When Mussolini fell, the advantages to be gained from a major assault nearer Naples became more attractive. The assault across the Strait was retained; in addition, the Allies decided to land the U.S. Fifth Army at Salerno on September 9th. Strategic intelligence on this operation should have been relatively complete. Certainly, the terrain analyses were quite adequate for planning purposes.

Enemy order-of-battle (identification and deployment) was, however, much less complete. Information that became available only after the war showed that the Italian *Seventh Army* H.Q., at Potenza, commanded three Corps – *IX* at Bari; *XIX* at Naples; and *XXXI* at Catanzaro, defending what was to be the invasion route for the British XIII Corps up the Calabrian Peninsula. *XXXI Corps* had four subordinate coastal divisions, *211*, *212*, *214*, and *227*; and a field division, the *104th (Mantova)*, in the Cosenza area. The H.Q. of *211 Division* was at Cittanova, and its battalions, together with some dismounted cavalry troops, were deployed along the Calabrian coastline for nearly a hundred miles, from the Gulf of Gioia to the Gulf of Squillace. A battalion of the *184th (Nembo) Division* and a battalion of *Blackshirt Militia* were in support.[9]

As the risk of Mussolini's overthrow grew, the German High Command strengthened its forces in Italy. Field Marshal Albert Kesselring, Commander-in-Chief South (i.e., of all German air and ground operations in Italy), organized a subordinate command, *Tenth Army*, to defend southern Italy. *Tenth Army* commanded *XIV Panzer Corps*, which commanded *15th Pz.Gr.* and *Hermann Göring Panzer Divisions* in Sicily; and *LXXVI Panzer Corps*, with *29th Pz.Gr. Division* and *1st Parachute Division*. Just before BAYTOWN, *26th Panzer Division* was sent to the Salerno area to reinforce the other formations withdrawn from Sicily. In addition, Kesselring had two divisions, *3rd Pz.Gr.* and *2nd Parachute*, near Rome, and *90th Pz.Gr. Division*, with an *S.S.* brigade, in Sardinia. North of the Apennines was *Army Group "B"*, under Field Marshal

8. THE OTHER SIDE OF THE HILL: I(A) IN ITALY

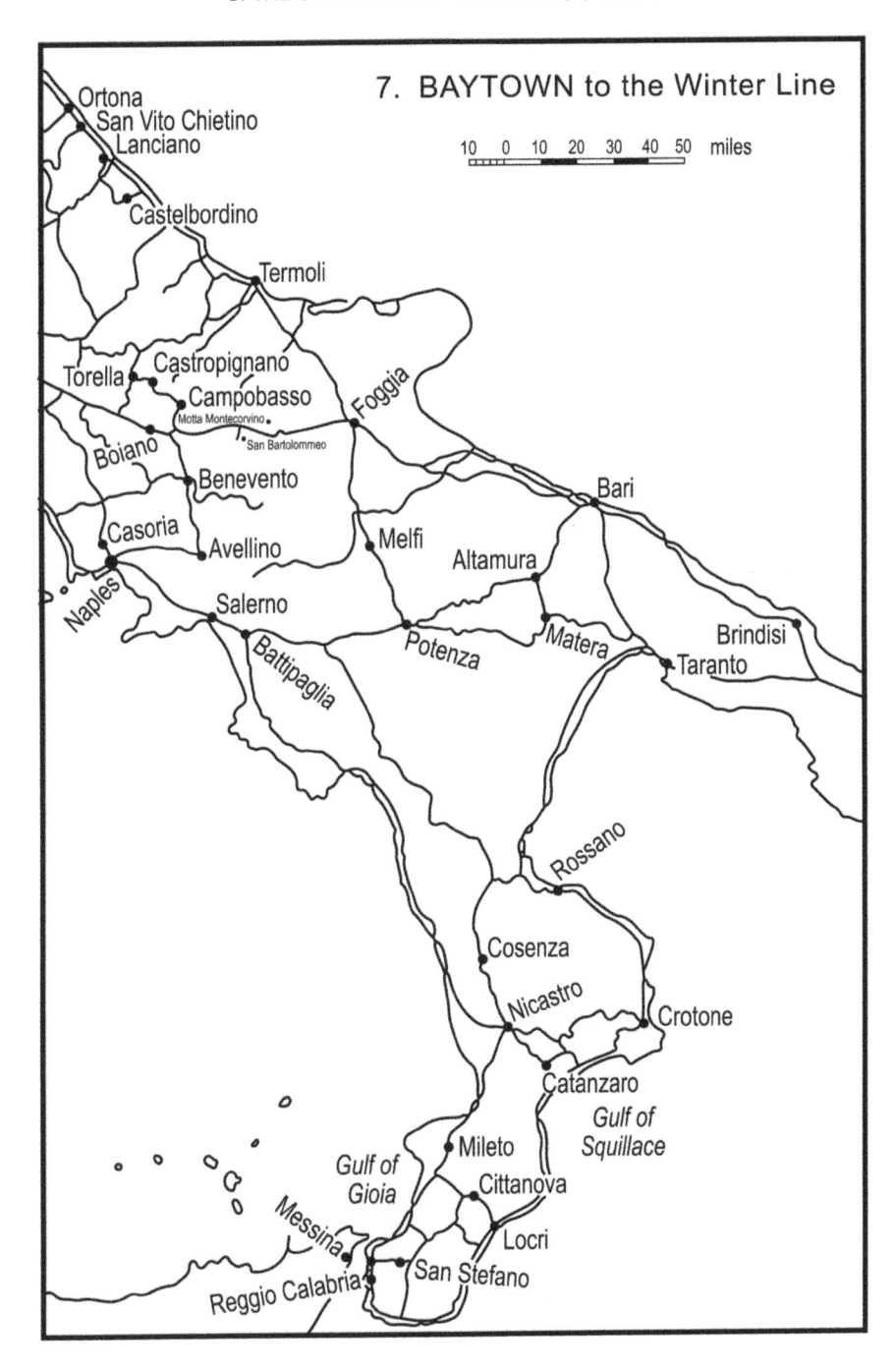

7. BAYTOWN to the Winter Line

Rommel, with three corps and eight divisions.[10] It must be emphasized that little of this was known beforehand.

Spike Sprung replaced Capt. A. Chambers as G.S.O.3. Because it was thought that the physical organization of H.Q. made it difficult for all its elements to work at peak efficiency, Sprung and staff from the Operations Branch fitted themselves into three 3-ton trucks, one of which was allotted to Intelligence. They sited the two office trucks about 12 feet apart, and parked the armoured Command Vehicle carrying the G.O.C.'s radio sets so that its side door was opposite the gap between the two offices. The side tarpaulins of the trucks could then be supported using a system of telescopic poles to make a more convenient and cooler office. Despite their ingenuity, the subsequent campaign showed that accommodation in buildings was preferable.

Planning for the invasion of Italy had started at Gen. Eisenhower's H.Q. in Algiers on May 26th. About July 23rd, XIII British Corps was assigned the Calabrian Peninsula. Ottawa gave its formal approval for Canadian participation on August 16th. It seems clear, however, that the forces in the field anticipated that approval, for the First Canadian Infantry Divisional Planning Summary No. 1 is dated August 11th. It dealt in detail with topography and beaches, repeating material provided by Corps. The attached order-of-battle map showed *211th Division* in Cittanova, and its units deployed along the coast. A coast artillery regiment was deployed on both sides of Reggio, and more artillery was possibly sited in the area. On August 17th, Gen. Simonds' outline plan selected 3 C.I.B. to lead the assault. Detailed planning began the next day.[11]

Planning Intsum No. 2, issued August 31st, warned that its information was two months old. It estimated five Italian and 10 German field divisions, but identified only six. The four evacuated from Sicily were: "*2nd (?)" Parachute Division* (wrong – *1st*), *Herman Göring* and *29th* and *15th Pz. Gr.* The German High Command was thought to be "sensitive about the 'toe' and the Pontine Marshes". One Italian and two German divisions were between S. Eufemia and Squillace, with most of their strength near Catanzaro and Nicastro (wrong – two battalions of the *15th Pz. Gr. Regiment* were astride the two roads leading into the area). Their position offered "greater possibilities for prolonged defence than perhaps any other in the whole of Italy." Conditions were ". . . favourable for the defence. . . . Forming-up places [from which an attack is launched] and gun positions . . . will be dominated by the enemy's guns. . . . The divisions in Catanzaro and Nicastro must reckon . . . against landings . . . on the West Coast and . . . the east." The Intsum saw these formations as "blocking the rapid advance and falling slowly back" to rear positions. Earlier estimates were that four divisions could hold all lines of advance in the Italian peninsula.

The Intsum continued: "In the face of specific ignorance, what is the general possibility of the German troops defending [the Canadian objective] and the hills behind it? Assuming that the Germans will only fight on ground allowing for a successful withdrawal, [a logical position is] the high ground between Reggio and Gallico *[just north of Reggio]*. Running east from each . . . is a good road. Air photos show the two roads going up around S. Stefano. Here, too, withdrawal is possible. The likelihood of our meeting Germans must be considered fairly high. South of Scilla the likelihood is less, though it must not be overlooked. South of Reggio, the 'dead-end' nature of the country makes the presence of Germans unlikely." Italian *XXXI Corps* H.Q. was correctly located at Catanzaro, with *211th Coastal Division* in the "toe", *212th* at Catanzaro, and *104th* north of the line Nicastro–Catanzaro. Minor Italian units were identified. The Canadian objective was defended by an estimated two platoons of infantry, possibly supported by a machine gun section and perhaps some 47 anti-tank guns on the high ground behind the beaches.[12]

What was not known at the time was the actual fighting strength of the German forces. According to the Official History, 39,569 Germans and 59,000 Italians were evacuated from Sicily. *Hermann Göring* and *29th Pz. Gr. Divisions* were at half-strength. The Italians were in an even worse state.[13] BAYTOWN took place on September 3rd. The enemy abandoned his positions. *II Battalion* of *15 Pz. Gr. Regiment (29th Pz. Gr. Division)* was identified; the Italian *55th Bersaglieri Battalion* and *78th Field Artillery Battery* surrendered. As the Official History states, the Intelligence evaluations had been highly accurate.[14]

Though the landing had been easy, the advance was not. An inadequate road system, and natural obstacles that had been reinforced by extensive enemy demolitions, allowed the German forces to break contact at will. All efforts were made to locate them and to identify new defence lines. Motorcycle-mounted patrols were used extensively. On September 7th, Spike Sprung realized that the enemy had, in fact, no real intention of holding the Calabrian Peninsula. "It is doubtful if they would stand and fight unless we close with them swiftly enough to interfere with their demolition plan. Even then they would probably commit nothing but their covering parties [the men protecting the demolitions experts]." He saw that the German infantry was withdrawing too quickly to give its rear parties support, which meant that the opposition would be light. In his view, the enemy was moving out of contact in order to regroup. (At the time he wrote, he could not have known of the Salerno landings, and that the Germans were, in fact, reinforcing that sector.) He identified the main enemy party north of Mileto, noted that 5th Division on the Canadian left was being slowed by booby traps, teller mines, and heavy fire, and warned that First Division could expect to meet the same obstacles.[15]

The Italians surrendered on September 8th, 1943. By the 10th, "the Italians are becoming more of a problem as a friendly force than as an enemy. The roads are swarming with Italian troops going home." The British Wireless Intercept unit overheard "one of the Italian generals . . . reporting to his Corps H.Q.

behind the German lines . . . a clear description of his visit to the British Corps H.Q. including its locality".[16] Field Security dealt with him.

By September 16th, the Allied line across the lower end of the Italian boot was complete. On the 18th, Col.-Gen. von Vietinghoff ordered his *Tenth Army* to retire its left or eastern wing until it held a line Salerno–Potenza–Altamura. The move was to be accompanied by an extensive program of demolition and mined obstacles. Gen. Montgomery's task was to hasten this withdrawal, and to try to push the Germans out of their new defences before they were firmly set. The Apulia (Puglia) region north of Taranto was garrisoned by the German *1st Parachute Division*, some of whose elements had been sent to the Salerno front.

The Canadians advanced to Potenza on the 19th. Lt.-Col. M.P. Bogert had received two completely contradictory reports on German occupation of the town and decided to accept the calculated risk. His attack was successful. Sixteen prisoners from a battalion of the *3rd Regiment* of *1st Parachute Division* said when they were interrogated at Division that they had been in Battipaglia, near Salerno, and had been rapidly moved to Potenza on the 19th, without supporting tanks or artillery. Their disclosures not only gave Intelligence an indication of the flexibility of German defence deployments, but also revealed that the speed of the Canadian advance had caught them unprepared.[17]

By September 21st, the Allied armies held a continuous line from Salerno to Bari. From this they intended to seize certain vital areas where they could reorganize and reinforce before the next assault. First, however, a mobile screen was to harass the enemy, keeping the initiative and gathering as much information as possible. The terrain was difficult; mountains that had very few roads or alternative tracks, and then a small river system, all favoured the defence. Most of the actions were small, with the unit I.O.s playing a major part in collecting and processing the information needed.

A vigorous patrol policy maintained contact. 3 C.I.B.'s Intelligence staff went a little further and recruited several Italian officers into a "reporting corps", dressing them in plain clothes and sending them through the lines. These were brave men who faced certain death as spies if they were caught. They reported on September 27th that Melfi was clear, but there were so many contradictory reports from the unit patrols, and from civilians coming through the lines, that a formal reconnaissance was necessary.[18] We do not know what happened to this particular reporting corps, but similar groups were operated by a senior branch of Army Intelligence; the unofficial agents were probably taken over later by Eighth Army; if they had been adequately cleared, that is!

An incident at Motta Montecorvino in early October 1943 illustrates another source of help. The enemy held a commanding position. Reconnaissance showed that the ridge he held was defended for four or five miles on each side of the Canadian axis and that a major assault would be necessary to dislodge him. But a detachment of No. 1 Long Range Demolition Squadron, better known as "Popski's Private Army", located a narrow track along which a squadron of the Divisional reconnaissance regiment could outflank the enemy's defences. This was the first of many close working arrangements between the "P.P.A." and Canadian units.[19]

The German casualties on the Motta Ridge were from the *3rd Regiment, 1st Parachute Division*; later at Baselice, on October 5th, they came from the *71st Regiment, 29th Pz.Gr. Division*. For the first time in some weeks, the G.S.O.3 began to feel he could make some sense of the enemy organization. The line from San Bartolommeo to Termoli was thought to be held by *1st Parachute Division*, organized into battle groups. Opposite the Canadians, west of Motta, was *Battle Group Heilmann*, headed by Col. Ludwig Heilmann, Commander *3rd Parachute Regiment*; it comprised his regiment and a battalion of *1st Parachute Regiment*, two troops of parachute artillery, four anti-tank platoons, a machine gun battalion, and anti-aircraft and engineer troops, with a total strength, less the machine gun battalion, of 1,350 men. It was acting as a screen to mask the withdrawal of *26th Panzer Division* and *29th Pz.Gr. Division* of *LXXVI Panzer Corps*. It was this practice of withdrawing a unit through the force deployed in the defence line behind it that caused the confusion in enemy order-of-battle identifications.

Intelligence discovered the tactical doctrine the Germans were following in a captured document – a directive dated September 27th, 1943, by Gen.-Maj. Heidrich, G.O.C. *1st Parachute Division*. (It later turned out to be a restatement of *Tenth Army* Order No. 4, of September 26th.) The aim was to delay, to cause casualties, and to deceive the Allies. The defence was to be based on a succession of lines, so sited that the Allied artillery would have to redeploy to engage each of them. It was to be based on outposts, strong points, reconnaissance to identify the enemy main thrust, and on mobility to ensure complete disengagement when forced back. Before withdrawal, which was only to take place under pressure by the Allies, German artillery was directed to intensify its fire. This was a signal Canadian troops learned to recognize as the first indication that an enemy position was being vacated.[20] The importance of the north-south roads – Boiano–Isernia and Castropignano–Torella–Cittanova – as withdrawal routes for the German divisions was very apparent.

Tenth Army's directive has to be viewed in the context of German grand strategy. Hitler, anticipating an Allied invasion of Europe in 1944, had ordered his forces to hold where they were in the west while accepting, as far as he was ever able to accept it, the loss of some territory in the east. In Italy, this was to mean a defence in depth, in a series of defensive lines, rather than a withdrawal to the northern Apennines. The first of these was the "Bernhard Line", running from Gaeta to Ortona. It was sited at the narrowest part of the Italian peninsula, and was to be held by five divisions, two of them infantry, on a front of 85 miles split into two sectors, with a division deployed in reserve behind each. It was based on two rivers, the Sangro in the east and the Garigliano in the west *(shown on Map 8)*. The rugged massif of the Abruzzi in the centre, with its few poor roads, formed a virtually impregnable barrier. In the west, the Liri and Sacco valleys led to Rome, but entry to them was limited to the narrow Mignano gap. German engineers' mine-laying and demolitions rendered almost impassable any avenue that nature herself had not already blocked, and the snow and rain of an Italian winter compounded the difficulties. Field Marshal Kesselring took command of all German forces in Italy, namely *Army Group "C"*, with *Tenth* and *Fourteenth Armies* as his subordinates. Rommel's *Army Group "B"* was then withdrawn.[21] In early November, despite ambitious planning, the Allied advance spent itself against the incomplete defences of the Bernhard Line.

The Canadians went into reserve in November. The Intelligence staff used the time to tidy up some of its procedures and to give further training to the battalion and brigade Sections. The combined scout and sniper platoon system that had been proposed in 1940* had been adopted by the battalions of 2 Brigade after their experience at Agira, in Sicily. The system was highly regarded by the units and by Capt. F.N. Pope, the Brigade I.O. Pope was replaced by Capt. W.S. Dewar, P.P.C.L.I., on November 16th. The 2 Brigade interpreter, Capt. H.S. Whitehead, offered Italian lessons to officers and N.C.O.s of the Brigade. Capt. Jack Robinson, who had recovered from the jaundice that laid him and many others low during the campaign, gave lectures on Air Photo. He and the Air Photo office were greatly encouraged when Brig. Hoffmeister, Commander 2 C.I.B., firmly stated that before any operation he wanted "air photos down to the lowest sub-unit possible". The brigadier was also insistent that Intelligence and large-scale maps must be made widely available.[22] We have mentioned only 2 C.I.B.; the other brigades were equally active.

Gen. Montgomery, faced with the task of taking Avezzano in order to threaten Rome, decided to feint a thrust through the mountains and to put the real attack along the coast road. The Canadians were to cross the River Sangro from Castel di Sangro to Ateleta, some 12 miles downstream, and then advance to Sulmona. The forward positions of the Bernhard Line were sited along this river, but information on it was scanty. All possible sources were exploited: escaped Allied P.W., civilian line-crossers, German P.W., air photos, and the data obtained by the artillery. *1st Parachute Division* was identified in the Line when a skirmish on November 17th left four of its men dead. The German engineers blew up all the bridges except two; wireless intercept brought Intelligence news of this omission.

By November 28th, when some degree of stability had been achieved on both sides, Army Intelligence was able to compile much more comprehensive

---

* An I.O., eight Intelligence men, and eight snipers/scouts; a normal section could have up to five in the Intelligence office, with scouts controlled elsewhere.

summaries on German identifications. *16th Panzer Division* "may by now have succeeded in extricating itself for refitting and possibly to follow its Panther tank battalion to Russia." *1st Parachute Regiment*, from Rivisondoli, covered its move. The road from Sulmona to Rivisondoli was the only one not yet blocked by snow, and *3rd* and *4th Parachute Regiments* were deployed to guard it. The *Hermann Göring Pz. Division* was the possible "lay-back" division.

In succession from left to right, the Canadian front, therefore, was faced by *3rd*, *4th*, and *1st Regiments, 1st Parachute Division*; *79th Pz.Gr. Regiment, 16th Pz. Division*; and *146th Infantry* and, with its left flank on the sea, *145th Infantry Regiments*. *Hermann Göring Pz. Division* was behind the *79th*, which was expected to be withdrawn. West of Mount Greco was the *305th Infantry Division*. *26th Pz.* and *29th Pz.Gr. Divisions* were then on the Fifth Army front; *3rd Pz. Division* was in the Cassino sector. "Thus it would seem that the enemy is so anxious that his main defences on the Garigliano should not be outflanked from the east before the Cassino position is complete that he has striven to make use of the mountains regardless of supply difficulties."[23] (This reference to the *305th Infantry Division's* deployment was essentially accurate.) The two infantry regiments on the east coast had not been identified as to subordination; they belonged to the *65th Infantry Division*.[24]

The Germans, however, recognized that the Allied attacks on the centre of the Bernhard Line were merely a feint, and began to reinforce their eastern sector. They replaced the *65th* by the *90th Pz.Gr. Division* (*200th* and *361st Regiments*), but were unable to repel a major assault by British Eighth Army, starting on November 28th. First Canadian Division replaced the British 78th Division; its mission was to push up the coast road to Ortona and Pescara. 2 C.I.B. led across the Sangro on the last day of November 1943.[25]

The Moro River was the next most likely place for the German forces to make a stand. V British Corps reported on December 5th that aerial photography did not reveal any "large-scale digging south of Pescara",[26] but it soon became obvious that the Germans were doing so. Interrogations and statements made later by senior officers emphasized the impact on their defensive doctrine of the massive Allied air support that had accompanied the assault at the end of November, and on their intention to protect themselves from its effects in future. First Division Intelligence forecast that the Germans would defend the ridge lines that lay across the axis of advance but would not have sufficient strength to counter-attack. Unit identifications were not easy. Most P.W. had no idea of the division their unit belonged to, although, much to the relief of Capt. Cottam, the I.O. (German), they were generally quite ready to talk.

Within the Division itself, the efforts that had been made to convince troops that they must report new equipment began to bring results. 2 C.I.B. found a new type of German anti-tank rifle on December 4th and, together with its projectiles, passed it back to Divisional H.Q. A 75 mm PAK 40 anti-tank gun on a 38-ton Czech light tank chassis, so new that it did not even have identifying marks painted on it, and a 12 cm (4.7 in.) mortar were also captured. Neither of these was previously known to the Allies.[27]

On December 5th, Capt. Bill Hall, a Canadian in the R.E. who had replaced Jack Robinson as I.O. (Photo), went up to H.Q. 2 C.I.B. to assist their advance. At about 0200 on the 5th, a heavy enemy shell severely wounded him and injured his driver. He was a man who worked well with others and had a valuable fund of common sense. Time was always precious, and one of his associates recalled a technique he was fond of using. If, when working for an infantry formation, he saw an object he could not identify, he would show it as "possible mortar". If it was an armoured formation, the object would be a "possible anti-tank gun". If he was right, the men would be prepared for the worst when they dealt with it; if he was wrong, no harm was done.[28]

The Moro crossing began on December 6th, and succeeded. P.W. interrogations conducted afterwards revealed that the enemy had been able to regroup his forces on the river before the first assault.[29] German forces were now identified as: *200th Pz.Gr. Regiment (90th Division)*, and *26th Pz. Regiment* with Mark IV tanks, "subordination not given but possibly a *90th Division* unit". The *361st Pz.Gr. Regiment* was at San Leonardo; the rest of the *90th Division* was astride the coastal road. Division did not learn until later that it had only two of its three regiments. The *26th Pz. Regiment* was not clearly identified, and Intelligence also learned later that the *26th* had replaced the Russia-bound *16th Pz. Division*.

The Divisional Intsum set the scene for the advance northward after December 10th. The confused enemy deployments that had followed the breach of the Bernhard Line had now been replaced by well-organized, if not well-prepared, "tank-proof" defensive positions. The enemy had five infantry battalions. Three were known to be committed: *I* and *II* of *361 Pz.Gr. Regiment*, and *III* of *200 Pz.Gr. Regiment*. Intelligence did not know where *II/361* was; *III/200* was probably in divisional reserve. *200 Regiment* was fresh; *361* had been in action and was not fresh. The full enemy divisional artillery (48 guns) was thought to be available, plus 10 infantry guns and two or three 17 cm guns. Two or three squadrons of Mk. IV tanks were standing by, one on 24-hour notice. The G.S.O.3 considered that the familiar pattern of "hold and withdraw" was likely to continue.[30]

The advance to Ortona, which began on December 10th, involved direct assaults across a succession of gullies at right angles to the coast road. Each was defended; each cost lives. By December 13th, *90th Pz.Gr. Division* had to be reinforced from *3rd Parachute Regiment*.[31] The slow, grinding advance was complicated by the fact that each of the artillery fire plans had to be individually surveyed. Italian maps were too inaccurate to use. By December 27th, the whole *Parachute Division* was identified. The Ortona garrison was known: *90*

Pz. Gr. Regiment and two battalions of paratroops. What could not be foreseen was the prestige factor that made fighting for that unfortunate town so bitter. Intelligence became very personal, low-level, and precise, aimed directly at the location and probable intentions of enemy sub-units, sometimes not even as far away as the next house. By December 28th, the German *Tenth Army* had had enough. And so had the British Eighth Army.

First Division had fought the entire range from the formal attack to the tedious grind of small infantry skirmishes. In the formal assaults, the detail and range of intelligence provided was, in general, sufficiently accurate for an attack to be planned with a better-than-average chance of success. Minor attacks depended on the information that could be obtained on the ground itself, by troops actually engaged with the enemy. Most data at this level is passed from man to man, from officer to officer, so that the immediate task can be done. This material is required to help junior commanders to plan, but it is equally important as the minor, but highly significant, direct personal information that helps men stay alive. Its nature is oral and ephemeral and it is rarely reported very far back. But experience taught all troops how important it was to observe, to evaluate, and to pass on to all potential users all items about the enemy, at every level of interest. First Division learned this lesson well and became a highly professional formation.

ORTONA TO ROME

H.Q. I Canadian Corps landed in Sicily on November 8th; Fifth Canadian Armoured Division and some Corps units arrived at Naples about the same date. Shortly afterward Eighth Army feared some sort of disturbance in the Bari–Taranto–Brindisi area. Fifth Division, ordered to put a battalion on stand-by, initially committed its infantry element, 11th Brigade. The order was signed by the Divisional G.S.O.1 but the instructions to the Brigade went out as an Intelligence, not an Operations, letter.

The staff at Corps was: Maj. C.D. Kingsmill, G.S.O.2; Capts. A.B. Laver, G.S.O.3 I(a); B.G. Foreman, G.S.O.3 I(b); and D.G. Molnar; Lieuts. D.M. Healy, W.E. Edwards, S.H. Foyer and J.A. Philip, I.O.s. Maj. D'Arcy Kingsmill lost no time. He spent some days with XIII Corps H.Q., whose staff was most helpful. On his return, and with full support of his Commander, Lt.-Gen. H.D.G. Crerar, he arranged for brief training attachments for his officers. On November 28th, Foyer, Molnar, and Philip were sent to Eighth Army; Philip went to the Combined Services Detailed Interrogation Centre (C.S.D.I.C.) at 307 (Army) P.W. Cage; Foyer and Molnar were to be employed at a Forward Interrogation Centre (F.I.C.). Even as late as January 11th, 1944, when Corps joined Fifth Armoured at Altamura, near Bari, it had no specialist Intelligence units. No. 1 Special Wireless Section arrived in late January; to get it, special pressure had been exerted by H.Q. Central Mediterranean Forces in Algiers.[32]

Corps arranged to issue a Most Secret Intelligence Summary daily, whenever one was justified. Part I was to contain information of interest to all: enemy ground and air situation, methods, equipment, tactics, and propaganda, together with intelligence from other theatres. Part II – specialty Intelligence data – was to be sent to "Corp Troops". Security was to issue a summary every two weeks. Maps in use included a "1:100,000", showing the enemy situation on the Corps and adjacent Corps fronts; a "1:250,000", kept to show the situation on the Army front; and a larger-scale map (not specified but probably 1:1 million) to show the general situation in other theatres. Eighth Army Intelligence would issue the overprints (maps marked with detail on the enemy). The first Corps Intsum of December 13th, 1943, gave a general review based on information from Eighth Army and V Corps. It listed the German *Tenth Army's* nine more or less severely mauled divisions, described German battle techniques, quoted extracts from captured documents, identified equipment, and gave a few personality summaries – assessments of the leadership characteristics of some German commanders.[33] Its principal purpose was to encourage the new arrivals to think seriously about local situations, to ensure that the Intelligence machinery was geared to meet the requirements of regular production during combat. The general format became the pattern for subsequent issues.

Gen. Sir Oliver Leese, Commander Eighth Army, planned to attack over the Arielli River *(just north of Ortona)*, to pin down German troops while operations were taking place against Anzio and in the Cassino area. The main German positions were sited on the Foro River, a small stream east of the Arielli, held by *LXXVI Panzer Corps* with four divisions; three were in the line: *1st Parachute*, *26th Panzer*, and *334th Infantry*. The other one, *90th Pz. Gr. Division*, was being redeployed to the Rome sector. Its strength was so seriously reduced after Ortona that *I* and *II Battalions* of its *361st Regiment* had to be combined, and only *II* and *III Battalions* of its *200th Pz. Gr. Regiment* were battle worthy.[34]

No. 11 Canadian Infantry Brigade (Fifth Armoured Division) was to capture several strong points, then exploit into the Arielli valley. No detailed record appears in 11 Brigade's Diary to show what information it had to support this, its first operation. But a good deal should have been available, for it took over from 3 C.I.B., then in the line north of Ortona. That Brigade H.Q. would have given whatever information it had to its replacement. After taking over, 11 C.I.B. units spent three days patrolling. Unit commanders were able to examine the area of their objectives from the high ground behind the Riccio; they should have been familiar with the strong points of the enemy defences. Two days before the operation there was an estimate of tank strengths: *1st Parachute Division* – 15; *90th Pz. Gr. Division* – 20; *26th Pz. Division* – 25–30. "On 11 C.I.B. front enemy appears to have three companies dug in with

8. Liri Valley

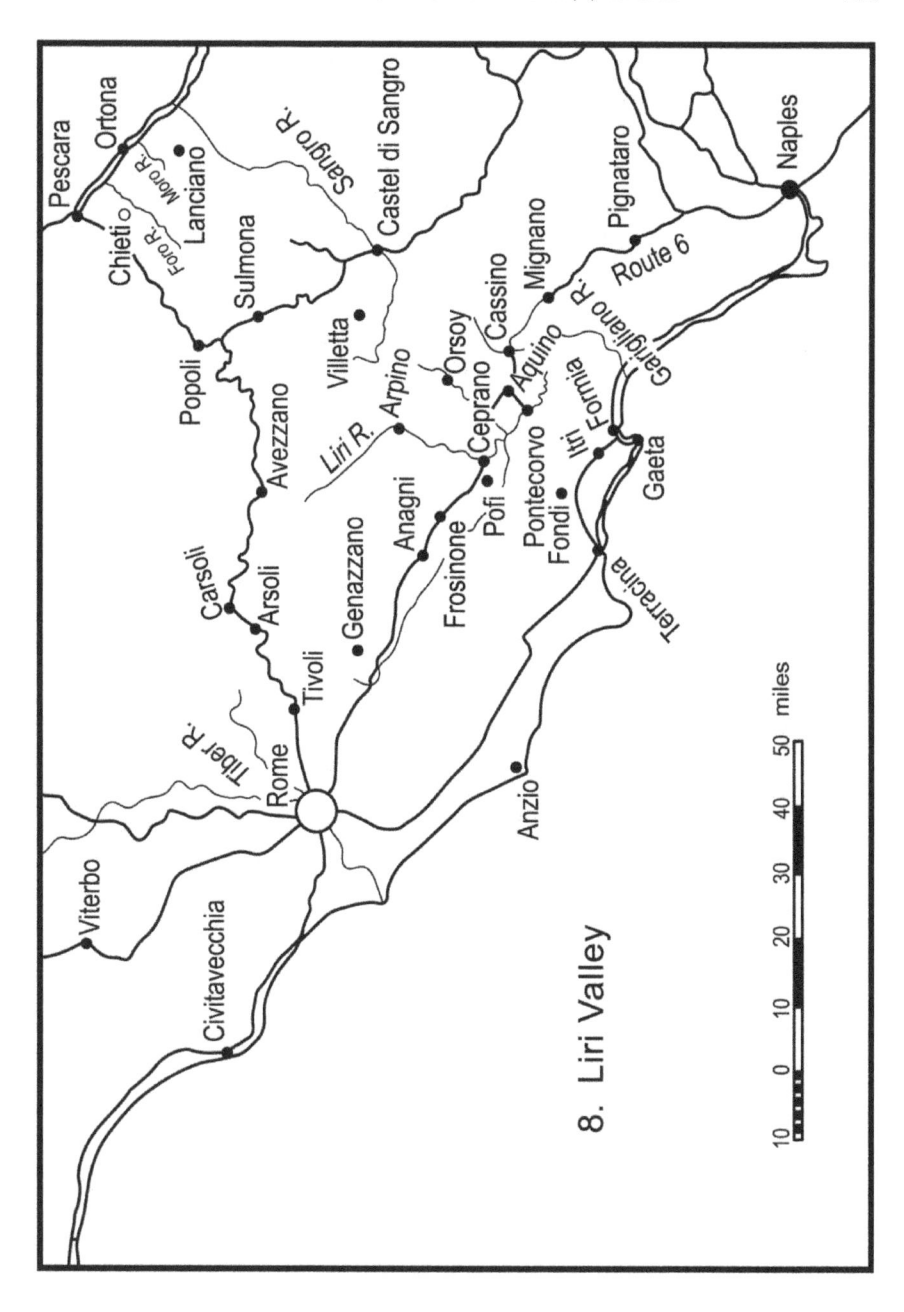

medium machine guns and mortars in support holding the line of the lateral road forward of the Arielli. Units were *I/1* and *III/1 Parachute Regiment*." It was thought possible that *90th Pz. Gr. Regiment* [sic] had been taken out of the line, although this was unconfirmed. It appeared that the line was being held lightly and that the remainder of the force was in deep dug-outs to the rear.[35] *90th Division* was in the process of moving out. By January 15th about half its strength was in the Rome area, according to the Official History.

The attack, which began on January 17th, failed. The maps were cited as one of the main reasons for failure. They were indeed inadequate. The printing was poor, the colours were poorly registered, and they were hard to read. In addition, they were highly inaccurate. A series of gridded air photographs was issued as a substitute; but failure to appreciate the effects of paper shrinkage and to notice errors in scale made these less effective than they might have been. The main reason for the failure was the inexperience of 11 Brigade. It was up against professionals; it learned the hard way, and its subsequent record was very good.[36]

On January 9th, the first Psychological Warfare "leaflet shoot" took place from the Canadian position. The leaflet reviewed Russian gains near Zhitomir and the Allied bombing of Berlin; quoted a Swiss newspaper estimate that 10% of the German population had died on the Russian front; drew *1st Parachute Division's* attention to the slaughter at Ortona; and suggested that men would be needed in the postwar period to rebuild Germany. Conditions were not particularly suitable for Psychological Warfare, especially against *1st Parachute Division*. The Commander *Tenth Army*, Col.-Gen. von Vietinghoff, issued an immediate threat, "in the event of a soldier . . . desert[ing] . . . the most severe measures against his family will be taken".[37] Occasionally German discipline was even more direct. First Canadian Division had already seen enemy machine-gunners shooting down a group of their own men who were trying to surrender.

After the Anzio landings on January 17th, 1944, it was imperative that Intelligence determine which German units were being sent to that bridgehead. *LXXVI Panzer Corps* was expected to send reinforcements; they would most probably come from *1st Parachute Division*. Positive identifications of the units opposite I Corps were needed, and the only way to get them was to capture and interrogate prisoners. Patrols set to work at once, co-ordinated by H.Q. 11 Brigade, specialists in using air photographs to control patrols, and helped by Major Jack Robinson, then at Corps. On January 25th, they caught men from *305th Infantry Division* and learned that *26th Pz. Division* had moved. Fifth Army, responsible for the Mediterranean coast sector, was the first to report that *III/1st Parachute Regiment* had been identified in action on January 31st. The Division's move, probably made on the 23rd, was not known to the Canadians, who had taken no prisoners since the 22nd. The aggressive Canadian patrolling policy now escalated into an expensive holding attack on

January 30th and 31st, designed to convince the enemy that weakening his eastern front was unwise. One very minor benefit was the identification of *I Battalion, 4th Parachute Regiment*.[38]

On February 2nd, I Corps Counter-Bombardment stated that it had identified 62 "fixed hostile troops (enemy gun locations) which included heavy A.A. 8.8 cm guns.... These ... guns are being used to do a small amount of ground shooting. The weight of the shell is 20 lbs. and the range 11,900 yards ... in this role". This was the first Canadian recognition of the famous "88". An amusing example of German camouflage was reported from another front: "One of our patrols was recently engaged by a haystack. On the return of the patrol the haystack was engaged by our artillery, whereupon it retreated in the direction of a nearby house and was shortly immobilized by a near miss."[39]

On February 4th, 1944, the Seaforths took a prisoner from *III Battalion, 3rd Parachute Regiment*; he told Intelligence before he died that the Division was still on the Corps front. On the 5th, Maj. Kingsmill reviewed the German deployments in a detailed and exemplary Intelligence Summary that listed accurately the units, weapons, and positions facing Canadian forces. The positional and organizational detail it gave reflected the skill and hard work needed to exploit and interpret the many sources on which it was based. It also reported a German practice of dropping shells into the Allied barrage, a ruse intended to make the infantry think that rounds from their supporting artillery were dropping short. It weakened their confidence, made the men hang back, and gave the defence time to react.

Prisoners taken on the morning of February 6th confused the interrogators by giving different but detailed locations for their unit, *578 Grenadier Regiment*. On the 7th, two skirmishes produced "a Pole who knows nothing and an officer who says nothing". By the 11th, a report that *I Battalion, 1st Parachute Regiment*, was near Anzio indicated that a move might have taken place, and the G.S.O.2 speculated that *II Battalion* might also have left. First Division, basing its assessment on proven form, disagreed. After the 11th, behaviour was reported which could not be satisfactorily explained. Civilian movements were being tightly controlled. Enemy patrols were becoming more active, and artillery was responding more readily. Air photos on the 17th showed strong points across the Arielli. Indications that the *Parachute Division* was thinning out were noticed on the 18th. An error in German signals security gave the Wireless Section a route and a rendezvous. First Divisional Artillery was accordingly given extra ammunition on the night of February 19th with which to speed the parting guest.[40]

The old adversary had gone. Intelligence now needed to know who had replaced him, and where he was. Air photos located a new line across the Arielli with which, for want of anything better, Corps had to be content. A Czech deserter "broke" the story to Capt. Bob Prince, who had replaced Spike Sprung as First Division's G.S.O.3. By February 24th, additional prisoners and four more deserters made the situation clearer. The *Parachute Division* had not been replaced; *305th Infantry Division* had taken over some of the line, followed, at least in part, by *146 Pz. Gr. Regiment*. Its units were badly under-strength, and some 25% of its complement were Poles, Czechs, Yugoslavs, and Lorrainers. By the end of February, the *146th* was withdrawn, and *305th Division*, slightly reinforced, took over opposite I Canadian Corps.[41]

By March 4th the overcast cleared enough to allow photo missions to be flown. Their coverage indicated that the "Foro Line" had not been built up significantly, and detailed its layout. Photographs at Pescara on February 28th had shown that the defences north and south of the river had been developed, and mines had been placed between the coastal road and the sea.[42]

The Canadians thinned out between the third week of April and May 5th, a move detected by the Germans. In preparation for the spring offensive, Capt. Bob Prince and his I.O.s, Lieuts. I.T. Burr and K.A. Cottam, arranged an Intelligence training course to cover patrolling and its problems, German organization, tactics and weapons, the duties of I.O.s at every level, including Engineer and Artillery Intelligence, P.W. control, and the use of air photos. The course was vital because many of the Intelligence staffs were new. It also gave the Division an opportunity to lay down policy, to discuss and resolve its problems, and to build the personal contacts that are so necessary in a good Intelligence team.[43] No similar course was reported in Fifth Division. Corps had long been concerned over the state of Intelligence in that formation, and, when they had finished a program of short exchanges of personnel between Corps and First Division, tried to set up a similar arrangement with Fifth Armoured. They were rebuffed. When Gen. Burns took over I Corps, Maj. Kingsmill tried again, and was asked to wait and see how the Division fared in the forthcoming actions.

In reply to the Anzio landings, the Germans deployed 17 divisions to bar the door to the Allied advance northward. The total strength of that Allied assault, concentrated on a ten-mile front, was to be eight divisions and three brigades. I Canadian Corps, with Fifth Armoured and First Infantry Divisions, was given the British 25th Tank Brigade, while 1 Canadian Armoured Brigade went to XIII Corps. German Intelligence had identified the Eighth Army boundary, and had deduced that its location in front of the Liri foretold a thrust up that valley. But it could not dismiss the possibility of a further seaborne landing. The Germans could see no reason why the Allies persisted in inching their way up the length of Italy when amphibious operations were more logical. They did not realize that there were never enough landing craft for these. Consequently, Kesselring's Intelligence made the most determined efforts to obtain any information which would suggest that such landings were being planned. Attempts were made to capture Allied prisoners. German radio intercept teams tried to identify units. But the enemy was virtually blindfolded; his air reconnaissance could not penetrate Allied air superiority, his agents were few and inept, and prisoners were difficult to obtain.

Headquarters Allied Armies in Italy decided to exploit the enemy weakness. A false landing was therefore "prepared" for the Civitavecchia area, some 40 miles north of the Tiber. The illusion of this preparation was to be created by using dummy signals traffic. First Canadian and 36th U.S. Infantry Divisions, and 5th Canadian Armoured Brigade, were to "assemble" under I Corps in the Salerno area, to train for amphibious operations in which they would be the assault element for the formations opposite the Liri and the southern front. The "operation" started on April 18th. Units "closed down", and "reopened" on the 22nd in Salerno (the "break" would be noted by German intercept). A "normal stream" of traffic was passed between I Corps and these subordinate formations; and between senior and rear H.Q. On May 2nd, a signals exercise involving the Royal Navy gave the illusion of a landing exercise in Salerno bay. The "target" was Ogliastro, some 25 miles down the coast from Salerno, an area that closely resembled the Civitavecchia region. Meanwhile, strict security masked the preparations for the real assault. Postwar examination of German records shows that this deception plan completely bamboozled German Intelligence.[44]

Terrain was significant in this sector. The Liri valley varies in width from four to seven miles throughout its 20-mile length. It is bordered on the north by the many spurs of the Apennines of which the best known is Monte Cassino; from its summit, an abbey dominates the whole eastern end of the valley. The Liri River and the streams running into it from the mountains present a series of natural obstacles to any advance up the valley. These obstacles were further strengthened by the German engineers.

The first of these defence lines was the "Gustav Line", which ran along the Gari and Garigliano to the sea. The fast-flowing Gari was 40 or more feet wide, and six to eight feet deep. Behind it were belts of mines and wire, covered by machine gun fire from concrete emplacements and semi-mobile pillboxes. Artillery fire could be controlled from the heights on both sides of the entrance to the valley. Deep shelters gave protection against Allied air or artillery bombardment, and ensured that troops were nearby to repel any assault. Behind this line was a switchline, the "Senger Riegel", best known to the Allies as the "Adolf Hitler Line", which branched from the main "Winter Line" at Monte Cairo, crossed the valley about eight miles west of the Gari River, and extended through the Aurunci Mountains to the coast at Terracina.

I Canadian Corps was not in direct contact, but it spent a great deal of time and effort trying to provide information on enemy units, their characteristics, tactics, defences, and equipment. About this time the Germans reduced the complement of their divisional infantry regiments from three battalions to two, with a corresponding reduction in the size of the support services. The total divisional establishment dropped from 17,000 to about 13,000. Intelligence learned that the reorganization affected about one-third of all divisions in the field, and was applied both to those which had been hard-hit and to new formations. It had identified only a few of these, and the staff had to assume that a division was at its old establishment until proven otherwise.[45]

A careful watch was kept on the enemy organization and deployments and the Intsums of the period are a catalogue of German units. On April 2nd, there were six enemy divisions between the sea and Cassino. Much redeployment took place during the first two weeks of April, and the Summaries attempted to keep up with it. It was a trying time for the order-of-battle staffs at Eighth Army, who had to make sense out of the reports. The Canadians could merely watch and try to keep up with the changes.[46]

By the 20th, it became clear that some of the enemy reserve battalions had been redeployed. Tactical Air reported much movement of small groups of vehicles toward the coast at Formia and Itri. *II/276*, attached to *15th Pz.Gr. Division*, had earlier been reported at Formia. Two battalions of *104th* and one of the *276th* were on the Rapido *(which merges into the Gari/Garigliano Rivers)* between a low ridge of hummocks and the Liri. By the 24th, the presence of all units of *114 Jäger Division* was confirmed, and on the 27th *15th Pz.Gr. Division* was reported to have been withdrawn.[47] In summary, the Canadian attempt to cross the Liri would be opposed by one machine gun and four infantry battalions, all from separate formations.

Though Canadian armour and artillery were to be in action in the breaching of the Gustav Line, the main weight of the Canadian assault was reserved for the Hitler Line. The defences of this line were first described in the Corps Intsum for May 1st, reflecting the great amount of work done by the Air Photo Interpreters:

> Camouflaged structures . . . clearly form the . . . main defence . . . increased to nearly two hundred . . . thirty five run roughly east to west . . . covering the approaches to Piedimonte San Germano . . . to prevent any outflanking movement from the Liri Valley up the wide reentrant commanded by Piedimonte. . . . Eleven . . . are staggered in depth behind the forward edge of the line north of Route 6. Between Route 6 and . . . where the line crosses the Liri south of Pontecorvo . . . about 9,000 yards . . . are . . . 114. . . . West of the Liri to a point just beyond San (Sant) Olivia . . . are 30. . . most . . . in the rolling country north east of San Olivia and only a few south west of Point 101 . . . [none] in front of the almost continuous line of wire except for the 35 forming the arc south of Piedimonte [where] no wire has . . . been detected. The average depth of the line . . . about 800 yards and only five . . . detected . . . west of the lateral road Aquino–Pontecorvo–San Olivia which runs roughly parallel to the front line of wire. . . . Machine gun and anti-tank gun positions . . . approximately 70 . . . also sited behind the line of wire, except in the Piedimonte area . . . a certain number found in front . . . in the triangle . . . the road Pontecorvo–San Olivia–the River Liri and the Rio Forma Questa and in the neighbourhood of the Aquino airfield.

It was not known if the Liri was an anti-tank obstacle or not.

> The wiring . . . except in the Piedimonte area, forms the front edge of the position . . . almost unbroken from the mountain slopes on the north side of the Liri to San Olivia except for the gap of Le Forme di Aquino watercourse. Small gaps . . . double apron. The anti-tank ditch is not continuous . . . connected to watercourses in the Piedimonte area.

It warned of the possible use of demolished buildings as defence works, and admitted that the location of the enemy gun lines was not yet clear but that several unoccupied sites were known. Reflecting the preoccupation with the enemy "camouflaged structures", the Intsum admitted that air photos

> do not show whether these . . . should be classified as concrete pillboxes or casemates . . . [more than large enough for two men] . . . very small elevation above ground level.

The reader could take his choice of

> emplacements with embrasures just at or above ground level, or converted cellars, or shallow emplacements with light camouflage-covered concrete pillboxes.

There were no communication trenches.

> This lack . . . and the size and known siting of the structures would seem to indicate that mutually supporting heavy infantry and /or anti-tank weapons will be . . . the structures' armament . . . the exact nature of such . . . cannot be determined from air photographs.

The Intsum's author speculated that the Monte Cairo and Torelle areas would be incorporated in the Adolf Hitler Line, and that a switchline would be set up, pivoting on Monte Cairo *(just north of Cassino)*. He suggested that the shorter "Valmontone–Avezzano Line", at the west end of the valley, would probably be used, but that the enemy would have to leave the Hitler Line first. In addition, the Intsum made the first mention of the "Gothic Line", which ran from Pisa to Rimini *(see Map 9)*.[48]

This was a good Planning Intsum. It covered enemy strength, positions, possible sources of reinforcement, and the special features of the defences themselves. The defence structures were completely new. Intelligence knew nothing of them, and it had learned to have a healthy respect for German field engineering ingenuity. The gaps in Corps' knowledge were openly admitted; lower echelons were warned to search for any clues that would help to fill them. The areas they were asked to cover may appear, with hindsight, to have been a bit broad, but the exact location of the Canadian attack was not yet generally revealed.

Canadian officer questioning a German prisoner near the Hitler Line, Liri Valley, 24 May 1944. (Canada. Dept. of National Defence/Library and Archives Canada, PA-114915)

On May 2nd, Corps thought *1st Parachute* and *15th Pz. Gr. Divisions* were out of the line, the latter in reserve. Maj. Kingsmill still had no firm information despite the P.W., civilians and Allied escapees who kept coming through the lines. Preparations continued. In First Canadian Division: "Maps by the thousand are pouring in. These are Capt. Prince's baby usually, but in his absence [he ran a course for the Divisional Intelligence Sections from April 27th to May 4th] . . . Capt. Lightstone is sorting . . . and arranging for their issue. . . . Grade 3 officers have not yet been [told] . . . but in handling dozens of planning and 'going' maps, it is hard not to come to conclusions."[49]

At 2300 on May 11th, the Allied barrage opened. Fourth British and Eighth Indian Divisions launched their assault boats at 2345. By the end of the first day there were shallow penetrations into the Gustav Line, but the bridgehead was still not won. The early batches of prisoners made the enemy deployment assessments clearer. There was one surprise – men from two battalions of "*Blocking Group Bode*", the *576th Pz. Gr. Regiment*, which Army thought had returned to its parent *305th Infantry Division* on the Adriatic. Eighth Army forecasts may have erred in small details, but their errors were relatively unimportant.[50]

Corps now considered that the enemy had two alternatives open to him: to eliminate the already well-established Allied bridgeheads across the Rapido, or to make a fighting withdrawal to the Hitler Line. It had seen elements of three parachute battalions, and anticipated a counter-attack (by *II/104th Pz. Gr. Regiment*). The *XIV Corps* strategic reserve (the regimental group of *200th Pz. Gr. Regiment*) was expected to be brought down from its location north of Frosinone, either to man the Hitler Line or to be committed in front of it. Tactical reconnaissance (Tac R) spotted an unusual amount of traffic on the roads.[51]

First Division's Intsum on the 15th identified 24 units in the area north of the Liri; many of them were battalions represented by only one company. Attempts were made to assess their strength. The words "hard hit" and "very hard hit" occur frequently. "The enemy defence is crumbling along the whole front." But still the Germans continued to hold around Cassino. The tank battalions of *15th Panzer, 26th Panzer,* and *90th Pz. Gr. Divisions* were reported on their way to the battlefield, but had not yet been encountered. "The enemy's main attention now seems directed at keeping *1st Parachute Division* and *100th Mountain Regiment* in the Cassino area . . . preventing any drive across Route 6 that could cut his force off. Second in his mind is a regrouping of his forces to fight a withdrawal to the Adolf Hitler Line. There is a possibility that he hopes to use the Line as a basis for his Divisional counter-attack. But he will have to hurry."[52]

German resistance stiffened. Pignataro fell on the night of the 15th. On the 16th Kesselring ordered a withdrawal to the Hitler Line. And on the 17th, Corps reported that contact had been broken. There were still no reports of reserves arriving to reinforce the new position. German deployments, reading from north to south, were: *3rd Parachute Regiment*, astride Route 6; *1st Parachute Regiment*; *115th Pz. Gr. Regiment, Schultz Group* (the regiment, less some components); two battalions of two regiments of *114th Jäger Division*; *95th Reconnaissance, 95th Anti-Tank Battalion (5th Mountain Division)*; *Alarm Company, Engineer Battalion (1st Parachute Division)*; *361st Pz. Gr. Regiment*; *576th Pz. Gr. Regiment*; remnants of *115th Pz. Gr. Regiment*; and *4th Parachute Regiment* (in reserve). Most of this information would have been obtained from prisoners, by identifying casualties and by making educated assessments. The mixture of units is significant; the German commander was clearly filling his defences with whatever troops he could get. On the 19th, Corps warned that "the momentum which had been lost . . . must be regained before the enemy has a breather to carry out the regrouping and reorganizing of which he is now badly in need".[53]

By the 20th, it was obvious that a set-piece attack on the Line would be necessary. Reconnaissance patrols explored the defences, lifting mines and checking tank routes. First Division was guardedly optimistic; the delay in the advance "gave the enemy 48 hours to move equipment and anti-tank guns up the Liri Valley. Withdrawal is imminent." On May 20th, Fifth Canadian Armoured Division issued its first and second Intsums. The first was a detailed trace of the Hitler Line sector they had been assigned; the second noted enemy movement toward Frosinone from Pontecorvo, and expressed the hope that the Germans were evacuating, swinging their defence line west of Pontecorvo to defend the Liri crossings.[54] But Corps had not made sufficient allowance for the strength of the minefield defences. Nor, although Intelligence forecasts were reasonably accurate, had it been anticipated that the Germans would move anti-tank guns to prepared positions near the "camouflaged structures".

On May 23rd, 1944, Corps saw the beginning of the end, a ". . . breach in the Hitler Line and the enemy . . . merely attempting to extricate himself". First Division, perhaps a little closer to the action, thought he was trying to hold the Canadians for 48 hours, to allow a reorganization into mobile battle groups to contain the Allied pursuit. Prisoners said that only about 80 Mk. IV tanks were deployed over the entire front. Capt. Bob Prince thought this meant that only about 25 could be deployed against First Division. That night the German order to withdraw from the Hitler Line was captured.[55]

On May 23rd, Fifth Canadian Armoured Brigade succeeded in seizing a bridgehead over the Melfa. On the 25th, an advance party from First Division also crossed the Melfa *(just east of Ceprano)*, downstream near its junction with the Liri. The Canadian Corps now had routes forward for each of its formations. Canadian patrols, which were clearing Aquino, found the withdrawal order for *1st Parachute Division's* artillery regiment. They passed it up through Intelligence to Eighth Army in time for action to be taken before the regiment had actually finished its move.[56]

The Canadians continued forward across the German front, and found themselves facing a number of "new" German units; but P.W. identifications meant little. "From now on the enemy will make our advance as difficult as possible by extensive demolitions . . . hopes to break contact with our forces tonight . . . the P.W. talk of a 15 km withdrawal." On May 31st, a sharp fight took Frosinone, held by a battalion of *134th Pz. Gr. Regiment*; four prisoners were taken. When they were interrogated by Capt. I. Tucker Burr, I.O. First Division, they spoke of a force of 200 men from *III Battalion, 721st Regiment*, who were stationed in the convent of Ticchiena, and were supported by heavy mortars.

They were supposed to have orders to hold until dark and then to withdraw. When the Loyal Edmontons attacked, they found the convent deserted.[57] On June 4th, the Canadian Corps went into Eighth Army reserve.

This phase of the Italian Campaign marked the "baptism of fire", as it were, of the Corps Intelligence Section. It was fortunate that it had a quiet period after Ortona to get established. Its best work was done in the period of preparing for the battle. As the action developed, the contribution that could be made by the higher H.Q. to the battle being fought by units in the line became smaller and smaller. This was normal. It was the Intelligence staffs at the lower levels who had to deal with the immediate problems. About May 21st, Corps, finding that its material was too voluminous, began to issue its Intsum by signal.[58] It was a short message giving estimates and movements, identifications, and short summaries of important items. It was some improvement; it reduced in volume the four pages of somewhat chatty and not always well-organized material that Army often passed still unsorted. Its transmission imposed a burden on the signals system.

It is hard not to be critical of the Intelligence component of Fifth Canadian Armoured Division. Until late May, there is nowhere in the formation's Diaries, or in those of its subordinate formations or units, either a copy of an Intelligence Summary or an indication that one had been sent out. On May 7th, following the usual morning conference ("morning prayers" in the jargon), an "I" meeting was held, chaired by the G.S.O.3. Its purpose was to keep the General Staff and the I.O.s in touch with the latest developments, as well as to "cut down on the amount of matter sent out from H.Q. and to ensure that a common "I" conclusion was reached by all". As we have seen, its first Intsum was a trace showing the defended localities in the Hitler Line. But this had no marginal notes nor any detailed assessment of the enemy deployment or his possible techniques. The written Intsum, issued later the same day, was quite short, not particularly informative, and of no relevance to the map issued earlier.

On May 27th, the G.S.O.3 ordered his I.O.s to record exactly when and where P.W. were captured, to evacuate them faster, and to try to acquire and pass back more documents and enemy equipment.[59] It surely should not have been necessary to hold the special meeting on May 7th to provide an Intelligence assessment; in every other formation H.Q. this would be done by the G.S.O.3 at each of the G.O.C.'s morning conferences. A meeting to ensure "a common 'I' conclusion" suggests that the G.S.O.3 did not control his staff. This may indeed have been the case. H.Q. Fifth Division used its Intelligence staff as a pool, detaching officers on liaison duties as needed. The G.S.O.3 never knew what staff he would have. P.W. evacuation, of course, was a constant problem, more acute in an Armoured Division than elsewhere because of the more mobile war it was designed to fight. But in the Liri Valley, the Fifth moved neither fast nor far enough to warrant special consideration. And such a reminder should not have been necessary at this stage in the campaign! It was this weakness that had been noted by Maj. Kingsmill. Now that it had become obvious, something could be done to remedy it, and Gen. Burns gave his full support to a program of training and cross-posting for the Divisional staff.

THE GOTHIC LINE TO THE PO

Except for a few individual units, the Canadians were not involved following the battle for Rome. Instead, they were taken back to the Adriatic coast. In Intelligence, Capt. W.S. Dewar left Corps on June 11th to go to the Staff College; he was replaced by Capt. J.M.E. ("Johnnie") Clarkson, M.C., from First Division. On the 20th, Capt. Burr and Lieut. D.G.E. Molnar formed the I Corps Interrogation Team, a valuable specialist unit designed to assist the small sub-section of Corps H.Q. Lieut. L.J. Pronger, of the Seaforths, came to Corps H.Q. as an I.O. (Learner). Later, in August, five Italians were attached as Intelligence Liaison Officers; three of them, Capt. U. Uieil-Perara, and Lieuts. A. Prato-Preride and C.P. Cigona, went to Fifth Armoured Division, and H.Q., 11 and 12 Brigades respectively. Lieut. Wally Lehman, from the P.W. Cage at Eighth Army, replaced Lieut. Molnar, who went to First Division as part of a switch that brought Capt. R.L. Hancock to Corps. Lieut. J. Flynn came to No. 1 Special Wireless Section.[60]

Most of the Summaries in this period covered the fighting much in the style of a daily newspaper. They gave a general review of the situation, together with items of more specific interest, such as captured equipment and enemy morale (examples of German reactions to events taken from P.W. Interrogation Reports, German propaganda, and letters). A defence overprint, which had been captured when Kesselring's H.Q. was overrun, was circulated within Corps in mid-June; it showed some of the detail of the Pisa–Rimini (Gothic) Line. Eighth Army preparations for the battle against that Line included a number of air photo sorties; the pictures were processed and circulated to H.Q. I Corps. The reports covered the entire Line but did not draw special attention to any one area. A detailed review, with corrections, was circulated on June 24th.[61] By July 26th, Corps Intelligence began serious information-gathering on the defences of that Line.

The construction of the Line, which was started in 1943 and then broken off, recommenced after Anzio, and accelerated at the beginning of June 1944. It extended some 200 miles from south of Spezia on the Ligurian coast to the Foglia River and Pesaro, on the Adriatic. It was too ambitious a project to be built in the short time available: in some places in the mountains construction had barely begun; in others, it was already a most formidable defensive work. The Official History quotes German figures for the entire Line: 2,375 machine

9. Adriatic Coast

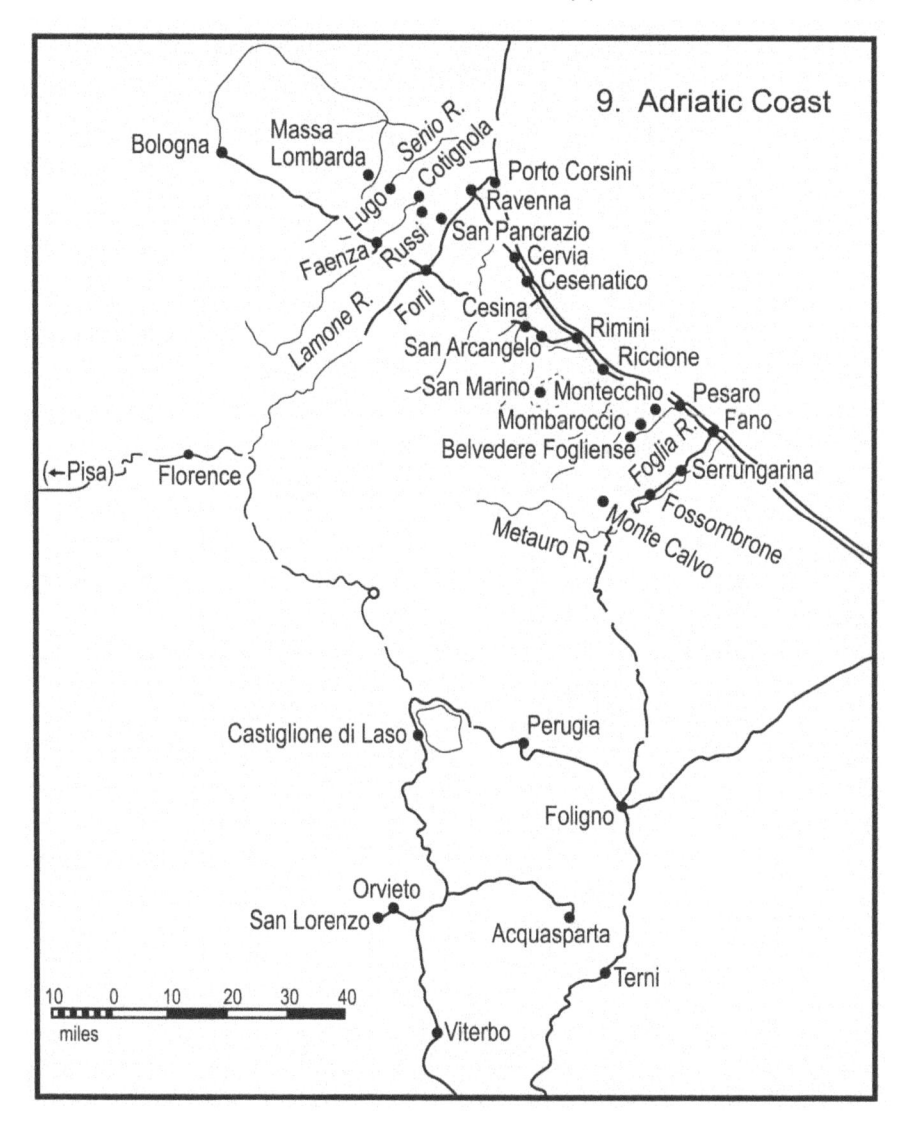

gun posts, 479 anti-tank gun, mortar, and assault gun positions, 3,604 dugouts and shelters, 16,006 rifleman's positions (of trees and branches), 72,517 Teller anti-tank mines, 23,172 "S" anti-personnel mines, 117,370 metres of wire obstacles, and 8,944 metres of anti-tank ditch. But of the 24 Panther tank turrets and 46 smaller tank gun turrets planned, only four and 18 respectively were in place.[62]

The Corps Intelligence Summary of August 14th provided Canadians with the first detailed survey of the Line:

> The past month has shown a notable thickening of the defences including the growth of outpost positions. Many villages . . . have already been cleared of civilians. . . . The eastern end . . . includes Pesaro . . . then . . . southwest, following closely . . . the road . . . Monte Calvo in Foglia then due west to Auditore and Bronzo. . . . This . . . follows the . . . Foglia River and air photographs reveal a close line of infantry positions in front of which an anti-tank ditch runs as far inland as [map reference] . . . troops available to garrison this sector are *278* and *71 Infantry Divisions* and *5 Mountain Division* with *1 Parachute Division* in reserve.[63]

The Summary listed identifications, discussed the weather that could be expected, and described captured enemy equipment. Johnnie Clarkson had obtained some of this information from the Intelligence staff of the Polish Corps, who were in contact along the coast, and who had made careful notes of fords, bridges, diversions around demolitions, roads, tracks, and minefields.

On August 18th, a Special Intsum gave more information on German units, minefields, and activities; some of it could not be evaluated. It also gave a list of the Canadian preparations: air photos of two major areas, photographed with a 20-inch lens; gridded maps of five areas; and completed seven-sheet mosaics on a scale of 1:1,500 of two other areas. Delivery was promised for between the 20th and 24th of August. The western half of a series of obliques from Pesaro to a depth of 15 miles had already been flown; the remainder was expected to be completed soon and would cover the whole Line. Maps were issued in four scales: 1:100,000, some of them layered (elevations in different colours for easy reading); 1:50,000 (not adequate for artillery but good for general use); 1:25,000, fully revised and accurate; and a few 1:25,000 with overprints of enemy defence data. On the 19th, Corps thought that the enemy "will withdraw to the far bank of the Metauro . . . though he may . . . fight rearguard actions to get his troops across. Otherwise he does not seem to be unduly concerned over what he evidently considers is purely a local push." Civilians crossing the lines on the left flank (the inland end of the line) were telling both sides what they had seen in the enemy camp. The Official History states that the confident feeling that the enemy would be surprised was justified.[64]

First Division, which would be directly concerned in the attack, detailed the enemy deployments: *278th Infantry Division*, with *278 Fusilier* and *I/993 Battalions* – from the coast to just short of Mondolfo; *II/993, I/992, II/994,* and *I/994 Battalions* – in succession to the left; *525 Heavy Anti-Tank Battalion, 914 Assault Gun Brigade*, and elements of *242 Assault Gun Brigade* were in support, equipped with 75 mm, 105 mm, and self-propelled guns; *71st Infantry Division*, with *II/ 211 Battalion* – on the seaward end of their line to Barchi; *II/191* held Montalfolto; *II/194* held the divisional right flank; *II/171* was the Army reserve in the area; *III/194*, mostly Russians, was digging in the Gothic Line. On the right flank, in the mountains: *5th Mountain Division*, with *85th* and *100th Mountain Regiments*. This Division had suffered least, and was believed to be well up in strength, with high morale.

Minefields were laid in the San Maria area, between the railway, Route 16, and the Foglia River, as well as along the right bank of the Foglia in the area of Montebakko to Chiusa Nova. The Line was anchored on Pesaro and organized for all-round defence. It was continuous, reaching as far as Caprazzino, and strongest from north of the flat valley of the Foglio to Belvedere Fogliense, where the foothills began. It had a long anti-tank ditch, casemates and pillboxes, wire entanglements, and minefields. But little concrete had been used, and it was not deep (i.e., from front to rear), especially in the sector east of Montecchio. The Division's objective was the 13-mile Pesaro–Belvedere sector; its defences overlooked the flat valley to the south and reminded Division of the Sangro. The river had few bridges, but was not considered to be a continuous tank obstacle; though it had broken stretches of steep banks, it was fordable at several points. The defences were described as of "the usual type"; sited either to cover the approaches to the Foglia from the south or the roads running through the Line itself. Reconnaissance had found 20 casemates and a three mile stretch of mines, laid at least three months earlier, running from just west of Montecchio to the river. This field was made up of over-lapping panels of mines, 50 feet wide and about seven feet apart, with 6 or 7 rows of mines, 7 or 8 feet apart, in each. A second small field was identified near the anti-tank ditch. The wire could not always be traced, but had probably been strung around all 11 groups of defensive positions. Additional wire had been erected, with indications that anti-personnel mines had been laid underneath it. Few mortar positions were found. Further defences were being constructed and those already started were nearing completion. Troops were warned about the Panther turrets and the 88 mm gun positions.[65]

Gen. Burns planned his attack in four phases: the establishment of a bridgehead over the Metauro; an advance to the Foglia; a breaching of the Gothic Line beyond it; and the break-out battle for Rimini. First Division was to handle the first two phases and be joined by Fifth Division at the Foglia. Exploitation was to take place as circumstances permitted.[66]

In the final days before the assault ". . . the Germans are pulling two full Divisions out . . . presumably to go to France . . . in reserve . . . north . . . divisions . . . in Italy are . . . about 60% of their normal strength." On the 20th, Corps reported a rearguard action south of Pesaro, mainly by the *994th Pz. Gr. Regiment*. But, what was more significant, it had heard reports that *1st Parachute Division* was in the area. On the 22nd, it focused attention on news that was very relevant to Phase 3 of the Corps Commander's plan: "The enemy are presumably on the high ground from Serrungarina to Saltara to the Monte Giove ridge behind the Via Flaminia [Route 72] . . . he will undoubtedly fight along the ridge if he wants to keep us forward of the Gothic Line defences for more than 24 hours . . . his only alternative unless he is willing for us to embroil his reserve *1st Parachute Division* before *278th Division* can be extricated. His

Canadians were ordered to stay and to maintain pressure. From late September through October 1944, they advanced steadily in a succession of small actions, seldom more than battalion-sized, fought to gain immediate tactical advantage.

Once again, these small actions shifted the weight of Intelligence analysis on to the battalion and brigade staffs while the higher formations tried to find a pattern that would enable Corps to throw its full strength at the enemy's weak spots. On September 27th, Kingsmill noted that: "for many days . . . the enemy has been picking a line which . . . he would permit us to reach without too much resistance. . . . If . . . the line of the day was threatened he would put up a stiff resistance to slow us down. During the night, he would withdraw." By resisting stubbornly on one flank and letting the other one withdraw, he was able to turn ". . . our line of advance . . . in other words, despite our preponderance, we were letting him keep the initiative. If we merely follow up his withdrawal he will succeed in extricating most of his forces. . . . If we push him back faster than he wishes . . . we will upset his time-table and bring disaster to some of his forces. We have not succeeded in doing this . . . we must hit hard at one spot, penetrating faster than his elastic front can stretch."[72]

On September 28th, the enemy had withdrawn to the Fiumicino, and by October 4th he had "succeeded in establishing himself . . . covered by strong outposts . . . particularly at Savignano" *(nine miles northwest of Rimini)*. Elements of nine divisions had been identified, none of them above half-strength and some below one-third. But despite this, "there is no sign that they are selling out the Italian theatre. . . . It would be logical to fall back to a winter line – the Garda–Adige." There were many rumours that the enemy intended to withdraw to the line of the Po or to a Venetian defence line in front of it, but these could not be verified. Some photo sorties had been flown on September 20th, but adverse weather now prevented them from being up-dated.[73]

On October 5th, Corps learned that the Fiumicino was merely the outpost line, and that the enemy was digging in in-depth behind it. Flooding was reported along the coast, and Kingsmill believed that he was probably hoping to use water to hold ground in places where he did not have enough troops to conduct a normal defence. The next four days were uneventful, but: "During the pause . . . due to bad weather the enemy has had time to [reorganize]. . . . The line-up [given in an earlier paragraph] is mostly theory." On the 11th: "due to our neighbor's advance [46th Infantry Division] . . . the enemy . . . readjusted his line in the Savignano area. . . . By tonight the . . . Line . . . will probably conform to the Scolo Rigossa. P.W. from *2 Company, 39 German Air Force Regiment* [think] that this is the start of a planned withdrawal behind the Po . . . two days ago the tanks and guns had been withdrawn. . . . The Po . . . is too long for his diminished forces to hold. . . . The Adige line offers him a better chance . . . is short and inland has the observation." By the next day, "a number of prisoners and civilians crossing the line reported paratroopers going to sea in barges [at Porto Corsini, near Ravenna].... If true, this may be a move back of 'B' echelon [logistics support] and other heavy equipment."[74]

By the 15th, P.W. had given Corps identifications for six divisions: *1st Parachute, 162nd (Turcoman), 26th Panzer, 90th Pz.Gr., 114th Jäger* and *278th Infantry*, and *39th* and *40th Luftwaffe (Field)* and *15th Gr. Regiment*. A P.W., a former steward in an officers' mess, explained their slowness in retiring. He had heard senior officers talking about the plan; they were so short of gasoline and transport that the withdrawal of the rear echelon troops and installations was behind schedule. The forward troops had therefore to hold until the others were clear.[75]

On October 28th, I Corps went into reserve. Intelligence summaries then adopted the format used after the fall of Rome, a newspaper-style review of the front. But the respite did not last long. Bologna had to be taken. Phase One required the Canadians to capture crossings over the river obstacles and to take Ravenna, on the Adriatic flank. During the first half of November, Canadian units operated south of Ravenna, where they came into contact with Italian partisans operating in the area; under agencies, however, that were outside Canadian control.

On the night of November 19th, the leader of the partisans in the marshes north of Ravenna, Lieut. Arrigo Boldrini, alias "Major Bülow", was brought into the Canadian lines by boat. Maj. Kingsmill discussed with him the advantages of working with Canadian troops. He was promised arms and ammunition, clothing, and food. Capt. D.M. Healy was given radio equipment and sent with him as Liaison Officer. After two attempts, he and the partisans with him were landed north of Porto Corsini and, with some difficulty, reached their camp on a small island in the marsh. As soon as the news that aid was on its way became known, co-operation was good and useful information was obtained, particularly from old and infirm persons who could wander more or less at will without exciting German suspicion. But their movements were uncontrollable, and Healy had to sift their reports carefully before radioing them back to Corps.[76]

Capt. Norman Rowe, O.C. I Canadian Corps Mobile Air Photo Interpretation Unit (West) Detachment, of Eighth Army's A.P.I.S. (nicknamed "Miaow"), was asked to get photographs showing the state of the Senio bridges near Cotignola and Lugo. No high-level photography was available. He therefore set off in the Corps "Whizzer" (Auster light liaison aircraft) with F/O Jim Rees. The plane crossed the lines at 1,000 feet, then dived steeply down towards Cotignola to circle over the town at 500 feet. The Germans were surprised and, for almost a minute, Capt. Rowe was able to take photos of the bridge and town without hindrance. Then the "Jerries" opened up. The "Whizzer" left in a hail of machine gun, 20 mm, and 37 mm anti-aircraft fire, made a quick turn over Lugo, dropped to 250 feet and hedge-hopped home. The photographs of the Cotignola bridges were excellent, but those of Lugo were a little blurred. Capt. Rowe was undecided whether it was the aircraft or himself that had shaken the camera.[77]

The Army plans for the resumption of the main thrust northward required the Canadians to cover the right flank, to capture Russi, outflank Ravenna, and then advance through Lugo to establish a bridgehead over the Santerno near Massa Lombarda. Two divisions lay opposite the Canadian front: *356th Infantry*, to about San Pancrazio; and *114th Jäger* holding the sector from Pancrazio to the coast. Both were part of a newly-formed *LXXIII Corps*, and both were believed to be under-strength in artillery and tanks. All known reserves had been assigned to *LXXVI Panzer Corps* in the Faenza Sector facing V Corps and the Polish Corps.[78]

The Planning Intsum for November 27th read:

> The enemy started [to prepare to evacuate] Ravenna and the area east of the Santerno, the next logical line . . . his guns started to go back several nights ago according to the civilians crossing the lines. Troops started thinning out in the coastal sector but . . . remained fairly strong directly south of Ravenna. . . . Then came the rains and our offensive stopped. . . . The threat of being cut off . . . diminished. He managed to stabilize the . . . line between the Montone and the Lamone Rivers, northeast of Faenza. As long as this . . . remains secure, and providing we do not cross the Montone north of this line . . . there is no need to evacuate Ravenna . . . no major change in . . . *114 Jäger Division*. . . . Due to the unsuitability of the soil for digging, a greater use of buildings and above ground field works may be expected. [He was not expected to fight in Ravenna; all his defences were in the outskirts.] If we attack north towards Russi we . . . endanger . . . *114 Jäger Division* . . . even now, according to civilians, troops are leaving the area between Ravenna and Russi. . . . It is therefore believed that the enemy will evacuate Ravenna when we capture Russi and our first indications . . . will be the sounds of demolitions.[79]

Attacks in the Albereto area gained Corps a marked map showing the headquarters of *356th Regiment*; it was duly dealt with by the artillery.

Since the only area in which the Canadians could attack was just as obvious to the Germans, Corps made several attempts to deceive them. In one such attempt, on November 29th, Maj. F.K. Reesor, then G.S.O.2 (Liaison), borrowed from Eighth Army Psychological Warfare Branch a set of "Sonic Warfare" equipment – phonograph, amplifier, and four loudspeakers. His G.S.O.3, Capt. I.A. Hamer, obtained stock recordings of tank noises, machine gun noises, launching assault boats, artillery concentrations, and so forth. It was taken up to 1 Brigade's lines, where its deployment and operation, with added pyrotechnics as gunfire simulators, provoked a violent German reaction. It was unpleasant for the Brigade; but Corps later learned that the display did draw German attention away from the main point of the attack.[80]

The partisans were to engage a German force, cause casualties, and draw the Germans from Ravenna. This would not only weaken the garrison, but would also give Corps some idea of the size of the German mobile reserve. On the night of November 29th, they deployed about 150 men in small boats down the canals, landed some 500 yards from the German billets at La Fabrica Vecchia, and crept up and opened fire. The Germans replied with machine guns, two of which were silenced by the partisans before they withdrew. They suffered one wounded; there is no record of German casualties. On a second occasion, on December 2nd, about 50 of the 900 men "Bülow" claimed as his strength fought hard but briefly before vanishing into the marshes. Another group destroyed the 60-man German garrison of Porto Corsini, a number of outposts, and some German patrols that had chased them into the marshes. By December 8th, they were exhausted and were withdrawn to Ravenna, where they added to the labours of the Field Security Officer. About 30 were then assigned as scouts to Fifth Armoured Division for the advance beyond Ravenna.[81]

One of the problems of planning the advance had been a lack of adequate photo cover. Because of the ground fog and adverse weather, no photo coverage could be flown between November 22nd and December 2nd, a situation which prompted a frustrated Corps I.O. to write:

> The R.A.F. is grounded / The Kitties and the Spits/ With mud up to its hub caps/ The air offensive quits/ All huddled on their runways/ The mighty Air Force sits/ Just as useful to the Army / As the well-known bull with tits.[82]*

On the 2nd, skies cleared sufficiently for a mission which, it was hoped, would give large-scale cover to a depth of about 15,000 yards. The pictures were rushed to Corps M.A.I.U., where they arrived about 0100. The interpreters produced target lists and engineer intelligence, and issued their reports on the afternoon of the 3rd. However, the attack, which had started on the 2nd, failed in the face of determined German counter-attacks. The Canadians regrouped and the plan was restudied. Ravenna fell on December 4th, and the subsequent advance against the left wing of *114th Jäger Division* reached the Lamone.

The second attempt to cross the Lamone took place on December 10th. It was successful. Advances were made against the *356th Infantry* and *114th Jäger Divisions*. The Commander, *LXXIII Corps*, had few reserves, but managed to muster a scratch force of the reconnaissance battalion of *90th Pz. Gr. Division* and a battalion of *278th Infantry Division*, which he threw into the gap between the *356th* and *114th*. Further elements from *98th Infantry Division* were sent in on the following day, and the front stabilized. Attempts to expand the bridgehead over the Lamone continued. Gen. Dostler, Commander *LXXIII Corps*, had laid down the principles applicable to the defensive battle he had to fight, in an order dated December 18th, but, although a copy of his order was captured, Canadian troops could not do much to counter them. The close,

---

* "Kitties" = Curtis P. 40B Kittyhawks; "Spits" = Spitfires

hand-to-hand fighting meant, once again, that every yard had to be won at a price. On the 20th, the advance reached the Senio and there it stopped, except for two areas east of the river which had to be cleared before the winter line could be established.

Intelligence carefully watched the many German order-of-battle changes, reported on developments discovered in the theatre and elsewhere, and speculated on possible German future plans. But its work was irrelevant, because I Corps was redeployed to North-West Europe. The directive covering the move was received on February 4th, 1945 (the Corps Commander, Gen. Foulkes, had heard of the intention in late January and had already started his H.Q. planning).[83] The last Intsum in the Italian theatre was a routine, short paper, No. 237, dated February 10th, 1945.[84]

Although the Canadian Corps had left, a few Canadians remained. One of these, Lieut. Ian N. Fleming, took part in an Intelligence coup that was anything but routine. Ian was with "R" Section M.A.I.U. West at Eighth Army H.Q., an attachment which had been authorized because of his detailed knowledge of the front.

One morning in February 1945, a heavy fall of snow occurred on the German front between midnight and 0300. When the photographic sorties, which were flown as soon as it was light enough to see, were brought in to the interpreters, they showed everything that had moved during the night. By careful study, R Section was able to pinpoint every gun, mortar, H.Q., telephone line, and dump – and even dugouts – by the tracks left by men and vehicles. With the co-operation of the artillery, and of course the R.A.F., M.A.I.U. was able to present a complete plan of the German front and rear. With this information, the resulting engagement cut all the line communications between battalions. These were unable to get in touch with their flanking units, and surrendered.[85] This is a classic example of intelligence gained and applied to contribute to a victory in the field.

The Italian Campaign was the first operation since 1918 in which a Canadian force had been in sustained action against a real enemy. It was highly trained, it was as experienced as it was possible for a force to be, but it had never been tested under continuous combat conditions. It is difficult to assess the contribution of the several components of Intelligence. Intelligence, by its nature, rarely sees the "big breakthrough", or suddenly discovers the one vital piece of information. Rather, it is the steady and painstaking compilation of small items of information, by keeping records within a unified and structured system that enables them to be compared, used, and built up into the larger, more accurate picture, that determines Intelligence efficiency. Each level is able to contribute something which adds to the sum of knowledge the commander needs.

Apart from a few errors which have been cited, in particular, those in Fifth Armoured Division's early experience, we find no indication that the I Canadian

Corps Intelligence organization was guilty of any major failure. It was a relaxed but alert organization. It enjoyed a close personal relationship with its respective commanders. If there was a weakness, it is the one that is always more apparent to hindsight than to the vision of the time. It is that the battalions and regiments in the line may not have had as much detail on their enemy as they should have had.

I Corps Intelligence was fortunate in its relationship with the experienced Eighth Army. Its procedures, and many of its assessments, owed a great deal to the assistance of its colleagues. When it moved to North-West Europe, it had to fit into a Canadian organization which had functioned as a team for nearly a year. Before we show how the Corps adjusted to that change, we must again return to 1943 to tell the story of Intelligence (b) and the security problems it met during the Italian Campaign.

9.
AGENTS AND REFUGEES: I(B) IN ITALY

British Third Division was originally selected for the invasion of Sicily. It had begun work at a Planning H.Q. at Norfolk House when First Canadian Division replaced it. Consequently, the Canadians inherited both the preparatory work and also the measures to protect it. Capt. Bill Cooper, No. 1 F.S. Section, was the Force Security Officer, with full responsibility for all Security arrangements. His assistant was Maj. Horatio (Con) Boddington, of M.I.5, who had been sent by the Inter-Service Security Board (I.S.S.B.) especially for the task. In Bill's words, Con was one of Britain's finest Security Officers. His advice and help were incalculable, his experience of Counter-Intelligence was phenomenal, and his contacts at all the ports, and with staff officers in the many H.Q. who were in a position to help, made Bill's Security task that much easier.

In all planning there is information for which distribution must be kept very limited. This is required by the nature of the task and has no connection at all with rank. As the Security regulations said: "No man is entitled solely by virtue of his rank or position to have access to classified material." To control this access, even beyond the protection that applied to the "Most Secret" category, warning codes were used; "XO" and "YO", the latter protecting the more important material. Capt. Cooper made sure that the persons who were to have access to this material had been cleared; that they had signed the special form acknowledging that they were aware of its importance and the regulations for its protection; and that they were issued the special identity tag permitting access to the Restricted Area in which the documents were held. Their names were recorded in the Intelligence Office at C.M.H.Q. Capt. Cooper ensured that the list was kept up-to-date. General access to the building was controlled through special passes. Visitors were escorted by six Canadian Provost Corps N.C.O.s under the direction of two F.S. N.C.O.s.

Capt. Cooper arranged for War Office passes for Planning H.Q. staff. He also maintained Security liaison with many officers at C.M.H.Q., Scottish Command, I British Corps, H.Q. First Canadian Army, the I.S.S.B. (which co-ordinated Security arrangements), M.I.9 (for Escape and Evasion information and equipment), M.I.5 Operations (for Counter-Intelligence), Civil Affairs (Military Operations 11) and with officers at the War Office responsible for cover plans. This list illustrates the wide range of Security interest and responsibility.

The units were too widely dispersed to conceal movement to a port of embarkation. Security therefore confined itself to protecting the sailing date, the objective, and the date of the actual assault. Units were assigned serial numbers and code names to cover their identity. They were ordered to load tactically, as though for an exercise. But if speculation became too accurate, or a leak had occurred, Capt. Cooper was authorized to release "Corsica" as the cover objective.

Censorship was an early problem. It was not imposed at units until the Force actually embarked; but prior arrangements had to be made through M.I.12, the British Military Censorship authority, for coverage of civilian mail in Scotland. The Canadian Army Postal Service arranged for base censorship of all mail that passed through its hands. When Capt. Cooper asked for a supply of Unit Censor Stamps, the Canadian Army had none. The War Office section responsible, C.2.C., told him that Stamps had never been issued to Canadian units; it, and the Canadians, had obviously forgotten 1940. Capt. Cooper asked I.S.S.B. for a block of Stamps (they were numbered) to be given to Maj. Walter at C.M.H.Q. He, in his turn, sent them to the F.S.O. Capt. Cooper then issued them to units, made a list of all the allotments, and sent it to Maj. Walter to pass to I.S.S.B. until after "D" Day, when it would be returned to C.2.C.[1] The control arrangements were complicated. They were designed not only to protect the Stamps, but also the order-of-battle of the units to which they were sent. The risk of information falling into unfriendly hands always existed.

Two Security instructions were issued to every officer and man involved in the planning of Operation HUSKY. The first, on April 25th, was general; the second, on April 30th, gave the cover story:

> All formations of First Canadian Army are in succession undertaking advanced training in combined operations in the following order: First . . . Division and 1 . . . Army Tank Brigade, Third . . . Division then Second Canadian Division. . . . Certain administrative units. . . . This is part of the training programme . . . to give . . . experience. . . . Staffs are in London for refresher "planning course".

The instruction emphasized that the story was perfectly normal and logical, that it was imperative that it be adhered to in all conversations with people not in the know, and that any action taken or instructions issued were to be given as naturally as though the story was factual. All requests for Intelligence were to be made through the G.S.O.3 (Int), H.Q. First Division. Everyone was warned not to buy pamphlets, travel guides, language books, etc., from book stores, but to order them through the G.S.O.3 (Int).[2]

A third instruction, on May 15th, told the troops that secrecy depended on the absolute discretion of every officer and man with respect to the port of embarkation, name of ship, sailing date, and destination. It warned that offenders would be punished. The use of public and other telephones and the despatch of telegrams from the port were prohibited, except under stringent controls. Censorship arrangements and the issue of special envelopes were explained. Letters could only be posted aboard ship. Personnel were warned not to talk to stevedores, not to use cameras or radio sets, not to receive visitors, and not to make any reference to their unit in any official message or on any packing case, beyond the serial it had been given. Divisional patches were to be removed from clothing. Equipment and vehicle signs were to be covered. (And, in fact, First Division's vehicles were left in a park in Scotland and driven back by drivers dressed as First Division men.) Rear parties were to deal with outstanding bills and contracts. Ships' Security Officers were assigned to control access to the ship and contact between the troops and dock staffs, to supervise markings and mail, to protect classified material, and, finally, to give lectures to the troops on security.[3] In spite of these many and stringent precautions, the people of Greenock and Gourock turned out in large numbers to wave the convoy goodbye.

Additional security training was given on board ship. All troops were cautioned not to take any Operations Order or any private papers ashore. 1st Army Tank Brigade made this point crystal-clear: "We do not want any Op Order captured after the Dieppe fashion". All ranks were reminded to give no more than "Name, Rank, and Number" to the enemy if they were captured and not to talk to other P.W., especially if they were strangers. Troops were reminded that civilians often pretended to knowledge that they did not have. Unit Security Officers were again reminded of their responsibilities.[4]

These warnings were essential. The Germans were known to have Intelligence networks in North Africa. If they had organized a similar system of "stay behind" agents in Sicily and Italy, it was clear that Allied Security would have to act alone, without help from any indigenous counter-espionage services until the Italians surrendered.[5]

No. 1 F.S. Section was briefed to rendezvous after the landing at H.Q. 103 Sub-Area, a beach command post. The men were told to get their motorcycles in order and on the road, to report to their brigades and, once there, plan to exploit the F.S. targets. They were on no account to get in the way of the attacking troops, but to help the Ship Security staffs check the ship and, if they were ashore, to pick up documents should a withdrawal become necessary. They were to remember that interpreters would be there to deal with civilians. As it turned out, most of their equipment went to the bottom of the Mediterranean during an Axis submarine attack on July 5th. In that sinking, Gunner Ruben Bennett, the O.C.'s popular batman-driver, was missing. Fortunately, he was picked up, and rejoined later at Modica.

Capt. Cooper's Section landed at "Roger" sector, Pachino Beachhead, with the Divisional reserve.[6] Bill Cooper was one of the first ashore on the 10th, with Cpl. Smith and L/Cpl. Freypons for 1 C.I.B.; Cpl. Robert Hubbel and L/Cpl. Carl Zunti went to 2 C.I.B. C.S.M. Dave MacAuley brought Sgt. Robert Fowler, Cpl. Peter Johnston and L/Cpl. Edel Direnfeld ashore on the 11th. Sgt.

Jack Porter, Cpls. Bruce Lefebvre and Bill Trueman, and L/Cpls. "Red" Burnett and Jack Hadden came ashore on the 13th. On July 11th, in mid-afternoon, 3 Brigade captured Ispica. On the 12th, Johnston and Direnfeld checked it, and moved on to Rosolini the next day. Because the surprise had been complete, a good deal of useful information was obtained. On the 14th, the Section H.Q. was set up in the Casa del Fascio in Modica, the first big town to be taken. But here the Fascist Security authorities had had time to clear out all useful documents before the town fell. They had disappeared at Ragusa also, as had the Segretario Federale of the Province, a man who was "wanted". The Section did pick up the Prefect of the Province and three men whose names were on the Allied "Black List" – a list of Intelligence agents, prominent Fascist officials, and persons likely to constitute an organized danger to Security. It had been compiled before the invasion and was kept up-to-date as new information came in to I(b). All prisoners were sent back to Corps H.Q. on the beach.

The round-up of Fascists inspired the leader of the local clandestine Sicilia Libra movement to propose to the Section that Britain should take over the island. Numerous dramatic meetings, usually at night, were held between Capt. Cooper and the group. C.S.M. Dave MacAulay trusted none of them and the Section became very nervous during the meetings. The proposal was sent to XXX Corps and nothing more was heard of it. The Sicilia Libra, however, were most useful in identifying wanted persons, many of whom would otherwise have escaped arrest.

In one episode, the Section found itself in the forefront of an advance. In the strategic plan, Enna, an important town south of Leonforte, was to be left to the Americans advancing on the Canadian left flank. This did not appeal to Gen. Simonds. Through his G.S.O.1, Lt.-Col. George Kitching, he ordered Capt. Cooper and two scout cars of 4 Princess Louise Dragoon Guards to do something about it. They went up the road, obviously mined at the edges, met and dealt with a German rear party (the F.S. on their motorcycles felt most exposed during the exchange of fire), and arrived in Enna. Here they hoisted the Union Jack and proceeded with their normal routine of checking C.I. targets. The Americans, who arrived at the same time, were greeted cordially.

Valguarnera fell to the Canadians on July 18th, after bitter fighting. The town was chaotic; no Civil Affairs staff was available, and Gen. Simonds ordered his F.S.O., on top of his regular duties, to sort things out so that the lines of communication were clear. Capt. Cooper got the waterworks and the smashed electric light plant going and, drawing on Italian government stocks, arranged for an issue of milk to the children and of "V.D. pills" to the adults. This Civil Affairs role was to become commonplace during operations. Quite frequently, also, the Sections had to provide food and shelter for refugees. This was normally a Military Government task, but many emergency cases had to be dealt with quickly, even before the A.M.G. staff arrived. As such, it became, in many ways, a valuable adjunct to their F.S./C.I. duties.

On the 20th, so many clashes occurred between Canadians and the civilian population that members of the Section had to assist the Provost town patrols. They moved to Leonforte on the 22nd. On the 25th they arrested "a professional informant and criminal". On the 27th, they were given four interpreters; also they completed the checks of their Black List, and visited Nissoria, which had fallen on the 24th. The next day they arrested prominent Fascists in Leonforte. When Agira fell on the 28th, two N.C.O.s went forward to set up Section H.Q.; they chose the Dopolavore Locale (a workmen's club) and spent the next 10 days there.

The Section was divided into three detachments, each with its own Italian Army interpreter. One detachment went to Regalbuto, which had been severely damaged during the fighting. Its Casa del Fascio (Party office) was almost completely demolished. In Agira the detachment arrested an Italian soldier and handed the civilian who had hidden him over to Military Government. An informer told them that German paratroopers were hiding in a disused sulphur mine. Taking the informer with them, and armed with tommy guns, they found the mine and shot into the mouth of the shaft to draw fire; it was deserted. They verified a report of black marketing, and gave the material they confiscated to Allied Military Government of Italy (A.M.G.O.T.).

The Section was delighted with the systematic way the Fascists had put all their useful information on paper; it greatly simplified their work. In their first month, they checked 153 names on the Black List; all had to be verified in consultation with some of the 109 White List Sicilians known to be friendly. Many of the suspects had fled and, in so doing, may perhaps have confirmed the reasons for their inclusion on the List. Often civilians not on either List would volunteer information, but this always had to be carefully checked. Arrests were almost a daily affair; every one of them, however, meant a dangerous night drive back to the Cage. F.S. even had to take charge of a load of German P.W. which the Americans turned over to them. Suspects were usually put in the local jail, guarded by Carabinieri working under A.M.G.O.T. Arrested civilians were sent to the special civilian compounds at the Divisional, Corps, and Base P.W. Cages.[7] No stay-behind agents were arrested in Sicily. The Allies subsequently discovered that when the Germans withdrew from Tunisia, they moved their entire apparatus directly to Italy.

The control measures imposed in Sicily closely paralleled those in North Africa. As soon as territory was occupied by the Allies, A.M.G. posted proclamations imposing regulations respecting movement, curfews, and surrender of arms, explosives, and radio sets, etc. These orders provided F.S. Sections with an additional and useful weapon and were continuously enforced, mostly through the agency of the Italian police.[8]

On August 10th, the Division went into rest with Divisional H.Q. near Francofonte. Swimming, catching up on minor personal administration – and the ripening grapes – made this an idyll long remembered. On the 15th, the Section, less one detachment, was moved to Aci Castello to work with XIII British Corps, then planning for BAYTOWN.

During their last few days before BAYTOWN, they took part in a multiple raid to capture a number of prominent Fascists. The procedures used were to become routine in the months ahead. They checked the villages around their H.Q. at Aci Trezza and arrested some low-priority suspects. A.M.G.O.T. issued an order prohibiting fishing, which the Section had to enforce. With no work to do, the local population had a lot of spare time, which they unfortunately spent questioning and complaining to the Section. One day the Edmonton Regiment reported through 2 Brigade Intelligence Section that they had picked up a civilian who had struck up an acquaintance with two soldiers, offered them drinks, and asked searching questions. They took the man to the Battalion I.O., but by the time Sgts. Lefebvre and Trueman arrived, he had been released. They borrowed the C.O.'s jeep, an indication of the co-operation between the units and F.S., searched the man's home, interrogated him – in French – and found nothing incriminating. It was a frustrating incident, which Sgt. Lefebvre appreciated even less when he discovered that his pack had dropped off his motorcycle.

At this time, Eighth Army had one G.S.O.2 I(b), Maj. George de Freitas; he controlled two G.S.O.3s and two I.O.s, assigned equally between military and civil security. They had one staff sergeant, one corporal, two clerk-privates, and four drivers. Corps had one G.S.O.3 I(b). Each Division, Corps, and Army H.Q. had its own Section. In addition, there were a number of British Port Sections. G.S.O.3 I(b) at XIII Corps, Capt. Frankenberg (an outstanding personality), had at his disposal Sections working with 5th British Division and with the Canadians, his own Corps Section, an Army Section, and an *ad hoc* Section headed by a Captain Interpreter with four F.S. N.C.O.s, attached to 231 (Malta) Brigade. The Divisional Sections were to land on "D" day, followed on D + 2 by the Corps Sections which would take over from them. No. 1 was allotted Reggio di Calabria, the provincial capital. It would move on to check towns as its Division cleared them.

During the Sicilian Campaign, Capt. Cooper had allotted detachments from his Section to Brigades.[9] This system had not worked, mainly because the Section targets were mostly in the towns, while the fighting took place in the open country around them. It was changed. For the invasion, Cooper was required to put his Section into more than one landing craft. Accordingly, he formed a reconnaissance party of himself, an interpreter, and one N.C.O., all in their new Section jeep. The C.S.M. brought over the main party in the Section vehicle, and a rear party of a corporal and two lance-corporals on motorcycles was to follow. The total strength of Cooper's group was two officers (himself and

Lieut. Morgan), 13 F.S. N.C.O.s, two batmen-drivers, three N.C.O. interpreters (Sgts. Champendale, Brattisany, and Ribolla), and one Italian fatigueman.[10] They were still short of vehicles, and were forbidden to take any of the Italian equipment with them because of the difficulty of maintaining it. They stripped the tires from six of their eight Fiats, and persuaded a friendly unit to load these tires, a stock of selected engines and spares, and one complete Fiat into an empty truck going to Reggio. Once there, they were easily able to acquire "new" vehicles.

Their duties were straightforward. The reconnaissance party had to contact the local police, get office space and quarters for the Section, contact the local A.M.G., if any, report the office location to higher authority, and have the Military Police place the necessary route signs. The Section would then search the objectives, putting their own guards on them when appropriate; there were no spare troops to call on. Their targets included Fascist Headquarters, where papers and files would give them the names of the local Fascists and, equally important, of those opposed to Fascism. The Municipio, or Town Hall, provided names of the local inhabitants, and advised them not only on who was important, but also on municipal problems that could have a bearing on A.M.G.O.T. affairs. In the larger towns, they would find political records at the Questura, or Detective Headquarters, in the offices of the Fascist Secret Police (O.V.R.A.) political intelligence organization, and even in the Carabinieri (CC. RR.) barracks. The Post Office would have material to interest the Censors. In camera stores, they often discovered films that were useful to the I(a) staffs. The Civil Prison often had political prisoners who were friendly to the Allies, and it could also be used to house suspects. The Royal Automobile Club of Italy (R.A.C.I.) had maps; garages augmented the transport pools. Until A.M.G. arrived, the Section had to protect public utilities, which were prime targets for sabotage. They "found" stocks of pistols, cameras, and, on occasion, vehicles, which were used to pay debts among the staff and units from which they obtained help.

Recording and filing the results of these varied activities were burdens that no small mobile Section could handle. When the Italians became allies, the Questura were given charge of records. But they first had to make a difficult mental switch from hunting anti-Fascists to hunting Fascists; and, as they were not completely trusted, their work had to be carefully verified. The Section was then billeted with Rear Administrative or Rear Divisional H.Q., an arrangement that had many drawbacks. Capt. Cooper began to negotiate for equipment and a cook to make him self-sufficient.

At Col. Felix Walter's request, Cooper prepared a paper describing his experiences. It was designed to give Canadian F.S. staffs in the U.K. and in Canada concrete facts on which to base more realistic planning and training. He stressed co-ordination, mobility, and centralized control; he pointed out that Sections could not operate alone and that they worked best in towns. He recommended that they should be controlled by Army instead of being tied to one formation. He made a number of suggestions for facilitating Section administration. Most, but not all, of his proposals were accepted officially and put into practice. F.S. owes a great debt to Bill Cooper.[11]

After clearing up Reggio di Calabria, the Section sent detachments to Gallina. By September 8th, it was relieved by the Corps Section, and moved on over narrow roads blocked by demolitions. That night, in Delianuova, it heard the news of the Italian surrender; "The people are wild with excitement and the streets . . . are thronged with hitherto hidden people . . . kissing one another, and usually accompanied by cries of 'Allies, comrades, *amici*'." No church bells rang, however, for Cooper had banned them; ostensibly to prevent signalling, actually to permit sleep after 0400. At Locri, where a report on an O.V.R.A. chief resulted in a 1 F.S. raid that arrived just too late to catch him, the Section heard of the imminent fall of Catanzaro, a major C.I. target. Losing no time, it reached the town as the enemy was leaving and before the P.L.D.G. It carefully cross-checked the Questura files, found in them evidence of a connection with the O.V.R.A., and was able to break the code both organizations were using. This was an important achievement, for since the Questura was on the Allied side, while the O.V.R.A. was opposed, it eliminated a serious leak in Security arrangements. The O.V.R.A. had employed tight security, but the finds enabled Eighth Army to arrest many people, and so eliminate that agency as a threat.

At Catanzaro, the Section arrested "a pro-German, Italian Colonel who had been the Maresciallo of Strongoli". As the Section drove to Rossano, through the small towns, it was welcomed with a "terrific reception from the populace, much of it mere curiosity as we were the first troops in." At Rossano it found a whole Italian division still carrying its arms. "Coming into town with a distinguished person under arrest has its good points – today everyone is nice to us . . . as they consider us the people with great powers".

The Section was beginning by now to feel the effects of the climate, the roads, and the pace. Spare parts for the vehicles were not available and there was a real shortage of inner tubes and patching kits for motorcycle tires. Mr Morgan, the attached interpreter, had sand-fly fever; the F.S.O., and Sgts. Porter, Johnston, and Trueman (who was already limping after hitting a dog with his motorcycle) all had jaundice and went to hospital. Most of them, in fact, were sick at least once during this period. But they had one idyllic day in late September: "It is a change being out here in the open after having worked in the towns for so long. The blue sky is speckled with cool, fleecy clouds; the rough mountains have been replaced by more regular large hills; some slopes are wooded and clothed in a variety of autumn colours . . . others lie bare. . . . Above us, half hidden in the trees and undergrowth, are the vehicles and bivouacs of Div. H.Q. and music from some signals radio finds its way to our little clearing; from below the tinkle of the bells from the peasants' goats comes drifting to us. . . . And now the best sound of all, the clang of the kitchen utensils, even if it does mean just another Army meal."

At Matera, the Italians, now allies, demanded equal status. At official levels, there was a good deal of misunderstanding and lack of co-operation; it came from ". . . these people feeling that they preferred to have an officer deal with them." At the personal level they were friendly "in a very sincere way". They were eager to tell horror stories of German atrocities and to claim that they themselves had rebelled and had suffered hardships. With the help of the local police, known Fascists were arrested, "with the populace following in dumb surprise; some with a look of satisfaction and always a few, naturally, with looks that make one say: 'I'm staying in after dark tonight'".

German *Sicherheitsdienst* (S.D.) agents first began to appear during the static period that followed the link-up of Fifth and Eighth Armies. After the failure of the Abwehr to obtain early warning of the Sicilian and Salerno operations, German Intelligence made many changes which were reflected in an increased use of *S.D.* agents in military espionage and sabotage. Many of them were captured, chiefly as a result of interrogations done at the Refugee Interrogation Posts (R.I.P.s) set up near Army P.W. Cages, to which F.S., Provost, and even the forward units themselves sent everyone who crossed through the lines. These R.I.P.s were staffed by a Security Officer, two F.S. N.C.O.s, and one or more S.I.M./C.S. (Italian Military Counter-Espionage). Refugees were given a brief interrogation on arrival. Those considered to be suspect were sent for more detailed interrogation, sometimes even as far as the C.S.D.I.C. On the whole, however, the quality of agents was poor. Many gave themselves up voluntarily; only a few maintained their story under close interrogation, and even these confessed when they were confronted with evidence obtained from other agents.[12]

Campobasso fell on October 4th. It had long been planned as a Forward Maintenance Centre for XIII Corps, a key administrative point, and a rest centre for troops. The security threat, therefore, was not only the usual danger of enemy espionage and sabotage, but also, as always where there were troops, subversion. The Section H.Q. was set up in the Casa del Fascio; since accommodation was in short supply, it had to repel frequent attempts to evict it or to billet other units with it. The Fascista Federale, who had occupied the house, was reported to have fled with the Germans; it took the Section four days to find and arrest him. His relatives protested, as many others did when more arrests were made. The Town Major (A.M.G.) succumbed to some of the pleas and tried to exert pressure on the F.S.O. Another prisoner, the former Maresciallo of the town, was released by higher authority, despite what the Detachment considered to be irrefutable evidence against him. Foolishly, he returned to Campobasso, was rearrested, and this time stayed "inside". Three female suspects were arrested, the first the Section had caught. The wife of one of the prisoners trumped up a charge that F.S. had stolen 4,000 lire from her house while they were searching it. She was very convincing, but the Section was able to prove its innocence.

Some forward troops turned in two men they had found in possession of radio transmitters; they produced conflicting stories and were jailed. A German officer deserter was arrested and turned over to I(a). Former Allied P.W. were collected and passed to I.S.9. A "well-informed journalist employed by the Badoglio government . . . anxious to serve the Allied cause . . . would like to have the selfish and anti-Allied intrigue going on . . . brought to light". The Section was prepared to believe him. The newly-appointed Prefetto of Campobasso became hesitant about co-operating. Eventually he went too far; a short interview with an annoyed F.S.O. changed his attitude – at least until the Section left. Around November 13th, the Section began the laborious task of vetting Italians who were seeking jobs with Allied Occupation, refugees left homeless by the German "scorched earth" policy, and those persons who wandered through Allied lines. Refugees were established in camps outside San Pietro and Carovilli, then trucked to Lucera and from there taken by train to Bari.[13] No one, however, wanted to go to Bari, and everyone wanted to carry the maximum amount of baggage. Prisoners, on the other hand, were taken back to 371 Army P.W. Cage in Foggia.

In November, I Canadian Corps arrived, with Capt. Basil Foreman, C.Int.C., a long-time F.S. officer, as G.S.O.3 I(b), and Nos. 7, 11, and 14 F.S. Sections. No. 14's transport, the *Santa Elena*, was attacked by a dozen German torpedo bombers about 20 miles north of Philippeville (now Skikda), Algeria. The ship was struck twice, and violent explosions plunged it into darkness. The 121 nursing sisters aboard were loaded into the life boats and lowered; the troops were told to abandon ship and take to the life rafts. By 2030 the ship was clear, and the men were picked up by the S.S. *Monterey* (11 C.I.B.). The *Santa Elena* was then towed into Philippeville, where she sank, taking with her the Section's kit and equipment.[14] L/Cpl. Watling became separated from the rest and, after the *Monterey* had left for Philippeville because of a submarine alarm, he was picked up by a U.S. destroyer.

No. 7 Section arrived in Naples on November 8th, and No. 14 on the 10th; No. 11 disembarked at Augusta, Sicily, on the 8th. No. 7 had no competent interpreter. However, it managed to recruit Michele Pignotta, a Canadian veteran of the First World War who had been living in Genosa (Genisi) and who spoke fluent English and Italian. He soon made himself useful. The men discovered an Italian in battledress, loitering around the Casoria railhead; they interrogated him and let him go – "less battledress" – an evocative image. On the 30th, the G.S.O.2 of Fifth Canadian Armoured Division reported a suspected illicit radio transmission; the Section raided the address but found nothing. A.M.G.O.T. asked No. 11 Section and No. 310 British Section to investigate

Interrogation of a German soldier caught entering San Leonardo di Ortona, Italy, in civilian clothes, 13 December 1943. Left to right: Pte. J.A. Eastman, 48th Highlanders of Canada; Lieuts. W.F. McLellan and A.V. Soley, both of the Loyal Edmonton Regiment. (Lieut. Frederick G. Whitcombe/Canada. Dept. of National Defence/Library and Archives Canada, PA-180098)

Every Section had its local troubles. The frequent thefts of signal wire aroused suspicions that they might be deliberate attacks on communications. No. 14 came across a newspaper, *Italia Libera*, that was publishing anti-Allied views and urging the population to begin a campaign of civil disobedience. A.M.G. was asked to suppress it. No. 11 Section arranged the arrest of the Brigadiere of the CC.RR. and the Capo di Guardia Campestre in Grumo, for black market dealings. The Brigadiere, an ex-Fascist Squadrista, had also been circulating pro-Nazi propaganda. At this time F.S. had to secure special permission from the Badoglio government before it could arrest suspects in the rear areas. When it applied, it always became involved in long, drawn-out negotiations and, not infrequently, suspects disappeared before these were concluded.

Personnel administration took a lot of time. The reinforcement stream was not satisfactory. N.C.O.s would go to the hospital, then be sent back to the Depot for reassignment. Despite direct orders from 2nd Echelon (the agency responsible for control of manpower), delays still occurred in getting the men back to their units. No. 1 Section's Carabinieri, who were supposed to report for duty fully uniformed and equipped, ready to go into the field, generally arrived in no more than their normal clothes, and for that reason alone were useless for anything except town patrol duties. Eighth Army agreed that each Section would be given 16 Guardia Stradale, to be used for manning control points 24 hours a day, two at each post, one spare and one supervisor. They were not very satisfactory. One group had been "bloody scared by our guns and we had to fire them"; they were convicted of leaving their posts, and the troubles ceased. In addition, cameras were a continuous security hazard. Cooper suggested that Corps establish a Base Photographic Development Unit, like the one that was operating in Cairo, and the one that Eighth Army was thinking of setting up in Bari.[17] The severe food shortages not only aroused hostility against the Allies but gave a great impetus to the black market. Capt. Cooper expressed in strong terms his conviction that Eighth Army did not have a true picture of the tasks of the F.S. Sections, nor had it any understanding of the administrative problems facing them. He argued that units should deal with their own military security, and that F.S. should be left to handle the civil side. He also considered that they should work not for the Divisional I.O., but for Corps.[18] Eighth Army, which had not had to deal with so many or such serious civilian problems in its earlier campaigns, may still have been feeling its way through them in Italy.

In February 1944, No. 1 Section arrested a priest for collaborating with the enemy. The Bishop of Lanciano tried to have him released by appealing to Army R.C. chaplains whom he had come to know. The appeal was successfully resisted, for the Section had irrefutable evidence to support his arrest. The Germans now began to use propaganda leaflets against Canadian units; the Section tried vainly to get samples of them. The railroad between San Vito and Ortona offered such an easy escape route for refugees that it soon vied in importance with the port areas as a control task. A.M.G. employed people without adequate clearance. New Anti-Fascist Party cells became so active in denouncing ex-Fascists that Security had to intervene. Personal dislikes were often used to condemn innocent men. Reports came back from Teramo, which was still in German hands, that a rebel group was active there; Psychological Warfare was informed.

No. 14 Field Company, R.C.E., employed an Italian interpreter. He was allegedly an artist who had escaped from a Fascist internment camp in the north, but his story raised F.S. suspicions. He was dismissed when F.S. discovered that he was "not as pure as he pretended and should not be seen in our uniform, much less mingling with the officers of a unit." The nature of his offences was not cited. No. 412 British Section then controlled access from Castel Frentano to Casoli. As part of an Eighth Army plan, No. 7 took over Lanciano on February 9th, although, strictly speaking, it was outside the Canadian Corps area. No. 11 took over from No. 68 British Section, and extended the system of control lines along the Sangro to include a new pattern of night patrols. Passes were given only to doctors, nurses, police officers, and Italian Army personnel on duty. Unfortunately, A.M.G. also issued passes, often relying on rather flimsy evidence of personal reliability. Passes that were issued outside the Army area were often inadequate. Some travellers had no papers at all; No. 14 Section estimated that 80% had no identification and 60% no valid travel permits. Many permits were forged.

The Sections worked also for War Crimes and for I.S.9. Their first investigation concerned the murder of an American bomber pilot who had parachuted into the area on July 27th, 1943. A local priest who had denounced the crime from his pulpit had subsequently been arrested. He made a useful first contact in the successful F.S. enquiry. Another investigation, which F.S. passed on to War Crimes, involved three New Zealanders who had escaped from a P.W. Camp. They had first been fed by villagers in Bracigliano and then shot at; one had been killed and the others wounded.[19]

Though the following incident is a little difficult to classify in terms of Intelligence responsibility, it caused some amusement in Corps Intelligence circles. Each German Infantry Regiment had had dogs on its establishment since 1939, and Allied patrols were hard put to know what to do with them. It was unlikely that they could be tamed; orders were therefore given to destroy them. On the 15th, the I Corps War Diary states that the anti-dog "campaign reached a peak when one Nazi deserter was secured. He was trapped by the strategic employment of an agent, a canine prostitute of Italian origin. She, with the aid of a light breeze, successfully carried out a long-range seduction. The P.W. showed no knowledge of English, but responded to words in German [a standard entry in a P.W. interrogation report]. It was impossible to send the dog back for further investigation and he was shot in an attempted escape".[20]

By this time, I(b) had pieced together a good deal of information about the German Intelligence Service (G.I.S.) in Italy. It did not know the identity of individual agents, but, after the first one was captured, the task became easier. For agents did not hesitate to tell all they knew. What was learned was passed to F.S. Sections farther forward, which picked up the next batch, who also talked, and so it went on. The G.I.S. of that time did not have high standards of security, and agents normally had plenty to divulge. F.S. did not capture all of them, and many carried out more than one mission. But many also had accepted agent duty solely to visit their families in the south. Those who were serious, and who were caught and convicted, did provide propaganda. Their identifications and subsequent fates were collated, published as a leaflet, and dropped over enemy territory in the hope that further volunteers would have second thoughts.[21]

Although minor frictions did occur, most A.M.G. officials and F.S. personnel worked well together at this time. No. 1 Section, however, became involved in an incident that considerably damaged its relations. F.S. investigated thoroughly, and then arrested, the Sindaco, the Segretario del Comune, and the ex-Segretario del Fascio Femminile of Lanciano (Mayor, Town Clerk, and ex-Secretary of Women Fascists). The next day the I.O. of a British unit in the town lodged a protest. Lieut. Pat Cole, F.S.O., went to V Corps to explain his action to its G.S.O.3 I(b); his explanation was accepted. That same evening, he was asked for a second explanation by the G.S.O.2, who also accepted his reasoning. A.M.G. at Corps, however, succeeded in having the F.S. decision reversed, and the three officials were released. After the somewhat heated exchange that followed, the Section was ordered to withdraw from Lanciano and Frisa.

In mid-March 1944, the Canadian Corps moved south to Larino, where the Sections found their work a little easier. They had 55 auxiliaries, spread over a wide area. About this time, the Allied Control Commission lifted travel restrictions. No. 14 Section tried to retain some control over movement, through spot checks on hotels and boarding houses, but was not very successful because of the rather loose registration system used in Italian hostelries. The populace felt that the Commission was filled with former Fascists, and were deeply suspicious of some of its decrees. People were just getting used to the more efficient distribution of goods, particularly of food, arranged by the Allies, and did not want to see the Fascist administrators return, even though they now wore new coats.

In April, No. 1 Section returned to Campobasso. No. 7 Section sent a detachment to the Polish Corps F.S. Section, including L/Cpl. Boyd and two of its British interpreters, Sgts. Buckibaum and Schlesinger. Lieut. Fleming took a small detachment of four men and the third British interpreter to 11 C.I.B., which was then readying for the Melfa River battles. Nos. 11 and 14 Sections moved to H.Q. Eighth Army, to control the Army rear boundary.

The detachments continued their work of exposing former Fascist officials, attacking black market activities, and supervising curfews. One interesting prisoner was picked up by No. 11's Carabinieri. He had no travel permit, and when Section H.Q. searched him, they found sewn inside his shirt, a map of Italy and two work permits. He was sent back to the R.I.P. when his cross-examination revealed discrepancies. He mentioned that civilians were crossing the lines in small boats from Pescara to Termoli; his information was passed to Army for action. The Allied Control Commission in Avellino issued a proclamation reducing the price of some essential items. The shopkeepers at once withdrew them from sale and the inhabitants, thinking the goods were being kept for the black market, became restive. The Section tried to have the policy changed. Reports of Fascist meetings increased in number but there was seldom enough evidence to permit the Section to act. The worst trouble spot was Ariano. It seems to have been a popular centre for absentees, a good many of whom became expert at holding up civilians to get money and food. No. 14 picked up two Canadians who had escaped from the Military Prison and gone "underground" there. In this town, Canadians had become their own worst enemies: "The practice of Canadians to drink too much and then knock on doors is a regrettable but apparently national characteristic".[22] The strongly anti-Allied feelings that developed in the citizens as a result of such incidents made effective F.S. work difficult, because it was from those citizens that much of the needed information had to come.

The burden of F.S. tasks became so heavy that Capt. Basil Foreman pressed for more personnel. By late March, A.F.H.Q. agreed, and recommended to the War Office that four Canadian Field Security Detachments be formed. Two were to be recruited in the theatre itself, and two were to be sent from the U.K. The message emphasized the fact that they were an additional reinforcement, not just a replacement for British Sections. On April 20th, Basil Foreman and Lieut. Molnar, his I.O., visited Avellino to arrange for even more trained reinforcements to replace the casualties expected to occur in the coming battles and from normal attrition.[23] Higher authority refused their request, and two smaller units, Nos. 8 and 11 Field Security Reserve Detachments (F.S.R.D.), were formed using available manpower. They were posted to Avellino and Ariano respectively.

The ruse that helped the Allies win the battles for the Hitler Line has already been described. Captured German Intelligence documents showed clearly that it had succeeded, but at the time it was being worked out the troops themselves were highly sceptical. The Diarist for H.Q. First Division makes this comment: "Corps has now ordered us to restore our Canadian and Divisional badges we have had on for eight days, all of which we have passed in an area where troops of the Division are well known to nearly all the inhabitants. Now just before the move to an area where we are not known and where there might be a possibility of remaining unidentified as a formation, if not as Canadians, we were told to put the identifying signs back up. There is no great opinion of the logic behind this around this H.Q."[24]

The Canadian advance to the Hitler Line battlefield began on May 15th. By the 19th, the roads, still under sporadic enemy shellfire, were blocked with refugees. No. 1 Section chose a point about four miles south of Pontecorvo and there, more or less single-handedly, attempted to establish a refugee control centre. But the situation was completely unmanageable. There was a temporary check in the refugee stream on May 25th, when the Hitler Line was broken. But on the 26th, "now that the enemy has been driven back they all think that they are free to move as they wish". On the 27th the Section moved up behind Divisional H.Q.; the 10 miles took them seven hours.

"There were more refugees ... than ever before. Thousands are coming in from their hiding places and caves. ... Some are locals ... we are allowing them to go home. One German in civilian clothes and 10 Italians sent to R.I.P." And, on the 31st: "Although we have our end of the refugee control functioning perfectly A.M.G. does not seem to be on their toes and the refugee centre that we have started is a mass of hungry refugees. Transport is the main problem."[25]

No. 7 Section was probably the only one that was not then troubled by refugees. From Mignano, where it had moved on May 17th, it sent three N.C.O.s, Direnfeld, Fitzsimmons, and Wiens, with 10 Italian soldiers, to establish a civilian control line in the Corps sector from Sant' Angelo to the Liri River. But the Germans had evacuated most of the civilians in front of the Rapido, and very few came their way before May 26th.[26] On the 27th, they were relieved by No. 11 Section, which was normally responsible for part of Eighth Army's area. Its men had also had their difficulties with A.M.G. They arrested three men carrying a large dynamo and its equipment, worth about $10,000; A.M.G. released them. F.S. re-arrested them and brought them to trial for theft; they were found guilty and were jailed.

But as May drew to a close, all Sections found themselves swamped by refugees. Despite continuous patrolling, it was not possible to keep the roads clear. No. 11 Section was moved to Pontecorvo on May 23rd and, assisted by CC.RR., Italian military, and a Section from the Sixth South African Division, took over a control line based on the Pontecorvo–Aquino Road. No. 14 Section, in the Morconi region, found that a great many refugees were trying to move into the Rome area. The congestion was so bad that A.M.G. had to issue a warning that anyone found in Rome without a permit would be sentenced to two years in prison. The control lines picked up many "wanted" persons. No. 14 caught two German soldiers wearing U.S. uniforms and turned them over to the C.S.D.I.C. at Torre Annunciata (Annunziata). It also caught three Italian sailors who had escaped from a P.W. Cage, and 37 Italian and five Allied deserters.

As the war moved up Italy, and as the liberated areas began to return to normal, political activity, often erupting in noisy civic unrest, emerged again. At times it was exacerbated by what seems, at this remove, to have been at best lack of tact and at worst stupidity. No. 14 reported that men of the Nembo Parachute Division at Fontelandolfo (Benevento) would sometimes drive into Benevento, gather together large numbers of civilians, and boast of their exploits. Their talk would excite people with Fascist leanings to demonstrate against the Allied troops. The same formation also clashed frequently with the Free French troops, many of whom still had vivid memories of the Italian occupation of part of their country. The Section strongly recommended that the Nembo be sent to a more active combat area.[27]

In June, the Allies captured many of the German *Fourteenth Army* files. These showed that the enemy had been able to identify the line units very clearly through their interrogations of prisoners, but their knowledge of subordination to higher formations was much less accurate. They had located H.Q. First Canadian Infantry and Fifth Armoured Divisions, but not I Corps H.Q. *Fourteenth Army* overestimated Allied reserve strength and hence assessed the seaborne threat as more of a possibility than it really was. Once battle began, they were able to pick up a great deal of information from radio intercept and captured documents, etc. The fact that Allied troops were not following the oft repeated "Name, Rank, and Number" drill was cause for real concern.[28]

At Frosinone, No. 1 Section found the first indications that a partisan movement had been organized, the *Comitato di Liberazione Nazionale*, supposed to have been formed spontaneously in September 1943, with the help of a Senator Croce and the B.B.C. Its aim was to assist the Allied advance in the hope that, after the liberation, it would become a nucleus on which a future government of Italy could be based. Its supporters were opposed to Fascism and to the German occupation policies; they wanted them replaced by a fair, representative, and capable administration. They had pledged their support to the Allies, worked to help British prisoners escape, and spread news and Allied propaganda taken from Allied broadcasts. Wherever possible they tried to help townspeople avoid the worst hardships. The Section found the senior control group of the movement a little hard to identify, but it seemed to have headquarters in the provincial capitals, and a central committee in Rome.[29]

The next move, to Genazzano on June 15th, 1944, brought No. 1 into direct contact with Communist partisans, who were much less tractable. They had taken the town over, and its people were rather dissatisfied. No. 7 Section had by this time moved to Anagni, where it ran into a similar situation. Many of these partisans joined their movement after the Allies had occupied the area; they expected to be given preferential treatment, including the right to bear arms, in exchange for the assistance they claimed to have given the Allies. The Section sent them south to join the Italian Army.[30] In Fiuggi, then the A.M.G. H.Q. for Frosinone Province, No. 11 Section encountered an even more sophisticated group which, under a certain Gen. Egio Paduani, was working for more immediate political power.

No. 1 Section arrested a Carabinieri lieutenant-colonel from Rome, carrying documents relating to the Republican Fascist Party. C.S.M. Fowler and two N.C.O.s escorted him back to Rome, where his material could be better exploited. Canadian troops in Pofi misconducted themselves; F.S. investigated and, as a result, Corps restricted entry to the town. After No. 7 Section checked Acuto, it informed I.S.9 that, since the signing of the Armistice the previous year and despite the rigours of the German occupation, many Acuto families had been actively aiding escaped Allied P.W.

No. 11 Section moved into the Ceprano area in early June. Here its men arrested two German deserters wearing civilian clothes, and several collaborators, including a few who were accused of betraying Allied P.W. They also found an ammunition dump and, among its contents, an intricate time fuse similar to one that had been used in a sabotage explosion in the Naples Post Office a few months before. Eighth Army and U.S. C.I.C. were interested in discoveries of this sort, both to further their own investigations and to develop measures to counter such devices. Eighth Army sent in an Italian officer who had led partisans in the region. He produced a diary of his exploits, which the Section translated before sending it back. Arpino, which the war had almost bypassed, had been the site of a German espionage headquarters, *Dienststelle Hans*; the Section prepared a detailed report on its activities. At Isola di Liri, the commune was composed of Guardia Nazionale Republicana (G.N.R.). These were arrested and a whole new slate was appointed. Many civilians brought in I.O.U.s signed by escaping P.W.; arrangements were made to have them paid. In some cases, the papers gave the location of the P.W. who had signed them, and the Section had to see if it was possible to retrieve him. Arpino had no A.M.G. office and the Section had to take over some of these responsibilities. A.M.G. was badly overstretched; it had set up temporary camps in the rear, but could not evacuate refugees to them because of the dearth of transport.[31]

The two new F.S.R.D.s, No. 8 under Lieut. A.S. Fleming, and No. 11, were sent to supervise the Rear Army control line along Route 6. Lieut. Fleming, who had acquired his experience with No. 7 Section, worked with 64 Italian soldiers and an officer. Soldiers were generally preferred to CC.RR. or Auxiliary Police, because they had no local contacts and were not so easily bribed. No. 8 set up its own R.I.P. to handle refugees moving southward. Fleming had to arrange food, not only for the Detachment, but also for Italians and refugees. He even became involved in distributing fertilizer to farmers, an A.M.G. task. By the end of June, No. 11 F.S.R.D., with 16 more Italians, had taken over the whole line.

The rapid advance past Rome left a lot of work for F.S. in the Army rear areas. The Eighth Army Section was needed for the occupation of Florence. No. 1 Section and No. 8 F.S.R.D. were therefore detached to Army control. No. 1 Section moved first to Orvieto and then to Castiglione di Laso. No. 8 F.S.R.D., unable to catch up, moved to Tivoli and reinforced the rear control line, which then ran from Castelnuovo on Route 3 to Tivoli – Route 5 to Arsoli–Carsoli–Avezzano to the east coast. The area had not had any F.S. Section for more than five days at a time; as a result, the succession of operations had been entirely without continuity of policy. People had been put in jail by partisans, Communists, CC.RR., F.S., and by the various units that happened to pass through. Some had been there for three weeks without investigation or trial. After it had made its first seven arrests, the Detachment tried to take its prisoners to the Allied Armies Italy (A.A.I.) P.W. Cage. H.Q. A.A.I. gave them the wrong location, Military Police could not give them directions, and they spent a whole day vainly looking for it. They had to return to Rome and then to their base, still escorting their seven unhappy prisoners. When they arrived there, the CC.RR. informed them that there were no keys to the handcuffs they were using! The next morning, they discovered that the nearest Cage, No. 371, was at Terni, 90 miles away. But it had not been intended that the Detachment form part of the control line and when Capt. Basil Foreman caught up, he sent it to Terni.

At Terni the confusion facing Lieut. Fleming was, if anything, worse than it had been at Tivoli. There were not enough guards on the ammunition dumps. The Army employed about 3,500 civilians; none of them had been cleared. The Italian Army was calling up all men between the ages of 20 and 30; these also had to be vetted before A.M.G. would give them travel passes. The Detachment arrested some German stragglers who claimed to have deserted in order to fight with the partisans. They felt that, as such, they deserved privileged status and were annoyed when they were treated as ordinary P.W. Sgts. Laing and Cheyne were told to arrest an Italian Army officer who had been running a police force made up of partisans. Since he had been in the G.N.R., his status was doubtful, but A.M.G. had unfortunately made the mistake of giving him and his *ad hoc* force a permit to operate. Laing actually picked up the man's brother in error, but found a way to use him by sending him as a messenger to persuade the band to disarm and halt its operations.

A day or two later, Fleming was confronted by a crowd of relatives of arrested Fascist officials clamouring for explanations. When he investigated, he found that the CC.RR. were just beginning to work on the 'automatic arrest' list compiled by the Control Commission and, without examining cases separately, were arresting people whom F.S. had already cleared. As a result, all the jails had to be re-checked; 12 prisoners were cleared at once, 20 still had to be vetted before the Detachment moved on. Finally, on the morning of the move, it found that its truck, four jeeps, and a motorcycle were missing – stolen, in all probability, by Canadians.[32]

Fleming was not, of course, the only F.S.O. beset by this sort of difficulty. And when one considers that a complete upheaval in local administration must inevitably follow a change in Occupation authorities, that those newly in power would have scores to settle with their predecessors, that the military moves themselves were bound to create an enormous dislocation, and that A.M.G. may not have been physically capable of meeting the demands made on it as quickly as desirable, it is indeed surprising that F.S. managed as well as it did. Soon afterwards the situation began to settle down of its own accord.

At Aquila, an area in which large Italian and German P.W. Camps had been located, No. 7 Section found many local people who had actively aided escaping

Allied soldiers; others had assisted the Germans. Feeling ran high, and the jails were full of prisoners who had been arrested on the flimsiest evidence. In Fiuggi, relations between partisans and Communists were bad. F.S. had to ask A.M.G. to arrest the partisan leader, which seemed to ease the pressures. In Campoli Apennino, near Sora, a political demonstration controlled by ex-Fascists posing as leaders of new parties took over from the A.M.G. appointees. F.S. arrested the ringleaders and turned them over to A.M.G.

Finally, the control line which had been "selected" by No. 8 Detachment – Route 5 – was established on a more business-like basis. No. 11 Section was given the sector from Tivoli to Avezzano; No. 7 from Avezzano to Pescara. No. 11 Detachment closed its control points on July 7th and joined No. 1 Section at First Division – just in time to assist in security arrangements for the visit of H.M. King George VI, on July 31st.

On July 18th, Security was ordered to cover the move to the Perugia area, which was part of the deception plan devised to facilitate the breaching of the Gothic Line. Eighth Army tried to convey the impression that the Canadian Corps was deployed behind the Polish Corps in the Adriatic Sector. But the Canadians were actually in the centre. All vehicle signs were to be painted out. "Canada" badges and all unit and formation identifications were to be taken off. Towns along the route were placed out-of-bounds, and the route signs, normally profusely posted and clearly identifiable, were replaced by a simple code letter. Code names were allotted, and everyone was forbidden to refer to senior personnel by name. Corps H.Q. moved to an olive grove four miles south of Foligno during the first week of August.

Security was horrified by what actually happened. Maj. Kingsmill, G.S.O.2 (Int), I Corps, a strong supporter of his C.I. staff, summarized the many breaches in a scathing report: "You were [told] what to do and . . . what not to do . . . the result was lousy, and we know the enemy knows we are here. He knew as early as 3 Aug 44. . . . Orders were to REMOVE all formation signs from vehicles . . . certain units . . . supply conscious – or just plain lazy – tried to blank out the signs with grease . . . and dirt . . . too lazy to take them off their greatcoats . . . it rained . . . cool . . . so some of these labour-saving specialists put on their greatcoats flashes and all . . . stretch of road practically paved with Canadian cigarette packages and the "Maple Leaf" [troops' newspaper] . . . day after first troops arrived civilians were seen carrying packages of Canadian cigarettes . . . some B.F.s have to blab . . . 'I no f-----g Inglese, me Canadese'. And it's not only the O.R.s . . . Canadian concert party sang 'O Canada'. . . civilians carried with units . . . will gossip . . . R.C.A.S.C. Coy . . . told the farmer they were Canadians and would be back in three days carrying the troops. . . . Canadian outfit on the air with wireless." The G.O.C. ordered F.S. to visit all the units to tighten up security. Despite Maj. Kingsmill's concern, postwar studies have shown that, if the G.I.S. did know of the Canadians' arrival, it was unable to disseminate the information to forward units.[33]

Early August saw all the Sections, including the Polish Section, working in the Corps area. Nos. 9 and 10 F.S.R.D. had arrived in late July. Capt. Foreman assigned the four Detachments to his four Sections, giving them a much needed reinforcement and him a chance to streamline his administration. No. 1 Section, in Galluzzo to cover the move of First Division towards the Gothic Line, established a strong roadblock, using local partisans, and cleared all Italians from the brigades, except the 40 soldiers they were using. No. 7 Section, covering the move of its parent Fifth Armoured Division, tried to ensure that troops would have as little contact as possible with the local inhabitants. This meant keeping them away from the towns, a policy which the citizens interpreted as permission to start looting. No. 11 Section tried to tighten control in the Army area, where security was so slack that Gen. E.L.M. Burns ordered the Red Shield Club and the Imperial Cinema in Spoleto to be closed, to reduce the risk of breaches. No. 11 Detachment was deployed along Route 3, to cover the boundary between V Corps and II Polish Corps; partisans and CC.RR. were recruited to man the posts.

Mombaroccio was cleared by First Division on August 26th. The sudden influx of refugees raised its normal population of 3,500 by about another 9,000, and water became very scarce. Once again F.S. found itself doing A.M.G. work to try to restore a semblance of civil administration. No. 1 Section had definite evidence of enemy agents. According to reports from two different units, light signals were being exchanged between two church towers. When they were raided, two Italians were caught in the act of hiding maps, binoculars, and a mirror, but interrogation failed to secure enough evidence to send them to jail.[34]

No. 1 Section stayed with its Division during the September advances. In addition to the usual road patrol work, it also had to watch the coast and deal with Port Security problems. On September 6th, with No. 8 F.S.R.D., it moved into Riccione and immediately contracted the senior members of the Comitato and the partisans. The town was still in no-man's-land; some shelling was going on, and Andy Fleming withdrew his Section except for Sgts. Hadden and Johnston. One story, that cannot be confirmed, relates that a Provost officer who went into Riccione a little early, and against the advice of two F.S. N.C.O.s, suddenly found himself confronted by armed Germans. Fortunately for him, the two F.S. shot the "Jerries" before they could react. After the town fell, there was an orgy of looting, which an increase in the allocation of Provost and A.M.G. did little to halt. The Section had a Black List, but could not readily check it because so many of the inhabitants remained for days in their shelters. However, it did pick up one suspicious character who, after interrogation at base, proved to be an agent.

Because Germans dressed in civilian clothes were infiltrating the lines, Gen. Vokes ordered all civilians to be evacuated. During the evacuation, which was done with the help of Section trucks, a German agent and two Italian nationals, whom an informer identified as Fascists, were caught. When the two Italians were interrogated, it became clear that something was wrong. The informant was re-interviewed, and finally admitted he had been lying. On September 21st, since Riccione was no longer sufficiently important to warrant the evacuation of civilians, the roadblocks were taken down. A.M.G. and the Section had many disagreements over roadblocks, refugee control, and the disarming of guards.

For the other Sections, September was a relatively quiet month, although Sgt. Moore, then with 11 F.S.R.D., was slightly wounded by shellfire, and No. 7 Section lost its H.Q. to a direct hit. Fortunately, no one was hurt. Sgt. Masinda, No. 8 F.S.R.D., found that his chief of Auxiliary Police had been changing personnel and altering permits to suit himself. Sgt. Masinda reprimanded and dismissed him, and seized the opportunity to warn the rest of the Auxiliaries that he expected improvement in their conduct. No. 14 Section, which was manning the Rear Army control line (Acquasparta–S. Lorenzo), found that by using Italian soldiers it reduced the north and south movement of civilians by 75%. But it had its own special problems. Men of the nearby Canadian units were looting, bullying civilians, and fighting with the Auxiliaries. And F.S. had to plead with C.O.s to get them to control their men.

In Terni Province, "Patriot Communists" tried to mete out their own justice to the Fascists, and caused unrest that had to be dealt with. At Avellino, the Italian government, concerned that the activities of black market and contraband gangs would cause a food shortage in the coming winter, requested Nos. 9 and 10 F.S.R.D., jointly commanded by Capt. J.M. James, to raid their hiding places. The first raid, on an isolated farm, brought in five prisoners, all prominent men; the most important ones escaped, however. The next night a second raid brought in 11, and three days later a third raid caught four more, all from the same gang. They were well-armed and well-supplied with money and transport. Their wealth of vehicles, in fact, annoyed the Detachments, who had to scrounge hard to get any themselves. On September 11, the ringleader was captured.

Not all criminals were Italian. In September 1944 alone, the number of Allied vehicles stolen by Allied soldiers and sold to civilians ran into four figures. Many were used in other thefts. On the night of September 15th, a 3½-ton American 6 X 6 truck, loaded with 30 quintals (6,613 lbs.) of contraband grain, was stopped at a roadblock on the Avellino–Ariano road. Two American soldiers sat in the front; four men were in the back, three of whom spoke only Italian. The truck was driven into a side road and put under guard by a Provost. Sgt. Durham, whose No. 312 (British) F.S. Section worked very closely with Nos. 9 and 10 F.S.R.D., began to interrogate the men. All of them got out of the truck except one in the back who, according to his friends, had malaria. They began a fight, the Provost was knocked unconscious, someone shot Sgt. Durham in the shoulder, more shots were fired, and the men ran into a nearby cornfield. Reinforcements arrived from the roadblock, but all the men escaped.[35]

Theft in some areas reached such proportions that the police, military as well as civil, could not cope with it, and F.S. was called in to help. For example, on October 29th, 10 cases of soap, 1,600 pairs of socks, 800 pullover sweaters, and 80 pairs of boots were stolen from the Canadian Ordnance Depot. The cost of the supplies was $1,800; on the black market, their value was in excess of $6,000.[36] Estimates of monthly losses in the Avellino area ranged from $20,000 to $100,000. There was a thriving market in military material. Cigarette prices were 2–2½ lire each; boots 1,000–1,500 lire a pair; blankets 700–1,000 lire; socks 100 lire. A purchaser could sell any of these items in rural areas for twice what he had paid. F.S. was interested, because the ease with which military uniforms could be obtained eliminated the chief obstacle an enemy agent had to overcome – that of blending into the military environment. It was a hard problem to solve, for the Canadian soldier had a superficially strong argument. Pay regulations in the theatre were such that he had no money for casual spending off duty. He felt he had to resort to selling equipment or cigarettes to obtain money for entertainment, for souvenirs to send home, and for essential supplies. A private soldier was paid $45 per month; $20 of this was deducted as compulsory savings. He was allowed to draw only one-half of the remainder, in order to build up a balance in his paybook for leave purposes. He actually drew 1,000 lire a month – about $10 at the rate of exchange then. His spending would be in the order of 270 lire for 900 cigarettes, 200 lire for laundry, 400–500 lire for razor blades, writing paper, hair tonic, etc., and 50–100 lire for stamps. The remainder was for entertainment. And soldiers commonly believed that the deferred pay was really a compulsory loan to the government on which they received no interest. This resulted in a serious morale problem.

On October 28th, I Canadian Corps went into Army reserve. The lull in hostilities, reflected in the reduced volume and changed nature of their work, gave the Sections time to attend to the administration and maintenance they had had to neglect in the more active periods. No. 11 Section had the *Comitato di Liberazione* at Viserba disbanded, a step which did much to restore calm. Boundaries between formations, and control measures imposed on them, became more formal. A new Corps Rear Control Line was established on the River Savio, under No. 7 Section. Crime continued, but the tighter control lines forced contrabandists to use the inferior back roads where the risks of accidents were greater; at least one man was crushed under an overturned load of grain. The local authorities had no records on the small boats operating in the Civitavecchia area, and every single vessel had to be registered. The Royal Navy tried, not very successfully, to control them.

Vast quantities of small arms were available. No. 14 Section was very annoyed when, in at least two communes, pistols it had collected were handed back by the CC.RR. The presence of small arms made Civitavecchia, in particular, a dangerous town because of their potential use in the heat of debate between Communists and anti-Communists. Political activity was: "wide and varied, with confusing aims and platforms, if any. The Communist Party in one commune appears to have the same platform as the Liberal or Christian Democrats in another... and vice versa. Frequently the platforms are entirely different from those expressed by the party heads of the province. Former Fascists appear as leaders or members of almost all the parties. Several new parties... being formed... a Democratic Workers Party at Bisaccia... with members recruited from ex-Fascists and property owners.... Another... Liberal Party of Teora... has 150 members who include all the former Fascist Secretaries and Squadristi of the area with a stated platform of combating Communism." There were many cases where Fascists were allowed to retain power: "It would appear that the anti-Fascists have just cause for many complaints... against Provincial Administrators who are former Fascists and who allow other Fascists to remain in control of the Communes. Allied prestige has suffered." Capt. James warned that the shortage of transport in the Italian Security agencies might make it impossible for them to control serious political conflicts.[37]

The Sections arrested many German deserters who were attempting to blend into the background; few had enough Italian to be convincing. German Intelligence also sent Italians on short-range missions across the lines to obtain tactical information on troop movements, military installations, etc. They were ordinary civilians, with no special equipment and little special training, who were instructed not to get too deeply behind Allied lines and to return quickly. The fact that the enemy was now reduced to getting results from the quantity rather than the quality of his sources indicated how completely the Allies dominated the skies over the battlefield. Without an aerial reconnaissance capability, the G.I.S. was virtually blind.[38]

No. 11 F.S.R.D., on its way back to Avellino, halted on the night of November 23rd at Pontecorvo. About midnight, local peasants brought in a German agent who had been dropped by parachute near the town on the previous evening. The Italians who picked him up convinced him that they were helping him on his way to Rome. Lieut. Cole, and two sergeants, Harding and Grunberg, went with him to search for the radio and parachute he had buried after landing. They had trouble locating them. The Detachment felt encouraged by the Italians' decision to turn the man in. On the other hand, the discovery that the spy had rid himself at once of the vital radio, probably the only link he would have with his control, and that he was not sure where he had hidden it made them wonder about his dedication. He may, of course, have judged it

Accused of collaboration by a woman partisan, a Signor Ghetti is brought before Maj. W.M. Harrison, A.M.G., and his interpreter, in Bagnacavallo, to plead his case. Sgts. W.J. Trueman, right, and J.C. Hadden, left, No. 1 Section, are the escorts. (Alexander M. Stirton/Canada. Dept. of National Defence/Library and Archives Canada, PA-173561)

too risky to carry the set with him; but in that case he would presumably have made certain that he knew exactly where he had hidden it.

Ravenna, a provincial capital, was an important C.I. target offering the prospect of finding records and even agents. It was quite possible that the enemy would leave an espionage network behind. A special I(b) task force was therefore created to counter that threat as well as deal with the overall Security problems. It was code-named BASFORCE (from Basil Foreman, G.S.O.3 I(b), I Canadian Corps). It comprised No. 11 F.S. Section; a detachment from No. 7 F.S.; Nos. 9 and 10 F.S.R.D.s; No. 47 British Port Security Section; a detachment of S.I.M./C.S.; and a guard force of 20 Italian soldiers, 90 Carabinieri and partisans and representatives from the P.W. interrogation centres.

The city fell on December 4th, and the first I(b) men in were the F.S.O. and a small detachment from No. 7 Section. No. 11 Section managed to get some of its vehicles over the Uniti River on the morning of the 5th. I(b) H.Q. opened in the Tribunale about 1330, but the operation was something of an anticlimax. Partisans brought in the only valuable find, an agent and his radio. The Germans had removed most of the records in places like the Casa del Fascio two months previously. Their Military H.Q. had been bombed out; its alternate was empty. The jail records contained the name of every inmate but not the crime for which he was incarcerated. At the Preffetura and the Questura the records were complete but they had little intelligence value.

Once again, I(b) tried to enforce some sort of refugee control; this was not easy, even though the bridges were not reopened until the 16th. The undisciplined partisans assigned to check points were not satisfactory. There was a food shortage and, until A.M.G. arrived on the 9th, F.S. had again to arrange for emergency supplies, using the partisans as porters. Some of these, with little valid claim to the title, quarrelled with the real partisans who had been fighting north of the town. They were paraded and disarmed; those who were found to be trustworthy were given an armband. Major Bülow was given responsibility for their discipline.

The partisans were not the only ones who were slack. Two agents, who had slipped out of Ravenna almost unchecked through a Carabinieri post on December 5th, surrendered to No. 7 Section at Cervia the next day. The radio they had left behind in Ravenna was picked up later by F.S. BASFORCE ceased to exist on December 8th, and the city was turned over to No. 47 Section.[39]

On January 5th, the I Canadian Corps advance was halted on the south bank of the Senio. The new area contained a number of towns notably Russi and Bagnacavallo, and a network of roads and river lines that could be used to assist in movement control. No. 1 Section with a partisan leader and about 140 of his men, moved into Russi. Knowing the region well, the partisans could identify strangers and wanted persons, in addition to doing their more usual tasks of manning roadblocks. This was far from being an unimportant duty; for at one of their check points, Eighth Army caught one "most-wanted" prize.

The presence of partisans raised many awkward administrative problems. In the beginning, Eighth Army merely armed them; they had to provide their own food and most of their own clothing. After they were overrun by the Allied advance, they also received pay. Then they demanded food from Allied stocks because there was none to buy on the market. In the end, they got neither money nor food, for Eighth Army stopped their pay. They were finally disbanded and, except for those who worked directly for an Allied unit, were treated as ordinary civilians. Their disarming led to some tense exchanges; Maj. D.M. Healy, who knew them well and had fought with them, had to be called in to help.

I(b) in the Corps area had the support of the people. The area, with its long, open coastline, was vulnerable to infiltration. No. 8 F.S.R.D. picked up a boatload of 12, and managed to obtain information about coastal traffic that the Navy found valuable. Two days later, two women came into the office to report that four soldiers had come to their farm near Cesenatico demanding lodging. Sgts. Brown, Sillanpaa, Cheyne, and three S.I.M./C.S. men went out and arrested an officer and three men. Interrogation revealed that they belonged to a German sabotage element – "X" *Flotilla* – and they were taken to the G.S.O.2 (Int) at Eighth Army. The next day the Detachment learned that five more of these men were in the area. Unfortunately, their raid was a half-hour too late; the birds had flown.

Men from No. 1 Section picked up an agent who was unkind enough to tell them how easily he had slipped through their fingers at Riccione at the end of October. On December 5th, No. 11 Section, on movement control outside Ravenna, picked up three German deserters and then assisted in disarming partisans. On December 26th, it received reports that enemy saboteurs were in its area. The next day the partisans found three men, whom the Section promptly sent back to Corps. Their interrogation provided Capt. Basil Foreman with descriptions of 10 others. No. 11 captured all but two of them. They caught three others in January, together with their parachutes and equipment.

The detachments stationed in Ravenna were next ordered to take over the area from Cesenatico to the Savio and, later, from there to San Pietro, in Campiano. No. 9 summarized its activities as follows: "With new lists of enemy agents continually arriving, the task of keeping index up-to-date and detachments fully informed represents a major portion of all work done. One list is no sooner completed when two or three more arrive. The Cesenatico Det [Detachment] under Sergeant Shook, plus three (attached) of S.I.M. are organizing controls for the area and commencing the compilation of local information files. [These contain] (a) Central Statistics, population and refugees; (b) Sanitary situation; (c) Alimentation situation; (d) Medical situation; (e) Conditions of residences, etc.; (f) Black List and White List."

The next day the Detachment reported: "several special investigations . . . amongst them Maria . . . one of the most presentable suspects ever encountered; which fact caused considerable rivalry amongst F.S. investigators." Shook won.[40] The area was reported to be well supplied with agents who spoke English, wore British or American uniforms, and had vehicles and weapons. Their mission was to attack small headquarters and their staffs. Security precautions were accordingly tightened, but none of these special agents was found.

The Black List contained some 1,500 names, including those of two women which had been provided by a British agent who was a waiter at the German "spy school" at Lake Como. Sgts. Hadden and Smith, No. 1 Section, at Bagnacavallo, arrested one "Katia Ansiloni", who finally admitted she and another girl, whom she did not know, had crossed the lines. Ten days later Eighth Army arrested "Clara" and complained that she held a pass for Faenza which had been signed by an officer in the Seaforths of Canada. The Germans had staged a "refugee linecrosser" act. They had taken "Clara" to the lines, and had told her to run screaming towards the Seaforth positions while they fired over her head and the Canadians would "rescue" her. And so it proved. "Clara", a Parisian prostitute, then spent a few days with the officer concerned, who gave her a pass "to visit her mother in Faenza". Capt. Andy Fleming tried unsuccessfully to find that "mother" and, on January 31st, "Katia" was confronted with "Clara": ". . . Katia confesses, giving so much information that the interrogator has to rest for a day with writer's cramp." A visit to the unit revealed that the officer had been taken to hospital with "a social disease". Considering he had been punished enough, the Section closed the case.[41]

On January 13th, 1945, No. 11 Section was ordered to evacuate all civilians from the forward area. After some initial hesitation, all 4,500 were moved. No. 11 took over the rear control line on the River Montone, and the Provost was instructed to arrest all drivers carrying civilians in Service vehicles. Although First Division's progress was handicapped by the accidental blowing up of a bridge over the Lamone, its disappearance actually benefited No. 1 Section, because it forced a great reduction in the flow of civilian traffic.

Operation GOLDFLAKE, the return of I Canadian Corps to First Army, began officially on February 4th. On the 13th, No 1 Section reported that the Italians knew the Canadians were leaving: "but that is all".[42] Despite strenuous efforts to halt careless talk, rumour and speculation were widespread. No. 7 Section, ordered to check Fifth Division through "Harrod's Staging Area" at Pisa, attempted, but almost in vain, to stop troops throwing away Canadian cigarette packets and *Maple Leafs*. Troops were confined to their camps, but men still reported for prophylactic treatment. It was found that they had not broken camp, but that two enterprising prostitutes had set up business in the camp area itself. They and their pimp were arrested and sent to American C.I.C. for detention until after the move. The Section was loaded on February 24th; those for whom accommodation had not been found had to sleep in the vehicles.

No. 10 F.S.R.D., minus an attached interpreter who had used his position to extort jewelry and sex, moved to control-line duties in the first week of February, and from there to Exercise PENKNIFE, the deception scheme that was intended to make the enemy believe the Canadians were moving to near Macerata, in preparation for operations in April. It was executed by a special organization, called 1st Canadian Special Basra Unit, made up of about 230 officers and men from many small units in the theatre. Formation and unit signs were put up on the roads into Macerata. Widely scattered Canadian signals detachments filled the air with dummy messages. All Canadian leave facilities were left open as long as possible and the *Maple Leaf* was published in Rome until mid-March. The cover was successful. As late as February 26th, German Intelligence thought that First Division was in the line, with Fifth Armoured Division in reserve near Rimini and Corps H.Q. located on the Savio. 12 Canadian Infantry Brigade was shown as being at Ravenna. About March 17th they began to be confused; they thought that both Divisions, and Corps H.Q., were in the Ancona area, and were doubtful about Fifth Armoured Division's location. It was not until April 19th that the Germans realized that the theatre was free of Canadian troops.[43]

Our last reference will be to the troubles that plagued No. 9 F.S.R.D. Just before it moved to San Arcangelo, it received information that German agents were infiltrating through Fifth Army's area to the rear of Eighth Army, via San Marino and the mountains. The Detachment set up roadblocks at Sogliano and Fiume Marecchia, but caught no agents, although they did turn up G.I.S. produced fake 1,000 lire banknotes. In their area, many of the village mayors were known Communists. On one occasion, Communists came to denounce a man because he had publicly carried a Fascist flag. No. 9 investigated and found he was actually the village half-wit, whom the Communists themselves had set up to cause trouble. His action provoked a small riot; he was arrested, charged as its instigator, recognized as an idiot, and released.[44]

The story of Canadian Security in Italy stops almost as if it had been cut with a knife. All the files and cases were turned over to the Allied I(b) agencies. No. 1 Section, the first in, was the last to leave.

In retrospect, what did Canadian Field Security contribute to the Italian Campaign? Because the Sections and the General Staff officers who were responsible for its day-to-day operations formed only a part of a much larger whole, it is not easy to identify individual successes and failures. Individual German agents did complete missions successfully. But the large number who failed did so because F.S. made their task so difficult they lost their will to overcome the obstacles facing them. The losses incurred by the German Intelligence Service so depleted its reserve of trained agents that it was forced to use untrained, inexperienced men hoping they would swamp the system through the sheer weight of numbers. Certainly, Canadian F.S. helped destroy that hope. But the greatest victories in the Security battle were won in Rome and by forces other than Canadian.

Security often had to call for control measures which conflicted with the views and intentions of staff and unit Commanding Officers. The individual Sections did their best to administer the measures fairly, completely, and in ways that would not impose unduly onerous burdens on anyone. Through good public relations and educational programs, they persuaded others to recognize that they were vitally necessary. They owe a great debt of gratitude for the consideration and cooperation they received from those whose security it was their duty to protect.

For the first time since 1919, a Canadian F.S. component participated in an extended campaign. The Italian campaign was fought literally in and around the homes of ordinary citizens. Humanitarian as well as military considerations required that their interests and their well-being be recognized. Field Security had an operational responsibility, not only to keep civilians out of the way of troop movements, but also to ensure that they did not provide cover for enemy agents. It was the first Security agency to arrive after an objective was gained and therefore the first to impose controls. It was an extension, as it were, of the Allied Military Government, but its responsibilities were not the same. On many occasions, the two agencies clashed. Their differences, fortunately, were usually short-lived and almost always resolved, for with time each learned to recognize and respect the other's point of view. The similarities and differences in the tasks that each was allotted should have been studied beforehand; the conflicts could have been anticipated and prevented by closer co-ordination.

The F.S. component had a task to do that, in practice, was hard to define precisely. Starting virtually from scratch, it learned quickly; it passed on what it had learned, and did it well. In the I Corps area, throughout the campaign, no major case of sabotage occurred. If there was espionage, it never gave the enemy more than a minor and short-term advantage. The Corps F.S. helped to make that possible.

10.
TO KNOW THE ENEMY: I(A) IN NORTH-WEST EUROPE

OVERLORD TO FALAISE

Third Canadian Division, the assault formation selected for the invasion of Normandy, came under I British Corps command on December 1st, 1943. The responsibility for gathering the intelligence required to support its landings lay well outside Divisional control, in the hands of the Planning Staff subordinate to the Chief of Staff to the Supreme Allied Commander (C.O.S.S.A.C.). This Staff had, as direct intelligence sources, agents, refugees, strategic wireless intercept, photographs (air, private snapshots, postcards), and reports of detailed reconnaissance of beaches and approaches. These sources were exploited by offices in Britain, some of which employed Canadians; two officers per month, for example, were assigned to the Engineer Section of the Theatre Intelligence Section (T.I.S.). C.M.H.Q. set up a special list (Q) to record these assignments.[1]

General Keller, G.O.C. Third Division, and his H.Q. Staff Officers were given their first detailed Intelligence briefing on May 15th, 1944. The brigade and unit commanders were briefed a week later. The junior officers and men were not told of their objectives until after they had embarked (June 5th), when the sealed packages of maps, which had been given to the units earlier, were opened. The officers of the supporting forces were briefed separately on models of the target areas. The remainder of First Canadian Army, which was to follow the invasion force and capture Le Havre and Rouen, directed its Intelligence planning and collection of information to support those future operations.

The German defence line in Normandy paralleled the coast, with strong points and fortresses in the major towns along it. It was not continuous and had little depth. The static divisions that manned it were reported to have had their best men replaced by youths, by men over 35, by frostbite casualties, and by Russian P.W. who had volunteered to serve with the German Army. Their equipment was believed not to be the most modern, and often included captured material. Many of the units were said to be under-strength and under-equipped, and to lack mobility and training.[2]

Over-all responsibility for the defence of western Europe in general and the French coast in particular and for command of the Army troops in those defences (*Army Group "D"*) was vested in Field Marshal von Rundstedt, whose H.Q. was at St. Germain-en-Laye, near Paris. But his control was not absolute.

10. TO KNOW THE ENEMY: I(A) IN NORTH-WEST EUROPE

ENEMY DISPOSITIONS IN THE WEST ON 4 JUNE 1944
AS KNOWN TO THE ALLIES ON THAT DATE

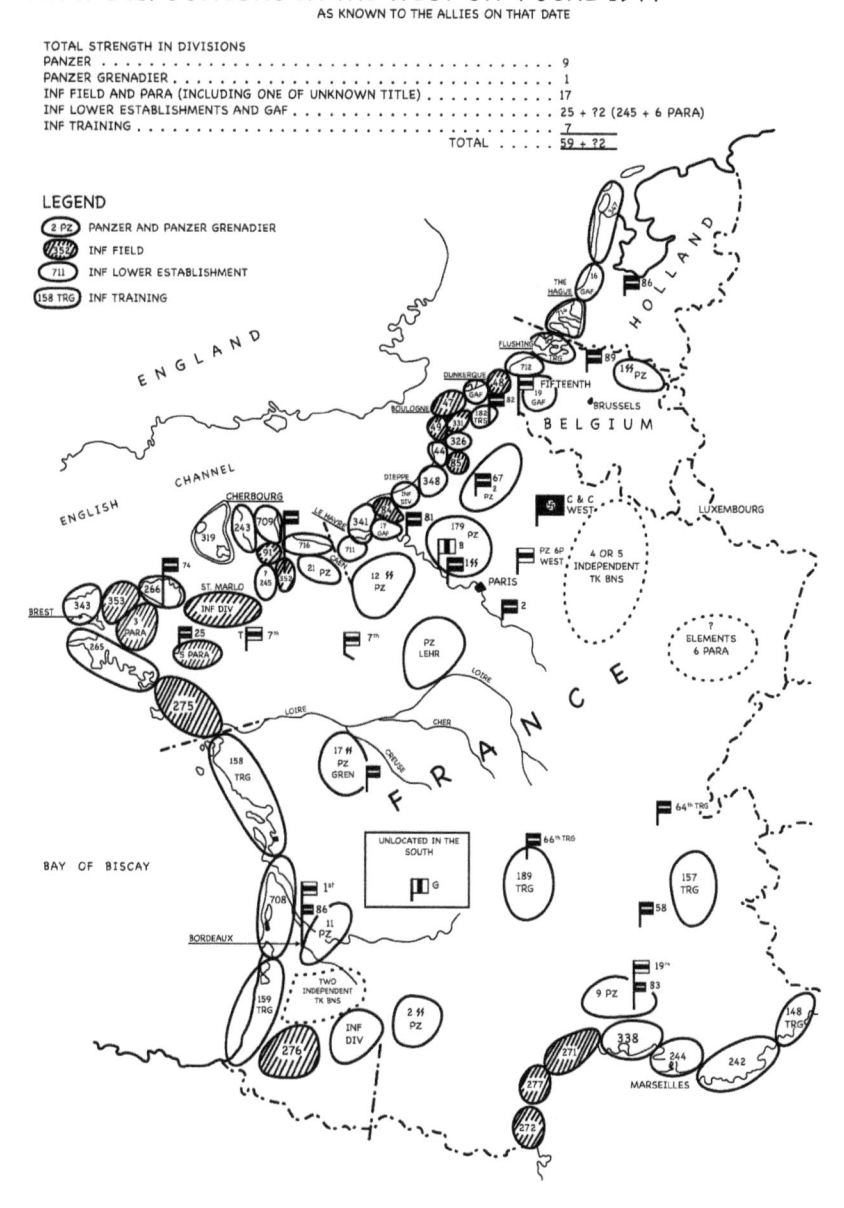

TOTAL STRENGTH IN DIVISIONS
PANZER 9
PANZER GRENADIER 1
INF FIELD AND PARA (INCLUDING ONE OF UNKNOWN TITLE) 17
INF LOWER ESTABLISHMENTS AND GAF . . . . 25 + ?2 (245 + 6 PARA)
INF TRAINING 7
                                                              TOTAL . . . . . 59 + ?2

LEGEND
- (2 PZ) PANZER AND PANZER GRENADIER
- INF FIELD
- (711) INF LOWER ESTABLISHMENT
- (158 TRG) INF TRAINING

Enemy dispositions, France, 4 June 1944. (Map has been reproduced based on a copy of the original that appeared in first edition of *Scarlet to Green*. Source of original map is unknown.)

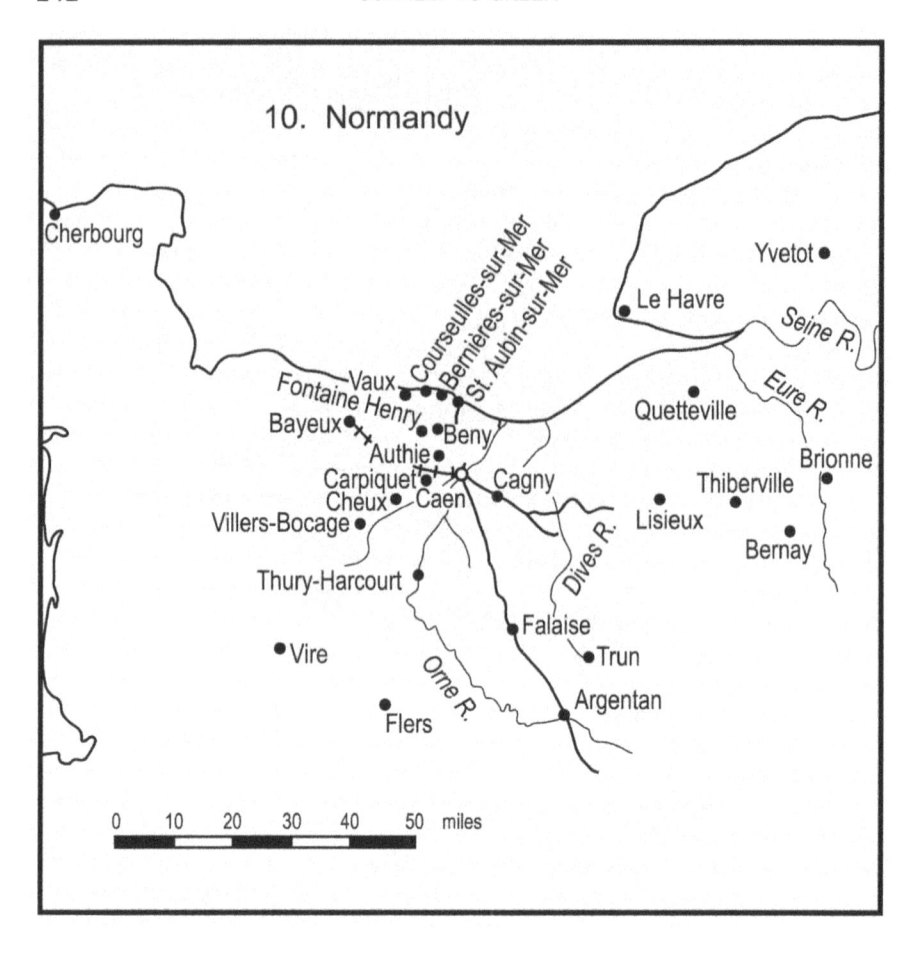

Some of the coastal artillery units belonged to the Navy, others to the Army; the *Luftwaffe* commanded the anti-aircraft units and the parachute divisions. All Services were controlled from Berlin, including Himmler's *Waffen Schutzstaffel (S.S.)*. Four of the mobile divisions – *1st* and *12th S.S. Panzer, Panzer Lehr*, and *17th Panzer Grenadier* – were subordinate to the *Oberkommando der Wehrmacht*, which was located in East Prussia. Even his nominal subordinate, Field Marshal Erwin Rommel, who commanded *Army Group "B"*, comprising *Seventh* and *Fifteenth Armies*, had a direct link to Hitler. In brief, although the German force was quite adequate to contain an invasion attempt, the divided command and the inefficiencies inherent in controlling units from H.Q. located great distances away from the theatre in which they were operating made it difficult for the enemy to react quickly.[3]

In the actual invasion area, *Seventh Army* was on the German left, *Fifteenth Army* on the right, with the high ground between the Orne and the Dives Rivers marking the inter-Army boundary. *Seventh Army* commanded *LXXXIV*

Corps in the Cherbourg Peninsula; a division in the Channel Islands; the *243rd Infantry Division* in the northwestern part of the Cotentin Peninsula; *709th Infantry Division* in Cherbourg; and the *352nd* and *716th Infantry Divisions* along the coast. All but the *352nd* were static. The *716th*, holding the area the Canadians were to assault, comprised the equivalent of two infantry regiments: six infantry battalions, two panzer grenadier battalions, and the anti-tank battalion from *21st Panzer Division* were in support some five miles inland. There were 16 batteries of artillery totalling 67 guns, exclusive of anti-tank guns or the guns in the beach defences. The beach defences in the Canadian sector held one 88 mm, three 75 mm, and six 50 mm guns, and a number of 81 mm mortars. Minefields running 300–800 yards inland formed an integral part of the defences. There were many obstacles on the beaches, almost all of them with mines attached to them.[4]

The Canadian beach objectives extended from St. Aubin-sur-Mer on the east to Graye-sur-Mer on the west *(less than one mile west of Courseulles-sur-Mer shown on Map 10)*. Courseulles-sur-Mer had the heaviest defences: an 88 mm gun and a 50 mm anti-tank gun guarded the eastern side of the harbour, and a 75 mm gun was located about 500 yards east of them. The gap between held six machine guns. On the west side of the harbour was another 75 mm, and two 50 mm guns. Six more machine guns and two 50 mm mortars were located in that general area, and another 75 mm gun was north of Vaux. Bernières held two 50 mm guns and seven machine guns; at St. Aubin there was a 50 mm gun, machine guns, and mortars.

Third Division's Commander issued his orders on May 13th, 1944; attached to them was a lengthy, unnumbered Intelligence Summary prepared by the Divisional Intelligence staff from C.O.S.S.A.C. material. Intsums Nos. 8 and 9 followed on May 16th and 18th. On "D" Day (June 6th), First Canadian Army produced its Intelligence Report No. 1, a comprehensive review of the enemy picture in depth, based on Wireless Intercept, Air Photo, and visual air reconnaissance (Tac R).[5] It was too late to be used in the assault, but it did give the follow-up pattern to Third Division and was the first coverage provided to the other Canadian formations.

The Divisional Intelligence Summaries described *716th Division* as "low category", with "two regiments of infantry and one of artillery (two field and one medium battery)". They identified and located the headquarters of the *736th* and *726th Grenadier Regiments*. Only one battalion of the *726th* was identified and although their presence was suspected, the two battalions of Russians were neither identified nor located. The locations of some of the sub-units were not entirely accurate. *716th Division* was estimated to be up to strength (13,000); it was actually at 7,771. The identification of the mobile reserve was also incorrect, but the Summaries did locate it in the divisional area and estimated it could move in about an hour and a half. *21st Panzer Division* was shown to be in the

Rennes area – two of its grenadier battalions, and its anti-tank battalion, were actually in support of the *716th*. The Summaries also discussed longer-term reinforcements and the possible presence of a *Parachute Division*.

The beaches – approaches, gradients, landing places, exits, and obstacles – were dealt with in detail. The offshore obstacles were: "80 to 250 yards from the coast. . . . Courseulles to Bernières . . . three and . . . four rows deep, some . . . diagonal to the coast. . . . In addition . . . are six staggered rows from the back of the beach . . . all . . . below high water mark. From the location and distribution . . . they are intended to be anti-craft rather than anti-vehicle." Artillery positions were given, and the coastal defences described in great detail.

"The coast is held by a system of linear defences. . . . A company area consists of several strongpoints occupied by either one section, two sections, or . . . a whole platoon. Each battalion has three companies forward . . . probably no battalion reserve. . . . Defences consist mainly of pillboxes and open machine-gun positions with open emplacements for 75 mm guns reinforcing the stronger positions. Strongpoints are usually set astride exits to cover the beaches with enfilade fire . . . assumed that each point will have a 2-inch (50 mm) mortar and that . . . six 3-inch (81 mm) mortars per battalion will be shared . . . [except] . . . in strongpoints in which there are infantry guns. Each strongpoint is surrounded by [its own] protective minefield and wire." In the three preceding months, observers had seen inland dug-out systems under construction, probably to house the heavy mortars and machine guns. In addition, the Summaries advised that " . . . all . . . wireless installations are organized for all-round defence although the allotment of automatic and heavier weapons is more meagre than for coastal strongpoints."

The Summaries also gave data on terrain: areas of flooding, suitability for cross-country movement, mines, cover, routes inland and the road system, river details, and bridges. Units were warned that the only civilians left in the area were those who were useful to the Germans, and that enemy agents could be expected. The location of the P.W. collection point was given. On May 16th, reports showed that *21st Panzer Division* had moved and had been replaced. *179th Panzer Training Division* was mentioned as being at La Roche-Guyon (actually Rommel's H.Q.). Two days later: "An excellent source reports an immense park of armoured vehicles . . . 600 in Forest de Cinglais [*sic*] . . . south west of Bretteville [-sur-] Laize on May 7th." It was *21st Panzer Division*. This report located four more guns and warned of mines at main junctions and bridges.[6]

The amount of information greatly exceeded that which Intelligence had provided before the Dieppe Raid. Deployments, unit identifications, and enemy weapons that could significantly affect the landings were all given in more detail, although the coastal gun positions were not located with sufficient accuracy. Intelligence was now much more aware of the real problems than it had been;

10. TO KNOW THE ENEMY: I(A) IN NORTH-WEST EUROPE 245

Officers of Canadian Air Liaison Sections in England, February 1944. Left to right; front row: Maj. W.R. Fysh, Maj. T.E. O'Reilly, Lt.-Col. Colin Rankin, Lt.-Col. R. Stockley, Maj. C.B. Gray; middle row: Capt. T.H. Lines, Maj. D.D. Sweeting, Maj. J.H. Mooney, Maj. Braithwaite, Maj. D. Corrigal, Capt. D.R. Griffin, Capt. K.G. Rice; back row: Capt. R.S. Forbes, Capt. G.G. Carter, Capt. R.H. Diplock, Capt. J.C. Stothard, Capt. T.R.F. Skemp. (War Diary, 1 Canadian Air Liaison Group/Photo collection Canadian Forces School of Military Intelligence, Kingston/Canada. Dept. of National Defence)

Maj. Odlum, with the aid of a stereoscope, studies photos taken by air reconnaissance flight over enemy territory. Date and location unknown. (Photo courtesy of MWO J. Moreno, Canadian Forces School of Military Intelligence, Kingston/Canada. Dept. of National Defence, PL6568)

its staffs were more experienced, and concentrated more heavily on discovering those facts that could affect success.

From April 24th until June 14th, First Canadian Army sent out a stream of fictional messages intended to make the Germans believe that the main thrust would enter France through the Pas de Calais. Attempts were made to seal the skies against enemy air reconnaissance. These appear to have been more successful than the deception scheme, but all these measures were enhanced by German uncertainties about the Allied capabilities. The German Intelligence Service had "identified" an extra thirty divisions in the Allied order-of-battle. It thought the Canadians had five infantry and three amoured divisions; it correctly identified Second and Third Infantry and Fourth Armoured Divisions in Britain; it knew that First Infantry and Fifth Armoured were in Italy, and it "tentatively identified" Sixth and Seventh Infantry – they, with Eighth Infantry, had been disbanded in Canada. It "suspected" two more to be in the U.K. and "failed to locate" another, the "First Armoured."[7]

Many Army A.P.I.S. officers worked at the Theatre Intelligence Section, while those remaining at the unit, averaging about six in all, were busy processing some 70 sorties. On May 21st alone, 11 sorties required about 3,000 prints to be plotted. Between 2015 and 0830 the following day, 12,000 copies were processed through the Mobile Field Processing Section. By 0600, the Air Liaison Officers were given a summary of the coverage.[8]

The Interrogation H.Q. Section and its four teams (Nos. 2, 3, 4, and 5) were mobilized at the beginning of May. On May 22nd, a meeting laid down procedures for handling P.W., and for reports, records, terminology, and content. On May 29th, No. 4 Team was sent to Hobbs Barracks, Lingfield. No. 5 Team was sent to Cannons Park (Wormwood Scrubs Prison, the British Interrogation Centre). The Document Section, and No. 2 Team, went to Kempton Park Race Course, a P.W. Reception Centre. No. 2 had its first "customers" on June 8th – a mixture of 175 young, arrogant Germans, and Poles and Russians who were talkative but who knew little. No. 4 Team was able to extract from its P.W. information that filled in a few blanks in enemy organization and strengths. On the 19th, No. 2 was sent to II Corps, to move to France. No. 5, in its role of dealing with French civilians, received some French employees of the *Todt Organization* in the U.S. Sector (Omaha Beach) on June 13th, but got nothing from them. On June 28th, it was given two self-confessed "stay-behind" agents of the *Abwehr*, and a well-known collaborator. The team had originally been formed to obtain I(a) information; this duty began its I(b) role.[9]

In answer to a British request, the First Canadian Army Interpreter Pool was formed on May 20th at 1 C.G.R.U., to facilitate dealings between H.Q. and the L. of C. units and the French civilian population. It had five officers, 39 N.C.O.s and men, and some 45 civilians, all of whom were fluent in French and English, but whose medical categories were too low for them to participate otherwise in the campaign. The unit was disbanded at the end of September 1944, after a short but useful life.[10]

The first day's fighting brought Intelligence no surprises. It reduced *716th Division:* ". . . of four German and two Russian battalions there remained in the evening one German battalion which had had about 20% casualties; otherwise only remnants".[11] Most of Gen. Richter's artillery had also gone, but it had given a better account of itself than had been expected. By June 16th, Third Division's advance had halted. The Germans counter-attacked at Authie with a new formation which was to become very familiar – *12th S.S. Pz. Division (Hitler Youth)*, commanded by Gen. Kurt Meyer, and manned by ardent young Nazis. It had one tank regiment of two battalions (150 Panther and Mk. IV tanks), an anti-tank battalion, and two Panzer Grenadier regiments, each of three battalions. At the beginning of 1944, its strength was 20,540.

No. 3 Interrogation Team landed on June 7th at Courseulles-sur-Mer. Mendel and Trasenko went forward to 7 Brigade, while the rest went to the Divisional P.W. Cage at Fontaine Henry. By the 10th, they had 140 P.W. to interrogate and were complaining that the units were also sending them civilians. To the units it was probably immaterial where the civilians went, so long as they got out of the way. On the 16th the Team had its tents damaged by shell splinters, but no one was hurt.[12]

No. 10 Air Liaison Section's L.C.T. was "torpedoed in mid-Channel". Capt. Dennison and Tpr. Gatchell were resting in a jeep which caught fire, but they managed to get out before the gas tank exploded. Capt. R.S. Forbes was asleep in an ambulance about 10 feet from the blast; he was picked out of the water with only a singeing and one small scratch. The Section was taken the rest of the way by motor launch. Once ashore, they scrounged a jeep and, for the next two days, explored abandoned German positions, collecting maps, traces, letters, and paybooks, which they turned over to Second Army Intelligence. Capt. Lines and No. 9 Section went to their designated concentration point, but retired quickly upon finding that the Germans had not yet left. Allied aircraft landed on the strip outside Rommel's former H.Q. on the 10th. No. 10 Section was given two replacement Air Force I.O.s who had never done Tactical Air, and Capt. Forbes felt somewhat aggrieved in consequence. By June 13th, six Mustang and five Typhoon squadrons, and the Air Support Signals Unit which controlled them, were functioning. "God, are we tired, but it's great to be busy." No. 8 Section arrived on the 14th, and set up with 17 Sector H.Q. at Pierre Artus. No. 13 Section was supposed to move to Beny-sur-Mer on the 14th, but, since the enemy were within 800 yards, some redeployment was necessary. No. 11 Section arrived on June 15th.[13]

The planning information was adequate only until battle was joined. The changes in enemy deployments and organization forced by battle had then to be mastered, a task which called for continuing efforts by the Divisional Intelligence staff. Enemy identifications reflected the direct contact of combat. On June 9th, Capt. Black, G.S.O.3 (Int), knew what was on his right flank, but was less sure of his left. Some of the enemy P.W. were from the *989th Coastal Division*, and another prisoner gave him the organization of *902nd Regiment Pz. Gr. Lehr*. On the 10th, Capt. Black "identified" *22nd S.S. Pz. Division* (probably a typographical error for *12th)* and *716th Infantry Division* as being on his front, with *352nd Infantry Division* deployed to Authie, and *902nd Pz. Lehr Regiment* and a reconnaissance unit on the Division's right. He summarized the action: "... 716... need no longer be considered a separate fighting formation."[14]

On June 12th there was "evidence of digging and for the first time an enemy artillery concentration... indicating... real co-ordination... and possibilities of a counter attack.... The enemy has been told to stay in his foxholes until the tanks are by and then attack the infantry following up.... A sergeant who had been cut off from our lines... returned... with information that the enemy appeared to have evacuated [Le Mesnil-Patry] village". A platoon of the Canadian Scottish was sent out and found it empty. Tac R reported that "a column of all arms ten miles long was moving towards Argentan" – either *116th Pz. Division* or *1st S.S. Division*. On June 17th, *716th* and *352nd Divisions,* and *30 Mobile Brigade,* had "had it"; ten divisions were left, and: "It would appear that the enemy, finding himself incapable of defeating the invasion on the beaches, is possibly preparing to fight a defensive battle." He would probably use delaying tactics south of the railway line between Bayeux and Caen, including mines and booby traps. The interrogation of a Polish deserter enabled I British Corps to fill three pages with data on enemy mining techniques, which were duly passed on to Third Division and then to the units.[15]

The Odon was crossed on June 30th. Tac R observed "much enemy movement between Thury-Harcourt–Flers–Falaise–Argentan–Vire–Villers-Bocage ... showing that enemy reinforcements are moving within striking distance of our most forward elements".[16] Confirmation was obtained when a German officer was captured making his reconnaissance, with notes of what appeared to be verbal orders in his pocket. An enemy attack at Cheux was repulsed.[17]

In Britain, the rest of First Canadian Army waited its turn. D-Day came as "a complete surprise to (almost) everyone". The G.S.O.3 I(a) "smelt a mouse... when the G.S.O.1 insisted on getting the Tac R Broadcast listening set arranged [by Lieut. C.M. Hayes].... German radio broadcast the news of paratroop landings in France and our own Tac R [controlled from Odiham and Middle Wallop] began to broadcast enemy moves in the Cherbourg Peninsula. The news ... precipitated a great flurry of activity... as innumerable items scheduled for the day were despatched. The planning room was... evacuated... superfluous planning material... destroyed or taken to the Intelligence Company... the I(a) Section set up in the Army Operations Room and the Intelligence Centre and First Canadian Army Intelligence Summary No. 1 produced.... It was a great source of satisfaction to find that the enemy deployment turned out almost exactly as we painted it." The Section established personal liaison with 21 Army Group. Second Army and 21 Army Group Summaries and Intelligence Logs, Wireless Reports, and Combined Operations Special Intelligence Summaries were obtained. Col. Wright arranged for a daily "morning prayers" at 1000 to inform all the Intelligence staff of the progress of the fighting. And now that the units were together, almost for the first time other than on an exercise, the "I" Mess was born, with 1 A.P.I.S. acting as midwife.[18] Its members included Canadians, British, French, and Belgians.

The Army Commander's party left for France on June 15th. "It had once been anticipated that H.Q. First Canadian Army should control a part of the assault on Europe."[19] Intelligence was to send an advance and a reconnaissance party, an "A Shift" and a "B Shift", on D + 10, D + 15, and D + 17 days, respectively. Instead, the Army Commander decided to station himself near 21 Army Group. The G.S.O.1 (Lt.-Col. Wright) was to be in his entourage to ensure that enemy data was available to assist any last-minute planning. An information centre was set up at Uxbridge with Majs. D.R. Morrice and R. Marks, Capts. P.P. Mustard and John Timmerman, and Lieut. D. Wiens. The available interrogators were concentrated, and the Wireless Intelligence Sections were assigned to British control.[20]

The advance and reconnaissance party which led the Commander's party over on June 16th contained Maj. J.W.G. (Bud) Macdougall, G.S.O.2 I(b), Capt. W.J.R. Wilson, I.O. I(b), Capt. J.M. Robertson, I.O. (Topog), Capt. W.E. Grant, G.S.O.3 I(s), and one of his Wireless Intelligence I.O.s, Lieut. K.L. Fawdry. They landed at La Rivière, and went to their assembly area south of Courseulles. On June 17th, they went on to Amblie, some of them via Second Army, to get the latest information. After a speedy crossing in H.M.C.S. *Algonquin,* Lt.-Col. Wright arrived on the 18th, and the small Section was set up.

Because the breakout had not gone as quickly as anticipated, the whole troop build-up timetable was delayed. General Simonds opened Tactical H.Q., II Canadian Corps, at Amblie on June 29th and main H.Q. at Camilly a week later. Second Canadian Infantry Division landed on July 7th. First Army did not assume tactical command until mid-July. Intelligence had three office trucks: the G.S.O.1 and Bud Macdougall shared one, the I.O.s had a tarpaulin against I(b)'s office HUP, and I(s) were half a mile up the valley to the south. But the main H.Q. did not get to France until late July.[21]

When No. 12 Air Liaison Section arrived in France on June 26th, the A.L. organization was complete. It comprised the Air Support Signals Unit control (A.S.S.U.) at Second Army H.Q., the Ground Control Centre (G.C.C.), the Visual Control Point (V.C.P.), and Air Liaison Officers at 22 Sector (Nos. 1 to 6 Sections), which contained No. 121 Airfield, No. 124 Airfield (124 Wing), No. 11 Section, and No. 125 Airfield (No. 143 Wing, 438, 439, and

11. Caen to Falaise

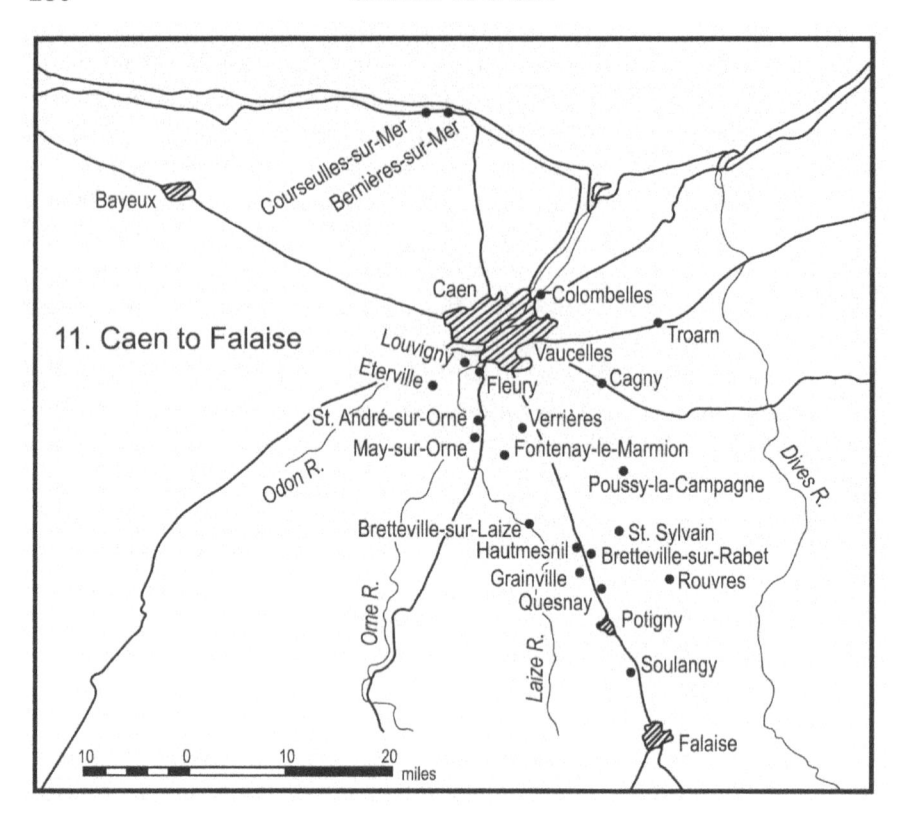

440 R.C.A.F. Squadrons), No. 12 Section. 17 Sector controlled Airfield B 2 (Bazenville), where No. 8 Section was based. No. 10 Section served 127 Wing, then supporting the battle for Caen, (EPSOM). No. 9 Section was with 126 Wing at B 3 (St. Croix-sur-Mer). No. 13 Section was with 144 Wing at B 4 (Beny-sur-Mer). They were busy; 17 Sector's three Wings flew 418 sorties on June 28th alone. During the preparations for EPSOM, 1 A.P.I.S. dealt with photography from 164 sorties, flown in 15 days flying weather – 22 of them on June 12th. They handled 40,000 prints, and the combined Photo Section ran off 250,000 copies. They prepared nearly 40 Interpretation Reports, which explained what the photos showed.[22]

On July 2nd, a deserter from the *46th Luftwaffe Regiment* announced the arrival of *16th Luftwaffe Division* from Holland. Higher authority identified *21st Pz.* and *12th S.S. Pz. Divisions* as the defenders of Caen. A captured map gave the boundary between them, and with its help Third Division produced a map showing the general areas of their positions for its lower formations. In the Order covering the capture of Carpiquet, the "Enemy" paragraph stated: "Recent patrol reports indicate the enemy may have thinned out. . . . There was no evidence that anti-tank or field artillery was located in Carpiquet. Heavy tracks, probably tanks [they could also have been self-propelled guns], had been noted but not in great quantities."[23] The movement forward of the assault force was observed by the Germans, and received heavy gun and mortar fire. Carpiquet itself may not have contained field artillery, but there was plenty within range.

Later information revealed that *1 Battalion, 26th S.S. Pz.Gr. Regiment*, had been in the village and part of the airfield, while the other two battalions occupied the rest of the airfield and the area east of it. But the senior staff officer of *12th S.S. Pz. Division* subsequently gave credit for the defence to 50 men of the *25th Pz.Gr. Regiment*.[24] There has been some controversy over this discrepancy and, inasmuch as all the identifications that follow reflect the *25th*, not the *26th*, there was probably an error in the original report.

Caen fell on July 9th. The heavy damage to the old city made so many obstacles that it was almost impossible to follow the retreating enemy. *16th Luftwaffe Division* was estimated to have lost 75% of its infantry; *12th S.S. Pz. Division* was left with only one battalion's worth of infantry, and just over half its tanks, after its encounter with Third Division.[25]

On July 11th, II Canadian Corps came into the line under H.Q. Second British Army, to hold about 8,000 yards of front on both sides of Caen and "by active patrolling to study the problem of gaining a bridgehead across the Orne south of Caen". The first Intsum, after cautioning against taking marked maps into forward areas, drew on Army material to locate the general areas of the five divisions opposing the Corps.

On July 12th, Corps admitted that it had no new information on the strength or dispositions of the *16th Luflwaffe* and *12th S.S. Pz. Divisions* that had survived Caen. It thought that *12th S.S.* (invariably called the *Hitler Jugend*) had lost most of its tanks, and that a Grenadier Regiment of *1st S.S.* (*Leibstandarte Adolf Hitler – L.A.H.* or *A.H.*) was in the area of St. André-sur-Orne. "The enemy will make a determined effort to prevent us crossing the Orne . . . harass our movements with mortar and artillery fire."[26] On the 14th, an unidentified Field Security officer picked up at St. Germain two P.W. from the *25th Pz.Gr. Regiment*, thus confirming the presence of *12th S.S. Pz. Division*.

Second Canadian Infantry Division issued its first Intsum on the 14th. It located *1st S.S. Pz. Division*, and elements of *1st S.S. Pz.Gr. Regiment*, in front of it, with *102 Heavy Tank Battalion* and some 150 rockets from the *Lehr Mortar Battalion* in support. Civilians had told Corps that the enemy had withdrawn from Colombelles, Faubourg de Vaucelles, Fleury-sur-Orne, and Louvigny. When Division sent patrols forward to verify the reports, they were found to be false.[27]

Second Army's plan to establish a firm bridgehead beyond the Orne required the Canadians first to capture Faubourg de Vaucelles, then to bridge the Orne and take the high ground north of St. André-sur-Orne, and the village of Verrières overlooking the Falaise road. Third Division was to attack through

Colombelles and Vaucelles. Second Division would exploit the breakthrough. II Corps identified *361 Pz. Gr. Reinforcement Battalion* of *21st Pz. Division* in Vaucelles. An Air Observation Post (A.O.P.) aircraft reported seeing 80 tanks southeast of Caen, but Corps thought its estimate too high. On July 17th, a tank regiment of *1st S.S. Division* was identified. The lack of information on units behind the enemy line was serious, and No. 2 Wireless Intelligence Section could offer little help, because "Jerry [was] observing almost a wireless silence in the battle area".

On the 17th, Second Division patrols were reporting nothing but stragglers and deserters. The German mortar positions were close to roads and tracks, and the Division surmised, correctly, that the enemy was ready to move rapidly. Third Division, which had been in close contact during the break-in battle, confirmed that *1st S.S. Division* held the western end of Vaucelles. It also confirmed the *361 Pz. Gr. Reinforcement Battalion* that Corps had reported earlier, and located elements of the *Luftwaffe* near the factory at Colombelles. Corps also located six German artillery support areas in the triangle of the Caen–Vimont and Caen–Falaise roads. Their 29 gun positions and over 80 guns were believed to be artillery of *346th Infantry* and *16th Luftwaffe Divisions*.[28]

Doubts concerning enemy identifications began to arise. A prisoner stated that the *S.S.* had been withdrawn on the 15th and that *271st Infantry Division* was now at Maltot. Capt. Stephens and Lieut. Fred Pollak of the Wireless Section, who were working as interpreters for Third Division, identified the formation as the *272nd*. *16th Luftwaffe* was confirmed at Cormelles. Third Division provided an explanation on July 19th: "The previous P.W. statement that *361 Erzatz Pz. Gr. Battalion* was holding . . . the railway yards in Vaucelles was technically incorrect. Actually, elements of *192nd Pz. Gr. Regiment* were . . . and . . . had received . . . companies from *361*. . . . Other reinforcement units were being used. . . . *271 Infantry Division* were . . . west of Eterville. . . . *980th Pz. Gr. Regiment* were astride the Orne, *982nd* were between it and the main Falaise road." There was nothing to identify the specific composition of the German force which had stopped II Corps' advance below Verrières Ridge in the bloody fighting of July 25th – excepting Dieppe, the most costly day for the Canadians of the Second World War.[29] But the German front was beginning to crack and swing back under American pressure, though the move came too late to prevent the bloodshed at Verrières Ridge.

The Interrogation teams had found it difficult to operate as units. No. 2 Team landed on July 3rd, and then moved, via H.Q. II Corps, to Second Division at Cairon. Its O.C., Capt. J. Stonborough, took two men to 8 C.I.B.; the rest went to the Second Division Cage. On the 21st they were moved to a new Cage across the Orne, and spent all of August between the two Cages or on assignment. Much of their time was wasted in unproductive travelling. Both Stonborough and Motzfeldt, O.C. No. 4 Team, were big men with good presence, disinclined to take arrogance from cocky P.W. such as *Hitler Jugend*. Both did excellent work. One of their N.C.O.s, Sgt. M.C. Silzer, looking for privacy for an interrogation, took his *S.S.* prisoner into a house. Once inside, he heard a noise, opened a cupboard and found two more Germans; "one had a luger, both had cameras". The Team Diary quotes a parody of a popular song of the period, "Luger luggin' Ludwig – Lay that Luger down!" When No. 3 Team, which worked for Corps from July 12th to 24th, was assigned to Third Division, it found that its P.W. simplified the task of identification by falling in as units when paraded in the Cages. But, as No. 2 Team put it, ". . . our air and artillery superiority makes interrogation difficult. The former forces the enemy to undertake all moves at night and the latter to remain below ground level all day. . . . P.W. have little opportunity to observe features of the terrain or dispositions of other troops."[30]

A.P.I.S. also suffered mixed fortunes. On July 23rd, Third Division reported: "The confused Order of Battle situation . . . has not been assisted by the past three days of bad weather which has prevented Photo and Tac R. Consequently we have been unable to determine movements of reserves or progress in the preparation of defences. . . . ground reports indicate digging in the area of Tilly-La-Campagne and . . . north of La Hogue [which was to be an early objective of the infantry of Fourth Armoured Division]." *(Tilly and La Hogue are just east of Verrières respectively on Map 11.)* Three days later, after Third Division had been stopped along the high ground Fontenay-le-Marmion–Garcelles–Secqueville; "although photo reconnaissance has disclosed the new [enemy] defensive position on the high ground south-east of Bretteville-sur-Laize, this would be too far back to form the main position of Fontenay–Garcelles. He has successfully held the latter today with comparatively little infantry and may be expected to continue. . . . Troops he is using to prepare the Bretteville line . . . may be . . . Panzer Grenadier Regiments of *9 S.S. Division* . . . he has 80–90 tanks and not all are committed."[31] No. 3 Special Wireless Section had earlier "overheard" the *S.S. Division*, and all formations were watching for evidence of its deployment.

By the end of July, changes began to appear in the enemy deployments. Second Division located *20th Pz. Gr. Regiment (9 S.S. Pz. Division)* from the east bank of the Orne to Fontenay-le-Marmion, with *1st S.S. Pz. Gr. Regiment* on its right. It thought that *272nd Division* had been withdrawn. Corps believed that its Fusilier Battalion might still have been in the line beyond *1st S.S.*[32]

II Corps admitted that it did not have adequate information on German minefields across the front. The Germans certainly had had enough time to lay mines, if they had the mines and the transport to bring them forward. The interrogators were asked to try to get this information from the P.W., and at the same time discover P.W. reactions to the assassination attempt against Hitler, which had just been revealed. Most P.W. had not heard of it. When they were told, the non-German members of four infantry divisions regretted that it had not succeeded; the Nazi hard core refused to believe the report, and reminded interrogators that loyalty to the Nazi oath meant that they would go on fighting. But the news did cause misgivings among those who were not fanatical members of the Nazi Party.[33]

Intelligence did not learn until later that the German High Command had been expecting a further attack in the Caen area. *XLVII Panzer Corps* had been ordered to send *2nd Panzer Division* to Tournebu, northwest of Falaise, on July 22nd to counter it. *9th* and *10th S.S. Panzer* were to assemble between the Laize and Orne Rivers. This meant that Second British Army faced seven enemy armoured divisions; one and parts of two others were west of the Orne. II Canadian Corps faced *1 S.S. Panzer Corps*, with *1st S.S. Panzer Division* between Cagny and Verrières, *272nd Infantry Division* (soon to be replaced by *9th Panzer*) with its left flank on the Orne, reinforced with a tank battalion and a Panzer Grenadier battalion from *2nd Panzer* and *9th S.S. Panzer Divisions*, and the reconnaissance battalion from *10th S.S.* Northwest of Bretteville-sur-Laize was the rest of *9th S.S.*, and northwest of Tournebu the rest of *2nd Panzer*. *116th Panzer Division* was located northeast of St. Sylvain, in *1 S.S. Panzer Corps* reserve. Second Army did not know that *2nd Panzer* had come forward, nor did they know the full story of the dispositions.[34]

This information was not easy to collect. The enemy was filling his line with whatever random reinforcements he could get. The moves and reorganizations he had to make in order to set up short-term defence positions produced for Intelligence an unconventional, varied, and puzzling mixture of identifications. Tight German radio security, and weather so adverse that it hampered air reconnaissance, made it difficult to detect moves and assess the strength of positions. Enemy P.W. interrogations did furnish valuable data, but much of it was after-the-fact and unsuitable for use in extended forward planning. Second Army gave invaluable guidance and help. II Corps and its subordinate Intelligence units learned quickly, and played a part in helping to resolve the uncertainties.

First Canadian Army took over from Second British Army on July 23rd. First Army's Intelligence advance party had "settled down to the, by now familiar, role of spectators . . . keeping in touch with the main developments of the enemy situation, advising the G.O.C. accordingly, and keeping the maps neatly marked . . . thanks to the friendly helpful . . . Intelligence staffs [at] . . . Second British Army, B Group, R.A.F, and First U.S. Army." They visited the latter and were "initially confused . . . all the officers are majors or more and . . . the enemy [is] marked in red and our own troops in blue on the maps [the reverse of British and Canadian practice at the time; it now is standard NATO usage]. . . . Later [they found] common grounds in mutual problems and speculation over a common enemy."[35] It was unfortunate that the Section at H.Q. First Army did not commence work earlier. Inaction had dulled their sharply-honed enthusiasm and it took a little while to regain it.

As we have seen, the two Wireless Sections arrived before mid-July; No. 2 went to II Corps on the 10th; No. 3 was held for Army use from the 18th. Capt. Riehle and his Document Team went to H.Q. First Army by the 12th, and fell heir to a vast volume of unprocessed material. Both Riehle and Rudi Aksim, who was responsible for Technical Intelligence, spent most of their time with the forward units. Army also received representatives from two British organizations, Security Control Unit 8 (S.C.U.8), responsible for links with line-crossers and clandestine units operating in enemy-held territory, and Intelligence Security 9 (I.S.9), responsible for Escape and Evasion. Army also at this time ran a "Beach Feeding Cage" for P.W., to which the Interrogation H.Q. was attached.

The air strength also was increasing; No. 400 R.C.A.F. and two R.A.F. squadrons arrived on July 3rd, bringing with them additional A.L.O.s and I.O.s. The A.L.O.s in each unit were then reorganized and separated into two groups. The Senior A.L.O. (S.A.L.O.) was to plan the missions, the Junior J.A.L.O.) was to brief the crews. Four Sections were disbanded – Nos. 8 and 11 "Type E" and Nos. 3 and 13 "Type F" – thus "saving" two majors, six captains, and 16 men. The change was supposed to streamline operations; in practice it meant more work for the Group Control Centre, which now had to deal directly with Fighter and Fighter-Bomber Wings, and, at the Section level, for three A.L.O.s who now had to cope with up to five squadrons per airfield. It was a reversion to an earlier system that had already proved to be unsatisfactory.

No. 10 A.L. Section, at 127 Wing, R.C.A.F., got from H.Q. Second Army a regular Situation Report (SITREP) of the forward troop locations and the positions of all H.Q. down to Brigade. About once a week they received Intelligence Summaries, from which they briefed the R.C.A.F personnel. From time to time they arranged to have the pilots taken up to the forward battalions for familiarization. "The close shelling impresses them (as well as ourselves) very much." An A.L.O. from Second Army stressed that "the Army are not sitting on their 'fannys' doing nothing. . . . The biggest job the A.L.O.s have to do is to keep the Army on the right side of the pilots . . . the feeling that the Army was wrong extended right to the top of the Air Force tree." The pilots, especially those in 39 (Reconnaissance) Wing, R.C.A.F., then at Sommervieu with Nos. 1, 2, 4, and 6 A.L. Sections, were frustrated by indifferent weather which often prevented them from flying. No. 12 Section, helping No. 143 Wing, R.C.A.F., to support the ground action in the Falaise area (Operation GOODWOOD), had to cope not only with the enhanced pressures of operations but also with those of reorganization and the posting of their O.C., Capt. A.W. Woodhouse.[36]

Gen. Montgomery ordered a further advance on the eastern flank on July 27th. The Canadians' part, Operation TOTALIZE, was a thrust south and southeast of Caen, intended to cut off the German forces from their withdrawal routes eastward. In First Army Intelligence, the "activity . . . was completely focused on the enemy and centered around the Intelligence Summary". This involved the G.S.O.1 and his assistants, Maj. Les Chater, G.S.O.2 I(a), and Capt. C.M. Tetrault, G.S.O.3 I(a), and the I.O.s (ORBAT), Capt. M. Shulman and Lieut. P. Pootmans. In his initial assessment on August 1st, Lt.-Col. Wright said: "The paramount need to stay firm on Caen is best shown by the forces . . . there . . . by the strength of the lines constructed. . . . To bridge the gap from the gorge of the upper Orne to the flooded flats of the lower Dives . . . the shortest distance . . . is the enemy's present position . . . May-sur-Orne to Troarn. The second line from Bretteville-sur-Laize to Aire appears from photographs to be equally strong . . . a third line has been found 2,000 yards in length two miles north of Potigny. Thus the enemy has a position as strong as nature and art . . . can make it which offers to his forces further west right flank protection as they are withdrawn behind the Orne."[37]

On August 6th, i.e., just before TOTALIZE started, Third Division viewed the situation: "It is not considered likely that the enemy will make a stand along the River Orne as no actual defensive line has been constructed. . . . It seems likely that he will withdraw to the line of the River Dives fighting a delaying action. The enemy forces south of the junctions of the Orne and the Laize are the *271 Infantry* [sic, 272], *9 S.S. Pz.* and elements of *10 S.S. Pz. Divisions*. The latter has been engaged in small battle groups over a rather large area leaving a state of confusion. . . . The enemy must hold any thrust southwards from Caen long enough to permit the withdrawal of his forces between the Orne and the Laize."[38]

The Canadians intended to attack in three successive phases: breaching the enemy positions first at Fontenay-le-Marmion–La Hogue; then at Haut-mesnil–St. Sylvain; and then enlarging their penetration. A Yugoslav deserter, picked up on the night of August 5th, told Intelligence that *1st* and *9th S.S. Panzer* had been relieved by *89th Infantry Division*. II Corps speculated that *1st S.S.* had withdrawn to Bretteville-sur-Laize, and identified its replacements as a Grenadier battalion each from *272nd* and *711th Infantry Divisions*. Second Division did not regard the change as significant. Fourth Armoured Division thought opposition on the present enemy line would be strong but that the Bretteville-sur-Laize position would be the stronger. There was a good deal of discussion regarding possible German reinforcements; as it turned out the Germans were kept from moving by a simultaneous British attack.[39]

1 A.P.I.S. had started work on a planning mosaic for TOTALIZE on August 1st. The copy was prepared, flown to Odiham in England for reproduction, and delivered on the 3rd, one full day ahead of the deadline. A second mosaic, to include Falaise, was ordered on the 3rd. It was finished by 0430 on the 4th, and passed back to 5 Mobile Field Processing Section in four pieces for reproduction. A third mosaic was ordered at 1800 on the 4th, and finished on the 6th. All three, of course, concentrated on the immediate battle area. The A.P.I.S.

appreciation on the 1st had spotted the defence lines and new battery sites two miles north of Potigny. On the 5th, A.P.I.S. reported the extension of the line and its defences in the Poussy-la-Campagne to St. Aignan-de-Cramesnil sector. Two days later: "Report of Panzer Division in Forêt de Cinglais can neither be confirmed or denied on excellent but incomplete cover". The next day, after a lull in which virtually no movement was seen, A.P.I.S. reported an extensive redeployment of A.A. units from the area northeast of Dozule and southeast of Troarn. On the 10th: "Today's sorties have been remarkable for the amount of movement seen. Excellent cover revealed nine new artillery positions in the area north east of Potigny. Many positive identifications were made by II Corps . . . rapid development of the Rouvres defence line was noted." (The Rouvres Line was based on the Laison River, the last obstacle north of the escape route from Falaise.) "34 new A.A. battery positions . . . on our front south of Mézidon." They included a new type of gun, and A.P.I.S. asked for help in identifying it. On the 12th: "Activity in infantry defensive works has increased considerably today on our immediate front from the Mézidon Railway south to our right boundary. It has been noted that Flak batteries are being more and more sited for an effective anti-tank role."[40]

On the 10th, "the picture is fluid. . . . Forward troops are not passing back information on tanks and guns knocked out or destroyed." The next day, Corps assessed *89th Division* at about 500 infantry, located *271st Division* at Placy Bois, and reported indications of withdrawal in the Mortain area. Third Division was somewhat more comprehensive; " . . . both of *[89th Division's]* regiments west of the Caen–Falaise road. *85 Division* is on the east with . . . left *1054* . . . right *1053 Gr. Regiments*. *980 Regiment* of *272 Infantry Division* is . . . north-east. These identifications seem to show that the enemy has shifted his infantry slightly west presumably to meet the new threat to his left flank and to bolster up the gap caused by the mauling of *89 Division*."[41]

Operation TOTALIZE advanced the Canadian line to a point on the Laison River just beyond Bretteville-le-Rabet–Langannerie–Grainville. It failed to clear the Germans from Quesnay and the wood behind it. When the battle joined, the Intelligence staffs could do little, ". . . apart from watching the map and the enemy's moves from it. During . . . the battle news tended to fall off and the future to become even more confused". On the morning of August 11th, Gen. Simonds cancelled all further advances and set planning in train for a new set-piece attack, using Second and Third Divisions. The new operation, TRACTABLE, was essentially the same as TOTALIZE, but with significant changes in the details of its execution. Unfortunately, notes of Gen. Simonds' orders given on August 13th were taken from the body of an officer of Second Division who had accidently driven into the German lines. With that evidence, the enemy re-deployed his defences and delayed the capture of Falaise by at least 24 hours.[42]

During this period Capt. Mark Robinson, A.P.I.S., noticed some "88s" in the photo coverage. Capt. Bob Wodehouse found more than "just a few", and took the information to Maj. Les Chater, who showed it at once to Lt.-Col. Wright. Later, Les told Bob Wodehouse that this was First Army's first indication of the whereabouts of a German Flak Corps earlier reported by Strategic Wireless Intelligence ("Ultra") – which had a link to Army H.Q. – to have left Berlin. It was a significant addition to German strength, especially since the 88 was often used in the ground role. A Corps contained three regiments of three, and sometimes four, battalions, each with up to six troops, each troop with two to four 88 mm guns and two to three 20 mm. An early estimate indicated a total in this case of 62 88 mm and perhaps 41 20 mm guns.[43]

The first suggestions of a projected enemy withdrawal appeared. On August 13th, Corps passed on Tac R reports that the enemy was beginning to move east through Falaise. Fourth Armoured Division made a number of minor identifications involving *85th*, *12 S.S. Pz.*, *272nd*, and remnants of *89th* and *271st Divisions*, which lay on the enemy's right, supported by at least one battalion of heavy (Tiger) tanks. Fourth Armoured Division's assessment was: "The enemy . . . appears to have formed an anti-tank screen pivoted on the area Quesnay–Potigny. The screen to the east follows . . . the river Laison."[44]

The attack began about noon on the 14th and, although the enemy had its route and frontage accurately identified, its weight was irresistible. The Laison River, however, turned out to be an unexpectedly difficult obstacle that A.P.I.S. had failed to estimate correctly. Its banks were sheer, and the river, which may have been a trout stream, had been blocked by weirs. It was just wide enough to let a Sherman tank belly in. By the 15th, Corps' assessment was: *12th S.S.* was in reserve; the *89th* could pretty well be written off; the *85th* was down to two battalions of 200 men; *271st Division* had two battalions left; and *272nd* had only one. Prisoners were reporting to Second Division that a general withdrawal to the Seine had been ordered. They cited as proof the withdrawal of *12th S.S.*, but the Intelligence staff hesitated to believe them. Yet Third Division, when it confirmed the identity of *85th Division*, reported that of 700 prisoners captured in three days, one only was *12th S.S.*; he was from *Battle Group Krauss*, which had been astride the Caen–Falaise road at Soulangy until the 15th. Tac R "has reported much enemy movement during the day in the bottleneck area. It would appear that the enemy stands little chance of establishing a firm line this side of the Seine". Second Division saw no threat of counter-attack except southwest of Falaise, and then only from one (named) battalion of *12th S.S.* and perhaps a Tiger tank battalion.[45]

Falaise fell on the morning of the 17th. Second Division now learned from one of its prisoners that *12th S.S.* had indeed withdrawn southeast from Falaise on about the 14th. Third Division passed on a Tac R report of "very heavy traffic through the gap [between the Canadians and the Americans] towards

Trun *[shown on Map 10]*. This target is being taken by air and artillery . . . estimated that 100,000 enemy are in the pocket to the west". Five named divisions seemed to have gone through the gap; two were inside; the locations of two others were not known. Second Division thought two panzer divisions were still there also, with remnants of three parachute and at least three infantry divisions. Intelligence did not know who was trying to keep the gap open, but Army thought it was *1st* and *10th S.S. Divisions*, supported by heavy mortars, 88s and Tiger tanks.

None of the identifications was, in practice, very useful, as a Canadian "Canloan" officer serving with the British pointed out. He had been taken prisoner and been marched through the gap at Trun, and had escaped to Canadian lines; "all roads and particularly byways were crowded with transport . . . there were no complete ordered formations on the move". First Army's most distinguished prisoner was Lt.-Gen. Erwin Menny, *84th Infantry Division*, a veteran of the *Africa Corps*. Col. Gerloch, Commander *708th Division*, was captured about the same time following a navigational error made by his senior operations officer. As Army said, "the battle for Normandy is lost. We can expect he [the enemy] will try to stabilize somewhere, possibly the Somme–Aisne–Marne line. His intentions after this decisive defeat are rather more political than military and, as such, even more unpredictable".[46]

During the advance, A.L.O.s of the Air Liaison Sections had to ensure that the "bomb line" – a prominent feature lying in front of friendly troops and behind which bombing was forbidden for safety reasons – was accurately marked on the pilots' maps, based on the latest information. In the last ten days of August, Allied units sometimes came under attack from their own aircraft. The A.L. Sections used scales of 1:500,000 for long sweeps and bomber escort missions; 1:250,000 to show the entire Allied front; 1:100,000 for all situation records and for bomb-line data; and 1:50,000 for close support missions. The errors that the maps unfortunately contained could account for some of the mistakes made by the pilots, but the weather, the haze, and the smoke and dust over the target areas often made navigation, not to mention accurate sightings of targets, a matter of luck rather than certainty. In addition, not all units made sure that their positions were accurately reported.

The Interrogation H.Q. Section moved on August 1st to the I British Corps Cage at Gazelle, where they pooled their facilities with that Corps and with No. 4 Canadian Interrogation Team. On the 10th they moved to Beny-sur-Mer, and the First Canadian Army Cage, just in time to receive their first batch of P.W. By the end of the month, 327 officers and 19,827 other ranks had passed through their hands. The sheer volume of prisoners forced them to streamline their procedures. They set up a No. 2 Cage about one half mile from the main No. 1. P.W. were first put through a preliminary screening at No. 2. Officers and any men identified as specialists were automatically referred to No. 1 for detailed interrogation by Capts. Cliff Webster, Ernie Skutezky, and Lieut. R. Geisler, an attached reinforcement officer. Lieut. D.H. Jones looked after segregation, W.O.II Denzler took care of documentation, and Capt. Kuhlbach was free to supervise the operation and to help where needed. The N.C.O.s were assigned tasks according to their qualifications. At the end of the month, Capt. Kuhlbach was replaced by a British officer, Maj. E.F. Williams, from Second British Army H.Q. Interrogation Section, and on August 27th the Cage was moved forward, near Lisieux *(shown on Map 10)*.[47]

After the Army Cage had become completely operative, No. 3 Team II Corps prepared a survey on P.W. for training in Canada. The prisoners were a pathetic lot; "their uniforms are torn and their boots in a pitiful condition, tired from marching, shocked by shelling. . . . Many . . . are glad to reach the Cage which means for them the end of the fighting". Even *S.S.* could be so thoroughly fed up that they would become "most co-operative". Russian prisoners, happy to be out of the war, sang in their trucks as they were being driven off. On August 15th, the Team had moved to Bretteville-sur-Laize. On the 20th, it had felt abused when it was given an intake of 2,000, and then on the 24th, it had to accept over 6,000. On the 31st, by which time they were sorting the P.W. by division, not by unit: "Officers . . . asked Capt. Motzfeldt what he thought of their possibility of getting back to Germany and if so when; they had obviously been under the influence of propaganda about reconstruction work in Europe."[48]

THE CHANNEL COAST

The Canadians were ordered to plug the gap until all the German forces in the Falaise pocket had been rounded up. They were then redirected towards the Seine. On August 20th, No. 2 Wireless Intelligence Section's site was bombed and one officer was slightly wounded. On the 26th, Capts. Grant and Stephens found they had inadvertently passed through the lines and were in front of the forward infantry. They were lucky; on August 7th, a composite detachment from No. 2, No. 3, and 108 British W.I. Section had gone forward to Bras, south of Caen, to test V.H.F. reception. They came under a bombing attack, and W.D. Coxson, of No. 3, was severely wounded.[49]

A.P.I.S. seized the opportunity offered by the lull after Falaise to verify some of its identifications by actually visiting the positions. This enabled interpreters to check their skills, and to identify items they had previously been unsure of. A large quarry near Hautmesnil, identified as active but not worthy of attention, turned out to be a large underground supply installation which, according to local inhabitants, had 10 miles of tunnels! Their main efforts, however, were directed to verifying information obtained from P.W. on ferry sites over the Seine.[50]

12. Falaise to the Scheldt

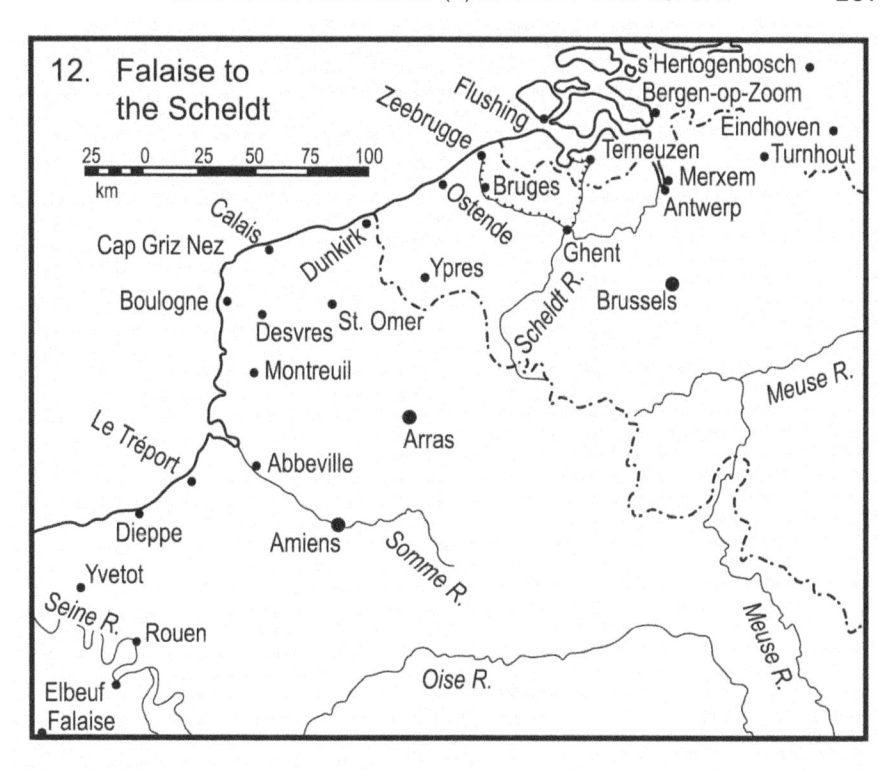

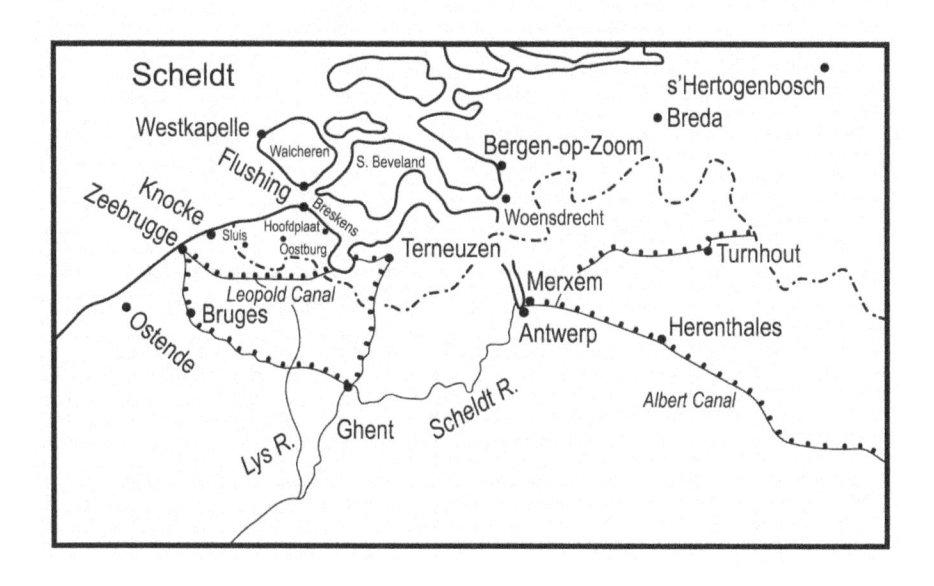

Scheldt

First Canadian Army's advance towards the Seine had I British Corps on the left to mask any enemy force along the coast. II Canadian Corps, on the right, was to cross the Seine between Pont de l'Arche and Elbeuf, and then be ready to cross in the Rouen area and establish itself north of that city. Photo coverage was provided in steps to a point east of Rouen. The first report, on August 20th, gave a number of isolated identifications. Coverage on the 22nd showed concentrations of flak batteries north and west of Lisieux, north of Thiberville, the departure of others which had earlier been seen near Quetteville, and unexplained camouflage south of Brionne *(shown on Map 10)*. On the 24th, coverage of the River Risle showed that, between its mouth and Bernay, which was on the axis of advance of the right-hand units, only two of the bridges were unserviceable but the approaches to five others had been cut.

"Photo coverage for 25 Aug., [which is] extensive, complete and of excellent quality . . . has shown a mad scramble by the enemy to get his vehicles across the Seine. Tail to nose concentrations of . . . vehicles in the Rouen bend of the river, particularly at the city itself. . . . Seven ferries . . . operating . . . other possible ferries had been noted . . . nine two to four flak battery concentrations have appeared." That night the area was heavily bombed but ". . . at only one point did bombing appear to have seriously affected the large concentrations . . . several fires were observed. . . . The enemy is still swarming across the river in more ferries than previously and . . . is believed to have the rail bridge . . . built up sufficiently to get motor vehicles and personnel across. . . . What appears to be . . . a new infantry defence line is seen south of Le Tréport." On the 28th: "Last night's Rouen air raids did a lovely job on MT [mechanical transport] concentrations but vehicles are still getting across. . . . There was very little activity at Rouen or the Seine Ferry crossings. The Le Tréport Defence Line has been increased by 10 machine-gun positions over one 1,000 yard stretch and another . . . is probably under construction 2,000 yards in front of this."[51]

The Intelligence staffs evaluated the new situation in these terms: "The hurried reorganization of an armoured force . . . beginning to show signs of an order of battle [of named units from] Orbec to Marelles supported by elements of *12 S.S. Panzer Division*. There is no information where he intends to make a stand. . . . [He] cannot hold the Seine [even with] 35–40,000 men and 80 tanks on this side." Civilians kept reporting concentrations of tanks in the Forêt de la Londe, a rugged area of thick woods lying in a loop of the Seine on the southern approaches to Rouen, but they were not taken seriously. Army Intelligence thought that a delaying action was possible, but saw no evidence that a major stand was being prepared south of the Seine. Second Division launched a somewhat optimistic two-pronged attack on the Forêt; it was repulsed with heavy losses.[52]

Third Infantry and Fourth Armoured Divisions swept through Elbeuf on the 27th and into and beyond Rouen on the 30th. Their Intelligence found it impossible to get confirmed identifications. Many enemy stragglers had been separated from their units for up to six days. Third Division speaks of one battalion commander who was quite willing to talk, but who did not even know what units lay on his flanks. Capt. Black appended a long list of possible units to his Intsum, but correctly forecast that Third Division would be opposed by a battle group of *271st Infantry Division*.[53]

Gen. Montgomery now ordered First Canadian Army to "operate northwards . . . secure . . . Dieppe . . . proceed quickly with the destruction of all the enemy forces in the coastal belt up to Bruges". I British Corps was to secure Le Havre, but the main Army advance was to be on the right, against the Pas de Calais and the north. Second Division was given the task of recapturing the port of Dieppe, to counter the memory of its defeat there in 1942.

The Le Havre garrison's strength was estimated to be 10,000, and was thought to include *711th Division*.[54] Army brought the air cover up-to-date on August 28th and prepared a defence overprint (a detailed representation of the enemy positions, overprinted on appropriate maps). From a P.W. who had been captured in July 1943, Army already had a detailed account of the northern sector; it was now carefully checked against the overprint. By using both sources, it was possible to calculate how many men and weapons would be required in the defence positions. Intelligence also received from civilians a great deal of information that was useful in locating H.Q., pillboxes, and other defences inside the town, but the data they had on the garrison itself was old and probably no longer valid. I Corps Intelligence staff, relying on deserters and P.W. picked up after September 1st, and on a document captured by II Corps near Abbeville, was able to publish on September 6th a strength estimate of between 7,350 and 8,700 fighting troops. On the 7th, another deserter brought with him a set of traces showing the exact section of the front that I Corps had selected for the assault. When the action ended on September 12th, the Corps had captured about 11,000 men. An enemy officer, who was shown the defence overprint during his interrogation, thought it more complete than his own and ascribed its accuracy to French treachery.

Second Division reached Dieppe on September 1st, to find that the Germans had abandoned it the previous day. Third Canadian Division took Le Tréport on the 2nd. Intelligence learned later that, on September 4th, Hitler had ordered the defences to be strengthened at Boulogne, Dunkirk, Calais, Flushing, Antwerp, and the Albert Canal as far as Maastricht. First Army had noticed very little activity around the French ports and had no idea that the Germans intended to hold them. They knew the identities of some fortresses and some field units from *64th Division* in Boulogne; nothing was known of Calais, but the remainder of *64th Division* was considered to be a possible garrison; the infantry and artillery of *226th Infantry Division* were at Gravelines; Dunkirk held the remnants of three Divisions.[55]

Capt. G.B. Shellon, Intelligence Officer of the 10th Canadian Infantry Brigade, and Lieut. R.C. McNairn of the Pioneer Platoon, Algonquin Regiment, talking with armed Dutch civilians near the Belgium–Netherlands border, 16 October 1944. (Lieut. H. Gordon Aikman/Canada. Dept. of National Defence/Library and Archives Canada, PA-144085)

Much of Third Division's information on Boulogne came from civilians. From it, and from other material including "innumerable captured documents", Capt. Black prepared a comprehensive study on the large, fixed installations and minefields: "The main belt of defences . . . are mutually supporting and command all approaches to the city. Coastal Defence Batteries, radar stations, infantry positions . . . mined and wired . . . linked by extensive minefields. . . . All roads have been mined and most bridges prepared for demolitions or blown. . . . [The enemy] undoubtedly will endeavour to deny this port . . . as long as he is able. However, he is fully aware of his plight and a strong blow might quickly appease his honour." He thought the total strength, including *Marines* and *Luftwaffe*, was between 4,000 and 5,000. His estimate was low. Army had thought that 10,000 was a more probable figure and, in fact, in the six days of fighting, Third Division took a total of 9,517 prisoners.[56] The last stronghold fell to a Psychological Warfare broadcast.

Third Division had also been given the task of taking Calais. Its defences consisted ". . . of islands surrounded by canals or dykes along whose banks strong points are located". The usual mix of mines, wire, anti-tank ditches, and water obstacles was identified. Strength estimates started at around 4,500, were increased to a maximum of 8,000, and the actual final count was about 7,500. After four days of fighting, a ceasefire was negotiated to allow the 20,000 civilians to be evacuated and the action was then resumed for a second short period.

Second Division's Intelligence staff located the Dunkirk outpost line, and completed a defence overprint on September 10th. On the 15th, the Division was ordered to turn over its task to No. 4 Special Service Brigade, but, before leaving, it decided to try Psychological Warfare. Gen. Spry ordered his G.S.O.3, Capt. Rodger Archbold, and his I.O., J.E. McEachern, to prepare a letter to von Kluge, the German Commander. The Mayor of Rosendaal, a nearby village, delivered it through the German lines on the 17th. When the ultimatum had expired the vigorous German reaction made it obvious that the demand had been rejected. It is quite possible that the Germans had learned that, in the interval, the Division had moved on.[57]

Against stiffening German resistance, Fourth Armoured Division reached the Ghent Canal on the 8th. Army had thought that the enemy would attempt to hold the line of canals Zeebrugge–Bruges–Ghent–Terneuzen. On the night of the 8th, 10 C.I.B. forced a small bridgehead, and the next day the Divisional Orders Group was told that the enemy was escaping north from the Ghent area into Holland. The canal positions were only an outpost line, and the main defences were on the general line of the Leopold Canal from Zeebrugge to Strooibrug and Haven; the bridges at Zoefendalle and Strooibrug were the main escape routes.[58]

The advance gathered in many P.W. and the Interrogators were extremely busy. At First Army P.W. Camp alone, over 200 officers and 19,205 other ranks were dealt with by Interrogation H.Q. Section, No. 2 Team, and any others who could be made available. In II Corps Cage, over 5,000 were handled by No. 3 Team, with assistance from Nos. 2 and 4 Teams. Detachments were also sent to duties elsewhere. Cliff Webster, for example, took a team to Le Havre and I British Corps, to work with the Highland Division. In addition to his normal detachment duties, Ernie Skutezky served with No. 2 Canadian Amplifier Unit to provide Psychological Warfare broadcasts in Boulogne and some of its outlying small towns. He claimed some success: 200 P.W. at St. Lambert, small groups at the River Liane, Outreau, St. Etienne and Herquelingue. He was employed by Brig. John Rockingham at the formal acceptance of the surrender of Lt.-Gen. Heim, commander of the German garrison at Boulogne. Ernie also discovered a French Naval Captain who brought in information useful to Third Division.[59]

On September 13th, A.P.I.S. was given their first detailed requirement to examine Walcheren. The material they had was incomplete. They therefore asked 16 Squadron, R.A.F., to fly a mission on the 14th over the area of South Beveland, including the Causeway. While they waited for the cover to be brought back, they completed a defence overprint for Calais, similar to those they had already done for Boulogne and Dunkirk, and did a careful check of the weapon sites at Flushing, on the south shore of the Scheldt. On the 28th, the Canadian Modelling Team demanded from them an accurate mosaic at the unusual scale of 1:5,000; a compromise was agreed on and a less accurate model produced at a larger scale.[60]

On September 19th, a fire, whose cause was never discovered, gutted the Army Operations Centre – four trucks backed into a canvas-covered square. At least one brave driver drove his truck away. Capt. Rudi Aksim, the Duty Officer, managed to save his own Technical Intelligence material, but Capt. Bob Wodehouse's Air Reconnaissance files, and a complete set of First Army, Second Army, and 21 Army Group Intelligence Summaries was lost. Since Intelligence relied on these Summaries for all its in-depth reference material, the loss was serious; fortunately, other copies were found. The Centre itself, of course, was back in operation the same day.[61]

First Canadian Army was next ordered to open the approaches to the Port of Antwerp. To do this it had to clear the main seaward approach, held by the German *Fifteenth Army*, with its three Corps, *LXVII*, *LXXXVI*, and *LXXXIX*, deployed on both sides of the Scheldt west of the port. The Canadians had two alternatives: to make a straight thrust, or to continue the British thrust that had taken the city of Antwerp. The Germans were well aware – and Second British Army stressed this point – that the extension of that thrust as far as Breda would cut them off. First Canadian Army estimated that the enemy had two choices: to go immediately, or to stay on the south bank of the Scheldt; the guns at Flushing would still protect their escape route. But 21 Army Group let the opportunity to cut this route pass, and an attack against the Scheldt by First Army became unavoidable.[62]

By September 13th, the enemy had withdrawn behind the Leopold Canal, the Caele River, and the railway line from Selzaete. His flanks were secure, his defence line was an obstacle to Canadian tanks, and yet "there were still no indications of an intention to make a determined stand south of the Scheldt".[63] On the 15th, Gen. Crerar assigned the task of clearing the Scheldt to II Canadian Corps, the Antwerp sector to Second Division, and the area up to the West Scheldt to First Polish and Fourth Canadian Armoured Divisions.

The Poles were successful, except at a corner erroneously called Savojaards Plaat. The Braakman inlet in front of them, just west of Terneuzen, to Zeebrugge, was covered by the Leopold Canal, behind which the enemy was well dug in. Fourth Armoured Division crossed the Ghent Canal at Moerbrugge *(just*

Schouen Island mosaic, 12 September 1944. (War Diary, 1 Canadian A.P.I.S./Photo collection Canadian Forces School of Military Intelligence, Kingston/Canada. Dept. of National Defence)

south of Bruges) with some difficulty, and then faced the Canal de Dérivation de la Lys, which is separated from the Leopold Canal by only a narrow dyke. The enemy was well entrenched and was able to repel the Division's attempts to cross.

The various Intelligence staffs, in a mood of apparent euphoria, tried to forecast the enemy's next likely course of action, all of it predicated upon withdrawal. On the 18th, hard reality brought them back to earth. From Corps: ". . . the enemy will defend the seaward approaches to Antwerp." Fourth Armoured Division was still soberly optimistic: ". . . the enemy withdrawal from the area bounded by the Canal de Dérivation etc., the Leopold Canal and the Ghent–Terneuzen Canal is still under way . . . pressure is necessary to ensure its continuation." The Division, however, was restrained, and was only allowed to patrol along the Leopold Canal, for the purposes of gaining information, of dominating the south side, and of preventing enemy penetration or infiltration of the area.[64]

When Second Canadian Infantry Division took over Antwerp from the 53rd (Welsh) Division on September 16th, the enemy still held the northern sector of the port. Civilians passed freely through the boundaries, a source of worry to I(b), but of aid to I(a). The Belgian Resistance (Brigade Blanche) brought Second Division a great deal of information, including a detailed order-of-battle. The Albert Canal was lightly held by pickets and patrols, except for three points (one of which was Merxem) which were alleged to be garrisoned by 500 men each. Some indications, however, seemed to show that the enemy was making a slow withdrawal northward. One enemy pocket at Schooten was thought to be a likely target for Psychological Warfare. Lieut. Henley, Second Division's I.O., prepared a suitable script, but the operation was later cancelled and it was not used.[65]

On October 2nd, Second Division moved northward to cut the long isthmus that forms the eastern approach to South Beveland. German resistance stiffened in the face of this threat to their escape route, and the Canadian advance became a unit and sub-unit battle. Fourth Armoured Division was brought from the Leopold Canal and deployed to the right of Second Division. The move was intended primarily to cover Second Division's flank and, in addition, to prepare the way for Second Army, which was then hoping to trap the German *Fifteenth Army* south of the Maas River.

Capt. Ted McMurrich, G.S.O.3 (Int) Fourth Armoured Division, found that ". . . [it was] difficult because of the fluidity of the battle to assess dispositions and strength." On October 23rd, he saw "remnants reinforcing remnants, inadequate reserves and indifferent morale . . . heavy losses . . . if counter attacks are made they will not be more than one battalion strength possibly supported by tanks. . . . Any advance from the tip of our present salient would threaten those troops [on our left] with encirclement. . . . Withdrawal would then mean sacrificing what little control the enemy has over future moves westwards of our forces. . . . He will therefore probably choose to use the strength he has built up in the Bergen-op-Zoom–Woensdrecht sector to deny us this coastal strip".[66] By November 4th, the Canadian forward patrols were on the coast; the other formations reached their objectives on the Maas and the Hollandschdiep *(the estuary of the Lower Maas)* by November 8th.[67]

The left flank of First Canadian Army was required to open the Scheldt. Third Division was moved from Calais to replace Fourth Armoured on the Leopold Canal. This obstacle had to be taken as a first phase in the capture of Walcheren. In the second phase, a waterborne assault by First Polish Division, from Terneuzen across the Braakman, would outflank the German defences, strongest in the Isabella Polder at the south end of the Braakman. When this Operation, named SWITCHBACK, was completed, another attack, called INFATUATE, would be directed against Walcheren itself.

Intelligence collection for INFATUATE had been going on since September 11th, initially under Lieut. E.H. Smith, I.O. (Defences), Lieut. D. Wiens, Capt. J.M. Robertson, I.O. (Topographical), and the Naval Liaison Officer, Lieut. Godfrey, R.N.V.R. They were fortunate to find a Belgian engineer who had been in charge of building the Walcheren fortifications. His memory and notebooks included details of guns and, under rigorous interrogation by Capt. John Gray and Dave Wiens, he provided a complete dossier which, when checked against air photos, gave one of the most accurate assessments of enemy deployments produced thus far. It was reinforced by the capture by a Canadian Recce Regiment of a trace showing the enemy dispositions. Their first paper was ready to go to higher authority on September 14th. On the 22nd, Engineer Intelligence was added. II Corps and Third Division had also started an informal study on September 16th, but their formal planning began on October 2nd. Corps' first report dealt with South Beveland in terms of sober realism: "There is every possibility that the enemy may hold. . . . A few days ago there was a Tac R report that flooding had started on . . . Walcheren. Photo R does not substantiate this. . . . [The enemy] has also been evacuating large numbers of troops across . . . the Scheldt and may be able to muster an effective garrison for the islands. Also there are very strong defences . . . with positions . . . along the beaches."[68]

Third Division's Intsum went on to describe the roads and the enemy dispositions that were known: ". . . the Leopold Canal to the coast is held in considerable strength. . . . Zeebrugge . . . Heyst . . . Knocke-sur-Mer . . . Breskens are believed to be garrison towns and are held by Coast Defence units such as . . . at Boulogne and Calais with elements of Flak and marine units. . . . The harbours at Breskens and Hoofdplaat were used by the enemy to evacuate troops across the South Zeeland islands where *70 Infantry Division* is . . . well established. Immediately east to Savojaards Plaat the area has been cleared to the coast. North of Antwerp a crossing of the Scheldt Estuary has been forced." (Antwerp lies north of the Scheldt; the G.S.O.3 meant that Second Division was on its northern shore.)

Two battalions from separate regiments of *64th Division* were located at Malentie and Eade. "Based on inundated areas on the flanks it seems probable to assume that *1037 Grenadier Regiment* is responsible for the right flank and *1038* for the left flank of the gap. Photo interpretation shows that this gap is held in depth in comparison to the inundated areas. Patrol reports from the extreme left flank, namely the eastern approach, indicate an immediate strong reaction to offensive activity. . . . The identity of the defending forces in this area is not known. The following are as yet unaccounted for: *1039 Grenadier Regiment*, *64 Fusilier Battalion* and possibly elements of *712 Division*, who originally withdrew through this area. It would appear more probable that *1039* would be held in a counter-attack role as a unit leaving *64 Fusilier* and/or elements of *712* responsible for the primary defence of the eastern approach. The artillery appears to be disposed (a) in the northwest portion of the central gap and (b) in the area behind the secondary line of defences. . . . The actual strength of the enemy is . . . difficult to estimate." Two days later, identifications showed the enemy units in a line from west to east along the island. The main weight of the defence was at the head of the causeway.[69]

This was a first-class Summary. It showed what was known, and admitted what was not. Units were identified and linked, where possible, to their formations. Sound, logical assessments gave possible alternatives. The nature of the threat posed by the enemy defence was clearly identified. The sources supplying the information were given and the reader therefore knew precisely to what extent the data could be trusted. It was the product of a continuous process of up-dating, correcting, cancelling, and re-assessing the enemy moves and deployments.

On October 6th, 7 C.I.B. established two tenuous beachheads across the Leopold Canal at Strooibrug. An amphibious operation by 9 C.I.B. near Hoofdplaat caught the Germans completely by surprise; 8 C.I.B. reinforced it. The enemy reinforced *64th Division* with detachments from the *70th,* but Canadian patrols found, on the 14th, that they had "withdrawn from the eastern end of the Leopold Canal and from the southwest coastal sector of Savojaards Plaat". On the 18th *64th Division* fell back to a secondary defence line, running from Breskens through Schoondijke, Oostburg to Sluis, then along the Sluis Canal to the Leopold. Third Division's advance halted before Fort Fredrik Hendrik. On the night of October 24th, a deserter reported that there were only 23 Germans left in the fort. He was sent back to tell them to surrender before they were wiped out; they came in next day. Oostburg fell on October 26th, and the enemy were driven behind the Uitwaterings Canal. Gen. Eberding, the German commander, was captured on November 1st, and Operation SWITCHBACK came to an end on the morning of the 3rd. Third Division had captured 12,707 prisoners; *64th Division* had been annihilated.[70]

Second Division began its move along the Beveland Causeway on October 24th (Operation VITALITY). By the 27th, it had reached the first major obstacle, the Beveland Canal, at the west end of the isthmus. An amphibious assault from Terneuzen turned the position and forced the Germans to withdraw into Walcheren. North Beveland was cleared next, on November 2nd, and another possible enemy escape route was closed. *When the Division finally cleared South Beveland, it found that the only access to Walcheren was over a 1,200-yard causeway, 40 yards wide and flanked on both sides by weedy mud flats. German artillery and small arms covered all its approaches. Units of 5th Canadian Brigade tried, but ultimately failed, to secure the far side.*

As a result, Canadians took no part in the final assault on Walcheren, which started on October 5th with an R.A.F. bombing raid on the Westkapelle dyke. This raid was very much a Canadian issue. Gen. Simonds wanted the dyke bombed and said it could be done. His Commander, Royal Engineers, said bombs could not break it. Lt.-Col. Wright, on the basis of information he held, said there were not enough enemy in Walcheren for their destruction to warrant the long term damage that would result. The Army Commander was adamant; the raid may have harmed rather than helped the operation. For a month Intelligence discussed the extent of the damage caused, while A.P.I.S. kept a watchful eye on enemy developments. On October 31st, it reported that demolition charges previously seen on the quays at Flushing had been detonated and the quays wrecked. After successful Allied attacks on Flushing and Westkapelle on November 1st, Intelligence was happy to find that, although they had missed a few alterations to artillery deployments, their assessments of the German strength and dispositions had been essentially correct.

Having witnessed the impossibility of fighting across the causeway, the British 52nd (Lowland) Division chose an amphibious attack on Walcheren. The 157th Brigade crossed by assault boat on November 3rd, secured a beachhead and, on the next day, linked up with forces at the end of the causeway. All organized resistance on the island ceased on the 8th, the Scheldt was cleared of mines by the 26th, and the first convoy arrived in Antwerp on the 28th. The first ship to moor was Canadian, the *Fort Cataraqui*.

---

*   Second edition note: The sentences in italics that follow, highlight changes to the first edition's account of Canadian operations in the lower Scheldt. These changes were kindly provided by Dr. Steve Harris, Directorate of History and Heritage at the Department of National Defence, Canada, on 18 January 2017.

THE WINTER "LULL"

With the end of the Scheldt operations, the Canadian Army began a three-month static period to reinforce and reconstruct. Experience gained in the fighting had shown that Intelligence had weaknesses in its procedures, its organization, and – in a gratifyingly small number of cases – its personnel. Now there was time to remedy these weaknesses. In the occupied area, the easy movement of civilians and agents from both sides gave Counter-Intelligence staffs a great deal of work. Their story belongs to the next chapter, but some of the things they did had a bearing on I(a). When, for instance, German wireless activity slowed down in late September, the Wireless Intelligence Sections were under-employed, and Maj. Bud Macdougall and the G.S.O.2 I(s), Maj. A.H. MacKenzie, arranged that Wireless Linguist personnel work temporarily with I(b). Enemy clandestine radios and the relatively free movement of civilians made a dangerous combination. Some of the linguists worked in their trade against these espionage radios; others were used as interrogators, often with mixed success, because not all linguists make good interrogators. Occasionally, they would be given an offbeat task, as when an Auster courier aircraft was lost between Army and I British Corps, possibly through enemy action, and Lieut. T. Pickup was told to make sure it was not carrying anything that would aid the enemy. Fortunately, the material was innocuous.[71]

A combined group of Nos. 1, 4, 5, and 6 Air Liaison Sections was formed in October at Diest, Belgium, to work for Second British Army. Squadron missions spotted the enemy digging along the Maas, and the group reported the incident: ". . . digging . . . to avoid disaster . . . trying to patch up each chink in the line as it occurs. All along the Front Tac R shows the Boche being forced to conform to our attacks." The group's biggest problem was adverse weather; it not only halted flying, but turned airfields and work areas into quagmires. Many of the squadrons worked principally on rail interdiction, which meant hitting targets of opportunity, which could not be pre-planned. The Section in these cases had to confine itself to debriefing and reporting.[72]

Between October 1st and November 13th, Interrogator H.Q. Section dealt with 847 officers and 37,201 other ranks at the Army Cage, whose location was changed twice during this period. Finally, when winter came, the Cages were set up under cover in large buildings. No. 2 Team was sent eight German naval personnel from the West Scheldt ferries on September 23rd and, at the end of October, another batch from Walcheren. No. 4 Team, with Lieuts. Skutezky, Jones, and Geisler, prepared a special brief on demolitions at Flushing, and on Schouen and Overflakkee Islands *(shown on Map 14)*, for which, in one day alone, they had to question over 1,500 prisoners. Some P.W. specialists, whose names were recorded on a "Watch List", were automatically segregated and interrogated. But, generally speaking, most of the P.W. had been rounded up well after the action ended, and the numbers were so huge that the interrogators could only make a rough selection from the Watch Lists and let the rest go unchecked.

On November 13th, the Teams were disbanded as separate units and reformed into 1 Canadian Army Interrogation Pool commanded by Maj. J.J. Stonborough; their duties did not change. Pool H.Q. remained at First Army P.W. Transit Camp, at Ruysbroek; detachments worked with 030 Civilian Interrogation Camp and at the Cages. The Pool had 42 men on strength: a major, 11 I.O.s, a W.O.II, five sergeants, 10 corporals (all Intelligence specialists), and 14 privates (two clerks, five batmen, two batmen/ drivers, and five drivers). On the 26th, they took up quarters in a cement factory in Ryckevorsel-Beersee.[73]

In mid-October, First Army prepared a study on P.W. based on Interrogation Team reports. Some were stragglers left behind in the retreat, others were from the Channel Fortresses, and still others had been picked up during the more static fighting of the early Scheldt operations. The men who had been captured during the retreat had practically nothing except what they wore. Those from the Fortresses had all the baggage they could carry – food, books, and musical instruments. In general, P.W. security was poor, although there were periods, obviously following careful briefings in their respective units, when they were close-mouthed. During the later phases, men had been so shuffled around between units that they really had very little to tell. They often held conferences in order to try to discover what unit they were in and where they had been. P.W. from the retreat were in poor physical condition, tired and hungry. Those from the channel garrisons were fat and soft, and were generally of lower medical categories. On the average, 10% were lousy and 5% had scabies, but infectious diseases were rare. The Polish and Russian prisoners often sang in their camps. Each evening, the Polish compound ceremoniously hoisted the Polish flag and sang national songs. Most prisoners were docile. They appreciated the food they were given; although it was usually only bully beef and biscuits, it was at least a change from their own rations.[74]

At A.P.I.S., in early October, Maj. D.R. Morrice, who had been G.S.O.2 (Air Recce), exchanged his position with Maj. Devaney, who had been the unit's first O.C. and who also had assisted in the formation of 30 Canadian Air (Survey) Liaison Section, later to be absorbed by A.P.I.S. On October 23rd, they moved from Antwerp Deurne Airfield to Gilze Rijen Airfield where they were able to find dry quarters for the winter and arrange for short leaves.[75]

Army H.Q. also found dry quarters, but took care to see that newfound comfort did not conflict with efficiency. Mr. Duncan Sandys, Parliamentary Secretary to the British Minister of Home Security, visited, and spent a lot of time with the I.O. (Tech), Capt. Rudi Aksim, discussing the German V-2 flying bomb. Later, a system was set up to co-ordinate information on all aspects of this weapon.

13. Crossing of the Rhine

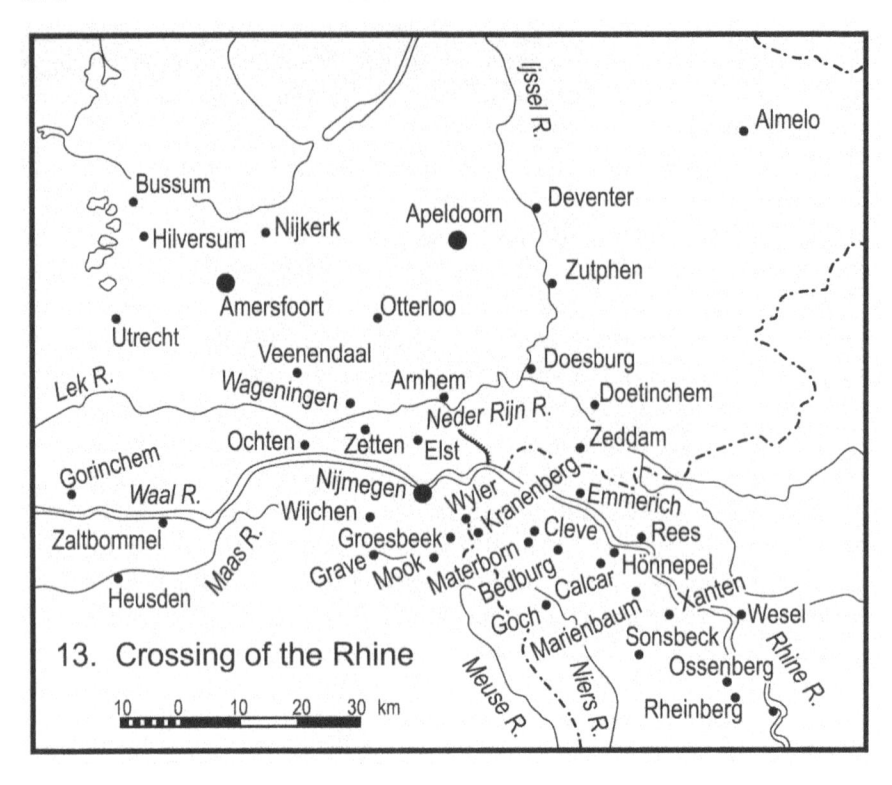

Intelligence set up a School in October, to train the officers and men of the entire Army Intelligence community. It had, as C.O., Lt.-Col. G.M. McLaughlan; as Chief Instructor, Maj. G.M.C. Sprung, M.C.; as Administrative Officer, Capt. W.S. Johnston; and a staff of 15 men. Col. McLaughlan was recalled to Canada on October 16th, and Maj. Sprung carried on to run four sessions of the course. Capt. P.A. Shultis was brought in as an officer-instructor.[76]

In early November 1944, First Canadian Army took over part of Second Army's sector. Lieuts. Waite and Strojich, I.O.s (Topography) were set to work on eastern Holland. By late November: "The static front . . . brought with it its own problems. . . . Intelligence sources tended to dry up. . . . The only fresh source was the civilian information which was turned to good use identifying enemy H.Q. for the Air Force to attack when a good day was available." On November 25th, the Topographers produced a summary of the Reichswald* for First Army Planners: "Events cast their shadows before", is how the Diary puts it.[77]

---

*   Second edition note: The Reichswald – meaning 'imperial forest' in German – refers to the heavily forested area generally located between the German towns of Kranenberg, Cleve and Goch shown on Maps 13 and 14.

While that battle was some way in the future, there was an immediate and urgent problem. Lt.-Col. Orville Eadie, G.S.O.1 of the Canadian War Intelligence Course at Kingston, Ontario, told Lt.-Cols. Wright and Walter that the Canadian Director of Military Training had ruled that Intelligence training in Canada would be restricted to battalion level and limited to six weeks. This meant that the supply of officers capable of filling the Battalion I.O. positions would continue, but that no replacement staff officers would be trained. First Army did not agree. The British had stopped teaching German Army material at both the Cambridge and the Matlock Intelligence Training Centres. To compensate for this lack, the School at 1 C.G.R.U. was running its own Divisional Intelligence course, and was accepting British students. There was no other source of officers trained for the European Theatre. Lt.-Cols. Wright and Walter also pressed for assurances that all C.Int.C. reinforcements would have a thorough grounding in German as well as in both I(a) and I(b). New men were not needed immediately, because three officers and 23 men were then in training and would graduate by mid-February 1945. Lt.-Col. Eadie warned, however, that no more German-language personnel were available.

On November 29th, 1944, First Army set up a new sub-branch, Intelligence Plans, under Maj. Sprung. Its task was to co-ordinate all Intelligence planning at First Army H.Q. on such matters as: operations in Germany; the disbandment of the German Army and its paramilitary organizations (Operation ECLIPSE); the Occupation of Germany; and the organization of "T" (for Target) Force, a special group intended to search specified German industrial, scientific, and planning offices. Spike Sprung was authorized to deal directly with all branches of the General Staff, at First Army and elsewhere, and told to work closely with Army Planners and with I(b).[78]

There were many Intelligence officers in the theatre who worked either alone, on detachment to H.Q. and units, or in small independent groups. To improve administration, No. 1 Canadian Army Intelligence Officers Pool was formed on November 10th, 1944, to absorb these officers. The original submission which led to its creation recommended that all these I.O.s receive the special I.O. pay. But the recommendation was not approved until February 14th, 1945, and only at that date could the officers technically be taken on strength. Authority was therefore sought, and granted, to do this as from the date the unit was originally formed. In effect, the decision granted these I.O.s three months back pay of their grade, unless they had been drawing it in the interval. Much paper work was needed to sort out individual "careers", since each assignment usually required at least two entries in the unit Orders.[79]

When the reorganization of 21 Army Group's front was complete, First Canadian Army held a sector stretching from about eight miles southeast of Nijmegen to the mouth of the Maas. I British Corps, on the left with Fourth Canadian Armoured Division, had the line from the boundary to Lith, east of

Maren; First Polish Armoured Division was on the south bank of the Maas. II Corps held the Nijmegen bridgehead, with 101 U.S. Airborne, 82 Northumbrian, and Third Canadian and Second Canadian Divisions under command. Across the Rhine *84th* and *190th Infantry Divisions* of *Fifteenth Army*, both well under-strength, held the front between the Maas and the Waal. The great Nijmegen Bridge was the key to any further Allied advance over the Waal. The demolition of dykes north of Elst and west of Arnhem flooded the area between the Waal and Arnhem. The Front was generally quiet, except for patrol incidents which occasionally escalated into bitter clashes.[80]

Allied strategic planning called for a major advance between the Maas and the Rhine, the final details of which were decided at a conference at Maastricht on December 7th. XXX British Corps, including Third Canadian Division, was to attack on the right of First Canadian Army. Its initial assault was to be followed by II Canadian Corps on its left. I British Corps was to create a diversion and, by so doing, to attract the enemy's attention away from the main thrust.

H.Q. First Canadian Army had anticipated this plan. On December 1st, Lieut. W.S. Strojich, I.O. (Topography), then just completing a map showing the flooding in Holland, was directed to prepare a topographical study of the Reichswald and, later, after some discussion concerning its scope, a detailed map of the order-of-battle and defences. The Intelligence Centre moved to Tilburg *(shown on Map 14)* on December 12th, but he still managed to prepare a fairly detailed basic overprint and a preliminary report. On the 17th, all preparations were disrupted when Army learned of von Rundstedt's attack in the Ardennes.[81]

At that time, the First Canadian Army Intsum format included a "General" section, which gave an overview of the war, followed by paragraphs containing reviews of activity on "Canadian Front", "British Front", and "American Front". Specific items of interest followed. The paper usually concluded with an estimate of the enemy's intentions. Annexes would report information on captured documents, order-of-battle, enemy tactics, equipment, propaganda, and the like. In the first two weeks of December, Army dealt with its own front in detail, and gave only a general review of the other two. On December 1st and 2nd, it twice gave information on enemy withdrawals from the area between the Maas and the Waal, and along the rivers to Ochten. *Fifteenth Army* had been replaced by a new *Army Group "H"*, under Gen. Student, whose H.Q. was at Hilversum, and had ". . . apparently moved east and south". Four divisions were no longer confirmed. Of these, only one was authoritatively reported to have left the area. After a review of the Reichswald positions, the Summary ended: "Movement is still continuing eastwards out of Holland." As far as Canadians were concerned, the chief threat stemmed from possible attack on the Nijmegen Bridge and a build-up in the Reichswald. The enemy was thought to be capable of mounting small raids, but these would not represent a significant threat.[82]

His withdrawal from between the two rivers was thought to be a preparation for more flooding, ". . . an effective obstacle behind which troops can most economically be placed". On December 3rd, 21 Army Group believed von Rundstedt had 50 relatively expendable infantry divisions. His tactical reserves were assessed at five Panzer Divisions, four Pz.Gr. Divisions, and six Parachute Divisions. His strategic reserve was *Sixth Panzer Army*. The infantry was to stop the Allies breaking through, the tactical reserve was to prevent the German infantry from leaving the line and to blunt the Allied assault, and the strategic reserve, which was under von Rundstedt's personal control, was to be used at the time and place of greatest effect. "Von Rundstedt is unlikely to use this precious guard over the Rhine [the five named panzer divisions] forward of a line Cologne–Bonn, until the Allied advance over the Roer . . . present[s] a threat not to be blunted by . . . tactical reserves . . . or [unless the Allies put themselves] off balance so that an abrupt counter stroke could put paid to future Allied prospects for the winter. This latter is unlikely for it demands four elements not usually to be found together: first, vital ground, and there is nowhere obvious for him to go. . . . The bruited drive to Antwerp . . . is just not within his potential. Secondly he needs bad weather else our air superiority would clog his intent. Third, he must find us tired and unbalanced. Fourth he needs adequate fuel stocks not only to sustain a full-blooded operation but also to guarantee a withdrawal in his own time when it fails. Lastly he needs infantry and of better quality. . . . To lose *Sixth Panzer Army* would . . . be . . . [an irreparable] disaster. . . . It seems more probable . . . that he will wait to smash our bridgeheads over the Roer."

The U.S. forces learned that the Division which left the Canadian front on November 23rd–24th had arrived in the Saar. On December 16th, First Army discussed the build-up of German strength and morale and quoted a captured document, allegedly signed by von Rundstedt: "The great hour has struck. Counter-attack forces are advancing."[83]

The German Ardennes offensive began on December 16th. Initially, First Canadian Army was perplexed. "The object . . . is not at first apparent. It . . . in theory might threaten our supply lines for Aachen or the Saar. . . . The development . . . follows . . . from the success . . . in holding and building up reserves. . . . [Is] *Sixth S.S. Panzer Army Group* . . . west of the Rhine as a reserve . . . or . . . to take part . . .? The answer . . . lies in the degree of success." Lt.-Col. Wright looked at the Canadian sector: "In any event the . . . northern . . . front is bound to be affected by . . . the Ardennes. . . . The Reichswald plug is more readily defended than the Caen hinge."[84]

By the next day: "Although he has the ability, the organization and the desperate spirit to mount an offensive of this kind he does not possess the resources to maintain or exploit it nor the long term position to make it worth while." Intsum No. 173 on December 20th noted the first check to the enemy advance. On December 21st, 21 Army Group admitted it had been caught in an error of judgement.[85]

From the evidence, therefore, it would appear that though First Canadian Army Intelligence perhaps could have made an educated guess that there was a build-up of some significance in the south, it did not forecast the attack. Granted, it was not directly concerned. Lt.-Col. Wright's team repeated 21 Army Group's assessment of the conditions that would make a German assault possible, but perhaps one question could have received more attention – whether or not those conditions did in fact pertain. The formation that should have drawn the correct conclusions was the U.S. Ninth Army. But the incident does highlight three Intelligence lessons. The first is that it is always dangerous to underestimate the opposition. The second is that, if that opposition requires certain conditions to be able to perform its mission, a continuing examination of those conditions is essential. Finally, and this is most important, when an Intelligence officer makes a mistake, he must admit it. No one is infallible; any I.O. who claims otherwise destroys his credibility.

By December 16th, First Army had correctly identified the enemy forces opposite it: *6th Parachute Division* now held the Neder Rijn from the Waal to Wageningen. West of it came successively *712th*, *711th*, and *346th Infantry Divisions*, all with *Luftwaffe* reinforcements. By the 20th, there was an indication that *LXXXVI Corps* had extended itself northward and now held the Reichswald.

On the 21st: "The evidence is reasonably conclusive that the enemy is preparing a large paratroop operation to take place very shortly to disrupt the communications of the armies dependent on Antwerp and Brussels." It was linked to the progress of the Ardennes offensive, and would provide assistance should the enemy forces cross the Meuse. Four proven, reliable sources supplied information covering the period December 15th–21st. They discovered that four parachute divisions were preparing for a large operation. They identified airfields, reported movements of paratroops, and reported the mission as being linked to the German thrust toward Antwerp, and the V-2 attacks on it. "Without a land operation, reasonably likely to reach the area, it is only a possible and not a probable operation. But it is being prepared and must be provided against." Lt.-Col. Wright set all his staff to work exploiting every possible source of information in order to determine the value of the reports he received. Of the two main sources, Wireless Intelligence was getting nothing, and A.P.I.S. was prevented by bad flying weather from getting photo coverage.[86]

On the 23rd, Army heard that a division equipped and trained to cross the Maas was now stationed between the Maas and the Waal, and between Biesbosch and the Isle of Alem. Tac R descriptions of the airfield conditions tended to discount any threat of paratroop operations, but photographs showed a great deal of activity in certain camouflaged installations. On the 24th, a P.W. report gave the impression that a feint attack would be made at Halderen. Interrogation of two captured agents, who had been given a specific task, helped identify the German objectives. Reports of increased German Counter-Intelligence activity suggested that the enemy was trying to protect his preparations for an offensive. A.P.I.S. made a determined effort to extract every possible item from photographic reconnaissance. It strained the capability of the Mobile Field Processing Section with 18 sorties on the 23rd, 33 on the 24th, and 23 on the 25th. Interpreters had to work from first rushes, i.e., the earliest possible prints they could be given, but they could neither confirm nor deny the reports.[87]

On the 26th: "The enemy appears clearly to have intended to cross the Maas between Geertruidenberg and Heusden. Whether in fact he will do so depends . . . on the issue of the Ardennes battle [which] must be taken to be pending." This Intsum also was signed personally by Lt.-Col. Wright rather than by his duty staff officer. At 1800, he told Gen. Crerar that, in his opinion, the threat was real, not fake. Gen. Cerar replied "I've been talking to Monty and he doesn't think there's anything in it." Col. Wright immediately called Brig. E.T. Williams, B.G.S. (Int), 21 Army Group H.Q., and told him of the pictures and his conclusions. He agreed and said he would speak to General Montgomery. Around 2000, Col. Wright was called to Gen. Crerar's caravan at Tilburg. He said "I've just been talking to Monty. He thinks there might be something to this threat across the Maas: We're deferring the move of Fourth Canadian Armoured Division to XXX Corps and the Guards Armoured Div. have been added to our reserve if need be and we're going to move Army H.Q. back from Tilburg to Turnhout." And in Col. Wright's own words: "That was the only time I can remember where any appreciation or fact from G(Int) at Army altered the disposition of the Army or its plans."[88] Certainly, it was a dramatic example of an Intelligence assessment leading to action. But Col. Wright does himself an injustice. There were many occasions, as we have shown, where Intelligence helped provide the knowledge necessary to make an operational decision. Admittedly, it is difficult to assess how much of any decision could be attributed to the assessment provided and how much depended upon the knowledge, instinct, ability, and good fortune of the individual commander. Without some understanding of "the other side of the hill", no commander can succeed.

The M.F.P.S. was still plugged with a week's backlog. The interpreters were swamped with requests for special traces of details like barge activity and build-ups in enemy assembly areas. Lt.-Col. Wright, in a broad review: "Over one hundred items of information dealing directly or indirectly with an attack south across the Maas have been received since 22 December. . . . Every effort has been made to prove or disprove the . . . reports. . . . Every day . . . evidence confirming the operation has been received . . . no evidence denying it . . . it must be accepted . . . [as] an impending attack." The Intsum also announced that a secret German planning H.Q. had been set up on December 5th at

Lt.-Col. P.E.R. Wright, G.S.O.1 (Int) H.Q. First Canadian Army from 21 June 1943 until the end of the war. Promoted to Colonel on 3 May 1945, his decorations include the Order of the British Empire and Commander of the Order of Orange Nassau (with Swords). (Photo collection Canadian Forces School of Military Intelligence, Kingston/ Canada. Dept. of National Defence)

Hilversum; it identified the formations available as the *711th, 6th Parachute*, and *346th Divisions, LXXXVIII Corps*, and possibly the *712th Division*.[89]

On December 28th Army learned that the island of Schouen had been reinforced: "We must expect an attack shortly on Tholen and points north coming from both Schouen and Overflakkee. The Gorinchem attacks stand . . . dependent upon the great battles in the south." On the 31st, some felt that the Reichswald coverage had gaps, and that therefore it was possible for the enemy to reinforce without Intelligence discovering it. On January 1st, 1945, as Army

H.Q. was moving to Turnhout (with all the disruption that a relocation always entailed), Intelligence received additional confirmation that a build-up was actually taking place. Yet, later on the same day, three new pieces of evidence suggested that, on the contrary, the enemy was beginning to withdraw. A reliable source reported an outward troop lift by train from Gorinchem; photo cover indicated a change in enemy anti-aircraft gun sites; and a P.W. reported that he had heard that the attack had been called off on December 27th. The Intsum of that night said: "Limited evidence . . . does not establish that the enemy has abandoned his offensive intentions . . . may still prove to be a relief or a comparatively minor adjustment."[90]

By the 2nd, Intelligence began to accept as a probability that the operation had been abandoned and, by January 7th, that the danger was over. At the time, many were sceptical regarding the threat. However, evidence found since the war reveals that the German Commander-in-Chief, West, had in fact ordered *Twenty-Fifth Army* to advance across the lower Maas in order to envelop the Canadian forces. The move was to be co-ordinated with the enemy thrust through the Ardennes towards Antwerp. *LXXXVIII Corps*, on the left flank, was slated to attack from north of the Maas. It started planning on December 16th, and issued its Operations Order on December 21st. Some diversionary activity was planned, and two parachute drops were to take place, one on First Army H.Q., which German Wireless Intercept knew was at Tilburg, and the other on the artillery positions north of Canadian Army H.Q. German forces in Schouen and Overflakkee were also ordered to attack. When intercepted Allied Air Force messages showed that their build-up was known, and when they realized not only that the Canadians were not being thinned out because of German moves in the Ardennes, but also that the Ardennes operations themselves had failed, *Twenty-Fifth Army* had to re-examine its planned attack. Finally, when *711th Division* was ordered to the Budapest front, the *Army* was so seriously weakened that the operation was no longer possible. Lt.-Col. Wright's stand is vindicated.[91]

VERITABLE AND THE RHINE

The enemy attacks had delayed but had not cancelled the planning for the crossing of the Rhine. Formal orders for that Operation – VERITABLE – were issued on February 1st, 1945. To facilitate planning, a preliminary report, issued on December 18th, 1944, had dealt with topography, defences, enemy order-of-battle, administration, communications, reserves, and dumps; other paragraphs treated the local conditions that might affect the attack. In summary, the so-called Reichswald plug closed the neck of the entire German "bottle" west of the Rhine. If it were cleared, the enemy's whole Maas position, the

14. Holland

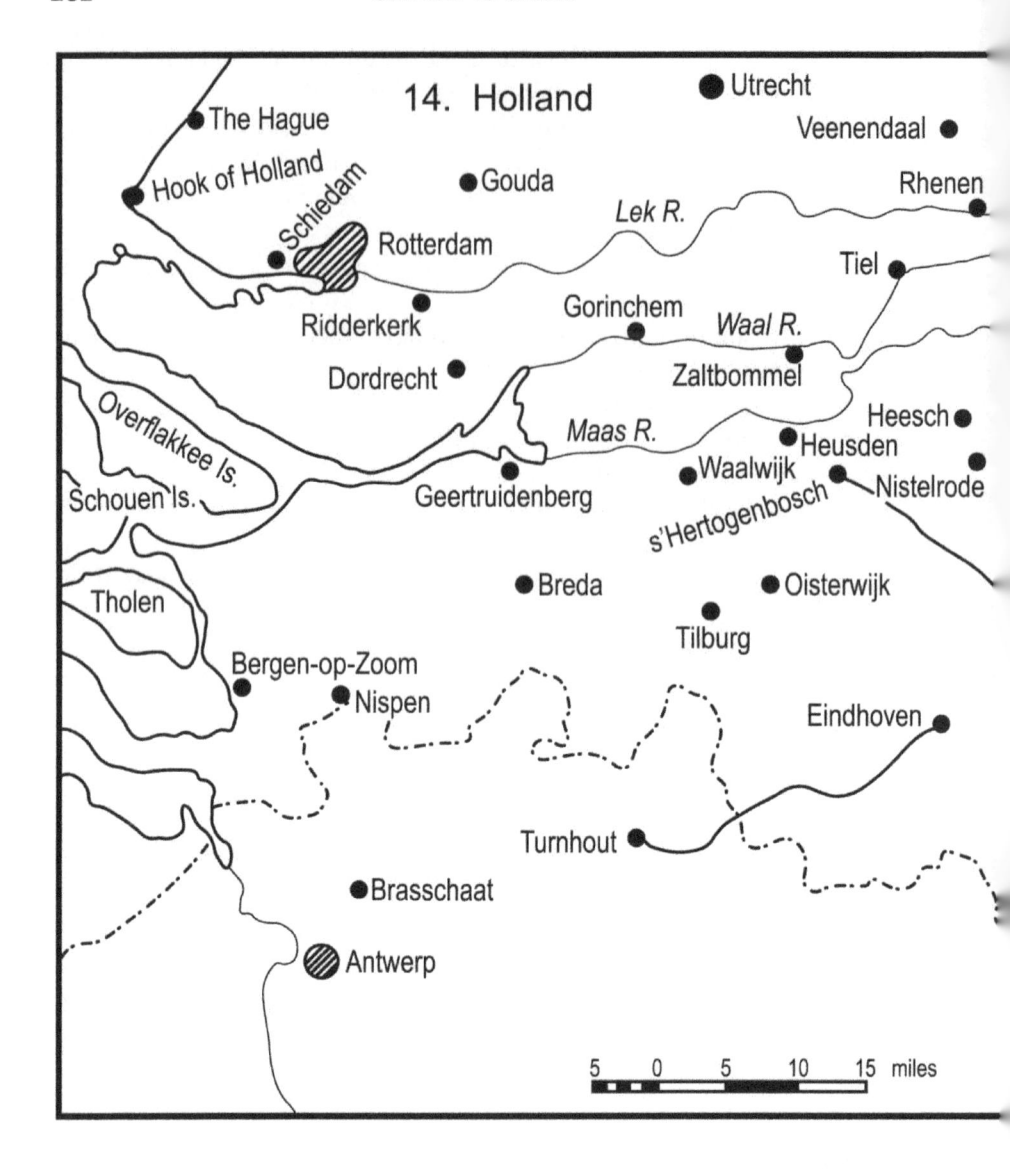

"West Wall" and all his new lines in Holland and east of the Rhine, would be outflanked. Wesel was judged to be the key location. Flooding in December was confined to the plains of the Rhine, Maas, and Niers Rivers; little increase was expected, except along the Rhine where the water was controlled by dykes. Lieut. Strojich described and pointed out the worst areas from Wesel to Nijmegen, most of them below water level, and made an estimate of the possible extent of inundation if the dykes were breached. He also discussed the upland areas that formed a low plateau between the rivers – the ridge Calcar–Xanten, an expanse of meadows, ditches, swamps, abandoned stream beds, trees, scrub, mud and, into the Reichswald, small woods, heathland, and reforested areas with trees set out in blocks separated by clearings.

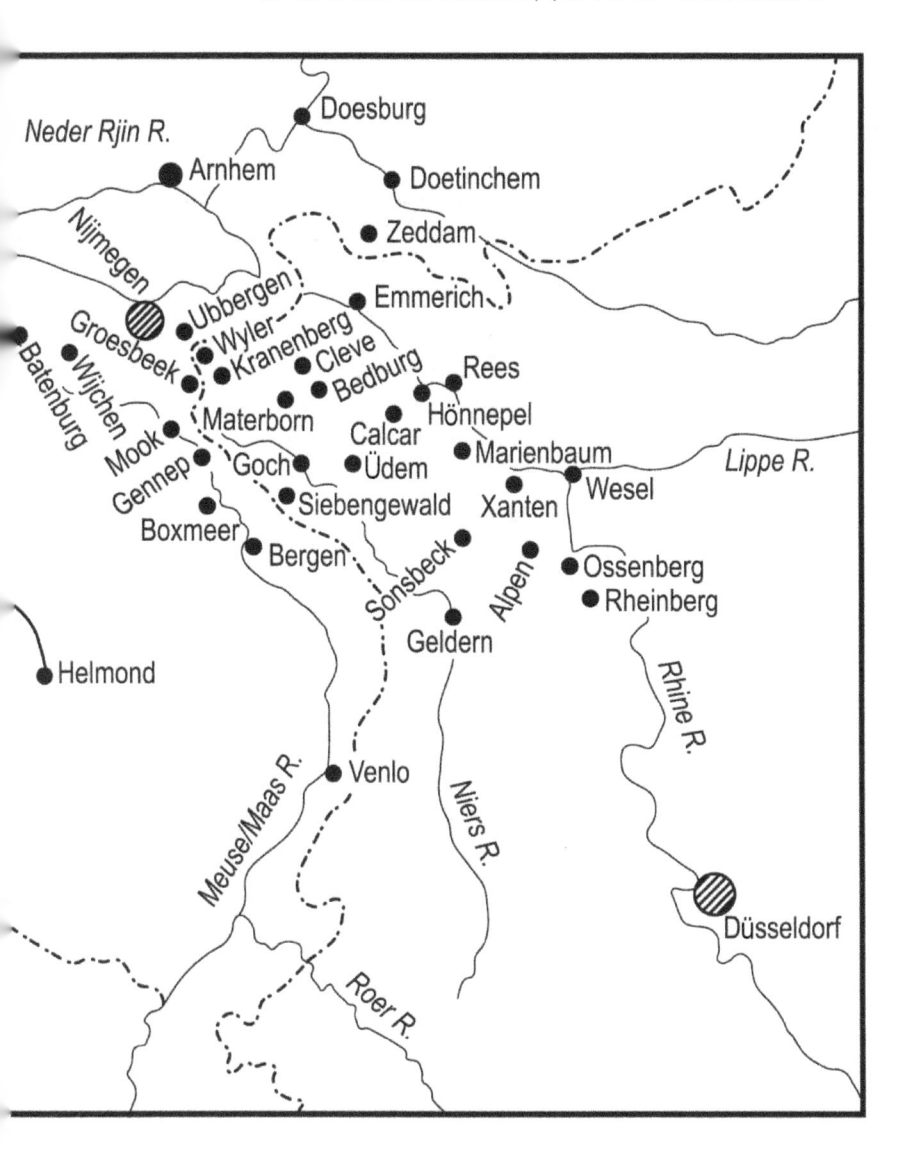

In mid-December, the German forces in the Reichswald and in Holland were believed to be under General-Oberst Student, commander of *Army Group "H"*. The *First Parachute Army* order-of-battle was fairly well known; it had two Corps, *LXXXVI* and *II Parachute*, but their actual areas of responsibility were obscure. *LXXXVI Corps*, with *84th* and *190th Divisions*, was thought to be responsible for the Reichswald.

There were three defence lines. The forward line, actually an outpost of the Siegfried Line, was organized into two belts. In the first, about 1,200 yards deep, each infantry battalion manned a frontage of about 1,200 yards; the weakest sector was north of the Nijmegen–Cleve road; the strongest was the Kiekberg woods. The second belt, also about 1,200 yards deep, ran from the Maas along the western edge of the Reichswald to Kranenberg. It was thought to be manned by about one-third of the enemy's infantry, positioned in the woods, in the houses, and along all the roads running at right angles to the front.

The Siegfried Line lay about three kilometres behind the forward positions. It comprised the original prewar pillboxes and bunkers, reinforced by new fieldworks, trenches, and a continuous anti-tank ditch. There were defences within the Reichswald, and a new defence line was under construction along its eastern side, between Cleve and Goch.

The Hochwald Layback ran about 10 kilometres east of the Reichswald, from the east bank of the Rhine opposite Rees, then diagonally along the southwest edge of the forest towards Geldern. With its two, sometimes three, continuous lines of trenches, often 600 yards to 1,000 yards apart, its anti-tank ditch, and an almost continuous belt of mines, it too was a very formidable obstacle.[92]

On December 31st reports came in that *190th Division* had been withdrawn. By January 8th, Army warned that the old enemy organization was no longer valid: "We have no modern or confirmed knowledge of what is behind the Reichswald." Three days later: ". . . his safety factor [in Holland] lies in the determination and vigour of his paratroops [which have been] allotted a wide sector. In the Reichswald and along the Maas he has weakened himself to provide forces elsewhere. . . . A strengthening of this sector or a reshuffle of divisions south of the forest along the eastern bank of the Maas allowing a reserve . . . would appear to be an essential part of a likely policy of safety." On the 20th: "In the Reichswald . . . *84 Infantry Division*, its odds and ends, and the *Parachute Regiments* [are] enough . . . to hold the fixed defences. . . . So far as we know . . . he has not . . . any substantial force in the rear areas."[93]

On January 26th, Intelligence assessed the enemy gun situation: ". . . since 14 Jan . . . an increase of about 35. . . . In early December . . . *190* and *84 Divisions* . . . total number of guns was approximately 100. The balance between . . . divisional artilleries and the total of 100 was made up by G.H.Q. artillery. With the present total of 70, 40 odd may be . . . *84 Division* with the balance . . . a G.H.Q. artillery battalion. . . . Photo coverage of 24 January showed . . . positions formerly occupied by the divisional artillery of *180 Division* were empty."[94]

A document taken from a P.W. described a number of enemy redeployments. The P.W. himself was suspect; although he wore no rank badge, he claimed to be an officer, and his story had gaps. But the document he was carrying contained just enough facts to make it worth studying, even if he were a "plant". Two days later, Maj. Les Chater considered that it was "probably authentic", but that the

German plan may have changed: "... the front line very thinly held by four divisions where there may have been seven and ten divisions previously.... There may be odd regiments or battalions lying back but only as local reserves." On January 30th: "There have been one or two signs of somewhat unusual activity.... Two nights ago ... a thick smokescreen ... and today again ... coincided with a slight increase in artillery activity ... movement ... suggest an increased attention to the Reichswald.... If he has divisions to spare we may expect ... something to bolster ... our northern front and some insurance in the Reichswald or behind his lines from there to Venlo."[95]

Tac R found more movement in central Holland, in the area Rees–Xanten–Goch; *7th Parachute Division* might have redeployed. Civilians were being removed from many of the towns. The official German propagandist, Sertorius, was pointing to the Reichswald as a possible location for future Allied operations. Les Chater's forecast read: "... enemy counts on being attacked in several places and north of Aachen." But he still had not specifically identified the Canadian intentions. First Army gave a comprehensive list of enemy order-of-battle. Under *Army Group "H"* were: in the north, *Twenty-Fourth Army*, with two Corps; west, *XXX*, east, *LXXXVIII*; and south and west of the Rhine along the Maas, *First Parachute Army*; north, *LXXXVI*, south, *II Parachute Corps*. Certain named divisions from *Twenty-Fifth Army* were in the line. Another division could conceivably have been in the Reichswald, but its identity was a matter of speculation.

On February 4th, Sertorius remarked that the mass of Allied troops was still in the north and that the Aachen sector was the most likely target. German moves fitted into that general appreciation. The flood patterns began to be an object of concern: "The level of the River Rhine at Nijmegen ... now stands at 11.32 metres. This ... affords some danger of ... flood ... west of the line Emmerich–Cleve." Lieut. Strojich had predicted his flood patterns on 10 metres in mid-December. Air reconnaissance also found enemy construction activity in the Hochwald, but the consensus was still that the three enemy divisions on the immediate front were not an adequate garrison against a determined assault.[96]

Senior Intelligence staff officers from Second and Third Divisions, and from Guards Armoured, 15th (Scottish), 51st (Highland), and 43rd (Wessex) Divisions met in the monastery at Boxtel on January 23rd for briefing on VERITABLE, for which the maps and models had been prepared by No. 1 Canadian Modelling Team in December. Maj. Les Chater reviewed the enemy situation on both the Eastern and Western fronts, and the G.S.O.2 (Int), XXX British Corps, gave the situation in the Reichswald. The meeting discussed an extensive program of defence overprints, and allotted responsibility for producing them to the various Divisions, with help, as required, from A.P.I.S.

Security precautions had to be improved. M.I.5 had identified an enemy agent with a transmitter in a Second Division unit (he was "turned around" and then sent back by Major J.A. Gray). Another, who also had been "turned around", was captured on his return by the unit which had picked him up the first time. Security had to accept, in silence, some caustic comments. And an amazing number of line-crossers had been caught. Carrier pigeons had been observed; Corps had no way of stopping them. XXX Corps vehicles were forbidden to go beyond the Grave River, and a Canadian Liaison Detachment, equipped with Second Division jeeps, was set up in Graves Barracks to take any of its officers who wished to go forward.[97]

The "subcontracting" of the maps was an excellent idea. The Divisions were able to concentrate on areas in which they were specifically interested. Each was asked to produce five 1:25,000 and five 1:12,500 sheets of the enemy forward areas; A.P.I.S. had to do five 1:25,000 of his rear areas. But flying conditions were still poor; only 12 days in the month were suitable and only 113 sorties were flown.[98]

The assault on the Reichswald began at 1030, February 8th, 1945. The main opposition was found in the south, where the Highland Division, opening the Mook–Goch road, ran into the *1222nd Grenadier Regiment* of *180th Infantry Division*, which had been deployed into that sector the previous evening.[99] The 53rd Division, astride the Groesbeek road, was hampered by mud; but found that the minefields in their sector were less extensive than had been estimated, and that the enemy anti-tank ditch had been imperfectly built. Second Division captured Den Heuvel and Wyler, and opened the Nijmegen–Cleve road. Third Division, on the left flank of the advance, had to contend not only with the enemy but also with the floods. The Rhine now stood at 12 metres, far higher than normal and, to add to the flooding, the Quer Dam, inside German territory, collapsed on the 8th.

In Army's Intsum that night,[100] Maj. Aris listed the units encountered and said: "It has not been possible until now to assess directly the enemy's reaction to attack against the Reichswald. Now we know *84 Division* . . . could not stand the hammering." Looking ahead: "P.W. who have been working in the forest report there is no concrete there and some state that . . . it is not manned. If that is so, the strength of the West Wall in the Reichswald is . . . forward defences, which we have already breached. . . . Where are the reserves? There is so far no evidence of any woodland garrison except *84 Division*." Tac R reported slight activity in the Hochwald Layback, "but it goes no further than to indicate that there are some troops in the area". If there were any enemy reserves they were more than a day's march away from the battle.

The weather closed in on February 9th. By the end of that day, however, the Lowland Brigade had taken the Materborn heights over-looking Cleve, just in time to repel *7th Parachute Division*. The Highland Division reached the northeastern edge of the Reichswald, overlooking the Cleve–Hekkens road, the main enemy supply route, and Materborn. Over 1,200 prisoners were

10. TO KNOW THE ENEMY: I(A) IN NORTH-WEST EUROPE   287

Mosaic of Kessel, Reichswald, February 1945. (War Diary, 1 Canadian A.P.I.S./Photo collection Canadian Forces School of Military Intelligence, Kingston/Canada. Dept. of National Defence)

taken on the 8th; 1,500 more on the 9th. "The confirmation of *7 Parachute Division* . . . fulfills previous speculation," which had appeared in Intsum 218 of February 3rd.

An assessment of enemy options followed: "He must now want first to hold us from crossing the Rhine at Emmerich and secondly to prevent us from deploying freely into the area Cleve–Xanten–Kevelaar–Goch. . . . The way left to stop us is to hold Cleve and Goch. . . . Cleve he has all but lost, but Goch is still in his control. If he has forces available either from the Hochwald or from across the Rhine he will be tempted to try to regain Cleve or at least to seal it off. If he cannot do so then he must hold Goch and also cover the nearest crossing of the River Rhine. These designs failing, he must rely on the Hochwald Layback position. Of the forces available, *84 Division* had dissolved . . . six battalions left out of 14. How much of *7 Parachute Division* is available we cannot yet determine, at present two battalions . . . have appeared." Aris thought that the *Parachute Division's* role was to hold Goch, and explored the likelihood of reserves moving in. *II/16th Parachute Regiment* was in Cleve, and a mixed group was in Materborn. Reserves were really only available from within the neighboring German divisions, and, ". . . *84 Division* has been stretched from 15,000 yards which it could not hold to 30,000 yards which it must hold. It . . . might now include as many as eight regimental groups. . . . A fresh staff and divisional troops are required and *7 Parachute Division* or possibly *180* offer the best. . . . The front now provides two potential divisional sectors, a northern one including Cleve and a southern paratroop one to the Maas."[101]

On February 10th, *Army Group "H"* was ordered to hold Cleve at all costs.[102] By the morning of the 12th, the advance had been checked by a German defence line along the Esels-Berg Ridge. A counter-attack by *15th Pz.Gr.* and *116th Pz. Divisions* was beaten off. On the Allied right, 51st Highland Division's capture of Gennep enabled Second Army to bridge the Maas. In the north, Third Canadian Division's 9th Brigade worked its way forward through the floods against a light defence.

First Army had succeeded in turning the northern end of the Siegfried Line, but the flooding of the Roer, which had hampered the U.S. Ninth Army in that sector, allowed the enemy to redeploy some of his reserves. Since the German defences were not designed to withstand an attack from the north, he would have to make some adjustments. "Notwithstanding our bridgehead over the Niers he may be expected to form his anti-tank line on the Niers and the line Goch–Calcar. He will move troops, possibly a regiment of *6th Parachute Division*, to hold against any attempt to cross the Rhine to the north."[103]

On the afternoon of February 16th, 7th Brigade, Third Division, advancing through Moyland Wood, ran against *346th Fusilier Battalion* and *60th Pz.Gr. Regiment* of the *116th Pz. Division*. The fight lasted three days and it seems that the actual enemy strength was not clearly appreciated at Divisional H.Q.[104]

16th Parachute Regiment had been expected, but not the heavier metal of the Panzer units. Second Canadian Division, on II Corps' right flank, also met heavy opposition from *116th Pz. Division*, including a battle group from the *Pz. Lehr*. Eventually the enemy was pushed back to the line Calcar–Hönnepel, but the engagement taught a bitter lesson that it was still unwise to take the enemy for granted.

On Army's right flank: ". . . to the west of our penetration towards Goch . . . *116 Panzer Division* is divided . . . *19 Parachute Regiment* . . . is a candidate for a counter attack against [us]. . . . *346 Division* and *II/21 Parachute Regiment* [which are] not firmly located . . . constitute his reserves. . . . We now hold the heart of the Bedburg–Calcar–Goch triangle and are poised over the whole enemy Maas position. . . . Either the enemy must reinforce further or he must plan on the basis that we will capture the land between the Rhine and the Maas and threaten his rear west of the Rhine . . . no evidence of any co-ordinated enemy plan to curtail our continuing success. We are at the stage where he has lost the battle but we have not yet won it. . . . Tonight [February 18th] the enemy situation is clear in its main features but obscure in detail . . . from the Rhine floods to the Maas we are opposed by parts of 10 divisions plus some odd units but it is impossible to sort them out." II Corps listed more than 50 units it had identified.[105]

Goch fell on the 19th. One of the P.W. was the garrison second-in-command. When interrogated, he stated that the Commander, *84th Infantry Division*, Maj.-Gen. Heinz Fiebig, had considered VERITABLE quite impossible because of the terrain. Von Rundstedt had warned that no reinforcements could be expected, except *7th Parachute Division*. The Intsum which reported all this warned that work was being done on the Hochwald Layback position (called by the Germans the "Schlieffen Line") and, although confirmation was still being awaited from the air photo cover flown that day, Wireless Intercept found strong indications that at least part of *116th Pz. Division* and *766th Volks Artillery Corps* were associated with it. "Clearly it would be premature to consider an immediate enemy withdrawal to this . . . layback but there are signs . . . that he may . . . attempt to defend it more stubbornly than ever he did the Siegfried Line proper."[106]

THE RHINE TO THE ELBE

The operation to clear the Hochwald was given the name BLOCKBUSTER. 15th Scottish Division was to assault on February 22nd, followed two days later by the 53rd (Welsh) Division; II Canadian Corps was to clear the Calcar–Üdem ridge on the 26th. Second and Third Divisions were to attack Calcar and Keppeln, to convince the enemy that the main weight of the attack would fall on the northern sector, which he could only reinforce by weakening other areas. Fourth Division would then push through. "His preparations in the Hochwald area are centred in the north and he is unlikely to abandon his left flank on the Maas until he is forced by catastrophe or until he does not lengthen his line by doing so."[107]

A.P.I.S. managed to collect a good deal of valuable information, despite poor flying conditions. Based on this and other material, Army thought the enemy had taken advantage of the lull to regroup; *Pz. Lehr* had probably moved south, *16th* and *18th Parachute Regiments* had withdrawn to Calcar and to the forward positions west of the Calcar–Üdem road. The two towns had become strong points, surrounded by anti-tank ditches and anti-aircraft guns sited for air and anti-tank use; 24 of the latter were at Calcar. Another line of as yet unoccupied positions lay one kilometre west of the high ground in front of the Hochwald. There were sites in the forest and along the Winnekendonk–Sonsbeck road, and self-propelled guns between Calcar and Üdem. Corps located two battalions of *16th* and *18th Parachute Regiments* north of the Cleve–Calcar road, and speculated as to the locations of the other four. Both H.Q. wondered where the enemy was going to get men for these positions.[108]

By March 1st, the advance of the U.S. XVI Corps as far as Venlo, only 18 miles from First Canadian Army's forward positions, made the enemy withdrawal increasingly necessary. He strengthened his Hochwald forces with two independent parachute battalions, which held until the night of March 3rd/4th. Now Army had to assess the escape facilities still available to him: "[a few] ferries are available east of Marienbaum and Xanten; the railway bridge at Wesel can still take foot soldiers. There are major ferries at Orsoy and bridges south of Homberg. To use these he must protect the axis Xanten–Rheinberg." On March 3rd: ". . . the enemy . . . has apparently appreciated that his greatest asset is [his] staunch front. . . . On this he can pivot back to the Wesel bridgehead and from it he can start his withdrawal." Two days later: "The major question is will the enemy stand this side of the Rhine. . . . Whatever his decision it is fair to assume that, by now, his heavy weapons and stores have moved to the right bank." Army did not know that orders from Berlin had made it impossible for the unfortunate German commanders to withdraw until it was so late that they were unable to remove their equipment.[109]

The Germans withdrew through Wesel. A lateral road linking the two flanks of the dwindling bridgehead ran from Xanten on II Corps' front, through Ossenberg, to Rheinberg. Covering this road in First Army's Sector were the three towns of Xanten, Veen, and Alpen. Xanten was the key. II Corps described it as: "bristling with A.A. and anti-tank guns. . . . This area . . . can be held by a . . . determined force to create a diversion . . . out of all proportion to the numbers . . . actually involved."[110]

Xanten fell on March 8th, and General Schlemm, Commander, *First Parachute Army*, withdrew his force on the 10th. First Canadian Army had taken 22,239 prisoners since February 8th. Maj. Bill Broughall, II Corps, had suggested on February 28th that enemy tactics "were not those of an Army planning to conserve his forces to fight another day, they were more . . . to stand where he is and inflict the greatest possible damage."[111]

The Canadian casualties in the battle totalled 379 officers and 14,585 men. They included two Intelligence officers. Capt. Certain de Beaujeu lost part of his left hand while trying to remove a fuse from a 40 mm A.A. shell on February 13th. Capt. Ken Fawdry, a British officer then employed as I.O. (Documents), was caught in shellfire at Üdem on February 27th, and lost a leg.[112]

The next phase in the Allied strategic plan called for the crossing of the Rhine and for thrusts up into northern Germany. The actual crossing of the Rhine – Operation PLUNDER – was to be made by Second British Army. II Canadian Corps would be involved for a short period after the crossing was completed. First Canadian Army was to hold the line of the Rhine and the Meuse from Emmerich to the sea, in order to ensure the security of the bridgehead at Nijmegen, and to safeguard the port of Antwerp. Preparations for the assault had been in hand in Second British Army for some time. Capt. Tetreault, G.S.O.3 (Int) Third Division, was given the enemy defences plan on March 17th and a topographical study on the 19th. Second Division received its briefing on the 21st.[113]

The outline plan of March 23rd stated: ". . . it is expected that once the Rhine has been crossed the enemy will be unable to hold a continuous line although parts will continue to fight very fiercely. We will be opposed by *First Parachute Army*, consisting of *6, 7* and *8 Parachute Divisions, 180* and *84 Infantry Divisions*, with in reserve *116th Panzer* and *15 Panzer Grenadier Divisions*." The enemy tank strength was estimated at 100.[114] During the preparatory phase, air cover revealed: "new positions from Emmerich to Zutphen with concentrations . . . at Doetinchem and on each side of the Hoch Elten feature" (which dominated the crossings at Emmerich). Field artillery was being emplaced around Hoch Elten, and A.A. strength was being reduced north and south of the Zaltbommel Bridge. On March 20th, Corps increased the count of guns in the area to 150, which, it learned later, was the exact actual count. Third Division cleared Emmerich and the Hoch Elten feature of elements of *61st Parachute* and *346th Infantry Divisions* on the 30th. The identifications turned out to have been wrong, but the type of opposition met was the same. In the meantime, Second Division moved northward through the gap between Emmerich and Doetinchem while, on its right flank, elements of Fourth Armoured Division moved northward toward Zelhem.

First Canadian Army regained control over II Corps on April 1st. It now had to fight two battles, in two different directions. The first was against the defence line based on the Ijssel River *(shown on Map 13)*, which the Germans had built to block any advance northeastward into Germany. II Corps, with Second British Army, would attack it through its unprotected rear, and then exploit northward along the coast. I Corps, which had rejoined First Army, had first to clear up a number of security matters that had arisen in the Army rear areas during the Reichswald assault. This gave Intelligence officers an opportunity to visit other H.Q. in the area and to build up their libraries. Their first Intsum, No. 238, issued on March 16th, contained a general description of the front, pieced together from the information they had just collected. I Corps was next ordered to clear a small "island" between the Waal and the Neder Rijn, to cross the Rhine (Operation ANGER), and then to send Fifth Armoured Division forward to join II Corps for the advance into northwestern Holland.

The operations between the Waal and the Rijn began on April 2nd. Arnhem fell to units of the 49th (West Riding) Division on April 14th and Fifth Armoured Division began to move through to the north. At Almelo, cleared on April 5th by Fourth Armoured Brigade, some units of *6th Parachute Division* were found to be using 14 to 16-year-old boys from the *3rd Parachute Training Regiment, Parachute Training Division*. Remnants of three divisions held firmly at Doesburg and in various small, isolated pockets, much to the mystification of II Corps.[115]

The reason for this became apparent on April 7th, when Army Intelligence discovered that the Germans had withdrawn into the Ijssel line as far north as Deventer, a strong town, well covered by canal bank defences. Army considered it to be: "the present pivot for the swing until we reach Zwolle where we face the Ijssel along its length. The value of Zwolle, Deventer, Zutphen and Doesburg as outposts and nodal points to an otherwise shallow . . . line will be . . . apparent". The enemy now faced action on two fronts, one eastward across the Ijssel, the other southwestward to block an advance towards Bremen.[116]

By April 6th, Fourth Armoured Division had reached the Ems River at Meppen. "The only serious obstacle to our advance is the nature of the ground . . . . Isolated parties of the enemy probably remain in some villages." Zutphen fell on the 8th, Deventer on the 10th, and the road into the "back door" of the Ijssel was clear. Numerous identifications were made, but they began to be somewhat meaningless. On the 8th, for example, Second Division reported taking prisoners from 15 different units. On the 11th, II Corps began the attack across the Ijssel and toward the town of Apeldoorn and the high ground beyond. By the 12th the crossing was secure: ". . . the light resistance along the dike itself from thickly armed but thinly spaced troops of *162 Marine Infantry Regiment*" was not enough. On the 13th: ". . . with our troops in Apeldoorn the enemy must withdraw to his next line or risk sacrificing Western Holland. Tac R and civilian reports show that he is beginning his withdrawal to a more economic line of defence further west."[117]

15. Rhine to the Elbe

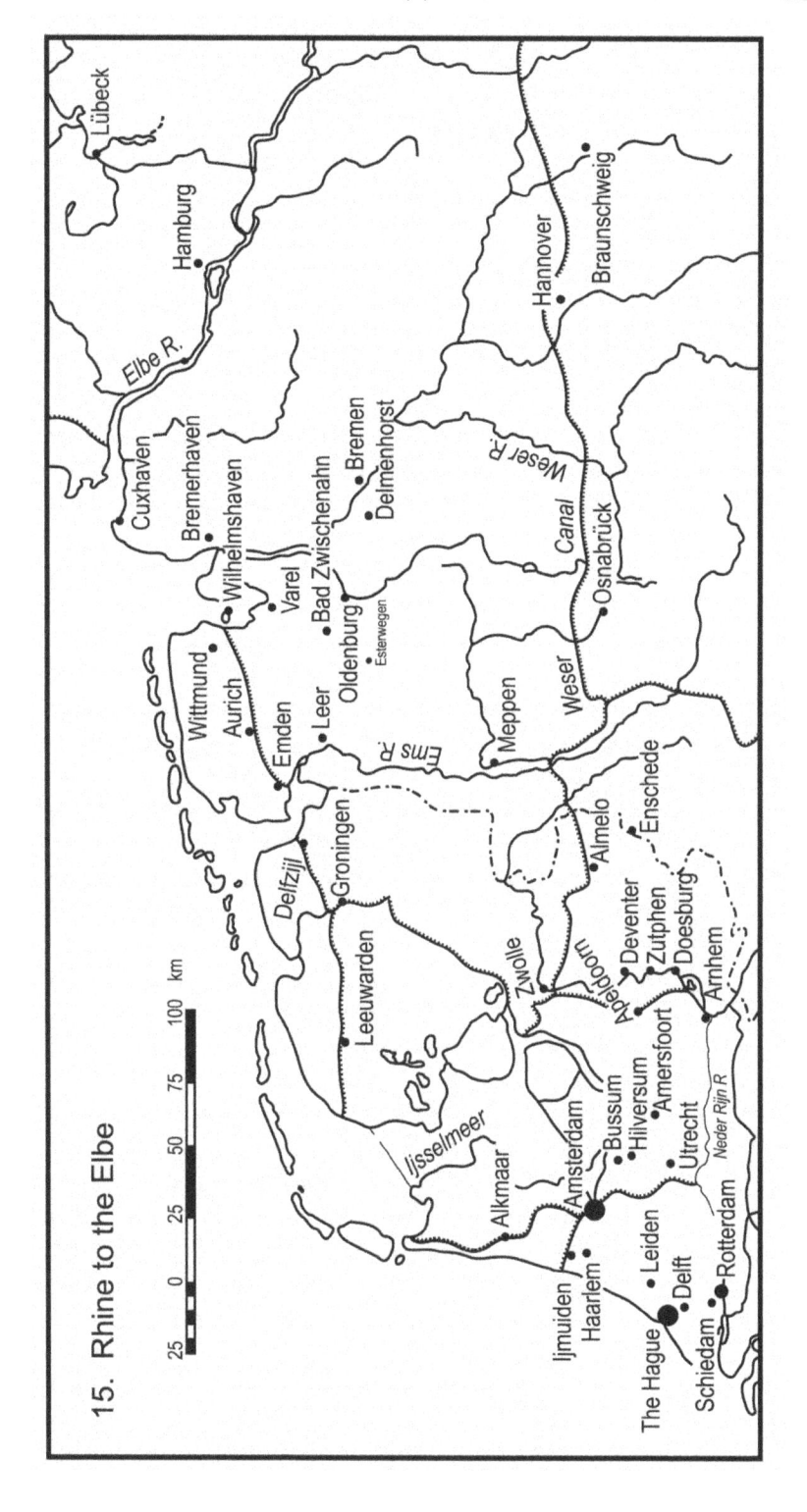

On April 15th, the Dutch captured a German courier on his way from *Twenty-Fifth Army* to *Army Group "H"*. His papers helped Army Intelligence to understand a little more clearly the local enemy organization, and to fit the German Navy units into his defence plan. Additional information, obtained on the 16th, explained how he was trying to form a line to defend the approaches to Bremen, Wilhelmshaven, and Emden. The key features were the town of Oldenburg and the Küsten Canal, garrisoned by remnants of *7th Parachute Division* and other elements, including a *Battle Group Gericke*.[118]

Groningen fell on April 16th. Fourth Armoured Division crossed the Küsten Canal near Oldenburg on the 18th, followed the next day by the Polish Armoured Brigade. Delfzijl and Oldenburg, the two strong points on the road to Emden, had to be reduced. Civilians told Corps that Delfzijl had a garrison of 1,500; photo reconnaissance had told them that Oldenburg had well-developed anti-tank and infantry defence positions astride the main roads leading into the town.[119]

Meanwhile, on the left of the Army sector, after the fall of Arnhem, I Corps deployed to clear west Holland. Because *Twenty-Fifth Army* lacked the troops, its commander had ordered the natural barriers it defended to be made as strong as possible: "Thus we find reports of the dykes of the Grebbe line and the New Water Line being prepared for demolition . . . and work is being done on the line of the Lek facing south." The Grebbe Line to which Army referred was based on the valleys of the Grebbe and the Ems (Eem) Rivers, together with the marshy polderland which bordered the Ijsselmeer (Zuider Zee) from the Ijsselmeer to Nijkerk, southwest of Amersfoort, southeast to Veenendaal, and thence to meet the east-west defence line along the Neder Rijn at Wageningen and Grebbe *(shown on Map 13)*. Local high areas near Amersfoort and Grebbe contained the strongest and most extensive defences. The New Water Line, which was even more floodable than the Grebbe, extended from Gorinchem in the south via these Merwerde Canal to the Lek River, thence north to Utrecht, then north and northwest to the Ijsselmeer.[120]

On April 9th, 49th (West Riding) Division moved down the north bank of the Rhine, beginning the clearance of the area in front of the Grebbe Line. Fifth Canadian Armoured Division moved northward, virtually cutting the Apeldoorn–Amersfoort road and the escape routes of German units withdrawing from II Corps' assault on the Ijssel Line. Those who tried to use boats or the damaged causeway to cross the Ijsselmeer became excellent targets for the Air Force. Some fled by road around the tip of Fifth Division's advance. Others attempted to cut across its axis. Intercepted radio messages had warned that these enemy columns might be dangerous, and preparations had been made to receive them. One fleeing group chose to try a break-through at Otterloo, then occupied by Divisional H.Q. Another group actually drove right through the I Corps P.W. Cage. The senior Interrogator, Lieut. Hanel, wakened by the din, leaned out of his "caravan" and shouted in German at the passing mob, "What Company, what Battalion, are you?" Back came the reply, "*2 Company, 858*". The first identification had been made. Of the 7,000 P.W. taken in the escape attempts, many came from *346th* and *361st Infantry Divisions*.[121]

On April 11th, Gen. Blaskowitz had combined his *H.Q. Army Group "H"* with *Twenty-Fifth Army*, to form *Fortress Holland*: ". . . every step is likely to be taken . . . to make [the Grebbe] line more secure . . . all within their power to increase the flooding since the artificial defences as such scarcely exist and what there are are facing the wrong way." Civilians reported that troops were "already concentrated in the Fortress with only a quarter of the total – though the best troops – in the line." Flooding was increasing north and south of Utrecht. *LXXXVIII Corps* held the north of that line, and *XXX Corps* (which had been holding the area between Arnhem and the Line) was in the south, with the remnants of *34th S.S. Netherlands Division* also in place. Behind these operational troops were the garrisons of the towns and the ports, the flak troops, and the administrative echelons. It was hopeless to try to estimate their strengths.[122]

At this point, non-military pressures intervened to stop further Allied advances into west Holland. The population was starving; simple humanitarian considerations required that it be given relief. Negotiations therefore began and, by April 19th, fighting on this front had virtually come to a halt. I Corps H.Q. concentrated on administration and famine relief. In order to allow food convoys to pass, a truce zone was arranged, running from the Ede–Utrecht railway south to the Neder Rijn.

In II Corps, on April 23rd: "The Delfzijl pocket is being reduced . . . the enemy has got safely behind the Leda . . . but he has left pockets behind in the marshes." Three days later: ". . . there are indications . . . that he considers the time ripe to fall back closer on Emden and Wilhelmshaven. . . . that Oldenburg will be the pivot. . . . Leer and Bad Zwischenahn [are key points]." On the 29th: "Leer is taken [by Third Division]. . . . Tonight he must block the main roads leading from Leer or retreat to Emden and Wilhelmshaven." But Bad Zwischenahn held out until May 1st.[123]

During the whole month of April there was a great deal of speculation about the end. Lt.-Col. Les Chater thought it would be Wagnerian, with "Der Führer" pulling everything down around him in a great, final cataclysm. The actual announcement, broadcast on May 1st by Admiral Dönitz, came almost as an anti-climax: "Hitler fell in battle at the Reichskanzlei in Berlin this afternoon." At First Army, normal business continued. Intelligence had to find out about the defences of Oldenburg and the location of the remnants of the *7th* and *8th Parachute Divisions*.

Second Division captured Oldenburg in circumstances that had all the elements of low farce. The G.S.O.1, Lt.-Col. P.W. Bennet, had ordered Intelligence to prepare and deliver a propaganda leaflet, since the roads were too bad for the "Psy. War." teams to come forward. It was written and, under the direction of the Dutch L.O., printed by a civilian printer in Delmenhorst. The leaflets were showered on the city at about 0915. A little later, word came back that the "civil populace and the burgomeister were anxious to surrender or at least to have the place declared an open city." During the day, 4th and 6th C.I.B.s reached the outskirts of the town and, that evening, both the Royal Hamilton Light Infantry and the South Saskatchewan Regiment succeeded in reaching the burgomeister by telephone. He assured them that there were no German troops in the city and that he was unable to find a German officer to make a formal surrender of the town. But he promised to cross the Canal in the morning and explain the situation to them.

Meanwhile, in Delmenhorst, the G.S.O.3, Capt. J.M. Robertson, and the Dutch Liaison Officer, went to see the British Military Governor, a British Regular Army lieutenant-colonel, in order to arrange a phone call to the Oldenburg burgomeister. They were joined by Capt. R.H. Noble, G.S.O.3 I(b), II Corps, an F.S.O., possibly Capt. Ray Shelley, and the Intelligence Officer, Engineers. "The Colonel took us to the Chief of Police. We were received with much heel-clicking and . . . deference, and arrangements were made for the telephone engineer to be fetched. Finally . . . arrived – a short pathetic little man. . . . The party proceeded to the telephone exchange . . . where a sleepy and startled night watchman finally shuffled to the door. . . . The batteries required charging. The party . . . drove to the electric plant to lay on a full current for two hours. The man protested that his written instructions from the Military Governor prohibited this but . . . was finally convinced that he was being given a legal order. In fact, he received one in writing and compared the signature with that on his original. So the group returned to the exchange and the little man proceeded to pull every switch in sight and change every fuse, but all his efforts were in vain. . . . Another visit to the power plant revealed . . . a break in one of the underground lines. . . . At 2350 the project was called off."

On May 3rd, the two Brigades entered the town unopposed. Robertson and his I.O., Lieut. C.J. (Johnny) Doerksen, went down to the Canal to meet the burgomeister, only to find that he had been out and gone home again. Maj. Tex Noble went into the town, called on the Chief of Police, whom he ordered to assemble and disarm his force, and was driven by the Chief's chauffer to a camp of Russian P.W., which he officially liberated. Tex turned it over to the two senior Russians, searched the German H.Q. for documents, and returned.[124]

The news of the German surrender appeared in First Canadian Army's last Intsum: "With the exception of Dunkirk, enemy forces on 21 Army Group Front surrender at 050800B hrs. This summary concludes the issue of the publication known as First Canadian Army Intelligence Summary, which has been produced nightly since 6 Jan 44." Its last major article was a review of the arrangements for supplying food to the starving Dutch. Maj. Bill Broughall of II Corps issued his contribution – a cartoon, filled with topical allusions, including a large crystal ball topped by a bowler hat and a lunar eclipse. Its routine contents, "En Sit, ORBAT, Notes, Int. Notes, Breakfast Int", were each followed with a "Nil". At I Corps, Maj. Kingsmill issued a one line item only: "It's all over———Except the shouting."[125]

But unfinished business still remained. As we have seen, a special Planning Branch had been set up under Maj. Spike Sprung, M.C., on November 29th, 1944, to co-ordinate the Intelligence requirements expected under ECLIPSE. On April 2nd, Army Intelligence issued a preliminary set of general Notes intended to guide the staff branches and Services on the workings of the German forces. They included detail on: *Army* and *Waffen S.S.* organizations; order-of-battle of the *Ersatz Army* – the force gathered during the final stages of the war to defend the German homeland; types of H.Q.; the garrison system; organization of staffs; administration and supply, including the administrative staff and Services organization; the system of supply; internal administration of German institutions and the Nazi Party; Counter-Intelligence and Civil questions, including the Nazi Party organization; Party influence in the Army; German underground; and associated problems.[126] Groups had also been set up to safeguard the vital installations and to occupy significant German industrial and research centres. Maj. G.G. Black, who had been G.S.O.3 (Int) Third Division, was one of the officers appointed to this T (for Target) Force.

In addition to the German troops, who were at first estimated to number about 120,000, I Corps area had many starving Dutch citizens. The German authorities agreed that the soldiers and Dutch *S.S.* would be disarmed, and that any criminals found among them would be jailed. The news of the surrender, however, had not reached all the German units, and Kingsmill reported on May 5th that: "In Utrecht tonight flags and joy . . . whilst laughing, well-armed Germans parade the streets sticking up posters announcing the . . . Armistice. However in other areas such as Delft, The Hague and in Rotterdam . . . the civilians want the Germans to surrender to them but the . . . Nazis hang on to their weapons . . . consequently the civilians believe that the Germans are not surrendering and will fight when the Allies arrive. . . . In other towns the Nazis are surrendering to the civilians . . . all military stores are open to plunder and when the Germans try to guard these stores shooting follows. . . . Adding to the confusion all the Dutch on this side of the line now think they can travel freely to Amsterdam and vicinity . . . forward units will . . . have to turn back such . . . travellers".[127]

No prisoners were taken after May 6th, although odd stragglers drifted in to the Cages until about the 8th. The Interrogators were divided into teams and set to help in the massive task of screening the prisoners to identify anyone in the 'automatic arrest' category. All teams had long lists of suspects who had been identified through information received on their activities during the Occupation. *S.S.* and police were to be concentrated in The Hague; Dutch *S.S.* were to be held in Otterloo *(shown on Map 13)*; the German forces would remain in their immediate areas. Allied formations and units were asked for guards to ensure that the screened and unscreened personnel were kept apart. All arrested persons would be sent to Rotterdam Prison.[128]

In Second Division, Robertson and Johnny Doerksen spent most of May 9th investigating the arrest of Gen. Straube, the former enemy commander on II Corps front. He had discussed surrender terms with Gen. Simonds on May 6th, and had later been picked up by a British Naval Field Security Detachment. "When interrogated . . . the General was still very shaken – his dignity had suffered a serious set-back after having to sweep out his cell – and he dissolved into tears."[129] One suspects that, after all poor Straube had been through, to be treated as a common felon was the last straw.

The screening process was not easily set up, although things seemed to improve once it was explained to the local commanders. The Dutch Resistance helped to identify 'automatic arrest' suspects and most of the *S.S.* still wore their uniforms. The checking, however, was not particularly thorough; two officers and four men worked through 100 prisoners in 15 minutes. Any individual segregated as a result of that preliminary check then received more careful attention. Some units turned on one another, and one, *149th Division*, persisted in retaining its Nazi bias. The Teams left *34th Dutch S.S. Division* to the last, so that they could devote more time to it. They completed their task on June 1st.

On the 2nd, by which time the only Germans left were odd parties from hospitals and administrative elements, the majority of the Team went up to Wittmund and to Wilhelmshaven. In Holland, the aim had been to screen the German units before they were returned to Germany. In Germany itself, screening took place at the Discharge Centres, in order to make sure that suspects were found before they vanished into civilian life. Anyone arrested at this stage was sent back to Esterwegen Internment Camp.

Discussions began on June 12th to decide the role of First Canadian Army Intelligence Pool during the Occupation. The Pool had already absorbed many of the smaller units, and acted as a depot for individuals waiting to be reassigned. Its chief immediate responsibility was for the I(b) personnel working under British XXX Corps, whose temporary prisoner compound, No. 1 Canadian P.W. Transit Cage, was closed at the end of June. Officers and men were constantly changing positions. Maj. Ernie Skutezky, for example, moved to War Crimes Investigation duty; his place was taken by Lieut. Laban. Forty-five Intelligence officers and six A.P.I.S. Interpreters were needed for the Canadian Army Pacific Force; 12 men from the Pool volunteered. Only No. 9 Canadian Air Liaison Team survived until March 20th, 1946. The rest of the units were progressively reduced and finally disbanded. Their officers were sent to 1 A.P.I.S., which acted as an officers' transit depot; the men went to H.Q. Counter-Intelligence, which performed much the same function. A.P.I.S. itself was disbanded on September 23rd, 1945.

As far as Intelligence was concerned, the two European campaigns were very different. In Italy, I Corps received wholehearted and expert co-operation, and had free access to all the agencies in the theatre. But it was still, to a certain extent, a guest in a larger house. In Europe, the analogy of guest and host was equally applicable, but the larger scale, and the fact that the Canadian Army was a senior entity in its own right, gave Intelligence proportionately more freedom to operate, and more control over its own operations than was possible at the Corps level. And finally, although First Canadian Army H.Q. commanded many Allied formations, with their own Intelligence staffs and units, all of whom worked well as a team, the heart of that team was almost entirely composed of Canadians, secure in their identity and confident in their proven skills.

Ideally, when writing a history of Military Intelligence, the author should be able to state the Intelligence Requirement levied at a senior I.O. by his Commander, and to show the steps taken to ensure that all possible resources are exploited to satisfy the requirement. At the beginning of an engagement, as, for example, the Invasion itself, or a new deployment into a sector it is possible to do so – at some cost in terms of space. But, during the later stages, it is rarely possible to identify the actual, specific contribution made by any one of the many components of the Intelligence organization. Some of the conclusions reached by the Intelligence staffs came not only from hard evidence they collected, or that was presented to them, but also from conversations with staff officers and technical experts. Evaluations often depended less on solid fact than on specialized personal knowledge and training. And, in addition, as the campaigns progressed, the questions he would be asked and the answers he could give, tended to form in the I.O.'s mind a continuous chain of interrelated facts and suppositions. It is his ability to report these and his conclusions, without grave errors, that makes the I.O.'s reputation.

As we have seen, Intelligence did make mistakes: wrong identifications of enemy units, or incorrect estimates of the strength of enemy defences, or of the actions an enemy was likely to take. Whether these were really important or not, they always seemed so at the moment. But, at no time throughout the War was an officer holding a senior field Intelligence appointment dismissed because he failed his commander. Very few junior staff, even, had to be replaced, and many of those who were moved performed adequately in environments that were better suited to their talents.

The Intelligence team was carefully selected, and as well-trained as the pressure of time and circumstances allowed. But Intelligence is a craft that can only be learned through practice. By 1943, because there had been time to learn and to experiment, training was relevant and adequate. All Intelligence officers are aware that they can never know everything there is to learn about the opposition facing their commander. But they also know that, to fill the gaps in their knowledge, they must exploit every possible source of information: that the better they are trained, the better will they be able to select those sources, and to ask the questions that will get them all the information that is available in time for it to be of use. A good I.O. must be able to work without supervision, to take responsibility, and to use his initiative. He must also have the strength of character to admit he has been wrong, or that he does not know the answer. The I.O. who attempts to hoodwink his commander and to cover up his ignorance is dangerous. These basic rules were drummed home during training. To Col. Wright's knowledge, no one forgot or transgressed them. Intelligence staffs worked hard, over long hours, under the strain of knowing that what they did had significance for other men's lives. Though formation Intelligence staffs did not suffer all the physical dangers their colleagues in the line units had to face daily, they were all at risk together. Some in fact were wounded. A few were decorated; most received no recognition, except within their own circles.

At the beginning of the war, the idea that the Intelligence craft must be treated as a separate, specialist discipline met a great deal of apathy and even downright hostility within the Army. At the end of the war vestiges of this attitude still remained, particularly among those who had had little direct contact with Intelligence. But, for the vast majority, Intelligence was widely accepted as a highly respected function, essential to success. Some senior commanders, indeed, became strong supporters of it – at times revealing precious secrets regarding the sources of their information in their enthusiasm.

Members of the Intelligence Community had brought into the Army specialized knowledge and qualities of character that made them potentially of value to Intelligence. But their abilities had to be recognized and reinforced by training and practice, and officers and men had to be welded into teams. Support for the programs that could train them was vitally necessary. For Intelligence is a two-way street. There must first be a general recognition within the senior ranks of the Army that the function is necessary, that its practitioners have to be developed through programs of individual training, and that it needs an adequate organizational structure. On the other side, the members of an Intelligence organization have to ensure that each of them is as fully professional as it is possible to be. Only if both conditions are met can there be a successful team of Operations and Intelligence to support commanders in future campaigns.

11.
LIBERATION AND OCCUPATION: I(B) IN NORTH-WEST EUROPE

No. 3 Field Security Section, C.Int.C., followed its parent Third Canadian Infantry Division into France on June 7th, 1944. It was organized into an advance party of the O.C., Capt. Rafe Douthwaite, Capt. Reg. Taylor, Sgts. Bordewick and Doyle, Cpls. Rempel, Weibe, Freypons, and Schasny, L/Cpls. J.M. Wright and Holland, and Pte. Watson; and a rear party under C.S.M. Rahn, made up of L/Cpls. Alcorn and Wallace, and No. 4 F.S.R.D., with Sgt. Plewman, Cpls. McGuire and Worsdall, and L/Cpls. Larouche, Baker, and Simmons. The advance party set up a temporary H.Q. at Graye-sur-Mer. The rear party came ashore on June 13th and, after a little confusion, rejoined the Section at Cairon.

The Section's immediate task was to establish control over civilian movement. The civilians were generally friendly, although they had been well-treated and well-paid by the Germans. They were told to remain in their homes, but local scarcities of food forced them to continue their habit of seeking it in nearby villages. They travelled, in particular, the Caen–Bayeux road, which ran through the front lines of the two opposing armies. This brought the very real danger that agents, using civilian traffic as cover, would be able to penetrate and return unhindered. The threat was countered by instituting a system of passes that Field Security had to issue, because the Civil Affairs officers were not yet in position, and then, by applying a screening system, making sure that applicants for them were legitimate and respectable local residents.

As the battle moved inland, the number of refugees increased. Late in the month, reports came in that many were hiding in caves in the area of Thaon (Fontaine Henry), but they could not then be reached. A camp was set up at Amblie to which refugees found in the Carpiquet area were evacuated.

The Section also had to arrest civilians known to have actively collaborated with the enemy. There were many denunciations which, when investigated, were found to be based on "political, family, or personal spite".[1] Only one arrest was actually made; the evidence was admittedly shaky, but the individual "was too dangerous to leave at large".

Four members of the No. 3 Field Security Section, C.Int.C., sharing a glass of wine with a French couple, Thaon, France, 20 June 1944. (Lieut. Frank L. Dubervill/Canada. Dept. of National Defence/Library and Archives Canada, PA-133956)

When Caen fell on July 9th, No. 3 Section and No. 4 F.S.R.D. went in with No. 33 British Section, which was responsible for the city. It was still under artillery fire, and the British Section dealt with the few civilians. As a result, the Canadians had very little to do and made much out of relative trivialities like the discovery of the diary of a German pilot, shot down and killed near the Detachment's billets. When Vaucelles fell, they found few civilians, and spent most of their time watching for line-crossers attempting to get over the Orne. Later they discovered a party of Spaniards who turned out to be forced labourers with strong anti-fascist leanings. At Lisieux, the Section set up a warm relationship with the local French Forces of the Interior (F.F.I.), who gave them a private jail, complete with the staff to run it, in exchange for food.[2]

No. 2 Section had landed on July 7th and had been assigned to checking for "stay-behind agents". On August 8th, the O.C., Capt. R.H. ("Tex") Noble, sent Sgts. Osipoff and Dummer with two Engineers to St. André-sur-Orne to check reports that civilians were hiding in the mines there. The party took a wrong turn, drove across some Teller mines, and all were killed. They were the first fatalities suffered by F.S. in North-West Europe.[3]

The Section continued, collected documents, and tried – unsuccessfully – to set up at Carpiquet. It moved on again to Fleury-sur-Orne, the location of humid underground lime quarries filled with refugees living in squalor. Tex Noble initially sent in Sgts. McVea and Szun, with Pte. Janssen. When they discovered about 5,000 people, they realized that the task of evacuating and relocating them was too big for a detachment. Eventually the whole Section had to be assisted by a detachment from No. 15 Section, by local gendarmes, and by members of the Resistance. The Section finally cleared Fleury-sur-Orne, Basse, Eteauville [sic? Eterville], Ifs, and the areas between these villages, sending all the evacuees back to a concentration centre at the Lycée Malherbe in Caen. In the process, C.S.M. Lefebvre and L/Cpl. Croll were both slightly wounded by shell fragments; Lieut. Bill Blane, No. 15 Section, was more seriously wounded and had to be evacuated. On July 28th, the proprietor of a Bernais brothel asked Capt. Noble to authorize gasoline, so she could go to Paris for new girls to restaff the facility; despite repeated blandishments he did not oblige. The Section picked up two German agents and missed a third; it discovered sabotage equipment, a large ammunition dump, and many Dutch and Russian forced labourers.[4]

No. 18 Section, which arrived in France on July 11th with No. 7 F.S.R.D. under command, joined with Nos. 8 and 273 British Sections to deal with the influx of refugees into Bayeux. Such large crowds of people were arriving from Caen and the surrounding areas that C.I. decided to control their movements first and get at the other tasks as time permitted. A report of three Germans hidden in a barn was investigated, and the three American deserters found there were arrested. In Caumont, where the Section was located, the inhabitants were sullen and unco-operative because Canadian troops had looted the town. The Military Police were given the details, and provided with all possible assistance.[5] Unfortunately, similar incidents were to recur in other places.

No. 17 Section, which had arrived in early August, lost Sgts. Kazakoff and McCarthy, injured by the explosion of either a booby-trap or a delayed-action bomb. Nos. 1, 2, 3, 5, and 6 F.S.R.D.s landed on August 2nd/3rd and set up at Chateau Cairon, near Caen. Their first task was to determine the level of Security among the troops, and discover to what extent the few civilians in Caen had knowledge of the impending Operation TOTALIZE. Gen. Crerar was pleased to hear that Security had been good. The Detachments were then formed into a pool "H.Q. F.S. Res. Dets." – under Capt. Graham Blyth, with Capt. Ray Shelley as his Operations Officer. This gave them more flexibility and control with less sub-unit administration.[6]

Local Resistance told a Detachment checkpoint in Caen that two men, claiming to be line-crossers, had attended a high-level Resistance meeting. After they had left, the local Resistance had developed serious doubts about them and had asked the "Res. Dets." to locate them and return them to Caen. They provided hazy descriptions and a report that the suspects were heading "home" to a village up the coast. Capts. Blyth and Shelley took two jeep-loads of men up the coast and started to search three villages. Just before dawn, the two were found and turned over to Capt. Antzonberger, the French Security Officer attached to Army H.Q.

About this time also, the German Intelligence Service (G.I.S.) attempted to use frogmen against the Orne bridges near Caen. These frogmen carried an explosive charge which they were supposed to place on the piers. They were then to swim downstream a safe distance, come out of the river, and make their way back to the German lines. Fortunately, the first swimmer was captured before he reached his target, and thereafter booms and nets were erected to protect important bridges. Later the Nijmegen Bridge garrison deployed light artillery and searchlights to cover the nets.

On August 9th, the Army Counter-Intelligence Staff reviewed the progress that had been made. Before the Invasion, a good deal of thought had been given to methods of operation; the planning had proved accurate. The experience in Italy – that the best way to catch German agents was to control civilian movement – had been repeated and confirmed. Forward units had been encouraged to send anyone they found suspicious to a Corps Forward Interrogation Centre. Behind these forward units, the Field Security/Counter-Intelligence Sections set up controls and arrested anyone who could not be vouched for or whose papers were not in order. This applied particularly to anyone moving at night. During July, movement by civilians had been restricted to six kilometres from their current locations, but despite this order many tried to move farther afield. The Sections were too small. They were short of interpreters, and had had little success in recruiting locally. The local gendarmerie were too busy re-establishing law and order in the newly liberated areas. The Resistance groups were the only other source, and these were not always reliable because of their political ambitions.

The greatest weakness of the system was that the Sections were too rigidly assigned to formations. Some Divisions moved two and three times in one week, and their Sections were unable to finish their work. As the Division's subordination changed, the Sections would find themselves working for different Corps. As a result, successive arrests and re-interrogations of the same individuals occurred too often. In addition, these constant moves prevented the Sections from building up a proper informant network. A compromise solution was reached. During the next phase of the campaign, when a major town was captured, the Section given responsibility for it was to be withdrawn from its parent formation, placed under direct command of Corps or Army, and replaced in the formation by a Reserve Detachment. After the town had been cleared, the Section would be returned to its formation. Uncommitted Sections were to be held, and used, as and where they were needed.

Before the Invasion, Allied C.I. had prepared lists of the names, with all available details, of persons who were either actively collaborating with the German

Occupation forces (Black List), or who actively opposed them (White List). This information came from men who had escaped or evaded capture, from agents, from civilians, and from the press and similar sources. Each Section had a copy of each List, which it was required to check and expand as the Invasion progressed. When a town was captured, the persons on the lists were checked by teams of a Section or more, reinforced by highly trained counter-espionage and military police officers of the French Service de Sécurité Militaire (S.M.), or Surveillance du Territoire (S.T.). Arrested collaborators were turned over to the French authorities. The S.T. took evidence and developed cases against anyone who had committed an offence under French law. For large operations, the teams were directed by a G.S.O.3 I(b) from Corps or Army, and appropriate additional staff was supplied – interrogators, auxiliary police from the Resistance, and any otherwise unemployed F.F.I. A team could be subdivided into groups, each of which would be responsible for some facet of the operation, such as the Black and White Lists, special investigations, and movement control.[7]

After the fall of Rouen on August 30th, 1944, No. 2 Section went to Boulogne, together with No. 4 F.S.R.D.; No. 4 Section remained on the L. of C., to move to Bruges when that city fell; No. 15 was assigned Dieppe, Dunkirk, Ostend, and, finally, an ammunition dump protection task on the lower Scheldt; No. 16 was held first on the L. of C. and then moved to Ypres; No. 17 was held with H.Q. First Army as far as Arras, and then was sent to Calais; No. 18 and No. 7 F.S.R.D. went through Rouen to St. Omer; H.Q. F.S. Res. Dets. was to be at St. Omer, and used as needed. No. 5 Interrogation Team, under Lieut. Jan Jezewski, was deployed at Camp 030 at Fontaine Henry.[8]

No. 15 Section entered Dieppe on September 2nd. Most of the suspects had withdrawn with the German garrison, but it did find a great deal of documentary evidence on the local Fascist or Fascist-sympathizer groups. The Section also found useful details on the port facilities and on demolition preparations, which it passed to the Navy. The Army Cage and Camp 030, swamped with prisoners, had to instruct the Sections to limit their "catches" to suspected or confessed members of the G.I.S., so anyone they found was turned over to the French.[9]

While waiting for Boulogne to fall, Capt. Noble set up H.Q. No. 2 Section at Montreuil. On September 6th, he sent Sgt. Cuthill to the crossroads near the town to intercept and guide the rest of the Section, travelling in the unit truck. About 1300, Sgt. Croll told him the driver had missed the checkpoint, by-passed the town, and could not be found. At 2100, he learned from Corps that the men had run into an enemy minefield and come under fire, had abandoned the vehicle, and were now with No. 3 Section at Third Division. C.S.M. Bert Sutcliffe had somehow managed to get them out without casualties. The Section had lost all its administrative transport and equipment but, much worse, it had lost all its records, including the Black and White Lists.[10] Their arrest of an important female agent at Montreuil was little compensation.

No. 16 F.S. Section, England, May 1944. Seated left to right: Sgt. A.S.A. Bake, W.O.II E.K. Skippon, M.M., Capt. D.K. Drury, Sgt. C.L. Davidson, Sgt. W.J. Brown. Standing: Sgt. R.J. Levesque, Pte. G.H. Douglas, Sgts. D.H. Massy, P. Weissman, T.J. Richardson, C.G.P. Playfair, J.E. Hyslop, J.R. Algar. (E.K. Skippon collection/Canadian Forces School of Military Intelligence, Kingston/Canada. Dept. of National Defence)

On September 10th, the Germans began a wholesale eviction of civilians from Boulogne. No. 3 Section, which had moved up to Saher on the 5th, manned checkpoints until the 14th, in an attempt to screen the hordes of people coming out. The Section collected 55 French sailors, 49 French marines, two Italians, two Russians, and a Pole who had been working for the *Organization Todt*, but was not able to pick out any of the people on either of its lists. (The *Organization Todt* was the construction agency of the Ministry of Armament and War Production, assigned to the *Wehrmacht*; it was named after Dr. Fritz Todt, its first head.) It finally entered Boulogne on the 20th, and at once arrested two Italians who had been working for the Germans, and three German deserters in civilian clothes. It released some 35 individuals who had been jailed by the Chief of the F.F.I. at Desvres on "evidence" based almost entirely on spite.

In Boulogne, the Section spent a great deal of time searching for a radio transmitter, which it finally found, but was unable to locate the agent who had been operating it. The Document Subsection had better luck. When it moved into the former G.I.S. office, it found No. 2 Section's office boxes and documents. There was no evidence that the Germans had exploited this material. It had been in their hands for three days before the mass evacuation of civilians, but it is possible that they decided to continue with the evacuation rather than make selective arrests.[11]

No. 17 Section, after an exciting time with the first troops entering Brussels, was pulled back and sent to its assigned mission, Calais. On September 17th,

Sgt. Weiss was wounded by a German sniper near Guînes while on patrol with his O.C., Capt. Graham George. The German Commander at Calais, hampered by some 20,000 civilians, requested a 24-hour truce to allow the town to be cleared. The Section, helped by the Calais police, processed some 10,000 through Ardres alone; many suspects were arrested.[12]

Army Main H.Q. sent an officer to Ghent, the day after it had been liberated, to arrange for accommodation. In his party was an ex-F.S. man who spoke French. About two hours after their arrival, this individual told his officer he had learned, on good authority, that a "severe security and spy problem existed in Ghent". Capt. Blyth was immediately sent to the city, where he contacted the White List. After much work, it was found that the reports, which were groundless, were based on inter-Resistance group rivalry.

No. 2 Section moved to Dixmude in Belgium on September 10th, and quickly established contact with the Belgian Forces of the Interior (B.F.I. = partisans). These provided information on Dunkirk's defences, which was sent to I(a). Two agents (No. 2 was unsure if they were *Gestapo* or *S.D.*) were arrested, and the information they gave included the names of some of their associates. Most of the suspects, however, were political, and hence of interest primarily to the Belgian authorities. The Section moved to Antwerp, where it recovered its transport and administrative records. It hired four interpreters, checked out "four individuals who had made a lot of money during the German occupation", and set up an Interrogation Centre at Schilde.[13] It also found some 250 hogsheads of rum and cognac, most of which was turned over to First Army.

No. 4 went to Bruges on the 10th, and Lieut. Dubois was chased out of the H.Q. he had selected by a German patrol. On the 12th, the Section took prisoner a German *S.S.* Unteroffizier of the *Flemish Brigade*, who surrendered to them rather than to the B.F.I. The Section was well received and was "swamped with invitations to dinner, etc." At Eecloo, Sgt. Laviola and the N.C.O.s from No. 3 F.S.R.D. found one *Gestapo* agent, two *S.S.*, and one *S.D.* Generally speaking, civilians showed little reaction when arrests were made. But feelings could run high. On one occasion, when Sgts. Davidson and Richardson from No. 16 Section had brought in a suspect they had arrested at Yvetot, near Rouen, the local citizens threatened to break into the jail and lynch him. On September 7th, at Hucqueliers, near Calais, the Section saw its first example of irate citizens cutting off the hair of women accused of having been over-familiar with the German forces. F.S. were under strict orders not to interfere. No. 18 Section, which had been at Rouen for most of September, picked up three Allied airmen who had been brought down behind the German lines and concealed by the French. They were returned to Britain, by R.A.F. rather than through I.S.9. No. 16 Section, then in Ypres, became host to the crew of a downed B-17, fed them, and also returned them via R.A.F. A few hours later, a second crew "dropped in" and were treated the same way. It is not clear whether the

Sections had forgotten the proper procedure, or were unable to make the crews follow it. No. 16 was very busy at the time investigating an *Abwehr* sabotage ring in Courtrai, Menin, Ypres, and Dixmude. Sgts. Playfair and Richardson went to Antwerp for more details, tracked down and arrested one individual, and passed the case over to the British C.I.

No. 15 Section, which had been earmarked for Dunkirk, worked in the surrounding area until September 29th. When 51st Highland Division assumed responsibility for the town's capture, the Section handed over to No. 13 British F.S. Section, and moved up to St. Nicholas to protect the ammunition dumps KING, QUEEN, and OOSTACKER, being prepared for the South Beveland operation, INFATUATE.

Between August 8th and October 1st, the Canadian Sections arrested 26 proven enemy agents. They delivered a total of 74 collaborators to the French and the Belgians, gave 14 others to the appropriate Sûreté officers, and held another 56 in custody either in the Divisional Cages or with other agencies. Five persons were cleared for enlistment in the indigenous Allied forces, and 50 others were released unconditionally. Everything, of course, did not run smoothly all the time. The Belgian Resistance was not united; each separate group tried to outdo the other, and people were arrested indiscriminately, often on very flimsy evidence. These groups were supposed only to pick up enemy documents and records. But when they did, the material generally disappeared.[14]

Calais fell at the end of September. No. 17 Section entered the town about 1100 on October 1st, and set up its H.Q. in the house of a millionaire collaborator. Sgts. Singer and Laperrière checked buildings; Sgts. Solomon and Rosen checked for Black List people. But they found little. On October 7th, the Section moved on to Ghent, where it worked with the Belgian White Brigade, a national Resistance movement that was most co-operative.

A truce had been arranged at Dunkirk to permit the 19,000 civilians to leave. They would have to be screened – a task which would require every available man on the checkpoints. No. 16 Section moved out to Esquelbecq on October 3rd; the flow started at 0600 the next day and ended at 2200 on the 5th. The Section made some arrests, and probably missed a number of agents, but its most lasting memory was of the many pathetic and emotional scenes that took place as the people moved out of German hands. For the rest of the month it worked on an *Abwehr* sabotage ring it had passed on to British C.I. a month earlier. The enquiries the Section made helped it locate a number of other low-grade agents. Eventually it was discovered that these had been a stay-behind network called "I" Net – 50–60 people between The Hague and Le Havre. Most of them were arrested.[15]

No. 15 Section spent October on the ammunition dumps, helping the guard units improve security. It caught five G.I.S. agents, who were passed back to Camp 030, then at Merxem, just outside Antwerp. The Section's greatest concern, however, came from reports of developing anti-Allied factions. It followed up these reports carefully, but was unable to uncover any concrete evidence. There was general criticism of Allied food rationing methods and serious fears of a winter famine. Such tensions, however, had obvious political as well as humanitarian connotations, in that they could be exploited by elements critical of Allied policies. The O.C. warned that a clear statement of Allied plans and intentions would be needed if the civilian population was to remain co-operative.[16]

No. 2 Section, by this time on the Dutch border, arrested an agent with a radio on October 5th. His interrogation led the Section to five more agents. On the 10th, the Section picked up another agent, also with a radio, who gave it two more names. A third came into its net on the 11th, six were arrested on the 12th. A woman agent was arrested on the 22nd. Another on the 23rd turned out to be an important link in the ring, and her interrogation revealed that, in addition to their radios, the agents were using pigeons; a large loft at Capellen was located and raided. The Section had to obtain assistance from the White Brigade to man the border control posts. This was no sinecure; on one occasion, four members of a White Brigade patrol were captured.[17]

C.I. was not the only duty. In early October, the remnants of 2, 3, 5, and 6 F.S.R.D., then in an Antwerp suburb, were charged with Security arrangements, including traffic control, in connection with the visit and investiture at Army H.Q. by H.M. King George VI. The occasion went off without a Security hitch.

Since future operations would take place in occupied territory, Army I(b) Staff decided to reorient Section training. Two one-week courses were set up in late October for all F.S. They consisted essentially of refresher lectures on the details of German organizations, and discussions of the methods that would have to be followed to obtain information in an environment that was expected to be, at best, unco-operative, and, at worst, openly hostile. At the same time, a number of officers and N.C.O.s from the Special Wireless Sections were attached to F.S. to intercept clandestine radio transmissions and provide a much-needed linguistic reinforcement.

During October, a control line was established along the Scheldt, which was manned briefly by the Canadian Sections. No. 2 covered the peninsula connecting South Beveland to the mainland; Nos. 4, 15, and 16 were at s'Hertogenbosch. About mid-month the three were moved to a new line controlling the Waal and Maas Rivers. Refugee traffic over the bridges was heavy, and there were many small boats which the Sections tried to remove. The bridges could be controlled; the boats could not. In addition, disputes arose between F.S. and the Civil Affairs offices, which were then issuing a wide variety of non-standard passes. The multiplicity of their often simple designs – which made them hard to recognize and easy to forge – made them impractical, as a control. There was some urgency to correct this. I(b) at Army had learned of a group of Belgians in the German-controlled *Flemish S.S. Brigade* who had been caught when trying to desert. They had been forced, under threat of being shot, to become expert in sabotage methods, and they were expected in the streams of refugees.

In an attempt to stop the Allies using the vital Antwerp port facilities, the Germans fired a reported 5,000 V-1s and V-2s against that city. An estimated 500 fell within the city and suburbs and caused many casualties. The only F.S. casualty was Capt. Graham Blyth, who was injured slightly when part of his house fell on him. But the local residents were firmly convinced that these missiles were being directed by agents with radios and pigeons. No. 15 Section worked with a Resistance group at Batenburg that operated two amateur direction-finding stations. They were able to pick up clandestine transmissions, tentatively identified as German, from many locations in the southern area of Antwerp Waas. One transmitter had three operators, each responsible for a short, coded message. The group never broadcast twice from the same location. It could perhaps have been housed in a three-ton truck reported seen at the transmission times in some of the suspected areas, but the operators were never caught.[18]

The security of the Port of Antwerp was a priority task. Supervisory responsibility was given to No. 18 Section, Nos. 322 and 325 Port Security Sections (British), and H.Q. F.S. Res. Dets. The area included the large towns in Holland south of the Maas River, between Walcheren and Nijmegen. F.S., supported by local auxiliaries, also began to supervise the crossing places on the Belgian–Dutch border. A general tightening up of controls was imposed under C.I. Plan No. 5.[19]

One task was to discover whether or not the enemy was receiving information on the results of the V-1 and V-2 attacks on Antwerp. Part of the answer emerged when the post at Nispen picked up an agent who had been ordered to establish a radio link; his priority mission was to send back damage reports. He was also to acquire samples of the revalidated Belgian identity cards and the new Belgian currency so that they could be copied for use by other agents. Obviously the G.I.S. was handicapped by Allied control and currency measures.

Many administrative questions connected with the use of Resistance personnel had not been satisfactorily resolved. Prominent among them was the matter of pay for work done for the Allies. The sums needed were considerable. By the end of November, No. 17 Section on the Dutch–Belgian border, for example, had 638 Resistance people on its establishment. Eventually, agreement was reached that the Belgian government would pay them, and that 21 Army Group would provide food, clothing, and transport. F.S. had mixed views on their value. Most of the Resistance men, in fact, wanted to hit back at the Germans and disliked spending their time guarding bridges.[20] No. 18 Section wanted to replace the ones it used with a regular, disciplined, and properly turned out Belgian Army battalion.

While much of the F.S. organization was engaged in what might be called garrison duties, No. 4 Section was checking F.S. targets in the town of Flushing, on the island of Walcheren. It found a few Black List people, and reported that it could not control the boat traffic to the island, which still continued. From its contacts with the Dutch Resistance, it learned that the morale of the German forces in Middleburg was low. It acted as the link with the Resistance through which the German commander offered to surrender. It could not collect the usual documents from such places as the H.Q. of the *Feld Gendarmerie*, the *Gestapo*, and the *Wehrmacht* Post Offices, because an Allied battalion that had billeted in the buildings had burned all the paper it found, in order to keep warm. But the Section arrested a Dutch agent who gave it maps of the German defences and photographs of the Gestapo agents on the island.

By the end of November, I(b) at Army had implemented a detailed plan to control civilians in the Army area from Bergen to Nijmegen. It laid out a restricted zone, about five miles wide, along the south bank of the Maas from the sea to s'Hertogenbosch, then along the Maas to the junction of the Waal–Maas Canal. Control points and patrols were deployed along the front, and in certain areas a system of civil passes was imposed. Civilians in the areas north of Nijmegen and around Tilburg were evacuated to Camp 030. Eight hundred Belgians helped to check the area from the Turnhout–Eindhoven road to the sea. A camp was set up at Vught to receive 5,000–6,000 German nationals and several hundred Dutch internees. When the Ardennes offensive began, 21 Army Group augmented this control line with a second line across central Belgium manned by eight to 10 F.S. Sections under the control of XXX Corps.

At the end of November also, Army reviewed the activity of the previous three months. No spectacular espionage or sabotage had occurred. German air reconnaissance was incapable of penetrating Allied defences. The G.I.S., instead, had tried during the early stages of the Invasion to flood the Allied areas, and, by implication, the C.I. facilities, with low-grade agents sent on short-range missions. It had tried also to penetrate the Maqui. In France, the average line-crosser had been a French man in his early twenties, with an unsatisfactory family background and a record of petty crime. He had membership in a Fascist-oriented organization, which he usually had joined either to avoid the call-up for forced labour, or a jail term. Many had trained at the Chateau Maulny, near Le Mans. After the break-out, however, and during the advance, the stay-behind agent replaced the line-crosser, a change which actually worked in I(b)'s favour; the number of refugees was so great that it was impossible to screen them efficiently, and the line-crosser would have had a better opportunity to penetrate. The stay-behind was usually identified as a stranger by the legitimate residents. In Belgium, the enemy turned again to line-crossers, most of whom were controlled by the *S.D. VI* Section.

Since the Invasion in June, some 530 suspects had been held at Camp 030. The total number of those who had been referred to it and released after a brief screening, though not recorded, was many times that figure. Between August and the end of November, 306 suspects went through the Camp. Of these, 39 were agents, 35 were active and significant collaborators, 67 had been handed over to the national Sûreté, 96 others were in custody on behalf of various agencies, and 60 had been unconditionally released. In that period, C.I. had caught, mostly through interrogation, a large proportion of the many German spies used in Belgium. Four main networks had been uncovered. One at Bruges had comprised 14 known agents, nine of whom were still at large. There was a second one in the Ypres–Courtrai area; 10 of its 30 members had been arrested. A third was at Ostend, where five of a known 14 had been arrested. For the fourth, at Heide-Brasschaet, the arrest-list was "nearly complete".

C.I. was plagued by the actions of certain elements in the several Belgian Resistance "movements". The Independent Front (O.F.I.) at Alst broke into the prison, released some "530 characters of all types" and stole the records. The O.F.I. leader was arrested, and all but 100 of the released prisoners rounded up. In early December, a Belgian Resistance captain, who had been attached to a Canadian Infantry Brigade for two months, was found to be a German agent. It was unwise to trust anyone; this man had come with the highest recommendation from the White Brigade.

The various Dutch Resistance groups represented in First Canadian Army's zone were divided by differing racial and national loyalties. Part of the zone at that time lay in the province of Noord Brabant, where there were seven Resistance groups. Prince Bernhardt (who headed the Dutch Resistance) had ordered them to unify under the name Nederlandsche Binnenlandsche Strijdkrachten (N.B.S.). Four of them did combine, and the Prince nominated a Provisional Commander for each area, set up a chain of command, and defined their role, which was to serve as guards and as shock troops.[21] National boundaries also complicated C.I.'s task. No. 18 Section was responsible for frontier control for the province of Antwerp and the islands of Walcheren and South and North Beveland. It had Belgian Resistance auxiliaries who aroused a great deal of opposition in Noord Brabant. On the other hand, No. 16 Section at Waalwijk in Noord Brabant, had a similar task, but was fortunate in having a Dutch ex-Service group, Orde Dienst (O.D.), on its establishment.

No. 2 Section, now in Nijmegen, found a number of German nationals who had not previously been investigated. On December 16th, the Section uncovered a German agent, interrogated him, and sent him back to Camp 030. Camp 030 then set up a Forward Interrogation Centre (two officers, one man) in Nijmegen to do preliminary interrogations. The lower farmlands along the river, and the islands in the estuary, had flooded, and all Civil Affairs staffs were working desperately to salvage what they could. Because of the sensitivity of the area, No. 2 and No. 15 Sections had to make sure that local inhabitants were vetted before being allowed to recover their cattle. Both the Sections also assisted in the salvage and, as No. 15's diarist observed, this "increase[d] friendliness between civil population and troops."

No. 15 Section reported that control of movement was proceeding satisfactorily, that the local Burgomeisters were accepting the fact that it alone was responsible for issuing passes, that telephone communications were being controlled, and that carrier pigeons were all registered and accounted for. It then turned to a rather difficult investigation. When the Section first came into the area, it heard that a local official, "X", had worked with the Germans against his own people. Its subsequent investigations revealed that, earlier, an Allied pilot had been shot down in the area, found, and hidden by the underground. "X" had learned of the incident and had gone to the German authorities. Also, unlike many other officials in his position, who were rather dilatory in such matters, he had actively sought horses for the German Army. After the Allies arrived, "X" had refused to authorize the return of confiscated radio sets to local citizens, allegedly saying "I will wait until we are allowed to call ourselves free to return [them]." He was obviously a strong character, with rigid, though misguided, ideas of duty, but there was no evidence that he had been, in fact, a collaborator.[22]

At Christmas 1944, every Section did its best to arrange some sort of celebration. No. 2 Section's Diary entry may speak for them all: ". . . all ranks, due to the forethought . . . of Army Staffs, were able to enjoy Christmas Fare such as Tinned Fowl; [C.S.M. Bert Sutcliffe had not been as efficient a scrounger as C.S.M. Paddy Doak, whose No. 15 Section had had goose] Tinned Fruit; Christmas Puddings and Cakes; Beer, Spirits; Candy; Oranges and Cigars, and to a certain extent were able to forget their intense desire to be reunited with . . . loved ones. Morale remains high. . . . Quarters, while not of the best, are still sufficient."[23]

Maj. J.W.G. Macdougall, G.S.O.2 I(b), moved C.I. Section, First Army, to Turnhout on January 2nd, 1945. Strict movement controls were enforced in all areas; a rigid curfew was imposed in the Army area and, much to No. 2's relief, the Senior Military Commander, North Brabant, completely prohibited all entry into the evacuated zone. No. 15 Section, on January 5th, discovered a German soldier alleged to have been concealed for over two months by the Resistance; it raised questions of other possible concealments. Line-crossers, among them escapers, evaders and Dutch refugees avoiding German call-up orders, used the frozen waterways to the control points. Before Christmas, three to six would cross per day on I British Corps Front; during the full moon holiday period the number dropped to zero; but between January 20th and 27th, in both I and II Corps sectors, the number rose to 347. Army also was trying to send out and bring back its own Allied agents, hiding them in the stream. Passage either way was relatively easy, because bitter weather and inadequate clothing often forced the Dutch guards to leave their posts.[24]

No. 17 Section came into conflict with collaborators in Helmond. Some of them had become very wealthy during the two occupations, and resented the enquiries the Section made into their former activities. One profiteer tried to use political influence against the Section. Official reaction to his protests took the form of a statement of intent only, which the Section quite properly ignored.[25]

C.I. areas were established along the Maas Control Line, with a Section or Detachment in charge of each. Counter-sabotage and spot-check C.I. groups functioned where they were needed. No. 20 Section came from England to H.Q. F.S.R.D. at Oisterwijk on January 24th, the day on which the first three members of the Sections from Italy also arrived. Cpl. C.R. Hubbel, formerly of No. 1 Section, went to No. 17. Cpls. H. Rempel and J.C. Weins, both of No. 5 F.S.R.D., went to No. 16, which was busy providing transportation and billets for families bombed out of their homes in Baardwijk. Concurrently all Sections began to prepare for their coming move into Germany. II Corps had revised and simplified file handling; the units had time to get used to the new procedures.[26]

A new C.I. unit was created about this time. At the planning sessions in 1944, no one had been able to assess the precise nature or extent of the opposition the Allies might have to face in Occupied Germany. The only precedent available was a report issued by the Joint Historical Research Section of the Commission which had been set up in 1918 to control Germany. This had said, in part: "The need for an adequate Intelligence organization had not been foreseen. . . . It was evident that the [Occupation] Commissioners were most seriously handicapped through lack of proper Intelligence." A Counter-Intelligence Headquarters was necessary to enable the Army Commander to build an organization which would advise on and enforce security directives, deal with informers, and direct C.I. personnel. The matter was given urgency in 1945 because of the achievements of the various Resistance movements in Europe, and the knowledge that a vast quantity of arms existed in Germany to arm a potential guerrilla movement there.

After discussions in January and February 1945 had led to its authorization, H.Q. Counter-Intelligence was set up at Rijessen (Risson) under Maj. D.F. Morris, with three officers, a W.O.I, nine senior N.C.O.s, and 14 men. It took over, in effect, the administration for all F.S. personnel in Holland and Germany, until it was disbanded in December, 1945. Its functions were then transferred to No. 3 Intelligence Pool.[27]

In the few days preceding VERITABLE, No. 16 Section, considerably reinforced by personnel from No. 20, was very busy. On February 9th, Capt. Paddy Bligh explained the reason for their activity. The 21 Army Group deception plan called for increased and obvious activity in their sector in order to induce the

Capt., later, Maj. C.R. Rafe Douthwaite, Field Security, was the most decorated member of the C.Int.C. during the Second World War. His honours and awards include Member of the Order of the British Empire, Order of Orange Nassau (with Swords), Croix de Guerre avec Etoile de Bronze, and Medaille de la Reconnaissance Française. (Photo courtesy of Capt. B.L. Carter, 3 Intelligence Company/Canada. Dept. of National Defence)

enemy to believe that the attack would take place west of Nijmegen. F.S. was told to be more active than usual in order to make possible agents think that important things were being protected. Rumours were "floated"; enemy reconnaissance patrols were allowed to penetrate the area and return; dummy guns were deployed; "ammunition" was ostentatiously dumped along the main roads; convoys of pontoon bridges were moved back and forth through the villages. Convoy directional signs were placed on the access roads leading into the area. Enemy reconnaissance aircraft were allowed to overfly the "concentration". One enemy agent was deliberately misled, allowed to gain the "information", and return. But east of the s'Hertogenbosch–Helmond Canal line, British formations enforced stringent security measures. Formation patches were removed, and what limited reconnaissance there was, was done in Canadian vehicles, with Canadian crews. Elaborate camouflage precautions were set up and dummy guns were replaced by real ones. The enemy network in Nijmegen, without radio, carrier pigeons, or line-crossers, could get nothing back to its Control.[28]

Operation VERITABLE opened on the morning of February 8th and, three days later, 29 German civilians, the first from Mehr, were brought to the Forward Interrogation Centre at Tuck School in Nijmegen. No. 3 Section moved forward with its Division. On February 16th, Capt. Douthwaite sent two British N.C.O.s, who had been attached to him from 1003 British F.S.R.D., forward to Cleve. One of their early targets was *Gestapo* H.Q., but German security had been too good. The office safe had to be blown open; it, and all other containers in the building, were empty. No. 3 spent the rest of February setting up area security restrictions and arranging to have them enforced. Bedburg, its H.Q., had a sanitarium with a normal occupancy of 3,000. It was turned into a Military Government Displaced Persons and Refugee Camp for the entire area. By the end of February, it housed almost 7,000 Dutch, Polish, French, and German refugees. After No. 3 had done the initial screening, these refugees were sent to Reese Camp, near Nijmegen, for a second interrogation.[29]

No. 2, which had initially taken over from No. 3 the same control points it had given No. 3 the previous December, moved to Cleve on February 21st, replacing No. 29 British Section. It was able to find some useful documents in the ruins. In Kellen, a suburb of Cleve, the Section found 500–700 civilians who had been cut off by the flooding for almost two weeks. It screened them on behalf of 225 Detachment, Military Government, and searched the houses they had vacated and those to which they were sent. Line-crossers again became a threat. In the two weeks ending on February 26th, 175 were sent to the Forward Interrogation Centre, who in turn sent 149 back to Camp 030.[30]

During the preparations for Operation PLUNDER, II Canadian Corps evacuated its area up to the Rhine. Twenty-four F.S./Provost/Signals/R.C.E. teams were used for a house-to-house search of all the towns, including Cleve. Between February 21st and March 20th, 417 line-crossers came into liberated Holland; 361 of them were sent to Camp 030, 14 to the Escape and Evasion agency, I.S.9, and the rest to local authorities. The increase in line-crosser traffic, attributed to worsening conditions in Occupied Holland and to intensification of the German labour draft policy, meant that fresh control lines had to be set up. One followed the railway from Katwijk to Boxmeer, to stop civilians moving from east to west into the evacuated area between the railway and the Maas; it was removed on February 26th. Another was set up between Ubbergen and Mook to prevent civilians evacuated from Groesbeek from returning, and to stop others moving between the control line and the frontier; it was lifted on March 12th. In the area from Millingen to Wyler Meer on the Dutch–German border, floods made movement impossible. Companies of the Dutch Grenswacht manned a line from Wyler Meer to a point southwest of the Reichswald; the N.B.S. manned the line from the Reichswald to the Maas at Bergen. There was no line from the Reichswald to Siebengewald. Civilians in the II Canadian Corps area were restricted to their towns, and curfews and blackouts were strictly enforced.[31]

For most of the Sections, March 1945 was a quiet month. Some men went on courses at H.Q. F.S. Res. Dets. at Oisterwijk, or at the British C.I. Centre at Brussels. No. 40 British Section took over the Frontier Control organization, and No. 20 Section at Waalwijk was responsible under it for the Maas. There was a good deal of line-crossing over that river in small boats, about 95 per cent of which took place near the town of Lage Zwalume. This "window" served both Germans and Allies and was used by agents of both sides. At times, the atmosphere was almost that of a carnival, with loud and careless talk on both sides of the river; strangely enough, only on two occasions did two opposing groups try to use the facility simultaneously. Anyone coming in through the "window" was sent immediately to Camp 030. The problem was even more complex because there was a considerable amount of other movement in the general region as well. No. 17, for example, during the week March 10–16, had some 2,770 come into their area and 2,686 leave, despite a curfew which cleared the streets after 1900. Two enemy escapees and an agent were captured.[32]

No. 20 Section reported one agent's story in detail. The 17-year-old man had been recognized in Waalwijk by some children who had seen him consorting with the Germans. While he was being escorted to Section H.Q., he tried unsuccessfully to destroy a piece of paper with an address on it. He then admitted he had been a spy, asked for a clergyman – evidently believing he was going to be shot out-of-hand – and then pretended to be an idiot. After four days in custody, he asked to be allowed to work as a cook, and was led to believe that this might be possible. He had joined the *Hitler Youth* when he was 12, enlisted in the *Wehrmacht* at 15, and was sent to *Stalag 1267632* in Düsseldorf as a cook. There he had learned a little English from the Canadian and British P.W. Five months later he was attached to the *S.S.* as a cook's helper, and had retreated with them through Waalwijk. He was then chosen as an agent, crossed the Maas in January, travelled to Oisterwijk, was arrested, and taken to the refugee camp in Tilburg where he was checked and released. He then made his way back to Waalwijk, built a raft of gasoline cans with one of his friends, recrossed the Maas, and went to Gorinchem. In March, he crossed the Maas again, this time with a party of 12 in two rubber boats, to look for ammunition dumps and H.Q. Two of the party were dressed in Canadian uniforms. In Waalwijk, he had tried unsuccessfully to sell two fountain pens, and was making his way back over the Baardwijk Bridge when he was arrested. No. 20 sent him to Camp 030 for further interrogation.[33]

Capt. Ray Shelley's No. 15 Section was ordered to clear civilians from an area along the Rhine, from near Emmerich westward to the German border. His Section divided the area into two zones, closed the border between them, and swept the eastern zone on March 17th/18th and the western on the 20th. It found some 1,500 civilians in the preliminary sweep, and set up a 24-hour patrol of four F.S. N.C.O.s, supported by men from other military units, to arrest anyone who had been missed. All civilians were moved back through a screening post at the monastery at Cleve, which was staffed by men from both No. 2 and No. 4 Sections. The evacuation had been assigned originally to the Military Government Detachment, but it did not have the linguists, the transport, or the support it needed from its superiors. The task was finally completed by the men and transport of the two Sections working with the Detachment.[34]

In the last big Canadian offensive of the War, I Canadian Corps' task was to clear the area between the Grebbe River and the Ijssel, while II Corps moved north and east to clear the area between the Ijssel and the Weser. I Corps' Sections, Nos. 1, 7, 11, 14, and 17, were in Oisterwijk; Nos. 3 and 5 F.S.R.D.s were in Belgium. No. 1 Section moved to Lochem on April 5th, sorted out the jails, which the Resistance had filled with "collaborators", and found two spies and two girls who were suspected of more than the ordinary level of collaboration. It rounded up Displaced Persons (D.P.s in the idiom of the day) and sent them back to Emmerich. When Hoven was clear, it set up road controls and pushed F.S. patrols forward to Voorst. This was not yet entirely clear of enemy, as Sgts. Smith and Hadden discovered almost too late. They did find one German in civilian clothes, interrogated him, and sent him to the P.W. Cage. The Section finally established a control line on the Ijssel between Hoven and Deventer, and persuaded the O.D. to run a ferry across for the military and for civilians holding F.S. passes.

No. 11 Section took over the Ijssel control line. No. 1 moved on to Apeldoorn on April 17th. Here it searched German H.Q. and produced an impressive pile of documents for I(a) specialists, and eight German P.W. On the 19th, it moved on to Voorthuizen, set up control posts on the roads, picked up many D.P.s, a line-crosser, and a number of P.W.; and, in addition, a set of German defence plans, and details of gun positions in Amersfoort, which it took to the G.S.O.2 (Int) First Division. It had dealt with the usual collection of problems: collaborators, members of the Resistance, and people at the control points who wanted to come into the area for what the Section considered to be frivolous reasons. Meanwhile, at Apeldoorn, No. 11 Section found a German hospital No. 1 had missed, complete with its original German staff; it also located and arrested a number of persons on the Black List.

No. 7 Section moved to Ewijk, near Nijmegen, to support No. 60 British Section (with 49th Division). At Otterloo, Lieut. Hank Hennie, Sgt. Lawton, and Cpls. Fitzsimmons and Direnfeld were wounded during the attempt by a German column to break through the line of the Canadian advance. The depleted Section carried on to Barneveld to check line-crossers and prisoners in the local jail; it found a typist who had been in the *S.D.* office in Arnhem, and four "spies for our side", who were immediately sent back to Camp 030.

No. 14 Section set up at Nestlerode, near Nijmegen on April 3rd. On the 13th, Capt. James, Sgts. Drysdale and Long, and their interpreter, L/Cpl.

Fawcett, moved in to Arnhem, where they arrested a police (*Sipo*) agent, a female propaganda agent, and a member of the *S.S.* On April 20th, they turned over the town to No. 3 Detachment and, in conjunction with No. 11 Section in Apeldoorn, No. 17 out of Nijmegen, and No. 60 to their west, took over a large sector north and east of the city. On April 21st, they found two large boxes of documents with "full particulars on all N.S.D.A.P." (*Nationalsozialistische Deutsche Arbeit Partei* = Nazi Party), which significantly augmented their Black List; on May 1st, the preliminary screening at a Dutch run D.P. Camp uncovered five German nationals.

Capt. Eddie Corbeil's No. 17 Section took over from No. 318 British Section in Nijmegen on April 4th. Two of his N.C.O.'s took over the Waal Bridge control point and four others, working with No. 40 British Section, patrolled the Maas. On April 10th, he set up a very busy checkpoint at Hees (Heesch); of the roughly 400 who passed through between 1400 and 2230, six were detained. About 0900 the next day, H.Q.C.I. warned the Section to expect two known agents; both were arrested and their cover story was quickly broken. No. 11 F.S.R.D., previously with No. 20 at Waalwijk, took over Wijchen and Leur as part of the Maas control directed by No. 17, and then moved on to Deventer and No. 3 Section on the 22nd.

No. 17 Section operated very much as a subordinate H.Q.C.I. responsible for all control and patrolling activities on Nijmegen Island. Nos. 40 and 60 British Section arrests were channeled through it to Camp 030, while a D.P. centre it established at Hees forwarded all suspicious persons to Dutch Security. On April 22nd, Army begged the Section to remove from the overcrowded Army Cage a group of 61 escapees from concentration camps, Dutchmen arrested for being in the wrong place, and others who were simply lost. These were duly collected, taken to Hees, screened, and sent to a camp at Bedburg. Two days later, No. 17 was put in charge of screening civilians at the First Army P.W. Cage.

At this time, No. 17 had no instructions on how to deal with German civilians. In most cases, the men merely took them to the line and sent them down the road, back into Germany. Suspected collaborators were handed over to the Dutch. On April 27th, the worst was over and the function was transferred to Hatert, a new camp with a capacity of 3,000.[35]

Emmerich fell on April 1st, and Third Division moved on to Zutphen and Deventer by April 11th. Sections 2, 3, 4, 15, 16, 18, and 20; and 1, 8, 10, and 11 F.S.R.D.s were deployed in the Corps area east of Nijmegen, in Germany, and in the rear areas near Tilburg. No. 3 Section entered Germany near Vrasselt, moved up to Emmerich on March 31st, cleared the F.S. targets, and handed over to No. 1 Detachment on April 3rd. For nearly a month this Detachment worked at the D.P. Camp at Speelberg, set up control posts manned by O.D. at two points on the border near Groenlo, and collected material on the local *N.S.D.A.P.*

After a rather fruitless search of Deventer, No. 3 Section moved to Weener; the N.C.O.s screened civilians at the Third Division P.W. Cage, while the office staff planned for the problems they expected at Emden. But instead of Emden, the section was assigned first to Oldenburg and then to Wilhelmshaven. Its replacement on April 24th, No. 11 F.S.R.D., reinforced the Ijssel control line. The Detachment caught some line-crossers, including an enemy soldier who gave the names of all the civilians who had helped him to escape. No. 18 Section left to take over Zutphen on April 4th; it had a narrow escape; the enemy had not yet withdrawn.

Along the Almelo axis, F.S. action was much more straightforward, although its control and direction grew increasingly difficult. No. 4 Section moved from Cleve to Ruurlo on April 3rd, with detachments placed in the nearby towns. Since other Sections had been in the area before them, the workload was light enough to allow them to provide extra staff at the II Corps P.W. Cage. At Bornebrock, about two miles south of Almelo, No. 16 Section's 15-cwt. truck came under mortar fire, and Sgts. Rempel and Levesque received facial cuts from its splintered windshield. On April 20th, Sgt. Massy ran into a party of about 20 German soldiers; fortunately, they "came quietly" to the Divisional Cage. At the former Dutch Fascist Party H.Q. at Almelo, the Sections found a lot of useful information. The flow of D.P. continued, and Sections had great difficulty sorting them into categories. Any interrogation of 'automatic arrest' category people always led to more suspects and more arrests, which, in their turn, meant more interrogations and fresh suspects. Although actual G.I.S. agents did turn up occasionally, their activities had by this time ceased to be a threat. But with all this, No. 4 Section, for example, was spread out from Gravensbergen (Gramsbergen) in Holland to as far as Meppen in Germany, some 37 miles.

May 1945 was probably the busiest month of the campaign for almost every member of both the Sections and the Detachments. The German *Twenty-Fifth Army* and *Armee Abteilung Straube*, which surrendered to I Corps in Holland and II Corps in Germany, respectively, numbered about 140,000 men. All had to be screened, so that men on the S.H.A.E.F. 'automatic arrest' list, i.e., who had been reported for crimes or atrocities, or who were members of the Nazi Party or of the German Intelligence and Security services, could be identified and segregated. In *Twenty-Fifth Army*, alone, were some 1,500 *S.S.*, about 100 *Abwehr*, and several small groups of other such individuals.

Col.-Gen. Johannes Blaskowitz, commander of the German forces in the Netherlands, was ordered by Lt.-Gen. Charles Foulkes, through Lt.-Col. Bud Macdougall, to parade all persons, including not only Army, but also Navy, police, and certain civil staffs, under his command, and to produce individuals in these 'automatic arrest' categories, at concentration points, at scheduled times on a certain day. His H.Q. did so, and provided a list of those concerned.

Field Security entering The Hague, 8 May 1945, with Dutch Resistance members on right. (Photograph by Capt. R. Shelley/Photo collection Canadian Forces School of Military Intelligence, Kingston/Canada. Dept. of National Defence)

Canadian infantry units provided guards and transport, and took their prisoners to the former German camp in Holland. In that one day, over 90 per cent of the people required, including complete *Abwehr* and *S.D.* units, Dutch Quislings and *S.S.*, and all *S.D.* and *Gestapo* officials up to major-general, were arrested.

As well as this clean-up, F.S. had to locate and arrest large numbers of deserters and agents, both in and out of uniform, within the Army area. There was concern that widespread guerrilla warfare might break out and that, if it did, these trained men might emerge as its leaders. F.S. support was also required in Holland, where there were many men and women whom their countrymen wished to bring to justice.

C.I. could draw on the following resources: one Section and two F.S.R.D.s in First Army; five staff officers and their immediate staffs in I Corps H.Q.; three Area Security Offices (A.S.O.), assigned to the three western provinces of Holland; three Interrogation Teams, each of two officers and six men; and 12 F.S. Sections and nine F.S.R.D.s. II Corps had five staff officers, seven Sections, two F.S.R.D.s, and an Intelligence Control Section. At Utrecht, 21 Army Group had deployed a Civil Security Liaison Mission for Holland. Its total strength was about 400 officers and men. Deployment of these units during May 1945 was as follows:[36]

First Canadian Army   H.Q. – Apeldoorn
H.Q.C.I. (Maj. D.F. Morris)   Rijessen
7 F.S. Section (Capt. H.H. Hennie)   Groningen (Det. at Assen)
2 F.S.R.D. (Capt. J.D. Steen)   Meppen (H.Q. First Army, Counter-Sabotage)
5 F.S.R.D. (Sgt. H.T. McIntyre)   Leeuwarden

I Canadian Corps
G.S.O.2 I(b) (Maj C.R.R. Douthwaite)   Utrecht (Area H.Q.)
I.O. I(b)   Hilversum

A.S.O. *Utrecht* (Maj. Basil Foreman)   Utrecht
1 F.S. Section (Capt. A.S. Fleming)   Gouda (To Berlin)
14 F.S. Section (Capt. J.M. James)   Utrecht
330 British F.S. Section (Capt. Caldwell)   Dordrecht (Port Security)
341 British F.S. Section   Ede (Grebbe Line – Zuider Zee to Rhenen)
3 F.S.R.D. (Sgt Vannier)   Utrecht
6 F.S.R.D. (Capt. J. Larsen)   Amersfoort

A.S.O. *South Holland* (Maj. J.M. Gray)   Rotterdam
15 F.S. Section (Capt. R. Shelley)   Buitenhoff
17 F.S. Section (Capt. M.G. Corbeil)   Rotterdam (west and south of the city)
336 British F.S. Section (Lieut. J. Knight)   Rotterdam (Port Security; rest of the city)
340 British F.S. Section   The Hague (west half)
7 F.S.R.D. (Sgt. J.L.O. Tarte)   The Hague (southeast part)
11 F.S.R.D. (Lieut. P.D.H. Cole)   Leiden

A.S.O. *North Holland*   Amsterdam (whole province)
11 F.S. Section (Capt. W.L. Robinson)   Amsterdam
16 F.S. Section (Capt. R.N. Bligh)   Amsterdam (Port Security)
8 F.S.R.D. (Capt. D.A. Hadfield)   Amsterdam
10 F.S.R.D. (Lieut. J.W.G. Langley)   Haarlem
60 British F.S. Section   Hilversum

23 British F.S. Section	Breda (Maas Control line, Walcheren, N and S Beveland to Bokhaven)
1016 British F.S.R.D.	Bergen-op-Zoom
9 F.S.R.D (Sgt. A.L. Gracie)	Zaltbommel
1 F.S.R.D. (Lieut. A.M.M. Dubois)	Utrecht (special screening)

II Corps

H.Q. (Maj. R.H. Noble)	Bad Zwischenahn
2 F.S. Section (Capt. R.R. Taylor)	Oldenburg (city)
4 F.S.R.D.	Oldenburg
3 F.S. Section (Lieut. D.M. MacAulay)	Wilhelmshaven
4 F.S. Section (Capt. H.J.L. Petersson)	Bad Zwischenahn
18 F.S. Section (Capt. F.G. Baxter)	Leer
20 F.S. Section (Capt. H.B. Brookhouse)	Aurich
325 British F.S. Section	Wilhelmshaven (Port Security)
327 British F.S. Section	Emden (Port Security)
1 Polish F.S. Section	Varel
1 Intelligence Control Section	Esterwegen Camp (special screening)

This deployment came about after some readjustment. In Holland, Capt. Eddie Corbeil's No. 17 Section described its move: "The Section left Epe (for Rotterdam] amidst much jubilation and flag waving ... children out in hundreds lining the streets, notices on main roads asking the liberators to pass through their village.... The Town Hall, Rotterdam ... was covered with police.... People clamoured around ... we signed hundreds of names. Nurses made us write on the corners of their uniforms. The people were tremendously happy but hungry. Hundreds stayed home, too weak to leave their beds." No. 7 Detachment, operating in the western sector of Rotterdam, reported witnessing its first food distribution and stated, with horror, that the death rate from hunger was 1,200 a day.[37]

No. 17 Section dealt with a case involving Werewolves, a German underground group whose reported aim was to carry on clandestine war against the Allies during the Occupation. Though there were many denunciations and some arrests, the movement never became a significant threat. By the 15th, the Section took over Noordsingel prison, miscalling it Camp 030, and used it as an Interrogation Centre for all arrested *S.S.* and *S.D.* On May 16th, it was sent 700 people for checking, and had to be given reinforcements from No. 15 Section, from Nos. 7 and 11 F.S.R.D., and from elements of No. 330 British Section. In a few days tempers began to fray. One diarist's reference to the fact that Holland was over-organized is probably a reflection of the difficulties the Section experienced in working with Dutch bureaucracy. The N.B.S. would bring in German prisoners whom they had to escort to the nearest P.W. Cage. They stamped passes for three Civil Affairs Detachments. They received steady streams of visitors asking for exemption from the rules, or cancellation of the arrest of some friend or relative. They screened around 600 Green Police (a German-organized force). On the 26th, elements of the official Camp 030 arrived to set up a Forward Interrogation Centre.[38]

No. 1 F.S.R.D. picked up an *Abwehr* agent and an *S.D.* agent who "turned his coat", and whom they kept as "Increment S.D." until his usefulness was over. (The usual "increment" was an extra clerk, authorized for each Section only after hard bargaining between First Canadian Army and C.M.H.Q. Very few were suitable.) It cleared the Hook of Holland and Ridderkerk (9,500 prisoners); checked Buren and Scheveningen (mostly German Marines); carried out a documents check on the prisoners in Hilversum for I Corps; and, on May 28th, managed to get together as a unit for the first time in nearly a month. No. 7 F.S.R.D. covered Schiedam and later Scheveningen. No. 10 F.S.R.D. found Haarlem quiet. No. 11 F.S.R.D. moved to Leiden on May 21st, where it found many suspects, including two women known to be involved with *S.D.*, who were in hiding. It checked hotels and boarding houses, discovered two men on the Black List, and asked the civil police to arrest them.

No. 11 Section interrogated the Chief and the Second-in-Command of the *S.D.* in Amsterdam. It checked a *Luftwaffe* hospital which seemed to be a collection point for German military deserters who wished to surrender, but which was suspected of harbouring *S.D.* and *S.S.* also. It gave lists of collaborators to the civil police, and ended the month by arresting an *S.S.* suspect wearing a Canadian uniform.

In No. 14 Section, Sgt. Watling picked up an *S.S.* man attempting to hide in the D.P. stream, and found he had much useful information about Werewolves. C.S.M. Smith arrested a Dutch *S.S.* man in a Canadian uniform, whom a Canadian unit had employed as an interpreter. It checked the jails; to give some idea of the magnitude of the task, its Diary entry for May 25th says that it had only another 15,000 to go! The first count had shown 12,000 Germans and 23,500 civilians. On the 30th, the Section found an Inspector Becker of the *Gestapo*, one of its "most wanted". Becker had been accused of breaking the jaw of a Dutch Resistance leader during her interrogation and was believed to be hiding in a Green Police Regiment. That regiment was paraded in a field under the guns of four Staghound armoured cars, and checked. Unfortunately, although a number of arrests were made among the thugs in it, Becker was not one of them. By the end of May five men were left in the Section; the rest were either on leave or repatriated.[39]

Both No. 6 F.S.R.D. at Amersfoort on the Grebbe control line and No. 9 F.S.R.D. on the Rhine–Maas line complained of the lack of standardization between F.S. and Civil Affairs passes, many of which were forged. No. 9 did not have enough men, and had to borrow some from nearby units. In the first week of May alone, apart from line-crossers and refugees, they arrested five German *S.S.* in plain clothes, one Polish deserter from the German Army, and a member of the Werewolves. On May 30th, it was announced that at 0500 on June 1st military controls would be lifted. By 1800 the N.B.S. were frantically looking for extra staff to handle the floods of people who had not realized that this lifting of controls did not permit them to cross the river at will.

June marked the end of the busiest post-hostilities period. Of the Sections, No. 14, in Utrecht, was perhaps the most active. Many "wanted" Germans tried to hide in the masses of people waiting to be repatriated. On the 1st and 2nd, the Section delivered 75 *S.S.* to Otterloo jail. On the 4th it handed over the Dutch No. 2 Nazi, Rost von Tonningen, to the Dutch police. The Dutch arresting party "used 35 men armed with sten guns, four motorcycles, one armoured car and the special staff [car]; we made the arrest with one sergeant and one interpreter armed with a revolver". On the 5th, it found 25 more *S.S.*, and two *Gestapo* who gave it leads to others. Sgt. Cheshire arrested two *Sipo* agents. Wim Sasson, said to be the head of the German stay-behind agents, was captured through a coincidence. Capt. Chown and Capt. Blyth met two Dutch girls. When discussing the girls later, their suspicions were aroused. They checked the Black List and found that one of them was Sasson's girlfriend. Capt. James of No. 14 Section had the girls picked up, and interrogation revealed Sasson's whereabouts. He was arrested, and a three-week investigation revealed that he was a propagandist rather than an agent. He was not treated as a war criminal by the Dutch.

On June 7th, a bride and a "very, very phoney" groom were arrested on the steps of their church. He was carrying forged documents. His first cover story was an obvious lie. His second, or fallback, story was an equally obvious lie, and he was jailed and later sent back to Germany. By the 14th, No. 14 felt it had settled the outstanding *Gestapo* cases, but the very next day it arrested 25 men who, after interrogation, turned out to be a complete sabotage ring. On the 19th, the Section took over cases from No. 3 F.S.R.D. (Sgt. Vannier). By June 23rd it was down to five men, enough to handle arrests but too few for the time-consuming checks and interrogation which had to be done also.[40]

No. 7 Section was in Groningen with No. 5 F.S.R.D., which had replaced No. 20 Section in Leeuwarden. The Section arrested 118 armed *S.D.* on the island of Schiermonnikog and, on June 26th, arrested and documented 22 G.I.S. No. 16 handed its Amsterdam files over to No. 11 Section and moved to Ede on June 11th, to screen prisoners in Apeldoorn jail and to interrogate others in Avegoor Camp, Arnhem. In the *S.S.* Camp at Otterloo, it caught a Dutch *S.S.* man accused of killing an American pilot, extracted a signed confession, and handed him over to the Dutch authorities. On June 2nd, No. 17 Section in Rotterdam found the former head of the *Abwehr* for North and South Holland. In the next few days, it had to investigate Werewolves, arresting three in early July, resolve a situation in which N.B.S. were protecting enemy P.W. in their custody, and make further arrests at Doetinchem. On the 25th it caught the *Kreisleiter* of s'Hertogenbosch, the builder of the defences of the Ijssel line and "a friend and advisor of the Finance Minister".[41]

No. 7 F.S.R.D. moved from The Hague to Zutphen on June 7th, and Sgt. Miller, the advance party, had a suspect waiting in jail for the Detachment. Sgt. Volpel picked up a member of the *S.D.*, formerly with the Dutch police, who took him to the graves of British officers allegedly shot and buried by the *S.D.* One grave was opened, but it was not possible, initially at least, to identify the several bodies it contained. (War Graves had a standing requirement that it be informed about all graves of Allied servicemen.) Sgt. Tarte went to Utrecht to determine the status of Dutch policemen who had received bonuses from the *S.D.* for good work. The Dutch decided that they had no interest in these men. In early July, the Section took over Security for H.Q. Canadian Forces, Netherlands (H.Q.C.F.N.), at Apeldoorn.

On June 9th, No. 8 Detachment was asked to deal with Communist-inspired activity in the N.B.S. H.Q. in Amsterdam. No. 9 Detachment, always busy, started June with a Werewolf, screened about 2,500 prisoners in Dordrecht, Gorinchem, and Tiel, and became the first to include among its unit transport "the Detachment motor launch". It heard that a certain Blankers, a *Gestapo* agent on the "want list", was working for a Canadian unit in Amsterdam. Sgt. McKay searched but did not find him. The Detachment spent the whole night of the 22nd interrogating another *Gestapo* agent, a "nasty sort of lad, specialty: man-handling of so-called juvenile delinquents". In July, it was given a case of suspected sabotage at Ridderkerk, a Port Security task, and an investigation into a Communist organization.

No. 10 F.S.R.D. screened German troops at Ijmuden, set up a control point in Alkmaar to handle the collection of all *S.S.* and *S.D.* north of the North Sea Canal, and sent many suspects to Camp 030. No. 11 Detachment handled many cases for No. 34 British F.S.S. in The Hague, and about 50 more for Dutch Naval Security. It always had a backlog of travel pet applications to process. On June 8th, Sgts. Moore and Greenberg made an arrest after a raid on a house in Leiden. Lieut. Cole investigated German disposal of Jewish property during the Occupation. Sgt. Greenberg arrested and interrogated two Dutch women, former mistresses of German *S.D.* agents; they gave him the names of two more *S.D.* whom he also arrested.

In these first few weeks after hostilities ceased, F.S. and its interrogators were processing 5,000 persons a day. In support of the Dutch authorities, they disarmed the Dutch Forces of the Interior (N.B.S.), some of whom wanted to keep their arms, without incident. The 1,700 wanted persons they arrested included: the bulk of the *S.D.* and the *Gestapo*, with their Chief, *S.S.* Brigadier Dr. Schoengarth, *Höherer S.S. und Polizei Führer* for Holland; two groups of *Geheimefeldpolizei*; Rost von Tonningen; and the majority of the *134, 360,* and *359 Frontaufklärungstruppe*, the *Abwehr* group responsible for line-crossing and radio agent work in North Brabant. Two *Abwehr* control agents captured at Bussum told F.S. that they had not been able to establish a successful radio agent in North Brabant after September, 1944. Line-crossers had been sent over at a rate of one to three a month until January 1st, 1945; from then on, ten a month were sent; only one had returned.[42]

As the Dutch authorities re-established their control, the Canadian responsibilities for Counter-Intelligence and Security in Holland became increasingly domestic in scope. Occasionally there were interesting cases, but unit Diaries for the summer and early autumn of 1945 contain mostly routine entries and minor administrative notes. Entries for July report the run-down of previous commitments, the conclusion of earlier cases, and several new incidents related to them.

No. 11 Section arrested a *Hitler Jugend* individual, a few Germans in Amsterdam with false identity cards, and Dutch suspects masquerading as Canadian soldiers. One prisoner committed suicide; the Section thought "it probably saved the Dutch Government the job". One of No. 14's wanted *S.S.* was picked up by Provost in Brussels; his arrest closed the books on three sabotage teams. No. 17 Section began to hand over its tasks to the Rotterdam C.I. on July 14th. In Apeldoorn, No. 1 F.S.R.D. investigated a local group of Dutch nationalists who were laying claim to a portion of Germany.

Generally speaking, the Sections now had three routine tasks. The backgrounds of Dutch girls wishing to marry Canadian soldiers had to be examined. Normally this was a chaplain's duty, but conditions were not normal and the volume of requests was too great for that Service to handle. Enquiries had to be made for Security had to be considered and both the man and the girl had to be protected. In late November "A" (Personnel Branch) staffs took over this function. The second and continuing task involved checks on applicants for employment with the Canadian Forces. Finally, C.I. was responsible for watching and reporting on the state of Army morale and on relations generally between units and the civilian population. No. 3 F.S.R.D. mentions this task as "requests to locate lost husbands, cars, and strayed animals."

When the war ended and demobilization plans were activated, F.S. felt immediately the effects of the first-in, first-out principle that had been agreed on. The system was eminently fair, but it deprived the Sections of men whose skills and experience could not be replaced easily, or at all. In addition, in a climate where everyone wanted to go home, motivation was weakened and administration became difficult. In short, the efficiency of the units began to be seriously affected.

The dismantling of the Intelligence organization in general, and Security in particular, required much discussion between Ottawa, London, and the Continent. C.M.H.Q., so as to keep as much expertise as possible, asked Lt.-Col. Macdougall, by now G.S.O.1 I(b) at H.Q.C.F.N., to find out which of his men would be prepared to serve until January 31st, 1946. His I(b) staff at this point consisted of a G.S.O.2, Capt. C.M. Tetrault; an I.O., Capt. J.L. Bourassa; and a captain's vacancy – later filled by Capt. J.E. McEachern. It was also busy collecting historical items for the Canadian War Museum and forwarding them under an escort of Capt. F.M. Mowat and Lieut. R.M. Donovan. Other C.F.N. officers included Lieut. Wally Lehman, serving with 1 Canadian War Crimes Investigation Unit; Lt.-Col. Les Chater, the G.S.O.1, and Capt. Milton Shulman, busy with the interrogation of senior German military commanders – a task that was to continue until October 31st. Capt. Shulman later went to the Kurt Meyer trial. Capt. G.F. Rogers was readying the draft of a *Manual of Air Reconnaissance* for the printers, in London. Detailed plans were being drawn up for disbanding the F.S. Sections and Detachments and such I(a) units as A.P.I.S.[43]

On October 4th, Third Division, C.A.O.F., announced that it wished to consolidate its Intelligence organization, so that it would have one system of records, one unit to control transport centrally, and a central control for personnel. C.M.H.Q. considered that the existing Intelligence Pool would be quite capable of accepting the new role. At Army, the position of Colonel G.S. Int., which had been filled since Normandy by Col. Peter Wright, O.B.E., was abolished on November 1st. Maj. J.M. Gray, G.S.O.2 (Int). at H.Q.C.F.N., was made subordinate to the Colonel A/Q (Administration), but was given a direct channel of communication to D.D.M.I. at C.M.H.Q.[44]

Maj. John Gray's task included the supervision and eventual repatriation of all C.Int.C. and Intelligence-employed personnel in accordance with the "Provisional Plan dated 16 Jul 45, and amendments". He also had to supervise F.S. work in Holland, prepare the Weekly Morale Report (on the Canadian Army in Europe), supervise the vetting of applicants for marriage to Canadian soldiers, and complete any outstanding overseas Intelligence matters. He was to transfer those responsibilities to other staffs as soon as possible. The last distribution of Intelligence reports would take place on November 15th, 1945. C.M.H.Q. undertook to direct the interrogations of senior German officers. In July, the Canadian Army in Europe totalled 65,000. By the time it was down to 26,000, i.e., by the end of 1945, all C.I. staffs and units in Holland had left; the ones in Germany remained.[45]

The F.S. Sections were brought under H.Q.C.I. control during the period mid-August to about October 10th, 1945. Disbandments began with No. 16 Section on August 13th and ended with H.Q.C.I. itself on December 8th. Many of the men had done work of the highest quality. It may be unfair to others to select any names for special mention, but Sgt. Tarte of No. 7 and Sgts. Gough and Gracie of No. 9 F.S.R.D.s were outstanding.

Before we turn to the activities of the units in the Canadian Army Occupation Force, we must mention those small units for investigating War Crimes, Missing Persons, and charges of looting by German commanders and units. Because of their size, they kept no individual records; they forwarded their reports to authorities other than Canadian. We therefore acknowledge their existence but must pass them by, except for two which had direct relevance to Security within First Canadian Army: No. 1 Canadian Army Photographic Processing Unit and First Canadian Army Refugee Interrogation Team.

The Canadian Army had learned that it was impossible to ban photography totally. As a compromise, sometime in June 1944, it decided instead to permit men to take photographs, but to insist that these be processed by an official agency where they would be censored. An *ad hoc* Army Processing Centre, set up under the H.Q. First Canadian Army Intelligence Section, drew complaints that the quantity and quality of the printed product was poor. As a result of a study by Lieut. T.E. Curry of A.P.I.S., a new unit was formed on October 4th with Curry as the first O.C. He obtained trucks which could be used as mobile dark rooms, but could not obtain any men who had had photographic training.

When the unit moved with A.P.I.S. to Antwerp Dourne, it had a backlog of 2,877 rolls of film to process, no equipment, and only captured stocks of photographic paper. Capt. Westaway, the A.P.I.S. Administrative Officer, ransacked civilian sources for equipment, and tried to recruit staff. He found four deep tanks and sufficient accessories to develop about 400 rolls a day. These were then censored, and the negatives passed – with Lt.-Col. Wright's concurrence – to a civilian firm for final processing. By October 31st, 1944, the unit – one officer and nine men – had the backlog down to about 1,000 rolls.

As soon as the new deep tanks were in operation, Lieut. Curry began training his inexperienced staff. He had to publicize the facility and to explain the new arrangements to the Army; he did this in the *Maple Leaf.* By November 15th, all his men had been remustered to C.Int.C. At the end of the month, the unit had to move, with sad results for productivity. In December, it fell still further behind because the Mobile Field Power Station, on which it relied for electricity, could not produce enough current. Complaints about the quality of the product were still being made; the unit attributed most of them to the camera user himself. Films were sent in improperly wrapped and without identification; the unit claimed that it managed to restore over half of them to their rightful owners. When, after waiting almost three months, the Unit finally received a supply of paper from Ordnance, it was wet and had to be carefully dried and tested to see if it was still usable.

The Unit's worst difficulties came in December, 1944. Most of the men were on guard duty. A.P.I.S. was handling more and more sorties as the weather cleared, and of course had priority for the electricity needed to process the results of these urgent operational photos. The fluctuating voltage burned out the unit's dryer motor, no replacements were available, and the supply of chemicals ran out. By mid-January, the Unit managed to rig up a temporary dryer, and finally, on January 27th, stock arrived that had been ordered five months earlier. The Unit cleaned up the backlog by February 4th and could promise a 24-hour service. Many of its men were unfit and were very severely tried by the noise of the V-bombs, but most of them preferred to remain in a useful job and in a group that was friendly.

By mid-June, after a short respite following V.E. day, more than 500 films came in every day for processing. The unit, short-staffed by reason of leaves, postings, and sickness, borrowed men from wherever it could. By mid-July, when it was using over 1,200 sheets a day, it also began to run out of paper and could not purchase supplies in the civilian market. By September, repatriation was taking its toll. It lost technicians, was told not to expect replacements of men or materials, dismissed the civilian staff, and finally disbanded on November 16th.[46] The Army Processing Unit, a small, very minor entity, performed a valuable Security function during hostilities and a convenient service when they ended. Its needs should have been foreseen, and a regular, properly equipped unit formed.

The First Canadian Army Refugee Interrogation Team, with Maj. Ernie Ofenheim as O.C., was formed on March 1st, 1945, to provide a support staff of Interrogators to augment the limited capabilities of the F.S. Sections. It spent much of the first month studying British techniques, and was ready by April 17th. On the 19th, Capt. Mendel and Lieut. Mang went to work checking 150 refugees at First Army's P.W. Cage.

On May 21st, the Team was moved to H.Q. II Canadian Corps, then in Meppen, Germany, to find out everything it could concerning structures and installations that could be used by the Corps Engineers. They worked also with the F.S. Sections. Capt. Jones, for example, went first to Groningen to interrogate one of No. 3 Section's enemy agents, then to Franeker and to Leeuwarden in Holland to interview repatriated Dutch workers; Capt. Mendel worked closely with Camp 030; the whole Team worked at the two civilian camps at Cloppenburg and Dalum and at II Corps P.W. Cage. Later they moved forward to Oldenburg.

From there the Team went to Wilhelmshaven where it found billets in the Marine Infantry kaserne, Mühlenweg, and was reinforced by men from the Canadian Army Interrogation Pool and the Intelligence Officers Pool. These included Maj. Ernie G. Kuhlbach, Capts. Cliff Webster, Ron Geisler, S.O.F. Evans, and Rudi Aksim (no longer needed for Technical Intelligence), and Lieuts. J.H.F. Laban, Wally Field, W. Sproule, A.H. Fast, and P. Faust. The Team's first task was to screen German officers before their discharge, using the German clerical staff to handle the release record procedures. It finished this task in two days and then did similar checks for postal and judicial officials and their staffs.

In early July, the Team noticed that the *S.S.* personnel coming through were trying harder to evade the controls. It therefore worked harder to find out every possible detail on the men screened so as to frustrate that evasion. Interrogation is terribly wearying work, and the pace, which permitted no breaks, left the Team's staff exhausted. At the end of July, the Team disbanded, with its members going either to No. 3 Canadian Intelligence Pool or to the F.S. Sections in the area.[47]

F.S. DETAILS – GERMANY

F.S./C.I. duties in Holland have brought us well out of our chronological sequence, and we must retrace our steps slightly to follow the fortunes of the Sections and Staffs in Germany itself. In Holland, the prospect of transferring Security responsibilities to a reliable civil organization had enabled the C.I. staffs to be flexible. In Germany, this did not pertain. Every former official was suspected of having Nazi connections, and the possibility of getting honest, unbiased answers from informants was remote, assuming they were willing to talk at all. In addition, the risk of guerrilla activity was considered to be very real. The Sections in Germany therefore faced a very different environment from that we have described for the Netherlands.

No. 4 F.S. Section moved out of Meppen over bad roads, under continuous rain, air bursts, and "Moaning Minnies" (heavy mortar bombs). At 1000, April 30th, it was part of the delegation sent to accept the German surrender of Bad Zwischenahn, a ceremony which included a cautious approach via the civil authorities. That afternoon, Capt. Petersson found them billets, but quickly abandoned them when he had to run the gauntlet of heavy machine gun fire as he drove away. As the fighting stopped, the Section tried to send detachments to cover the neighbouring villages, but found the roads virtually impassable. II Corps H.Q. arrived on May 6th and set up a tent camp in and around the town. The camp created a public relations problem for the Section – they lived in a house.[48]

No. 2 Section, with No. 2 and 4 Detachments, F.S. Document Teams, a Counter-Sabotage Detachment, and interrogators and guards, went to Oldenburg. In their house searches they caught many persons named on their lists, including six of the town's leading policemen. Capt. Jake Steen closed down a German clandestine communications circuit and arrested its personnel. However, much of their time was spent preparing to hand over to the C.A.O.F. No. 4 Detachment's territory included Delmenhorst, where it found that, although a British Section had paused there briefly, no records had been kept and the 'automatic arrest' personnel, including the Burgomeister and the Chief of Police, had not been attended to. It widened its investigations and arrested two particularly unsavory characters; one, posing as a British Intelligence officer, had used his false identity to terrorize Polish workers' camps in the area; the other had been a *Gestapo* agent in Russia.

No. 3 Section, with Sgts. Simmons and Harder from No. 2 Detachment and men from the Documents Section and Counter-Sabotage, explored Wilhelmshaven. The town was "about 80% kaput", but the Navy-controlled port installations were in good working order. The Section rounded up the *Kreisleiter* and 35 of his staff by summoning them to a "conference." They were rather proud of a ruse that saved them the labour of house raids and night-time arrests. They also picked up members of William Joyce's ("Lord Haw-Haw's") organization, a nephew of the Chief Scout, and one Dietze, who had been the English-language announcer at the 1936 Olympics. Cpl. Froggett acted as interpreter between a German Submarine Flotilla Commander and the Senior Naval Officer, in negotiating the surrender of eight U-boats in the harbour. The Section screened 300 Naval and Air Force women at a German Women's Service camp; the Diary does not speak of arrests being made. Sgt. Simmons, working in the suburb of Fedder Groeden, heard reports that people were recruiting for the Werewolves, but found no real evidence. The Section sent a number of other suspects to the Internment Camp newly set up at Esterwegen, where No. 12 Detachment was located after it had been formed on May 9th. On May 26th, with a section of Royal Marines, they raided a hideout in the country and caught three *Gestapo*. On the 29th, in another raid in which Cpl. Alcorn was accidentally wounded in the foot, more *Gestapo* were caught. They also caught some *S.S.* who had been guards at the *Reichskanselrei* in Berlin, who gave them "eyewitness" accounts of Hitler's death – the first such detail to be obtained by the Canadians.

In Leer, No. 18 Section's experience was similar: arrests of Nazi Party officials, and continuous struggles to get vehicles, clothing, heat, and light. No. 20 moved to Aurich on May 6th. It checked a German Army H.Q., found few documents, arrested people on its Black List, and checked leads on others; by the 18th, it had caught 66 persons. It heard rumours of Werewolves but found no concrete evidence. At first the situation had looked hopeless: everywhere hundreds of D.P. and unattached German troops were freely wandering about. To control them, it set up a P.W. Cage on the 7th and a D.P. centre a day later. It had no problems with the civilians, who obeyed without protest the control and curfew regulations it imposed.

Esterwegen Internment Camp, June 1945. (C.H. Richer/Canada. Dept. of National Defence/Library and Archives Canada, PA-159382)

Five other F.S. units were in Germany; Nos. 1, 3, 4, and 18 Sections, and No. 6 F.S.R.D. Capt. Andy Fleming's No. 1 Section left Hindenburg Barracks on July 4th, en route to Berlin. It had a tedious trip during which "Russians held up the convoy and we were delayed up to two hours on two occasions" before it found temporary quarters on the football field of the Stadium in which the 1936 Olympics had been held. The next morning, the men searched the city for billets, "thinking the R.A.F. has done a good job". The Russians had "stripped the city of almost everything", but eventually C.S.M. Smith and Sgt. Bosca found and occupied an ideal billet, ignoring the owners' claims that they had always been anti-Nazi.

On July 12th, the Section was sent to Potsdam to control the perimeter security of the Palace where the Big Three Conference was to be held. As part of his task, Andy Fleming was responsible for the passes giving access to the area. On the 16th, when Stalin arrived, the "Russians closed the roads and wouldn't let anyone through, not even Monty's [Field Marshal Montgomery's] car". Capt. Fleming was in Prime Minister Churchill's sightseeing party in Berlin that afternoon.

The Conference ended on August 1st; on the 2nd, the guards were withdrawn from the Palace and from all posts except Mr. Bevin's house. Capt. Hank Rennie replaced Andy Fleming on the 3rd, and the Section moved back to Berlin on the 6th. About that time, they made a recording for a radio broadcast to Canada and were interviewed for the Army newspaper *The Maple Leaf*. They were most indignant when the story identified them as Military Police. On

August 18th, the Section was given a D.P. Camp to check. It remained in Berlin through September, returned from there to H.Q.C.I., and was disbanded on October 17th.

No. 3, finding that the screening of women *S.S.* staff was not enough to keep its men busy, spent the entire last week of June getting ready for a routine move to Aurich, from which it covered Leer, Oldenburg, and Wittmund. By the 16th, it had 16 suspects to send to Esterwegen, and in the next week collected important documents which were used at the trial of *Reichskommissar* of the Netherlands, Arthur Seyss-Inquart. On the 27th, it located a man with the unlikely name of Lotto who was on its wanted list because he was an important organizer of the Werewolves. Section personnel had to chase him almost to the Danish border before they could capture him. His initial interrogation resulted in a twenty-five page report, which was completed on August 2nd.

No. 4 Section operated between Meppen and Cloppenburg. It was fairly busy; as well as the town itself, it had four *Kreise* (districts) around Cloppenburg to look after. The wartime Section was reorganized to its C.A.O.F. establishment on June 30th, and there was a short hiatus between the departure of Capt. "Pete" Petersson and the arrival of Capt. Eddie Corbeil. No. 4 was not always on good terms with the Polish Armoured Brigade and its Section, probably because of differences of opinion concerning treatment of defeated Germans. The Poles certainly tended to be less flexible and to react more quickly – "trigger-happy" was the way No. 4 described it.

No. 18 Section was at Leer, on one of the major repatriation routes to Germany. Security in the town appeared dubious when, on June 2nd, its citizens were heard cheering a passing German convoy. The Section therefore arrested on the 9th "the leading personality, head of the Werewolves, etc.", and locked him up "with proper theatrical effects for benefit of the local townsfolk". It set up road controls and, since half the population did not have documents and passes, clogged its detention facilities within 48 hours.

No. 20 Section in Aurich examined about 630 persons between May 18th and June 18th, 375 of them from *Armee Abteilung Straube*, and sent them to Esterwegen Internment Camp. In the last half of the month it caught an additional 104 in the 'automatic arrest' category. The Section vetted another 1,500 or so who were seeking positions with the Military Government, and also covered the military hospital at Sandhorst and the discharge centre at Wittmund airport. Its secondary task was to operate a Control Line along the Ems–Jade Canal from Emden to Wilhelmshaven, which was designed to contain the *25th Army* prior to its documentation and discharge. Much of the information the Section used came from local Communists. Capt. Brookhouse, however, viewed this group with suspicion, and believed that, though it was not active, ". . . it could be the basis for a strong movement if it were given a free hand". One of the many rumours, taken so seriously by the citizens that it drew several volunteers, was that Germans were being recruited by the Canadian Army to help fight the Japanese.

At the end of June, No. 20 moved to Cloppenburg, where it had the residue of No. 4's cases to complete. It tried to clear the prisons, a difficult task because of its own arrests and the 43 made by its Vechta detachment. By July 25th, it turned over to No. 2 Section and was on its way to H.Q.C.I. and repatriation. It was proud of its work; it had made 925 arrests, "a large percentage ... important from a C.I. view-point".

No. 4 F.S.R.D. spent the first few days of June hunting *Ortsgruppenleiters* (township clerks), minor Nazi functionaries, and similar 'automatic arrest' people. On June 21st, it had a harrowing day interviewing the inmates of a former German civilian concentration camp; their testimony was recorded for use as evidence at later Military Government trials. The Detachment found that many Germans in their area were unhappy because "the same Nazis are still running the town".

No. 6 F.S.R.D. patrolled Wilhelmshaven and Cuxhaven, and worked with 307 Infantry Brigade at Altenwalde to control the concentration area at Krupps Range, an historic ammunition proving ground. As its guard staffs became more skilled, the Detachment's duties declined, and it was withdrawn to H.Q.C.I. on October 16th.

C.I. IN THE CANADIAN ARMY OCCUPATION FORCE (C.A.O.F.)

The decisions reached at Yalta on February 11th, 1945, divided Germany into five zones. The British occupied the northwest, the United States the south, France the southeast, and the U.S.S.R. the east; Berlin was to be occupied jointly, as the H.Q. of a four-power Allied Control Council. This Council was to formulate joint occupation policies which the new German central government was required to put into force.

It so happened that the surrender was signed by the German High Command, not by a civil government. The Allies never recognized Admiral Dönitz' civil regime which followed Hitler, and S.H.A.E.F. continued to function as an operational H.Q., while governing Germany through its own Military Government organization. Field Marshal Montgomery, C.-in-C. of the British Zone, was appointed British Representative on May 22nd; he too controlled his Zone directly through the German military commander who was subordinate, in his turn, to the German C.-in-C., North-West Europe, Field Marshal Busch.

German Army boundaries were altered to coincide with Allied boundaries. The British Zone was then subdivided into Corps districts, in which division, brigade, and regimental areas coincided with the local civil administrative areas, and their H.Q. were located near their corresponding German military H.Q. In every case, the British H.Q. had a double task: to administer the areas through the appropriate civil authorities and, at the same time, to control the associated German military formation. But the civil side of the Military Government organization, consisting of the civilian department heads and their small staffs, could not assume its duties until the Control Council actually came into being, which did not take place until the first week of July. S.H.A.E.F. was disbanded on July 13th, and the Western Zones functioned under their separate Military Governors.

The British Zone Corps District, under the command of XXX British Corps (Gen. Sir Brian Horrocks) and based on the provincial capital of Hanover, comprised three divisions and one armoured brigade. The Third Canadian Infantry Division, C.A.O.F., commanded by Maj.-Gen. Chris Vokes, was one of the three divisions. This new formation had been organized on an establishment strength of 568 officers and 15,477 men, i.e., about four-fifths of the operational ceiling.[49] It took over from Second Canadian Infantry Division in northwest Germany during the first week of July 1945.

Military Government (Mil. Gov.), which the Division was intended to support, had four major duties: to purge the German administration of all active members of the Nazi Party; to ensure that the Allies' requirements were met; to direct the reorganization of the civil administration along democratic lines; and to collect, control, and ensure the welfare of Displaced Persons. These duties were performed with advice from an advisory branch at Corps District H.Q. by Detachments which, varying in size and importance, were located with the respective civil administration headquarters. 229(P) Provincial Detachment at Hanover had a strength of about 150 officers. The C.A.O.F. zone was served by 223(R) Detachment, which had two Sub-Detachments – 821 *Land* (rural) at Oldenburg and 613 *Regierungsbezirke* (administrative district – county) at Aurich. Aurich had five *Kreise* (districts, roughly equivalent to a township) and 319 *Gemeinden* (local self-governed areas – municipalities). The normal Military Government Detachment at a *Kreis* was four officers. Oldenburg, however, a more rural area, had seven *Kreise,* but only 33 *Gemeinden*. In addition, there were detachments of the Displaced Persons Executive to deal with some 25,000 D.P.s in 30 Camps.

Gen. Vokes' directives were designed to manage the control, disarmament, and disbandment of the German Army in his Zone. Since the immediate task was to control the forces themselves, he deployed his three brigades along the Ems–Jade Canal, which was lit by searchlights, constantly patrolled, and had control points at all crossing places. He had to maintain security in his Divisional area, a Mil. Gov. responsibility, and be responsible for the security, organization, and administration of the Internment Camps in his area. Using his own Engineers and German labourers, he also had to destroy or to concentrate

German war material. Finally, he was responsible for controlling displaced persons, P.W., and refugees. This last category included many foreign nationals.

Mil. Gov. staffs were responsible for the formation of a military government administration; the protection, care, and evacuation of Allied P.W.; displaced persons; rehabilitation of German refugees; prevention of starvation and disease; control of Information Services; re-education of German youth; and ensuring that Germany had no opportunity to revive its enthusiasm for going to war.

The Counter-Intelligence staffs were responsible for the elimination of the Nazi Party and its affiliates, the *S.S.*, the *Waffen S.S.* (the 22-division military force of the *S.S.*), and the *Hitler Jugend*. They paid particular attention to the *Abwehr;* the *Geheimfeldpolizei;* the *Reichssicherheitspolizei* (Security Police-Political) *(Sipo)*, and its branches, the *Geheimstaatspolizei* (State Secret Police) *(Gestapo)* and the *Kriminalpolizei* (Criminal Police) *(Kripo)*; and the *Sicherheitsdienst* (*S.D.* – the *S.S.* secret service, the Nazi Party Security force). They also feared that paramilitary groups like the *Grenzpolizei* (Frontier Police) could have links with the Party. 'Automatic arrest' categories included all higher *S.S.* and police leaders; all members of the *Gestapo* and *S.D.*; members of the civil police who had served with the *Gestapo* or as special investigators, and certain other senior police officials; all Nazi administrators at the *Kreis* level, and all officials of the *Hitler Jugend*, German Labour Front, Transportation Corps, and Nazi University Students League.[50] But it must be remembered that the Nazi Party had so controlled the nation that every public position equivalent to foreman and up was filled by a Nazi or a person acceptable to the *N.S.D.A.P.* It was not possible, nor was it desirable from a practical administrative point of view, to jail them all. A balance had to be struck between the risk of leaving an individual at large and the needs of the country.

The British tried hard to get the Canadians to take a major share of this commitment; they themselves had to be prepared to move their forces to the Far East, where the war was still going on. Any acceptance of a major role by the Canadians would mean, however, that a separate organization would have to be formed. Ottawa eventually agreed and, when the detailed establishment was laid down in May, it called for an additional G.S.O.3 I(b); three Area Security Offices, each with a major, a captain, and four men; three normal F.S. Sections; and No. 3 Intelligence Pool, a new unit of 16 officers and 26 men which had been formed as a Holding Unit on June 16th, 1945 – a total of 26 officers and 76 men. The G.S.O.3 (Int) at Divisional H.Q. looked after German order-of-battle, interrogation, search lists, and political intelligence; the I.O. dealt with German deserters and the staff aspects of interrogations; an additional G.S.O.3, with a clerk, was responsible for all aspects of civil and military security. Finally, four Document Control teams were deployed to Aurich, Oldenburg, Wittmund Airfield, and a small hamlet near Osnabrück.

Movement control on the Aurich road, 26–27 August 1945; spot-check of identity documents and travel permits. The men are from a nearby infantry unit; the post was under the control of No. 1 Area Security Office, C.A.O.F. (Lieut. Barney J. Gloster/Canada. Dept. of National Defence/Library and Archives Canada, PA-151759)

The Security Service was responsible for protecting the Force from subversion and sabotage; collecting information about underground intelligence, sabotage, or subversive organizations; advising on measures to frustrate the operations of such organizations; detecting and arresting security suspects; liquidating the German Intelligence Services; and assisting by Intelligence means in the elimination of the Nazi Party and its paramilitary organizations. The long-term aims of the Security Service were to acquire Intelligence information on individuals and organizations considered dangerous to Allied interests, and to investigate all political and other movements which might work against Allied control or which fostered underground Nazi or military organizations.

The methods used by the Security units were very similar to those they had employed before VE day. A system of controls was designed and put into force. It restricted communications and movement, censored the press, required individuals to carry identity cards and obey a curfew, and forbade them to possess firearms, pigeons, explosives, and similar items that could be used by clandestine organizations to foster their aims. Active enquiries were conducted into the background of public officials.

The Area Security Offices (A.S.O.) were put under the control of XXX British Corps, but were permitted to deal with any case that came to their attention within their own Areas. They received support from other Intelligence units which examined captured records and documents and checked names they found against the list of known undesirables. Security was responsible for collecting evidence against individuals who, in the text of the Potsdam Agreement, were "more than nominal" members of the Nazi Party or who had "... committed serious acts of cruelty or oppression against nationals of the United Nations in violation of the laws of war". Military Government prepared and presented the cases for prosecution. Information was obtained from the records of Nazi or Nazi-affiliated organizations, and from denunciations, confessions, or previous identification. The Military Police helped to enforce security controls and, on request, carried out arrests, raids, and house searches. They also acted as the link between Security, garrison troops, and the German police, who were sometimes brought in to reinforce the small C.I. and Provost sections.[51]

No. 2 Area Security Office, Maj. D.F. Morris, G.S.O.2, which was the first to form (on June 16th, 1945), was located in Oldenburg with No. 624 Military Government (*Stadtkreis*) Detachment. It had under command No. 2 F.S. Section, No. 1 Polish F.S. Section, and No. 325 British F.S. Section (Port). It also controlled No. 20 Section and No. 4 F.S.R.D. No. 2 Section was responsible for *Stadtkreis* Oldenburg and *Landkreise* Oldenburg, Vechta, Cloppenburg, and, later, Delmenhorst. No. 1 Section at Varel was responsible for *Landkreise* Ammerland and Friesland. No. 325 Section at Wilhelmshaven worked with the Naval Security Officers and was responsible for the Port. No. 20 Section and No. 4 F.S.R.D. were soon to be withdrawn from Cloppenburg; No. 16 F.S. was at Oldenburg, No. 15 at Aurich, arid No. 17 at Osnabrück.

No. 3 Area Security Office, with Maj. R.H. Noble, M.B.E., as G.S.O.2 and Capt. Bill Blane as G.S.O.3, opened at Osnabrück on July 20th. No. 1 A.S.O. was set up at Aurich on July 25th, with Maj. Rafe Douthwaite as G.S.O.2. Unfortunately, Rafe was injured in a car accident on the 30th; his place was taken by his assistant, Capt. R.J.G. Weeks. Reg Weeks was to end his military career in 1977 as a major-general, Director General, Intelligence and Security, in Ottawa.

No. 2 Office managed to persuade XXX Corps to simplify procedures for handling detainees and evacuees from *Land* Oldenburg. By mid-August it had studied the histories of pro-Nazi officials holding office under Mil. Gov. and, too optimistically as it turned out, hoped to have these men dismissed by the end of August. The large number of arrests of Black List suspects made this a very busy area. The local detention facilities and the new concentration camp at Westertimke were full and the Esterwegen Camp (one of the two in the British Zone) could accept a few very serious offenders only. A single example will show the size of the intake that could occur. On August 15, No. 2 Section raided a barn dance, really an illegal *Hitler Jugend* gathering. It took 150 names, made 25 arrests and, with other suspects it had to deliver, took 85 prisoners to Esterwegen by August 23rd. But many evaded the controls by working as casual labourers and moving around from farm to farm.

No. 3 Office spent until August 19th setting up. By the end of September, Maj. Tex Noble could see signs that the German people were beginning to be much more active in meeting the challenges of reconstruction. The left-wing groups thought that the Mil. Gov. was not drastic enough in enforcing the denazification measures; those on the right naturally felt that moderation was required. Most D.P. were Poles, but some were Russians and some were Yugoslavs. The Poles were not openly bitter towards the Allies but were worried because they were not being kept informed of Allied intentions towards them. During September, the Osnabrück *Regierungsbezirk* Office recorded 245 arrests: 221 Nazi Party members, among them the Bishop of Osnabrück, seven German Intelligence Service, three *S.S.*, and 14 paramilitary and civil service. A large stockpile of weapons was discovered in Meppen and traced to its owner, a former *Kreisleiter* named Eggert. Young children were hard to control; they continued to sing old *Hitler Jugend* songs and tried to put obstacles in the way of Allied troops. The most time-consuming task, as always, was the pre-employment vetting of public officials, police, telephone operators, and railway officials. Teachers had a special priority; of 31 examined in September at Osnabrück, three were not acceptable. Refugees from the Eastern Zone were not vetted but would go to a facility set up at Lustringen, where a German clerk would write on a card all the refugee's personal particulars, and the name of the village to which he was assigned, and then arrange his transport to it. The refugee would exchange his card for a ration card at the village, and would normally stay there.[52]

Security had to work among a population that was disturbed by privation, discipline, rumour, and lack of information, factors which, whether they were real or fancied, seemed important to those who had to live with them. No. 3 A.S.O. believed that boredom was one of the principal factors, and recommended an expansion of recreational leisure activities for youth. Doctors did not have enough gasoline to make their rounds. Political parties reproached Military Government and C.I. for real or imagined benefits they were suspected of giving to the parties' opponents. Differences in attitudes towards D.P., particularly in the Polish Division, meant that some of them were being described as difficult. Rumours abounded, especially the one that suggested that an East-West conflict was an immediate probability and that, if it did break out, Germans would side with the West. Some of the vettings that had been done at speed in the early days had now to be restudied and, in a few cases, different conclusions were reached.

On October 17th, 1945, Col. Wright obtained approval for Security staffs to prepare a weekly Political Intelligence Summary which would deal with conditions in Germany, particularly in the Canadian Zone; and be distributed to Ottawa, London, and the High Commissioner. The Summary was regularly issued during the period of the Canadian Army's stay in Germany. By the end of 1946, it had become a routine diplomatic document on German political parties, economic matters relating to Occupation conditions, illicit organizations, subversion, sabotage, terrorism, rumours, and details of D.P. difficulties.[53]

November and the onset of winter brought further crises. The food shortages were blamed on the distributors. Coal shortages were blamed on Allied demands on the coal industry, not, as was the fact, on the shortage of skilled labour. The denazification policy still got a mixed reception. Some Germans seized on differences in Allied statements regarding the Nuremburg trials of war criminals to declare that they were simply a device to allow the victor to humble the vanquished. Other Germans called for revenge on their former leaders for involving the country in a war on two fronts, and particularly for not stopping it sooner. Those who feared that war with the Soviet Union was probable also believed, with the majority, that if Hitler had waited he would have had Allied help. They entirely ignored the fact that he had attacked the West first.

The people interpreted the meeting of the Big Three Foreign Ministers in Moscow in December as an attempt to lessen tension. There was, in fact, a marked decrease in the number of rumours of imminent conflict, and a greater concentration on domestic affairs. The Sections and Offices themselves had a quiet but traditional Christmas; the officers served the men and manufactured a little merriment amongst themselves. Don Prowse of No. 3 A.S.O. put together a slick and professional souvenir booklet illustrated by photographs and sketches of the personalities in his Office, which may have made up for the loss of their Christmas pudding, stolen from their kitchen window.[54]

Public reaction to conditions during January 1946 showed a marked increase in self-confidence, and a sense of national pride, despite shortages of every kind. Teachers and teaching facilities were woefully scarce; refugees still lacked bedsteads, mattresses, and stoves. A new attitude appeared. Because people quite generally believed that Hitler had been insane, they felt that the Allies could not, with justice, hold a country guilty just because its supreme despot had been incapable of making rational decisions. Their reaction to the stories of returned P.W. suggested a possible resurgence of the post-1918 myth that the Germans had not lost the war because their armed forces had been defeated in the field, but because the Allies had had overwhelming strength in numbers, resources, and finance. This could be interpreted as conducive to a revival of German militarism, and so was carefully watched. Capt. Hank Hennie succeeded in having 29 proven Nazis dismissed from public office in Leer.

By the end of January, the sheer volume and nature of the documentary evidence presented at the Nuremberg trials began to influence public opinion. People sent to Internment Camps after the Surrender now began to return. Their reaction to their enforced holiday was encouragingly favourable. When people applied for jobs, they had to complete questionnaires which the Sections had to check; men in the railway service were asked to complete a second questionnaire. Each of these was compared with the earlier submission and significant discrepancies were explored, particularly those relating to dates and details of membership in certain organizations; they could be used to reveal a possible cover.[55]

Minor, but troublesome, affairs were never lacking. No. 1 A.S.O. received an accusation against a German Police Chief alleged to have shot 100 Poles. It received threatening letters from an organization calling itself *Führer Freiheitsbewegung Deutschlands*. A new underground organization was discovered and given the code name NURSERY; XXX Corps ordered all C.I. offices to investigate it, and selective arrests were made.

No. 2 A.S.O. found two Italian Army renegades in a local Internment Camp and handed them over to Italian Security. It apprehended a British adventurer wearing the uniform of a Canadian naval officer. In mid-February 1946, a week of bad weather caused rivers and canals to overflow, with resultant widespread flooding. People tried to rescue as much fuel and food as they could; but grain, vegetables, and cattle suffered heavy losses. Families had to be evacuated. Communities made a concerted effort to overcome the disaster. The civil administration was criticized for not paying sufficient attention to the rising water, but as not even the local residents had believed there was any danger, this was ignored. Rumours abounded. They included: "The Dutch had damaged the dams at Nijmegen and Arnhem as revenge for German flooding of Holland during the War;" and "Atom bomb trials had taken place in the North Sea between Norway and Iceland."[56]

In March, No. 1 A.S.O., with a company of infantry in support, conducted a successful sweep of the island of Norderney followed by a house search that brought many arrests. The news of the Gouzenko case in Canada reinforced the popular local belief that the West and Germany would soon combine against Russia. Former Nazis held that Winston Churchill's statement at Fulton, Missouri, "From Stettin in the Baltic, to Trieste in the Adriatic, an iron curtain has descended across the Continent," implied a further stage in the diplomatic war between Russia and the West. Workers looked on it as a warning against aggression, but they did not believe that it implied war. Intellectuals believed that the British government was endeavouring to preserve peace but had been compelled by Russia's attitude to issue a warning through an unofficial mouthpiece. A more immediate complaint against the Soviet Union arose over the inflationary effect on the German mark caused by an unchecked influx of currency from the Russian Zone. Domestic concerns continued to occupy most Germans' attention. A ration cut, imposed at the beginning of March, hurt the larger towns, but did not bear as heavily on largely rural Osnabrück. Rumours again abounded: "the cut was to build up stocks for the war against Russia . . . the wartime Allies were attempting to reduce the population of Germany by 25 million . . . fear of hunger riots was forcing the Allied troops to go about armed". And the black market prospered.[57]

Field Marshal Montgomery ordered his Corps Commanders to hand over their responsibilities for civil administration on April 15th, 1946. The first serious postwar challenge had been passed successfully. There had been no epidemic, no mass starvation, and, although there had been some shortages, coal had been available. German reconstruction had begun; it was time to let the Germans go their way.[58]

The Canadians transferred the responsibility for vetting to the Military Government. No. 3 A.S.O.'s last "Canteen Sitrep" was issued on April 27th, 1946 and the offices were handed over to their British replacements. No. 1004 F.S.R.D. took over Aurich from No. 1 A.S.O., No. 13 British F.S. took over Oldenburg from No. 2 A.S.O., and No. 74 took over Osnabrück from No. 3. On May 18th, all Sections and A.S.O.s moved to Maple Leaf Transit Camp at Delmenhorst where they were inspected the next day by Gen. Vokes. They left on the 20th for No. 4 Canadian Repat. Depot, Witley. There, on May 22nd, 1946, they were paraded, documented, and divided into drafts, either for duty with the Allied Control Commission (for which volunteers had been sought for some time), or for repatriation. That afternoon all C.I. units that had served in Germany were disbanded.

Counter-Intelligence forms a very small part of the total operational responsibility of an Army in the field. It can be argued that, even if it had not been used, the overwhelming Allied power made German counteraction, in effect, impractical. But this is an oversimplification. It was proved in both theatres that our Security measures hampered German Intelligence when it tried to obtain information on our forces. Up until the very end, the Germans were physically capable of mounting a local attack and of catching an unwary unit at a disadvantage. But they had to know when and where to direct it. C.I., and the Security training given to units and H.Q. by the Field Security units, helped to prevent the Germans from acquiring this knowledge. At the end of the War, G.I.S. staffs, captured in Holland, admitted that not one of the 100 agents sent across the line in the winter 1944–45 had been able to become established in First Army's area, and most had been captured by the Canadian C.I. After active fighting had ceased, the controls that C.I. imposed helped to accelerate the denazification of Germany.

It was fortunate that Canadian Security forces had so much time in which to prepare. No. 1 Section went to France in 1940, virtually untrained and certainly inexperienced. The duties assigned to No. 2 Section at Dieppe had been unrealistic and, with a little more experience, it would have known them to be so. Even Canadian units and formations were less than helpful until they learned what C.I. wanted to do and was capable of doing. It took a long time to achieve the complete co-operation that was fully attained by the end of the war.

The senior Intelligence staff officer had, and still has, as it were, a split personality. He has to advise his Commander on all the aspects of I(a) and, almost simultaneously, give him guidance on the complexities of I(b). Few are equally knowledgeable of both. Always that staff officer has to rely on his subordinate staff officers to provide accurate and timely advice as to existing situations. A recognition of the responsibility such an officer carried was the well-deserved promotion to lieutenant-colonel given Bud Macdougall late in 1944.

There is much evidence that no one in the field force had studied beforehand the function, role, and best employment of Counter-Intelligence forces. In consequence, some support functions were provided only at the last moment. Wireless Intelligence is one outstanding example. The important field of counter-sabotage had only one F.S.R.D., and it had to be specially trained by M.I.5. There was not enough preparation for Refugee Control. There were never enough linguists, not only in enemy but also in friendly languages.

It was soon found that a Section could not remain always with its original formation. But it took a long time to understand that all F.S. units had to be centrally controlled and administered, and that this is not possible with a very small staff. Eventually, as a partial solution, the H.Q.C.I. and a Pool were formed. A major unit from which detachments could have been deployed would have solved problems of both operational dispersal and administrative control. In their role, the Sections themselves had to be self-contained, particularly when they, in their turn, had to control large numbers of indigenous attachments. But in both campaigns, they had to wait a long time before they were given adequate personnel and enough equipment. Much praise is due Col. Peter Wright for the efficiency of the staffing and training arrangements that did apply. As soon as it became apparent that casualties were going to be lower than feared, Col. Wright managed to get officers and men forward where their training could augment the Section. The Army I(x) officer, Murray Paulin, controlled this, and many units benefited from this "double-banking". But it was the policy initiated by Lt.-Col. Pat Henderson, of holding a large pool of reinforcements that gave him the flexibility he needed.

C.I. had many other difficulties. The C.S.M. was responsible for administration. A C.S.M. who had a firm understanding of the operational side of C.I. and who, at the same time, was a competent administrator, was always hard to find. There were many good sergeants, but few who had this needed combination of talents. From the beginning, C.I. needed competent clerical assistance at all levels, but extra clerks were provided only at the very end of the North-West Europe Campaign and many of them were unqualified. Selection and training of F.S. personnel, by and large, was good, but their treatment during their service life had one significant weakness. Many of them wore three stripes, but only two sergeants in each Section received pay for their rank; they were the Sub-Section commanders, heads of Detachment, or others similarly employed. F.S. personnel were often given responsibilities which required qualities of leadership, maturity, and judgement at and above levels normally expected of a senior N.C.O., but they were paid at the level of a lance-corporal. The Canadian Army expected a lot of these men. It did not do much for them in return. Yet despite this, the men worked hard, willingly, and without serious complaint. It was an interesting life, with a good deal of what has since become known as job satisfaction. This, and the companionship and co-operation that existed within the units, led to an efficient C.I. system that more than held its own in the Allied C.I. operation. Their wartime association is recalled by F.S. veterans as a happy and profitable time, filled with memories that lose nothing as time moves by.

12.
FIELD PRESS CENSORSHIP

The Field Censor Teams, which were used to reinforce Security by supervising correspondence and material released to the press, were properly part of the I(b) organization, but they did not operate within the normal Intelligence circuits. Until 1943, the function was carried out by the Public Relations (P.R.) staff at C.M.H.Q. When, in March of that year, D.N.D. asked for a Censor unit to be trained, the P.R.O., First Canadian Army, recommended that it be made a G.H.Q. unit; the Army Commander thought it would be more logical for Censors to become a part of Army H.Q. establishment than to be formed as a separate unit.

There were to be 10 Censors, six of them Canadians. Without them, Canada would have no representation on the British Press Censor establishment in the Italian Theatre. D.M.O.&I. at C.M.H.Q. laid down their terms of reference: they were to establish liaison with the French African Press News Agency and Radio, with Military Base Censorship, and with Service des Contrôles Techniques de l'Afrique Française; to censor all material from accredited war correspondents, including articles, broadcasts, photographs, and sketches; to supply guidance to Press Censorship Liaison Officers and to local Intelligence staffs within the Force, including Psychological Warfare; to assist Military Base Censorship in handling mail and cables, and to act as a channel to the French Contrôles Techniques.[1]

H.Q. First Army sent Lieuts. J.F.A. Calder, D.A. Robbins, and L.W. Taylor, all former newspapermen, and asked that a small reserve be trained to support them. Even with their backgrounds, they were required to do the five-week War Intelligence Course followed by another five weeks at the Ministry of Information. The Press Censorship load they would have to carry depended on the number of war correspondents to be assigned to the Canadian Force. First Army proposed seven, two to each infantry brigade and one to each tank brigade. Of these, two each would be allotted to the Canadian Press, the Canadian Broadcasting Corporation (C.B.C.), and the independent agencies; the remaining one would go to British United Press. C.M.H.Q. asked for a total of 12, one to Canadian Press, three to the C.B.C. and eight to the independents. The increase was intended to ensure that rear areas and airfields could also be covered.[2]

Lieut. W.E. Austin was sent to the Mediterranean to study British organization and techniques. His report gave C.M.H.Q. a good insight into the duties and potential problems of Press Censorship, and eventually became a planning guide for North-West Europe. The final arbiter was to be the Military Advisor to the British Ministry of Information; units in the field were to follow his directives. The first responsibility of a Censor was, of course, to stop information getting to the enemy. But he also had to stop anything that would lower the morale of Allied troops and civilians, cause ill feeling between Allies, hold an individual up to ridicule, or be "horrific or inaccurate". Even speculation over future plans was to be avoided. Movie film was not developed in the theatre, but copies were to be checked there. A 48-hour stop was put on reports of visits by distinguished persons. Canadian correspondents were, however, given a little more freedom than others in reporting unit identifications.[3]

In December 1943, Ottawa asked C.M.H.Q. to review its general policy on Censorship and Security, particularly on unit shoulder titles, pictures of senior officers, breaches appearing in the American press, and some apparent anomalies in British Censorship procedures. London pointed out that the field commanders had accepted the risk arising from the wearing of unit patches (but did not add that commanders had ordered them to be taken off during moves). Information was protected by "Zoning and Timing", the name given to a system that held up items for a period of time and then released them in accordance with a regulated schedule. C.M.H.Q. felt that there was little value in putting a Canadian stop on what had already been released elsewhere.

When he was asked to comment, Lt.-Col. R.S. Malone, Deputy Director Public Relations, Canadian Mediterranean Forces, pointed out that Censorship often had to conflict with the politicians' desire to give Canadians the widest publicity. It did not release a unit's identity unless Intelligence knew that the enemy was aware of it. It did not release unit locations. Sometimes its releases were deliberately wrong, in order to mislead the enemy. Lt.-Col. Malone felt that the delay between the time an article was written and the time it appeared in print in Canada afforded sufficient protection.[4]

Capt. Robbins, Senior Canadian Press Censor in Italy, moved to H.Q. Eighth Army in March 1944. Capt. Taylor, who had been employed at A.F.H.Q., Algiers, returned to England to organize Canadian Press Censorship participation at Supreme Headquarters, Allied Expeditionary Force (S.H.A.E.F.), at the time when the final polish was being given to the Invasion preparations. He was replaced by one of the reserve officers, Capt. E.C. Lamothe. On November 30th, 1944, No. 4 Special Press Censor Section, C.Int.C., was formed at Forli. It absorbed Maj. Robbins and Capts. Curran and Elliott-Smith, with their batman-driver, E. Marchand. They had been employed with advanced A.F.H.Q., both forward at Eighth Army and at Base in Rome.[5]

In the meantime, Postal Censorship in the Mediterranean Theatre was also having its peculiar difficulties. British Postal Censors, unfamiliar with Canadian geography and idiom, had difficulty in judging the material they saw. The directives they had received did not allow them to give any individual the benefit of a doubt. On November 7th, 1943, A.F.H.Q. advised London that it was now

No. 1 Field Press Censor unit. © Government of Canada. Reproduced with the permission of Library and Archives Canada, 2017. (Library and Archives Canada/Canada. Dept. of National Defence fonds, MIKAN 930114)

essential that a Canadian Base Censor Section be formed to censor Canadian mail.[6] Two officers and four men would be sufficient to cover the mail of 20,000 troops, but Canadian planning had not included training in Censorship. No trained men were available, therefore, and C.M.H.Q., in refusing the request, recommended that the British continue to provide the service. The reasons given were: Censorship had not been included in the original intention, and London did not wish to increase the manpower totals nor set a precedent. (It is worth noting, however, that a Special Wireless Section, together with seven officers and 61 Field Security personnel, were being sent to or were already in the theatre.) The real reason for the refusal was that C.M.H.Q. felt that responsibility for Censorship properly fell within the British terms of reference.

A little gentle pressure was applied and, in March 1944, C.M.H.Q. agreed to support a demand for more Censors if the need for them could be demonstrated. It even wrote out a list of the arguments that could be used. A.F.H.Q. resubmitted the request, and approval was formally granted, on April 15th, 1944, for the establishment of No. 1 and No. 2 Censor Sections, each of two officers and four men; Nos. 3 and 4 Sections were to be formed later.[7] They were given experienced staff. As early as December 6th, 1943, Lieuts. R.M. Bell, R.J. de Mille (infantry), and D.E. Ross (R.C.A.C.) had already been sent from Algiers to Bari as attachments to No. 6 Base Censor Group, to work exclusively on Canadian mail. De Mille moved to No. 7 Base Censor Group at Naples on January 3rd; in March, Ross was replaced by Lieut. R.G. Lancaster, R.C.A.C. On April 21st, 1944, they all moved to Naples with the Canadian Post Office. When the new Sections were finally formed, Bell was given No. 1 and de Mille No. 2. Their fortnightly Summary and Appreciation, with its list of trends and breaches, gives the impression that, by and large, the Canadian standard of Security in their area was good.

During the winter of 1942–3, Public Relations, the link with Press Censorship, was removed from the Intelligence Section at C.M.H.Q., and the new D.P.R. took over the Censorship function. The Censors, however, were still shown as Intelligence, and the staff work involved in assembling them still fell on the Intelligence Section. On May 5th, 1944, Lt.-Col. Walter, unhappy with this arrangement, pointed out to the D.C.G.S. that, from early January 1944, he had been working on the assumption that Press Censors and Psychological Warfare units were part of Public Relations and that, in fact, they were so located within 21 Army Group. They were now posted as Intelligence. He had had nothing to do with their selection or training and did not see, therefore, that he could recognize them as Intelligence personnel. (There was also the question of graded pay.) Using as examples the British and the American systems, neither of which linked them with P.R., he proposed that they become a self-accounting and separate unit under Maj. L.W. Taylor, Senior Field Press Censor. After a great deal of discussion, the problem was left in abeyance until some specific difficulty actually arose.[8] Despite the anomaly of a situation in which two parts of the same organization were given two different goals, both sides seemed to reach a satisfactory working understanding.

The administrative arrangements made in preparation for the Invasion included Routine Orders for Censorship control and for the proper handling of unit addresses. Special Postal Censorship arrangements were made with M.I.12 at the War Office for priority to be given to units slated to go into action first, and for languages other than English and French. On May 10th, 1944, Ottawa was told that for the preceding month all civilian mail leaving the U.K. had already been placed under rigid censorship. A two-week stop on mail from the troops was to start slowly and be gradually extended; in practice the delay was later shortened to 10 days. The only publicity allowed was the bare statement: "There may be some delays due to operational requirements." Mail entering Britain from the Mediterranean, however, would not be affected. On May 25th, C.M.H.Q. reported the suspension of civil air service to Gibraltar, Portugal, the Azores, Cape Verde, Madeira, Spain, the Canary Islands, Switzerland, French and Spanish Morocco, Tangiers, Algeria, Tunisia, and Corsica. D.N.D. agreed to make no public comment on the restrictions unless an emotional reaction from the Canadian public obliged them to do so. The stop was successfully enforced and was lifted on June 21st.[9]

No. 1 Field Press Censor Section was formed in June 1944; it included Maj. L.W. Taylor, Press Censor at S.H.A.E.F., and Capts. Duckett and Gallagher. Capt. Duckett landed in France on June 6th and Gallagher on June 8th, and they began to operate in the former German Kommandantur office at Courseulles-sur-Mer. On July 21st, Capt. Duckett took over Censorship at H.Q. First Canadian Army P.R. Group under Lt.-Col. R.S. Malone; Gallagher remained with 21 Army Group, No. 5 P.R. Service, then at Bayeux.

In mid-July 1944, Maj. Taylor gave advance warning to Col. Walter that S.H.A.E.F. would be asking for two more Canadian Sections of 15 officers and an unspecified number of other ranks for work in France and at the Ministry in London. In his opinion, one of the Sections should be French-speaking, for assignment, together with the British and the Americans, to French civilian Censorship. Both should be under S.H.A.E.F., but the Canadians should be administered by their own separate H.Q. He pointed out that the initial demand for Censor Sections had been based on the assumption that there would be 452 correspondents. There were already 632. (The total ultimately rose to nearly 1,000.) Coverage was needed for S.H.A.E.F., Forward and Main H.Q., H.Q. Communications Zone, and 21 and 12 Army Groups and their subordinate forces, as well as for a number of subsidiary outposts in London and on the Continent. S.H.A.E.F. was short by 100 Censors, and had no one to deal with the liberated areas; it therefore asked for an increment of 20 British and 10 Canadians. The S.H.A.E.F. request was not approved. Of course, since it was not made officially it was not formally rejected, and any extra Censors who were available were indeed provided. Early in August, Capts. J.C. Taschereau and J.C.G. Chartrand were sent to France to work with the French press and radio. Chartrand reached Paris as soon as it was liberated. No. 2 Section, formed in September, was split up; some of its members went to Paris, the remainder stayed at the Ministry of Information. No. 3 Section, under Maj. Lamothe, went from Italy to Brussels, where its personnel worked with Belgian Censorship.

Taylor again presented his views in November 1944, and this time they were accepted. But the Headquarters he thought necessary was not finally approved until three days before the end of the war. In January 1945, the Advisor to the Chief Press Censor, S.H.A.E.F., Maj. J.A. Willoughby, a Canadian original, asked Lt.-Col. Walter for an extra increment of German-speaking Censors. He was told that, in the absence of a firm Occupation policy on which a demand of this kind could be based, he would have to argue his case formally. His brief, which reached C.M.H.Q. on May 3rd, proposed that the Canadians should be employed on a Psychological Warfare establishment, and that they should operate under the Director of S.H.A.E.F. but not be on S.H.A.E.F. or Control Commission establishments.[10] Approval was granted, but the positions were never filled.

The Section files form a sort of diary of the war. They list the stories that were breaking, the correspondents involved, the stops, and the press directives that formed the basis for the stops. Wordage reports are incomplete; but between September 7th and December 2nd, 1944, No. 1 Section received 2,675 submissions, totalling 866,531 words. In one day it handled 1,418 submissions, 404,492 words. Stops were placed on the names and techniques of Resistance and Escape and Evasion groups; casualty figures and atrocity reports were passed if there were no over-riding Security considerations. The greatest fear always was that an atrocity story might be false, and the correspondent had to produce conclusive evidence of its truth before his item would be passed. In the Kurt Meyer case, the Censor was wrongly criticized for releasing the Canadian Commander's name; the release was, in fact, only given in answer to a direct question from the Prime Minister. There were delays in clearing news of the Walcheren landings; they were due firstly to a hold order from First Canadian Army, secondly to delays in transmission; but finally also to a regrettable but real delay in Censorship. 21 Army Group created problems for the Section because it persisted in releasing Canadian stories before the Canadians gave them clearance. In November 1944, No. 3 Section had a few awkward moments when a speech by the Belgian Prime Minister cut across certain guidelines on the release of information on Belgian ports. Fortunately, because relations with press and radio were good, the reports of the speech that were published omitted the offending references. Another stop, intended to hold back all news stories on the cease-fire until the official statement that ended the war in Europe was received, did not inhibit the Belgians. They talked about the event and decorated their streets a day or two before the actual release arrived.[11]

When censorship was eased on May 30th, 1945, Taylor outlined a plan for the rundown. The order that implemented his plan returned No. 3 Section to Canada, and placed No. 2 and the small element intended for the Allied Control Commission in Berlin under C.M.H.Q. Canadian Army Routine Orders on censorship were cancelled on July 6th, except for news stories on the Far East and for secret items. The units themselves were disbanded during August. The U.K. lifted its censorship in early September. The G.S.O.2 position at C.M.H.Q. Intelligence was vacated on September 5th.[12]

Canadian Censorship was, on the whole, successful. It protected security adequately and supplied valuable aid to the planning elements. Of course, it made mistakes. Gen. Crerar said harsh things about some of its releases. Censors unfortunately passed one story about the Resistance that contained enough information for a whole group to be identified and annihilated. But many other breaches of security were caught in time and their publication prevented. It is unfortunate that the requirement was not more clearly foreseen, so that early steps could have been taken to recruit, train, and deploy the necessary field personnel.

13.
SUBSIDIARY OPERATIONS

Several minor campaigns and actions are almost forgotten today, but some did require an Intelligence contribution.

GREENLAND ("X" FORCE)

An operation to send a Force to Greenland to protect the vitally important and rich cryolite mines at Ivigtut was planned in Ottawa in March 1940. The planners were given little supporting Intelligence material – the initial instructions given "X" Force contained the statement that "as far as is known at present, fuel will not be available"; and an assumption that there would be no accommodation. By April 16th, the Force had received a little additional information on the population – 3,000–4,000 persons at Julianehaab, and on the climate, the jetty, and the water and local lighterage services;[1] all of which could have come from published sources. In any event, the Canadians did not go; Washington sent a small force in 1941.

ICELAND ("Z" FORCE)

In 1940, Britain's invitation to participate in the occupation of Iceland raised a serious internal problem for Canada. If a large force were sent, adverse Icelandic political reaction and perhaps internal security unrest could be expected; but the force had to be large enough to deal with any eventuality. After debating the dilemma, Ottawa decided on June 16th, 1940, to send one Brigade under Brig. L.F. Page; his I.O. was Capt. R.T. Bonnell. A.H.Q. prepared maps and short descriptions of Iceland and sent them to the Brigade on June 28th. The delay in forwarding this material argues that Intelligence played little part in the initial planning.

The first unit to land was the Royal Regiment of Canada, with Lieut. M. John as its I.O. He became responsible for arranging accommodation in Reykjavik, while Capt. Bonnell worked closely with British Force Intelligence. On a British ship he found much uncensored mail, and a quantity of rum, stolen from medical stores, which was being sold to the troops. In August, he went to the Vestmann Islands to arrest a German suspected of links with the pro-Nazi elements on the island. Most of the Brigade left Iceland on October

Brig. L.F. Page, centre, Capt. R.T. Bonnell, I.O., left, unknown brigade major, right. (Photo collection Canadian Forces School of Military Intelligence, Kingston. Original source of photo unknown.)

31st.[2] During the operation, Intelligence carried out only routine tasks; Capt. Bonnell's discovery of the censorship evasion was perhaps the closest to F.S.; the stolen rum was properly a police affair.

SPITSBERGEN

The British War Office planned this operation "to prevent the enemy from utilizing . . . its rich coal mines". An initial briefing, held on July 26th, 1941, could give little more than general information on German activities, a forecast that there would be no German opposition to the landings, and a geographical description summarized in the phrase "barren and rocky". The islands had two industrial regions, one inhabited by 1,200 Russians, the other with a population of 1,500 Norwegians. The force to be sent consisted of the H.Q. and two battalions of 2 Brigade, commanded by Brig. A.E. Potts. His I.O. was Capt. R.L. Proctor; he had as staff one W.O.II, and three sergeants for high-grade cipher duties, and a Security Officer and two interpreters on loan from the British. A further naval reconnaissance told Brig. Potts on August 20th that there were no enemy troops, and only one civilian policeman. The inhabitants were expected to be pleased to see the Canadians. The War Office supplied details

16. Greenland-Iceland-Spitsbergen

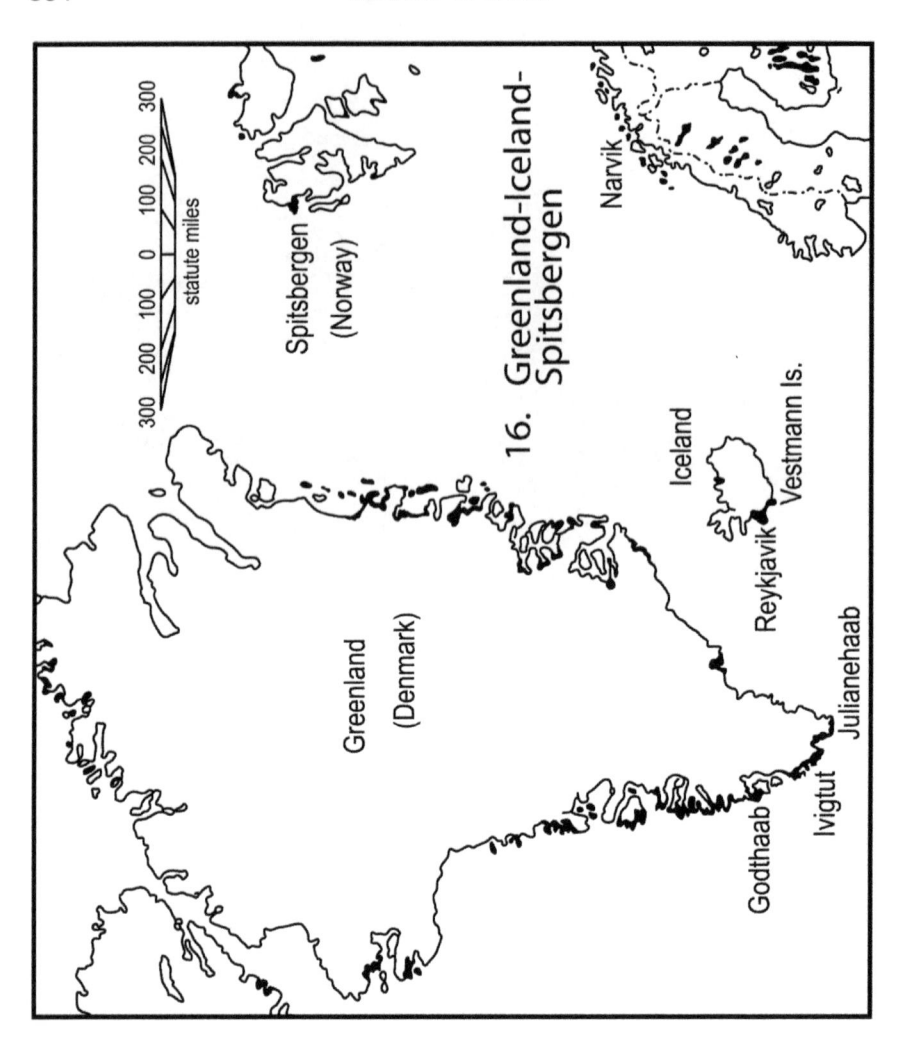

on beaches and roads. The only Security report suggested that the Norwegian mine manager might be operating on behalf of the Germans. Capt. Proctor and Cpl. N. Toseland, the Brigade Intelligence Corporal, spent August 22nd preparing a map on a ping-pong table, from which to brief the troops. On September 8th, a Security instruction was issued: troops were warned not to discuss the expedition with anyone, particularly the press; cameras could be taken but films would not be despatched until official permission was given.[3]

The Intelligence about the absence of a German garrison was accurate; the estimates of the Russian and Norwegian populations were not. The Force Signals Detachment, helped by the Norwegian staffs, continued transmitting meteorological information. To mislead the Germans and to discourage air reconnaissance, they reported fog during the period the troopship *Empress* was at Spitsbergen. When the Force left, the radio station was put out of action, and it was not until September 7th that the German command in Norway was able to confirm that the coal dumps that had been set on fire were still burning.[4]

HONG KONG

In October 1938, a 40,000-man Japanese force landed at Bias Bay, 20 miles north of Hong Kong, moved southward across the Si River, captured Canton, and thus cut the link between the interior and the last major Chinese port. From that time on, the only hope Hong Kong had of escaping attack by the Japanese was that Chinese pressure would keep the Japanese Army occupied elsewhere. In 1939, the Japanese occupied the remainder of the South China coast and the island of Hainan.

When Holland and France fell, on May 14th, 1940, and June 25th, 1940, respectively, reinforcements to the Dutch East Indies and Indo-China were stopped. An agreement with Vichy France, negotiated in late September 1940, permitting Japan to station troops in northern Indo-China, enabled the Japanese Air Force to interdict the Burma Road, China's last link with the West. As early as August 1940, the British Chiefs of Staff, having decided that Hong Kong could neither be reinforced nor relieved, recommended that it be considered an outpost to be held only as long as possible. At that date, there were estimated to be 3,000 Japanese troops on the frontier, and there were rumours of impending attacks by the Japanese-sponsored *National Peace and Regeneration Army* of Wang Ching Wei, and inconclusive reports of troop movements in the Canton area. The lack of accurate Intelligence induced Maj.-Gen. A.E. Grasett, G.O.C. British Troops in China, to send a special mission to Chungking to obtain what information it could from the Chinese. In October, the Governor of the colony, Sir Geoffrey Northcote, recommended that the garrison be withdrawn. The Foreign Office was unwilling to accept his advice on the grounds that withdrawal would encourage Japan, discourage China, and have an adverse effect upon American public opinion.[5]

On March 11th, 1941, Japan signed a second agreement with France and Siam (Thailand). In return she received permission to station troops and aircraft in the southern provinces of Indo-China, to use existing airfields, to construct others near Saigon, and to use the port in Camranh Bay. This placed a Japanese presence astride the British routes between Singapore and Hong Kong, and provided a base for further Japanese operations in the south. Japan secured her northern flank on April 13th by signing a neutrality pact with the Soviet Union. On the Allied side a conference was held on April 22nd, 1941, between the British Commander-in-Chief, Far East, and representatives of the Netherlands East Indies and the United States. The Intelligence Appreciation they were

17. Hong Kong

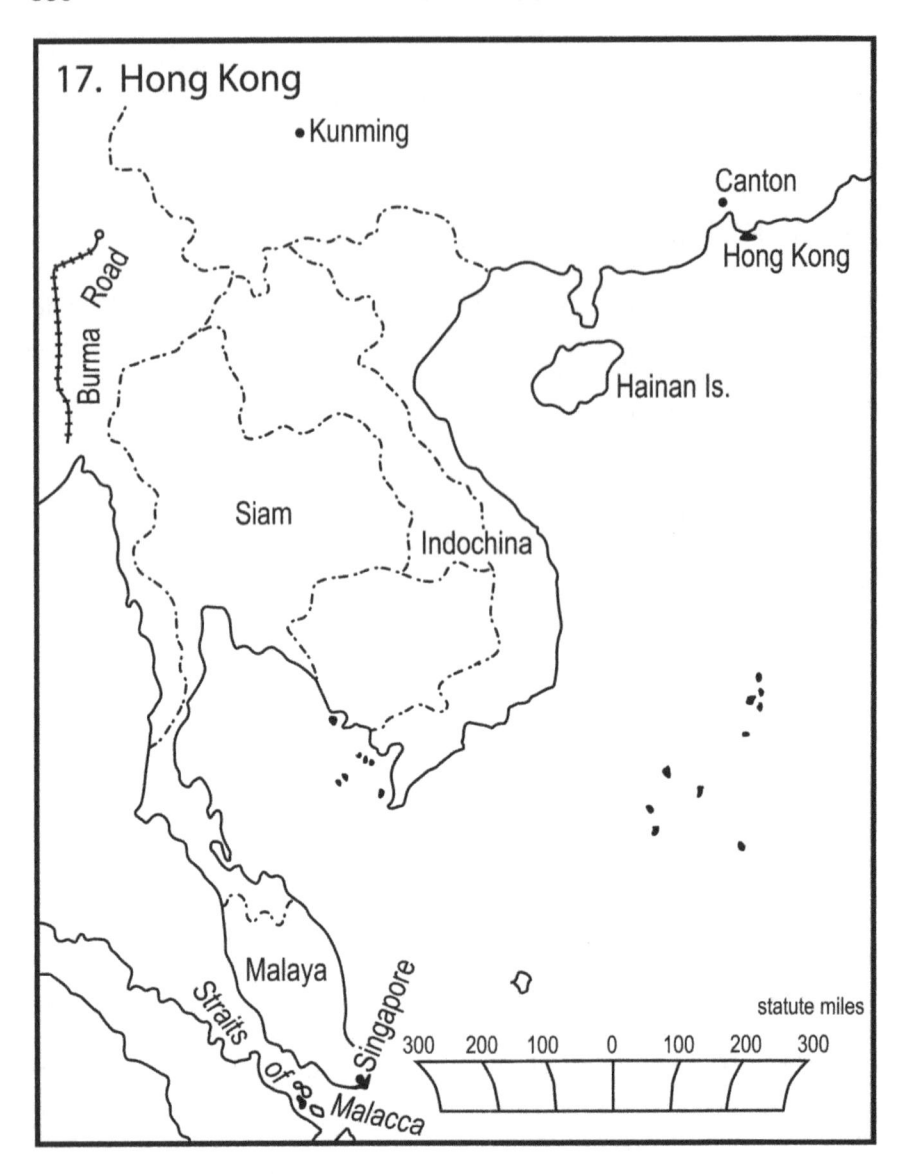

given foresaw that a simultaneous attack on Hong Kong and the Philippines, Malaya, and North Borneo would take place after Siam had been taken over.[6]

Gen. Grasett handed over to Maj.-Gen. C.M. Maltby on July 20th, and returned to England via the Pacific and Canada. In Ottawa he told the C.G.S., Lt.-Gen. H.D.G. Crerar, that, in his opinion, two more battalions would make Hong Kong strong enough to withstand a Japanese attack for a prolonged period. In London he told the Chiefs of Staff that, despite the almost total lack of aircraft and the weakness of the anti-aircraft defences, a small reinforcement would bolster civilian morale and would serve notice to both Japan and China that Britain was resolved to hold the colony. He thought Canada might be prepared to provide one or two battalions. The British Chiefs of Staff approved this report and, in recommending its acceptance to the Prime Minister, reviewed the Far Eastern situation, defences, and policy. Diplomatic relations with Japan were considered to have improved slightly. But while this review was being made, Japanese propaganda was shrilly protesting, amongst other things, the British alliance with Chiang Kai-shek – in the same newscast in which the Japanese ambassador in London reportedly assured Mr. Churchill that "Japan's programme in the Far East offers no threat or cause for worry on the part of Great Britain", a contradiction noted and commented upon by Col. Murray, G.S.O.1 (Int) at N.D.H.Q.[7]

On September 19th the Secretary of State, in a message to Canada, reviewed the background of British policy on Hong Kong, pointed out the improved defences in Malaya and the signs of weakening in Japan's attitude toward the U.S. and Britain, and stated his opinion that a small reinforcement would reassure Chiang Kai-shek and have a great morale effect throughout the Far East. He asked Canada for two battalions. Mr. King, in his capacity as Secretary of State for External Affairs, advised the Dominion Office that Canada agreed in principle to the request.[8] And the Winnipeg Grenadiers and Royal Rifles of Canada were duly sent to the Far East.

At that time, information was being received in External Affairs, in D.M.O.&I., and in the other Service Intelligence Directorates, but nowhere in the Canadian government was it consolidated and discussed. Most of what was received in M.I.1 was forwarded by C.M.H.Q. as part of its periodic Appreciation of the world situation (see Chapter 4). Mr. Anthony Eden had made an abortive attempt in May 1940 to establish a link between Ottawa and the Far Eastern Combined Intelligence Bureau at Singapore. This Bureau dealt mainly with the safeguarding of the local armed forces from espionage, sabotage, and subversion, and sought assistance in those fields from the rest of the Commonwealth. Since Canada had a link to Singapore through the R.C.N., the D.M.O.&I. suggested that relevant extracts from his own Summaries, together with any material from Pacific Command, could be added to the R.C.N.'s material. Both the R.C.N. and Pacific Command supported the idea, but nothing seems to have been done about implementing it.[9]

The Department of Transport radio monitoring service on Canada's west coast had been intercepting Japanese news broadcasts since December 22nd, 1940. Its reports were passed to the C.G.S., External Affairs, Naval, Air, and R.C.M.P. Intelligence, the Director of Public Information, the Districts, and, after May 1941, to the United Kingdom. In addition, at least one Intelligence Report was sent from Hong Kong. The C.G.S. did receive individual Intelligence items, but there were no regular and systematic Intelligence briefings. Nor, according to Col. C.P. Stacey, was a Far Eastern Appreciation ever requested of, or prepared by, the Canadian General Staff. If one had been prepared, it would have included an Intelligence paragraph, which is an essential part of any General Staff Appreciation. Intelligence available to Canada up to late September 1941 held that an outbreak of hostilities with Japan was not imminent. Prior to the departure of the force, no information was received to change that view. In fact, on October 26th, the day the force sailed, a wire from C.M.H.Q. said "Consensus opinion that war in Far East unlikely at present". That same wire provided a list of Japanese deployments in the Canton area, and gave the assessment that the most probable move by the Japanese would be against the Russians.[10]

This assessment was British, and there was no one at Army H.Q. who could have challenged it. In fact, the only man in the Canadian Army Intelligence Community with even the slightest claim to Far Eastern expertise was Lt.-Col. B.R. Mullaly, a former British Military Attaché in Tokyo, who had joined Pacific Command H.Q. as G.S.O.2 (Int). In late August 1941, he wrote a number of reports: the first dealt with the Japanese armed forces; those that followed contained general analyses of the Japanese situation. In his last report, written before the Canadian force sailed for Hong Kong, he discussed the implications of the appointment, on October 16th, of General Tojo as Premier. "Japan was standing at a cross-road." The Premier called for unity "to cope with the encirclement of Japan by foreign powers". Mullaly interpreted such rhetoric as the typical cry of an aggressor, and believed that, in the power struggle going on, Tojo and his government represented a victory for the Army over the moderates. He pointed out that:

> The ... war in China ... failed ... and the subsequent ... steps which Japan has taken ... have forced the British Empire and the United States to adopt measures which, if put into full operation, would threaten Japan's very existence. ... Japan finds herself enmeshed in the toils which her soldiers have woven about her and these same soldiers, who constantly preached that the only way out of the net is to cut the strands, are now seated more firmly than ever in the saddle.... The danger of direct action precipitating entry into the war ... is, therefore, undeniably great.

He went on to observe that it was late in the year for operations in Manchuria, and that the Japanese were vulnerable to air attack by the Russians. He saw indications of increased pressure on Thailand, and thought that Japan was continuing a war of nerves against the United States and Britain. But "... there are still grounds for hope that ... the new government will confine itself to all measures ... just short ... of war, while ... continuing redoubled efforts to arrive at a settlement of Japan's principal and most urgent commitment, namely the conflict with China."[11]

To criticize today the lack of a Canadian Intelligence contribution before deciding to send Canadians to Hong Kong is futile. Canada had neither the domestic resources nor the necessary machinery for obtaining information on foreign affairs. All assessments came from the British who, almost to the end of November, discounted the probability of an attack. Hindsight has proved them wrong, but Canadian Intelligence was in no position to do so at the time. The decision to send troops to Hong Kong was political, and it was taken in spite of reservations as to the dangers they might have to face.

Once committed, however, the troops should have had the best possible support and, in this regard, Intelligence was sadly remiss. Brig. Lawson, the Force Commander, in a report written shortly after he had arrived in Hong Kong, told the C.G.S. that they had arranged a series of lectures for officers and warrant officers on "conditions likely to be met in the Far East, races and religions, military geography, health in the tropics, characteristics of Indian Army troops likely to be met, and the Japanese Army". Shortly after they landed, they were given a briefing on the Japanese Army's weaknesses. British agencies in Hong Kong estimated there were only 5,000 enemy troops, ill equipped, with little artillery, unused to night fighting, and supported by obsolete aircraft flown by myopic pilots unable to dive-bomb. The Australian High Command, on the other hand, had taken quite a different look at the evidence. Before sending its forces to Malaya, it had issued a pamphlet warning that the Japanese were ruthless, and had good armament and technical training, great physical endurance, and few bodily requirements compared with British troops. Clearly the British error was not due to lack of evidence:

> The Military Attachés in Tokyo had for many years sent accurate reports to the War Office showing that the Japanese Army was a most efficient force. . . . It may have been the fact that they appeared unable to subdue the poorly-equipped Chinese forces that led to the belief, widespread throughout the Far East, that their armed forces were inefficient.[12]

In short, the Canadian troops were not provided, as they should have been, with adequate, accurate information on their opponent.

Toward the end of July 1941, Hong Kong learned of a large concentration of Japanese artillery in the area of Nam Tau and the Sham Chun River. Later Japanese successes further north led to claims at the end of October that 10 Chinese divisions had been lost and that "all the east coast railways, rivers and communications" were now under Japanese control. In early November, unusual activities were noted in the Canton area. The Japanese defensive perimeter was reported to be drawn in as if in expectation of an attack. What Allied attack could have been expected by the Japanese was not discussed, nor was mentioned the more likely possibility that the forces were being regrouped.[13]

On November 6th, the Japanese High Command ordered Gen. Hata to attack Hong Kong. Four days later a British agent reported that 18 tanks and 52 armoured cars, accompanied by motor transport, had moved near the frontier. On the 29th, Gen. Maltby's staff identified the presence of the Japanese *18th*, *48th*, and *104th Divisions*, with one medium brigade (regiment) of artillery and one tank battalion. He thought they had enough landing craft for a force of that size, but admitted that their actual numbers were unknown. No movement had been reported near the frontier. The actual Japanese force was the *Twenty-Third Army*, comprising *18th*, *38th*, *51st*, and *104th Divisions*, and one independent mixed brigade, a total of perhaps 90,000 men. They had additional artillery which Gen. Maltby's sources had not spotted.[14]

On December 3rd, the Japanese forces on the frontier withdrew slightly. On the 4th, Gen. Maltby stated his belief that they did not have sufficient forces in South China to attack the colony. On the 6th, three Japanese divisions were said to have moved to within eight miles of the frontier. "Despite this fact and other indications General Maltby was not yet convinced that war was imminent." He felt that reports that 10,000–20,000 troops were expected to move into the Nam Tau–Sham Chun Hu area for an attack on the colony were exaggerated; that they appeared to be propaganda spread by the Japanese to cover up their weakness in South China. He considered that their defence preparations around Canton indicated Japanese fears of attack. He did anticipate some reinforcement of frontier posts. In fact, the figure of 10,000–20,000 was surprisingly accurate. It comprised *38th Division* and a number of independent support units. The air support consisted of the *45th Air Regiment* and a detachment of the *5th Air Division*. In addition to this attack force there were four divisions in Canton, two in Indo-China, and one in Hainan. One infantry regiment, the *66th*, was deployed 40 miles northeast of Hong Kong to defend against any Chinese interference with the operation. It did not come into action.[15]

In the early morning of the 8th, Gen. Maltby's G.S.O.2 (Int), Maj. Charles Boxer, heard the Tokyo Radio announcer warn all Japanese nationals that war was imminent. Reports began to describe Japanese activity along the Sham Chun River. By 0730 all road and rail bridges over the river had been blown. The first Japanese air attack at 0800 destroyed the few British aircraft. The Japanese crossed the river using *230th* and *228th Regiments*, supported by three mountain artillery battalions in the west, and the *229th* in the east. A Japanese news broadcast on the 14th said: "It is anticipated they will have little difficulty in capturing the city."[16]

The Chinese talked of providing three Armies (each roughly equivalent to a British Division), but not until about January 10th. In the colony itself, there was no apparent reaction from the Chinese population to Japanese air-dropped propaganda leaflets, but there were reports that subversive elements were spreading alarmist rumours. On the 13th, Gen. Hata called on the garrison to surrender. The Japanese radio said: ". . . The offer was rejected and today the one million inhabitants of Hong Kong are subjected to the horrors of war due to the stupidity of the British Governor." On the 18th the radio announced that Japanese troops had landed on the island and were "attacking in all directions. . . . Japanese air units . . . caused much confusion among the populants [sic]". On the 25th, Station JZJ reported: ". . . the guns . . . ceased firing at five o'clock." On the 31st, Gen. Sakai (the intercept misheard his name as Takai), who then commanded *Twenty-Third Army*, was quoted as saying that the Indians and Canadians did all the fighting while all the British did was to "raise their hands and surrender."[17]

The British Official History points out that the Japanese had made full use of Strategic Intelligence:

> The Japanese assault on the Colony . . . was based upon accurate and detailed knowledge of the defences, troop dispositions and communications both on the mainland and on the island. This the enemy owed to his efficient Intelligence service, which had been in action for many years before the war and which took full advantage of the inadequacy of the British Security measures.
>
> The Japanese consular staff can have had little difficulty in making a full and accurate survey of the whole defense system including the detailed dispositions of troops when manning exercises were carried out. The special branch of the Hong Kong police was weak and the civil administration was slow to arrest or deport suspicious characters, some of whom were known to be enemy agents.

The History cites one example of this lack of ordinary caution. A Col. Suzuki, an exchange officer in Hong Kong to learn English, was not taking his lessons. When the British military authorities pointed this out, the Japanese Consul-General admitted that the colonel did not have time to study because of the pressure of his duties as an Intelligence officer working in the Chungking and South China areas. Asked whether he should be expelled, the Foreign Office, fearing that the Japanese might take an actual expulsion as an affront, suggested that action be delayed until Col. Suzuki went on leave. It would be easier to prevent his return than to evict him.[18]

During the battle, the Japanese had almost undisturbed opportunities for air reconnaissance and for artillery observation. Gen. Maltby lacked all means of reconnaissance and the means to use information he did receive. He was compelled to disperse his garrison over the whole of the perimeter because he could not identify the axes of the enemy advance. Such significant casualties occurred during the action that it was impossible to control and to direct his counter-attacks.

The Intelligence failure to protect the military secrets of the colony before the outbreak of war and to evaluate correctly the situation as Japan moved towards war, and the political decision which left the Hong Kong garrison unsupported in an untenable position (rather than withdrawing them), were

British, not Canadian. D.M.O.&I. knew too little of the situation because Canada had no means of obtaining its own unfiltered information on potential combat zones. Ottawa could not and did not provide adequate information to the men it sent there to fight, and that, in itself, is a condemnation of our lack of preparedness during peacetime.

NEWFOUNDLAND ("W" FORCE)

Newfoundland was an area of great strategic importance because of its forward position in the Atlantic and its use as a landfall for international communications. A Canadian force was stationed there from June 1940. In September, the Americans were given leases on the bases in the colony. Both national Commands continued to function independently while agreeing to co-operate in any emergency. First it was made a major-general's responsibility and then, in March 1942, a sub-command of Atlantic Command. The Commander had a Joint Intelligence Committee (J.I.C.) that included representatives of each of the Services. The U.S. Army and Navy I.O.s failed for some time to attend meetings of the J.I.C., and steps had to be taken to get them to do so.

Capt. R.H. Haskins, the first G.S.O.3, was responsible for an Operations Room at Command H.Q. as well as for recruiting and training its staff. Their principal duty was to maintain a Submarine Location Map. Because submarine sightings produced an increase in radio transmissions from the Portuguese fishing fleet, Capt. Haskins instituted, in July 1942, his own Wireless Intercept Service of amateur radio monitors to augment the regular Navy coverage. He was also responsible for Passive Air Defence. Each major Defence area and major unit had its own I.O., but unit I (a) duties were minor: stereoscopic examination of aerial photos to check the camouflage of gun positions and the supply of maps, mostly based on air photographs.

Security was busy. It handled postal censorship, counter-subversion, control of photography, control of prohibited areas, rumours, and morale. In Newfoundland, the regulations and the ways of interpreting them differed slightly from those in force in Canada. In the case of Censorship, a close working relationship had to be developed with Maj. Haig-Smith, Chief Censor of Newfoundland. A later G.S.O.3, Capt. J.C. Baker found himself in disagreement with the Newfoundland Secretary for the Department of Justice over areas where photography would be prohibited. In such cases, a compromise was reached by taking the best from both sets of regulations.

On October 7th, 1942, Capt. Haskins began to issue a Weekly Intelligence Summary. It gave submarine locations, ship torpedoings, and rumours, cited civilians who had come to the attention of Intelligence, and reported on breaches of Postal Censorship, passes, and morale. His "parish" included St. Pierre and

Miquelon (held by Free French forces) where the Aluminum Company of Canada's fluorspar mine was a potential target for saboteurs. He also had to watch occasional labour unrest for enemy agent overtones. When the Command was abolished on October 30th, 1944, the Section was disbanded.[19]

KISKA

The capture of Kiska, on June 11th, 1942, was part of Tokyo's grand strategic plan to widen the Japanese defensive perimeter and to forestall the use of the Aleutian Islands as stepping stones to the Kurile Islands. Its subsidiary aim, more political than military, was to provide propaganda showing that American territory had been occupied. Strategically, Kiska was a dead end. The weather makes air and sea operations difficult at best. It was not a base from which to launch a serious attack on the North American west coast. Similarly, even if the Americans had attempted to strike at Japan from it through the northern islands, conditions would increasingly have favoured the Japanese defence. The enemy presence, however, caused the inhabitants of Alaska, British Columbia, and the American Pacific Coast states to exert a great deal of political pressure to ensure that forces were available for their defence.

The U.S. decided instead to contain the islands and, except for air operations (in which the R.C.A.F. played a role) and minor naval activity, nothing was done until 1943. On May 11th, the American Seventh Division attacked Attu. The Japanese defenders, resisting bitterly, lost 2,350 killed and 24 prisoners. Operations against Kiska were approved at the "Trident" Conference in Washington, on May 24th, 1943.[20] The possibility of Canadian Army assistance had already been broached by Gen. De Witt, the American commander responsible for the theatre, when he visited Maj.-Gen. G.R. Pearkes, V.C., in Vancouver on April 19th. Gen. Pearkes merely reported the conversation without comment. A suggestion that Canada might participate came also from Mr. J.D. Hickerson, Secretary of the American Section of the Permanent Joint Board of Defence, in a conversation with Canada's representative in Washington, Lieut.-Gen. Maurice Pope; it was reported to Ottawa on May 10th. On the 11th, the C.G.S. asked Gen. Pearkes if it was "too late to consider some form of army participation". On May 24th Gen. De Witt asked for an infantry battalion and a light anti-aircraft battery to be available by June 15th, and a brigade for offensive operations to move to Alaska on August 1st for training. Formal approval for the despatch of the brigade group – 13th Infantry Brigade – was given on May 31st; the request for an additional infantry battalion was not pursued. The expedition was given the code name GREENLIGHT and Brig. H.W. Foster was brought back from England to be its commander.[21] Pacific Command did most of the planning for the actual move and M.I.1 supplied some of the information.

18. Kiska

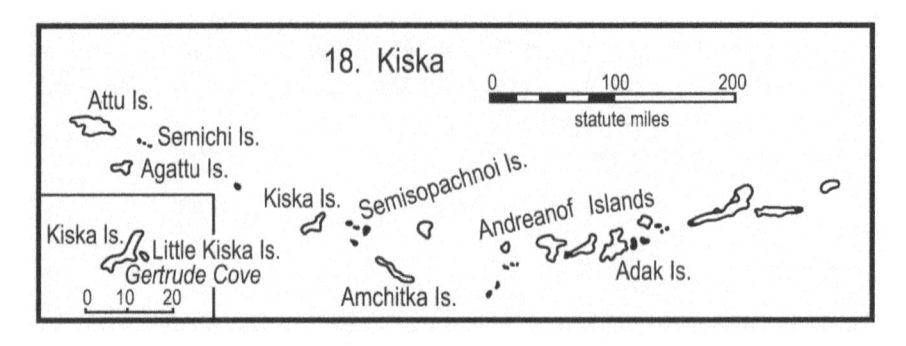

Attu Is., Semichi Is., Agattu Is., Kiska Is., Semisopachnoi Is., Andreanof Islands, Kiska Is., Little Kiska Is., Gertrude Cove, Amchitka Is., Adak Is.

0 100 200 statute miles

On June 12th, Col. Murray asked Gen. Pearkes for information on the security arrangements, the cover plan, and the links already established with the United States. He suggested that Security be included in the training program, that Security Officers be appointed in each unit, that mail censorship be imposed on all ranks up to platoon commanders, and that 100% censorship should be imposed in the Courtenay area (where the force was to concentrate and train); he also pointed out that it would be necessary to brief the Regional Press Censor at Vancouver. He suggested that a Deception Committee be established to work with N.D.H.Q. in order to produce fictitious messages from Operations, Signals, and Intelligence. Col. Murray was invited on the 12th to discuss his points in detail at Pacific Command. His advice was acted upon immediately. The already tight security was at once reinforced. "A" Branch, Sixth Division, for instance, forgot to classify a message; the offender received a personal reprimand from the C.G.S. through Gen. Pearkes. On the 14th, Ottawa was told that the training program included a deception plan "to test certain U.S. equipment and to find how a brigade group could fit into U.S. Combat Teams", and that it had been cleared with Gen. De Witt. The first phase would soon be completed and "it was hoped to train further with a group now at San Diego". They knew that this deception plan might not be entirely effective, but that Security could more easily be imposed in Alaska. Unit censorship was already in force as a training measure and Pacific Command asked that civilian censorship be advised.[22]

On June 15th, 1943, M.I.1 issued Japanese Information Extract No. 25. This contained what was known about order-of-battle and weapons estimates; the size of the Aleutian task force was thought to be 10,000. On the same day, the Pacific Command Intelligence Section used American material, dated May 1943, to produce a well-documented and detailed eight-page Summary, complete with maps and sketches; it included the six areas where Japanese were known to be stationed. Five were around the perimeter of Kiska harbour, one was at Gertrude Cove. There were also a few installations on Little Kiska. The Summary gave a history of these defensive positions and warned that they were being continuously developed. No detailed order-of-battle was available until mid-July and no position /manning estimates were provided.[23]

On June 16th, Col. Murray arrived to prepare the Security plan with Col. Mullaly; they requested air photo coverage, additional maps, and gridded photo-mosaics. Capt. E.S. Gladwin, the first F.S.O. selected, was not able to pass the medical examination; he was replaced by Capt. H. Peter Grauer of 6 F.S. Capt. Grauer's new Section, No. 13 (later renumbered 19 F.S.S.), had a C.S.M. (J. Mills) and five N.C.O.s from Pacific Command S.I.S. Unit censorship was imposed on all units in Nanaimo, Courtenay, and Comox. On the 19th, officers were ordered to carry identification cards. On the 22nd, Pacific Command made arrangements with Washington for Japanese linguists (Canada had none). On the 23rd, the Americans advised that all the Japanese aircraft on the island had been destroyed, and raised the estimate of total enemy strength to 11,000. On the 24th, Pacific Command agreed that the senior Canadian I.O. would be, in American terminology, an S-2. Maj. J.L. Black was appointed, with Capt. A.F.P. (Pat) Freeman as his I.O.; Black, however, was soon moved to a liaison post at the Military Task Force H.Q. and Pat Freeman covered the vacancy.[24]

Embarkation began at Nanaimo on July 8th, and the force sailed on the 12th. The Pacific Coast S.I.S., working closely with the R.C.M.P., sent patrols to collect personal mail and to keep close watch on the port area. Similar precautions were taken at the camp at Chemainus. Rumours of multiple desertions and of coercion of embarking troops were so frequent after the move that the Prime Minister demanded a report. On August 5th Brig. Macklin, acting for the Adjutant-General, was able to deny categorically that any troops had been marched on board at gunpoint (equally ill-founded report had them in handcuffs). All men carried their own weapons and only normal guards were posted in the dock area. Other stories spoke of multiple desertions from the Régiment de Hull; in fact, it had the smallest number, six in all. In the entire force, a total of one sergeant and 164 other ranks deserted.[25] Press Censorship was successful. Once the force arrived in Alaska, it became a U.S. Navy responsibility.

The Brigade disembarked at Adak on July 21st to begin its advanced training. Intelligence began to issue a daily Summary on the 27th, giving the enemy situation. It also gave information on activities in other theatres, to counteract the feeling of isolation. On August 8th, Gen. Pearkes arrived to set up his advanced Command H.Q. Fog continuously hampered air reconnaissance and, on July 26th and August 2nd, made all flights impossible. The Japanese were assumed to have their main positions in the hills, but reconnaissance had found new earthworks and foxholes around the beaches and in the centre of the island. Air reconnaissance had not been able to "determine which, if any, of these positions" were actually occupied "as the enemy has kept himself concealed and withheld his fire whenever our planes have been over".[26]

On the night of August 10th, no return fire was observed; on the 11th, some A.A. fire was reported; on Little Kiska, some movement and flak were observed on the 12th; on the 13th, no enemy activity. The invasion force landed on the 15th in fog. There was some confusion, tension led to shooting, and it took some time for the force to realize that the island was empty. In fact, the Japanese had slipped away on July 28th. Contrary to statements made at the time, Japanese records show that they had not even left a rear party, although they did leave delay-fused demolitions. Force Intelligence should have noticed the halt in normal wireless traffic from the island. The Official Historian excuses the Intelligence lapse by saying that the Japanese were ingenious and tricky. But Intelligence is only as good as its human sources, and it is well known that men often report what they expect to see. The A.A. fire the pilots reported was expected, and any enemy positions seen would quite honestly have been assumed to be occupied. On November 27th, 1943, Pacific Command was advised that the advance party would return to Vancouver on December 1st. Gen. Pearkes asked for a Censorship stop to be maintained until the whole Brigade was back.[27]

In its post-operational analysis, the American Intelligence community and the U.S.A.A.F. felt that interpretation should have started earlier and that more and better maps should have been available. They recommended that a Joint Intelligence agency be formed to coordinate the Intelligence from all three Services. As a matter of fact, Canada had had one in Ottawa since November 24th, 1942, and another on the Pacific Coast to perform precisely that function. On the whole, however, and despite the obvious mistakes, the pre-operational Intelligence participation was markedly better than it had been for Hong Kong. The fact that the tactical Intelligence was still so poor must be attributed principally to lack of experience.

CANADIAN ARMY PACIFIC FORCE (C.A.P.F.)

About the beginning of 1944, Ottawa began seriously to discuss what contribution might be made to the war in the Pacific. In May 1944, Mr. Mackenzie King went to the Conference of Commonwealth Prime Ministers with a rather vague General Staff Appreciation, which suggested that Canadian troops could be used in Burma, Malaya, Hawaii, or the Aleutians, but the discussions it provoked were inconclusive. About the end of June, the British War Council asked if Canada could provide one division and some corps troops, including one divisional and one corps F.S. Section. It repeated the request, in broader terms, in an aide memoire to the Canadian Chiefs of Staff on July 24th.[28]

The Chiefs reviewed the aide memoire, and on September 6th, 1944, recommended that one division, with ancillary troops, be employed under American command in the northern or central Pacific area. The Cabinet agreed and, by the end of November, approved a force of 30,000 to be drawn from men serving overseas. A recommendation on September 16th that it be reorganized on

American lines was submitted to the U.S. in April 1945. The War Department agreed, and the restructuring was started. The new formation, designated as Sixth Division, began to recruit volunteers from First Canadian Army.[29]

The American Table of Organization and Establishment called for a divisional Intelligence component of 22 officers and 94 other ranks, plus six artillery observer pilots and a military interpreter team of two officers. Lt.-Col. P.W. Cook, in Washington, warned that the force had to be trained and concentrated by September 15th. He asked for a cadre of 19 officers and 27 other ranks to take courses in the U.S., starting on July 15th. This was quite impossible; trained people could not be brought back from Europe by that time, and there were none in Canada. Nor was there a school. D.M.I. had to find new personnel and send them to Camp Ritchie, in Maryland, for basic Intelligence training. Ottawa advised London that the total requirement was 46 officers and 83 other ranks, and asked that as many men as possible be sent back.[30]

An Order-of-Battle Team of one officer and two other ranks, and a Photo Interpreter Team of two officers and five men were formed, effective June 12th, 1945, and were concentrated at Brockville. On July 9th, it was discovered that in an American division even the Medical Battalion had an officer who did nothing but Intelligence. The D.G.M.S. was asked to appoint someone to this onerous post and send him to Camp Ritchie. Col. Felix Walter was somewhat overwhelmed by the total requirement, by now 201 all ranks, and, though promising help, frankly stated that men in Europe showed little enthusiasm for service in the Pacific.[31]

On July 25th, the Division learned for the first time that all personnel for Intelligence duties did not have to be Intelligence Corps. Specialists were needed only in the Counter-Intelligence, Field Security, Language, Order-of-Battle, and Photo Intelligence Teams. Some of these personnel were now named: the Order-of-Battle Team comprised Lieuts. C.T. Penny and B.H. Fleming, both R.C.E.; and Sgts. G.C. Cook, R.C.A., and J.J. McDougall, C.A.C. The Photo Interpreter Team comprised Capts. E.A.R. Sutton and D.F. Cameron, and Lieuts. J.D. Sutherland and F.C. Sehull; all had overseas experience, but none had served with 1 A.P.I.S. The linguists were to be provided by the Americans as there were none available in Canada.[32]

The Japanese surrender on August 4th brought all preparations to an abrupt halt. The Canadian contribution in the Far East did not end, however, with the demise of the C.A.P.F. For the most part it involved individuals, not formed units (their activities will be described later), but there was one formed Intelligence unit, the Special Wireless Unit, which served in Australia.

SPECIAL WIRELESS UNIT – AUSTRALIA

In May 1944, the Commander-in-Chief of the Indian Army asked Canada to supply a special Signals and Intelligence Unit, with its equipment, "to intercept transmissions from Tokyo which could not be heard in Canada" (actually Japanese military radio messages). The Indian Army was not qualified, or able to qualify, in the field. The request was approved by the War Cabinet on June 7th; the War Establishment was approved on June 5th and authorized by the Minister on July 19th. The Signals element establishment was 13 officers, 278 men; the establishment for the Wireless Group Intelligence Section component was six officers (captains or lieutenants), one W.O.II., one staff-sergeant clerk, four sergeants, 15 corporals and 15 lance-corporals (all clerks, Special Intelligence), two batmen, and one driver, R.C.A.S.C., for a total Section all rank strength of 45. Some of the specialists came from the first course at S-20, the Army Japanese Language School in Vancouver (see Chapter 15); the remainder had to be trained, and a short course was arranged for the others.

The Group was to form by July 1st, 1944, and to move overseas in two stages, one on October 1st and a second one two months later. On June 30th, the Directorate of Organization asked that formation of the first group be deferred until August 15th, and that formation of the second group be delayed until March 1st, 1945. This request reflected, quite clearly, the current pressures on the manpower pool; the Signals personnel were simply not available. The Intelligence unit at Ottawa from which the specialists were to come (No. 1 Discrimination Unit) was already understrength, and had many low-category and over-age men who could not be sent abroad; the few who were available could not be released until replacements were found.

In late August, the War Office complicated matters further by asking that their despatch be deferred until after two opposing demands by Australia and India were reconciled. Approval to send them to Australia instead was sought on October 3rd and granted on October 23rd. The Adjutant General managed to select three Intelligence officers (two of them, Burns and Larkin, were still unqualified), five senior N.C.O.s, and 13 junior N.C.O.s. After some training in Ottawa, the group went to Victoria, where the Signals element had been located since mid-August.

On January 13th, they left via Seattle, and Camp Stoneman, where on January 20th they were embarked on the U.S.A.T. *Monteray*. On February 4th, they entered Finschafen Harbour, New Guinea. From there they went to Hollandia, where they were transferred to the U.S.A.T. *Shawnee*. The ship was filthy with lice, bedbugs, and cockroaches, and their first two days aboard were spent disinfecting and cleaning their quarters. On February 16th they docked at Brisbane, where they were met by the advance party under Lieut. Larkin.

They spent the next two months in Chermside camp, organizing and training, and on April 4th set out for Darwin. Their first shift went to work on April 30th and, on May 18th, they took over from the Australian Special Wireless Group intercepting and analysing Japanese military morse. The rear party, consisting of 12 Intelligence Corps specialists, left Vancouver April 9th, via Los Angeles and Melbourne, and arrived in Darwin on May 31st.

After the war in the Pacific ended, arrangements were made to have the unit returned to Canada. At that time, as we shall see, the Department wished to investigate crimes against Canadian P.W. who had been in Japanese hands. In September, six members of the Intelligence Section – Capt. K.C. Woodsworth and Lieut. A.C. Burns, S/Sgt. L.P. Van Ert, Cpls. C.D. Barrett and R.M. Ewing, and Pte. O.K. Hartwell – went to the Canadian Repatriation Group in Manila. Four N.C.O.s, Sgts. T.H.H. Bourne and L.D. Olmstead, and Cpls. D.M. Rogers and W.S. Veale, were sent to the Canadian Recovery Team, Japan, to assist in investigations; they returned to Canada late in 1945. The cryptographers, traffic analysts, and administrative personnel were returned to Canada at various times. On February 27th, 1946, the unit was disbanded, and Pacific Command took over the administration of the few personnel still in Australia.

14.
OFF THE BEATEN TRACK

CLANDESTINE OPERATIONS

British clandestine operations were controlled by three agencies. The largest, the Ministry of Economic Warfare's Special Operations Executive (S.O.E.), also called Special Forces, dealt with active sabotage and subversion within enemy-controlled areas. The Chiefs of Staff controlled its operational deployment, but, when the preparation for D-Day began, they delegated some of their control to Gen. Morgan, C.O.S.S.A.C. After the landings, Gen. Koenig, commander of the French Forces of the Interior under S.H.A.E.F., took over from C.O.S.S.A.C. Elsewhere, S.O.E. operations were decentralized to theatre Supreme Commanders, so that they could co-ordinate clandestine activities with regular operations.[1] The second agency, formed under M.I.9 at the War Office during the winter of 1939–40, recovered and evacuated Allied servicemen who had evaded, or escaped from, capture by the enemy. It began to operate in 1941 and to develop agent networks in neutral and occupied countries. A third agency, controlled by the Political Intelligence Department (P.I.D.) of the British Foreign Office, was responsible for all aspects of psychological (political) warfare. As far as Canada was concerned, the P.I.D. worked with the Department of External Affairs, through the Canadian High Commissioner in London.[2]

On March 12th, 1940, a representative from the War Office asked C.M.H.Q. if it would care to nominate personnel for duties "as irregular leaders or guerrilla warfare jobs". They would be taught the political and social background of certain European countries and would serve as a pool of trained men for political missions into foreign countries, "especially at the end of the war when conditions may be somewhat chaotic". After discussing their legal status, Gen. McNaughton ruled that Canadians would not participate in the program.[3]

In 1941, the British secured an agreement allowing them to recruit Canadians from units in Britain. For Security reasons, their only link was to be the senior Intelligence officer at C.M.H.Q. Later, the British Security Co-ordinator in New York was allowed to deal, through the Department of External Affairs, with the Directorate of Staff Duties at N.D.H.Q., which, in turn, worked closely with D.M.I. The administration was also unnecessarily complex. Originally, volunteers were discharged from the Canadian Army, and re-enlisted into S.O.E. However, in the interests of Security, the British kept their paper work to a minimum, and volunteers subsequently found themselves neglected in matters such as pay, promotion, and medical attention. By the end of 1942, a more reasonable arrangement attached such volunteers for a six-month "loan", which could be extended if required. In May 1944, the Canadian Treasury accepted the responsibility for their pay. Additional allowances, peculiar to the clandestine organization concerned, were paid by the organization itself, and were not considered by Canadian authorities either as pay or for record.

Most volunteers were trained both in Canada and in Britain. Those who were to be employed in the Mediterranean area had additional training in North Africa and in Italy. Those who went to the Far East received instruction at special schools in India, Ceylon, and Australia. The nature and length of the training depended on the duties and experience of the individual, but unarmed combat, explosives, small arms, parachuting, and detail on the operational area were included. Other rank volunteers who were to be dropped into Occupied Europe were commissioned on graduation, because it was thought the *Gestapo* would be more reluctant to torture or execute agents who were officers. The assumption was found to be wrong, but it was wise to ensure that no reasonable safeguard was overlooked.

The Canadian School, S.T.S. 103 (HYDRA), was set up at an old farm outside Oshawa in December 1941, as a result of discussions between Col. Lindsay of the British Army and Commissioner Wood, R.C.M.P. Subsequent negotiations brought it under the wing of the Department of National Defence (Staff Duties). Its initial establishment called for seven officers and 26 other ranks. The instructors were British, and Britain paid the costs of running the School, so the courses were based on and closely followed the British doctrine. Oshawa's main advantage was the fact that, unlike the British schools, instruction in all aspects of the operative's duties could be conducted in one area. Also, if the recruit was not suitable he could be easily returned to the Canadian Service environment. The first group, who were to go to the Balkans on S.O.E. duty, totalled 16. The courses were also attended by members of the F.B.I., Office of Wartime Information (O.W.I.), and selected Canadian and American Service officers and men. Until 1942, when the American Office of Strategic Services (O.S.S.) was formed, and before it built its own training facilities, Oshawa also trained American operatives, and briefed O.S.S. staff officers on the nature and requirements of special operations.[4] By the end of the war some 500 had gone through, on 52 courses. By August 1944, the School had a strength of three officers, 60 other ranks, and 27 civilians, and represented an unnecessary expense. It finally closed in September 1944, and all its material was passed to the O.S.S.

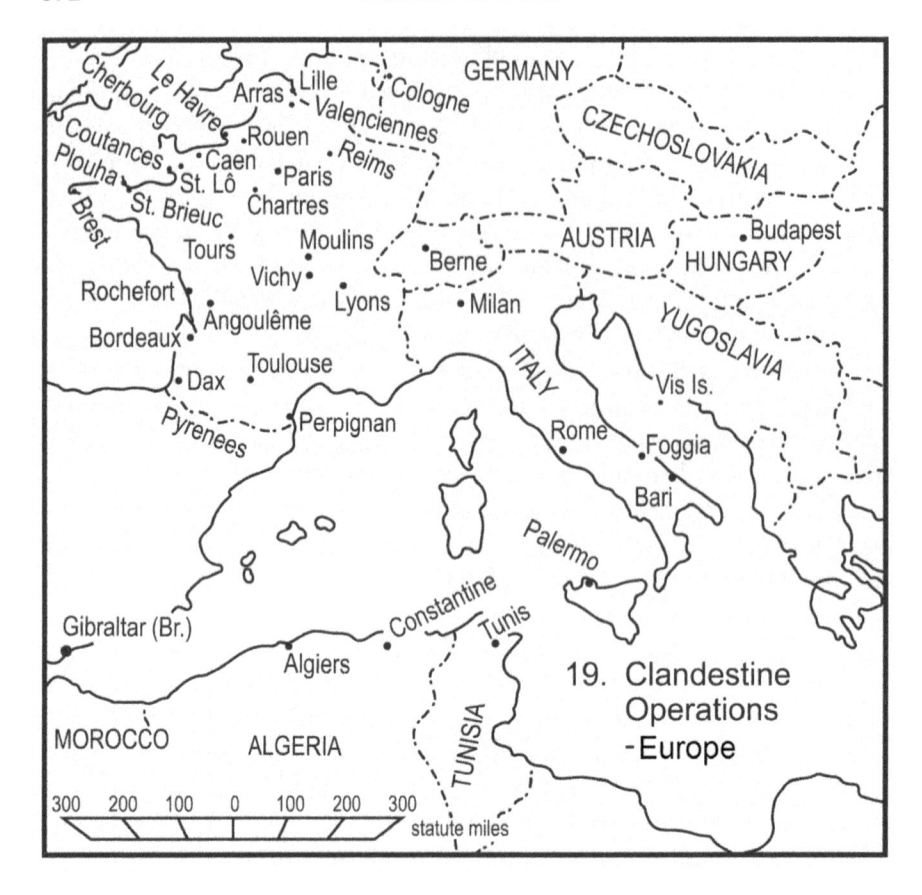

S.O.E. – France

The first Canadian to serve on S.O.E. operations, was Capt., later Maj., Gustave "Guy" D.A. Biéler, of Le Régiment de Maisonneuve.* Guy joined S.O.E. in early April 1942, completed his training, and, with Capt. Michel Trotobas, was dropped on November 25th near Montargis, in the northeastern part of the Ile de France region. Unfortunately, he made a bad landing, injuring his back on rocky ground. Unable even to walk properly, he spent the first months of his brief career in a Paris hospital under an assumed name. In February 1943, though still not well, he made his way to his district – Lille–St. Quentin–Arras –Valenciennes – derailing a troop train at Senlis on the way. Though still in pain

---

* Second edition note: Deployed to the U.K. with his regiment in 1940, Capt. Biéler "became his battalion's intelligence officer." He was talent-spotted by a member of the S.O.E. while liaising with the British War Office in this capacity. See Roy MacLaren, *Canadians Behind Enemy Lines 1939–45* (Vancouver and London: University of British Columbia, 1981), p. 29.

Maj. Gustave "Guy" D.A. Biéler, D.S.O., M.B.E.; below is the 'French identity card' issued by the S.O.E. before he parachuted into Occupied France in November 1942. In memory of his wartime exploits and sacrifice, a new training facility at the Canadian Forces School of Military Intelligence in Kingston was formally named in his honour on 12 September 2014. (Photos courtesy of Jacqueline Biéler/Canada. Dept. of National Defence)

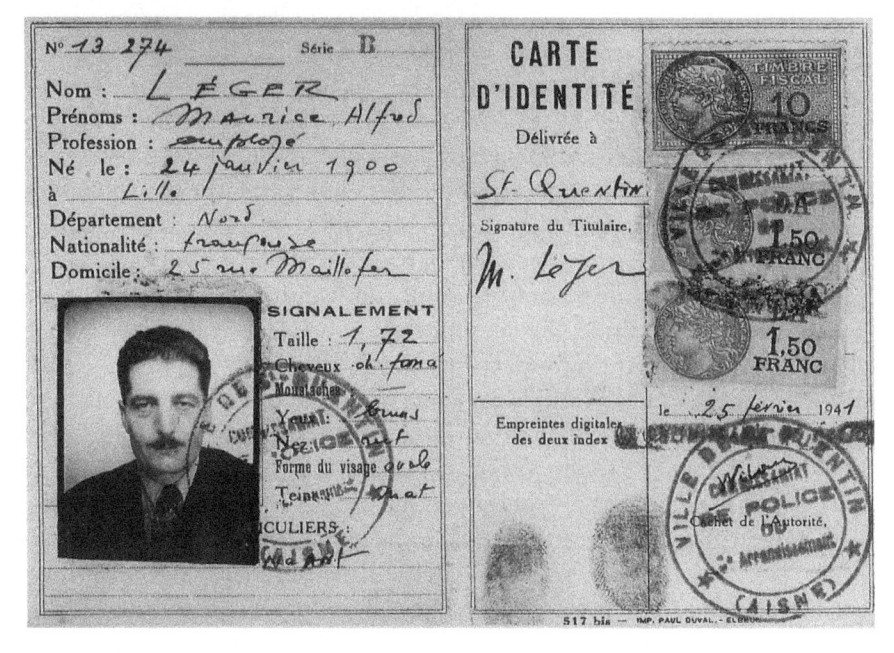

and unable to stand for more than five or six hours a day, he refused an offer to fly him out, and concentrated on building up his sub-network. In May, he and his French colleagues cut the rail lines between Paris and Cologne 13 times. By the second half of 1943, his teams were cutting the St. Quentin–Lille lines about once every two weeks. The close liaison he formed with French railway officials enabled him to identify those targets that would cause the greatest delays – signal boxes, switches, and communication links. Since St. Quentin lies in the heart of the canal system of northwestern France, Capt. Biéler was dropped a supply of limpet mines and explosives. He attached them to three of the principal locks near St. Quentin and, with two assistants, successfully laid time fuses and explosives in about 40 loaded barges. During the autumn of 1943, Guy and his team concentrated on the preparation of future targets; they hit a few minor installations, mainly to keep in practice. His abrasive greases crippled 10 locomotives during this period.

Biéler's radio link went out when his own master network closed in June 1943 and, although his action increased the security risk for both groups, he used the facilities of another one. On September 17th, he was sent his own operator, Yolande Beekman, a Swiss. Early in October she set up her transmitter in the home of Mme. Odette Gobeaux, 18 rue de la Fère, St. Quentin.

Yolande had been given a rigid transmission schedule. She came on the air from the same spot at the same time on the same three days of the week. The theory was that it was less dangerous to use a well-hidden set than to attempt to move it about. Also, strict schedules were helpful to the monitors at H.Q. The German Security Service Direction Finding (D.F.) teams pinpointed her location and began surveillance. On January 13th or 14th 1944, Guy and Yolande were in the Café Moulin Brûlé in St. Quentin, when the *Gestapo* struck.

They were taken to Paris, to *Gestapo* H.Q., located, ironically enough, at 13 *bis*, Place des Etats-Unis. Here Guy was tortured, brutally and repeatedly, but gave no information to his captors. In April, he was taken to Flossenbürg concentration camp in Germany, where he was locked in a narrow cell in solitary confinement, denied writing materials or reading matter, and fed daily on two cups of black ersatz coffee, a bowl of soup, and slightly less than six and a half ounces of bread. He made such an impression on his jailers that when, on or about September 5th, he limped to the firing squad, the *S.S.* mounted a guard of honour to escort him. Yolande Beekman was detained at Fresnes, Karlsruhe, and finally Dachau, where she also was executed in September. Major Guy Biéler was awarded the D.S.O., the M.B.E., and the Croix de Guerre with Palm. In the little village of Fonsommes, near St. Quentin, a street now bears his name.

Chronologically, the next Canadian to see service in Occupied France was Lieut., later Capt., J.C.G. Chartrand, also of the Régiment de Maisonneuve before he became Intelligence (Censorship). He was taken to France by *Lysander* aircraft in mid-April 1943, with his organizer, Philippe Liewer. They set up in Rouen, but Chartrand later joined another group working the region from Rouen to Le Havre. The *Gestapo* was active in this area, and he was spotted. He managed to escape, and moved to Paris. His companions were arrested in early September, and Chartrand was withdrawn via one of the escape lines. He left France on the night of November 15th.

Between June 1943 and March 1944, no fewer than eight Canadian agents were sent in. They were: Lieut., later Capt., F.H.D. Pickersgill, C.Int.C.*, Capt. J.K. Macallister, Lieut. Beauregard (General List, formerly R. de Mais.), Lieut. (later Capt.) R.M. Caza (formerly R.C.C.S.), Capt. F.A. Deniset, R.C.A., Lieut. (later Capt.) L.A.J. Sirois, R.C.C.S., Lieut. R. Sabourin, R.C.C.S., formerly F.M.R., and Lieut. R. Byerley, R.C.C.S., an American.

Pickersgill and Macallister were dropped on June 15th, 1943, at Sologne, in the Cher valley. On the 21st, with two French companions, they set off by car for Beaugency on the Loire, intending to take the train from there to Paris. They were stopped by a police control at Dhuizon village, their two companions tried to run, and the party was captured.** *They were taken to Gestapo prisons in Paris and tortured. Pickersgill, during one of his interrogations, stunned his guards with a bottle, killing two of them, and jumped from a second-storey window and ran off. He was chased, shot, badly wounded, patched-up and eventually sent to Rawitsch concentration camp in Poland in April 1944.*

During this period, the Germans, using Macallister's wireless transmitter set, and others that had been captured, lured S.O.E to drop more men, including one Rabinovitch, and Lieut. Sabourin at the beginning of March 1944. They heard German voices, slipped into the nearby woods, killed two Germans, and were wounded and finally captured.

Having become increasingly suspicious over time that Pickersgill and his transmitter had fallen into enemy hands, S.O.E. devised a test; a message was sent to Pickersgill, directing him to use an S-phone – essentially a walkie-talkie – to contact an overhead aircraft that would be circling near Châlons-sur-Marne on May 8th. The Germans hoped to use Pickersgill's 'voice' to reassure S.O.E.; they even later brought him to Paris to entice him to cooperate. However, he steadfastly refused to do so. He was finally sent to Buchenwald on August 8th. The trip took seven days, spent entirely without food or water and, to add to the horror, the train

---

* Second edition note: Frank Pickersgill was commissioned in November 1942 as a Lieut. in the C.Int.C. A civilian living in France at the time of the German invasion in 1940, Pickersgill was interned as an enemy alien for nearly two years before managing to escape and making his way to Britain via Vichy France, and neutral Spain and Portugal. Impressed with his story of escape, the British War Office approached him in October 1942 to join S.O.E. and subsequently asked Canada to grant him a commission so that he could be "loaned" and begin his training in January 1943. Roy MacLaren, *Canadians Behind Enemy Lines 1939–45* (Vancouver and London: University of British Columbia, 1981), p. 44–49; Jonathan F. Vance, *Unlikely Soldiers: How Two Canadians Fought the Secret War Against Nazi Occupation* (Toronto: HarperCollins Publishers Ltd, 2008), pp. 100–106.

** Second edition note: Sentences in italics highlight updates to the first edition's account of Capt. Pickersgill's days in captivity, based on Vance's, *Unlikely Soldiers*, which was published in 2008 in the wake of newly opened S.O.E. files. See pp. 228, 234–236.

was attacked by R.A.F. aircraft near Châlons-sur-Marne. On September 9th, *with Macallister* and 14 others, he was hanged. Capt. Pickersgill was awarded a posthumous Mention-in-Despatches (M.I.D).

Lieut. Beauregard, dropped in either January or February 1944, served as a wireless operator in the Tours area until June. London had become aware that the *Gestapo* were making efforts to D.F. his set, and he was ordered to stop transmitting. Choosing to take the risk, he and his assistant were surrounded and overpowered after a ten-minute fight, during which they destroyed their set and all the codes. He was executed at Fort Montluc, near Lyons, on August 20th, 1944. He also was awarded a posthumous M.I.D.

Capt. Deniset was dropped on the night of February 7th. Until July, he operated near Chartres, and was particularly successful in harassing railway communications. Lieut. Byerley had been dropped near Deniset in February, but his reception committee had been *Gestapo*-infiltrated, and he disappeared. No confirmed report of his fate could be found.

Capt. R.M. Caza was dropped into the Lyonnais area early in February 1944. His station was to be at Toulouse, but the Germans were becoming terribly proficient at 'DFing' S.O.E. wireless transmissions. Caza found he had to move every 10 days, even though each move entailed heavy risks and a need to build up contacts in a new area. He was awarded the M.B.E. and the French Croix de Guerre, with Palm. Capt. Sirois was dropped near Tarbes on March 2nd, 1944. He helped rebuild a network that had been badly damaged, joined it to another group, and operated between Angoulême and the coast near Rochefort until the Allied forces arrived on October 4th. He too was awarded the M.B.E.

Eight Canadians were dropped into France just before and just after D-Day. They were: Maj. John H. Wickey (R.C.A.C.); Capts. J.P. Archambault (General List), P.C.M. Meunier and P.E. Thibeault (Fusiliers Mont-Royal), and L.J. Taschereau (Régiment de la Chaudière); and Lieuts. J.H.A. Benoit, L.G. D'Artois, and M. Veilleux.

Archambault and Meunier were both dropped in the first two weeks of April, the former near Lyons and the latter near Bordeaux. Capt. Archambault was successful in forming and leading sabotage groups in the Department of the Ain until his groups were overrun by the U.S. 7th Army. He was awarded the M.C. Capt. Meunier changed his cover story and assumed the role of an Inspector of Police. This gave him wonderful opportunities for travel, and enabled him to train sabotage groups as far south as Arcachon and Dax. However, his entanglement with local Gascon political issues ultimately forced him to beat a hasty retreat over the Pyrenees. Before doing so, he successfully blew up cables in Bordeaux harbour. With the blessing of Gen. Koenig, he was dropped again, this time near Vichy. He achieved his objective, which was to induce the German garrison of Moulins to surrender, by persuading the Swiss Ambassador to go with him to help convince the German Commander.

Maj. Benoit was dropped into the Rheims–Epernay area at the end of May 1944. He successfully reconnoitred the V-1 dumps in the Champagne area and, on two occasions, cut the important Rheims–Berlin telephone cable. He came within a hair of being captured when his driver talked too much in a tavern and was arrested by the *Gestapo*. Maj. Benoit was awarded the M.B.E.

The activities of Maj. John H. Wickey offer one of the few examples of deliberate clandestine Intelligence collection. John Wickey, a Swiss who spoke fluent French and German, was recruited by S.O.E. in early 1944, and assigned to M.I.6 (the agency responsible for such collection). In May 1944, he was landed south of Sieze, in the Department of Sarthe. He then went to Argentan on a collection task that is still classified, and then to subsidiary tasks of obtaining information on troop trains and V-1 launching sites, and on courier duties. His information resulted in the destruction of two troop trains. He was withdrawn as a refugee through the Régiment de la Chaudière, then near Cairon, on June 10th. Maj. Wickey was subsequently sent to Holland and ended his war with the Military Government, as Governor of Wuppertal in West Germany.

Lieut. Guy D'Artois, who received his early training in Canada, was dropped in late May near Amberieu to act as Lieutenant to a Resistance leader near Lyons. When his leader was put out of action, Guy replaced him and, at one period, commanded three battalions of Resistance troops, 2,400 men. Not content with leading this force in a number of pitched battles (a practice normally contrary to guerrilla tactics), he established an efficient counter-espionage net which caught 115 collaborators. D'Artois once found himself very short of funds. To raise the million francs needed to enable his group to carry on, he successfully held a number of wealthy collaborators to ransom.

Guy subsequently married a charming British agent, returned to Canada, and was awarded the D.S.O. Thanks to the *Toronto Star*, his romantic story was given wide press coverage, which aroused the ire of Security authorities on both sides of the Atlantic. M.I.3 (Ottawa) had to warn him not to discuss his exploits, and to report to the British that the newspaper accounts were inaccurate and exaggerated. The publicity, however, delayed him so much that he was too late to be sent to the Far East, as he had requested.

Capt. Taschereau, also trained in Canada, landed by parachute in early June 1944 near Montvilliers in the Aube Department. He dropped almost literally into the middle of a battle between Resistance forces and German L. of C. troops; the enemy were driven back. Losses were 26 German, and five French Forces of the Interior (F.F.I), killed. He next took command of the Maquis in the Forêt de Soulaines, and led them in an even heavier battle where the enemy lost 300 killed to the Maquis 51. When the U.S. 3rd Army arrived on August 30th, he remained with them to organize an Army Intelligence Service of 50 agents who roamed the country on bicycles ahead of the leading American troops. By the time he was returned to England, he was responsible for all agent

Intelligence in three Departments: Aube, Cote d'Or, and Haute Marne. He was awarded the M.C. His assistant, Capt. Thibault, worked with him and, in addition, served as an arms instructor in the Aube. He was awarded an M.I.D.

Lieut. Veilleux was also dropped in early June, and found himself at once involved in a German air and artillery battle to disperse F.F.I. concentrations. His prime task as a trained operator, however, was to ensure that wireless communication with London was kept open constantly and at all costs. He kept his link active, and often was on his set for 18 and 20 hours at a time. He was withdrawn in November, and was later awarded the M.B.E.

In the critical weeks immediately following D-Day, six Canadian officers from First Canadian Division in Italy were sent to France: Capt. P.E. Chassé, R.22e.R., and Lieuts. P.E. Labelle, R. de Mais., and J.H.M. Dehler, L.J. Durocher, J.E. Fournier, and F.J. Lapointe, all General List. They were attached to Allied Forces H.Q., Algiers, to supplement the S.O.E. efforts being made in Southern France, particularly in the Rhône valley, in co-ordination with Operation ANVIL, the August 1944 invasion by the U.S. Seventh Army.[5]

Shortly after the liberation of Paris, S.O.E. set up an advanced H.Q. in the city. It was codenamed JUDEX, and had five duties:

> to investigate and clear up cases of victimization of people who had worked with our officers;
> to meet the French colleagues of these officers;
> to establish and check lists of citations for decorations;
> to collect radio and other equipment still required for the Japanese war;
> to settle outstanding financial problems and to hand over dossiers on pensions to the established French military command, as agreed in London.

During the seven months of its existence, JUDEX visited nearly every liberated Department; in many cases, Canadian officers were members of its teams.[6]

Italy and the Mediterranean

Allied clandestine activities in Italy were never mounted on such an ambitious scale as they were in France. Canadians participated mainly in subsidiary S.O.E. schemes in the Balkans, but also in North Africa and in the Dodecanese, under Political Intelligence Directorate control. In late 1941, the British Security Co-ordinator (B.S.C.) in New York obtained permission from the Canadian government to enrol Canadians of Yugoslav origin.

The men were enlisted in the British Pioneer Corps and given anglicized pseudonyms. Some were tough hard-rock miners from Northern Ontario; others, fishermen from the B.C. coast. A few had seen service in the Spanish Civil War. In all, 48 were despatched from Canada. Only 11 of them had

Canadian citizenship when they volunteered, 12 appear to have been in this country illegally, and the rest were United States citizens.

The first draft was torpedoed in the mid-Atlantic. They were picked up, fortunately without loss, and, together with later recruits, were eventually concentrated in Cairo and in Bari, Italy. One of the liaison officers with them in 1944–45 was Lieut. J.H.F. Laban, C.Int.C., an I.O. with Fifth Armoured Division.

They were generally attached as interpreters to teams of British agents who were dropped blind in areas believed to be dominated by Yugoslav Resistance elements. At first, they were sent into Chetnik territory but, after December 1943, when support had been withdrawn from Mihajlovic, drops were made only to Marshal Tito's partisans. Because of the secrecy that surrounded their employment, individual careers could not be traced. An exception is Nicola Kombol, who was recommended for the Military Medal and later commissioned in the field "for excellent services" under the cover name of "King". The British authorities had great difficulty when they tried to recover these operatives. Some flatly refused to return either to their parent unit or to Canada.

Six Italian-Canadians were recruited in Canada in 1941. Only one of them actually accompanied a field party; Cpl. Ralph Vetere did an operational tour of the upper Val d'Aosta and was commended for his services. Three Hungarian-Canadians who originally enlisted in the Canadian Army served with S.O.E. in Hungary: J.J. Gelleny, Andrew Durovecz, and Mike Turk; their noms-de-guerre were Lieuts. J. Gordon, Daniels, and Thomas. Gelleny/Gordon parachuted near Pecs in September 1944, where he organized Resistance groups among the local industrial workers. He was captured, but escaped and hid in Budapest until the city was taken by the Russians. Two Romanian-Canadians, Victor Moldovan and George Georgescu, were also released from the Canadian Army to go to S.O.E. They spent some time as administrative officers with the Executive in Italy, but the plan to send them to Romania was cancelled when, at Yalta, the country was allotted to the Russian sphere of influence.

The tale of Canadian participation in S.O.E. activities in Europe would not be complete without a mention of one accidental, but most valuable, recruit, Capt. George Paterson. He was taken prisoner while serving with the British Army, escaped to Switzerland, and was recruited by the S.O.E. in Berne. He became their expert on the vigorous Resistance groups in the Val d'Ossola, and visited them frequently as training liaison officer and chief technical advisor. Captured no less than three times, he was finally liberated by his own partisans when Milan fell.

Far East

The S.O.E. component in South East Asia, Force 136, had a much broader task than S.O.E. in Europe, for it combined the normal Special Force duties with those of Special Intelligence and Political Warfare. Its tasks included the raising and training of native levies, all tactical and strategic Intelligence to support Special Force operations, sabotage of industrial and military targets, Psychological Warfare, and deception schemes. It covered Burma, Siam (with O.S.S., who were responsible for that country), Indo-China, Malaya, and the western portion of the Dutch East Indies (Sumatra, Java, etc.). The Force was organized into a number of country sections, each responsible for its own region.

The Canadian contingent was originally intended for service in Indo-China. It consisted for the most part of veteran volunteers from the French Section who had returned to England when their tours were completed: Majs. J.H.A. Benoit and Pierre Chassé; and Capts. J.P. Archambault, J.E. Fournier, P.E. Labelle, F.C. Meunier, L.J. Taschereau, and P.E. Thibault. They were sent first to Canada for 30 days leave, then returned to Britain; they flew to Bombay on February 28th, 1945.

Capt. Labelle became a casualty almost immediately; he was returned to Canada to be replaced by Capt. R.M. Caza. The party was sent on a short course at the Jungle Warfare School, near Kandy, Ceylon. While they were there, it was learned that the early parties sent into Inda-China had been turned over to the Japanese by the Annamese nationalists (later known as Viet-Minh). Since the general view was that any further parties would probably meet the same fate, and because the Burmese Section had become sadly depleted through casualties, Force 136 decided instead to use the Canadians ahead of the southward advance of Fourteenth Army.

Accordingly, early in April 1945, Maj. Benoit and Capts. Archambault and Taschereau, followed, after a brief interval, by Capt. Meunier, were dropped into the Karenni region close to the Siamese border. They were to harry the enemy Lines of Communication which, in this sector, passed over narrow and tortuous jungle trails. One method used was to lay explosives by the route and detonate them as Japanese columns of pack animals and porters passed by. Fire support, to take advantage of the confusion, was provided by small detachments from the Burmese National Army under the command of the team commander. Each unit had its own radio set and could provide operational Intelligence to H.Q. Force 136. On May 17th, Capt. Archambault discovered that the monsoon moisture had damaged his stock of explosives. He took them into his tent and was trying to dry them out when they exploded. He was mortally wounded and died two days later.

In the meantime, another Canadian, Lieut. (later Capt.) C.C. Dolly, a Trinidad-born officer whose parents had emigrated from the Assam border

20. Clandestine Operations - Far East

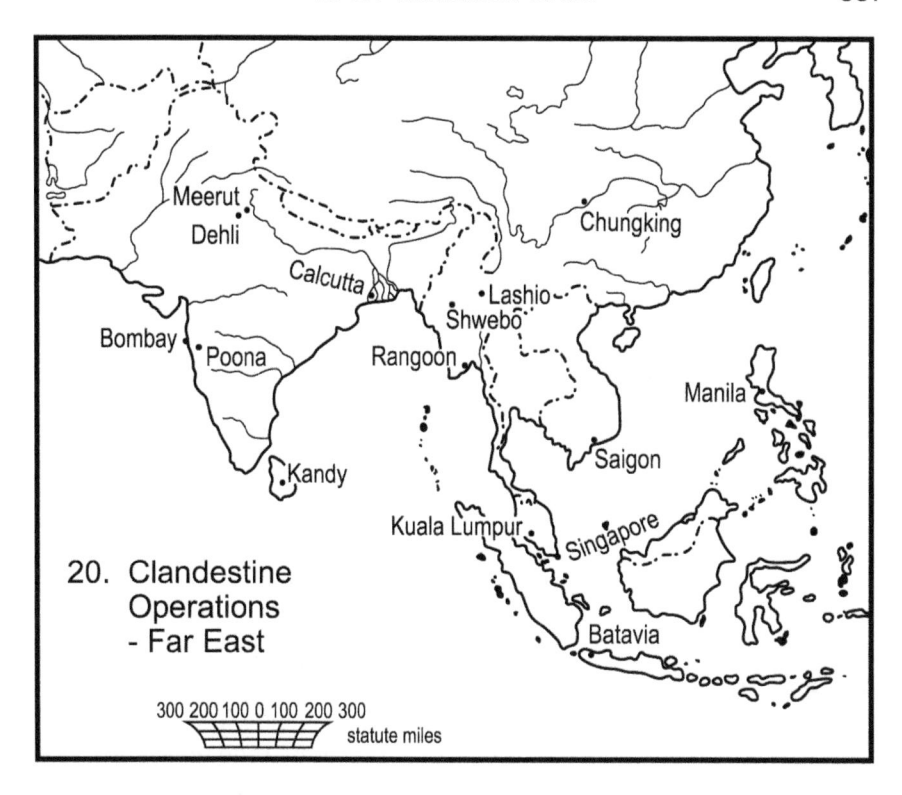

region, was working north of Shwebo. Capt. Dolly spoke several Burmese dialects with considerable fluency, and was a valuable addition to the Force. At the end of February, after only a month's training, he was dropped in to report on the movements of the Japanese *4th* and *41st Infantry Divisions (Fifteenth Army)*, and, if possible, to collect information on elements of the Japanese-sponsored *Indian National Army*. Dressed sometimes as an Indian coolie and sometimes as a native Burman, Capt. Dolly calmly drove bullock carts for the Japanese Supply Service from February until long past the ceasefire on August 15th. From time to time he had members of the Burmese National Army under his command, but he preferred to work on his own. Movement in Burma was difficult, even for him, because the Japanese had established an ingenious system of village political officers who reported the presence and movements of all strangers. Despite their vigilance, Capt. Dolly was able to sabotage rice storage areas and communications, and to send radio messages to Force H.Q. every three days. In July, two Japanese Army officers, disguised as Buddhist priests, attempted to assassinate him. Dolly had heard they were coming and had planted some 808 explosives on the only path to his cave. The weapons they had concealed made such a noise as they came up the path that he was able to control the detonation so as to kill them both.

A group of 12 Canadian-Chinese volunteers was also attached to Force 136. Ten were used in Malaya as interpreters: Sgts. K. Louie, Charley Chung, B.C. Lee, B.K. Lee, V.J. Louie, O. Wong, F.C. Ho, H.W. Fung, R.W. Lew, and B.L. Chinn. During the Liberation they gave valuable service, often under conditions of great personal danger; the Malay population was not always able to distinguish between a Canadian-Chinese and a native Chinese Communist.

In the latter part of July 1945, Force 136 formed a Canadian Jedburgh team, a small unit consisting of a commanding officer, his assistant, a wireless operator, and an interpreter; in this case: Maj. Benoit, Capts. J.E. Hanna and R.M. Caza, and Sgt. K. Louie. Hanna was a Chinese-speaking Canadian. Benoit's team was to drop into the northern part of Johore State, Malaya, to contact the Malayan Peoples Anti-Japanese Army (M.P.A.J.A.). This was an army of the largely Chinese Malayan Communist Party. The most aggressive of the Malayan Resistance movements, it was organized into seven regiments of five patrols of about 100 men each. The team was to provide day-to-day information on the Japanese forces in western Johore, some 85 miles from the dropping zone; to block three highways in the area; and, at the same time, to train and equip the M.P.A.J.A. The team was dropped on August 5th, and was getting nicely established when news came of the Japanese cease-fire.

The surrender began a nightmare period of three months in which the British gathered the Japanese, disarmed the M.P.A.J.A., released and repatriated Allied prisoners of war, and tried to restore normal civilian activity. Force 136, with its Canadians, dealt with the M.P.A.J.A. who, armed with weapons provided by the Force or from captured Japanese stocks, considered themselves in some areas to be the dominating power. Disarming them required tact and courage. Although intensive efforts were made, arms and explosives were successfully concealed, to emerge later during the period of terrorism that followed the surrender.

One of the most experienced Canadians in the area was Lt.-Col. Arthur R. Stewart, a Vancouver B.C., city policeman who had served in the Shanghai police force, and who spoke Chinese. He had been loaned to S.O.E. in January 1944 as a W.O.II. After training, he was assigned to Escape and Evasion duties, first on the Yunnan–Burma border, then in the Salween River area until February 1945, and finally near Lashio. In July, he was in Malaya; when Japan collapsed, he was with his team of five officers and one N.C.O. on Singapore Island. One of Col. Stewart's first tasks was to raise the Union Jack over the Singapore Municipal Buildings to greet the first Allied troops to return. He later served in Sumatra on operations with the Release of Allied Prisoners of War and Internees – R.A.P.W.I. – organization.

Maj. C.D. Munro, R.C.A., left England for Ceylon in early April 1945, and was ready for duty by the end of May. When Annamese activity caused the cancellation of Indo-China missions, Colin went to Malaya. In October, he was sent with his assistant, Sgt. Charley Chung of Chilliwack, B.C., to the northern part of Kedah, where trouble had developed with the local guerrilla forces. He later joined Maj. Pierre Chassé in Perlis. As a change from disarming recalcitrant irregulars, the two officers turned their attention to the Siamese pirates operating along the coast; it was not long before the incidence of the forays of these gentry declined notably.

Early in the war, S.O.E. employed at its Washington office Capt. Mary Dignam, C.W.A.C. Towards the end of 1943 she was transferred to its Indian H.Q. at Meerut and, when S.E.A.C. H.Q. was set up at Kandy, acted as second-in-command of the S.O.E. Liaison Section operating between the two H.Q. Later, in spite of ill-health, she became assistant to the S.O.E. officer in Chungking.

Canadians also served in the Pacific. Capt. Roger Cheng and Sgts. James Shiu, Norman M. Low, and Raymond Y. Lowe, who had been trained in the Okanagan Valley in B.C. by the B.S.C., arrived in Australia on November 2nd, 1944; nine others arrived on March 17th, 1945, and a final group of 15 a week later. Fifteen qualified as parachutists by April 8th. Seven of these were sent to the Services Reconnaissance Detachment (cover name for S.O.E.) at the end of May. On July 13th, Capt. Cheng was dropped into the Rejang River district of Sarawak (northern Borneo), followed three days later by A/W.O. Shiu and Sgts. Roy Chan, Louie King, and Norm Low. Sgts. Chan and King organized and led Dyak guerrillas, and blocked the Japanese supply route along the Rejang. Sgt. Low and W.O. Shiu maintained the radio links to the Australian Ninth Division in Labuan, providing Intelligence, sometimes under fire, of Japanese activities in the region. Eventually the Japanese withdrew to the coast. After the surrender, the team recovered arms and equipment that had been dropped, concentrated Japanese troops for repatriation, and conducted War Crimes investigations. All four N.C.O.s were awarded the M.M.

By 1944, S.O.E. had a total strength of around 12,800; 7,500 in Britain; 4,000 in the Mediterranean; and 1,300 in the Indian Ocean area.[7] Men were often recruited hurriedly, under conditions of extreme secrecy, with little attention to selectivity and without adequate provision for administrative support. Because of the strict security, recruits often did not clearly understand what they were volunteering for; as a result, withdrawals were frequent during the early training period. There were exceptions. One prospective agent, who had been turned down by I.S.9 after he had completed his training, was sent back to Canada, accepted by S.O.E., and acquitted himself gallantly in the field. The Force that implemented the S.O.E. concept made a brave and sometimes even decisive contribution to the war. Canadians played a small but useful part in it.

ESCAPE AND EVASION

All armies consider it the duty of every soldier to try to avoid capture and to escape if captured. During the Second World War, a differentiation was made between "Evaders" – those who had avoided being captured – and "Escapees" – those who had broken custody. Common to both, however, is the fact that each is only the first step towards a freedom that may have to be reached by travelling long distances through enemy or enemy-held country, amongst natives who may be hostile and difficult to avoid. The War Office set up the M.I.9 Section to assist evaders and escapers by providing networks of "friendly natives". Its operational arm was I.S.9 (Intelligence School 9 – a cover name), which established and operated links into Occupied Europe and the Far East. It also set up offices in selected neutral countries for recruiting operatives, for research and development of items useful to evaders and escapers, and for training men to use them.

Canadians first heard of this activity in a lecture given at Minley Manor in March 1940. The speaker mentioned a "Scarlet Pimpernel" organization – an obvious reference to I.S.9. On July 11th, 1941, when Maj. John Page visited I.S.9, he was offered enough escape equipment to supply I Canadian Corps. Corps did not then need it, but John Page was ordered to keep abreast of developments. On April 30th, 1942, he asked the War Office to instruct all Canadian troops in Britain in Escape and Evasion. His request was granted. Second Division (earmarked for Dieppe) was given a course on May 19th and 20th. This course stressed the undesirability of allowing oneself to be captured, how to avoid capture, and conduct if captured; it also demonstrated escape aids. Every escaper was sternly reminded not to discuss the circumstances and details of his escape with anyone except authorized Allied interviewers. In December 1944, Canadians were made responsible for their own training.

The instruction bore fruit at once. After Dieppe, three Canadian escapers, C. Lafleur, R. Vanier, and C. Joly, were picked up by I.S.9's "Pat O'Leary" escape line. While they were waiting to be passed along the network, an "O'Leary" agent, Val Williams, took them to a movie in Perpignan. The newsreel had pictures of captured Canadians, and they were amused when they recognized themselves. All were awarded the M.M. After they had returned, they were given basic Intelligence training at 1 C.G.R.U., followed in March 1943 by four months special training. In the summer, Cpl. Lafleur was dropped into Belgium as a radio operator. On October 21st, 1943, he was sent on a second tour, dropping at Fismes, in the Rheims area, with his team leader. Their task was to locate a field suitable for Lysander aircraft; near Coucy-le-Château, they found one capable of taking two planes a night. Lafleur reported the details and an R.A.F. Photo Reconnaissance mission was flown to confirm them. The team leader collected a number of airmen from Paris.

While a second operation was being planned, Lafleur's set was located by German DF. His house was surrounded; he opened fire, killed or wounded two Germans, jumped out of a window, left Rheims, and contacted another escape net which returned him to Britain. He was awarded the D.C.M., and later commissioned. Lieut. Vanier served as a radio operator in Brittany until February 1944. Evacuation from this area was by sea. On one occasion, he and his associates found themselves stranded on the beach with 26 evacuees and no ship. With amazing skill, he got all 26 back to Paris in 36 hours, unmolested, for later evacuation through the "Shelburne" network (Dumais).

The British agent, Val Williams, was paired in early 1943 with Sgt. R.J. Labrosse (later Lieutenant, M.C., Croix de Guerre avec Etoile de Vermeil, American Medal of Freedom), and sent to Paris to set up a new base for hiding and clothing escapees before their evacuation through Brittany. Because their network ("Oaktree") was new, Williams and Labrosse were dropped blind. They had to make nine separate attempts before they finally managed to land, on March 22nd, 1943, in a field in the forest of Rambouillet, 15 miles south of Paris. Both were equipped with a large sum of money, identity cards, revolvers, and folding bicycles, the first time this useful form of transport was used. Unfortunately, one bicycle was damaged in landing, but a farmer who had seen them drop was persuaded to let them hide their kit in his barn while Williams rode off to Paris. Ray Labrosse tried to contact London but could not get his radio working. At the end of May, they arranged for a pick-up from Brittany. Their radio communications were still poor, and Williams tried instead to move 90 "clients" across the Pyrenees. He was arrested at Pau on June 4th. Labrosse decided he could not go on because Williams had the only copy of their code. He handed 63 of the escapees to a French group ("Burgundy"), and took the other 27 through Spain himself, in July 1943. On his return to Britain, he volunteered to rebuild the network with another team leader. This time he was paired with L.A. Dumais, another Canadian.

P.S.M. Dumais (later Capt., M.C., M.M.) had conducted himself with particular gallantry at Dieppe, and made a singlehanded escape following the surrender. I.S.9 recruited him but, fearing that his strong accent would betray him, sent him to North Africa as an observer with British First Army. While there, he set up an Intelligence-gathering, irregular cavalry, private army that was so successful that I.S.9 decided his accent was sufficiently similar to ordinary Breton speech for him to be able to operate in Brittany.

His "Shelburne" network was to deliver escapees to Anse Cochat beach at Plouha, in Brittany, where they would be picked up by motor-gunboats from Dartmouth. Small rowboats would first bring in equipment, arms, and supplies, and then ferry the men from the beach to the MGB. The network would ask London for a pick-up, receive confirmation from M.I.9, which had the B.B.C. transmit an appropriate coded phrase, and would then move its escapees toward the rendezvous. Dumais and Labrosse were landed by Lysander in November 1943, at Chauny, northwest of Compiegne. Labrosse set up his radio in a private home in Paris, with the help of his host's daughter (whom he later married). When an operation was scheduled, he would travel to Plouha with his radio in a suitcase. To lessen the risk of detection en route, he managed later to obtain two other sets, one of which he could leave permanently at Plouha, carrying only the small frequency crystals.

The rendezvous was the Maison d'Alphonse, owned by the Giguel family and located about 1,500 metres from the beach. It had one room, and an attic in which the evacuees could be hidden until it was time to take them down the steep narrow path to the beach. Once a detachment of White Russians, who were part of the local German garrison, raided the house, but were so drunk that one of them shot a fellow guard. The others were so alarmed that, while they were thinking of how to get the wounded man back to their unit without being discovered, they forgot the reason for their raid. It was fortunate for them that they did so, for Dumais and one of his assistants had heard the noise and were getting ready to attack them from the rear. The Russians returned the next day and burned the house out, on suspicion that it harboured Resistance. This was the only casualty "Shelburne" had.

Weather delayed the first operation. Planned for December, it had to be postponed until January 29th, 1944. The party, supplied with false papers and wearing locally made clothes, was brought to Plouha via St. Brieuc, and met by guides. It included 13 U.S. and four R.A.F. airmen, and Val Williams, who had been helped to escape from prison. A second operation, on February 28th, evacuated over 20, including 16 American airmen. During it, a truck carrying the men to the rendezvous ran over a tank trap being erected by the Germans. While they were pulling their vehicle off, two gendarmes arrived and began to question the driver-guide. Fully intending to kill them at the slightest indication that his judgement was wrong, he told them the truth; they waved the party through. During a third operation, on March 18th, 24 men were taken out; their MGB 503 was fired at, but not followed.

In July, to save his evacuees, Dumais, an aide, and a group of Bretons had to fight a whole German battalion at Châtelaudren; they killed 80, and took 100 prisoners. In August, with the help of a Maj. Thornton, Canadian Army, they recovered 132 airmen from the Forêt de Fretval, near Châteaudun; the airmen had been sent there after the fall of Paris. Dumais evacuated 98 others through a Spanish escape route that he also developed. During its existence, his organization was responsible for the return of 365 airmen and seven agents. In July, he and Labrosse organized a Maquis near Plouha and attacked a Normandy-bound convoy, killing 54 and taking 166 prisoners.[8]

A Canadian casualty of these operations was Signalman G. Rodrigues. He was sent to North Africa early in 1943 to be trained for Corsica, an operation that was never mounted. In August, he was dropped instead into Northern France. On October 15th, he was arrested and eventually transferred to a concentration camp in eastern Germany. When the Russians advanced in early 1945, the camp was hurriedly evacuated. Rodrigues was by this time gravely ill with tuberculosis and died in or near Schwerin on May 26th, 1945.

Mediterranean Theatre

The first Canadian I.S.9 operative in this theatre was Cpl. A.D. Yaritch. Recruited from the C.M.S.C. in London in December 1942, he was sent to the Middle East in June 1943 and then, after further training, to Italy in November. He worked on the enemy-held island of Vis, in the Adriatic, from December until January 8th, 1944, when the boat in which he was travelling from Italy to Dugi Otok was machine-gunned by enemy aircraft, and he was killed.

Sgt. R. Bozanic (Bozanich), a 40 year old Canadian of Yugoslav extraction, volunteered for an operational tour despite a fractured spine incurred during his parachute training in Palestine. He completed one mission on Vis in November 1943, but his injuries limited his activities so greatly that he had to be returned to an administrative post in Italy. Another Yugoslav Canadian, Sapper J. Maystorovich, was trained and served in the theatre, but was not employed on operations.

One Canadian was recruited in the capital of Italy itself. Capt. H.J. (Barney) Byrnes, R.C.A.S.C., was a prisoner who escaped in September 1943 when his small party was being marched through Rome; he obtained sanctuary and was interned in the Vatican, where he remained until Rome fell to the Allies. With a fellow escapee, Sub.-Lieut. R.C. Elliott, Byrnes compiled a card index of all escapees in Italy. His purpose was to ensure that they received assistance and that information of their fate was relayed to their relatives at home. He was later awarded a most deserved M.B.E.[9]

After the Invasion had started, it was hoped that escapers and evaders would continue to hide behind the German lines until the Allies could pick them up. I.S.9 was therefore attached to the Counter-Intelligence Section of S.H.A.E.F. and re-named I.S.9 (WEA) – for Western European Area. Its British G.S.O.1, Lt.-Col. J.M. Langley, M.B.E., M.C., controlled a British and an American Section, with four Field Sections, one Canadian, one British, and two American, which did the actual recovery work. Each Army also had an Interrogation and Intelligence Section. One had been attached to H.Q. First Canadian Army since May 1944; it landed in France on July 10th, as did British Second Army's Section. These two Sections, neither of which had a very clear idea of its duties, agreed to set up a joint office in Bayeux and to standardize their methods of handling escapers.

Capt. J.A. Gray, C.Int.C., commanded the Canadian Field Section, with Capt. G.E. Lévesque, Sgt. Burns (later Murphy), one signalman, two drivers, and two jeeps with trailers, two motor-cycles, and a 22 set. From its first static H.Q. at Caen, established about July 11th, it contacted members of the underground, obtained names and locations of important contacts in areas that would later be overrun by the advance, and established "Ratlines" to help Allied personnel slip through the enemy lines.

The Interrogation Section was responsible for interviewing all evaders and escapers in order to be certain that enemy agents had not been introduced into the stream, and that operational information and information on other escapers was obtained and followed up at once. Escapers were also sent to the London District Transit Camp, which worked with Personnel Branches of the Allied Services. Canadian I.O.s, the best known of whom was Capt. K.G. Surbeck, dealt with Canadians. Their interrogations were intended to reinforce the Army Sections and to identify both those ex-prisoners whose conduct deserved reward and those who were suspected of dishonourable behaviour. They also sought evidence of enemy brutality against Allied P.W.

Initially, the First Canadian Army Interrogation Section was supposed to have been located at and administered by the Army Reinforcement Transit Camp. But the five officers (two Army, two R.A.F., and one R.N.), one clerk, and a driver/batman could not attend to the rations, quarters, clothing, medical examination, and the evacuation to Britain of the men it processed. Extra staff – No. 15 Administration Increment, I.S.9 (W.E.A.), First Canadian Army – was authorized, and on August 1st, 1944, the combined unit was attached to 030 Civil Internment Camp, then located at Fontaine Henry. The officers drew clothing, rations, and tentage sufficient for 40 evacuees; shortly after, they drew stores for 100. On August 3rd, the unit moved to the Olde Abbeye at Brienne, formerly occupied by the *S.S.*, which it shared with 030, a number of Field Security Reserve Detachments, and the G.S.O.1 I(b), H.Q. First Canadian Army. Waiting for it were a few escapers/evaders, and 17 S.O.E. personnel anxious to be returned to Britain; the unit arranged for their evacuation by 84 Group Communication Squadron, Tactical Air Force.

After the airborne landing at Arnhem had failed, the Dutch Resistance and I.S.9 agents managed to make contact with the units by using the telephone circuits serving the German-held power station and transformer system at Nijmegen. About 150 survivors were brought over the Waal River in small boats manned by an R.C.E. Company. They were met and interviewed by a massed group of interrogators drawn from Canadian Sections and Second British Army, and as many others as could be found in the I.S.9 organization. Following this they were treated at No. 6 Canadian Casualty Clearing Station for exposure and, in a few cases, minor wounds, and then evacuated to London. Unfortunately, the press heard and made much of the story. In late December, a second attempt to evacuate escapees across the river was made. The weather was bad, German vigilance had increased – the press reports were blamed for this – and only seven of the 120 waiting came through safely; the others were either captured or forced into hiding.

Capt. Leo Heaps, who had escaped the Germans by swimming the Rhine, and who had been a leading figure in the December operation, was awarded the M.C. and placed in charge of I.S. activities in the Maas estuary. He had a new Field Section, staffed mainly with British men, which was known as "The Water Group". This was not controlled by H.Q. First Army, but worked closely with the Canadian Section operating the ratlines across the Biesbosch. The Germans used these ratlines in reverse. On two occasions, two opposing parties tried to use the Biesbosch facility at the same time. The resulting dogfight closed it.

During the advance into Germany, the Canadian Field Section moved near Emmerich and operated forward with II Canadian Corps. When I Corps commenced operations in Western Holland, the Section was split. Capt. Lévesque was hurt, and Sgt. Murphy took the two remaining men with him to I Corps. Capt. Gray and his driver stayed with II Corps. After the surrender, Al Gray went to Lübeck and Schwerin, leaving his Section at Utrecht. All prisoners were warned, through as many channels as could be found, to remain in their camps after the collapse of the *Wehrmacht*, so they could be contacted. P.W. however, had one idea only, to get back to Britain. So many succeeded that teams had to be deployed at airfields and ports to screen them as they came through.

To check the camps themselves, a small additional group of interrogators was formed, trained, and held in readiness to investigate charges against prisoners alleged to have co-operated with German P.W. Camp authorities to the detriment of other P.W. (Operation ENDOR). An H.Q. group under Capt. K.G. Surbeck, then G.S.O.3 (Liberated Prisoners of War) on the staff of M.I Section, C.M.H.Q., coordinated these interrogations and, when the early rush had been dealt with, collected evidence which, in due course, led to the conviction by court martial of three Canadian P.W.

The Field and Interrogation Sections which, during the time they were active, had interrogated almost 1,000 Allied troops, were disbanded at Bad Salzuflen late in May 1945. The information they had obtained was often useful to Intelligence and Planning staffs. They had provided the special security arrangements for the evacuation system, often transported special high priority persons, and set up a simple, secure Transit Camp facility for them in the Army area. The only evacuation mishap occurred in January 1945. Lieut. S. Nichols of the Black Watch (R.H.C.) made his way through the Canadian lines after having been in captivity for a week, but was killed when his aircraft crashed on landing in England.

I.S.9 investigators identified a number of those selfless men who had courageously assisted others to escape. In the Mediterranean, C.S.M. N.L. McLean not only escaped himself and engineered the escapes of others, but set up an escape line leading through central and southwestern Europe to the Yugoslav partisans. He was awarded the M.B.E. Sgt. L.K. Pals, Field Security, Second Canadian Infantry Division, was captured with 6th Brigade at Dieppe. A fellow P.W. wrote of him:

> On our arrival at Lamsdorf September 1942 Sgt. Pals at once associated himself with the escape committee and in the spring of 1943 took over the operation . . . until January 1945 . . . of 28 escapes. . . . Without Sgt. Pals' knowledge of not only the German language but also of the people . . . the above result could not have been achieved. He was responsible for acquiring civilian clothes, passports, photographs, the organization of wire breaks, the successful operation of a tunnel for . . . three months.

He was also involved in directing sabotage by the work parties, Intelligence gathering, and in reporting this activity through safe channels back to Britain. He escaped himself on May 17th, 1944, and found en route that a "safe house" which he had been told to use was closed. He permitted himself to be recaptured, in order to be sent back to his camp to warn the others. He was able to assist in the escape of about 400 prisoners, and had directly contributed to the preparation of documentation for about 250 of them. He was liberated April 22nd, 1945, at Hohenfels (*Stalag* 383), awarded the D.C.M., and commissioned. After the surrender, he was employed with I(b) in Germany, and then with the Missing Persons Bureau.

Rewards for the civilian population were laid down by joint policy statements, and each case was separately investigated. Capt. H.J. "Barney" Byrnes reported on the situation in Italy on May 1st, 1945:

> The Allied Screening Commission (Italy) was formed in June 1944 from . . . the Rome organization . . . to deal with problems left behind by Allied escapees and evaders . . . and to recompense and to recommend those civilians . . . who had assisted and sheltered them. . . . Since June 1944 there have been some 30,000 claims of which 12,000 have been paid. Standard scales have been worked out to indicate the average cost of food, of shelter and of clothing for different areas – smallest was 1,000 lire ($10.00) and the largest 400,000 ($4,000) with the average 6,500 lire ($65.00). Special payments were made on the death or disability of a helper, which were based on the abrogated five year pension of a second lieutenant. Property was not paid for except, for example, a small vessel sunk while carrying evaders to safety. Three Canadians were involved in this together with 29 British, 38 Americans, 13 South Africans and one Greek.[10]

Germany captured 142,319 Allied prisoners; 7,310 died in captivity, 150 escaped to Sweden, Switzerland, and Russia, and 7,046 were recovered by I.S.9. About 4,000 were liberated in France, Belgium, and Holland before D-Day, and about 600 afterwards. There were 4,937 evaders. The speed of recovery was such that a substantial number of the aircrew shot down towards the end of

1943 and in early 1944 were being returned within a month of their landing. This helped morale, but, more significantly, it meant that a large proportion of trained, experienced aircrew were able to return to the fight. Over 1,000 of the escapers and evaders who returned to the Allied side before the end of hostilities – roughly 10 per cent of the total – passed through Canadian hands. Though Canadians played little part in the over-all concept, control, and direction of the service, they participated fully in both its clandestine and its overt operations.

PSYCHOLOGICAL WARFARE

Psychological Warfare (Psy. War.) was controlled by the Political Intelligence Department of the British Foreign Office (P.I.D.). Canadians were not involved in the over-all direction of these operations, but they served in the agencies that carried them out.

Psy. War. functioned on three levels. The first level was the obvious national information agency, such as the B.B.C., which commented on events from a national point of view, enhanced reports of its own victories and minimized its set-backs, and denigrated enemy gains and magnified his defeats. Its reports were calculated to exploit known enemy weaknesses, to divide loyalties among the enemy's people and his allies, and to lower confidence in his leadership. Because the agency's statements were deliberately and identifiably biased, they were known in the trade as "white propaganda".

The second level, called "black propaganda", was information sent out as though it came from agencies purporting to be enemy-official, or at least neutral-official. The P.I.D. agency masqueraded as an official source, and issued reports so carefully written that they appeared to be genuine but which actually were significantly different from the enemy official line. This spread confusion and cast doubt on the credibility of that official line. Black propaganda was, of necessity, clandestine.

The third level was the overt, tactical field operation: loudspeaker broadcasts, leaflets, and safe-conduct material directed against troops in the field. Its purpose was short-term, to convince the troops on the other side that surrender was preferable to continued fighting. This appeal was consequently especially strong toward the end of the war. When the war was drawing to a close, and the need to re-educate P.W. away from Nazi ideologies to a more democratic frame of mind grew greater, propaganda programs were also introduced into P.W. Camps.

P.I.D. recruited a number of Canadians: Capts. A.E. Altherr and C.V. Beaudry (later Major, Croix de Guerre avec Etoile d'Argent, Order of Nichan Iftikhan, 3rd Class), both General List, and J.M.R. Belisle, P. Lieven, R.C.A. (later Lt.-Col., M.C. and Bar), and J.M. Marcotte; Lieuts. G.R. Parry and J.D. Siddons; and Cpl. G.M. Saritch.

French-speaking Canadians with broadcasting experience were trained for teams which were to set up clandestine broadcasting services before the Allied invasion of French North Africa. This project was known as the "Accra Mission", as the teams were to be grouped at that city and sent on their assignments from it. When the success of Operation TORCH made this unnecessary, the Canadian members of the Mission, who by this time had received both S.O.E. and P.I.D. training, were sent as Political Warfare Officers to various North African centres: Capt. Beaudry to Tunis, Capt. Belisle to Constantine, and Capt. Marcotte to Algiers. After the invasion of Italy, Capts. Altherr and Parry filled similar appointments in Palermo and Foggia, respectively, broadcasting to Central Europe.

A Canadian who enjoyed a varied career in Psy. War. was Paul Lieven. He had served with I Canadian Corps as a G.S.O.3 (Int), was an Interpreter in 1941 interrogating captured *Luftwaffe* crews, and was loaned to P.I.D. on October 13th, 1942, to serve as the co-ordinating officer for the Accra Mission. At the last moment, he was sent on Operation TORCH. He landed on the beaches with the Commandos, and thus became the first Political Warfare Officer to serve with a front-line unit. His service during the first weeks of the campaign gained him a wound and the Military Cross. After convalescing in England, Maj. Lieven was sent as a training officer to the newly-organized Political Warfare School (Middle East), near Cairo. During the ill-starred British attempt to recapture the Dodecanese Islands, he went with a Commando Detachment as Political Warfare Officer to the island of Cos. He was again wounded, and won a Bar to his M.C. When the British force he was with surrendered, he escaped with the Commandos and made his way to Syria. He then served a second tour as a training officer, this time at Bronsbury Park, near London. His injuries precluded his serving in front-line duties, and he was returned to D.M.I., Ottawa. He eventually returned to North-West Europe to command No. 4 Information Control Unit, working on the overt side of Psy. War.

The Psy. War. Branch of Force 136 in South East Asia, also had a number of Canadians. Two of them had been instructors at the S-20 Japanese Language School. (A Canadian Army establishment in Vancouver, B.C. See Chapter 15.) Capt. Paul V. Halley, who spoke a number of Chinese dialects as well as Japanese, arrived about May 5, 1944; C.S.M. (W.O.II) A.S. (Tony) Kato arrived on August 21st. Paul Halley was tragically killed in a jeep accident on Christmas afternoon 1944. Tony, promoted W.O.I, refused a commission. A third man, Lieut. J.J. Harding, joined Force 136 from the R.C.O.C. Unfortunately, no details have been discovered of his activities.

A group of graduates of S-20, eight officers and two W.O.s, arrived by air in March 1945; a second group, 18 all ranks, left Canada in October 1945, and arrived in S.E.A.C. on February 1st, 1946. A third group, 22 all ranks, left Halifax on February 1st, 1946. Capt. Hugh Stephen, from the first group, and

Tony Kato were sent to Rangoon, to broadcast and to produce leaflets used in controlling surrendered Japanese. Lieut. Ed. Ripley went to Saigon, via Kandy. The others went by sea to Malaya to serve in the radio station at Kuala Lumpur, and in Psychological Warfare "consolidation" duties in the city's markets. Lieut. Bob Elliot went on to Batavia (now Djakarta), to similar duties with Radio Java. Most of the first group returned on October 25th, 1945, but Capt. D. Davies, Lieut. Elliot, and a number of Canadian officers from the S.O.E. branch of Force 136 and Canloan returned via India at the end of 1945.

Fifty-six Canadian-Japanese enlisted directly for special service as linguists for Psy. War. Thirty-five were sent out early in 1945 to work with Davies and the first S-20 group, in the Indian Field Broadcasting units that were formed during the summer of 1945 for service in Malaya. None had had any serious military training, and it was just as well they never saw action. They did face some hazards; George D. Suzuki was one of two survivors when a flying boat in which he was travelling crashed into a hillside on take-off from Singapore harbour in 1946.

The second group was assigned to the South East Asia Translators and Interpreters Corps (S.E.A.T.I.C.) to screen surrendered Japanese in Burma, Siam, Indo-China, Hong Kong, Malaya, and Java (not a Psy. War. role). Their activities are recorded purely for convenience. One of their officers, Capt. C.C. Brett, R.C.A.S.C., prepared a detailed study of the infamous Burma–Siam Railway. Nearly 25 years later, he and Bob Elliot discovered that each had worked on different aspects of the same project; Elliot had translated the questions put to the Japanese High Command in Malaya on the number of cemetery locations in the area, only to be told that there were none at all. Capt. Brett identified their locations.

The third group arrived in Singapore on April 4th, 1946, also for screening duties. By that date, Ottawa had decided that Canadians would not be employed in Java. By the end of April, work in Burma and Indo-China was completed; however, screening continued in Malaya until early June. By August 1946, all activity in S.E.A.C. ended and, on March 11th, 1947, the Canadians were ordered to return. Two officers and five sergeants were left in Japan and Hong Kong; the rest of the group sailed from Singapore for Britain on April 7th.

Three Canadian-born Japanese were selected for service in Australia: H. Mori, N. Tomiyama, and G.T. Uzawa. On August 13th, 1945, they were attached to the Short-Wave Division of the Political Warfare Section of the Australian Department of Information. Sgt. Tomiyama monitored the Japanese transmissions; his team transcribed, translated, and typed them; he then prepared simple Japanese broadcast texts. Mori and Uzawa, who had less knowledge of the language, were allowed to broadcast simple, carefully prepared scripts. On October 1st, the Australians asked for their services to be extended for another six months. The Canadian Army agreed, but warned that only one extension would be granted. They were returned to Canada on February 8th, 1946.[11]

Overt Psychological Warfare

The planners decided that, for the Invasion, Psy. War. would be controlled through Public Relations, and they set up a sub-agency, Publicity and Psychological Warfare Division (P.W.D.). Intelligence at C.M.H.Q. protested this decision, but was overruled. Years later, Gen. Morgan wrote: "the basic conception that brought P. and P.W. into being proved faulty when we really got down to business".[12] On January 20th, 1944, a Canadian field component, No. 2 Public Relations Group, was formed; on April 4th, it was renamed No. 3 Public Relations Group (Type C).

Its formation did not pass unnoticed in Canada. External Affairs, learning from the High Commissioner's office that Lt.-Col. Gibbs had been appointed Psychological Warfare Officer for the Canadian Army, pointed out with some asperity that, in making such an appointment, Canadian Military Authorities Overseas should have consulted the Psychological Warfare Committee of the Under-Secretary of State: "Under Cabinet direction the Psychological Warfare Committee was responsible for Canada's activity in this field." D.P.R. asked for full details of any links with D.P.W. and for Lt.-Col. Gibbs' terms of reference. C.M.H.Q. replied that Public Relations duties in 21 Army Group included Censorship and Psychological Warfare as well as publicity, and that Canadian participation was limited to leaflet and amplifier units. Canadian officers were posted to those staffs of Army Group H.Q. that dealt with policy, production, and dissemination. The Canadian Army had no Psychological Warfare Officer, and Lt.-Col. Eric Gibbs, A.D.P.R., C.M.H.Q., was performing the duties only until it was known whether Lt.-Col. R.S. Malone could be brought back from the Mediterranean theatre as A.D.P.R., 21 Army Group. Col. Clark, D.P.R., who was a member of the Psy. War. Committee in Ottawa, had been in London when the appointment was made, had discussed it, and had concurred in it. A Maj. Payne would be the liaison officer with Gen. McClure, Head of P.W.D., and Mr. Cadieux, in Canada, was acting as the link between Gen. McClure's office and External Affairs.[13]

The first S.H.A.E.F. policy directive, issued on March 20, 1944, stated that Psychological Warfare would carry on constant propaganda against the enemy and towards civilians behind the enemy lines. Leaflets distributed from April 1st to D-Day were to exploit war themes to try to increase the feeling of war-weariness. From D-Day to the end of the assault phase, they would cover current operations and stress the utter helplessness of the enemy position.

Maximum use was to be made of interrogators, and information was to be passed to civilians by means of loud speakers in the amplifier units.[14]

On D-Day, G (Psy. War.) Branch at 21 Army Group Main H.Q. consisted of some eight officers and 10 other ranks. First Canadian and Second British Armies each had a Psy. War. Officer, who controlled three and five Amplifier Units respectively. The Canadian Psy. War. Officer was responsible to three chiefs: the Colonel, G.S., at H.Q. First Army, the A.D.P.R., Public Relations, 3 P.R. Group, and G (Psy. War.) at 21 Army Group. 3 P.R. Group H.Q. provided the necessary administrative machinery. Intelligence had operational control of the Units. Each Unit had an Intelligence Officer, a sergeant linguist-clerk, a Signals corporal who looked after the loudspeakers, amplifiers, and radios, and one private, a batman-driver for general duties. Each of the three Leaflet Units had one corporal and two privates, one to assist in leaflet distribution and the other a driver. In practice the units were combined, and the leaflet corporal looked after day-to-day administration.

The C.Int.C. officers commanding the Units were trained at the Intelligence Company; all spoke fluent French and English. The sergeants, all of whom spoke fluent German and English, were given a three-week course at the Intelligence Company, 1 C.G.R.U., and all were given the British-run Political Intelligence course at Bronsbury Park. Each unit had a converted Austin ambulance to carry the generator, amplifier, pre-amplifier, radios, gramophone, and ten fifty pound loudspeakers; the Leaflet Unit had a jeep with a trailer. The converted ambulances were unsatisfactory. They were unarmoured ("soft" was the term used), top-heavy, lacked power, and had to be replaced by better, though still not completely adequate, White scout cars. The loudspeaker equipment, built by Paremko, of Leicester, had a maximum range, in perfect weather conditions across flat ground, of approximately 1,200 yards. In operations, they were rarely used over 1,000 yards and often under 800.

If the enemy force was within 1,000 yards, broadcasts were made directly to it. Usual targets were troops who were cornered, and particularly those whose morale was known to be low because of lack of food, length of stay in the line, inadequacy of support, absence of mail, shortage of ammunition, recent heavy casualties, etc. When they were too far away or too numerous to be contacted by the loudspeakers, leaflets were used. These were fired by 25-pounder artillery, 400 to a shell, could either be pinpointed or used to blanket an area, and could involve any number from 10,000 to 150,000. Where shells were impractical, fighter-bombers were used. The most popular types of leaflets were the news sheets, which kept Germans informed of what was actually happening, and the "Safe Conduct" leaflets, which helped them to surrender easily.

Consolidation was the term given to the work required to convey Allied policy to civilian populations in the liberated areas. As soon as a town had been cleared, a Psy. War. unit went in and made public announcements for

Amplifier van of No. 2 Unit, 21 Army Group, giving a news broadcast in a Caen suburb, July 1944. The sergeant may be Sgt. Garvey; the other soldiers are not part of the unit. (Donald I. Grant/Canada. Dept. of National Defence/Library and Archives Canada, PA-136044)

Civil Affairs, for the Mayor, or for the police. It distributed pamphlets, stuck up posters, prepared photograph displays, and made newscasts, often over the amplifiers. It restarted the local newspaper, if necessary with a new staff, and arranged to supply newsprint and, at the beginning, the news as well. It opened movie houses, if they could function, and provided films. When the town could be left to its own devices, the unit moved on.[15]

The units landed in France on July 12, 1944.[16] No. 1 Amplifier Unit was attached to First Canadian Army; No. 2 to II Canadian Corps; No. 3 to First U.S. Army. No. 2 Unit's first task was to provide the sound system for the 51st Highland Division's church service at Manoir de Greully, at which Gen. Montgomery was to read the lesson. No. 3 Unit went into action with 35th U.S. Division. With added Polish and Russian linguists, it was taken to a location roughly one-quarter of a mile behind the actual fighting line in the St. Lô area. Conditions were ideal for broadcasting; the area was clear except for low trees and hedges; there was virtually no wind and no moon; artillery was light, and there was no air action. The American officer in charge of P.W.D. in U.S. First Army, Col. D.B. Page, warned the U.S. troops in the vicinity that an appeal was going to be made to the enemy. Sgt. Suessman addressed them in German, pointing out the hopelessness of their situation, the vast superiority in arms and men that they faced, and the folly of carrying on. He then passed on Col. Page's instructions, which were: not to approach the lines before dawn, and to come forward without weapons, in small groups, with their hands up. He emphasized their brave defence, and tried to convince them that surrender in the face of such odds was entirely compatible with their sense of personal honour. The Polish and Russian linguists repeated both the appeal and the instructions. The whole performance took about one half-hour, from 0300 to 0330 on the 16th. It brought in nine Polish deserters.

That same morning, No. 1 Unit was asked to go to Bayeux to support a British action. They had trouble finding their contact, but eventually moved to about 200 yards from the enemy lines and set up in the courtyard of a small farm, sheltered by a slight rise in the ground. Their first transmission was hurried and unsatisfactory, "probably due to insufficient time being given the equipment to warm up"; the second was better. Their War Diary mentions that they had a hard time putting their loudspeakers on the roof of the van and removing them afterwards; had they taken longer about it, they would have had a much harder time – just after they left, the Germans mortared the farm where they had been sited. They never discovered the effect of their broadcasts.

On the 18th, No. 1 and No. 3 Units went to assist H.Q. First U.S. Army. This H.Q. had a monitoring room where a French news sheet was prepared for the Amplifier Units. These were given, in rotation, one of the four routes into the surrounding countryside. The Units visited the towns, read out news and announcements from the Mayor or from Civil Affairs, displayed posters, and turned over their newspapers to vendors who bought them at 75 centimes and sold them for one franc. No. 3 next went to 83 U.S. Division outside Carentan. But here it was obvious that a Psy. War. broadcast would be quite useless. The target Panzer Grenadier Regiment facing them had already repulsed two American attacks, was high in morale, and had an escape route. The assignment was refused. No. 3 Unit loaned its linguist to the P.W. Interrogation staff and moved to La Hays du Puits to support an American 8 Corps attack – which, in the end, did not go in. No. 2 Unit broadcast on the 24th to 5,000–6,000 refugees living in caves at Fleury-sur-Orne. The next day, No. 1 came under harassing fire from an 88 while supporting an American attack west of St. Lô. The Leaflet Unit, for their part, spent most of this time packing shells.

What the civilian population wanted most was news, but they were sceptical of the ability of French authorities to supply it. French editors had no paper, civilian distributors had no gasoline. The amplifier vans could and did satisfy the basic need for news, but civilians clamoured for any reading material – papers, pamphlets, books, and maps of the war fronts. No. 2 distributed 2,400 copies of a Caen newspaper, *Libération de Normandie*, published by a Monsieur Noisy, and considered bringing forward to Caen the official paper, *La Voix des Alliés*, then published by No. 12 British Amplifier Unit in La Déliverende. After they had set up their vans and made their announcements, officers and N.C.O.s would also take advantage of the opportunity to do what was, in effect, a minor survey of civilian public opinion.

On the 29th, No. 3 Unit was asked by 4th U.S. Armoured Division to take on a mission between St. Lô and Coutances, where *2nd Panzer Division* was trying to halt the American advance and permit other German troops to withdraw. Once again, the mission had to be refused. The amplifier van could not operate on roads out of St. Lô that were already being used by the vehicles of an armoured division; the situation was too fast-moving and changeable; the noise of battle was too great; and finally, there was no chance of finding a group of surrounded German troops. These were examples of the circumstances that made an operation impracticable.

Lieut. D.A. Stickland, the Psy. War. Officer, First Canadian Army, reported to H.Q. on July 24th to find two of his units with the Americans, and the other with II Canadian Corps, which was not then under Army command. He also had a vague responsibility for No. 12 British Amplifier Unit. In addition, he had to contend with a veritable torrent of Psy. War. directives from 21 Army Group, few of which were relevant to his problems.

He therefore began to organize leaflet shoots, and on several occasions obtained targets for air-drops of leaflets. Army Intelligence would give him pinpoint target references of troop concentrations, and 21 Army Group would arrange for the bombs to be packed with the appropriate leaflet. A liaison officer then took the bombs to the fighter airfields chosen by Tactical Airforce H.Q., and briefed the pilots. At first the arrangements took a day to complete; as the campaign progressed, the time was shortened to about four hours.

On August 4th, their O.C.s successfully requested A.D.P.R. to bring the three units under First Canadian Army control. Three days later, Nos. 1 and 3 Units joined No. 2 at the main Press Camp at Rots. No. 2 took over the consolidation role, the other two handled the support operations; the N.C.O.s, when they had time to spare, were employed on P.W. interrogations.

By this time, the escape route from Falaise was being closed off, and thousands of demoralized German troops were milling about in the pocket. It was a made-to-order opportunity for "surrender" leaflets. Unfortunately, the Amplifier Units were not far enough forward, and the 25-pounder leaflet-firing batteries were changing positions three and four times a day and were therefore out of reach. In their place and for the rest of the month, daily fighter-bomber sorties to drop pamphlets on enemy troops retreating across the Seine were flown whenever weather was favourable.

On August 18th, Lieut. M.P. Thomas replaced Capt. Stickland. He inherited many problems. The leaflet teams, for example, were loading the shells (they used a special tool the R.C.E. had made up for No. 1 Unit to simplify the process). But there was no guarantee that the artillery units were picking up the loaded shells. Thomas ordered the Amplifier Unit to collect, pack, and

14. OFF THE BEATEN TRACK

SIE KOMMEN
mit ihren Stahlkolossen, Jabos und Flammenwerfern.

SIE KOMMEN
denn jetzt kann nichts und niemand sie mehr halten.

SIE KOMMEN
denn jetzt liegen auch Nord- und Mitteldeutschland offen vor den Anglo-Amerikanern und Russen. Der größte Betrug der Weltgeschichte ist bald vorbei:
WO BLIEBEN die deutschen Wunderwaffen?
WO BLIEBEN die operativen Reserven?
WO BLIEBEN die Parteigenossen und „Hoheitsträger", die immer zum fanatischen Widerstand aufgerufen haben? Die alliierten Armeen nehmen Deutschland im Sturm.

SIE KOMMEN
um den deutschen Militarismus endgültig auszurotten.

SIE KOMMEN
um die Kriegsverbrecher ihrer Strafe zuzuführen.

SIE KOMMEN
um den Rechtsstaat aufzurichten, damit der Weltfrieden nicht wiederum gestört wird.

WG. 50 / A strategic leaflet of the attrition type, dramatizing the inevitable advance of the Allied tidal wave and the consequent disintegration of the German defenses. The reverse presents a hopeful picture of a possible solution to the dire outlook for the German people.

Propaganda leaflets, North-West Europe. Left, a leaflet dramatizing the inevitable advance of the Allies and the consequent disintegration of German defences. Below, a surrender leaflet translated. (Photo collection Canadian Forces School of Military Intelligence, Kingston/Canada. Dept. of National Defence)

TRANSLATION OF ZG 108

ONE MINUTE
which may save your life

Read the following six points carefully and thoroughly. They may mean for you the difference between life and death.

1. In a battle of material, valour alone cannot offset the inferiority in tanks, planes and artillery.

2. With the breaching of the Atlantic Wall and of the Eastern Front, the decision has fallen; Germany has lost the war.

3. You are not facing barbarians who delight in killing, but soldiers who would spare your life if possible.

4. But we can only spare those who do not force us, by senseless resistance, to use our weapons against them.

5. It is up to you to show us your intention by raising your arms, waving a handkerchief, etc., in an unmistakable manner.

6. Prisoners-of-war are treated decently, in a fair manner, as becomes soldiers who have fought bravely.

You must decide for yourself. But, in the event that you should find yourself in a desperate situation, remember what you have read.

deliver them directly to the battery designated for the shoot. The amplifier vans were useless, and he started a campaign to have them replaced by more suitable vehicles. He asked No. 3 Unit to take over the printing of *La Voix des Alliés* from No. 12 British Unit on the 17th. Its circulation soon rose to 10,000 copies per day, and it came to be regarded by civilians as superior to *Libération de Normandie* because it was more factual.

Units were now assigned to specific senior formations. No. 1 Unit, under Lieut. Watson, went to I British Corps; No. 2, under Lieut. Janisse, to II Canadian Corps; No. 3, under Lieut. Benoît, formed an Army Reserve Unit for use chiefly in consolidation, but also for deployment when needed. It became obvious that one man could not cover all the subordinate formation H.Q., keep up with the situation at Army H.Q., execute the numerous and voluminous directives from 21 Army Group, and at the same time look after normal unit administration. Lieut. Cowie became Thomas' assistant. 21 Army Group was providing a daily review, or digest, of enemy broadcasts picked up from civilian stations. The units studied it carefully for information on morale, shortages of material, order-of-battle, and other things they could exploit in their leaflets. Maj. Broughall, G.S.O.2 (Int) at II Canadian Corps, reported on the 18th that some P.W. at the Corps Cage were carrying the leaflets. A week later, at least 50 per cent of the prisoners at the two Corps Cages were carrying them.

At the end of August, when it seemed that the Germans would defend the Channel ports, Psy. War. was ordered to prepare leaflet operations against their garrisons. No. 1 Unit was asked to broadcast to the major towns in the Le Havre region, urging evacuees to stay where they were until they were told it was safe to return to their homes. Civil Affairs asked the Unit to visit Montvilliers, to advise its citizens not to be worried if their town was shelled by the Germans, for "the situation was in hand". The Unit found that the population had left the previous night, and that the Germans were still on the outskirts. "Having no one to talk to, we left." The Mayor had misinterpreted the order. Told to tell the townspeople that anyone who wished could leave, he announced that everyone should leave. By the 10th, some had returned, and the unit broadcast to them.

On the 11th, No. 1 left Criquetôt for Le Havre, to support 49th (West Riding) Infantry Division. They arrived at about 1030 on the 12th, and made the mistake of entering a square before hostilities had quite ceased. "The Churchill tanks were a little upset", and the infantry also resented a large van "poking around the front line in full daylight". One half-hour after the new sous-préfêt had taken over from the ousted Vichy representative, that van was touring the city, led by an F.F.I. guide, announcing its liberation, distributing leaflets, and making broadcasts which brought in about 60 deserters; their low morale was attributed to the bombing, which killed few except in the outpost positions, the activities of the Amplifier Units in telling the garrison that their positions were betrayed, and the lack of communications with the outside world.[17]

On the 15th, No. 2 Unit, now equipped with its new scout cars, organized a drop which fighter-bombers delivered one day late, on the 17th. No. 3 Unit, which had been working under fire with the Highlanders, joined No. 2 on the 18th. Their broadcasts brought in 150 P.W. The next day the Units supported the Highland Light Infantry and, despite fire directed on the loudspeakers which cost Sgt. Garvey a fractured cheekbone, were responsible for the surrender of 75 P.W. Two hundred more came in on the 20th, 10 others the next day. Third Canadian Infantry Division then asked for and were supplied with, leaflets for 91 shells.

Broadcasts to Boulogne began about 1140 on the 22nd; the final attack was scheduled to begin at 1300. The enemy was urged to surrender, and told which route to take. Desertions started about 1345 and, in a period of two hours, almost 500 came in. In this operation alone, surrenders which were directly attributed to Psy. War. totalled about 1,000.[18]

No. 2 Unit was to prepare next for the assaults on Calais and Dunkirk. Corps and Army arranged for a fighter-bomber drop, and for a special leaflet to be written expressly for the Dunkirk garrison. 21 Army Group promised to provide an additional 80,000 general leaflets. The Unit then went to Andres, near Calais, on the 24th, to broadcast a deception simulation of a regiment of tanks going into harbour east of Calais. Its purpose was to give the impression that the mass of the attack would come from that direction. It succeeded. The enemy shifted his defences to meet the assault he expected, while the main attack went in on his southern flank.

An attempt against the garrison of the island of Guernsey about the same time was less effective. A leaflet drop on September 21st called for a meeting between the German commander, reported as Gen. Graf von Schmettow, and a mission from Psychological Warfare Division, S.H.A.E.F. This mission, headed by a Canadian, Maj. Alan Chambers, and including a captured German officer, General Bassenge, sailed boldly into Peter Port about 1400 on the 22nd. They were stopped by the German duty patrol vessel and asked, somewhat incredulously, what they wanted. After somewhat guarded explanations – Chambers did not want to reveal that he had a German general aboard – the control station ashore was told that the party wished to "discuss the general war situation" with Graf von Schmettow. The German Commander of the Channel Islands, Vice-Admiral Hüffmeier, replied that he was fully conversant with the general war situation and the party had to return, somewhat shamefacedly, to Cherbourg. It was later learned that the leaflet drop had been off target.[19]

Lieut. Benoît of No. 3 Unit was asked to broadcast in support of 9 C.I.B. at Cap Griznez. The wind was against him, but some of his coverage was successful. A little later, 47 Commando asked him for armoured car-mounted loudspeakers to soften up a group at Ghyvelde. En route, his Section was unlucky enough to blunder into a minefield, managed to emerge unharmed, had to broadcast at 0515 under very poor atmospheric conditions, and only realized five surrenders.

By October 4th, Benoît had had 50,000 leaflets fired against Dunkirk; on the 7th and 8th, fighter-bombers dropped 180,000 more; later still, Flying Fortresses based in England dropped them in millions. The result was negligible; when the Germans realized that the Allies merely intended to contain the town, they had little incentive to desert. The garrison had plenty of food, comfortable billets, and secure bunkers. Its Commander promised that the harshest measures would be taken against the families of any who did desert, and the junior commanders were able to maintain strict control.

But there were many civilians in Dunkirk, and the garrison commander sent a French Red Cross worker through the lines to request that he be allowed to evacuate them. Maj. G.M.C. Sprung, H.Q. First Canadian Army, had been visiting the Calais area checking coastal defences with Sgt. D.R. Saran of the Documents Section, and was then with No. 3 Unit. He and Capt. Benoît were sent in as the Allied negotiators.

They set off "feeling somewhat self-conscious under a Red Cross flag and a white flag, held as conspicuously as possible". They soon saw a German flag, and two German officers marching out to meet them about half way. Courtesies were exchanged, "and in the first moment of embarrassment hands were shaken, credentials and cigarettes appeared, the Germans successfully outfumbling the British". The Germans produced neatly laundered blindfolds and apologized for requiring they be used. The masking was not easily accomplished, for the Germans were short men and both Canadians were over six feet tall. They were taken by car into the town, the blindfolds were removed, and Sprung and Benoît found themselves being stared at by a mixed group of curious townsmen and German troops, obviously amazed at the unexpected sight of Allied officers in the heart of the German fortress. Entering through a door bearing the sign Area Commandant, they were received by one of the fortress Commander's staff officers, a tall major "immaculately turned out with a variety of Iron Crosses and gleaming riding boots". Introductions were effected in the German manner. Both sides fumbled for cigarettes but the "lion suffered his first minor reverse by being manoeuvred into a position where he could not but light the cigarettes of the Canadians".

The Germans argued that they could not possibly be ready by 0600 the following morning, for the civilians were scattered over a wide area, and they needed twelve hours to lift mines and repair crossings. They wished the truce to remain in force during the entire proceedings. The Canadians decided that the request for time to put the route in order was legitimate, but that the other demand was not acceptable. They firmly insisted that the engineer work begin that very afternoon, and that the evacuation start at 0600 the next morning. The Germans were nonplussed, but accepted the terms offered. The question of the choice of routes to be used was discussed only in veiled allusions and vague references, because neither party wished to state clearly which bridges were blown and which were usable, which roads were mined and which were not.

The general plan was accepted by both sides, and the Mayor of Dunkirk and the head of the Red Cross were then called in: "The semi-dignified atmosphere of an Anglo-Teutonic parley was rudely shattered by the influx of numerous Latins, each striving to make himself heard above the others." The French assured the delegates that the evacuation would be completed in the time laid down and by the route chosen. The burly Mayor and his excited friend sealed the agreement with a warm handshake, their backs conveniently turned to the Germans. Outside, the citizens could be seen lining the sidewalks in their eagerness to learn what was being decided in the conference room. Several gave variants of the "V" finger sign. One even climbed to the window to take two quick photographs.

Both sides agreed that military dispositions in the area would not be changed during the temporary cessation of hostilities. The German negotiator tried, but failed, to have Cassel and St. Omer included in the zone of no movement, and then asked the Canadians to define what they considered to be the area of the force investing Dunkirk. He received a short, and quite rude, answer that caused a ripple of laughter around the room; everyone, except the major, was happy. The Canadians did agree to supply 400 litres of petrol for evacuating civilian wounded, but rejected a German proposal to fly the Red Cross flag over their P.W. Cage.

The agreements were to be drawn up in writing, signed by the British Officer Commanding the investing forces, and returned to the German H.Q., where they would be exchanged for an identical, written undertaking signed by the German Commander. The Germans had 12 hours to de-mine and clear an evacuation route which would remain open for 24 hours. No. 3 Unit's van would be stationed on the route to control traffic and to warn members of the *Wehrmacht* who tried to escape in civilian clothes that they would be treated as spies. Despite the warning, 24 deserters were arrested. The refugees included some F.F.I., and many of the civilians were quite willing to talk about the situation inside the city. On the 6th, the Czech Armoured Brigade took over the sector, and arrangements were quickly made to continue to give them support.[20]

When the units reached Belgium, they were badly in need of a refit. No. 2 Unit's jeep and van had become unserviceable just after Calais. No. 1 Unit's van hit a Churchill tank. Sgt. Dyck nonetheless managed to do a broadcast and leaflet shoot in support of 6 H.L.I., near Sluis. Four P.W. came in immediately and five more a day later, all saying that morale was low but opportunities to desert were limited by the threat of harsh reprisals. No. 3 Unit arrived in Brussels on October 23rd, loaded shells, provided Public Address facilities at a demonstration on the 26th, and supported the 104th U.S. Infantry Division with leaflet shoots into enemy pockets near Roosendaal and Breda. This Division used 105 mm guns, which fired rounds that could hold 1,200 to 1,600 leaflets, compared to the 25-pounders' usual 400. During the softening-up operations against Walcheren, drops were made in the rare periods when the weather was favourable. As Operation SWITCHBACK – the Breskens operation – drew to its bloody close, No. 1 Unit worked with 9 Canadian Infantry Brigade at Knocke-sur-Mer, and with the North Nova Scotias at Heyst.

Meanwhile Civil Affairs at I British Corps asked for an Amplifier Unit to do consolidation work. Capt. Janisse, of No. 2, went to Breda, established newspapers, found editors and paper, organized censorship, and, because of the newsprint shortage, arranged areas so that they did not overlap. No. 3 went to Roosendaal to cover Bergen-op-Zoom and Rucphen. On the 4th, it found meagre crowds, but the next day it covered 14 towns and villages and was received with considerable enthusiasm.

Although one of the newspapers, the *Brabantsch Niewsblad*, was approved by the Militar Cezag (Military Command) and by the local administration, its revival violated a Royal Decree forbidding the reappearance of papers that had operated during the German Occupation. Capt. Benoît therefore went to the Dutch Press Commission at Eindhoven to point out the importance of the *Niewsblad* as a paper that covered the whole of western North Brabant. He won his case only by agreeing to change its name to *Medeedelingen Blad*. No. 3 then went on to Middelburg, on Walcheren Island, and arranged for the local paper to resume publication.

November 19th was the day on which the Belgian Resistance was to be disarmed. The authorities, anticipating serious dissatisfaction, ordered the Amplifiers to be ready to explain to the people why their arms were being collected. No. 1 was still out of action, No. 2 went to Ghent, and No. 3 went to Bruges. No trouble developed, and the units returned to their routine duties.[21]

All the units had to be re-equipped. In December, Sgts. Neufeld of No. 2 and Suessman of No. 3 Units were loaned to the Interrogator staff for duties in Vught, a former German concentration area, now the H.Q. of 4 Canadian Armoured Division. No. 2, because of delays in its conversion program, was sent on leave; it was replaced by No. 12 British Amplifier Unit from Second British Army, under Capt. Waluch, for more consolidation work at Goes, on South Beveland, and on the island of Walcheren. The many moves of the units at this time accentuated the problems they had with equipment. No. 3 blamed a good many failures on the springing of the new Scout Car, that was too stiff for their delicate amplifiers; whatever the reason, the failures were never remedied.

In early October, C.M.H.Q. had discussed and made recommendations for controls over all media in the zone of Germany that 21 Army Group was scheduled to occupy. New establishments were proposed, and some argument ensued over the number of Canadian vacancies in them. Finally, a decision was reached that existing Psy. War. staffs and amplifier units were quite capable of taking over normal supervision and guidance, and that operational requirements would always take precedence over consolidation duties.

By January 1945, the front was static, and Psy. War. decided to discontinue the use of both safe-conduct and threatening leaflets. On the other hand, interrogations showed that many of the German troops opposite First Army had not been told of the failure of the Ardennes offensive, and were unaware of the Allied successes in the South. 21 Army Group produced a small newssheet, entitled *Die Lage*, for distribution by the 25-pounders. It contained a map showing the front and the Allied gains, with a brief review of the situation on the Western and the Russian fronts. It contained only straight news; truth was now the most deadly propaganda of all. The leaflets were first fired in mid-January 1945; other up-dated editions followed at intervals ending in mid-April. They were popular with German troops, and some prisoners complained because they were not fired often enough; they were the only source of news they had.[22] Leaflets that had been prepared and packed earlier in readiness to announce the expected fall of Warsaw were also distributed, as soon as that surrender became a reality.

On January 24th, 49th (West Riding) Division asked for a broadcast to support 146 Brigade in front of Hams. The target was *II/23rd Parachute Regiment*, in a position about 300 yards away. Weather conditions were perfect. The O.C. of No. 2 Unit, which did the broadcast, reported that his men were "quite sure we were heard because they machine gunned us on the road we were speaking from. Everyone went to ground and we finished giving the broadcast from under the car. The Germans got up and booed and jeered. Our work was somewhat hampered by the shooting incident". Another broadcast on the 27th in Zetten was similarly unsuccessful.[23]

In February, No. 2 Unit fired 68,800 pamphlets in support of 2nd Canadian Infantry Division and 49th Division. Civil Affairs asked No. 1 to conduct a public opinion survey to discover how much civilians knew about Britain's and Canada's share of the war effort. Black market activity had to be repressed. Units produced posters for Civil Affairs to publicize the penalties for it. No. 3 announced a shortage of milk in a special broadcast to farmers in the Breda area; within three days receipts increased by 50%.

The Psychological Warfare plan for the battle for the Reichswald originally called for broadcasts and air drops of a mixture of half "safe conduct" and half other leaflets. The tremendous artillery concentrations, however, made leaflet shells impractical. No. 2 Unit made several broadcasts and lured a few deserters, but success was not equal to what had been achieved in France. No. 3 was sent to support 49th Division in front of Arnhem. A Dutch agent had reported companies of *84th Dutch S.S. Regiment* located at Ochten on the opposite side of the Waal. Capt. Benoît, with his Dutch L.O., shot tactical leaflets at them and broadcast in Dutch on the theme of the futility of a hopeless fight; they provoked a number of desertions. Both teams then joined forces to consolidate Bedburg.

Until almost the end of March, No. 1 was grounded with vehicle trouble. Its men packed shells, helped other units, and did administrative duties. On the 12th, London asked No. 2 Unit to find the wife and daughter of the Polish General Koplanski, who were believed to be at Sonsbeck; they had been there, but had since left. On the 13th, the Unit broadcast an appeal at Üdem for able-bodied citizens to help clear away rubble. There was no longer any hope of encouraging desertion over the broad river barrier that formed this battle front. No. 2 therefore spent the rest of the month in consolidation, interrogating P.W. at the Corps Cage, and planning a newspaper intended to serve the interests of foreign workers in Germany.

The attack on West Holland commenced on April 3rd. Psy. War. not only had a low priority on aircraft, but also was handicapped by very bad flying weather. It therefore placed greater emphasis on leaflet shoots and broadcasts. No. 2 Unit moved into Zeddam and Lochem, along the approaches to Zutphen, where it worked in support of Le Régiment de la Chaudière, netting 37 deserters. In the three days it spent at Deventer, which was under attack by 7 Canadian Infantry Brigade, it claimed a total of 60 prisoners. On the 16th, it answered a request from Brig. J.V. Allard, 6 Canadian Infantry Brigade, for a broadcast telling civilians that he had imposed a 2230 curfew; there was no reaction, because, as they discovered later, the town was already deserted. The 75 miles of rough road back to Meppen so severely damaged the equipment that the unit was out of action due to a shortage of spare parts.

No. 2 had been out of action since April 16th with faulty vehicles. No. 1, in northeast Holland, had no serviceable microphones. The only unit more or less ready for action, No. 3, was packing bombs with leaflets that stressed the futility of dying when the war was so obviously close to its end. On May 4th, it was in the middle of its *Radio Oranje* news broadcast at the Raadhuis in Apeldoorn when, at 2015, it received the newsflash of the unconditional surrender. The announcement was immediately broadcast in English to cheering Canadian troops and then in Dutch: "The scene was terrific. We went round the town broadcasting the news while crowds everywhere were cheering and yelling and walking ten abreast in the streets. We broadcast it in all about 50 times."

The next day, No. 1 was told to provide the equipment for the G.O.C.'s address to the troops. No. 2's interpreters were used in the negotiations between Gen. Erich Straube and Gen. Guy Simonds, G.O.C. II Corps, in Bad Zwischenahn. No. 3, with two radio technicians, was sent to forestall any looting of the important Hilversum Radio station. En route, it met an overpowering reception. When it arrived, it learned that the station's prewar directors had arrived and were already busy resuming control. The Unit interviewed the German Foreign Office representative, F. Vennekohl, who told them that Herr Taubert, the chief

German director of the station, was in The Hague with the English-speaking female propagandist, "Mary of Arnhem". "Mary" was, in reality, two persons, Helene Sensburg and Gerda Wakko. Taubert and the two women were found on the 11th. "Mary" had spent 10 years in England prior to 1939, and spoke good English; her "other voice" spoke it less well, but was quite capable of reading a script. Not surprisingly, both wanted to change their allegiance and work for the Allies; their services were declined. Sometime later, the other notorious radio propagandist, William Joyce, alias "Lord Haw Haw", was also discovered, and arrested by officers of Lt.-Col. Paul Lieven's No. 4 Information Control Unit. Col. Lieven restored radio service at Radio Hamburg in 36 hours, and newspapers within three days, of his arrival.

In their last four months, the Canadian Amplifier Units helped local newspaper offices to resume publication, printed posters, did broadcasts and opinion surveys, assisted in preparing a souvenir booklet on Canadian Army operations in Holland, and acted as an intermediary, providing National Film Board and C.B.C. material for use by the Dutch. However, the change-over from military to civilian control was not always smoothly effected, and the Units had many disagreements on policy with S.H.A.E.F. As soon as Canadian diplomatic representation to Holland was restored with the arrival of a new ambassador, Mr. Pierre Dupuys, increased emphasis was at once put on presenting Canadian information. Capt. Benoît organized a touring display, "Meet Canada". He was in considerable demand as a public speaker; the War Diary shows that he was chosen to address the first meeting of the Netherlands-Canada Society, held on July 28th, 1945. The three Units were disbanded on August 23rd.

Because Psychological Warfare is only a support weapon, it is difficult to evaluate the results it achieved. 21 Army Group, however, claimed that the Units were directly responsible for the surrender of close to 2,000 prisoners. What cannot be statistically verified is the indirect effect that continued exposure to Psy. War. had on the enemy. Millions of leaflets were distributed, but no German ever said that he surrendered because of a leaflet. On the other hand, thousands who did surrender carried them on their persons, and reason suggests that they were at least conscious of Allied propaganda. The vigorous reaction of German Army leaders, who published many orders promising harsh penalties to anyone caught picking up leaflets or listening to broadcasts, must be interpreted as indicating that they had to treat Psy. War. as a very real threat to their troops. And perhaps this is the best indication we will ever have that it did have a significant effect.

In the consolidation period the Units were, strictly speaking, not waging war, but they performed a useful role in reducing the enormous effort needed to control areas as they were liberated. The Units would have been more successful still, had they been provided with sturdier, purpose-built vehicles and equipment, able to stand up to the strains put on them.

15.
ORGANIZATION AND TRAINING: OTTAWA 1939–45

On August 25th, 1939, the C.G.S., Maj.-Gen. T.V. Anderson, D.S.O., asked the Minister, the Hon. Ian MacKenzie, for authority to introduce the "precautionary stage" of the preparations for war. Approval was granted within the half-hour, and a wire to all Military Districts (M.D.) called out the units earmarked to protect the designated Vulnerable Points. On the 26th, at 0910, the Minister was asked to authorize Censorship. About noon, however, a message announced that the British had cancelled their General Censorship. The D.M.O.&I. had to retrieve his submission, and the Minister agreed that a draft censorship Order-in-Council should be submitted, but not implemented until complete Censorship was re-introduced in Great Britain. On September 1st, after the Germans had begun their attack on Poland, the Canadian Privy Council issued a number of Orders-in-Council, including one which authorized the formation of a Canadian Active Service Force (C.A.S.F.). At 1235, the order to mobilize the Force was sent to all D.O.C.s. An hour later the D.O.C., M.D. 1, asked: "Was the calling out of units to be kept secret?" He was advised that, in view of the large numbers of people involved, secrecy would not be possible. The first wartime problem with which the A.D.M.I. had to deal was therefore Security and, specifically, Censorship.[1]

At this date, the N.D.H.Q. Intelligence Section comprised the A.D.M.I., Maj. J. Preston, M.C., R.C.A.; a Military and Air Force Section under a G.S.O.3, Capt. A.H. Fraser, P.P.C.L.I., with F/O W.I. Webb; a Cipher Subsection with one of its two positions temporarily filled by 2/Lieut. John Buchan of First Division; W.O.II George Bolingbroke; S/Sgts. Bert Goldie, a notable cartoonist[*], and Alec Potter; Sgts. Steve Potter and George (Griffy) Griffin, R.C.A.F.; Ptes. G.B. (Bud) Gray and Beverly Prette; eight military clerk-stenographers; and two civilians, Miss Paule Chartrand and Mr. C. Turner. An Information Section of four officers and six clerks, under Maj. H.G. Scott, was being formed to handle translations from foreign languages and information received from intercepted code and cipher material. The Section's Security responsibilities included the protection and custody of classified material and the enciphering of outgoing H.Q. radio messages. The R.C.A.F. component, as we have seen, was withdrawn in late 1939.

---

[*] Second edition note: See Chapter 3 for one of S/Sgt. Bert Goldie's perceptive cartoon drawings.

On September 19th, 1940, the Minister approved a reorganization of D.M.O.&I. Each of the Operations and Intelligence staffs was placed under its own G.S.O.1. Intelligence was divided into three Sections:

M.I.1. (G.S.O.2):	Intelligence from the Districts; Foreign Armies; issuing Intelligence Summaries; Codes and Ciphers; custody and distribution of "Secret and Security documents"; administration (deputy to G.S.O.1). (The Cipher responsibility was passed to the Directorate of Staff Duties in November 1940.)
M.I.2 (G.S.O.3):	Intelligence from radio interception; Censorship.
M.I.3 (G.S.O.2):	Field Security; link with R.C.M.P.

This was a creditable first attempt to set up a Directorate of Military Intelligence as a functional organization *(see Annex 5 for line diagram)*. The linking under M.I.1 of Intelligence from the Districts with Foreign Intelligence was a holdover from prewar thinking; it was too early to see that Security would form most of the Districts' problems. M.I.2 was set up on its own largely because the information with which it dealt was very sensitive; its channel to Censorship soon became confused with that of another Section. Finally, M.I.3's functions were not sufficiently appreciated.

The D.M.O.&I. controlled two other major Sections with Intelligence links. One was Operations – Military Operations 3 (M.O.3) – responsible for liaison with Press and Radio Censors as well as for policy and co-ordination of maps and surveys. The other was the Chief Telegraph Censor, who dealt with all cables going abroad and with designated inland telegraph and telephone services. In December, another change in Operations moved responsibility for liaison with Censorship to M.O.1, and gave reaction to Intelligence from Districts to M.O.3, working closely with M.I.1.

At mobilization, no provision had been made for District Intelligence Officer appointments. Even as late as October 1940, only five Districts had I.O.s. D.M.O.&I. sought, and with some difficulty obtained, approval for a G.S.O.3 (Int) in each District. In the same discussions, the assignment and duties of Cipher Officers were also explored. By mid-October, M.D.s 6 and 7 were being combined with part of M.D. 5 to form Atlantic Command, and M.D.s 11 and 13 were being formed into Pacific Command. New organizations had to be devised to deal with their increased responsibilities.[2] *(See Map 21 in Chapter 16 for Army Commands and Military Districts.)*

In early 1942, it was found that "the A.D.M.I. was at a disadvantage in dealing with his opposite numbers in the Navy and Air Force", which had reorganized into separate Plans, Operations, and Intelligence Sections. In addition, there had been a marked expansion of both Operational and Intelligence duties, particularly with respect to Wireless Intelligence, liaison with Britain and the U.S.A., and "increased demands for Operational Intelligence".[3] As a result of the submission presenting these points, a separate Directorate of Military Intelligence (D.M.I.) was formed on June 27th, 1942. Lt.-Col. W.W. Murray was appointed to the post and promoted. The Director was to be responsible for advice on all aspects of recruiting, training, and deploying Intelligence personnel, and for many details of Intelligence and Intelligence-associated administration. One notable omission from his control was the British Security Co-ordinator's Special Operations School (HYDRA), located near Oshawa, which remained with the Directorate of Staff Duties. The B.S.C., located in New York, was the British Intelligence "window" in North America. It had a Canadian Security component, mostly comprising clerks and cipher personnel but including some officers, which rose to just under 400 by the end of the war. Though unofficial links were quickly established, it was only much later that liaison with the B.S.C. was made an official D.M.I. function. The D.M.I. organization, expanded slightly, remained in force with only minor changes in detail until the Canadian Armed Services were integrated in 1964. The functions of recruiting, deploying Intelligence personnel, and Intelligence-related administration were duly carried out, and while some of them are discussed in the four chapters which follow, most were fairly straightforward, routine matters involving discussions with the appropriate branches in N.D.H.Q., accompanied by the usual and ever-increasing flow of paper. Training, however, was a different story.

Though the new organization gave Intelligence its own training function, it did not give it a facility to conduct that training. As we have seen, the Canadian Army Overseas made arrangements with the War Office for courses to be given Canadians, and later opened its own facilities. In Canada, the initial impulse to conduct training did not, ostensibly at least, stem from the G.S.O.1. On July 2nd, 1940, Maj.-Gen. V. Odlum, then Inspector General of Second Division, pointed out to the Minister, firstly, that the General Staff, aided by officers and soldiers with special qualifications and training, was responsible for Intelligence; and, secondly, that the British had formed their specialists into an Intelligence Corps. He claimed that H.Q. was receiving applications from many specialists, and that most of them had no military knowledge. Since it was essential to have a trained reserve, he recommended that such volunteers be enrolled and sent on a course of study, and even listed the subjects:

Lectures:	*Practical:*
Principles of Intelligence work	Physical training and simple drill
Military vocabulary and abbreviations	Field observation and reconnaissance
Organization of the Canadian Army.	Map reading
Situation maps.	Filing of information.
Air photographs and their interpretation.	Writing of Intelligence Reports [and] Summaries.
Security.	Language practice.
Etc.	Military terms in other languages.
	Etc.

This would be only a preliminary to "an Intelligence course proper, which would include details of enemy organizations, tactics, equipment, methods of interrogation of prisoners and similar subjects", like the ones conducted by the War Office.[4] The detail in his submission would suggest that Maj.-Gen. Odlum had been well primed, although there was no evidence of a connection between him and a senior I.O. seeking allies.

The D.M.O.&I. agreed, and, on July 11th, with support from the Directors of Military Training and Staff Duties, obtained ministerial approval to arrange such a course; it was held at R.M.C. from November 17th to December 14th, 1940. The first candidates included two Command I.O.s, four from Brigades, N.D.H.Q., and the Districts, and 35 others, ranking from second lieutenant to major, from artillery regiments and infantry battalions: ". . . it was therefore apparent that their general military knowledge would be uneven and in some cases meagre". It was also expected that I.O.s would "have to act for adjutants and brigade majors". So almost half of the 225 periods of instruction offered were to be devoted to Canadian organization, staff duties, administration, military law, drill, revolver practice, and anti-gas training, i.e., subjects that should already have been covered. The Intelligence subjects were to have three periods on German Army organization, 20 on map reading and topography, four on air photo interpretation (on which little information was available), 30 periods on principles, organization, duties, security, filing, handling of information, reports, summaries, and situation reports, and 18 periods on foreign military terms in French, German, "and other languages available in handbooks of various armies".

The actual course bore no resemblance to the proposed syllabus; it was, in effect, a normal company commander's tactics course instead. Lt.-Col. K.C. Burness, in charge of training at R.M.C. (and a former part-time D.M.I.O. in M.D. 6), admitted that "this was the first Intelligence course . . . and no officer on the staff had any intimate knowledge of the subject. Some difficulty was

First Intelligence Officers' Course, Royal Military College, Kingston, 1940. (Photo collection Canadian Forces School of Military Intelligence, Kingston/Canada. Dept. of National Defence)

experienced... partly due to the lack of experience and partly due to the short time available for preparation". He recommended that an instructor be sent to the British course, and he asked for more time to prepare his own courses and for a special course to be held for Intelligence officers and sergeants. His remarks contain a strong indictment of the current situation in the Army: "There are commanding officers who do not appreciate the importance of a well-trained Intelligence Section. In some cases, Sections [had] not been formed, while in others the Intelligence officer [was] used for odd jobs and as a relief for other officers, thus preventing continuity of training of his section." Col. Burness recommended the issue of a training circular to include the following points:

1. The Intelligence Section is a specialist organization which requires continuity of training until it is efficient, and subsequent refresher training.

2. A reserve must be held to replace casualties.

3. All ranks in a unit must be aware of their responsibility for passing information.

4. Intelligence training is a full-time job for the Intelligence Officer, who should not be used except as a unit security officer and as an understudy for the adjutant [sic].

5. Every opportunity should be taken to exercise Intelligence personnel during collective training.[5]

The official policy that Intelligence was not a job for specialists had inevitably led to a situation where there was no high-level understanding of the problem, nor – which was even worse – any facility through which the situation could easily be remedied. There was no one at R.M.C., a major Army training centre, with any knowledge of Intelligence, a year after war had begun! Col. Burness' letter, highlighting obvious weaknesses, is a key document in the rehabilitation of Intelligence in the Canadian Army.

The G.S.O.1 next arranged that D.M.T. run a Field Security Course. On February 10th, 1941, Maj. Orville Eadie, Chief Instructor of the Intelligence Wing at R.M.C., who was then at Matlock in Britain, was ordered to study the methods there. The 10 students at the first R.M.C. course, from May 25th to June 21st, were the F.S.O.s from First Armoured and Third Infantry Divisions, the G.S.O.3s of M.D.s 1, 4, 6, and 7, and four officers from M.D.s 4 and 11, and the Kent Regiment. This course, based on British material, was ostensibly designed for F.S. duty in the field, rather than for Canadian domestic Security. The principles, procedures, and techniques were in fact common to both; though there were differences in detail, training for one was quite adequate for the other. A similar commonality of training in fact occurred at the postwar Canadian School of Military Intelligence. But confusion concerning its purpose continued to pertain. In mid-1941 there were 37 I.O.s in the Training Centres, and 37 in Coast Defence units in Atlantic and Pacific Commands, the Port of Quebec, and Arvida District. Lt.-Col. Murray proposed that these 74 officers be trained in a series of eight Security courses, run over an eight-month period. The D.M.O.&I. supported him, and added six vacancies for the reserves before sending it to D.M.T. Even at this late date, he still thought ". . . that the Field Security Course is designed primarily for officers . . . on Intelligence duties . . . in Canada in contrast to the Intelligence Course which deals with Intelligence duties in the field".[6]

Interrogators were also required. Interrogation was one of the responsibilities of the Divisional I.O., but interrogators were specialists who were appointed only after they had qualified at the Interrogation Course at Matlock. D.M.T. thought such a course would be difficult to run. Lt.-Col. Murray advised the D.M.O.&I. that R.M.C. had a good deal of material, but no instructor. D.M.I. was compiling a list of servicemen proficient in German and Italian, and suggested that the Auxiliary Services be asked to give German courses to interested persons "as part of their regular training". In October 1941, R.M.C. proposed that an Interrogation Wing be set up to provide four-week courses in German and Italian, with course loads of eight and four candidates, respectively, and that other branches be established to teach Spanish and Japanese. When the War Office offered 10 vacancies on courses it would give in February and March 1942, and, in addition, an exchange of instructors between R.M.C. and Matlock, the plan to begin a course at Kingston was shelved until 1943.[7]

After war broke out in the Pacific, Maj. Orville Eadie, then G.S.O.2 (Int) at R.M.C., suggested that the Veterans Guard of Canada (V.G. of C.) be given a two-week Intelligence and Security Course to prepare them for their increasingly important role in Home Defence. The Officer Administering the V.G. of C. thought that a five-day course would be especially useful for the "extracting of valuable information from Ps. of W". The D.M.T. saw no apparent reason either for the course or for interrogating P.W. who "presumably have been fully interrogated before reaching Canada". The V.G. of C. were already given occasional vacancies; the D.M.T. thought this should continue.[8]

Until 1942, the Section Intelligence Officer in Canada trained his own men. The practice produced close personal links in the Sections, but it precluded uniform standards. To overcome this weakness, Maj. Eadie proposed on March 31st to centralize F.S. N.C.O. training, and he pointed out the many advantages that would accrue if their course could coincide with that of the officers. The D.M.O.&I. supported R.M.C.'s proposal.

To Lt.-Col. H.A. Sparling, D.M.T., quartering and training other ranks at R.M.C., "a centre for higher military training", was anathema. Maj. Eric Acland replied that not only was adequate alternate accommodation available within marching distance, but that training had to take place at R.M.C.; the

Students on the first Field Security Course, 25 May–21 June 1941, conducting a field exercise. (Capt. C. Chauveau collection/ Canadian Forces School of Military Intelligence, Kingston/Canada. Dept. of National Defence)

D.I.O.s and Security Intelligence Officers (S.I.O.s) had neither the time nor the facilities to train their men themselves. The G.S.O.1 seized the opportunity to propose, unfortunately without success, that a separate Intelligence Training Centre be established. In the end, the candidates were accommodated at Fort Frontenac in winter and under canvas nearby in summer.[9]

In May 1942, C.M.H.Q. asked for 12 German-speaking officers for I.O. posts, and six men for the Type "B" Wireless Intelligence Section. Lt.-Col. Murray reminded the D.M.T. that the Army had no policy on linguists. In practice, people with a knowledge of a foreign language would approach an I.O., who would arrange for them to be tested at the nearest University; the test was always performed conscientiously, and without fee. Some of the candidates who failed the test would have been able to qualify after further practice, but there was no official way of helping them to gain this practice. In Lt.-Col. Murray's opinion, German and Japanese language training was as important as weapons training to the Army, and he thought the Service should provide the facilities needed to bring a suitable man to the desired level.

The Section had received no guidance with respect to Japanese linguists and had been forced to make its own estimate of what the requirements were likely to be. The G.S.O.1 foresaw that Chinese and Russian (as well as Japanese) interpreters would be needed as Interrogators, Translators, Wireless Intercept Section staffs, and Liaison Officers, if Canada had to fight in the Pacific. He considered that only a few could be obtained from the United States, and that Canada would have to provide its own, that it would have to be self-sufficient. He suggested that the regulations be relaxed to permit the enlistment of Canadian-born Japanese "who are adept in reading and speaking the language and who have completely severed their ties with Japan". He pointed out that this was the current, but unpublicized, American policy, and also that former students from the Canadian Academy at Kobe were being enlisted in the R.C.N. and the R.C.A.F., with ranks with which the Army could not compete. Col. Murray then asked for authority to conduct a census of linguists, offered to ask the G.O.C. Pacific Command for his views, recommended that an offer from the American Japanese Intelligence School at Camp Savage (near Minneapolis, Minnesota) be accepted, proposed to run a refresher course for German-speaking personnel at R.M.C., and recommended that linguists be commissioned immediately on entry to the Service.[10] D.M.T. supported most of the proposals, but delays in arranging accommodation and instruction deferred the German course until July 1943. Japanese language training became a responsibility of Pacific Command, and will be discussed later in this chapter.

The whole question of training coincided with steps then being taken to form a Canadian Intelligence Corps, and with attempts by the D.M.I. to expand his own facilities. Preliminary instructions for the forming of the Corps were issued on November 6th, 1942. Formal approval was not received until March

Col. W.W. "Jock" Murray, O.B.E., M.C. and Bar, Director of Military Intelligence, 4 July 1942 to 16 Februrary 1946. (Photo collection Canadian Forces School of Military Intelligence, Kingston/Canada. Dept. of National Defence)

1st, 1943, mainly because the office of the Director of Mobilization mislaid the policy file. On April 8th, Maj. H.D. Adamson (Mobilization 2) was made responsible for the new C.Int.C. He was to locate and keep track of personnel passing through the Security courses at R.M.C.; set up Corps records; compile the General Lists with the help of the Directorate of Personnel; deal with postings, transfers, selection, and despatch of overseas reinforcements; calculate overseas requirements; provide a Corps badge; and consider establishing an "N.D.H.Q. Details Intelligence Corps", in which personnel in transit for

D.M.I. Staff, Ottawa, July 1945. Seated in front row, from right to left are: Lt.-Col. E. Drake, M.I.2, Col. W.W. Murray, D.M.I., Lt.-Col. E. Acland, D.D.M.I., Lt.-Col. P.W. Cooke, M.I.1, Maj. C.G. Jones, M.I.3.

overseas could be held. D.M.I. had no nominal rolls for overseas units, but it did have rolls and record cards of all C.Int.C. personnel in Canada as well as those who had graduated from the Canadian War Intelligence Course.[11]

By May 4th, 1943, 24 Security and Intelligence units were already formed, one additional unit was authorized, and four others were awaiting authorization. They were distributed across Canada as follows: Security Intelligence Sections at both Pacific and Atlantic Commands, one Detachment with the Embarkation Commandant at Halifax, Sections at M.D.s 2 and 3 and at Camps Borden and Petawawa, a Divisional I.O. and an F.S. Section at Sixth, Seventh, and Eighth Divisions, and No. 1 Discrimination Unit and miscellaneous personnel at N.D.H.Q. Command H.Q. had small Intelligence staffs; N.D.H.Q. was in the process of forming a Holding Unit of 85 men. Including those overseas, there were 11 F.S. Sections, 11 formation Intelligence Sections, four Security Intelligence Sections (Canada), two Wireless Intelligence Sections, and the Discrimination Unit.

The new C.Int.C. needed its own distinctive badge. There was a good deal of speculation in the Intelligence Community as to the form of this badge, and those with artistic talent in D.M.I. sketched suggestions for it, some of them vulgar. At that time, there was a reaction against the use of Latin in mottos, and a number of alternatives appear with the sketches. They were passed to Col. A.F. Duguid, who rejected them, suggesting instead the old Corps of Guides badge with new titles. One of these was finally found in the Royal Canadian Military Institute and used as a model. On May 11th, 1943, Lt.-Col. Eric

15. ORGANIZATION AND TRAINING: OTTAWA 1939-45

Seated left to right in first row: Lt.-Col. W.A Todd, M.I.3, Lt.-Col. A.C. Wygard, M.I.4, Maj. D.D. Cameron, M.I.2, Maj. E.L. Williams, M.I.3, Maj. A.N.K. Hobbes, M.I.3, Maj. J.H. Moorehouse, M.I.3. (C.G. Jones and C. Chauveau collection/Canadian Forces School of Military Intelligence, Kingston/Canada. Dept. of National Defence)

Acland, acting for his Director, informed D. Adm. that the D.M.I. wanted the Corps of Guides badge with its centre open, and backed by green cloth. The Latin motto VIRTUTE ET LABORE on the bottom scroll would be replaced by CANADIAN INTELLIGENCE CORPS; the scroll around the magnetic bearings would retain the words GUIDES, CANADA. The cap and collar badges, and buttons, in silver or white metal instead of brass, would be those of the Guides. The proposed new design, with one change that replaced GUIDES, CANADA with ACTION FROM KNOWLEDGE, was approved and brought into use at once, although it was not given Royal Assent until April 30th, 1947. As an aside, silver was selected for the insignia ostensibly because it was distinctive and needed little polishing, but actually to honour Col. Murray, the D.M.I., whose First World War regiment wore silver.[12]

On January 4th, 1943, Col. Murray asked the C.G.S. to authorize a major extension of Intelligence training at what had become known as the Canadian War Intelligence Course (C.W.I.C.). Instead of the three courses then being given, he asked for seven, for increases in instructional and administrative staffs, and for the use of R.M.C. as an Intelligence School. He obtained agreement in principle on January 28th, 1943, and began at once to work out the details. Col. Murray based his submission on three outstanding requirements: Commands and Districts needed additional courses in German and Japanese Army organization and tactics, Intelligence duties in the field, and Security; more linguists had to be provided; and a remedy was needed to counter serious deficiencies in numbers and quality of Intelligence officers and men in Canada and overseas. The Canadian Army Overseas had 68 officers and 255 men in Intelligence positions. The British were then changing their Intelligence establishments and, although the precise total was not yet known, increases were expected. In Canada, the Department had recently taken over the P.W. Camps, and additional I.O.s were needed for them. Even at this early stage there were indications that the supply of reinforcements would be limited. The Army as a whole suffered from these shortages, but Intelligence was especially vulnerable because many graduates of the R.M.C. Intelligence Courses were not being placed in appointments for which they had qualified.[13]

On April 22nd, 1943, Lt.-Col. G.P. Henderson, G.S.O.1 (Int), First Canadian Army, prepared a comprehensive memorandum on the training and reinforcement of Intelligence officers overseas, in which he carefully differentiated between a "non-Corps" officer in an Intelligence Staff post and a Canadian Intelligence Corps specialist. Of the 41 officers and other ranks he had received as reinforcements from Canada, nine (22 per cent) were unsuitable for reasons that ranged all the way from over-age (3) to mentally unbalanced. He had found that training in Britain had progressed to the point where he was able to fill all vacancies except those in the Wireless Intelligence Section Type "A" (Army). The fact that personal suitability could only be gauged after, not before, a man had been trained, together with the difficulty of finding any reinforcements at all, was ample cause to hold a larger reserve in the Intelligence Training Company in Britain simply to cover normal wastage and casualties. The 30 officers and 105 other ranks he needed could not be procured from field units, since these were preparing for their Invasion roles.

Col. Henderson compared Canadian training courses unfavourably with those given in Britain. He assumed that the Operational and Security Intelligence Course was the equivalent of the British War Intelligence Course. The R.M.C. four-week Photographic Interpretation Course could not produce the same result as the two British courses of nine weeks, followed by a one-to three-month attachment to the Photographic Unit for practical experience. In his opinion, the Other Ranks F.S. Course was the equal of British courses, but it had only sent him 10 men. He felt that the Other Ranks Intelligence Section Course was similar to that at the Intelligence Company, and should be eliminated. The All-Ranks German Refresher Course was excellent, but he considered that the Interrogation Course should only be given by experts working under realistic conditions. The British were doing precisely this, and he thought that Canada would be wise to use them for it. The U.K. also gave training in Special Wireless, an area which R.M.C. did not cover.[14]

The D.C.G.S.(a) concurred, and enjoined the D.M.I. to ensure that future candidates for Intelligence received basic military training first, and that trained men were not lost in the reinforcement stream. On June 22nd, the C.G.S. rejected the proposed Interrogation Course, but ordered two instructors to be returned from Britain for the German Language Refresher Course and for the Photographic Interpretation Courses, which were open only to men serving in Canada. Approval was also granted for a larger reserve, and for the School to be retained, without, however, any increase in staff. The School was to graduate around 140 men a year, divided equally between Canada and overseas, a figure well within its capabilities.

The instructor in photo interpretation was Capt. H.J. Basso; he had been associated with Interpretation from its early days in Britain, had performed well in Exercise SPARTAN, and was a knowledgeable and hard-working officer. Unfortunately, the British training material he had sent ahead had not arrived; he did not even have any Photo Interpreter Kits – the boxed collection of scales, magnifying glass, and stereoscope that are vital to instruction. He tried unsuccessfully to find some in Washington, while collecting material from the Central Film Library. As a result, a suggestion was made, but rejected on administrative grounds, that he be attached to an American school to which Canadians could be sent.[15] His candidates first completed the Intelligence Course, and were then given a study program and ultimately a photo course, which ran from September 27th to November 20th. Four of its eight students went overseas.

In early November 1943, Ottawa allowed Pacific Command to form a Photo Interpretation Wing at its Divisional Jungle Warfare School at Prince George. The Command decided shortly afterwards that it was preferable to run the course closer to its H.Q. at Victoria, with a staff of three officers and nine men, and a course load of 20. It gave two-week courses for senior officers (essentially a photo-reader's course to enable them to use photos in planning), and a four-week course for junior interpreters.

On October 5th, 1943, Col. Murray tried again to secure authorization for the Japanese Army courses. He asked for two officer-instructors, with recent experience against the Japanese, to give four-week courses at R.M.C. Their classes would average 15 staff and regimental officers; the syllabus would include Japanese organization, tactics, equipment, and doctrine.[16] D.M.T., misreading both purpose and content of the course, thought that it should put its emphasis on the study of Allied armies instead, and that it should be co-ordinated with the current Jungle Warfare training. In his rebuttal, Col. Murray pointed out that the course did not need to be tied to Jungle Warfare, and that it could be run in any classroom. What was essential, in his view, was that the Canadian Army should recognize and should remedy its complete ignorance of everything Japanese. He was convinced that ". . . we are obliged to get ahead of G.S. policy and make provision for what we reasonably and logically feel are going to be the demands made upon us once G.S. policy is crystallized". He won his case, and an Australian Army officer, Maj. R.W.T. Cowan, was attached for six months as instructor, from January 31st, 1944. Canadians sent on exchange to Australia included Capts. M.M. Perrault, instructor at R.M.C., R.L. Archibald, M.I.1, and R.M. Baldwin, C.Int.C., Canadian Army Staff, Washington.

Lt.-Col. R.O. MacFarlane replaced Lt.-Col. Charley Krug at R.M.C. on May 16th, 1944. By that time the C.W.I.C. was divided into three wings: Military Intelligence, with a G.S.O.2 and four G.S.O.3s; a German Refresher Wing, with one G.S.O.2 and three W.O.IIs; and a Field Security Wing with one G.S.O.2, one G.S.O.3, two W.O.s, and two S/Sgts. On November 24th, 1944, D.M.I. advised C.M.H.Q. that, in view of the suspension of all specialist training in Canada, Intelligence training would be halted at the end of the current courses unless there was an urgent demand from Britain for its continuance. The Military Intelligence Course ended on December 20th; the German Refresher, F.S. Officers; and Other Ranks, on January 17th, 1945.

The C.W.I.C. was the only general instructional unit for Intelligence personnel in Canada. Yet records on its activities are incomplete. It ran 23 War Intelligence, 32 F.S. (Officers), 23 F.S. (Men), and 12 German Refresher courses between May 1941 and January 1945. (Other than the one Photo course cited, there is no record of training in that field.) In that 182-week period, it conducted a total of 434 course-weeks, with a maximum potential course-loading of about 1,550 students. The actual total was well below that; we have seen that in 1944 only 140 candidates were to be trained. Most early graduates did go to Intelligence appointments, particularly in Canada, but the later ones did not, partly through the deficiencies in the reinforcement system, partly because they were employed in their units and did not go on "in the trade". It was obvious that First Army preferred training in the U.K. to that of C.W.I.C., and yet there was a need for a Canadian-based, domestic-oriented training facility.

It is possible that the duplication of training facilities had an adverse effect upon the establishment of a formal School in Canada. But a more basic reason was the fact that the program neither began soon enough, nor did it produce a graduate who was clearly a man doing a job for which such training was essential. Proficiency in Combat Intelligence in Canada was largely academic; exercises rarely provide the true flavour of battle. The proficiency of Security staffs could only be judged by their superiors, and remedies taken as appropriate. Standards of instruction were not, therefore, apparent to outsiders.

The late development of a training establishment stemmed in turn from the slow growth of D.M.I. as a separate Directorate, coupled with the fact that it was not until well into 1942 that it began to be regarded not merely as a staff function but also as the head of a far-flung and complex Service. As such, its function was as much administrative as operational. But even D.M.I. itself was slow to recognize this. It never had sufficient staff to deal with administration, which includes training.

JAPANESE LANGUAGE TRAINING

Most Canadian Army linguists owed their capability to what the Service described as "inherent skills" – knowledge of a language gained from parental backgrounds or acquired in other ways before entering Active Service. The political decision not to employ people of Japanese ancestry in the Army had virtually closed the door to recruiting men with these inherent skills. At the national level, interest in Japanese already had a long history. As early as 1921, the Commissioner of the R.C.M.P. had said that the effectiveness of his Force, which had to police Asian communities, was lessened by the fact that almost no one in Canada knew the languages. The same thing was true of the Armed Forces, and of those Departments dealing in external relations and trade. He recommended that a School of Oriental Languages, assisted by a grant-in-aid, be set up at the University of British Columbia. Col. Sutherland Brown, D.M.O.&I., strongly supported the project, suggested that textbooks be free, instructors be paid, and an annual proficiency grant be authorized. The C.G.S. asked Maj.-Gen. J.S. Ross, G.O.C., M.D. 11, if he had any interested officers. A small class of six students was started in Victoria; they included Maj.-Gen. Ross, who joined, in his own words, "to set an example". The cost, $30 per month for three lectures a week, was defrayed by the officers themselves. On September 9th, 1921, the C.G.S. reported to the Defence Committee, and suggested that successful students finish their training in Japan.

An unsigned, undated, but contemporary memorandum, which was obviously intended to answer possible questions regarding further training in Japan, estimated the cost at £700-800 ($3,500-4,000) per officer, over and above his pay. It discussed the desired personal characteristics of candidates, gave its firm opinion that one year was not adequate for real proficiency, and added a suggestion which, if it had been accepted, would have guaranteed recruiting: ". . . firms should be urged to make it worthwhile for their young men to learn Japanese . . . even at the cost of keeping a Japanese mistress". As late as 1930, unsuccessful efforts were still being made to develop a policy for sending men to Japan; in 1939, there were virtually no Japanese linguists in the Canadian Army.[17] By 1942, the requirement for them was urgent.

The Military Intelligence Service of the United States gave a Japanese Language Course at Camp Savage, Minnesota, and a preliminary course at Ann Arbor, Michigan, for men, usually Nisei, who already had a basic knowledge of the language. In July 1942, when Canada was offered 20 positions, no suitable Canadian candidates could be found. In late June 1943, D.M.I., working through the Canadian Army Staff at Washington, sent four officers, an officer cadet, and 10 other ranks to Camp Savage.[18] Curiously, no effort seems to have been made then or later to send candidates to the Japanese courses at the

London School of Oriental and African Studies, which trained most of the British linguists.

The D.M.I.'s action prompted Lt.-Col. B.R. Mullaly, G.S.O.1 (Int), Pacific Command (which was responsible for the Pacific front), to ask N.D.H.Q. for official facilities for language training. He had a quite inadequate civilian school, and wanted a better one, capable of giving students enough grounding in Japanese to profit from any more advanced courses that might be open. He estimated the cost at $400 per month, for two Canadian-born Japanese instructors to handle a course capacity of 20. Col. Murray supported his proposal, the C.G.S. obtained Ministerial approval on June 2nd, and Pacific Command asked for an advance of $500 on the 8th. It was granted on the 16th, and, at long last, Japanese language training in the Canadian Army was officially launched.[19]

In mid-October 1943, the Commandant of the School at Camp Savage sent the D.M.I. a rather discouraging report, stating that only eight of the 15 Canadian students showed potential, and that even they needed six months additional training. He was convinced that only Nisei could benefit fully from the instruction given at his school; it was learned later that those Canadians who did have some knowledge of the language were in the top third of the class. Col. Murray pointed out to the C.G.S. that this raised the issue of the extent to which Canadian Nisei should be enlisted or employed in the Canadian Armed Forces; he acknowledged the difficulty of assessing their loyalty, and dealt at length with the existing prejudice against Japanese. He went on:

> ... the question of such enlistment is, however, governed by the character of the employment envisaged for them; and that ... can only be determined after promulgation of a policy ... covering our contemplated participation in the Far East campaign. Until that has been determined, it is difficult to advise whether Nisei should or should not be enlisted and trained for such Intelligence work. ... Should such a policy be decided ... without preliminary warning, we may be caught unprepared.[20]

On November 13th, Col. Mullaly had nine officers and 13 men taking unofficial language instruction at a branch of the Vocational Training School on Inverness Avenue in Vancouver. The O.C. was Maj. A.P. McKenzie, M.C., who had taught school in Japan from 1920 to 1941. His Chief Instructor, 2/Lieut. Paul V. Halley, who had a very good knowledge of Chinese as well as Japanese, and an instructor, David Bee, had been recruited from Postal Censorship. When his first two Nisei were recalled by their parent firms, they were replaced by a Mr. Griffith, a Welshman who had been employed in the British Consulate General in Yokohama, and his wife, a Korean graduate of the Imperial University. They were ostensibly giving vocational training, and so were paid by the Dominion-Provincial Youth and War Emergency Training Plan. To ensure that his graduates had a job to go to, he suggested that a Corps of Interpreters should be organized, to be used for immediate tactical interpretation purposes at Brigade H.Q. and below. To provide them, he recommended that the Camp Savage course, which he thought inappropriate, be replaced by a Pacific Command course lasting one year, divided into a Junior and a Senior Wing, with intakes spaced every six months. Prospective students would be carefully screened to ensure a high standard of physical fitness and education. He proposed an initial course load of 24, and subsequent intakes of 20. As a result of his submission, the group at Camp Savage was withdrawn; some men returned to their units while others formed the basis of the first Canadian course in September 1943.[21]

The course was reorganized on January 26th, 1944, as a Pacific Command School, which meant it was outside D.M.T.'s jurisdiction. It was later placed on Active Service by Order-in-Council and, on October 1st, 1944, was re-named the S-20 Japanese Language School. Its purpose was to turn out interpreters in the shortest possible time. Its course, which remained basically the same during the life of the School, was divided equally between written and spoken work, and was followed by six months of intensive study of military terminology, P.W. interrogation, geography, and military doctrine, organization, and tactics. The course was both sound and practical, shorn of non-essentials, built up after carefully analyzing the British and American systems, coloured by Maj. McKenzie's personal experience, and modified by the results of the first few months of experimentation.

It had many administrative challenges. It had to endure changes of location and attempts by higher authority to house other rank students in ill-lit and inadequate barracks; it struggled hard, but in vain, to secure promotion and/or Trades Pay for other rank graduates; it also failed to achieve pay raises for its civilian instructors. Perhaps its greatest handicap came from the fact that, in spite of frequent requests, it was never given a clear statement of the number of students it was expected to train. In view of the time it took to train a Japanese linguist, this lack of direction militated against an efficient instructional program.[22]

The estimated total Allied translator requirement for the force to occupy Japan and the islands was 5,487 by January 1946, and 7,502 by January 1947. Canada was expected to provide 135 and 235 respectively. Both figures were unrealistically high, but the School might have trained enough people to meet the 1947 quota. In mid-August 1945; 114 students were under instruction; 26 were to be available at the end of September, 18 by mid-December, 38 by the end of March, and 32 by the end of June. D.M.I. knew that the U.S. Navy was continuing to keep its school open, and suggested that Canada should do the same, "not only to meet the requirements of all three armed Services, but also the diplomatic and commercial requirements of the Dominion, the Pacific interests of which can hardly fail to expand and evolve".[23]

It was decided that the courses should continue until the end of the Junior Course in June 1946. The male students were encouraged to complete their program, and would then be given the option of joining the Interim Force, or of taking their discharge; the female students were discharged. Minor administrative problems were to be referred to the appropriate D.N.D. Directorates, the civilian personnel would be retired, and the training material would be collected and stored. A few outstanding matters relating to other variously employed Canadians, including C.W.A.C. in Washington with the Pacific Military Intelligence Research Section (P.A.C.M.I.R.S.), were passed to the Directorate of Organization. The School was closed on July 15th, 1946.

A total of 232 students attended S-20 between August 1943 and July 1946: 202 male members of the Canadian Army, 62 of them Nisei, 14 C.W.A.C., 9 R.C.N., 2 R.C.A.F., 4 R.N.V.R., and one R.A.A.F. Of these, 137 completed the full course and were qualified; 16 were given a special three months course before they were sent to No. 1 Special Wireless Group Intelligence Section; three C.W.A.C. were posted to P.A.C.M.I.R.S. after their six months Junior Course; seven R.C.A.F. and R.C.N. were transferred to duty before graduation; 24 resigned, six left for medical reasons, six Nisei transferred to other duties, five were taken on the School staff before graduation, and 28 who would have graduated left to return to school.[24] This was a new, rather daring but not unsuccessful venture in Canadian military training. Many of its graduates found themselves in strange places, doing jobs they had never known existed, but which were demonstrably necessary. It was also very economical; the staff worked terribly long hours to make it so. At minimum cost in men, and without political commitment, it offered the Canadian Government the opportunity to make a significant contribution to victory in the Pacific, and to postwar reconstruction. It is possible that had this training been given in Eastern Canada, where its results were more obvious, the opportunity might not have been missed.

At no time did S-20 train for clandestine operations. But it did become involved in the provision of some Japanese linguists for them. The Allied forces had both overt and covert requirements for Japanese and Chinese linguists. The use of Chinese raised no great issues, but the political and social considerations involved in recruiting Japanese in Canada were not understood abroad. Other Allies seemed to think that the large numbers of them who lived in Canada and who, presumably, could be considered loyal to democratic principles, would be an excellent source. We have seen in Chapter 14 how some of them were used. Here we shall see how they were provided.

The first Japanese linguists were E. Matsuyama, R.C.C.S, and F. Yamamoto, U. Tsubota, and later S.P. Yamauchi, all R.C.O.C. and all members of the Service before December 1941. On July 15th, 1942, the War Office requested the loan of the first three for duties at the School of Oriental and African Studies at London University. C.M.H.Q. made them available, but apparently did not advise N.D.H.Q. In lieu of Trades Pay, they were given the rank of Acting Corporal; in December, Yamauchi joined them, and they became Acting Sergeants. Unsuccessful attempts to have them commissioned continued up until June 8th, 1945, by which time they had been promoted to A/W.O.II. C.M.H.Q. was then told that there were no vacancies for them, and they were returned to Canada in August 1945.[25]

On April 26th, 1944, the D.M.I., Melbourne, asked D.M.I., Ottawa, for assistance in obtaining Nisei for the Australian Translator and Interpreter Section. Col. Murray recommended that Canada provide 20–30 thoroughly vetted, fluent men, willing to serve anywhere. The C.G.S. refused because of the political difficulties involved, but he asked D.M.I. to find out if Australia would enlist them directly and, secondly, if S-20 could provide them. The D.M.I. explained the situation to the Australian High Commissioner, and undertook to find out how many could be recruited; he offered four Caucasian S-20 graduates, and suggested that Australia should send its own students to S-20.[26]

On June 23rd, the D.M.I. circulated, somewhat prematurely, an instruction that applicants for enrolment "from Japanese of British ancestry" would be interviewed. On June 28th, the British Security Co-ordinator told D.S.D. that H.Q. South East Asia Command (S.E.A.C.) needed Canadian-born Japanese, if possible by September 1st, for front-line propaganda work with the Indian Army. He already had six names, and hoped for 35 more; they would be sent in uniform to India, either to remain in the Canadian Army, or to be discharged and re-enlisted in the Indian Army. An alternative was to send them to England as civilians, and to enlist them into the Indian Army there.[27]

Opinion varied as to the actual availability of Japanese-Canadians. On July 6th, 1944, Maj. Bray, G.S.O.2 (Int), Pacific Command, told D.M.I. that he had had no applications for two years. Since Bill 135, then before the Senate, proposed to disenfranchise all persons of Japanese ancestry, he thought that the Japanese would want to be sure of their position before they would enlist. On the other hand, Lieut. C. Thomas of D.M.I. interviewed nine applicants in Toronto on July 20th, and thought there would be more once the word got around.

The C.G.S. advised the B.S.C. to consult the Secretary of State, because Canadian regulations still did not permit such enlistments. The War Office, anticipating a favourable response to its request for Nisei, answered Admiral Mountbatten, Supreme Commander S.E.A.C., with the following suggestions: that S.E.A.C. should set up its own training facility on the model of Camp Savage, that a force should be organized to provide two officers to every 10 Nisei corporals, that it have a Canadian administrative staff, with a ceiling of 200, including officers and the administrative cadre, and that it be attached to South East Asia Translators and Interpreters Centre (S.E.A.T.I.C.). The copy that was sent to Ottawa asked also for an additional 10 instructors for London.[28]

Lt.-Col. Acland asked Pacific Command if it could provide basic and advanced training at S-20 and, if so, how many students could be accepted. At N.D.H.Q., the D.C.G.S.(c) first separated the two demands into translators and propagandists, and then attempted to telescope the training time. He suggested that some students could be trained by the Special Wireless Group then being prepared for S.E.A.C., that the Nisei should be carefully selected to ensure that they really were linguistically competent, and that S-20 officers could be used. But he considered that the commitment Canada had made to India governed the number of translators who could be sent to Australia. This meant, of course, that for the present the Australian request had to be held in abeyance.

The submission that finally went to the Minister asked for authority to enlist Nisei. It proposed also that S-20 be moved to a normal camp, where recruits could be given their basic training; its authors seem to have forgotten how much such a move would interfere with language training, its primary role. Eight two-officer, 10-man teams were to be sent to India and two to Australia. When the decision became known, the Japanese-language *New Canadian*, of Kaslo, B.C., published a speculative article that bothered the Censors. In the end, however, the Cabinet War Committee decided not to enlist Nisei, but to allow them to enlist in Allied forces. B.S.C., which by this time had received 12 applications, was prepared to take them to England, but wanted assurance that they would be allowed back into Canada afterwards. External Affairs could "see no objection to this".

These complex negotiations confused the R.C.M.P., who asked plaintively on October 30th for clarification, "in view of an apparent conflict in policy". Lt.-Col. Acland assured them that there was no change in policy, but that he expected one. On January 17th, 1945, the War Cabinet, reversing its earlier decision, permitted 100 Japanese-Canadians to be enlisted, and at the same time authorized direct contact between the District H.Q. and R.C.M.P. Divisions. Two additional linguists, George Tomita and Eiji Yatabe, were assigned to D.M.I. By February 17th, 119 applications had been received, and 74 were accepted. Fifty were sent to do their basic training in Ontario, and the other 24 were sent to the B.S.C.; they were to wear Infantry badges, not Intelligence. On March 9th, D.S.D. advised the C.G.S. that a Joint Intelligence Committee meeting in Washington had agreed to pool the limited Nisei resources, and that the War Office would act as co-ordinator within the Commonwealth. This agreement did not affect the previous commitments to the B.S.C. or to Psychological Warfare (External Affairs), but it did have a bearing on the Australian request for 200. By April 6th, 12 had already left for India. On May 17th, the Minister was asked to authorize an additional 150 for Australia; he did so on July 10th.

On August 1st, D.M.I. reported that 125 Japanese-Canadians had been recruited; 52 were at S-20, 35 had gone to S.E.A.C., three were in Australia, and 35 were at the Basic Training Centres. The Pacific Force, however, now needed 19 translators, later raised to two officers and 28 men. Australia asked for 200, S.E.A.C. needed 200 including the 35 already there, the War Office wanted 186, and P.A.C.M.I.R.S. wanted 20. The D.M.I. doubted that he could find more than 250 of this total of 625; only 135, in fact, were ever recruited. He blamed the poor response on the lack of publicity; the only public statement was made by the Prime Minister on April 25th, when he said that enrolment was sufficient to meet U.K. and Commonwealth requests. The Japanese-Canadians, who were already resentful as a result of their treatment by the Canadian government, disliked the secrecy surrounding their enlistment, and the strictness of the loyalty guarantees required. In addition, and this seems to have come as a surprise to the recruiters, many Nisei were not fluent in Japanese. No one seems to have realized that the average young Japanese-Canadian entered the work force early, and tried hard to integrate himself into the anglophone environment, rather than following traditional family patterns. Few language courses were given in Japanese-Canadian communities, and many Nisei spoke only the simple colloquial speech used in the home. It was ironical that, while the Nisei were suspected of disloyalty, most had worked so hard to integrate with the Canadian way of life that they had lost their ability to use the language of their parents.

There may also have been opposition within some family groups. Censorship stopped one most heart-rending letter from a girl to her soldier-brother. She called him a traitor to his race, and invited him to forget that he was a member of her family because, she assured him, the family was going to forget him. Personal mail was rarely stopped, but the Censor rightly regarded her letter as likely to foster disaffection in the Service. At the same time, one cannot avoid feeling sympathy for the young sister, torn between her love of her brother and her love for her family and its background.

The actual employment of these potential Chinese and Japanese specialists was a considerable disappointment to most of them. Their tasks had been arranged at the highest level, but their administration and control at lower levels were bad. They were never properly trained, few of them were usefully employed, and, by the time an adequate program had been worked out, the war was over and they were returned to Canada. So much more could have been done so easily, if only the problems had been recognized early enough for positive action to have been taken. The political obstacles in the case of the Japanese-Canadians were admittedly great, but they were far from insurmountable.

At the same time, these incidents show how necessary it is for Intelligence staffs not to get too far ahead of the immediate mission. They face a perpetual dilemma. If they do not look far enough ahead, and in matters of long-term training that can mean many months, they may find that a skill does not exist at the time it is needed. The planning and preparation must always be flexible enough to compensate for changes in direction. In their preparations for providing Intelligence support in the Pacific it is just possible that the desire to develop unique expertise, and their own enthusiasms, may have taken Cols. Murray and Mullaly a little further than their very pronounced common sense should have allowed. Canada was still a long way from being Pacific-oriented – and they knew it.

16.
STRATEGIC AND OPERATIONAL INTELLIGENCE IN CANADA 1939–46

As had been the case in 1914, no serious attempt was made in 1939 to provide the Canadian force being sent overseas with useful background information on the enemy. N.D.H.Q. had no directly controlled sources abroad and no Intelligence staff capable of handling more than the most general data. The A.D.M.I.'s office had not kept abreast of current foreign developments in weaponry and tactics. The second C.E.F. may have thought it was in a better position than the first, for at least some of its members had served in France in 1918. In reality, there was little to choose between the state of unpreparedness in Intelligence at Defence H.Q. in 1914 and its counterpart in 1939.

An Intelligence staff at any H.Q. supplies the Commander with the information he needs for his task. The Canadian Active Service Force (C.A.S.F.) was intended to support the army of a major power on whose greater development of Intelligence sources it could rely. Once overseas, therefore, it needed no Intelligence support from Canada. Ottawa needed Intelligence for long-range planning and development, and to assist political decision-making. As we have seen, Col. E.L.M. Burns at C.M.H.Q. realized this rather more quickly than either his immediate superiors or D.N.D., and instituted a program of collection which provided Canadian Defence H.Q. with most of its Intelligence material. The only operational commitment within Canada itself was the defence of the two coasts, a function which was soon delegated to the respective Command H.Q.

The Strategic Intelligence Staff in A.D.M.I. was therefore in a somewhat invidious position. It knew that it was required to collect all the information it could about the war, the enemy, and potential enemies, and yet it seemed that the C.G.S. did not really need the few items it could offer. These were very few indeed; it had no direct access to adequate and relevant information; almost everything it received had already been filtered through other agencies.

The prewar Intelligence collection system, based on news reports, was now inadequate. Censorship had eliminated many of its sources, and news from enemy territory was suspect. The Staff turned instead to examining the speculative assessments in the press. On January 25th, 1940, A.D.M.I. produced a paper, entitled "Trends of Opinion connected with the War". It so impressed the C.G.S. that he ordered it to be continued and, by the end of 1940, Capt.

R.E.L. Ste. Marie and his two clerks had turned it into a Weekly War Review. Ultimately, M.I.1 was clipping 3,500 to 4,000 items taken from 66 newspapers and magazines every week, and circulating them through a widely distributed Daily Press Service. In mid-February 1943, its responsibility for domestic coverage was transferred to the Chief of Information Services. When the war ended, the files were used to compile a detailed review of the period as seen through the public press. The magazine index formed the basis for the very wide selection now kept in the Departmental Library.[1]

The original Book System required the Districts to participate. The A.D.M.I. soon realized that this was leading to excessive duplication. But when he tried to stop the allotment of subscription monies, the Districts protested, arguing for their continuance on the grounds that the press was a useful source of information on weaknesses in morale or Security, and on "matters likely to bring the Service into disrepute"; a fact most had really only just realized. Because it was responsible for centralizing and controlling expenditure on periodicals, the Printing and Stationery Branch was caught in the middle of this feud. In the end, the Department agreed to pay for one paper in each major Canadian city, for a $150 subscription in each District to the *New York Times*, and $166 for magazine subscriptions. The time and effort the Staff officers concerned expended on the dispute through most of the war, if costed, would probably have paid for all the publications wanted by everyone.[2]

The Section also received a good deal of official material. The earliest was "Intelligence Summary No. 1 on the General War Situation", which, as we have seen, was prepared from British material by C.M.H.Q. in early February 1940. The C.G.S. had it reproduced in two copies, one for himself and the other for the A.D.M.I./D.M.O.&I. The first British Technical Intelligence publications arrived in July 1940; they were given wide distribution. By early 1941, M.I.1 was receiving the British Intelligence Summary, the War Office Weekly Intelligence Commentary, the Weekly Political Intelligence Summary, the G.H.Q. Intelligence Summary, the War Office Summary, and the Daily Digest of World Wireless Propaganda. By that summer, it was also receiving Press Surveys, particularly of Central and South America, Canadian Consular Reports, Trade and Political Intelligence Summaries, arms production and transportation studies, Censorship extracts from other than Canadian sources, and reports of Japanese radio broadcast intercepts.[3] All this material was broken down into its component items, collated, and used as the basis of subsequent studies and reports.

By mid-1941, Latin America was recognized as a potentially dangerous channel between Nazi Germany and the Western Hemisphere, through which threats to Canadian internal security might slip. Until it declared war on the Axis in March 1944, Argentina, with its somewhat Fascist administration, was thought to be a prime avenue for German infiltration; Brazil, Chile, and Cuba

M.I.1 Section, 13 December 1944. Front row: Capt. J.K. Ross, Capt. R.F. Macey, Maj. R.L. Archibald, Maj. P. Geymonat, Lt.-Col. O. Eadie, Maj. C. Chauveau, Maj. A.F.P. Freeman, Capt. A. Hutchison. Centre row: Lieut. R.W. Jones, Cpl. B.G.C. Millar, Pte. M.E. Porter, Sgt. C. Feingold, Pte. G.L.M. Deeks, L/Cpl. C. Hartz, Miss P. Chartrand, Sgt. K. McCormack, Cpl. E.L. Rice, Pte. M.E.A. McLaren, Cpl. C.N. Clark, Lieut. G.T. Scott. Rear row: C.S.M. H.W. Warner, Sgt. O.A. Smith, Cpl. J.H.P. Dorval, S/Sgt. W.A. Hicks, Sgt. C.W. Cameron, Sgt. G. Sequin, Cpl. J.H. Wright, Cpl. V. Beaudin, Sgt. T.J. Kennedy, Sgt. M.J. Dunlop, Pte. H.B. Francis. (Photo collection Canadian Forces School of Military Intelligence, Kingston/Canada. Dept. of National Defence)

were also suspect. Since South American information was much more valuable to the Americans and the British than it was to Ottawa, anything D.M.I. obtained was at once passed on as a very small quid for the very large quo that Canada received from them.[4]

Interest in the Far East increased after the fall of Hong Kong. M.I.1 tried hard to obtain, at first from Singapore and later from the U.S., information on the Chinese and Japanese forces, and was able, occasionally, to offer something in return. Early in 1942, the G.S.O.3 (Int), M.D. 4, Montreal, Capt. Charles Chauveau, received a large TOP SECRET parcel containing copies of Japanese maps of that country's cities. He was asked to contact missionaries and businessmen, some of them British, who had managed to get out of Japan just before Pearl Harbour, and get them to identify any establishment they knew that could have a direct bearing on the Japanese war effort – powerhouses, railroad stations, naval, military, and air installations, dockyards and munition plants – to plot the locations on the maps, and to add as much other information as they had. Fortunately, he had as his assistant a Japanese-Canadian R.C.N.R. Petty Officer, for very few of the people he consulted could read the language well enough to translate the maps. The marked maps and Chauveau's 50-page report were sent to Washington, and were most appreciated.[5]

In early 1943, the general public, the press, and public libraries were asked to contribute pictures of Europe, Japan, Burma, Singapore, the Pacific islands, and the Australian Northern Territories. The intent was to index this material and key it to topographical Intelligence research. However, no staff was available to support such an ambitious program and, though a Combined Services Photographic Library was set up to do that research, it became largely an R.C.N. project.[6]

Although it was responsible for obtaining general military information from the Allies, M.I.1 was not the only channel. In March 1941, the Director of Engineer Services sent the Quarter-Master General a bulletin on "Engineer Information" which he had obtained through Engineer, not Intelligence, facilities. He suggested that his officers could assist by explaining new technical developments, by making arrangements for practical demonstrations, and by publishing extracts from articles dealing with the role of Engineers in modern warfare. But the U.S. War Department advised that such a link was "not legal". Much of the information had been passed to the U.S. by the British and, though this was not specifically stated, probably contained a restriction on disclosure to a third party. After some negotiation, the difficulty was resolved and a steady flow of material began to arrive from the Engineer services of both Allies.[7]

The Medical Services had similar requirements. On February 19th, 1943, the D.G.M.S. asked D.M.I. for a comprehensive list of diseases, poisonous reptiles, insects, and plants, together with details of climate, water, and food in China and the adjacent territories, including Burma, Indo-China, Manchukuo, and the eastern Russian seaboard. M.I.1 prepared, and sent on March 9th, a 77-page report, together with a list of further possible sources of information outside D.N.D. control. The D.G.M.S. was very appreciative, and asked them to get additional data from the U.S. Surgeon General. M.I.1 did so, the first item of record arrived in November, and the exchange continued until March 1947.[8]

Negotiations to obtain U.S. Intelligence began shortly after the U.S. came into the war. By May 1st, 1943, Maj. P.W. Cook at C.A.S.(W) had made satisfactory arrangements with the U.S. War Department for access to enemy order-of-battle and movements, and for amendments to this information to be forwarded daily as they became available. This exchange made possible the Information Room, which was set up for Intelligence briefings of senior officers in the later years of the war. It also marked the official beginning of the long, pleasant, profitable, and not entirely one-sided relationship between the two countries that exists to this day.[9]

M.I.1 controlled the Military Intelligence Library. This was not the collection of books that had been the A.D.M.I.'s charge and which became the Departmental Library, but rather as described in the first order sent to Washington on December 8th, 1942: ". . . to give circulation to such American publications as might assist Canadian Intelligence Officers . . . and to establish an Intelligence Lending Library for suitable publications". It was not an expensive operation; the first shipment, containing 70 books, cost only $27.14. The Americans intended to bill Canada through Lend-Lease, to which, as Maj. Cook explained, Canada was not a party. He established a routine system of purchases which continued throughout the war and resulted in a most useful reference collection. It was, of course, training material only, with little or no security classification.[10]

In late 1943, M.I.1 became involved in a rather unusual and, perhaps, ineffectual activity. The Political Warfare Committee headed by External Affairs, a satellite of the Political Warfare Board of the British Foreign Office, set up a "Sub-Committee on Political Warfare against Japan". Its first meeting, held on September 17th, with Dr. E.H. Norman and Mr. A.R. Menzies, from External, and representatives of the Services, including Capt. R.L. Archibald, M.I.1 (Order-of-Battle), decided that the Services would compile Intelligence material for use by Psychological Warfare. This meant, in effect, that in addition to the operational data they were already collating, desk officers were to extract any information on internal conditions in Japan, and in Japanese-occupied territories, that could be used to attack enemy morale. No evidence has been found that any significant data were actually forwarded to the Sub-Committee, or indeed that anything unique or valuable emerged from the studies made.[11]

M.I.1, the channel to Canada's Allies for information on enemy forces, was also required to obtain training material. This was a difficult assignment. In the early days of the war the Schools overseas could spare very little enemy equipment, and a large backlog of unfilled requests soon accumulated. Further, some of the Arms and Services tried to secure material through their own contacts. Situations often arose where these contacts were competing with the Intelligence Office at C.M.H.Q., for the same piece of equipment, for the same ultimate user. In January 1944, after discussions with D.M.T. and D.M.I., the Army Technical Development Board (A.T.D.B.) was made responsible for co-ordinating this procurement. It immediately cancelled all earlier requests, some of which dated from 1942, and it received from C.M.H.Q. a promise of two-month delivery on German and Italian equipment. D.M.T. wanted enough to permit firepower demonstrations to be held once a month. But at this stage in the war, suitable material was available in quantity only from the Mediterranean Theatre, whose Commander-in-Chief was not convinced that the captured artillery munitions were safe. He was unwilling to allow them to be exported, and the demonstrations had therefore to be curtailed in number and restricted in character.[12]

Japanese equipment was controlled by the U.S. Army. A.T.D.B. tried to get at least one working item of each of the principal weapons of a Japanese Infantry Division, to be held in a central training facility. After interminable correspondence, a first exchange was made. In an extremely generous gesture, the American Ordnance Intelligence Unit at Aberdeen Proving Ground, Baltimore, Maryland, gave Pacific Command about one-third of their holdings. In exchange, Canada sent them some British material – and a Ross rifle, a weapon which might perhaps have had some souvenir value.

A good deal of abandoned Japanese material was captured in the Aleutian campaign. Unfortunately, very little came back to Canada through official channels; the troops, on the other hand, brought in a great deal as personal souvenirs, much of it damaged. Le Régiment de Hull had a very impressive collection that included a complete Type 92 Heavy Machine Gun (the A.T.D.B. had tried unsuccessfully to get three of these from the U.S.), a Type 96 25 mm twin anti-aircraft/anti-tank gun with its mount, and a long list of minor items. N.D.H.Q., however, had not received a single gun of any kind in working order – due entirely to its own error in not assigning a Technical Intelligence Officer to the Force. The Americans searched all ships returning from the war zones, and confiscated many interesting souvenirs. The method was not always satisfactory, for a great deal of the material they obtained in this way was damaged through amateur packing.[13]

In November 1944, Pacific Command asked that every effort be made to provide "a minimum of four sets" of uniforms and basic rifles, machine guns, and small "knee" mortars used in Japanese infantry units. The Command, which was to be the staging area for troops to be used in the Pacific, had no official sources for procuring the Japanese material that was essential for training. After a whole winter of frustration, Lt.-Col. Orville Eadie, Operations and Intelligence Officer to the War Department, was told bluntly at a meeting on April 16th, 1945, "that it was improbable that Canada would obtain any equipment for training purposes until such time as D.M.T. were prepared to say how many men it was proposed to train", and where. But the C.G.S. had directed Canadian officers not to discuss Canada's participation in the war against Japan with members of the U.S. Armed Forces. As a possible alternative, Col. Eadie told the A.T.D.B. that Japanese equipment could be obtained in India, but that it would have to be collected. D.M.I. was asked to begin an immediate search. In order to organize the acquisition of enemy material, the members agreed to form an Enemy Equipment Collection Unit and to set up a central controlling agency that would assign priorities and rationalize distribution.[14]

Enquiries made in the U.S. showed that a great deal of Japanese material had been captured, but that very little had actually reached North America. Enough, nevertheless, had been brought back to enable the U.S. Army to assemble an "enemy demonstration team" of Japanese-Americans, dressed and equipped to put on firepower demonstrations, and give lectures on the Japanese Army, the medical aspects of the Pacific Theatre, and Intelligence courses. It was not practical to have a team come to Canada at once, but it was hoped that one would come later. But the end of the war with Japan came, and neither the equipment nor the demonstration team ever arrived in Canada.[15]

Our account of the training requirement has moved the M.I.1 story a little ahead of chronology. The invasion of North-West Europe led to an increase in the demands for briefings on the military situation. At 0830 each morning, C.M.H.Q. received an advance copy of the Chief of the Imperial Staff Summary that was delivered daily at the War Room of the War Office at 0900. It also received reports from Rear H.Q. 21 Army Group and from the E.T.O.U.S.A. All were forwarded to Ottawa. Col. Eadie asked London to provide, in addition, a daily Situation Report that he could take to the Prime Minister, to Col. Ralston (a strong supporter of D.M.I.), the C.G.S., and the Deputies. He asked for specific order-of-battle information, a résumé of the Allied and enemy situations in both Italy and North-West Europe, the total Canadian casualties, and the total strength in France. All this material was made available to him.[16]

The system seemed to be working smoothly, until just before the Minister's morning conference on December 27th, 1944. At this meeting, Gen. McNaughton stated that he was not satisfied with the N.D.H.Q. Intelligence Information Room, an M.I.1 responsibility. He wanted not only more information, but also assurance that it was being fully used and properly interpreted. The C.G.S., Gen. Murchie, reminded the Minister of the dangers of making appreciations that were based on insufficient data, and pointed out that, in his view, Intelligence was doing all it could with the scanty input it received. Gen. McNaughton agreed that his instructions had been that Intelligence should develop sources of information to the limit of practicability; to do this, it was essential that the Branch should be staffed by officers capable of assimilating and making forecasts on the data passed to them.[17]

This seemingly serious accusation of inefficiency developed out of an unexpected visit the Minister had made to the Information Room for a briefing. Because M.I.1 was relatively short of staff, because First Canadian Army was not then in action, and because of the Christmas lull, it had so happened that, on the day he arrived, the Information Room had been staffed by an officer who did not work in I(a). He had been given adequate instructions for him to perform all the routine tasks, but he had no knowledge of the detail he needed to answer the very searching questions put to him, and Gen. McNaughton was annoyed. The C.G.S. personally directed the Secretary, Chiefs of Staff Committee, to arrange for the Daily Summaries to be supplemented by Appreciations and maps, and M.I.1 saw to it that its procedures improved.

On January 2nd, 1945, the American authorities informed the Canadian Military Attaché that a mysterious balloon weapon, believed to be Japanese, had been found in Montana on November 4th, 1944, and that, since the first report, seven more had been discovered. Did D.M.I. know anything about them? While M.I.1 was looking for information, M.D. 13 reported that a similar balloon had been found near Minton, Saskatchewan, on January 12th. Another one – it is not clear which of the eight it was – had been seen near Kalispell, Montana. It had been reported through the F.B.I. to the R.C.M.P. in Saskatchewan, and to the G.S.O.3 (Int) in Regina, Capt. Jim Morgan, who informed the neighbouring Districts and M.I.3. The balloon at Minton, the first sighted in Canada., was equipped with two flares, or incendiaries, and a 20-lb bomb. One of the flares had exploded; the balloon escaped, but a farmer recovered the other two devices intact. When Jim Morgan went to collect them, he found them in the local crossroads store, near the stove. They contained enough high explosive to obliterate the structure – a fact unknown to the finder and his admiring audience. Jim himself was very careful when he was carrying them back to Regina, but he also did not take all the precautions that today would be mandatory.

Neither D.N.I. nor the Directorate of Intelligence, Air, had any knowledge of these weapons, but what little was discovered was put in a memo for the C.G.S. on the 18th. On that same day, a balloon was seen drifting east by an observer in Bella Coola; other sightings followed on the West Coast in the next few days; then there seemed to be a lull. When the U.S. reported on the 19th that a balloon they had found may have carried bacterial matter, serious concern developed. D.M.I. (M.I.3) and the R.C.M.P. were told to control information on the devices; this was no easy task, because observations and recoveries soon ranged from the Northwest Territories southward and as far east as Manitoba. Most landed in British Columbia, where it was feared that they might cause widespread forest fires. By careful planning, and by plotting the normal incidence of fires, everything possible was done to ensure that maximum force would be available at the site of any outbreak. Fortunately, the fire season passed without mishap.[18]

Intelligence examined the recovered components to try to establish where they were made and the probable pattern of future attacks. But it was only when enquiries could be made in Japan itself, after the end of hostilities, that the full story emerged. The project had begun in the spring of 1944. Japanese school children were organized to produce glued paper panels that could be assembled into 33.5-foot diameter balloons, capable of carrying three or four bombs. Each balloon usually had two incendiaries and one anti-personnel fragmentation bomb, fused to explode on impact with the ground, a control device, and sometimes a small transmitter, for a total weight of 25 to 65 pounds.

The balloons were released from the Kantu district of eastern Honshu and crossed the Pacific on the prevailing winds at an altitude of between 30,000 and 35,000 feet which they maintained by means of a barometric control device for valving gas or dropping sand. None was designed to carry bacteriological warfare materials. Of the some 9,300 that were released, between 900 and 1,000 are known to have reached North America, including 92 in Canada, where one of the three known rubberized silk variants was recovered. The balloon weapons caused no casualties in Canada, but killed six in Oregon. The only certain damage in Canada was one large grass fire. Their lack of success, however, should not be blamed on a conceptual weakness. They cost very little – about $800 each – and their simplicity gave them many advantages. Their defeat can be credited in large measure to Censorship which, from the very beginning, enforced a close "stop" (prohibition) on the publication of any information about the threat. When the Japanese heard absolutely no reaction from either the U.S. or Canada, they assumed that the weapon was a failure. In May 1945, they ordered the officer responsible, Gen. Kusaba, to stop launching them.[19]

For a long time, M.I.1 was responsible for "Intelligence from the Districts", which required it, in effect, to keep a watch on the state of Army morale in Canada. Morale checks were part of the regular duties of Unit I.O.s and Security Sections; they reported to M.I.3, which would relay relevant information to M.I.1. Some of the early reports were very superficial. In March 1941, for example, M.D. 5 reported ingenuously that there was "an absence of subversion, morale was good, morale in the training camps was dull, discipline and relations with the civilians were both good. Reactions to the French cause and de Gaulle were mixed". In May, "the N.R.M.A. were listless". The A.C.G.S. Gen. Pope, was critical: ". . . the original idea was for a balanced picture. Intelligence is inclined to search for villains and to paint black pictures. While the former is an essential part of their duties, they are duty bound to report such gratifying features as exist." The D.M.O.&I. invited D.M.I. to be mindful of this comment.[20] The responsibility for assessing morale was later passed to M.I.3, which was in a far better position to evaluate reports and to relate them to Security coverage. With all respect to Gen. Pope, good morale should not be news; poor morale and the situations that bring it about must quickly be drawn to the attention of the higher Command.

In November 1943, an article in D.M.T.'s monthly Canadian Army Training Manual encouraged unit I.O.s to set up an Information Room where they could collect, file, and display information about the enemy for familiarization purposes. They were urged to use unit training films, models, and similar aids, and to be alert to the advantages of arranging map, air photo, and other displays from material already sent to the Districts, including especially M.I.1's newly published *Handbook on the Japanese Army*. In September 1944, D.M.T. praised the system as a training aid and encouraged the unit Education Officers to enrich it with press reports and photographs. When D.M.T. once more reissued his instruction in February 1945, he clarified the roles of the two officers, about which confusion existed.[21] The Information Room, when it was well supported, made a useful contribution to training, but its chief weakness was a lack of sufficient material to permit displays to be renewed frequently. When the novelty wore off, the Room was seldom visited.

In 1946, a reorganized M.I.1, soon to lose its wartime staff officers, became the nucleus of the Strategic Intelligence component of D.M.I. Its task had been difficult and relatively unrewarding. Some critics have said that its Information Room served merely to repeat the newspapers, and that its briefings had no real impact on decision-making at Army H.Q. But they did show what extra information was available, and theirs was the most factual. The fact that its data had been so processed that it could not readily be checked by M.I.1, was not a serious drawback to an agency without adequate resources of its own. M.I.1's briefings did, hopefully, give the staff officers at N.D.H.Q. a clearer understanding of the worldwide nature of the conflict towards which their daily efforts were directed.

It must be admitted, however, that M.I.1 was not the only agency involved in assessing information on the threat to Canada. On July 22nd, 1938, the Joint Staff Committee had estimated that an attack against Canada could take the form of "bombardment by fast armoured ships . . . air attack as far from the coast as Toronto". Prior to that date, the Pacific coast had been thought to be in the most danger; thereafter it was the Atlantic coast. In early 1939, the assessment reappeared in more detail: bombardment by "one capital ship", amphibious raids of "up to 250 all ranks", and air attack by "one airship or . . . 12 ship-based aircraft". These assessments were not unrealistic, although the air threat appears now to have been somewhat overstated.

Reinforcement of both coasts followed the outbreak of war. Details may be found in Volume I of the Official History, but essentially the Maritimes were initially given Third Division, deployed as a Mobile Reserve to contain any attack that might occur. A senior Command was created on August 1st, 1940 – Atlantic – to co-ordinate defensive measures with the other two Services, to control Army elements, including those in the Fortresses and Defended Areas, to be responsible for Internal Security and Vulnerable Points, and for training. The G.O.C.-in-C.'s area included M.D.'s 6, 7, the eastern part of 5, and Newfoundland and Labrador.

Pacific Command, comprising M.D. 11, M.D. 13, the Yukon, and the District of Mackenzie, was formed on October 17th, 1940. Defences were grouped into three areas; Victoria-Esquimalt Fortress, Vancouver, and Prince Rupert. With the outbreak of war with Japan, the Command was progressively reinforced, until eventually it contained two Divisions, Sixth at Victoria and Eighth at Prince George. (Seventh Division, formed at the same time, was based in Debert, Nova Scotia.) By 1943, the Army strength in Pacific Command was about 35,000. The maximum enemy threat was estimated at two brigades, slightly less than one-third of that total. The defeat of the

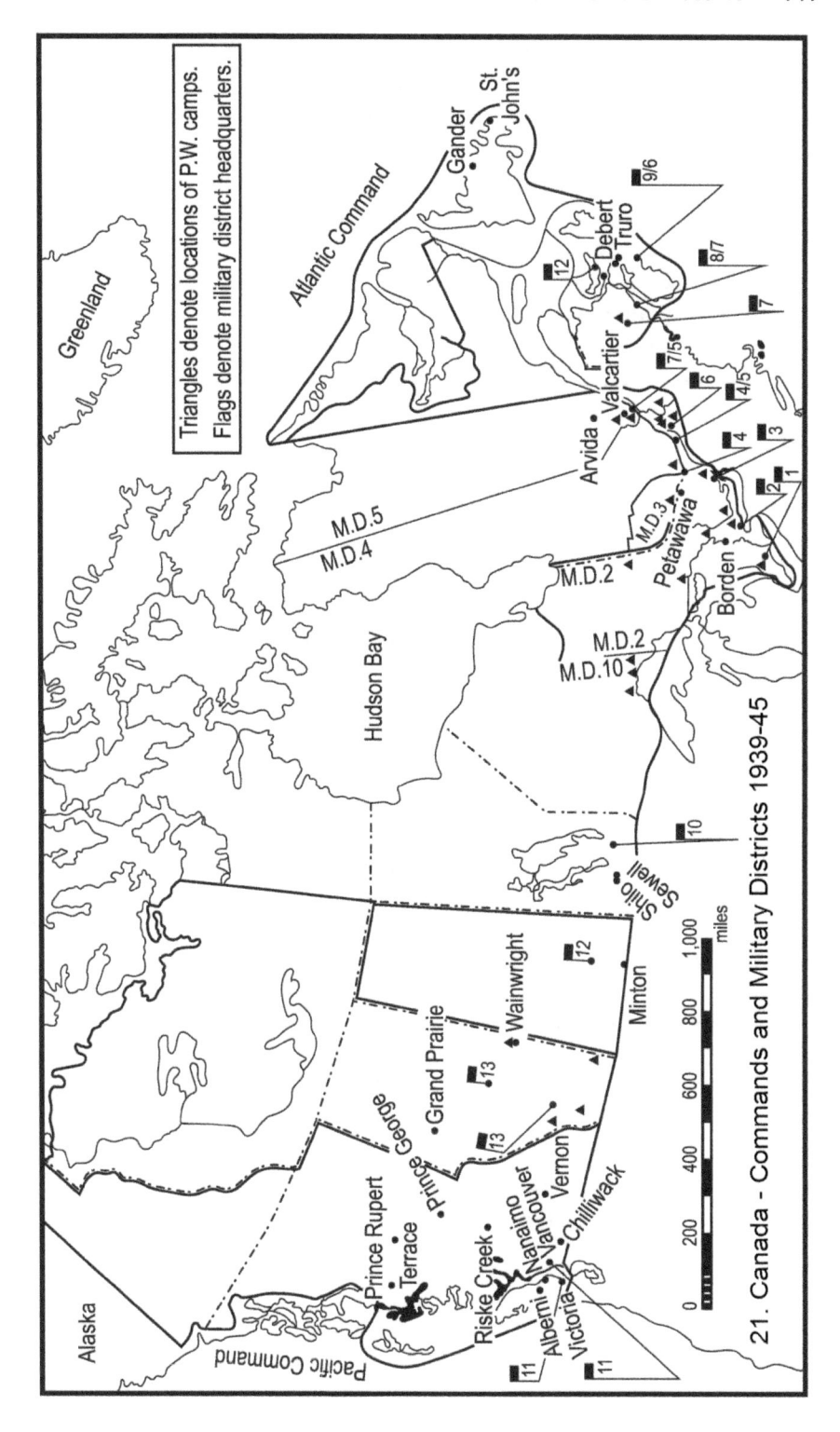

16. STRATEGIC AND OPERATIONAL INTELLIGENCE IN CANADA 1939-46   441

21. Canada - Commands and Military Districts 1939-45

Japanese in the Aleutians that summer marked the beginning of the ebb of the perceived threat, and the forces were slowly withdrawn. The Japanese, in fact, had never intended to attack the West Coast in strength. American and Canadian military judgements had clearly identified the enemy limitations but, despite appeals from the Chiefs of Staff Committee, political considerations supervened, emotion replaced logic, and a large number of men and their equipment were expensively misemployed.

Intelligence within the Commands was very much local and tactical. Both H.Q. had small Intelligence staffs; the one on the West Coast was headed by a G.S.O.1. Each Fortress and some Defended Areas had their own I.O.s, as had all major units and formations. Each received regular Summaries from D.M.I., and the H.Q. worked closely with their opposite numbers in the Navy and R.C.A.F., through the medium of the respective Joint Intelligence Committees which met formally once a week but whose members were in daily contact. They seem to have done an adequate job of keeping the respective G.O.C.-in-C.s informed; distribution downward may have been more sporadic. Both suffered from a lack of long-range information-gathering agencies, although, with its links to Britain, Atlantic Command was adequately provided for. Atlantic Command closed in August 1944, Pacific in January 1946.

Intelligence staffs were formed at Sixth, Seventh, and Eighth Divisional H.Q. on March 18th, May 12th, and June 11th, 1942, respectively. During their brief existence, their duties, like those of their opposite numbers in the Fortresses and Areas, were routine – training, managing maps and air photos, routine briefings. Their officers made a number of arduous trips into remote areas to select sites for training. Occasionally their instructions had an amusing side. The G.S.O.3 (Int), Eighth Division, Capt. J.O. McNamee, once ordered the units to conceal their Secret List equipment. Commander 19th Canadian Infantry Brigade asked him, with some asperity: "How do you expect me to hide an engine and six cars?" McNamee had forgotten that the Brigade had on its List Canada's only armoured train. The Divisions were disbanded in 1943; Seventh on February 20th, Eighth on October 15th, and Sixth on December 2nd.

The sole independent I(a) unit, No. 7 Air Liaison Section, was formed at Debert on April 1st, 1943, and moved 12 days later to the large air base on Sea Island, Vancouver. It handled its first photo sortie on May 10th, but had difficulty obtaining aircraft. It had to switch missions between *Bolingbrokes* and the ubiquitous *Harvards*, was sent to Camp Wainwright on September 1st, and was disbanded in late October 1943.[22]

M.I.2

Communications have always been vital to the command and control of armed forces in the field. Armies have always tried to intercept enemy communications and to protect their own. The Guides were required to include all possible information on telegraph and telephone facilities in their reports. In the First World War, the emergence of electronic communications led to electronic methods of intercepting them, and special units to handle the intercept equipment. But in the years before 1939, Canada made no provision for these skills to be preserved and developed.

In 1930, a small Signals sub-committee was directed to collect and study information on existing systems of Signals communications, their operation, control maintenance, management, and the procurement of technical equipment. The intent was to improve operational capability, not to explore Intelligence applications. Staff shortages and priority conflicts limited the sub-committee to asking telegraph and telephone companies for information they could use to meet the domestic operational needs of the Army. Canada had no intercept capability until just before the Second World War, when a small Signals Intelligence unit was formed in a basement at Rockcliffe Air Station, Ottawa. Gen. Macklin once said, when he was recalling forming the unit: "... the Wireless Organization Radio Intelligence, Signal Security and cipher was really in hand in the War Office when the War began – we were nowhere".[23]

In September 1939, D. Signals asked that either Maj. M.T. Megill or Capt. S.F. Clark be sent to London to obtain information. On December 6th, D.M.O.&I. asked the War Office for Cipher Intelligence, for the codes used by other nations, particularly Germany, and for technical help to break them. The dual responsibility of Intelligence and Signals was never entirely resolved. The expansion of both the field units and the Wireless Intelligence service generated great and conflicting demands for equipment, accommodation, and men, throughout the War.[24]

Canadian Intercept facilities were in service by early 1940, using British techniques, including code-breaking material. They were of considerable value, particularly as peculiarities of radio wave propagation meant that receivers in eastern Canada could intercept military transmissions originating in Europe which were beyond the capabilities of British-based equipment. The opening of the B.S.C. in late 1940 facilitated the exchange of this information.

Ottawa developed a great deal of expertise in the interception and exploitation of German espionage control messages, particularly from Hamburg and Lisbon to South America, but also to Canada. A German agent in Canada passed shipping information, which, in enemy hands, resulted in heavy loss of life and tonnage. A fortunate lapse in late August 1941 enabled M.I.2 to initiate the action that led to his capture. The enemy radio transmission (WER) happened to come on the air during a violent thunderstorm in eastern Ontario, Quebec, and New England. Every time it was interrupted by the storm, any groups that might have been lost in the static were patiently repeated. This helped the monitors to narrow down the search area to a radius of 200 miles from Ottawa, and the agent was located and arrested. What might have been a similar incident in the following September turned out to be simply a British merchant ship employing a private code. Counter-measures were taken in many areas with the assistance of a number of veterans of the First World War, recruited by M.I.2 and working with M.I.3. Counter-action taken abroad was handled by the B.S.C. through its own facilities and contacts.[25]

In October 1941, the G.S.O.1 offered officials of the U.S. Federal Communications Commission (F.C.C.) in Washington free access to the results of Canadian monitoring activities. Almost immediately the Americans offered, in return, technical D.F. data that were invaluable for pinpointing the location of a transmitter. This was particularly useful to Canadian stations because they were still two months away from being operational in this field, and the R.C.N. had too many commitments of its own to guarantee help. Canadian material given the F.C.C. included transmissions from "foreign units" in Africa, and the isolation and breaking of *Gestapo* codes used in transmissions from either Cuba or Central America to Hamburg and later between Italy and Latin America. The lack of a D.F. capability had made it impossible up to this time to locate the sources with enough precision. The arrangement, however, was soon terminated, because the F.B.I., which controlled the F.C.C., thought it an unnecessary duplication of its own exchange service with Canada. In its place, and with the help of the R.C.M.P., a direct legal channel between D.M.I. and F.B.I. was established.

By the end of 1941, M.I.2 had assembled detailed information on Nazi activities and organizations in Chile, Cuba, Mexico, Colombia, Argentina, and Brazil. It had identified 52 separate agents in Latin America and, in some cases, had even been able to pinpoint the location of their transmitters. In addition, some ciphers had been broken. The information was useful to the U.S., but some material made D.M.I. very conscious of the nature and extent of the threat to Canadian security.[26] Much care had to be taken to protect this material against disclosure.

In August 1940, the Chief Telegraph Censor reported to the D.M.O.&I. that carrier pigeons were being used to carry messages across the U.S.-Canadian border. M.I.2 pointed out that "ham" radio operators were also potential evaders of control measures. On August 30th, Capt. Ed. Drake, the former head of the Rockcliffe unit and now a staff officer under Maj. Scott, proposed to the Director of Signals that some 20 amateur operators could be selected, checked by the R.C.M.P., trained, and formed into an organization to work under D.M.O.&I. to monitor German propaganda, U.S. amateurs, and possible illegal

16. STRATEGIC AND OPERATIONAL INTELLIGENCE IN CANADA 1939–46   445

German espionage equipment, 1944: suitcase, code books, and emergency food supply. The suitcase contains a 40-watt transmitter, accessories, and a code slide rule. (Photo collection Canadian Forces School of Military Intelligence, Kingston/Canada. Dept. of National Defence) transmissions. The "hams" themselves had been making similar proposals since the outbreak of war, but the Department had instead advised the operators to dismantle their sets, and cancelled all but 19 licenses: four in M.D. 1, six in M.D. 2, one in M.D. 3, three in M.D. 10, four in M.D. 11, and one in M.D. 13. The Minister approved Maj. Scott's proposal on September 5th and, on December 26th, D.M.O.&I. instructed District Signals Officers to contact the 19 operators.[27]

Short-wave fans who, unlike the "hams", only had receivers, searched the wavelength bands on their own, and ably assisted the Radio Division of the Department of Transport. Although they did occasionally pick up illegal transmissions in Canada, they provided a particularly useful back-up for the D.O.T. monitoring station at Point Grey, Vancouver, which had begun to listen to Stations JZ1 and J2J of the Japanese Broadcasting Service, on December 22nd, 1940. D.M.O.&I. passed copies of their transcriptions to Washington when their content warranted. In March 1941, M.I.2 reviewed and forwarded to the Americans a particularly bitter propaganda attack on Britain and the Empire. The covering letter said that "the impression here is that the United Kingdom . . . authorities listen closely to the Japanese stations; and it is assumed that these particular broadcasts would not escape them". They were wrong. The British did not routinely monitor the transmissions and, even as late as May 1941, thought that it was not "necessary at present to take steps to procure a record of them". But when they learned of the propaganda attack, both the British and the Canadian attachés at Washington came at once to Ottawa and arranged for regular deliveries of copies. After this incident, M.I.2 reviewed the material it received very carefully, and underlined all items it thought important.[28]

The admission that the British had not intercepted the Japanese broadcasts made obvious the unpleasant fact that the British Empire did not have a station capable of covering the North Pacific. Japanese intentions were suspect, and worst-case analysis suggested that Tokyo would probably honour its commitments to the Axis. In October 1941, therefore, D.M.O.&I. asked the C.G.S. for authority to build a new station on the Pacific Coast; he warned that it would probably take six months to build, but that it would be "indispensable in the event of hostilities". At that time, Army Wireless Intelligence effort was focused on Europe, and eastern North and South America to the 90th meridian (approximately the longitude of Thunder Bay, Ontario); the Navy and D.O.T. were responsible for the Japanese Navy, and for merchant shipping. The C.G.S. obtained approval for a new station on November 11th, and Capt. Ed. Drake went out to the West Coast to arrange for temporary accommodation for a Detachment of one officer and 14 men at Work Point Barracks, Victoria. The Detachment was administered by No. 11 Fortress Signals Company, and reported to Col. B.R. Mullaly, G.S.O.1 (Int) at Pacific Command. When the station was completed, about April 1942, it established its own detachment at Point Grey.[29]

By January 11th, 1942, three stations were authorized: Ottawa, Amherst, Nova Scotia, and Victoria, each of them intended to monitor and "D.F." foreign transmissions. The only D.F. component actually operating was Ottawa, but all three had an operational intercept capability. Since the work of the Amherst station, built to support the Battle of the Atlantic, was being done elsewhere, the C.G.S. asked that its planned expansion be applied to Victoria instead. Equipment was in short supply, and often had to be specially made by the Canadian Signals Experimental Establishment. Two days later, the C.G.S. asked for and received permission to acquire the old Northwest Territories Control Station at Grand Prairie, Alberta. It opened for service on May 4th, 1942. In March 1944, No. 4 Intercept Station was authorized at Riske Creek, British Columbia.[30]

In April, a special cipher was introduced to protect the material passing among the Wireless Intelligence agencies in New York, Washington, the U.K., Australia, India, and Canada. It was controlled by M.I.2, under extremely tight supervision. As a result, the administrative burden soon grew beyond the resources of the Section. After February 1945, control was assumed by No. 1 Discrimination Unit (D.U.) in Ottawa, a branch of M.I.2 which had been formed in 1943 as a translation bureau, and which became a linguist pool. Its establishment was increased by one major, three captains, five lieutenants, one W.O.I (Special Intelligence), a second W.O.I as superintending clerk, five W.O.IIs, 10 staff-sergeants, 15 sergeants, and 10 corporals. They were reorganized into three Sections: Machine Records, Teletype, and Cipher.

In addition to its primary mission, M.I.2 became involved in areas which were properly Security. The most direct example occurred in July 1941. The A.C.G.S., Gen. Maurice Pope, learned that there were no cable links with some of the East Coast ports, and that units there were using the radio telephone. He had heard of one case where messages passed by similar means in Britain had been overheard by one of our stations. Signals had informed him that the gun positions were also linked to the headquarters by radio telephone and, further, that the guard vessels checking ships coming into port used sets whose transmissions could also be intercepted. He therefore suggested to D.M.O.&I. that these links should be strictly supervised. Pacific Command suggested that a simple operational code should be used, and M.I.2 obtained and introduced, with appropriate restrictions, a code used for similar purposes by the British.[31] It appears to have been satisfactory.

A less direct contact lay in the field of propaganda. This started much earlier. The Canadian Broadcasting Corporation also had a "wireless Intelligence" agency of its own to monitor and locate unlicensed radio emissions. In June 1940, it informed Maj. Scott, who then headed M.I.2, that it had intercepted

"The New British Broadcasting Station", with a transmitter located probably in northern Scotland or in Norway. It was transmitting "anti-government and anti-Churchill but not pro-Nazi . . . [material and] what they claimed to be uncensored news" on frequencies and at times the C.B.C. had verified. Maj. Scott sent the report to the Deputy Minister with a request that the Department of Information warn the public of its origin.[32]

Enemy Psychological Warfare tried to make use of P.W. Both the Germans and the Japanese offered inducements to their Canadian prisoners to broadcast messages home. Intelligence regarded this practice as "giving aid and comfort to the enemy", and frowned on it. An early, but erroneous, report was received in August 1941 that a Canadian soldier had participated in a German broadcast; he turned out to be an interned merchant seaman. But the hope of hearing news of loved ones would naturally impel Canadians to listen in eagerly. Intelligence therefore planned to monitor and to publicize all such transmissions, so that Canadians would not have to waste time listening to propaganda while they were waiting for the broadcast that interested them. Unfortunately, lack of staff prevented the plan from being implemented.

The system for obtaining information on Canadian P.W. in Germany was well developed and relatively efficient. But the men who fell into Japanese hands after Hong Kong virtually disappeared. The Point Grey Station was therefore directed to monitor and to report every item of P.W. news, no matter how minor it might seem. An intercepted report on March 30th, 1942, of the death on February 24th of a Cpl. Green, Winnipeg Grenadiers, led to a formal policy decision. D.N.D. would tell the next-of-kin, but would warn that the news had been received through unofficial channels and that its accuracy could not be guaranteed. On August 1st, 1942, Point Grey reported that six Canadians had taken part in a propaganda broadcast. Their action reopened the earlier discussions on the propriety of such conduct. It was found that there was nothing in the Army Act, the King's Regulations and Orders, the Defence of Canada Regulations, or the Official Secrets Act that would make such acts illegal. To repair the omission, a Canadian Army Routine Order forbidding broadcasts of this nature was prepared and published in February 1943; it was never applied, however, to the Hong Kong prisoners.[33]

In November 1944, External Affairs asked the Army to provide a small Section, which it promised to administer, to exploit the Japanese commercial transmissions that were then being dealt with by an overworked staff in the Chief Telegraph Censor's office. D.M.I. agreed but decided that the Section would probably have to be larger than External had planned. No. 1 D.U. had seven men available; three N.R.M.A. at S-20, who could not be used overseas, could be added. In early January 1945, the D.U. began to analyse, translate, and prepare weekly Summaries of Japanese material. The Americans were advised, and Col. Murray arranged to pass their demands directly to the Unit.[34]

Lt.-Col. Edward Drake (C.Int.C.), M.I.2, July 1945. After the war, Lt.-Col. Drake was named Director of Canada's first peace time cryptologic agency, the Communications Branch of the National Research Council, which would eventually become known as the Communications Security Establishment (CSE). He served as Director until he died in 1971. In recognition of his leadership of Canada's Signals Intelligence community for over three decades, the newly constructed CSE headquarters building in Ottawa was named in his honour in 2015. (C.G. Jones and C. Chauveau collection/Canadian Forces School of Military Intelligence, Kingston/Canada. Dept. of National Defence)

The intake was about 2,800 messages a week, but the flow was expected to increase as reception improved and the intercept operators became more practiced. If the equipment also was improved, M.I.2 was sure that even better service could be expected. Success, of course, would depend mostly on the operators available. By this stage in the war, these were difficult to find. Canadian stations were too understaffed to be able to monitor all the Japanese broadcasts. M.I.2, which initially had been well ahead of the Americans in its coverage, continued to fall behind. Eventually, by arrangement, specific coverage tasks were assigned to each of the stations in the two systems, resources were better utilized, and the staffs suffered much less from overwork.[35]

M.I.2 and its associated units did not long survive the end of the war, although the title was reassigned to quite a different function in the 1950s. Riske Creek station, with one officer and two other ranks, closed in April 1946. The Discrimination Unit disbanded on August 31st, 1946. We cannot leave, however, without a tribute to the officer who built and directed this service through the war; Lt.-Col. Ed. Drake. His imagination, zeal, and flair made this very demanding branch of Intelligence the international success it was. It was his efforts, although he would have been the first to pass the praise to others, that made it possible for D.M.I. to provide some original material, in partial payment for the valuable and willing assistance given Canada by her Allies.

17.
SECURITY AND COUNTER-INTELLIGENCE IN CANADA

For the first few months of the war, Security was merely one of A.D.M.I.'s many functions. But Security duties developed so rapidly in extent and complexity that, in November 1940, a separate Section had to be formed. By the end of the war, under its head, Eric Acland, it was the most active and important component of D.M.I., as his title, D.D.M.I. (Security) indicated. It was, in fact, the Security experience and reputation gained by D.M.I. during the war that preserved the C.Int.C. in the immediate postwar years.

Military Security dealt with matters ranging from the mundane to the most politically and socially sensitive. Take, for example, two fairly simple incidents which occurred, coincidentally, on October 30th, 1939. Intelligence drew the C.G.S.'s attention to a find of Secret letters and memoranda in a wastebasket, and had him sign the first of many circular letters warning all officers to destroy such papers, and forbidding the discussion of secret matters in public. In the other incident, a new "Committee on the Security Aspects of the Alien Problem" was formed, with Maj. C. Vokes as one of its members. On November 9th, it issued a paper restricting the enlistment of aliens. The first incident marked the beginning of a program of education and control that has lasted to this day. The second was the beginning of attempts to counter a specific perceived potential threat, which was to receive attention throughout the war as conflicting pressures arising from an increasingly critical shortage of manpower were measured against the Security assessment of the possible risks.[1]

Methods of enforcing Security were to change. On December 2nd, 1939, M.D. 6 asked for permission to display Security posters. This request was granted, but the posters had to be signed by the Minister of Defence, or the Commissioner of the R.C.M.P. The reasons for this were technical and legal, for the posters were, in effect, announcements of a regulation, and of the penalties for non-compliance. Two thousand were ordered and distributed in March 1941. Later posters were designed to warn and to teach, rather than to proclaim.[2]

Recognition of the need to co-ordinate national planning of the means to counter threats to Security took many months. It was not until June 8th, 1940, that the Minister appointed Maj. Scott as his representative on a new Committee, organized "with the objective of discovering the total field of probable enemy operations within Canada", to advise on espionage and

Lt.-Col. Eric Acland, O.B.E., E.D., Deputy Director of Military Intelligence (Security), circa 1945. (Strathy E.E. Smith/ Canada. Dept. of National Defence/Library and Archives Canada, PA-152129)

sabotage. Representatives came from the Secretary of State, External Affairs, Mines and Resources, Finance, National Revenue, Post Office, Trade and Commerce, Transport, Munitions and Supply, Labour, Pensions and Health, Justice, R.C.M.P., National Harbours Board, National Defence (Air) (W/C. C.C. Walker), and Army (Scott). The Committee decided that it first had to co-ordinate the exchange of information between Departments and to establish guidelines as to what this information would comprise.[3]

It issued its first report on August 1st, 1940. The Army had developed "some machinery within the Directorate of Intelligence, whereby any indication of suspected subversive activities on the part of any members of a unit would, by arrangement between the District Intelligence Officers and a few selected personnel of such units, be available for transmission on to the R.C.M. Police for investigation". The report discussed the protection of installations in Ottawa, and made recommendations, which the R.C.M.P. thought quite adequate, on finger-printing, security for sensitive Departments, Press Censorship, Refugee Security, Security of personnel in military units, and the protection of key material. A week later, the Committee proposed that the R.C.M.P. Intelligence component be brought under Defence control, on the grounds that the Force had not been able to keep pace with developments, either in terms of its manpower or of its efficiency. The Defence Department considered that the Axis threat to Canada was military, and that therefore the military should control the measures taken to counter it. It suggested that the component's officers should be drawn from the three Services and the police, and trained in all phases of Intelligence counter-measures to meet enemy activity at home, and in active offensive methods of irregular warfare against an enemy in his own country. The R.C.M.P. representative was probably too overcome to reply, as no rebuttal was recorded. Fortunately, this half-baked expansionist proposal was eventually forgotten.

In August 1940, the D.C.G.S. proposed that the Army should have a Secret Service to watch for subversion. The proposal was rejected: "Such matters could adequately be dealt with by the unit officers and N.C.O.s." That "such matters" were actually occurring became evident in October when Communist literature was found at Camp Valcartier; it was turned over to the R.C.M.P., and arrests were made and convictions secured.

The perceived need grew and, in response, Security Sections were formed at Atlantic Command, M.D. 2, M.D. 3, and Pacific Command during early 1942. M.D. 2 also asked for a Section at Camp Borden, basing its request on "subversive activity... reaching alarming proportions". Its original request was rejected, but later both Borden and Petawawa were given small Detachments under a Warrant Officer who reported to the Camp I.O. Pacific Command took its control measures a little further. On May 5th, 1942, it formed a Joint Services Intelligence Bureau, which met every second Tuesday to discuss, among other things, careless talk, prohibition of photography, and counter-sabotage. Its members also worked closely together between meetings. The Command had a field agency, the Pacific Command Militia Rangers (P.C.M.R.), which was loosely organized into Companies throughout British Columbia. Though primarily a guide force, with a role similar to Wellington's Corps of Guides, its local knowledge often resulted in early reports of suspicious incidents which could then be investigated. Relations with the R.C.M.P. were, of course, very closely maintained, particularly in the Yukon.[4]

Nos. 6, 5, and 8 Field Security Sections were also formed in the summer of 1942, for the Sixth, Seventh, and Eighth Divisions, respectively. They contained some N.R.M.A. men, who were excluded from the formal Security courses. No. 5 Section was responsible for Security at Camp Debert, Nova Scotia. A fire broke out at the Camp Ordnance Railhead on January 14th, 1943. Many illegal photographs were taken, and mortar bombs were stolen as souvenirs; the latter were recovered later. One reported female Nazi turned out to be a year-old girl. But No. 5 did identify and isolate a group of men in one unit who were effectively dissuading others from "going active". Their Commanding Officer managed to disperse them.

No. 6 F.S. Section was formed on July 5th, 1942. It worked closely with the P.C.M.R. on Vancouver Island, was transferred to Seventh Division at Prince George in October 1943, and to Camp Wainwright during the summer of 1944.

It provided an officer and some N.C.O.s for the Kiska operation. No. 8 was formed on June 15th, 1942, and sent on November 6th to Prince George. Its principal duties were to check leakages of information to officers' wives, security of movements, "loose talk in staff cars", formation training, and training of its own men. Nos. 5 and 8 were disbanded on October 15th, 1943.[5]

In early 1942, D.N.D. agreed to provide soldiers to be directly attached to the R.C.M.P. who were forming four Special Security Service Sections. On August 18th, 1943, but with effect from June 1st, formal approval was given to deploy Sections at Sydney, Nova Scotia, Saint John, New Brunswick, Quebec City, and Trois-Rivières, Quebec. They were to be employed under R.C.M.P. direction, with special pay, travel allowances, and civilian clothing. The Force provided food and clothing; the Army looked after discipline, pay, clothing, and equipment. The men were sworn in as special constables, and used as examiners for incoming passenger and ships' crews and in the apprehension of suspects. The Sections were disbanded in September 1945.[6]

The Directorate of Military Intelligence was formed in July 1942. M.I.3 was subdivided into M.I.3(a) – Security of Personnel – and M.I.3(b) – Security of Information. Although these and other Security functions (some of which continued after the cancellation of the Defence of Canada Regulations on March 18th, 1946) will be discussed separately, it must be remembered that if Security is to be efficient, it must be closely controlled, integrated, and directed from the top. Eric Acland was keenly aware of this, and the various functions worked closely together under him.

M.I.3(A) – SECURITY OF PERSONNEL[7]

The R.C.M.P., whose duty it was to preserve Canadian Internal Security, was asked to ensure that the First Canadian Infantry Division contained no subversive individuals. Although there were exceptions, former members of the Mackenzie-Papineau Battalion were not normally acceptable. Nor, obviously, were members of the Nazi Party itself, with its known links to German diplomats in the United States. D.O.C.s were given the names of reported agitators; they kept some men off overseas drafts and discharged others. But efficient screening was impossible. The D.O.C.s were preoccupied with the mobilization and despatch of troops overseas. None had an Intelligence staff with experience, and many had no Intelligence staff officers at all. Indeed, domestic Intelligence duties in the Districts tended to be neglected, and Maj. Preston had to obtain a C.G.S. Directive urging that they be attended to with greater zeal.[8]

The Army had to face a unique Personnel Security threat. The U.S. border was open and, before Pearl Harbour, many enemy-controlled organizations operated freely. Many aliens enlisted, and only by penetration of the subversive movements themselves was it possible to identify the dangerous ones. Information obtained through the wholehearted co-operation of Cable, Postal, and Telegraphic Censorship, did identify some pro-Nazis. Fortunately, by the outbreak of war, the R.C.M.P. had succeeded in penetrating these Nazi and Fascist organizations and had identified and interned many of their leaders.[9] Some members, however, did escape the net, and enlisted in the Army, where they caused trouble. Some Army personnel falsely claimed to be Party members in the hope that this admission would result in their discharge.

The Communist Party of Canada and some 10 of its front organizations were declared illegal under the D.O.C.R. on September 12th, 1940. This Party attacked the war as "imperialist", worked against the war effort supporting it, distributed propaganda, and attempted to subvert troops and to incite men to take part in disorders. In February 1941, the Service was estimated to have enrolled about 100 men who either were members of or strongly supported the Communist Party. They had two aims; to weaken the Army's effectiveness by damaging morale, and to create support for eventual social revolution. They exploited the host of normal minor grumbles about food, clothing, equipment, quarters, absence of leave, and actions of officers, that are a part of Service life, and exaggerated them until they became major grievances. Communists themselves rarely came into direct conflict with authority, worked hard, and gave the appearance of being good soldiers. Consequently, it was increasingly difficult to discharge them on the usual grounds as "unlikely to make an efficient soldier". Even when released, they merely re-enlisted in another District. The best that could be done was to ensure that they had no access to classified material. When Germany invaded Russia in 1941, the Party reverted to the anti-Fascist line it had promoted from 1938 until the Nazi-Soviet Pact of August 1939. It began to advocate support both for the Canadian war effort and for increased aid to Russia, a theme which eventually culminated in the 1943–44 propaganda campaign for the Second Front.

Other groups posed a potential threat to Security. *Technocracy Inc.*, for example, was declared illegal because it openly opposed the war effort; its members declared that they could not be trusted not to send confidential information out of the country. War resister groups, "Peace Now" programs, and some groups such as the U.S.-based pro-Nazi "Deutsche für Kanada" were obvious threats. Less obvious was "Petainism", which emerged after the establishment of the Vichy Government in France. This took the form of propaganda, directed mainly against French Canadians, stressing the "imminent defeat" of Britain and the effect this would have on Quebec. It created some front organizations, most of them U.S.-based, and recruited a few politicians and some young intellectuals, but it lost ground as the war progressed. Eventually, M.I.3 detailed an officer to work closely with the R.C.M.P., watching, recording, and studying such groups, and making data available to Section investigators. By the end of the war, his list contained the names of over 300 of them.

Effective control, the key to successful measures to counter the covert threat, could only be achieved by a system of positive identification. The C.G.S. and the Minister approved a fingerprinting system for the Army in January 1941, but administrative problems prevented it from being introduced until more than a year later. M.I.3 began to keep a card index of persons coming to its attention through Commanding Officers' reports, Censorship, other agencies or casual complaints, and passed its information on suspicious characters to the R.C.M.P. By the end of 1941, the first year of operation, M.I.3 had over 7,000 cards, and was adding 60 to 80 new names each week. Files were opened on about 800 serious cases; 484 of the men were cleared, 103 were released from the Service. By the end of the war, some 2,400 soldiers had been placed under observation because they were suspected of being, or known to be, members of a subversive organization. Both Col. Ralston, then Minister of National Defence, Army, and the D.M.I. were opposed to putting men in a labour battalion, a concept used by our Allies and by C.M.H.Q., and attempted to control the potential threat by enhanced Security within the Army. Each of the two methods had merit; the latter was the more risky, but that risk was probably less acute in Canada.

When a soldier was alleged to be untrustworthy, he would first be put under observation in his unit. His Commanding Officer would be required, at regular intervals and over a period of three months, to submit reports that would be compared with information received from other sources. If at the end of this probationary period he was declared to be a serious risk, he was discharged. Otherwise he was either placed where he could not have access to classified matters or cleared outright. It was not easy to investigate such suspects. Like all reporting systems, this one was subject to human error. Men were sometimes accused out of spite, through an informant's excess of zeal, or through ignorance of the man's ethnic, social, or political background. Witchhunts had to be avoided at all costs, and it was, of course, of supreme importance that every fit man should be retained in the Service.

As the duties became more sophisticated and more deeply involved with technical equipment, the threats of hostile ideology made guarantees of individual loyalty, integrity, and discretion vitally important. Intelligence was the first branch requiring background checks, and was followed by those Directorates that handled the new and secret radar devices, then known as Electrical Methods of Fire Control. These checks, and those required in other government departments, produced a workload that the R.C.M.P. could not possibly handle. The District G.S.O.3 (Int) who short-cut the system by doing his own checks not only duplicated work but also invaded an area properly belonging to the R.C.M.P. In July 1942, Commissioner Wood suggested that the Army deal with its own cases.[10] The Army, however, also lacked investigators, and was not able to accept the responsibility until January 1943, by which time the volume of cases reached almost 100 a month. By May 1st, Army investigators were handling all radar, Field Security, and Cipher personnel clearances. On May 11th, the Military Members of the Defence Council decided that officers working in those fields should be investigated not only for subversion but also for suitability and discretion. By April 1944, officers going to the Staff College, C.W.A.C. officers, and all officer candidates had to be cleared, and by January 1945 there were 15 separate categories requiring clearance action.

Even the 100 cases per month represented a significant work load when we realize how few investigators there were, their lack of experience, the wartime restrictions on travel, and the constraints facing men in uniform trying to make discreet enquiries. By 1945, when the monthly rate had risen to 500, more investigators were available. But the enquiries had become more sophisticated by that time, and took longer. The Sections were also active in non-investigatory tasks and a steady build-up of the backlog continued.

M.I.3(C) – SECURITY OF PERSONNEL: ALIENS

The potential threat posed by aliens has been mentioned. Because both the threat itself and the regulatory legislation were complex, a specialist sub-section under Maj. A.N.K. Hobbs was formed in 1943 to monitor it. By that time, the U.S. was in the war, the 1,200,000 German-born residents of that country were under surveillance or interned, and the many German consulates near the Canadian border were closed. But before 1941, M.I.3 had to get its information on foreign nationals unofficially through personal contacts in G2 (U.S. Army Intelligence), the Office of Naval Intelligence, and the various State police agencies.

When the British Security Co-ordinator's office was established in New York, M.I.3's contacts could be arranged legally. Special tribute must be paid to Supt. E.W. Bavin, who resigned from the R.C.M.P. to join B.S.C., and who played a vital part not only in setting up this liaison for M.I.3 but also in organizing a wide range of Security and Intelligence-related functions. D.M.I. worked closely with him, and he is remembered with warmth and respect; some say that B.S.C. would have been much less successful without him.

On January 22nd, 1942, the Adjutant-General's Branch directed units to discharge immediately aliens of German and Italian racial origin who had been called up. If they were naturalized, they could remain in the Service, but they could not serve on either coast. Unfortunately, the circular did not define the term "racial origin". The result was that even third and fourth generation Canadians of German and Italian stock were returned to Depots for re-allocation, simply because of their names. Some of the confusion arose in National Registration records from errors, sometimes deliberate, but most often caused through understandable ignorance; many men had not the remotest idea of their correct nationality. The Army was also at fault; attestation papers contained nothing that could be used to establish correct citizenship.

Order-in-Council P.C. 5842, issued on July 9th, 1942, gave military personnel the right to obtain naturalization on the basis of a simple application, without going through the courts. But, by March 1943, only six soldiers had availed themselves of the privilege. Many thought that the Oath of Allegiance they had taken at enlistment was sufficient, and it was very hard to persuade them otherwise. The Order provided another concession; an alien who had gone overseas – many had slipped through the rather loose screen of the first few years – could apply for and be granted citizenship at once. But a man who had been caught by the earlier system, and had had to remain in Canada, was not eligible to apply and, until this anomaly was resolved, the Office of the Secretary of State decided to place all applications in abeyance. Many volunteers were therefore held in Canada, unable to go overseas because they could not get the piece of paper which would change their status and allow them to go. On August 1st, the Adjutant General's Branch made the problem even more complicated by using in an order a phrase that was widely misunderstood: "Foreign nationals and Canadians of foreign origin". On the premise that the only persons to whom the order did not apply were North American Indians, even men born in the British Isles were removed from both coasts.[11]

C.M.H.Q. advised that, in Britain, allied aliens could serve in any unit, neutral aliens were banned from some units, and enemy aliens were permitted to serve in the Pioneer Corps and, in certain circumstances, in the Medical and Ordnance Corps. No neutral or enemy aliens were recruited until they had been vetted.[12] In November 1942, the Minister of National Defence required all recruits other than those born in the British Empire and the United States to answer a questionnaire, to give all particulars about themselves, and to be fingerprinted on records to be marked "alien".

There was some disagreement among the Departments on the detail and application of the Regulation. Defence, for its part, decided that individual alien recruits would be enrolled, but only for employment in "non-sensitive" units, i.e., units in which access to secret apparatus or documents was not required. A list was prepared in which units were designated as either "sensitive" or "non-sensitive"; inevitably, the distinction irritated the pride of those who were placed in the latter category.

The Adjutant General defined the kinds of employment open to aliens on June 14th, 1943, and on July 12th enrollment began. The potential intake was 26,000 alien males of military age in Canada. Enemy aliens were now legally eligible for enrollment if their completed "Declaration of Intention" had been accepted by the Secretary of State; many of them were actually being enrolled before they had the official receipt. A revised order was sent out on November

30th, and the combined 1944 amendments were reissued as an overall instruction on January 20th, 1945. In March and July 1945, two new amendments were added: alien applications for service in the Occupation Force were to be rejected, those for service against Japan were to be accepted.

By late 1944, the pressures on the Adjutant General's Branch to find reinforcements forced him to send aliens overseas to non-sensitive units. The criteria used were: 18 months of satisfactory voluntary service, eight years of Canadian residence, and a clear police record. D.M.I. was required to take clearance action and to issue a formal certificate in each case. By the end of November, the Department of the Secretary of State was able to use the D.M.I. files to facilitate the naturalization of returning ex-soldiers. D.V.A. officials were given access to those held by the D.I.O.s, who had been handling cases in their areas since October 1944. Finally, the regulations that had permitted aliens to serve overseas were invoked to permit them to acquire the Canadian citizenship they had earned.[13]

Two random examples will illustrate the cases that passed through M.I.3(c). One young man, born in Romania in 1906, had come to Canada in 1911. His father became naturalized in 1922, but somehow neglected to put his son's name on his application. Thinking he was a Canadian citizen, the young man enlisted, went overseas, married, returned to Canada in April 1944, and was discharged. Because he was not legally naturalized, his wife was legally a citizen by marriage of Romania, an enemy country. She was pregnant, unable to comply with the administrative procedures required for an exception to be made, and was refused entry to Canada. Maj. Hobbs received the report on July 10th, dealt with it on the 12th, and, by the 14th, Immigration had sent her clearance to the U.K.

The second case appeared during First Canadian Army's advance to the Scheldt. Hans Wolpe, a Jew brought up in France after his parents had been liquidated by the Nazis, had joined the Resistance, had been deported from France by the *Arbeitsdienst* to work with the *Organization Todt* in Germany, had crossed through the lines, and was picked up by the Royal Winnipeg Rifles. He then voluntarily pinpointed the locations of pillboxes and weak points in the German defences. The Rifles' attack was successful, and Wolpe fought with the "Little Black Devils" throughout the Scheldt, Nijmegen, Hochwald, and Deventer actions. He was fed and clothed, but received no pay and would have had no protection if he had been captured. Submissions were made to the Secretary of State and to Immigration, who ruled that he should be allowed to enter Canada, and that the effective date of his naturalization would be the date when he first came into the Canadian lines.[14]

M.I.3(B) – SECURITY OF INFORMATION

The Planning Staff had hoped that the D.O.C.R. would be sufficiently detailed to make separate Censorship Regulations unnecessary. When war broke out, however, the D.O.C.R. were not ready and, on September 1st, Censorship Regulations, 1939, were authorized under P.C. 2481 to meet the emergency. Censorship of cables, transoceanic radio communications, radio-telephony, and telephones, all of which were controlled by D.N.D., was applied under P.C. 2499. Postal Censorship was authorized by P.C. 2506 on September 2nd. Cable Censorship was imposed at Vancouver on September 2nd, effective at 2400; on the 3rd at Montreal at 0147; and at Toronto at 0917. Because the D.O.C.R., which were approved on the 3rd, introduced a second and different set of Censorship regulations, the Privy Council ordered a Censorship Co-ordination Committee, of a Chairman and six members, to be set up to direct and co-ordinate the censorship activities of the various government departments concerned. The Department of Transport and the acting-Secretary of State each had two representatives; Defence and the Postmaster-General had one member each. Mr. Walter S. Thompson, C.N.R., Montreal, was appointed as its Chairman. The D.N.D. temporary representative, pending the appointment of a Chief Cable Censor, was Col. Pope.[15]

The first recorded stop was made on September 4th by the Cable Censor in Toronto who held up a message to Japan from the Japanese Legation in Ottawa. After this incident, a ruling was made to allow diplomatic messages to be passed, provided that they were franked by an official whose signature had previously been lodged with the Chief Cable Censor. Col. Pope suggested that the ruling be brought to the attention of all neutrals.[16]

On the 5th, Vancouver asked whether internal messages were to be censored. It also asked for authority to censor domestic subversive telegrams. The Censor was told not to interfere with internal messages and not to censor subversive ones, but to pass all useful information to the Chief Censor for transmission to A.D.M.I. From this beginning, Censorship and Security remained linked in a close and profitable relationship. On September 9th, Col. Pope, pointing out the conflicts between regulations, recommended to Mr. Thompson that the Orders-in-Council be revoked and the differences resolved, and that revised orders be issued. On September 20th, Lt.-Col. W.W. Murray, M.C., of Canadian Press, was appointed Chief Cable Censor and, on October 7th, Lt.-Col. R.P. Landry became Chief Radio Broadcasting Censor.

On October 19th, 1939, D.M.O.&I. drew to the attention of the C.G.S. an article that had appeared in the *Toronto Star*. From the very beginning of the war, this paper's attitude regarding military information caused D.N.D. to regard it with suspicion. In this case, it gave information on Canadian unpreparedness that an enemy would find very useful. The C.G.S. ruled that, in such critical matters, the danger of providing information to the enemy outweighed the need for informing the Canadian public; this became a basic Press Censorship policy guideline.[17] On October 24th, the question of clearly defining the areas in which photography would be banned was brought up; Halifax was the first area to be listed. On November 17th, the Q.M.G. forwarded a sheaf of press clippings containing information on troop movements; Press Censorship was asked to issue a directive to prevent leaks of this kind. Brig.-Gen. C.H. Mitchell, a former Guide, was appointed Senior Cable Censor, Toronto, with Capt. Eric Acland, a former Defence columnist with the *Toronto Telegram*, as his assistant. Brig. Mitchell's office was located on the 14th floor of the C.P.R. building; he was given a full time staff of three, with two others for occasional service. At Montreal, Mr. H. Yuill had a staff of 14, and one 10-foot x 23-foot room in the C.P. Telegraph building. Col. T.E. Powers manned the station at Halifax and handled 75 items per day relating to warships, convoys, and military movements. Mr. Victor MacLean, in Vancouver, had four censors on duty at a time, and the C.N. donated his quarters rent free.[18]

Lt.-Col. "Jock" Murray was appointed G.S.O.1, Censorship Section (D.M.O.&I.) on November 25th, 1940. On December 9th, Mr. Thompson left to become Director of Public Information and Col. Pope, who had become D.M.O.&I. on October 15th, assumed the post of Censorship Committee Chairman. Under Col. Pope's guidance, the various Orders-in-Council were re-drafted and reissued and a new handbook was issued to the Censors. Until May 1942, Cable, Telegraph, and Telephone Censorship remained under D.N.D., Postal (Mr. F.E. Joliffe) under the Postmaster-General, Radio under the Minister of Transport, and Press (Mr. Wilfred Eggleston) under the Secretary of State. All branches were then co-ordinated under a single Minister of National War Services, and a number of advisory committees were set up.[19] The Advisory Committee on Censorable Communications of Military Interest met every four weeks, and was of great use to Intelligence; the Advisory Committee on Publication of Military Information met only rarely.

The close co-operation between all departments of Censorship and M.I.3 did more than add to the security of military information. From the thousands of intercepts that Censorship received, M.I.3(b) was able to cull a wealth of information involving subjects as varied as economic warfare and counter-espionage. The harvest was particularly rich while the United States was still neutral. For some inexplicable reason the enemy assumed that the cable links between New York, Berlin, and Rome were safe. M.I.3 people were placed in strategic New York City cable offices and, with assistance from the R.C.N., the Chief Cable Censor, and some good fishermen off both coasts, the offshore cables were lifted and tapped. The resulting windfall was staggering in more senses than one; the difficulty was to find a government department geared to digest and handle it. Much was passed to British Intelligence.

PRESS CENSORSHIP

Canadian newspapers printed accounts of the departure of First Canadian Division. The breaches of security were not quite as extreme as they had been in 1914, but they still gave the enemy much useful information. On February 20, 1940, the press even linked the names of the units to those of their ships.[20] The regulations were so loose that when a stop was ordered to protect the names of the formations to which troops were being allocated, the authority had to be signed personally by the Minister of National Defence. On July 1st, D.M.O.&I. tried to explain why it was necessary to deny information to the enemy. His press release was so progressively watered down that when the C.G.S. finally issued it on July 22nd, it permitted only "general information not containing sufficient detail to provide Order of Battle information", which was valueless as a guide.

On June 12th, the Press and Radio Censors were warned that "the Department considers it desirable that no references should be made to First Division for the time being". This was to cover the Division's move to France, but it was not appreciated that a complete stop would have been just as revealing. On June 29th, Press and Radio Censors were urged "in future" to prohibit information on the full order-of-battle of Canadian units then being mobilized. Two days later, the Director of Public Information, who had already been asked to publicize the need for security, was told that no announcements should be made of the arrival of troops in Great Britain and Iceland, no photos should be published, and no mention should be made of troop movements to ports of embarkation or of embarkations for overseas except when they were specifically authorized.

In November, all mention of the names of Canadian units was banned. A ruling of January 20th, 1941, ordered infantry regiments to be referred to only by their territorial affiliation (e.g., a western battalion); other units could have a broad classification added to the territorial identification (e.g., a medical company from the Maritimes). In some areas, photography was an obvious security hazard; orders were publicized, posters were displayed, and, on occasion, cameras and film were confiscated in attempts to exercise control. The G.O.C. Vancouver Defences had his I.O. issue permits to local newspaper staff photographers working in restricted areas. Press photographs had to be submitted to the Regional Censor, who, in doubtful cases, would refer them to the Service concerned. In mid-June 1941, officers were said to be talking to the press about matters affecting coastal defence. They had already been forbidden to publish articles without clearance; now they were also told that they were not allowed to talk to the press.[21]

When Japan entered the war, Canadian Censorship in the Pacific had to be co-ordinated with that of Canada's allies. The British Chief Censor visited the United States and Canada in December 1941, and successfully laid the foundation for common Censorship action in the western hemisphere. Policy was to be closely supervised at the higher levels; day-to-day operational details were to be worked out by liaison officers in the respective capitals.

At the domestic level, co-ordination was still far from satisfactory. The function of Press and Radio Censorship was not legally defined until May 1942. In June of that year Ottawa set up an "Ad Hoc Committee on Stops and Releases", comprising the three Directors of Intelligence, representatives of the Censorship organizations, and government departments. Its first secretary was Capt. E. Williams, later an officer in M.I.3.[22] It soon consolidated a number of minor Committees, including the Advisory Committee on Intelligence and Security, and it was very active.

Canadian firms engaged in defence contracts were slow to realize that they now had to protect not merely their own industrial secrets but every aspect of their defence production. In July 1939, the British Committee of Imperial Defence sent Canada a Board of Trade leaflet on trading with the enemy. External Affairs later compiled from Postal Censorship records a list of persons whose import/export trading was suspicious. In March 1942, the Inspector General's Branch obtained another British policy statement on the release of information on military production. In early 1942, The Master General of Ordnance, Mr. Victor Sifton, reported that one engineering firm with a contract for anti-tank guns had printed a detailed picture history of the weapon it was producing. The Directorate of Technical Requirements (D.T.R.) pointed out that, while such practices were not actually prohibited, they could reveal to any enemy agent what was being made at a particular plant, and perhaps its rate of production. In this case, the D.M.O.&I. took no action until the D.T.R. informed him that the gun was on the Confidential List. He then ordered all copies of the publication to be impounded, and the Ministry of Munitions and Supply directed that, in future, material intended for publication by a supplier should first be submitted to its publicity branch.[23] But a continuing education program was necessary.

On September 18th, 1942, responsibility for liaison with Censorship agencies was relinquished by D.M.O.&P. and handed to D.M.I. Its appropriate Section, M.I.3(b), interpreted its role as that of an advisor and guide to the press. The abundance of sometimes confusing regulations often led newspapers to make mistakes through ignorance of the precise meaning. In July 1942, Lieut. C.G. (Cec) Jones of M.I.3(b) prepared a brochure entitled "Editing against the Enemy", that was printed by Press Censorship and widely circulated. It showed a number of typical items in the form in which they might appear in the press and then demonstrated how they could be compared to produce order-of-battle. M.I.3(b) then tried to make the regulations and directives more practical and up-to-date, to co-ordinate them with U.S. and British practices, and, by keeping in daily contact with the Censors and the press, to ensure that they were workable. It circulated the British list of Stops and Releases, and drew attention to differences between them and Canadian practices.[24]

The Section also maintained the only copy held in Canada of the "Secret List" of classified equipment. D.M.O.&I. had received only one of the two amendments that had been made to it; the other was obtained only after strenuous effort. The three voluminous documents were laboriously consolidated into one massive List, and then, of course, Amendment No. 3 arrived. Since the List contained only items of U.K. origin, M.I.3(b) compiled a parallel List of Canadian equipment. It also prepared and held in D.M.I. a list of classified Canadian projects, similar to the one maintained in London. A joint Canadian-British-American Secret List, completed on September 1st, 1943, was not as useful, for its amendments never succeeded in keeping pace with the changes.

The Section had charge of liaison with the Directorate of Public Relations, a task which kept some of its staff working 17 to 18 hours a day, seven days a week. They had to vet each and every D.P.R. release, including news, films, features, and photographs. In a single month, they examined as many as 328,000 words of written copy, 450 still photographs, and 47 motion pictures. To be sure their decisions were sound, they constantly referred to other Directorates for advice. In addition to D.P.R. material, they had to clear all copy prepared for official Canadian Army and Wartime Information Board publications, everything sent in clear through the Canadian Army Signals System, and all material produced by the artists of the Directorate of History.

Maj. Eric Acland wisely made certain that the Sub-section contained a high proportion of newspapermen. Its Head, Maj. Cec Jones, was an excellent example; he was a well-trained and experienced Intelligence officer with Infantry experience, and he had been the editor of his own weekly newspaper. He understood the conflict between news and Censorship, and could discuss them in terms that both sides could understand. He was meticulous and careful, had an excellent grasp of language, and the ability to remain "unflappable" in crises. His M.B.E. was richly deserved.

In August 1942, in the course of a survey of Censorship breaches and of trouble areas, Atlantic Command discovered that a number of technical publications, sold openly on newsstands, contained information of the most recent kind: *Canadian Aviation*, *Iron Age*, the *Army and Navy Journal*, and particularly *Model Airplane News* (which some years later was to publish a drawing of the U.S. U-2 plane well before the Gary Powers incident). Through the appropriate channels, the Command asked both U.S. and Canadian Censors to have all technical magazines censored at source.[25]

When Canadians were deployed in North Africa and in the Mediterranean Theatre, press officials were quick to complain that the Security protection provided was excessive, and that information of public interest was not being released. This was not a simple problem. Should Canadian units be named or designated merely by their territorial affiliation? How soon should casualty lists be published? Should War Correspondents' despatches be censored by both Britain and Canada? The War Office replied that Allied Forces H.Q. was releasing the items from Sicily with appropriate stops. Casualty returns, for instance, were being held for 30 days to prevent identification with any specific action. On October 5th, M.I.3 was able to inform the Chief Censor of Publications that Canadian units in Britain could now be identified by name rather than by territory, but that identification with a place or an event and any indication of future plans were still prohibited.[26]

The first Escape and Evasion stories appeared in January 1944. These were unusual, interesting, and exciting, and journalists were eager to report them as fully as possible. They were told that the stories had to be delayed and that, above all, nothing could be said about the assistance an escapee may have received. M.I.3(b) received excellent co-operation from the newspapers on this. In March 1944, it had a little more difficulty persuading the press not to publish the story of the Commando group led by Lord Lovat, that had trained in Canada during the winter 1943-44. It was eventually agreed that its activities would be filmed, but that the processing of the film would be supervised, vetted, and held, and that formal promises of silence would be demanded from everyone involved in its production. The National Film Board was annoyed because it thought itself competent to handle the Security. Lieut. Ross of M.I.3(b), who supervised D.M.I.'s interests, was sceptical. Enough breaches occurred in the immediate vicinity of the Commando Camp for it to be commonly said that the activity was "well-known west of Winnipeg". But the stop was maintained and the story was not made public until it appeared in the *Journal of the Alpine Club of Canada* after the war.[27]

By the early fall of 1944, D.N.D. could assume that the enemy had samples of most, if not all, Canadian items of equipment in service. There was therefore no real reason to restrict publication of descriptions of it. It was essential, in order to maintain good relations with the press, to lift these restrictions as soon as possible. Editors, who were well aware of the progress of the war, tended to ignore directives which were outdated, and to question others which still applied. The Military could not understand the need to be flexible, and the Censors and M.I.3(b) had a great deal of trouble operating between the two.

One of the Censor's difficulties stemmed from the fact that breaches of the D.O.C.R., which was the authority for Censorship, could not really be prosecuted. Section 16 and five sub-sections, prohibited, under a penalty of $5,000 fine and/or five years imprisonment, the publication of any material "likely to prejudice the safety of the State or the efficient prosecution of the war", or of "information . . . which would or might be directly or indirectly useful to the enemy". But this penalty was too strict, even for the bad days of the war, and was never in fact applied. With victory almost in sight, a conviction was even more unlikely, and the Censor and M.I.3(b) had to rely upon the co-operation of the newspaper editors in order to get items stopped. These editors, in turn, had to rely on the good sense of the officials concerned. Capricious demands only weakened this mutual trust.

The news that Canadian forces had been transferred from Italy to Germany in early 1945 was ordered withheld until the move was completed. The normal flow of mail was interrupted, and the public instinctively realized that something important had happened. Under strong pressure, Prime Minister King asked British permission to release a statement, since "our Press silence is only maintained through Censorship". He was told that there were strong reasons for believing that the enemy had not yet fully appreciated the extent of the reduction of forces in Italy, and that Gen. Eisenhower considered that the release should wait until the enemy had identified Canadians in the line. The Canadian Press, however, broke the story on April 3rd, 1945: "All Canadian infantry and armoured forces are together once more as an army under Gen. Crerar." When the official announcement was made on April 23rd, it was no longer news.[28]

Generally speaking, the Intelligence Directorates of all the Services worked with the Censors "in a spirit of mutual confidence and respect". But some officers saw the Censor as an ally of the press, intent on destroying military security. The Censor, for his part, often found it difficult to get the sort of confidential information he needed to make rational decisions on what things he had to stop; he often looked on the soldier as a "hide-bound brass-hat who considers it his business to say no". Senior officers would often object to the release of an item, give reasons quite irrelevant to the needs of Security, and become extremely annoyed when they were told that the story could not be stopped on Security grounds. In such cases, M.I.3(b) would simply try unofficially to persuade the Directorate of Censorship to advise against publication. There were also many other occasions when D.N.D. would not clear a story which neither it nor the Censor could legally stop a newspaper from printing if it chose to do so. Once again, the impasse would be resolved by negotiation. M.I.3 often gave helpful advice to the Censor and, equally often, the Censor saved the Department from falling into situations which could have been embarrassing.[29]

TELEGRAPH AND POSTAL CENSORSHIP

Most Telegraph Censorship breaches were probably the result of ignorance. Many others were deliberate attempts to evade the controls through the use of private codes and veiled allusions. One system which permitted Service personnel to send personal messages at a reduced rate soon became a prolific source of leakage of information on future moves and plans. The messages were always examined for peculiarities of phrasing which, by prearrangement, could reveal information to the recipient. One of the earliest and most blatant of these attempts occurred when a unit moved to Iceland in June 1940. An officer wired his wife: "I send love and nature did everything". It was stopped, because the initial letters of the words in the message spelled the name of the officer's destination. Where a code was suspected, the message was paraphrased, unnecessary words were deleted, and it was held for at least a week. Safe-arrival messages were held for at least 96 hours, and released with the date and office of origin deleted. Messages announcing the departure of drafts from ports in Canada were blocked for varying periods, up to as long as five weeks after filing. At Halifax, all public telephones on the pier were disconnected to make last-minute messages virtually impossible. All overseas messages were transmitted by cable to prevent enemy interception.[30]

In May 1940, a Canadian Active Service Force Routine Order forbade correspondence between soldiers and strangers. Its purpose was to check the activities of "pen pals" and "lonely hearts clubs" which were being used to provide contacts through which information on order-of-battle could be obtained. The order was never successfully enforced. Pen pal correspondence problems continued throughout the war, and M.I.3 even failed to persuade Press Censorship to ban their newspaper advertisements.[31]

In mid-January 1941, Postal Censorship intercepted a letter from a Canadian Communist internee asking for information about his sons who were serving in the Canadian Army. The request was reasonable, but it raised deeper issues of the possible effect of such correspondence on the military efficiency of the sons. The Minister directed that, except where the internees were enemy aliens, communications would be permitted between blood relatives; their letters would be censored and the privilege withdrawn if abuses occurred.[32]

In August 1941, Maj. J. Haig-Smith, Chief Censor for Newfoundland, drew up a lengthy and comprehensive report in answer to enquiries and complaints about Censorship there. All telegraph and cable traffic inland, entering, leaving, or in transit, was monitored. Outgoing international mail, including items addressed to the U.S. and other neutrals, was scrutinized. Only letters from Gander Base sent by suspects or aliens were censored internally. Newfoundland had no Press Censorship, but the Telegraph Censor's Office system checked the wire services. Radio broadcasts were examined before they were transmitted. In August, however, the D.O.C., M.D. 5, reported that "W" Force troops were having their letters mailed by friends returning on leave to New Brunswick. Intelligence first suggested to D.M.O.&I. that the hole could be plugged if unit censorship were applied, and then, in 1942, urged that all mail should be sent to Moncton for processing. In the end, the Chief Censor took over part of the flow, and the Postal Censor at North Sydney accepted the rest.[33]

When Canada agreed to take German prisoners and internees from Britain in July 1940, their mail was to be collected and sent back to the U.K. for censorship.[34] This was impractical, and the postal censorship system already applied to the Italian Reservist internees was extended. This decision was reached partly because the system had successfully uncovered information on Italian order-of-battle, which turned out, after the Italian invasion of France, to have been surprisingly complete and accurate. But the procedures of Military Censorship and Intelligence were sometimes not as well planned as they should have been. On April 22nd, 1942, for instance, the D.N.I. reported a marked decline in the amount of information he was obtaining from German naval P.W. mail. He said that, in order to eliminate duplication of effort, Postal Censorship officers had been sent to the Camps to discuss duties with the Camp Censors. While there, they had talked to P.W., who, in turn, had warned the other P.W. Another curious Censorship incident involved about 30 aliens, sent to Canada early in the war and later released, who were employed to censor German P.W. mail. The Director of Censorship thought it advisable to ask M.I.5 in London to review their files, and D.M.I., perhaps with tongue in cheek, asked for an opinion on the advisability of using aliens as censors. M.I.5 replied that nothing detrimental was known about those particular aliens mentioned, but: "The employment of enemy aliens on P.O.W. Censorship duties is . . . entirely undesirable. Not only are such persons given the opportunity of direct communication with the enemy, but if they are ill-disposed it is possible that they may allow information which should be condemned to pass to enemy countries, or may disclose to undesirable persons information which they may have derived." No one will know if information which should have been stopped escaped through their employment, but, as we shall see, much was available.[35]

By the end of the war, 10 million P.W. letters had been checked, close to 100,000 were condemned; 400,000 more were released only after items had been deleted. A separate Censorship Advisory Section was set up to review not only the mail of P.W. in Canadian hands, but also that of Canadian P.W. held by the enemy. It had a staff of five officers and seven men, drawn from the P.W. Intelligence Section, M.I.4. It succeeded in gathering from P.W. correspondence a great deal of information about German order-of-battle in the Mediterranean and on the Russian front. It included field post numbers (cover numbers to hide the actual identity of a unit), and locations, dates, installations, and distribution of components of the German forces. A full dossier was compiled on a German underground movement, including the ramifications of its foreign financing. D.M.I. learned of Nazi cells abroad from P.W. correspondence, and obtained information on the escape plans of German leaders; it made this knowledge available to the Occupation authorities. From civilian information, it also learned of the effects of air raids, the efficiency of air raid precautions and relief measures, the relocation of industrial plants, the dislocation of transportation, and of morale, privation, health, social problems, and reconstruction. P.W.

letters also helped to identify the more ardent Nazis in the Camps as well as in Germany itself.[36]

Censorship also concerned itself with clandestine methods of evading its scrutiny. It formed a Special Examiners Section to deal with suspected subversion and espionage, codes, ciphers, and veiled speech. Secret inks were first noticed in January 1943, and from then on, a watch was kept on suspected P.W. In 1944, one prisoner alone used such inks 35 times. No evidence of two-way correspondence was found.

In August 1943, the various executive officers of the Allied Censorships met in Miami, Florida, with Intelligence officers of the Services, the police, and other interested government agencies, to make sure that Censorship was playing its full role in counter-espionage activities, and to develop a single correlated Allied plan. They established a special central office for Counter-Intelligence tasks within Censorship; its role was purely liaison, with no executive or investigative functions.

We have seen that M.I.3 was the link between the Chief Postal Censor and the Army. The Section kept the Censor advised on Army policy and was directly responsible for seeing that unit censorship arrangements were correct. It issued and accounted for Unit Censorship Stamps, a relatively small task in Canada itself. It put specific stops on the troops' mail during the Kiska expedition and during cold weather trials at Prince Albert in the winter of 1943–44, and on certain other special projects. Postal Censorship itself applied specially stringent controls in areas where morale was bad, but it believed strongly that these measures worked best when they were undertaken by units themselves, for units were more aware than any others of their own local problems.

Censorship did not attempt to stop normal grievances, complaints, or service grumbles. On one occasion, a draft of airmen refused to go overseas in a transport because of its filthy condition. The story had to be stopped in order to protect the ship's departure. The Department felt that refusal to board the ship was a breach of discipline, and that publication of the airmen's action would encourage others to follow their example. The Censor, thinking mostly of the condition of the vessel, sided with the men. D.M.I. said that "this was not a matter on which he could properly advise them". The Censor correctly interpreted his statement to mean that there was no Security objection, and feared that if he suppressed the story, Censorship could be accused of covering up administrative abuses. The controversy between the Department and the Censors was resolved only about an hour before the ship was due to dock in Britain. The Minster released a statement admitting that conditions aboard her were bad, and promised a thorough investigation. After this incident, inspectors always checked vessels before the troops were loaded.[37]

By 1945, Censorship had increasingly to turn its attention to protecting activities connected with the war with Japan. It succeeded reasonably well in controlling information on the very sensitive matter of the enlistment and employment of Japanese Canadians. Its work ceased on August 16th. M.I.3(b) closed shortly afterwards.

SECURITY – COMMANDS AND DISTRICTS

Commissioner S.T. Wood asked D.N.D. on October 2nd, 1939, to report all incidents of suspected sabotage to the nearest R.C.M.P. Detachment for investigation. Sabotage occurred in the aircraft industry, and in mills making uniform cloth. On October 26th, Maj.-Gen. Constantine, D.O.C., M.D. 3, reported that a prowler near Fort Henry, an alien internee camp, had been challenged and shot at, but had disappeared into the wilderness that then was Barriefield Common. On November 6th, one of the sentries at the Signals Training Centre, Barriefield, discovered two men near the camp water tower. One ran away immediately, the other threw stones at the sentry and then ran away. The sentries were at once doubled, and issued with rifles and five rounds of ammunition. The camp was known to contain Communists, and a mysterious fire that broke out on November 9th was thought to have been a sabotage attempt.[38]

In May 1940, the A.D.M.I. decided to reinstitute a prewar reporting practice. The D.O.C.s were reminded that Germany was prepared to use subversion to further its aims; they were warned of possible threats and advised that, though the police were primarily responsible for maintaining law and order, the military could be required to help. The District I.O.s were required to become thoroughly familiar with conditions within the Districts, including the presence of aliens, their attitudes towards the war, the presence of Nazi, Fascist, or Communist organizations, and the possibility that they might hold arms and explosives and be disseminating anti-British literature. The A.D.M.I. warned that the R.C.M.P. was engaged in similar studies and demanded close liaison with it. Finally, the D.I.O.s were required to produce a monthly Security Report covering these matters, and special reports whenever any significant items came to their attention. This document, the first wartime definition of the D.I.O.s' duties, formed the basis for all Intelligence activities in the Districts throughout the war.[39]

In April 1941, the G.S.O.3 (Int)s in the Districts were told to forward all details of suspected incidents at once, without waiting for the usual Board of Enquiry, or even the routine District Weekly Report which had replaced the Monthly Security Report. On May 27th, 1941, the C.G.S. directed all Militia units to receive training "designed to meet contingencies arising from 'Fifth Column' activities in support of the enemy". This was to include training, but not action, in the protection of Vulnerable Points, the clearing of places "seized by enemy sympathizers", and other duties laid down in the still relevant pamphlet of 1932.[40]

Rumours of all kinds abounded. On March 16th, 1940, a disturbing but quite false, Communist-inspired story advised that the students at the Brandon, Manitoba, Technical School would shortly be "grabbed" by the Army, and that some had already been conscripted. On March 23rd, an accurate rumour was received from Camp Petawawa. Its very pro-German internees were supposed to be planning to escape as soon as the warm weather returned; the Guard Detachment officers were said to be so lax that they allowed the internees to retain axes with which they could easily overpower the guards who supervised the work parties; the Camp C.S.M. was allegedly smuggling beer to the internees; and the Military Police in Pembroke were supposedly often drunk. Reaction was swift; prisoners were deprived of their axes, the C.S.M. was caught at his smuggling, and the M.P.s were dealt with by the Camp Commander.[41]

In January 1943, M.D. 3 heard many "reports", firstly, that all the schools in Canada were to close by Easter so that the students could work on the land to relieve the labour shortage and, secondly, that the Army Trades Pay structure was to be increased as a result of pressure on the government by labour unions. M.D. 1 heard that U.S. troops were being moved to Canada to force "Zombies" overseas; this may have been a distortion of the real U.S. moves through Canada to Alaska. Rumours of pregnant C.W.A.C. grew to the point where the girls were reported to be entitled to two free abortions a year, to be on a regular roster as "duty bed-fellow", etc. Public Relations tried to counter these lies but they refused to disappear.[42]

Undoubtedly the most sensitive area in Canada was Halifax. And here Security was bad. Because of the seriousness of the reports received in D.N.D., Maj. Acland was sent in September 1941 to check personally and to report to Lt.-Col. Murray. His findings strongly criticized the arrangements in force in the docks area. As this was an R.C.M.P. responsibility, the report was construed as an attack on that Force, and relations between it and D.M.O.&I. cooled.

In his subsequent submission, Lt.-Col. Murray stressed the obvious fact that, since Atlantic Command was the terminus of the transatlantic route for all reinforcements, leakages of information on troop movements were completely unacceptable. He proposed a Command Security Section of an officer and 12 men, with a power of arrest that it would exercise on rare occasions only. Its duty would be to admonish offenders and to supervise Security generally. When the Section was eventually formed, it grew to two officers, one W.O.II, seven sergeants, eight corporals and two clerks, and its area of responsibility included Newfoundland.

The operations of this Atlantic Command Section, No. 5 F.S.S., and a steady stream of advice, comment, and reprimand, were still not enough to curb the torrent of security breaches. Fundamental to the problem was the fact that, even by August 1942, there was still no clear-cut allocation of Security responsibility. The Command Section was subdivided into detachments in order that the Fortress Commanders might have a small security force. Their reports went to the Military District, not to Command Intelligence. Even if they had, the G.S.O.2 (Int) was fully employed on I(a) and had no time for Security duties. The Embarkation Area was commanded by an R.C.N. officer, who was willing enough to take advice but saw no need for a trained Security Officer on his staff, nor indeed, for giving the local H.Q. Security Officers access to "his" port. Command H.Q. could not co-ordinate policy, and there was no Joint Service Security Intelligence Bureau, comparable to the one on the west coast, where policy could be decided. Finally, many units would arrive in transit overseas without even the most basic Security training. The incidence of illegal photographs will serve as an indicator; within the Restricted Areas of M.D. 6 alone, up to 60 films were being confiscated each day.

Major Acland's recommendations dealt successively with all three aspects to this problem: over-all control, supervision and reinforcement, and training. They were accepted. Atlantic Command's powers were enhanced. A G.S.O.2 Security was appointed at the H.Q. The Command Section was placed directly under Command, with its Detachments reporting to it, not the subordinate H.Q. A Joint Services Security Intelligence Bureau was formed (it held its first meeting on November 10th, 1942). Finally, Maj. Acland and the D.M.I. convinced the D.M.T. to allot time during unit training for short Security lessons. But this did not begin to take effect until well into 1943.[43]

Action was mandatory. Repercussions of the poor state of security at the Port of Halifax had reached Cabinet level. British naval authorities were concerned lest the extensive Security arrangements they had established to protect their transatlantic convoys, and which bore directly on the use of the "Queen" ships, were being rendered useless by breaches committed in Canada. These also were limiting American transatlantic traffic through Halifax. Col. Ralston, after consulting with the British High Commissioner and his own Air, Naval, and R.C.M.P. colleagues, decided to call in British experts. Their criticisms were scathing. When the *Queen Elizabeth* visited Halifax in December 1942, unlimited access to the pier was permitted before her arrival. Movement Control passes were unsatisfactory because they carried neither photograph nor fingerprint; there were too few guards on the pier entrances and gangways, none at all on the ship before embarkation began, and guards only on the central staircase while embarkation was in progress; the "No Smoking" orders were not enforced; no firemen were on board, and the nearest fire engines were fully a half-mile away from the ship; finally, her departure time was widely known in Halifax well before she sailed.

The British report provoked an argument between the Minister of Defence and the Minister of Justice, Mr. St Laurent. Col. Ralston supported the D.M.I.'s demand for better Security. St. Laurent supported Commissioner S.T. Wood, who still believed that Security, for which his O.C. Halifax Division was directly responsible, was good. Entirely apart from the bureaucratic politics involved in this interdepartmental controversy, there was the considerable doubt in many minds that the citizens of Halifax would accept the very stringent measures normally imposed in British ports. But a compelling counter-argument came in January 1943, when the Admiralty told Ottawa that the "Monsters" would not be used as troop ships from Halifax until effective military security was applied. This meant that, in addition to the loss by the Services of their troop-carrying capacity, Halifax itself would lose the revenue that always came at a turn-around. After studying a searching and critical report prepared by Det. Sgt. Thomas Scrogg, which had also been sent to D.M.I., Commissioner Wood accepted D.N.D.'s criticisms. A meeting shortly thereafter between Sir Conup Guthrie, Brig. Stratton (British Intelligence), Mr. St. Laurent, the Minister of Defence (Navy), the D.N.I., R.C.M.P., and Col. Ralston, resulted in M.I.3 being ordered to put the necessary measures into operation. Sgt. Scrogg's action cost his career with the police dearly. But his unselfish service probably saved thousands of lives and many thousands of tons of shipping.[44]

When the *Queen Elizabeth* returned to Halifax in late March 1943, the British Security Co-ordinator was there to watch. He stated in his report that the Canadian authorities had made a serious and successful attempt to put every one of the January recommendations into effect and, although some of the controls were still not operating as they should, they were being rapidly improved.[45]

The Americans were equally alarmed. An American unit, travelling by train through Nova Scotia to Halifax, stopped at "a small town about 250 miles out". One of the townspeople, making casual conversation, told an American officer that "the unit was going to sail on the *Louis Pasteur* [sic], which it did". The Americans, with considerable understatement, reported: "there is every indication of some very bad information leaks in Nova Scotia". This was sent, unchanged except for an additional comment that things were also bad in Newfoundland, to the Canadian Military Attaché in Washington, with a request that a joint, tri-national Board of Enquiry should be set up. The Canadian Attaché asked Ottawa for guidance.[46]

In Newfoundland, it was discovered that the Port Security Officer (P.S.O.), Capt. Eld, really had very little power in a system also weakened by divided authority. The Newfoundland government was responsible for the harbour of St. John's, but R.C.N., Canadian Army, U.S. Navy, U.S. Army, and the civilian Merchant Navy convoy administration each had a responsibility for its own traffic within the harbour. Capt. Eld estimated that proper access control to the docks would mean that the town of St. John's itself would have to be divided, that 50 dock gates would have to be built and guarded by 250 policemen, with an additional 200 on patrol, and that entry permits would have to be issued to about one-quarter of its population. In any case, since the town was completely surrounded by hills, an agent sitting on any one of them could watch everything that went on in the harbour.[47] In the end, Canada had to tell Washington that it had no jurisdiction whatever on the island of Newfoundland, and that complaints could only be resolved by that British colony's government.

Col. Murray then told the C.G.S.: "It all leads back to the responsibilities of the Port Security Officer who, although functioning most conscientiously, does not have the backing of regulations that have teeth in them . . . an utter impossibility to obtain any sort of a conviction under the present Regulation 16, D.O.C.R. A joint Board of Investigation might . . . have the support not only of the military authorities but, particularly, of the political authority on the very top level. Previous enquiries have been too low level and though . . . an improvement, Security was still unsatisfactory".

In the end, neither Col. Ralston nor the Minister of Justice felt that a Joint Board was necessary, and the Americans decided not to take any further action. The R.C.M.P. report on the case stated that the U.S. information lacked many essential facts, including the correct name of the ship. It established the date and route of the movement, and the numbers of American troops, and suggested that Truro was the probable site of the incident. The investigator felt that, as a matter of routine, Auxiliary Services would have been given information on the numerous troop moves through Truro on that date, so that they could have refreshments ready. In his opinion, this system was an open invitation to breaches of security, but he admitted that the risk had been discussed and considered acceptable. Leakages could also have come from the extra crews required by the railway company and the personnel of Auxiliary Services, who were "ladies of the best families in the communities concerned, but serious doubt is entertained as to their capacity for keeping entirely secret the information received by them in connection with their charitable work". Finally, the identity of the ship, particularly one as large as the *Pasteur*, could not have been kept secret from the people of Halifax, and any extra troop trains would almost automatically be linked with its arrival.[48]

This and similar incidents were undoubtedly attributable to poor Security training. In May 1943, a Censorship report covering a move of reinforcements on the *Queen Elizabeth* stated that, in a random examination of 456 letters, Censorship found mentions of the port of embarkation, the name of the ship, the duration of the voyage, the number of troops on board, and many other less important items that should have been protected. The Director of Military Training agreed to provide time for Security instruction for everyone during the training cycle. Questionnaires, posters, reprints of Security Orders, reminders about Orders, and other publications were produced in great quantities for use in Security classes right to the end of the war. But as the German naval threat was countered and the movement of troops became more routine, the requirement to stress protection also declined until, by the end of the war, good Security was almost a normal part of life.

The Sections sent to H.Q. voluminous reports of Security incidents of lesser moment than those that dealt with overseas troop movements, but which still had considerable importance at the time. In October 1941, for instance, Districts were asked to report on such varied matters as the reactions of troops to conscription, recruiting, Active and Reserve Force training, public comment on equipment and health of the Armed Forces, the Canadian Women's Army Corps, relations with the U.S. and American press comments on the Canadian war effort. But the major focus of interest among the troops was morale. One of its factors was the battle dress. Never a glamorous uniform, its appeal was further limited by the fact that in the early days soldiers were not issued with low shoes or light socks, and had perforce to go to dances in anklets and boots which, with their steel heel plates, were downright dangerous. Further, issues were limited in quantity, and men found themselves working and playing in their one and only uniform. The R.C.A.F., on the other hand, had a walking-out uniform of shirt, tie, low shoes, and light socks. They also had the added prestige of the Battle of Britain, of being "Gentlemen with Wings", and of the King's alleged address: "Men of the Navy and Army, Gentlemen of the Air Force". In mixed stations, ugly scenes sometimes took place between junior members of the two services. The D.M.I., supported by the Adjutant General's own morale-watching Branch, the Directorate of Special Services, made strong recommendations, and eventually the Army did get a walking-out uniform – cotton shirts with collars, neckties, low shoes and socks, and battle-dress jackets designed to be worn with a collar and tie. A soldier could not compete with R.C.A.F. glamour, but at least his dress was now reasonably comparable.[49]

A District I.O. was required to report on all factors affecting the morale of men in local units. In December 1942, the I.O. of M.D. 13 reported of one of the Training Centres that: "The Chaplain did not appear to be adapted for duties with a Western Unit". The Adjutant General complained to the D.O.C. that the I.O., a training officer detailed to perform Intelligence duties, had no business making reports on a Chaplain, and should be disciplined. The D.O.C. pointed out that the Chaplain was the person to whom the men normally took their complaints. Because the men found him unsympathetic, the I.O. was quite properly attending to a problem of simple morale. His report was approved by the Senior District Chaplain. The unsuitable Chaplain was transferred, and the D.M.I. mollified the Chief Padre.[50]

In that same month, Capt. Clear, A/G.S.O.3 of M.D. 12, received a report from another Chaplain commenting on: "considerable loose talk . . . about the relation of the C.W.A.C. to the troops . . . tough, as they smoked cigars instead of cigarettes." He investigated this himself, and discovered that the source of the rumour lay in a simple misunderstanding. One of the girls on Regimental

Police duty had entered the shop of a military tailor in downtown Regina for a rest and a chat, a quite normal practice. She asked the tailor for a cigarette, which he did not have; jokingly, he dared her to smoke a small, cheap cigar, and she accepted the challenge. Without any intention of speaking disparagingly of the C.W.A.C., or of starting gossip, the tailor had casually mentioned the incident to his wife and to a civilian friend. This was one of the very few times that a rumour could be traced to its actual, trivial source.[51]

Rumours, and morale, always matters for Security concern, take on an enhanced risk if enemy agents can encourage the first to impair the second. And the presence of enemy agents in Canada was very real. In November 1940, a notebook was found on the east coast. It contained two addresses, and parts of a letter referring to military and police deployments, to details of navigable approaches to the coast, and to a radio receiver. Its author told how he had successfully used a false National Registration Card, and he described an arms cache. The material was accepted as genuine, and the R.C.M.P., with technical assistance from the Army, verified the exact location of one of the approaches cited, and found that the addresses given were those of a German front organization.[52]

In November 1942, a Veterans' Guard Company heard that a German spy had been landed in the Gaspé; on December 3rd, Censorship stopped a civilian letter saying that there were two spies. Another letter a day later brought the total up to 22, with five captured. The G.S.O.3, M.D. 7, explained on the 12th that these were rumours only, spread by a failure in local liaison arrangements. He was, in fact, quite wrong. A spy *had* landed from a German submarine and, thanks to the alertness of a cafe proprietor in New Carlisle, he had been arrested by the Provincial Police. Interrogated by Inspector Harvison, R.C.M.P., and threatened with hanging, he was "turned around", given the cover name of WATCHDOG, and operated for about nine months in Montreal as a double agent under the control of a special committee of the Chiefs of Service Intelligence, British Intelligence, and the R.C.M.P. The information he was sent to acquire showed them the gaps in German information. He was obviously only allowed to send unimportant information – minor details of military units in the Montreal area, vessels in port, anti-submarine nets, National Registration Certificates, ration coupons, and the like. To reduce its value still further, his material was usually held back for about two months before being released.[53]

WATCHDOG was not the only agent to be uncovered and turned around. R.C.M.P. in Toronto found another, whom it used with WATCHDOG to curb a known Montreal Fascist group which was being allowed to operate in order to discover its current and possible postwar Nazi contacts in Canada. In late March 1943, M.D. 1 was told that an agent from the U.S. had approached the guards at the Neys P.W. Camp to ask for the name, number, rank, and address of certain P.W. His questions seemed to be linked to reports of a shipment of "parcels" from Brazil, and of trafficking in P.W. letter envelopes. M.D. 1's investigations failed to produce any concrete evidence, but it forwarded the address of the supposed agent to the B.S.C. In 1944, a third spy landed in northern New Brunswick, made his way to Montreal and Ottawa, failed to establish himself, and surrendered a year later.[54]

Intelligence was also involved in a few cases of public disorder. In June 1943, a strike at Galt Malleable Iron, Ltd. threatened to lead to violence. The D.O.C., M.D. 1, sent his I.O. to Galt in plain clothes to watch the situation. He also asked the D.C.G.S. for authority to place the infantry battalion at Niagara on a six-hour alert in case the strike became violent; by the 11th, the danger was over. In April of the following year, the D.I.O. went to Windsor, and troops at Ipperwash were readied to meet a second outburst, which lasted until mid-May. This time there was no doubt that the unrest had been stimulated by Communist activity.[55]

On November 24th, 1944, after the announcement of the Order-in-Council authorizing overseas service for 16,000 N.R.M.A. personnel, a member of the Pacific Command Security Intelligence Section at Vernon overheard plans for a N.R.M.A. protest parade. He informed Vancouver and the nearest Provost Company, and stood by to watch what would happen. The demonstration was held, and the press reported it with sensational details: "1,000 in the parade, an officer trying to stop them had been injured, 37 men armed with machine guns, under an officer, standing by", and so forth. The 200-man parade was noisy but orderly, although an officer did receive a skinned face. At eleven points in British Columbia, F.S. were ordered to watch carefully for any changes in attitude among the N.R.M.A. Parades were held on the 25th at Terrace, Prince George, Courtenay, and Chilliwack; on the 26th at Nanaimo; on the 27th at Alberni and again at Prince George. The marchers carried slogans expressing N.R.M.A. objections to being sent overseas, calling for total conscription and for wealth to be conscripted, and protesting that the government did nothing for returned men, and that the Wives' Allowance was inadequate; some attacked Gen. McNaughton and Defence Minister Ralston. The Section learned of other parade plans in time for higher authority to take steps to control them.

There was no evidence that these demonstrations were being organized by a central authority, although some of the slogans were the same. There was, however, ample proof that there was in each case a small group of ringleaders. Maj. Bray believed that many of the later parades were patterned on, and perhaps stimulated by, the rather wild and sensational newspaper reports of the earlier ones. The C.N.R. arranged for troop trains to pass through Prince George without stopping; all public telephone and telegraph service to Prince George, Prince Rupert, and Terrace was monitored to ensure that no central subversive H.Q. would be able to control demonstrations in those towns. The Chief Censor of Publications paid a flying visit to Vancouver and, with some difficulty, persuaded the local press to verify its facts with Pacific Command before publishing; he also got Headquarters to give the press all items not requiring protection. The earlier sensational items had not been cleared with his office before release. Generally speaking, the protests had their origins in three alleged inequities: French-Canadian units feared they were to be sent directly overseas and not back to Quebec, as they had been told; N.R.M.A. men in British Columbia saw no reason why they should be the group selected to go overseas – they felt everyone should be asked to go; non-French Canadians feared they were going overseas, while the French Canadians would never leave Quebec. When the moves did take place, they passed without incident, and the unrest subsided, although F.S. continued for some time to observe that girls still often refused to dance with N.R.M.A. men at social gatherings.[56]

As the numbers of returning veterans increased, the nature of the complaints reported by F.S. drastically changed. The Army wanted demobilization to go smoothly, partly for morale reasons, and men had to be protected against the vagaries of the system and the cunning of those who tried to exploit them. Some complained that certain depots seemed to be delaying releases unnecessarily. Their complaints were countered by publicizing examples of other men who were well satisfied. Men fell victim to rackets and confidence schemes designed to separate the veteran from his gratuity, to knockout drops, and to pickups that would be followed by the "unexpected" intervention of an irate "husband/father" and then an attempt at blackmail. F.S. helped to investigate these, and the Service tried to protect the troops in the only ways possible, by warnings and by publicity.

The extent, the variety, and the burden of a Security Section's normal wartime duties can be seen in a report from M.D. 2. In the last quarter of 1944, with only a W.O.II, a sergeant, and two corporals, it reported on 35 active organizations and radical groups, carried on "close surveillance" of 50 individual servicemen, had 566 active Alien files, completed 478 character investigations and had 63 pending, did 120 record checks with City of Toronto or Ontario Provincial Police records for other Districts, and completed some 40 special investigations and four P.W. Camp searches. In addition, with Provost assistance, it did surveillance duties in hotels, dance halls, and amusement places. What it was not doing, because it did not have the men, was the tasks it was supposed to perform – tightening up Security on troop moves, providing proper surveillance of suspects, training men, and supervising Unit Security measures.[57] The M.D. 2 Section was busier than it should have been, but it was merely typical of all those others who were equally overburdened by what must have seemed a never-ending task.

18.
PRISONERS OF WAR

Earlier we have shown that it was often possible to obtain tactical information from enemy and returned Allied P.W. But the idea that it was worthwhile to maintain a continuing watch over P.W. in the Camps took some time to be accepted. It is true that Censorship, with the help of M.I.2, studied enemy P.W. correspondence, and that M.I.3 dealt with what little general P.W. Intelligence there was. But there was no one Canadian agency in a position to exploit this information. Released prisoners returning to Canada often had information on missing persons, on P.W. collaborators and war criminals, and also on the selfless and heroic devotion that other Canadian P.W. displayed. It was not until mid-1942 that Canada began to formulate a standard policy for collecting information from these sources.

When the Swedish repatriation ship, S.S. *Gripsholm*, arrived in Cape Town from Hong Kong in early August 1942, one of its passengers, a Canadian who had evaded capture and taken refuge in the British Embassy in Hong Kong, made serious allegations to the Canadian High Commissioner about the conduct of Canadian troops. Another Canadian evader categorically refuted the charges in an interview with the D.M.I. and other Intelligence officers. After this unfortunate incident, the Special Advisor to the Adjutant General (S.A.A.G.), Lt.-Col. F.W. Clarke, recommended that all government servants should be forbidden to make any public statements until they had been interrogated by Intelligence at Ottawa.[1]

As a first step towards this, officers were sent to meet the 69 Canadians who were among the 1,500 repatriates in the *Gripsholm* when she docked at New York in late August – Maj. Orville Eadie, A/G.S.O.1, M.I.1; Capts. J.F. Browne, M.I.1, and C.G. Jones, M.I.3; Lieuts. M.M.K. Perrault, M.I.1, and L. Hébert, G.S.O.3, M.D. 4, and officers from the R.C.N. and R.C.A.F. They carried a draft questionnaire which they were told to alter, if necessary, after discussions in Washington. When Maj. Eadie arrived, he discovered that he would not be allowed to board the ship at Quarantine, although External Affairs had cleared his visit with the Canadian Minister to the U.S. and with the New York authorities. As the repatriates came ashore the Americans proposed to divide them into 45 groups for interview by Immigration, F.B.I., Customs, and Security. The 69 Canadians would pass through four selected Boards, which would each have one officer from Eadie's party. Eadie protested that Canadians were not subject to U.S. Immigration and Customs, and should be sent straight to Ottawa on what amounted to a bonded train. The U.S. War Department agreed, and notified the New York military authorities.

But the U.S. Customs, not the military, controlled the docks, and they refused Maj. Eadie, and U.S. Army Intelligence, access to the pier. The Ottawa group were confined to ". . . protecting External Affairs [which had guaranteed Canadian Press that no news reporters would interview repatriates in New York] by shooing away newspaper reporters and standing guard around the train and the route along which the repatriates moved from taxi to train". The system broke down, and the Canadians were cleared through any available Board, a process that took about 15 hours. They reached their train at 0300 on the 26th, and arrived at Montreal at 1600. Because of meal times and other necessary interruptions, the officers had only six hours for interrogation. One unfortunate Canadian, who missed his party in the confusion and spent seven days in the Immigration Detention Centre at Ellis Island before he was recovered, was the subject of a diplomatic protest.[2]

To avoid repeating this conflict of jurisdictions when the *Gripsholm* brought in her next load of repatriates in December 1943, D.M.I. sent Capt. R.L. Archibald to meet her and her 221 Canadians at Rio de Janeiro. The questionnaires they were asked to complete provided useful information on their contacts with the international organizations responsible for looking after them.[3]

The first medically unfit Canadian P.W. to return from Germany arrived on November 24th, 1943, on the S.S. *Lady Nelson*; they were immediately sent to their homes after a simple low-level interrogation by Col. Clarke's office on their treatment in the camps. On December 6th, M.I.1 asked Intelligence at all the Commands and Districts to obtain from these men answers to a list of questions about enemy Censorship and Psychological Warfare, and about Escape and Evasion. External Affairs asked D.M.I. for information on War Crimes, which the latter was able to supply from Intelligence files and from the Judge Advocate-General's office.[4]

Two further groups were returned in May 1944, one through Britain where C.M.H.Q. dealt with them, the other through New York, where D.M.I. interviewed them on behalf of the Directorate of Records and the S.A.A.G. By this time, the British and the Americans also had questions, and D.M.I. found there was barely time to talk to the 48 men in the group. The D.M.I. later proposed that the D.I.O.s be asked to give each returned prisoner a long questionnaire about German tactics, equipment, and history, from which useful training information could be gained. The Directorates of History and of Operational Research, and C.M.H.Q. felt that this was going too far; the potential product, of course, was soon overtaken by actual field experience.[5]

The men in this group had found enemy propaganda very anti-Semitic. They also found it and its emphasis on the mutual need to fight against Russia quite ineffectual. The Germans they had spoken to expected that their country would lose the war. The group had also heard rumours, but without details, that members of a Canadian unit had been shot and wounded when they tried to escape. This may have been a reference to certain Air Force prisoners who were recaptured after escaping from *Stalagluft 3* in 1943. The questions put to the September *Gripsholm* group dealt with matters that would be useful during the Occupation: military and paramilitary organizations, German ministries, research depots, training establishments, ordnance, and medical resources.[6] The Director of Repatriation, feeling that the range of enquiry was now entirely too unorganized, called a meeting in November to rationalize the requirements and streamline the procedures.

A new, consolidated, and reduced list of questions was tried out on a group in January 1945. When it uncovered evidence that rackets were being operated in the camps, another special questionnaire from the War Crimes Advisory Committee was drawn up, and given to P.W. who claimed to have direct knowledge. The Committee was also concerned that its investigations could miss some men who were being repatriated through other channels. D.M.I. assured the Committee that the problem had not yet arisen, and that future repatriations could be carefully controlled.[7]

When war ended in the Pacific Theatre, M.I.9 at the War Office sent D.M.I. the repatriation routes and asked that all P.W. be interrogated on casualties, war criminals, collaborators, particularly praiseworthy acts, escapes and evasions, and other matters of interest. Col. Murray told the C.G.S. that there were about 400 Canadian P.W. in Hong Kong, about 1,100 in Japan and, in addition, 9,000 Americans and up to 10,000 British. He understood that they would come in small mixed groups through Manila, but he did not think they could be intensively interrogated because of the poor state of their health. They could, however, be interviewed en route if they were brought back on the C.N.R. ship *Prince Rupert*, which was due to sail with relief supplies to Hong Kong, and to return via Manila. Three of Murray's officers – Capts. K.C. Woodsworth and D.E. Neelands, and Lieut. A.C. Burns, attached to the Australian Central Bureau (Intelligence) – were already stationed in Manila.[8]

External Affairs asked the Acting High Commissioner to Australia to go to Hong Kong. Before he left he sent word that Capt. Graham, Lieut. Mason, Canadian Radar Detachment, and three sergeants, J.K.O. Bong, R. Lowe, and W. Wong, then attached to the Services Reconnaissance Detachment (S.O.E.), would work in Hong Kong; others were available from the Radar and Special Wireless groups then in Australia. The Canadian P.R.O. in Manila, Brig. R.S. Malone, reported that he had five N.C.O.s available. D.M.I. also sent Capt. W.E. Braun and Lieut. C. Thomas, and asked the Americans for Gen. MacArthur's permission to admit six additional I.O.s to Manila.[9] By September 3rd, the four officers and 13 men in Manila were formed into a small Canadian

Repat Liaison Group. Woodsworth, Neelands, and Burns later went to Japan with recovery and interrogation teams.

Canada declined a British request to set up an Interrogation Centre at Vancouver, preferring instead to send men to their homes as quickly as possible, but gave Britain permission to send its own Interrogators if it so desired. As it turned out, Maj. H.C. Bray, G.S.O.2 (Int), Pacific Command, handled all P.W. sent through Vancouver, and by October 3rd, 1945, he had dealt with 146 men altogether. He described their physical condition, enumerated the many deaths from malnutrition and disease, commented on Japanese beatings, often of men virtually dead on their feet, cited the "particularly vicious Japanese known as the Kamloops Kid", and also mentioned the many acts of kindness shown by individual Japanese. He related a 1942 attempt at escape, and gave examples both of collaboration and of heroism.[10]

D.M.I. identified the "Kamloops Kid", and provided the names of one British officer, two British N.C.O.s, and one Canadian believed to have been possible war criminals. The Canadian was accused of theft from Red Cross parcels, beating fellow P.W., and acting as an informer. However, the preliminary reports were so charged with animosities that Lt.-Col. Acland warned that they should not be accepted at their face value. Altogether, 82 returning P.W. missed the initial interviews. D.I.O.s were asked to locate them for questioning, and by early 1946 all those thought to be useful had been processed.

While the full story of Canadian P.W. in Japanese hands does not belong to this history, D.M.I. was involved in at least one incident that could have had value. Many Canadian P.W. tried to pass information in their letters, disguising it as innocuous gossip. The wife of a Canadian officer, Mrs. D.G. Philip, was sure that one of her husband's letters contained a hidden meaning. He called his father, for instance, "a shadow", when in fact he was a heavy man; he said that he himself was now "up to 161 pounds", when he had weighed nearly 200 on leaving Canada. And he referred to a mutual friend, Brig. Orville Kay:

> Talking about weight, how is Orville doing? Better drop him a line and suggest that he be sure to move this herd in No. 2 pasture to No. 3 this fall. The field they are now in must be in pretty poor shape. It will be a long hard drive but well worth it. Sandman is a pretty good scout and I'm sure will lend a hand if asked nicely.[11]

Mrs. Philip understood "this herd" to mean the Winnipeg Grenadiers, the "move" to be a move to another camp, and the "Sandman" to refer to the song "The Japanese Sandman". The G.S.O.3 (Int), M.D. 10, passed the letter to M.I.3, which agreed with her interpretation, identified the field "in pretty bad shape" as Camp A, Hong Kong, and thought its situation must have been extremely serious "to impel this officer to make this attempt to get the information out". D.M.I. at once recommended action by the Protecting Power, but warned that the source had to be protected. Unfortunately, his letter, dated July 2nd, 1942, had taken 14 months for delivery, and other moves had occurred in the interval.[12] Many P.W. tried in similar ways to send bits of information home. Each was an example of extreme devotion to duty, for each represented a sacrifice of one of the very small quota of monthly letters a P.W. was allowed to write. Lieut. Philip's attempt was a notably gallant one; if it had been detected, it would have brought him real risk of injury or death.

On May 16th, 1943, D.M.I. formed a new Section – M.I.4 – with three sub-Sections: M.I.4(a), to deal with information obtained from enemy and internee correspondence; M.I.4(b), to deal with information obtained through interrogations; M.I.4(c), to stop disclosure of Army information useful to enemy Intelligence or for propaganda, and to collect information about the enemy from Canadian P.W. M.I.4(a) and (b) exchanged information with Censorship on enemy organizations, activities, and Service slang, and kept Censorship informed of D.M.I. requirements. The new Section used a comprehensive German order-of-battle index begun by M.I.1. Its linguists had to possess a thorough knowledge of the German language, including dialects, idioms, and slang, as well as of geography, customs, military organization, and doctrines. M.I.4(c) gathered as much information as it could on North-West Germany, Westphalia, Oldenburg, Hanover, Schleswig-Holstein, and Hamburg and, most particularly, on German Army equipment and ammunition depots, and on civilian attitudes to the war and to the Allies.[13]

M.I.4 was closed shortly before V.E. day, and Lt.-Col. Alex Wygard took Sub-Sections 4(a) and 4(b) with him to his new post as head of M.I.7. M.I.4(c)'s functions rapidly declined as the Allies captured enemy P.W. Camps. The collection of evidence on war crimes and the identification of war criminals was given to M.I.3(a), with links through C.M.H.Q. to S.H.A.E.F. The situation in the Japanese camps, however, was still a matter of great urgency.

M.I.7 owed its creation to a fairly blatant bit of empire-building by the Intelligence Community. Originally, Internment Camps had nothing to do with Intelligence but were the duty of the Directorate of Internment Operations, which reported to the Adjutant General. Even after the function was transferred to the Office of the Secretary of State, in June 1941, the A.G. continued to be responsible for the establishment, maintenance, and administration of the Camps.

German military prisoners captured during late 1939 and early 1940 were held in England. However, after the fall of France the British asked the War Committee of the Canadian Cabinet to hold them in Canada. The first group of 153 officers and 323 men arrived on June 29th, 1940, and were accommodated at Camp "C" (later called No. 20), at Calydor, near Gravenhurst, Ontario. Six hundred internees were already at Camp "F" (Fort Henry, Kingston) and 1,149 at Camp "R" (Red Rock, Ontario). Camps "E", at Espanola, and "Q", at

Monteith, were established to receive the second P.W. groups. Canada opened 26 Camps in all, but not all simultaneously. *(See Map 21 in Chapter 16 for P.W. Camp locations.)* In the peak month of October 1944, 34,193 P.W. were in custody. The final group arrived in December 1944. By December 1945, the number had declined to 1,916 officers and 27,358 other ranks and, by December 1st, 1946, to 1 and 59 respectively. The last group left in January 1947. During the entire period, there were 14 successful escapes.[14]

Initially, Intelligence merely watched the Camps to ensure that they did not present an Internal Security threat. Interest in them was limited; M.D. 2 recommended in November 1940 that more I.O.s should be posted to them, but the Adjutant General rejected the proposal, saying that the Provost Sergeant was able to perform the duties adequately. Censorship of P.W. mail was also ineffective. Its laxity became apparent in February 1941 when German postal propaganda led some internees to believe that the invasion of Britain was imminent. Two months later, M.D. 2 discovered a brochure containing a card which P.W. were invited to complete and return to Berlin. The information it asked for would have helped the enemy to establish useful contacts for planning escapes to the United States. All D.O.C.s were alerted to watch for the cards.[15]

In May 1941, the Veterans Guard of Canada (V.G. of C.) took over from C.Pro.C. the task of guarding the Camps. The P.W. Section of the Directorate of Administration became a separate Directorate in January 1943. It then had two sub-Sections: P.O.W.2(a)(ii) was responsible for Intelligence, punishments, complaints, welfare, and education; P.O.W.2(a)(iii) handled Censorship, translations, and interpretations.[16] The Camp Administration tried always to keep ahead of the prisoners and their attempts to escape, by reading their mail and by using German-speaking guards, called "scouts". Some P.W. regarded the scouts with suspicion and reserve, while others tried to make friends with them, either to gain information or, in extreme cases, to seek protection from their fellows. The scouts were successful in detecting a number of planned escapes.

The daily life of the individual P.W. in a Camp was directly influenced by the Camp's internal administration. This was headed by a Camp Leader, usually, though not always, the senior German officer or N.C.O. He controlled a structured subordinate staff whose numbers and organization would vary from Camp to Camp. This staff conducted an unending battle of wits with the Camp Administration. The strong ideological hold of National Socialism meant that, for the P.W., their war was not over but merely interrupted. The Nazi Party tried to make sure that everything possible would be done to aid the German war effort. In doing this, they exercised strict control over the P.W., enforcing it by terror against those who refused to conform.

The effects of Nazi discipline were well known, and steps to counter it in Canadian Camps began in late 1941 or early 1942. At that time, the Political Warfare Executive in London had agreed that a Canadian Political Warfare

Grand Ligne P.W. Camp, Quebec, 1943. (E.N. Jungbluth collection/Canadian Forces School of Military Intelligence, Kingston/Canada. Dept. of National Defence)

P.W. Camp, Sherbrooke, Quebec, November 1945. (Canada. Dept. of National Defence /Library and Archives Canada, PA-114463)

Committee should be formed, headed by External Affairs and with the D.M.I. as its military member. The Committee accepted the British view that the release of a disciplined body of Nazis into a defeated and disorganized Germany would militate against a lasting peace. All three Service Intelligence Directorates regarded the need to curb Nazism in the Camps as urgent, and criticized D.P.O.W. for what they felt were its inadequate efforts to obtain and to control useful information from the P.W. themselves. For its part, D.P.O.W., with its experience, considered with some justification that it knew more about these matters than did its critics. It was also very unwilling to do anything that could lead to reprisals against Canadian P.W. But, about this time, the British D.M.I. managed to obtain authority to re-educate enemy P.W. in Allied hands, thereby providing the precedent for a similar program in Canada.

The Committee decided first to obtain information from P.W. for use in Psychological Warfare against Germany, and then to study the problems of re-education. It proposed that a special Joint Service unit be formed and, on July 22nd, 1943, External sent to the C.G.S. a detailed outline of its requirements. In discussing this with the C.G.S., the D.M.I. stated that the 30,000 P.W. then in Canadian Camps were not being adequately examined and that the External Affairs concept was too narrowly political; he also repeated the criticisms earlier charged against D.P.O.W.

Col. Murray and the other Intelligence Directors were perhaps a little less than fair to D.P.O.W. Its small Intelligence staff did provide regular reports based on information caught by Censorship, on conversations with P.W., and on interpretations of events that took place in the Camps. They were circulated within the Intelligence Community, but they were certainly not exploited. The D.P.O.W. staff, which was in effect a simple collection agency, had been given no Intelligence requirement or directive other than to watch local Camp problems, unrest, and escape attempts. It had not extended its horizons to include breaking the control of the Nazi elements, or obtaining information of wider usefulness. In his rearguard action, the D.P.O.W. strove to have judgement deferred, by asking that the British and Americans be contacted for advice and for specially trained Intelligence personnel to augment his own overworked Camp Intelligence and Censor officers.[17]

The three Service Directors of Intelligence then met with D.P.O.W. to draw up a tentative plan. This envisaged a staff of 60, mostly Army, to provide operational, Security, and general information for Political Warfare, and to make recommendations on segregation, re-education, morale, and Camp newspapers. D.M.I. asked the D.P.O.W. to provide detail on his organization, its strength in Intelligence officers and Interpreters, their duties, qualifications, and training, and whether their numbers were properly proportional to the numbers of P.W. held.[18]

D.P.O.W.'s senior I.O. was Capt. V.E.K. Waldie, who functioned as a Senior Translator, Censor, and Intelligence Officer. His staff consisted of one officer, 2/Lieut. G. Ladner, and two sergeants. This single small office was responsible for all P.W. Intelligence, Censorship, and translation, for dealing with all correspondence from Postal Censors, for material despatched to and from all the Camps, and for complaints and Red Cross Forms. At that time, Canada had 15 Camps, with 12,839 Army, 2,603 Navy, 4,353 *Luftwaffe*, 3,453 Merchant Seamen, and 1,244 civilians, for a grand total of 24,492. Ten Camps had one Interpreter/Censor each; three had one Interpreter/Censor Officer and one Translator; Camp 132, Medicine Hat, had five officers, one W.O.II, and three men, all Interpreter/Censors; and Camp 133, Lethbridge, had eight officers, one W.O.II, and one man – in all, 18 officers and 22 men.

Their duties added liaison between the Canadian Camp Director and the German Camp Leader, interrogations of P.W., Intelligence Summaries, "and such other duties as may be delegated to them", to Capt. Waldie's listed duties.[19] They were required to have a knowledge of German, Italian, or Japanese, and a good basic education, and to be unfit for overseas service. They were given no special instruction except for in-job training in the Postal Censor's office, a somewhat peculiar place to teach men to be used on Security duties in a military environment, when the C.W.I.C. was available. Clearly, errors had been made on both sides. The A.G.'s Branch should have realized the nature and magnitude of the task, and assigned to it a staff of suitable size, composition, and qualification. The D.M.I. should have made sure from the outset that men who were to be called Intelligence Officers had the basic training necessary to perform their duties.

The submission recommending the creation of a Prisoner of War Intelligence Directorate received Cabinet approval on April 14th, 1944, but was never implemented. The D.M.I., however, did not lose the whole of his argument. On May 9th, he received the Minister's approval for a new Section "... to develop and disseminate Intelligence derived from P.W. in Canadian custody and to provide facilities for the Psychological Warfare Committee, Ottawa, to carry on its functions in conformity with the policies and programmes of the Psychological Warfare Board, London, and with its own policy regarding the re-education of P.W."[20]

He created a new Section and a new sub-Section. The Section, M.I.5, under Maj. R.H. Pender, was required to study and report on the attitudes of P.W. and their reactions to the influence of Nazi pressure groups and educational programs, and to provide the Committee with guidance for its segregation and re-education policies. It was to assist in the latter if required, and to collect material for broadcasts to Germany. Prof. Pender was ideal. A graduate of Edinburgh University, he had first-hand knowledge of German psychology and of prison camp life, much of it gained through his internment in Germany between 1914 and 1919. One of the original officers of the Directorate of Military Intelligence, he later, as head of M.I.7, established a high reputation in the field of Allied Psychological Warfare. On VE day, the Canadian government borrowed Lt.-Col. Pender to work on veterans' education. Recruited a few months later by the Allied Control Commission, he was put in charge of restructuring all German universities.

M.I.3(d), under Maj. J.H. Morehouse, collected information on escapes and attempted escapes, and was responsible for detecting codes and secret writing equipment, for P.W. Security, and for liaison with the other Security Services (which its position within M.I.3 simplified). It had two officers: Maj. Morehouse handled Security, and Lt.-Cdr. G.A. Feilman, secret information. External Affairs offered to provide selected and trained educators to reinforce and support the Army. Each Camp Administration retained its Interpreter/Censor Section and added two others; a Security Section for information on escapes, clandestine radio, and liaison through the District Intelligence staff to D.M.I., and an Intelligence Section to report on P.W. attitudes and to act as a vehicle for Psychological Warfare activities.

The War Office protested – unofficially – the designation of the Section as M.I.5, on the grounds that it would be confused with the British M.I.5 Counter-Intelligence agency. The D.M.I. had never followed the British numbering system, but he accepted their stand, foreseeing a similar objection to M.I.6, another famous agency. But when he renamed the Section M.I. (P.W.) someone immediately pointed out that the name revealed the function. It was again officially changed on October 14th to M.I.7.[21]

By that time, the D.P.O.W. had only 21 officers and nine men to serve 11 P.W. Camps and 30 Department of Transport Labour Camps. Because the new Intelligence officers had to be drawn from those already employed by D.P.O.W., and because their departure would disrupt the operation of the Camps, the change-over was, at the beginning, largely a paper transaction. But changes were made; the D.O.C.s, not Ottawa, now had charge of Security in camps lying within their Districts; and Camp I.O.s reported to D.M.I. through their Camp Commanders and the D.I.O.s. To limit misunderstandings, the D.I.O.s were brought to Ottawa for careful instruction on their new responsibilities. The D.M.I. also asked the D.P.O.W. and the Director, Veterans Guard of Canada, to become members of an ad hoc Advisory Committee to review Intelligence procedures.[22]

By July 6th, 1944, Camp Commanders had been given a three-day briefing; all D.I.O.s and Directorate of Internment Operations officers from Districts where camps were located had had a four-day course in the management of the new system; six Interpreter/Censor Officers from the camps and three similarly employed Naval officers had been given a two-week course; and 10 German-speaking N.C.O.s were ready to take a two-week German language refresher course. All the courses were arranged by Lt.-Col. G. Skilbeck, who had been Chief Instructor of the B.S.C.'s Special Intelligence School at Oshawa. Additional special courses, using local facilities, were being given at the Lethbridge and Medicine Hat Camps.[23]

In May 1944, the Chief of the British Secret Service discussed with D.M.I. the possibility that P.W. Camps in Canada were linked to an espionage network, and that some P.W. were being recruited as Nazi undercover agents and organizers to go into action after the defeat of Germany. There were indications that Himmler, who now controlled the reorganized *Abwehr*, might have formed a special section to direct this work. This threat added a new dimension to the existing challenge of separating the Nazi elements from those other Germans for whom re-education might have some appeal. Once again, M.I.3(d) found itself without Canadian precedents, direction, or experience. The Camp I.O.s and the District staffs were given courses in *Abwehr* and *Gestapo* espionage and terror techniques, methods of body searches, and other procedures. M.I.3 arranged close links with British agencies and with the Technical Chemist in Censorship. In Pacific Command, where there were no P.W. Camps, and at N.D.H.Q., Security Section personnel were trained to be used as a "flying squad" to augment District staffs when major searches had to be made. The situation gained heightened urgency when the interrogation of a P.W. who had been placed in protective custody revealed that one of the more co-operative and capable Camp spokesmen, who had originally been captured in the Stavanger raid of 1940, was actually an important German agent. He was subsequently handed over to the Norwegians.[24]

D.M.I. had long suspected that P.W. were obeying orders and directives issued and transmitted by some central agency. The first break came in February 1944. A Maj. Kurt Mueller, in Camp 20, sent a photograph through the mail on which, in invisible ink, was a message about secret tribunals held in his Camp. On August 29th, his quarters were raided. The ingredients for secret inks were found, together with a large haul of notes and diaries, proving that Mueller was an organizer and administrator in an official Nazi disciplinary system that controlled German P.W. in Canada. Messages were being passed in books exchanged between Camp libraries, and by P.W. being transferred to other Camps. The orders came directly from Lt.-Gen. A. Schmitt, the Senior German Officer. The Camp he was in at Bowmanville was linked with Gravenhurst, Lethbridge, Medicine Hat, Grande Ligne, and possibly, but not certainly, with several other Camps. M.I.7 also suspected that short-wave radio sets were being used, some of them perhaps even capable of reaching Germany. After these discoveries, strict instructions were issued for thorough body searches of transferred P.W., for all books and parcels moving between Camps to be carefully checked for secret writing, and for searching the rooms and possessions of 17 key people who had been identified.[25]

Confirmation was soon obtained that the active enforcement agency was the *Gestapo*. Kangaroo courts, operating under the German Penal Code and in direct contravention of the Geneva Convention, tried P.W. known or suspected to be co-operating with the Canadian authorities. Conviction could mean death, camouflaged to make it appear that the victim had committed suicide. If the offender could not be dealt with summarily, full particulars were to be recorded and taken to Germany for action after the war. The Camp Leader in each Camp was made personally responsible to Gen. Schmitt.

The *Gestapo* ran compulsory Nazi courses. It forbade all religious instruction. It selected books in the Camp libraries that would reinforce Nazi Party ideology; Lethbridge was even reported to have a copy of *Mein Kampf*. It carefully ensured that only good Nazis were allowed to use the escape program. P.W. who escaped and were recaptured were interrogated in detail by the Escape Committee; parallel interrogations by the Canadian staffs were seldom productive. The Committee carefully prepared maps of the surrounding terrain, and sketch maps of the Camps showing their strengths and weaknesses. It taught the proper pronunciation of the names of North American towns and cities, and kept data on rail schedules, bridges, tunnels, and routes. The *Gestapo* maintained its power through a variety of vicious measures. It tried particularly to control incoming mail, partly to ensure that information about adverse conditions in Germany would not reach P.W., and partly to reinforce its own position. When this was discovered, mail was simply handed to the P.W. directly, which annoyed the German Camp Administration intensely. Food was similarly withheld. *Gestapo* members dictated what prisoners could say in their letters. The only non-Nazis to come to the attention of Intelligence were those who had fled the system in terror; even these men were convinced that their action had destroyed their rights as Germans, and would bring punishment to their relatives. Suicide often seemed a simpler alternative, but this also was denied them by their *Gestapo* masters.

Two proven "executions" took place in Medicine Hat, on July 22nd and September 10th, 1943. In the first case, R.C.M.P., D.M.I, Pacific Command S.I.S., and D.P.O.W. investigated. Three men were arrested; one was hanged, another sentenced to life imprisonment, and the third acquitted. As a result of the second murder, four P.W. were convicted and hanged. M.I.7 learned that a similar murder had taken place in Pietermaritzburg, South Africa, on June 6th, 1942. The victim, who apparently had already been considered unreliable, had been so unfortunate as to learn of an escape attempt. Other P.W. who knew of the incident had been transferred to Canada. They were sent back to South Africa, where their testimony helped convict the murderers.

In a fourth case at Camp Gravenhurst, the German Camp Leader acted quite differently. One P.W., who may have been a *Gestapo* agent, accused another named Stoepel of defeatism, anti-Nazi behaviour, and fraternization with the

Canadian enemy. When the German Camp Leader ignored the accusation, the P.W. recruited a coterie of rabid Nazis who tried to ostracize Stoepel; this also was vetoed by the Camp Leader. The gang then decided to hang Stoepel, but once more the Camp Leader intervened. They then planned to carry out their sentence clandestinely. Fortunately for Stoepel, his friends after first trying to have him placed in protective custody, arranged a surveillance system in such a way that any attempt to carry out the sentence would be bound to lead to a disturbance and attract the Canadian guards. Their interference was so effective that, after about 18 months, the gang abandoned its efforts.

Control of communications between Camps became effectively a battle between chemists. The usual method, secret writing, was curbed by issuing a special paper on which chemicals would be revealed. Until 1943, a British white paper was used; it was later replaced by American stock. Then the formula for a second and much superior British paper was obtained: unfortunately, as we shall see, its production in Canada was not fast enough to meet the growing urgency.

On October 27th, 1943, material sent from Germany to Camp 42 at Sherbrooke, Quebec, was intercepted and found to contain secret writing. In March 1944, a P.W. in Camp 132, Medicine Hat, tried to pass a clandestine message. When he was caught and questioned, he convinced the interrogator that the ink had been smuggled in by a personal friend for a harmless message, and the incident was not pursued. The Mueller raid in August led to another in September. The Security team was severely manhandled by the P.W., but one N.C.O. succeeded in bringing out more of the same secret ink, with instructions for use and a code word. The ink, a solid material known as "AV Putty", was one of the most significant Counter-Intelligence finds of the year. It confirmed that the reorganized *Abwehr* was taking greater interest in P.W. More critically, it meant that the special sensitized paper used in Allied Camps was no longer proof against secret writing.[26]

The AV Putty was first found on the door frame of a ship's cabin occupied by a suspected enemy agent. It looked like a wad of well-chewed gum. When the suspect was offered a stick he refused it. "Never use the damned stuff!" His mistake. It was so serious a discovery that there was even talk of postponing D-Day until its use could be controlled.

There was little doubt that it was being used in the Camps, but how? And in what form was it being brought in? Thorough searches revealed nothing. The only way to get the answer was through penetration. The D.D.M.I.(S) knew that the senior German general most likely to be in charge of *Abwehr* operations in Canada had bizarre sexual inclinations, so an effort was made to find a person who might appeal to him. The volunteer was a young Romanian who hated the Nazis; the *Gestapo* had killed his parents because they were "gypsies". He had watched the killing from hiding.

German P.W. using the library at internment Camp 42, Sherbrooke, Quebec, 18 June 1944. (Canada. Dept. of National Defence/Library and Archives Canada, PA-213869)

He was thoroughly schooled to meet all eventualities and, in due course, was moved to the General's camp. His face was beaten, with his approval, to show that his Canadian captors did not approve of his inclinations.

He succeeded in his mission, but during the last stage the Camp *Gestapo* became suspicious. He was "executed" by hanging, arranged by the *Gestapo*, as usual, to suggest a suicide. As pre-planned, he had inserted the evidence in his body, to be reclaimed at the autopsy. The AV Putty was being sent into Canadian and other Allied P.W. Camps in the stones in plum conserves. His sacrifice was not in vain; the Security authorities were able to block the route and so control the threat. He was a valiant man. Regrettably, at his own request, he must be nameless.[27]

The new improved Canadian paper was tested in September 1944. It provided visible reaction to liquids, aided the detection of solid inks, and gave some reaction to wax-based inks; this latter capability was very important, because P.W. had ready access to candles and waxed paper. It now became vitally important to introduce these new aids to detection. As a result of the battles on the Continent, prisoners were arriving in such large numbers that the few people available to censor P.W. mail were overwhelmed. Neither the Civil Service Commission nor the Army could supply enough additional qualified linguists. Those that were available did not have the time to subject every document to detailed scrutiny. Any new paper that would facilitate detection would therefore greatly ease the workload.[28]

By February 22nd, 1945, German prisoners in Camp 44 were proved to be using a new, most advanced solid ink, and Censorship urged that the new paper be introduced at once. But its production had been delayed, and in some cases the new and old papers were being issued together. D.M.I. protested that the simultaneous issue of two quite dissimilar papers would lead P.W. to suspect a new form of control. D.P.O.W. was still not convinced, although its representatives had been kept fully advised of the need for additional protection and the obvious advantages of the new paper. Its main concern was to avoid complaints that paper was not being issued in sufficient quantity, for these could lead to reprisals against Canadian P.W. The decision to issue old paper until stocks were exhausted made control of clandestine correspondence unnecessarily difficult.

Until the Nazi control over P.W. was destroyed, no re-education program could succeed, for the *Gestapo* were in a position to counter it. Those whose views were so strong that any attempt at re-education was bound to fail had to be identified and segregated. Those whose views were anti-Nazi, or at least neutral, had to be grouped together, on the theory that the "white" would help to influence the "grey". Information from documents, from the Camp staffs, and from Censorship, was pooled and used as a basis for a selection process that began in August 1944. By December 1944, M.I.7 claimed to have identified 341 pro-democratic P.W., 9,030 passive, 23,073 mild Nazis, and 1,360 ardent Nazis, a total of 33,804 out of an over-all total of about 35,000.

The rather haphazard method of selection that was used was not considered reliable. A more complex method – the PHERUDA Report – was devised to reduce the subjectivity of the individual interrogators to a minimum. It derived its name from the initials of six areas of major interest, each of which was subdivided into numbered categories: Political, attitude to Hitler, Education, Religion, Usefulness for labour, Dependability (the only area where the Interrogator had much room for judgement), and a subjective section called Attitude toward the Allies. P.W. were evaluated under each of the area headings, and graded according to the intensity with which they displayed the individual characteristics. For example, a violent, pro-Nazi, pro-Hitler, illiterate, atheistic trouble-maker might have a PHERUDA profile of P5 - H5 - E5 - R5 - U5 - D5 - A1 (anti-Allied). Each prisoner in the smaller Camps was "PHERUDAed"; the 13,400 in Lethbridge and the 12,300 in Medicine Hat were not. Camps were given a classification depending on the political colour of their inmates. Camps 20 at Gravenhurst, 130 at Seebe (officers), 100 at Neys (other ranks only), 133 at Lethbridge, and 132 at Medicine Hat were "black" (pro-Nazi). As individuals were categorized, they were sent to an appropriately coloured Camp. D.P.O.W. did not like what seemed to them a retrograde development, liable to confuse their own policies and to be a source of unrest in the Camps.[29]

The program was delayed while the Camps were prepared. Britain was now asking Canada to take an additional 50,000 P.W., and Bowmanville Camp had to be returned to the Ontario government, to house juvenile delinquents. Moves between the Camps were begun in January 1945. P.W. were permitted to carry two suitcases each; they were searched by the Intelligence Sections, with R.C.M.P. assistance; additional baggage was searched, labelled, and then forwarded. At least one man attempted to use a packing case as a means of escape. Some "whites" were deliberately left in "black" Camps, to obtain information and to assist the Camp administration.

A good deal of Intelligence material and many escape aids were found. In one Camp, searchers discovered a short-wave radio that could be played through a gramophone or earphones; all Camp gramophones were quickly checked. Aerials were found; in one case a copper wire threaded through a clothes line; in another case, a fine wire unravelled from bed springs and stretched around the room. Despite four years of careful searches, four compasses were found, one of them a very fine oil type. Paper, pencils, typewriter ribbons, carbons, bottles of ink, patent medicines, and the like were all suspect; after one move, about eight tons of materials were sent to N.D.H.Q. for testing.

The escape aids included maps and forged U.S. and Canadian registration cards, some of them poor copies when compared with the original but quite adequate when seen alone; Czech shoulder titles; and a genuine R.C.A.F. serge uniform with crude Flight Lieutenant rank badges. Written documents usually contained errors that could be caught: forged letters of recommendation, for instance, many with excellent hand-lettered letterheads but containing phraseology not normally used in the business world; a forged Army discharge certificate which, according to the four-time loser who had carried it, "was all the documentation you need". A second Canadian Active Service Force discharge, on the correct linen paper, was wrong in almost all other respects, particularly in that it was made out to an officer; they were never issued to officers. Yet its bearer had managed to use it to get as far as Halifax. Another loser was caught only because an alert officer recognized the signature of a well-known girly artist on the bottom of the pass form he was using. Messages were concealed in dried fruit, censored letters, book bindings, linings of wallets, briefcases, collars, seams of uniforms, tins of tobacco, false bottoms of suitcases, and cigar boxes. During the searches, evidence was found describing in full detail the Camp thought-control apparatus already discussed.[30]

Just after the main moves, on March 28th, a scout at Camp 100 at Neys noticed suspicious activity. The raid that followed uncovered a cross-bow powered by bed springs and rubber bands, with a 35-lb pull; it was capable of shooting a sharpened steel rod accurately to about 10 yards. The weapon was probably intended either for killing "white" P.W. or small game, and is now in the National War Museum.[31]

Morale checks were done in the Camps shortly after the transfers were complete. They showed that the news of the progress of the war, which was carefully passed to the P.W., had lowered their spirits. But in those Camps from which "blacks" had been removed, the men appreciated their new freedom of expression, and an active anti-Nazism was even slowly emerging. In Camp 40 at Farnham, for instance, three anti-Nazi groups were believed ready to co-operate in rehabilitation programs. In the "black" Camps, however, the checks showed that P.W. were talking of linking up with Communism, and of forming *hara kiri* and *Götterdämmerung* (Twilight of the Gods: the Norse-German-Wagnerian legend of self-immolation at the fall of Valhalla) clubs. Some officers were using their military oath as justification for refusing to join in any re-education program. At the same time, and in most Camps, religious observances increased visibly, despite the strong opposition of the Nazi elements.

Sorel Camp was established in March 1945 for "whites" willing to co-operate actively with the Allies in post-surrender Germany. P.W. who were selected assumed that they would be used by the Occupation authorities, and were disappointed to learn that their sole task would be to produce pamphlets and lectures to counter Nazi propaganda. It was not easy to convince them that, in doing so, they were usefully serving the anti-Nazi cause. When the time came for them to be repatriated, Lt.-Col. Wygard warned that they had become marked men. He recommended that they should be segregated and integrated into similar schemes in Britain, and sent back to Germany as early as possible. It seems, however, that nothing was done, and they were merely re-absorbed without differentiation into the normal stream of repatriates.[32]

When the news of VE day was received, the Commandant of the "black" other ranks Camp at Lethbridge announced it at a normal roll-call. There was no outward reaction. A memorial service was held next day for Hitler; there was no attempt at propaganda and no display of anti-Allied antagonism. In some Camps, the wall poster giving the details of the German surrender aroused resentment; in others, there was obvious relief that the war was over. Some P.W., fearing reprisals, asked to be placed in protective custody.[33]

Prior to VE day, the re-education program had merely tried to sow seeds of doubt as to the future of Nazism. After May 8th, it tried to instil an actual abhorrence of Nazism, a respect for the democratic life, and a desire for more international co-operation. Not all of the Nazis could be convinced, of course. The initial classification was completed by the end of May, but the urgent need to rehabilitate Germany physically made the re-education program too time-consuming and too unwieldy. M.I.7 asked all Districts on May 30th to find men in the "white" or "grey" categories who could be employed as State, Provincial, or Municipal officials in Germany, in administration, transportation, law, public health, and food and fuel distribution, or who were qualified engineers, architects, and teachers. The Occupation Force needed communicators and was prepared to take men of any political complexion. But translators and men with experience in the mass media, who were also desperately needed, had to be politically reliable.

At the end of July, some P.W. began to fear that they would be sent back to areas that had come under Russian control; they reacted by denying having any connection with them. The shifting of frontiers raised difficult questions of nationality for other P.W., particularly for the 1,353 Austrians. Ideological Austrian Nazis were arbitrarily deemed to be only those who had joined the Austrian Nazi Party prior to the union with Germany in March 1938. After the union, such draconian measures had been taken against anti-Nazis that many had had to join in self-defence. There was such a strong anti-German and anti-Russian feeling that the PHERUDA system was of little value in assessing their reliability.

Towards the end of November 1945, London, which badly needed "whites" for the Allied Control Commission and was concerned that the re-education schemes were not moving fast enough, suggested to Ottawa that, if the British card system was introduced into Canada, demands for certain special categories of P.W. could be quickly and easily filled. This would mean that Canada would have to redraft its 33,866 P.W. record cards. The British Political Intelligence Directorate classification system was less complete than its Canadian counterpart, and there were significant differences in detail. A month later, the British asked for all P.W. to be returned by March 31st, 1946. They suggested, through External Affairs, that all ardent Nazis be kept together and separated from the other P.W., that officers be repatriated after the other ranks, and that any prisoner under sentence by Canadian courts complete his sentence before being returned.[34]

By the end of March, nearly all the P.W. had been processed. The final classification gave 6,531 (18.7%) "white"; 15,343 (44%) "grey"; 10,563 (30%) "black"; and 245 (0.7%) ardent Nazis. For one reason or another, 2,318 (6.6%) had not been classified. The figures showed a greater percentage of "whites" (by 17%) than had originally been estimated, a lower percentage of Nazis (by 3.3%), and a corresponding redistribution of the other two totals. One wonders if all the effort to double-check the original estimate had really been worth while.[35]

M.I.7 was disbanded on February 28th, 1947. By May 15th, only 25 P.W. had not been returned to Germany; 14 were still at large, one presumed to be in Mexico and two presumed dead. Four were in hospital, six were employed pending repatriation to countries other than Germany, and one was serving a life sentence for his part in a murder.[36]

With the closure of M.I.7, the story of D.M.I. during the war comes to an end. Its history was that of many other N.D.H.Q. directorates; duties which barely existed and which were ill-defined, if acknowledged at all, grew in size and scope, and staff increased to deal with them. The Intelligence Directorate differed from its predecessor of the First World War most significantly. On the I(a) side there was a greater interest in international affairs, even though the support for it was still lacking: it reflected, however, the increased participation by the Canadian government in external relations. Similarly, I(b) expanded to deal with an ideological threat that was virtually unknown before 1918, at least in Canada.

During the early war years, the Intelligence organization in Ottawa was less dynamic than it should have been. One can overlook the slight confusion in defining the duties of the (a) and (b) wings. But it should have been clearly apparent from the beginning that recruiting, training, and administration of Intelligence was at least as important as the other functions. Instead, they were virtually ignored. D.M.I. seemed to be used solely as a staff directorate, whose chief mission was to support Army Headquarters; it did not adequately turn its attention to the support of the forces in the field. On the other hand, it must be remembered that it had a very large responsibility insofar as Security within the forces in Canada was concerned. And this role was discharged thoroughly and efficiently.

It is relatively easy to identify and to document a weakness; but it is much more difficult to determine the reasons for that weakness. Part of it may have been due to a lack of understanding at the D.M.O.&I. level – a legacy of the years of virtual neglect. As time went on, the need for professionalism in the Directorate, and later in the Districts, became accepted, but the pressure for the creation of a specialist professional Corps had to come from the field commands which needed it. It is entirely possible, though it cannot be proved, that, from the G.S.O.1 down, the varied peacetime backgrounds of the non-specialist officers meant that the need for trained specialization was simply not understood. This, in its turn, was a product of the prewar view that specialization was not necessary. If that is so, the price of specialization, finally achieved nearly five years after the war had broken out, was high in terms of wasted manpower and avoidable errors.

The postwar organization of Intelligence at Ottawa and, to a lesser extent, in the Districts, was based on the framework developed during the war. The large Security element, which had been visibly active and efficient, met fewer obstacles to survival and recognition than it might have during the difficult period of retrenchment. On the other hand, the small Foreign Intelligence Section did not seem to have an obvious and clearly defined reason for existing, and tended to be overlooked and neglected immediately in 1945.

Many D.M.I. officers stayed in their posts almost throughout the war, in spite of repeated attempts to obtain operational posts overseas. D.M.I. was one Directorate where the strength of the organization depended more than in most on the experience, skills, and proven reliability of its members. Throughout the Directorate, but particularly in the Security Sections, an intimate knowledge of the background and interplay of the forces at work in given situations was vital, and could only be gained after long experience. Difficulties often seemed to be self-induced, created more by conflicts of interest than by operational demands. There was seldom the excitement of the operational theatre, although M.I.s 2, 3, and 7 had challenges of their own to meet. There were times when the officers and men in D.M.I. must have wondered if their work had any meaning. Yet it had to be done and many did it well.

19.
PEACE AND RECONSTRUCTION

The end of the war in Europe did not bring any significant reduction in the work load in D.M.I. The prospect of Canadian participation in the war against Japan involved a good deal of administration, planning, and recruiting. Security was an ever-demanding responsibility. The program of P.W. re-education was just getting into full stride. Even after VJ day, the momentum of projects in hand required staff action to continue. But it was obvious that the switch from wartime to peacetime operations was imminent. Many staff wanted to return home and rebuild their lives. It was necessary to record their experience and knowledge before they departed, and this was started during September and October 1945, as far as it was possible to do so. At the same time, efforts were made to induce many of the better officers and men in the Directorate and the Sections to make the Service their career.

These efforts were met with mixed reactions. The future of Intelligence specialists was by no means assured. Postwar defence planning assumed that Canada would work closely with the United States. Defence H.Q. was required to have the capacity both to plan and supervise a general mobilization, and to work within the framework of mutual defence planning in international combination to preserve peace. The idea of universal compulsory military training was rejected. In 1945, the government set the Army strength at 27,000; by 1947 it was reduced by 25%, and the actual figure in 1950 was lower still. The Regular Army comprised three parachute battalions, two armoured regiments, and a regiment of artillery at approximately full strength, plus a cadre to reinforce them.[1] The Militia, which on mobilization was to form the Field Force, was to consist of two armoured and four infantry divisions. Headquarters establishments were expected to be reduced proportionately.

The competition for the few vacancies on the Establishments became intense. In this competition, those in the Arms (Armour, Artillery, and Infantry), particularly those with prewar Regular connections, had friends in high places and, although the horse-trading and in-fighting for vacancies was sometimes vicious, managed pretty well to maintain control not only of power but also of the levers to it. The mechanized sophistication of the Army had created a need for specialists capable of supply, operation, and maintenance. The technical Corps survived, although reduced significantly in numbers. But the smaller Corps which existed to provide a service, rather than a technical function, had great difficulty.[2]

The first threat to the continued existence of the Corps appeared in August 1945. But by October, hard work and much lobbying by Col. Murray and Lt.-Col.

Eric Acland won an interim decision to retain the C.Int.C. to handle the Security and Counter-Intelligence functions. It was a decision forced, to some extent, by necessity; the R.C.M.P. was not yet in a position to reassume this function within the Services. D.M.I. had long been pressed to eliminate the small Security Sections across Canada, which presented an administrative burden far in excess of the number of men involved. Part of the price paid for the preservation of the Corps was the incorporation of these Sections with the H.Q. of the respective Districts. At the end of the war there had been 14 Sections, including one at N.D.H.Q., one at Camp Petawawa, and one at Camp Borden, with a total strength of 22 officers and 91 men. A submission in September reduced the officer strength slightly and the other rank total considerably. The Section at M.D. 13 (Calgary) was held at its wartime level because of the large P.W. Camp populations in Lethbridge and Medicine Hat. That at N.D.H.Q. was reduced only slightly because of the vast amount of classified waste which had to be destroyed as offices cleared out their accumulations of files. A November 5th submission incorporated all those proposals and added a vital one – that the identification of Security people with the Corps be continued. At the same time a peacetime policy regarding character investigations was established. The C.G.S. had assigned this duty to Security on February 5th, 1943, and had laid down the principle that everyone employed on Secret duties would be cleared. By now, the list was quite extensive, mostly because the circulation of classified material had become more widespread.[3]

With the continued existence of the Corps at least a probability, it was possible to try to lay a firm foundation for the postwar era. During October and November 1945, Colonel Murray prepared a lengthy argument to the C.G.S. under five headings: the need to concentrate the Army Intelligence effort; to establish a Security Section; to establish Signals Intelligence; to establish a School; and to maintain links with the Reserves.[4]

He dealt first with Foreign Intelligence. He considered a 1935 recommendation stating that "all political and military activities of an important nature, wherever they occur, are of interest to this country", to be even more important in 1945, and that new experience and knowledge made it possible to study these activities properly.

Illustrating his theme with a lengthy list of subjects based mainly on the Book System but updated and in more detail, Col. Murray pointed out that Canada would not engage in clandestine acquisition of information but would perform the legitimate military function of collecting it openly. He listed sources, some of them with Canadian control, such as diplomats, travellers, foreign press and radio, and those sources under Allied control which might be available to Canada. The material collected had continuously to be evaluated and correlated with material already acquired. It would be impossible to study ". . . the 50-odd nations of the world. In most of them we have no present or potential interest. . . . Where we have common defensive interests with the Commonwealth and the United States we should, within our limitations, exploit our own facilities ... to [make] an acceptable contribution on the basis of *'quid pro quo'*." This last point is perhaps the most important single item on his list.

Col. Murray stressed the implications of the geographical contiguity of the Soviet Union (D.M.I. had long noted that the Soviets always seemed to want a lot and were not forthcoming in return), and observed that we really did not know much about our own North. He was concerned lest Germany be still a potential source of trouble, and drew the C.G.S.'s attention to the Crerar Library of military works at R.M.C. He foresaw trouble with China: "War in the Orient will inevitably affect Canada ... perhaps ... including active participation," and suggested two troublesome but minor areas. He touched upon some of the political and military considerations that exchanges of information with Britain and the United States would raise, and mentioned that our reputation was good – the British Army was just then basing much of the content of its new manuals on First Canadian Army's Intelligence Report. He reviewed the nature of the information required and the sources from which it could be obtained. He saw a continuing need to "study, correlate and assess Intelligence in order to equip ourselves for the future", and saw a secondary value in Intelligence duties "as an antidote to irksome regimental duties" for young officers.

Colonel Murray then discussed Security. The Army had a right to protect itself against dishonest and unreliable elements – a right normal in commercial establishments – and he listed areas where clearances would be required. Wartime experience had shown that between four and six per cent of applicants for sensitive employment would be rejected. He reviewed the question of aliens, then still within his purview, and commented upon "organizations whose practices were not designed to aid in the prosecution of the war". Under "Security of Information", he detailed the need for control over Canadian information, and for the protection of future plans and operations, and material still on the Secret list. He stated, very clearly, that at no time had D.M.I. been responsible for the physical security of material. He saw a continuing requirement for close liaison with the British and American authorities in the area outlined, and in the allied field of Counter-Intelligence.

Minor aspects of Colonel Murray's paper included the preparation of Security in Intelligence planning as part of the over-all "Readiness of War" concept, the control of Military Attachés, who should be Intelligence-trained and whose assistants should have had previous attachments to D.M.I., and the control of foreign Attachés accredited to Canada. He argued that a D.M.I. officer should handle all aspects of training, and that Canadian manuals should be prepared by Canadians, geared to Canada's particular situation, and used also by the Reserves, who would be concentrated once a year. Believing that Intelligence learners should be attached to D.M.I., he outlined an imaginative and useful study program which, although it would have given the individual valuable training, would have greatly added to the burdens borne by the Section Heads. He recommended the expansion of the Inter-Services Topographical Section, which had been formed in 1944 mainly as an extension of the Naval Photographic Library, and the absorption by it of a number of minor similar organizations, so that it would be the repository of the topographical, geographical, and economic information held by all the Services.

Col. Murray considered that the Canadian Intelligence Corps' role was that of an administrative cadre within the Regular Force, with its main strength in the Reserves. In direct response to Colonel Peter Wright's *Report on Intelligence within First Canadian Army*, he recommended the establishment of an Intelligence Battalion as part of a mobilized Field Army. This was an attempt to streamline and simplify the Field organization. He concluded: "The Canadian Intelligence Corps could be used as the organic structure to retain all specialist personnel . . . [naming the units]. . . . Little revision of authority is needed. D.M.I. could quickly estimate the number and rank of personnel . . . for specialist tasks in both Active and Reserve armies and set down an establishment necessary. . . . It would be fatal to have Intelligence specialists administered and trained in any other way." The Army H.Q. Intelligence organization he recommended had three Sections, each headed by a lieutenant-colonel, with a total strength of 24 officers and 43 other ranks.

Col. Murray believed that the emphasis on specialization required some Regular Army personnel to have a thorough grounding in Intelligence subjects. The Intelligence portion of the Staff College curriculum was not sufficient. He was convinced that Staff Officers, particularly those in "G", should be clearly aware of what Intelligence could provide, and to this end he recommended a special Intelligence course. After the course, they would be able to produce more realistic exercises, because they would understand, firstly, that a Commander's tactical moves depend upon his Intelligence, and, secondly, that some operations are required to obtain Intelligence.

He recommended that a self-contained School be established, which would offer courses at every level from battalion to N.D.H.Q., and which could devote time to the evaluation of the doctrine and methods of other countries. He foresaw the need to rotate Regular officers through the desks at D.M.I., but emphasized that these had to be "particularly competent young officers who have shown a flair for Intelligence and whose experience it was desired to enrich", before moving them on to higher things. He warned that the D.I.O., often employed as an "odd-job man", would be fully employed in Intelligence training. He made the following recommendations: that the D.I.O. appointment be restricted to Corps officers, rather than being a staff vacancy, open to all corps; that the appointments in M.D.s 2, 4, and 11 be majors, with captains in the other Districts; that each infantry battalion and armoured regiment have a Captain I.O. with one sergeant and six men, all personnel to be trained at the Intelligence School; and that all be required to teach both in their units and at the Reserves' summer camp. The officers were to be regimental, not Intelligence, and would form a pool of frequently changing officers from which the Military Attaché slates could be drawn.

He discussed the Reserve Army at length. He reminded the C.G.S. of the pitiable state in which Canada had gone to war, pointing out that there had been no Regulars in Intelligence posts either at D.N.D. or overseas, and that even though First Army had had four years to get ready, it had had difficulties. He recommended a Signals Intelligence program for eight officers and 20 men, enough to give a team for both sides of any field exercise, and an Air Photo Intelligence program to train men down to Brigade level. At the time, he was prepared to accept training at only three of the six Divisions planned – Halifax, Toronto, and Vancouver – linked to the three functioning R.C.A.F. Commands. He pointed out that co-operation between Army and Air was vital. He thought a case could be made for an additional divisional headquarters for the Arctic at Edmonton, which would require an Intelligence component of 36 officers and nine draftsmen. He repeated an earlier recommendation for linguists, with a total of 60 officers and 60 men to receive language training at different centres – German in Toronto, Russian in Montreal, etc. He thought that the District Security Intelligence Sections could teach Counter-Intelligence to the Reserves. The Security-trained Militia Intelligence could then conduct Security training within the Reserve units. He recommended three Divisional Counter-Intelligence Sections, one at each Divisional H.Q., for a total of six officers and 66 men. He proposed discussions between D.M.I. and the R.C.E., for Engineers' Intelligence training. He recommended that the Division establishment include a G.S.O.2 (Int), a Staff Learner, and three N.C.O.s.

For the six divisions, his total manpower requirement was 116 officers and 209 other ranks, as follows:

	Six Divisions			*18 Brigades*	
	Officer	Other Ranks		Officer	Other Ranks
H.Q.	6*	18	H.Q.	36	36 (C.Int.C)
Wireless	8	20	Units (x54)	108	378
Photo	36	9			
Linguists	60	60			
Counter-Intelligence	6	66			
Not mobilized		36			
Sub-total	116	209	Sub total	144	414
			Total	260	623

Total Intelligence Personnel in Field Force - 883
*He had disregarded the six Intelligence Learners

To a considerable degree, Col. Murray was a prisoner of his own concept of the Corps as an administrative cadre on the Regular establishment. He had asked for a three-Section organization in D.M.I. and for Corps officers at the Districts. He had recommended the formation of a School. But he neglected to put this, a first peacetime proposal for his entire establishment, in tabular form so that the actual cost could be quickly seen and discussed. Above all, he did not stipulate that those who were responsible for the detailed direction of the Sections at N.D.H.Q. and at the School should be officers who had considerable Intelligence training and experience, in short, Corps officers. And he made no attempt to ask for additional officers to offset those on courses, attachments, non-Intelligence employment, and so forth. The numbers involved were small, perhaps an additional 12–18.

Failure to secure for Intelligence the senior D.M.I. positions – major and up – meant that they were open to all comers, regardless of their experience or interest in Intelligence. Another disadvantage lay in the fact that, with insufficient officers to draw on, the tendency was to keep capable individuals working within the organization; when under consideration for promotion, these were regarded by the Personnel Branch as having insufficient general background to warrant advancement. The other side of this coin was one which had been identified in the Guides before 1914. Those officers who were not very good, and there were some, tended to be more "visible" than officers with similar faults in larger arms or services. These were retained in the Corps because it was believed better to use a more or less inadequate individual, whose faults were known and could be compensated for, than to have to fill a vacancy with an untrained unknown. This situation led in turn to difficulties in recruiting, and in keeping some of the better officers who wearied of the frequent moves that were required to bolster weakness.

In December, 1945, D.M.I. suggested that the Security organizations of the three Services be combined in a Joint Services Security Bureau (J.S.S.B.). The removal of the War Measures (the Defence of Canada Regulations, Censorship, etc.) had increased the Service's responsibilities for Personnel Security, for the physical protection of information, for Security education, and for declassifying material. Standardized procedures between the Services would result in tighter control all round. Lt.-Col. Eric Acland, who was the prime force in this attempt, managed to obtain approval from the Chiefs of Staff Committee on January 10, 1946. The J.S.S.B. was to report to the Joint Intelligence Committee, to have a permanent staff, and to set standards and maintain appropriate indexes. On July 9th, the Minutes of the Security Subcommittee revealed that the R.C.N. and the R.C.A.F. were alike reluctant to serve under an Army officer. The R.C.A.F. was forming its own Police and Security force. At the end of July, all agreed that the Services should co-ordinate their Security policy, attempt to make their procedures "as uniform as possible", and perhaps centralize their records.

No one body would be responsible for investigations. A J.I.C. sub-committee recommended that the J.S.S.B. be replaced with a permanent Secretary who would attempt to co-ordinate policy. The Chiefs of Staff Committee "approved this with regret" on October 17th, 1946; the Joint Security Committee and Joint Security Staff which were formed as a result functioned until Integration. The Secretary's job became progressively more routine, but the two bodies were useful forums for co-ordination.[5]

Col. "Jock" Murray retired on February 16th, 1946, to be replaced by Colonel W.A.B. (Bill) Anderson, whose father had been one of the original Guides. Though never employed in it, he was not a stranger to Intelligence. He had a realistic and fundamental appraisal of the professionalism required of his staff, and a clear understanding of postwar trends within the Canadian Army. He lost little time getting to know his people, warning them that there was little real future for the specialist, and advising his officers to get out into the broader world of the Service. There was a good deal of criticism of this at the time. Admittedly, there was some deadwood, but Intelligence also lost many good officers. This led to the introduction of increasing numbers of non-professionals, only a few of whom were good; most had no specialist qualifications and often little interest in the job, and some were unashamedly hostile to their temporary employment in the field. What was most significant was that many were quite senior and became responsible for the direction and form of some aspect of Intelligence. On the plus side, Col. Anderson's daily "coffee break" briefings and discussions encouraged a camaraderie and an exchange of views which led to better understanding and work.

Despite his views on the professional Intelligence officer, Col. Anderson implemented Col. Murray's suggestions to support the Intelligence function. He concentrated his few professionals in Security and Counter-Intelligence. In April 1946, he removed the administrative function from the Foreign Section, a step that was at least six years overdue. By that time, Command H.Q. had been established at Halifax (Eastern), Montreal (Quebec), Oakville (Central), Winnipeg (Prairie), and Edmonton (Western). A Security Section was assigned to each of these, and Col. Anderson recommended that these Sections be headed by a G.S.O.2 who, though primarily responsible for I(b), could also be used in the I(a) role when needed. He recommended that the Section personnel be Corps, considering this adequate to guarantee the perpetuation of the Corps and its skills. But, at the same time, he did not consider that the positions of G.S.O.2 at the Commands or G.S.O.1 in D.M.I. should also be Corps, although some of them were. He was also having difficulty obtaining officers. Not only did some leave after his advice, but the Selection Boards, reviewing applications for the Interim Force, were rejecting most of the Intelligence Corps officers who came before them. There was no guarantee, therefore, that he would get the qualified staff officers he needed to fill the positions. These obviously could not remain vacant, but if he had added the caveat, "To be filled when possible by C.Int.C.", the Corps would have had some protection. As it was, his proposal also would have closed the door to promotion beyond major for all but very exceptional officers.

The C.G.S., General Foulkes, thought that the rank structure for the Sections was too high, and dropped the vacancy at Command to captain, and at the District to lieutenant. He also considered that the Sections should be kept at Command H.Q., not decentralized to the Districts. But economy dictated that this be changed, and Detachments were soon assigned to the District H.Q. Corps officers were posted to some Command G.S.O.2 (Int) positions as they managed to enter and to pass Staff College.[6]

At N.D.H.Q., the former M.I.1 (its name was changed to Military Intelligence (Int) in 1946 and to Foreign Intelligence Section (F.I.S.) on August 11th, 1953), headed by a G.S.O.1 (lieutenant-colonel), was divided into area desks. Most of these G.S.O.1s were adequate; two, Lt.-Cols. L.E. (Joe) Sarantos, R.C.A.S.C., and C.D. (Ced) Haynes, R.C.O.C., were outstanding. Responsible for certain selected countries in depth, and for a watching brief on the rest of the world, F.I.S. staffs became prime exponents of the spirit of "the impossible only takes a little longer". F.I.S. Sections frequently produced relevant assessments which compared favourably with those of the larger partners. These assessments were passed upward within the Department through the Joint Intelligence Staff (J.I.S.) and the Joint Intelligence Committee, where they contributed first to Departmental and then to Interdepartmental decision-making. A series of agreements between the Department and its counterparts abroad led to work on narrowly specialized subjects, often using voluminous raw material provided by those other agencies. These paid for much of this work D.M.I. had received from them, although there were occasional disagreements with Treasury over the free distribution of the finished product. Though the F.I.S. assessment record was good, with much of its material being quoted abroad, any success it enjoyed was largely due to the hard work and skill of a few professionals, who were able to see a situation developing and did not have to go through the bureaucracy of a larger agency. F.I.S. never was successful in limiting the scope of its coverage, and often was spread too thin to do the job properly.

Security did not really change from the late wartime period. Again, this Branch was headed by an officer who was only occasionally C.Int.C.; the clever ones learned early to rely upon their Corps officers. Perhaps the best of those was Ced Haynes, who filled the post as a major until he was assigned as Military Attaché to Scandinavia. Experienced officers such as Bill Braun, Jake Steen, Ken Hope, Dave MacAulay, and Leo Knoop, worked much as a relay team through Military Intelligence (Security), which had, as its chief function, the Security Clearance of Personnel program. One officer, with occasional help, handled Security of Information. The imperturbable Maj. S.O.F. Evans was perhaps longest in that post. The staff officers knew the investigators, and kept them closely controlled. They were well aware of individual bias – some of the N.C.O.s were "down" on alcoholism, some on promiscuity, others on financial irresponsibility – and were able to make appropriate allowances when reviewing their cases. Corps investigative standards were as high and as thorough as any. In all the many cases that were submitted, there were none of wrong identity.

A few investigators tried falsifying their reports to claim more money for temporary duty. There were invariably caught, generally sooner rather than later, and were immediately transferred out of Intelligence. *All* the cases they had worked on were rechecked. It must be stressed that any indications of subversion were passed immediately to the R.C.M.P., both by the Detachments and by M.I.(S). D.M.I. may have been lucky – or skilful – but there were no cases of proven unreliability of persons in highly classified posts.

After the Hungarian Revolt in 1956, many expatriate Hungarians were admitted to Canada through Saint John, New Brunswick. Capt. George Parry, C.D., C.Int.C., was the Area Security Officer at that time. As good fortune would have it, George was a fluent Hungarian linguist. In addition to providing advice and guidance, and acting as interpreter between the Hungarians and Canadian officials, George went to great lengths to try and ensure that the Hungarians' transition to Canadian life was as painless as possible, even to supervising the Canadian cooks in the preparation of Hungarian food.

The period following 1949 was marked by a general willingness on the part of authority to support requests for more officers and men, for additional funds, and for permission to engage in more international Intelligence discussions. A number of officers who had returned to civilian life after the war rejoined, a few were commissioned from the ranks, and some, under a variety of arrangements, transferred from other Corps. For the first time in many years, the D.M.I. began to hope that he could fill the Intelligence appointments in the Commands and Areas, plus a more generous portion of the N.D.H.Q. posts, with career Intelligence people. Considerable credit is due to Lt.-Col. R.H. (Tex) Noble, whose tour of duty as G.S.O.1, Military Intelligence (Organization and Training), coincided with this trend. To a degree Tex may have "ridden the wave", but he was tireless in ensuring that its force was turned in a career direction, and that others could reinforce what he had gained.

Tex was also very active in promoting Canadian participation in the development of new and better techniques of obtaining information over the battlefield, and, to a lesser extent, in handling it after it had been provided. The early stages of the CL 89 Drone, which is now in use abroad, owe a great deal to Intelligence advice provided by him. Finally, he was responsible for having John Gayfer write the Corps March, "Silver & Green".

The last D.M.I., Col. Tommy Fosbery, C.D., R.C.O.C., was appointed on August 6th, 1962. Theoretically he should have had an easy tour. Virtually all of

Col. Murray's 1946 recommendations had been adopted. Of his three G.S.O.1s, Lt.-Cols. Haynes and McShane had had many years in Intelligence; the latter was a professional. The third, Lt.-Col. Guy Robitaille, M.C., R.22e.R., had only been in his Security post a year, but, though still learning his job, was competent, and had a good staff and the other two to call upon for advice and guidance. Most of the Corps officers were very experienced, providing a solid phalanx of knowledge and skill. But there were not quite enough junior officers to replace wastage, and most of these were at various stages of their early training. The men followed a similar pattern. On the international scene, the Cuban Crisis of late 1962, the Sino-Indian war of 1962, and the U.N. Peacekeeping Operation in Cyprus (discussed in Chapter 20), required action by the respective F.I.S. Sections. The Security duties were routine. Relations with Allied Intelligence agencies were good. F.I.S. was then engaged in a number of projects whose results provided the international Intelligence Community with some relatively high-standard material. Both the D.M.I. and his G.S.O.1, F.I.S.., were very aware of the dictum that the better the contribution the better the exchange.

Nevertheless, Tommy Fosbery had a most difficult tour. The early stages of Integration/Unification called for changes on three main fronts. Firstly, all H.Q. establishments were to be reduced by one third. Secondly, the three Service functions were to be amalgamated. In Intelligence, this principle was extended to include the civilian manned Joint Intelligence Bureau and the Directorate of Scientific Intelligence. And finally, the vastly different trades and career structures that existed among the three Services were to be reconciled.

Col. Fosbery held that the desired personnel savings could be achieved by curtailing the administrative echelons, necessary when the various Intelligence Directorates occupied separate locations, but superfluous when they were combined. By such curtailment, the Intelligence staffs proper could be left untouched. He was outvoted in favour of a policy which sacrificed junior staff to preserve a virtually untouched officer rank structure. This preserved vacancies for three full colonels, and added a brigadier as branch head.

An ad hoc committee of three officers, none of them with significant Intelligence experience, studied the subordinate staff organization. This committee totally ignored the directive of the Intelligence Planning Committee which had met annually to decide upon priorities and trends. The directive would have shown them which priority areas needed staffing. Predictably, its findings confirmed the steps toward Integration that already had taken place. The loss of most of the sub-staff forced the desk officers to do the clerical work their N.C.O.s had formerly done, and significantly reduced the time and effort available for their primary function, analysis. A time-and-motion study would have shown the true cost of this "saving", but none took place.

Amalgamation of the Foreign Intelligence and Administrative components was relatively straightforward. The desk officers in D.N.I. and D.A.I. had always worked closely, and generally happily, with those in D.M.I., and many analysts, particularly those older professionals who had been in and out of the H.Q. for some time, were close personal friends. The hope that, through reorganization, more productive use could be made of the limited manpower, was most appealing.

But the Security component was different. The R.C.A.F. had combined its Police and Security functions and wished to continue to do so. Col. Fosbery, rightly of the opinion that Police and Intelligence were not compatible functions, fought this, seeking as best he could to continue the separation of the Security Intelligence function from the Police. Ably assisted by Lt.-Col. King McShane, he succeeded in getting agreement from both the R.C.N. and the R.C.A.F. that this would be the arrangement. Regrettably, he had to visit Washington during the discussion. On his return, he found that, during his short absence, his opponents had obtained approval for the incorporation of the Police function with Intelligence. Col. Fosbery was told that his arguments had been countered by better ones; that he had been denied the opportunity to present his himself was disregarded. The Army Provost Marshal, who had been conducting his own fight for survival, took over first the Security side of Intelligence and then the Air Force Police. As the "Director of Security", he was now responsible concurrently for all aspects of Military Police and Counter-Intelligence. Canada is the only country in NATO where this pertained.

This was the culmination of a long-standing and often-expressed ambition of the Canadian Provost Corps. That Corps held that Security and Police were common trades, and used the R.C.A.F. example to bolster its presentation. The operational role of Field Security was ignored. Provost did not understand, nor did they particularly want, the Strategic side of Intelligence. But the proposed removal of the Security element left an even more unviable rump. The entire Intelligence organization was therefore merged with Military Police.

This decision had far-reaching effects. In the Regular Force, it combined the Command Security Intelligence Sections with the Provost Detachments and Air Force Police Security Investigation Unit (S.I.U.) Detachments. Some saving in administration was achieved. In the Militia, Intelligence Training Companies and the Military Police were combined and, eventually, became part of the Service Battalions created at each Militia Command and named "Security Platoons".

During 1964, the position of Corps Director was abolished. Again, Col. Fosbery (strongly supported by other Directors) protested, pointing out that, without a Corps Director, the individual had no one to whom to take his professional and personal problems. As a rather weak compromise, it was agreed that the Schools would assume this function. How the Commanding Officers of these establishments were supposed to handle such matters was never satisfactorily explained, perhaps because it was not studied, and the increasingly complex command structure in the Forces made their new task impossible. Private complaints against inequities were particularly difficult to pursue, particularly as the Intelligence Community did not have adequate professional representation in the Personnel Branch. And, with Directors who had little or no Intelligence experience, the immediate result of Integration was a marked falling off both of morale and of efficiency.

At the end of the war, the Intelligence N.C.O. had been expected to be competent in three branches of the profession: Collation, Investigation, and Photo Interpretation. The progressive trades structure demanded that he pass tests in all three in order to qualify for higher trades pay and promotion. But the concept was too rigid; not all could qualify, or were suitable, for employment in all three fields. By 1956, a new system, designed to provide progression in all fields, was introduced in its place. Although this limited flexibility in planning postings, it was fairer to the individual. What turned out to be the final polish to the system – the incorporation of the recruit assessment training – was provided by Capt. Elliot and Lieut. Bachand in Organization & Training in 1962–63.

With Integration, similar trades in the three Services were to be combined under one category, based on commonality of function. This was a simple matter in the case, say, of a cook. But the R.C.N. had no comparable Intelligence trade. The R.C.A.F. had two: Intelligence Operators and Investigators, the latter a Police trade. The R.C.A.F. considered the Army men to be over-qualified, and made little attempt to understand the Army's need for the specialists it had produced. With the merger of Security and Police, part of the problem was resolved. Intelligence investigators were placed in the Investigator category; all other Intelligence tradesmen became Intelligence Operators. Sub-branches of the latter category were later developed. Even at that, there was conflict within the Security environment; the Intelligence N.C.O.s' duties called for more responsibility and, in consequence, they were paid at a higher rate than their policeman counterparts. The trend, however, was to "level down" rather than to bring the members of the other two Services to a higher standard of training. This wholesale amalgamation effectively met the requirement to reduce trades. But it was effectively a revision to the "One Big Trade" concept which Army Intelligence had found to be unworkable and which it had spent 10 years replacing.

The confusion, and apparent lack of concern for subordinates, that seemed to prevail at the higher command levels, led some Intelligence personnel to leave the Service early. This was particularly noticeable in the Security Sections. But all components suffered from the disorganization and frequent changes of personnel, and from the departure of experienced individuals. This placed a strain on those who were left, both to fill the vacancies and to carry the load which increasingly fell upon those with experience. Some stayed because they felt it their duty to help carry the organization through difficult times, when every experienced man could contribute something to the good of the whole. Others stayed because they just could not afford to leave. But all found that knowledge and experience seemed to be ignored, except when a crisis ensued, and that most of the time their needs were overlooked and their efforts unrecognized.

Col. Fosbery remained for a few months to provide advice and guidance to his successor, Brig. Lloyd Kenyon. But there was no place in the new organization for the ex-D.M.I. This was a great pity. Tommy Fosbery's proven ability and skill in administration, his knowledge of the Corps with which he had so closely identified himself, and his sympathy for and understanding of the problems of the junior members of that Corps, would have been a tremendous asset during the early days of Integration. He left Intelligence in 1965, and the Service some two years later, and, regrettably, to this day is of the opinion that the senior officials, military and civilian, of the Department were unaware of the problems of Intelligence, and unsympathetic to proposals intended to solve them. He was presented with the Colonel Commandant's Award, a token given only infrequently by the Colonel Commandant himself to the individual who has done a great deal for the Corps; a sole, small gesture of appreciation for all the work done on behalf of professional Intelligence by a man who, two short years before, had come to that profession as a stranger.

INTELLIGENCE UNITS

The need to train officers and men without wartime experience was recognized early. It was met in part by the summer camp concentrations held at a temporary school at Petawawa, for both Regular and Militia. But a more permanent establishment was required, and Col. Murray's recommendation, supported by pressures from D.M.I. and the Canadian Military Intelligence Association, resulted in 1952 in the formation of the Canadian School of Military Intelligence (C.S. of M.I.) – the "College of Knowledge" at Camp Borden. Headed initially by Major Tex Noble, it comprised an H.Q. and three Wings, responsible respectively for Combat Intelligence, Field Security, and Photo Reading. It was an entirely self-contained unit, with its own Quartermaster, graphic artist, and carpenter staff. Though small – there were only six officers, a W.O.II, five N.C.O.s, and eight civilians, all housed in four "I" huts – it was the training centre not only for the Corps but also for a number of other Security and Intelligence courses serving the other Arms and Services, and both government and civilian agencies. The course load was, in fact, its most serious weakness. The few instructors and assistant instructors handled teaching responsibilities of a number and variety which greatly exceeded those demanded of staffs in other Corps Schools. Since Integration, the School has been amalgamated with the Provost School to form the Canadian Forces School of Intelligence and Security.

Staff at the Canadian School of Military Intelligence, Petawawa, Ontario, summer 1949; standing, from left: Lt.-Col. R.L. Raymont, Capt. J.R.G. Suprenant, Capt. G.M. Paulier, Capt. R.R. Dixon, Cpl. S.E. Fisher, Capt. M.G. Corbeil, Sgt. J.A. Wall, Capt. G.G. McDermott, Capt. W. Tenhaaf, Capt. F.A. Pollak, Capt. J. McCrossan, R.C.R. Kneeling, front: S/Sgt. D.G. Kirk, Sgt. R. Henderson, W.O.II A.W. Reid, Cpl. R.O. Conover, S/Sgt. J.E. Martin, W.O.II Wheatley, Capt. W.I. Binkley. (Photo collection Canadian Forces School of Military Intelligence, Kingston/Canada. Dept. of National Defence)

Brigade Intelligence Section on night duty during an exercise at a Militia Summer Camp Concentration, Petawawa, 1954. (Photo collection Canadian Forces School of Military Intelligence, Kingston/Canada. Dept. of National Defence)

Lt.-Gen. G.G. Simonds, C.B., C.B.E., D.S.O., C.D., Chief of the General Staff, inspecting a C.Int.C. Guard of Honour, comprised of a mix of Militia and Regular Force, during the official opening ceremony of C.S. of M.I. Camp Borden, July 1953. Accompanying the inspection party is Maj. "Tex" R.H. Noble, Cmdt C.S. of M.I., third person back. (Photo collection Canadian Forces School of Military Intelligence, Kingston/Canada. Dept. of National Defence)

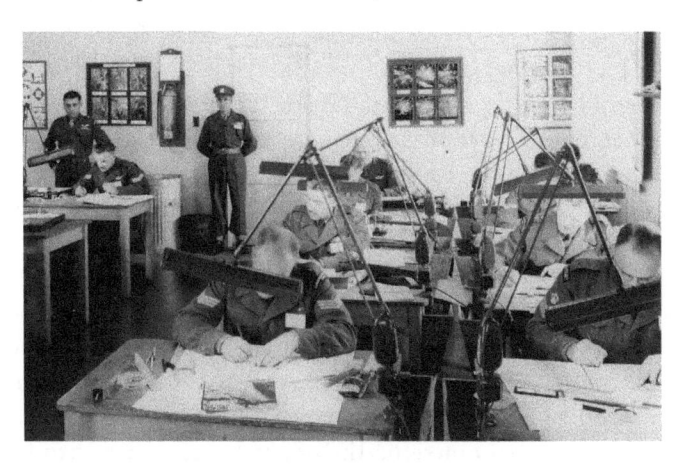

Students at C.S. of M.I., Borden, conducting a practical exercise as part of the Photo Reading Instructors Course, October 1955. (Photo collection Canadian Forces School of Military Intelligence, Kingston/Canada. Dept. of National Defence)

Following the closure of S-20 Japanese Language School in 1946, there was no domestic program for linguist training in the Regular Force.[7] Those who wished to qualify were either sent to commercial establishments or to the American Army's language school in Monterey, California. In 1954, it was decided to open a Canadian language school, and a small tri-Service unit was set up in Ottawa. Its main language was Russian, and attaché training in the less common languages was handled commercially, with the School responsible for administration. Militia training was also controlled by the School, through a staff officer in D.M.I., Organization and Training. The School did not become involved in the French language program.

Concern was expressed after the war that the skills of aerial photography in Intelligence would be lost. After representation, a Joint Service Air Photo Interpretation School (J.A.P.I.S.) was formed in 1948 at the Canadian Joint Air Training Centre at Rivers, Manitoba. The army component comprised C.Int.C. personnel, under Capt. C.I. (Charley) Taggart. This unit was responsible for providing air photo support for the field units, and for all air photo training. In 1953, the First Canadian Division A.P.I.S. was formed in Rockcliffe, under the command of another wartime Intelligence officer, Capt. Mark W. Robinson, M.B.E. Primarily responsible for support to the Division and its units, 1 A.P.I.S. also became a library and general support unit. In 1960, J.A.P.I.S., A.P.I.S., and an Air Force interpretation unit were amalgamated and the resultant unit renamed the Joint Photographic Interpretation Centre. In 1965, it was redesignated Defence Photographic Interpretation Unit.

Not only did it perform air support for the H.Q. and field units, but it arranged for air photo cover of exercise areas for the Regular and Militia forces, provided significant support for Army H.Q., and acted as a link with other national and allied agencies. It maintained a library of air photo coverage and acted as a training establishment for advanced specialists. A small unit – 12 officers, 14 N.C.O.s, and a civilian – it was seriously pressed to fill the many demands on its services.

There were also a few field units, in addition to those in Korea and Cyprus. One, a small Wireless Intelligence Section, suffered from a lack of purpose or direction, stemming in large degree from an imprecise understanding, in almost all quarters, of its actual function. The original requirement had been based on an assumption that two Sections would be used during field exercises. But few of the wartime W.I. specialists remained in the Service. It was never used in its true role. Eventually it became a pool for linguists who were needed for short periods on a variety of tasks, which was a gross mis-employment of these specialists. Its main purpose lost, it became an "orphan" unit, too small to be viable. Both it, and the responsibility for its function, were absorbed by the Royal Canadian Corps of Signals unit with which it was based. Its linguists,

An unidentified C.Int.C. corporal and Army aircrewman servicing an underwing camera on a Cessna L-19 Bird Dog, most likely in Gagetown, New Brunswick, circa 1964. (Photo collection Canadian Forces School of Military Intelligence, Kingston/Canada. Dept. of National Defence)

No. 1 Canadian Field Security Section, Soest, West Germany, summer 1957. (Photo collection Canadian Forces School of Military Intelligence, Kingston/Canada. Dept. of National Defence)

unable to use their skills, left the Service, and another expensive investment was lost.

A second unit, formed in 1951 to support Canada's brigade group in NATO, was No. 2 Field Security Section. This unit went overseas from Montreal under Capt. W.E. "Bill" Blane, and its first task was to teach Security to 27 Brigade. On February 1st, 1954, it was renumbered No. 1, a designation which had become vacant when that Section returned from Korea. The Section remained at full establishment for about six years, but was thereafter progressively reduced in strength until it became only a small Detachment, headed by an officer, and then part of the combined police unit.

20.
PEACEKEEPING

Since the Second World War, the Canadian Army has served in a number of United Nations peacekeeping operations and on two International Control Commissions in Vietnam. Servicemen assigned to these missions often received briefings from Intelligence at Army H.Q., but only in Korea and in Cyprus were Field Intelligence Units assigned to support U.N. operations. This was a result of decisions made at the United Nations H.Q. itself. U.N. field forces have an obvious requirement for the Intelligence function but, for political reasons, are compelled to conduct most of their operations without specialist units and with only a minimal H.Q. staff.

KOREA

On June 25th, 1950, eight full-strength divisions and some 250 tanks of the Democratic People's Republic of Korea crossed the 38th Parallel into the Republic of Korea. The South Korean forces opposing them were about 50,000 strong, organized into eight weak divisions, without tanks, heavy guns, or aircraft. They were virtually untrained, and were still forming and organizing the H.Q. staffs they needed. After the North Korean forces had paused to regroup on the Han River, just south of Seoul, President Truman ordered American forces to go to the aid of South Korea. They went into action on July 5th, and finally stopped the Communist advance along a small perimeter around the port of Pusan. American air attacks and naval shellfire, including some from Canadian warships, were directed against the North Korean lines of communication in order to reduce their re-supply capabilities.

The United States, which had deployed an Occupation Force to South Korea at the end of World War II, declared that the area was no longer strategically significant and, in 1949, withdrew its troops after the Russians had withdrawn theirs. In consequence, Intelligence coverage of the area had a low priority. The American Intelligence office in Tokyo, for example, thought that the North Koreans were only capable of carrying on subversion against the South.[1] In Ottawa, the responsible Section in M.I. (Int) received all its information from either U.S. or U.N. sources. Its head, Maj. Jim Leys, had China as his primary target, and had little time to watch Korea. The assessments he did make on North Korean capabilities were more cautious than the reports from Tokyo and Washington. But there was little information on North Korea and its forces.

22. Korea

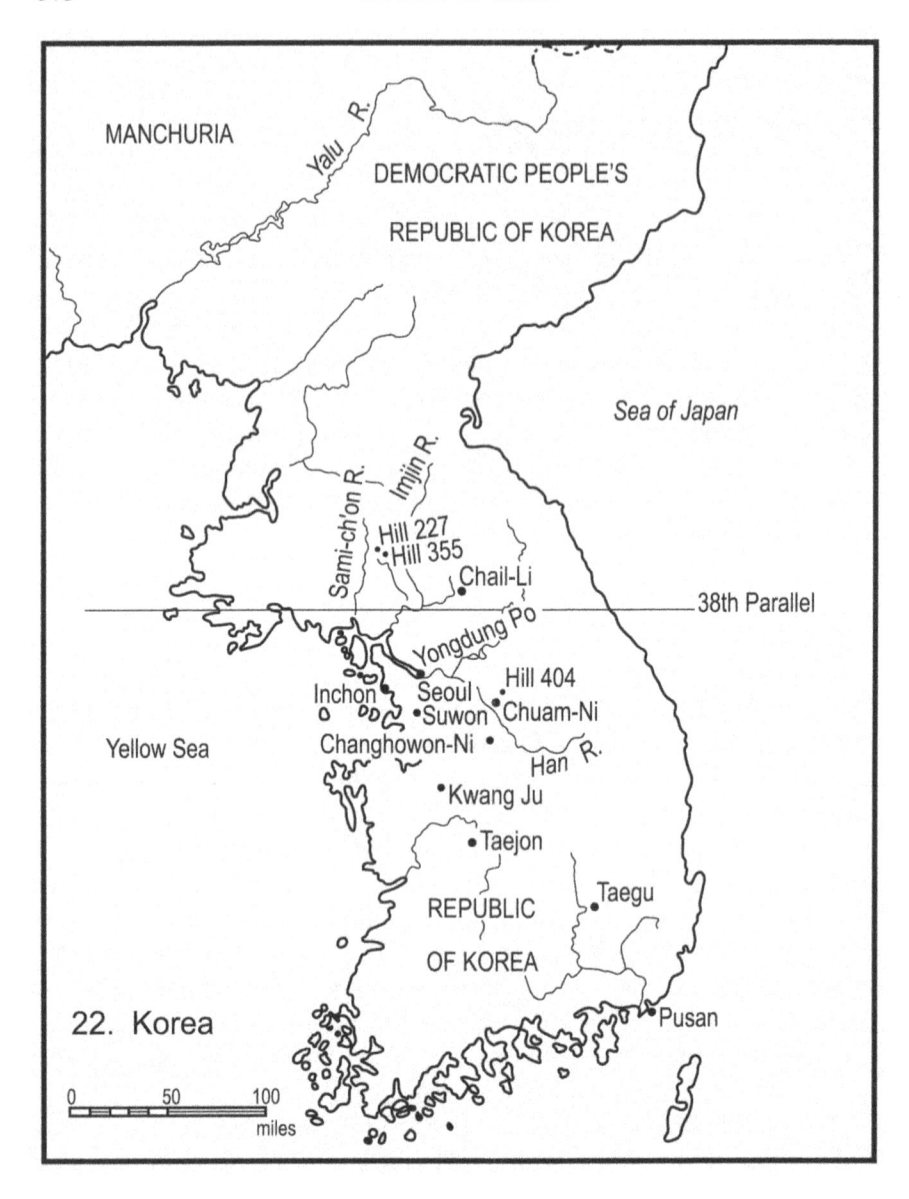

In Ottawa, the Joint Intelligence Committee, of which the D.M.I. was a member, obtained an estimate of North Korean strength and capabilities, studied the situation, and, on June 29th, recommended that the South be given aid. On August 7th, the Minister announced the formation of a Canadian Army Special Force, to consist of one brigade specially recruited for service in Korea. Officers of the H.Q. and technical units were mostly Regulars; those in the battalions were mostly Special Force. The I.O. at Brigade H.Q., for example – Capt. N.A. Buckingham, from M.I.1 – was a Regular; his men were all Special

Force. The battalion I.O.s, Lieuts. E.J. Mastronardi, 2 R.C.R., A.P.P. McKenzie, 2 P.P.C.L.I., and M. Côté, 2 R.22e.R., and all their men, were Special Force.[2]

The counter-offensive, which pushed the North Koreans back across the 38th Parallel, seemed to make the need for Canadian participation much less urgent. As a result, only 2 P.P.C.L.I. was sent to Korea, while the rest of 25th Brigade went to Fort Lewis, Washington, for training. The picture quickly changed; for while 2 P.P.C.L.I. was actually en route, the Chinese People's Republic came into the war. American Intelligence was still reluctant to accept the reports that Chinese forces were massing, and even moving across the Yalu River from Manchuria. Maj. Bill Braun, on exchange to this particular desk in the Pentagon, had great difficulty in getting the warning signs he detected to higher authority. When the attack did start, he was reassigned, and his work handed to a greatly enlarged American staff.[3] Chinese prisoners later admitted that they had actually been crossing the Yalu on October 19th. By early November, U.S. air reconnaissance confirmed a massive enemy movement southward along the roads in North Korea. On the 17th, the British Commonwealth Occupation Forces identified three Chinese armies and an extra division. An American offensive began on the 24th, and was repulsed by a Chinese counter-offensive. By December 16th, the U.S. Eighth Army held positions along the Imjin River, north of Seoul. 2 P.P.C.L.I. arrived in Pusan on December 18th, 1950.

Lieut. Peter McKenzie had been taken on strength of 2 Battalion on September 19th. He spent six weeks recruiting and training a Section, and giving map-reading and photo-reading courses to junior officers. His Section boarded the U.S.N.S. *Private Joe P. Martinez* on November 25th, went ashore with the C.O.'s group at Pusan, and moved to a training camp near Suwon, about 20 miles due south of Seoul. There, Peter's first problem was a Security matter. December 22nd: ". . . all companies desire . . . Koreans . . . as interpreters, mess and kitchen help". Since vetting was impossible, he had to issue passes to these employees and ask the regimental police to make simple spot checks.[4]

The Intelligence Section was then used on route reconnaissances. Peter McKenzie's comments on the only maps he had indicate the kind of problems his men faced: "Black and white maps printed in 1923 and with a 1950 Army Map Service grid overlay do not provide a very accurate source of map information. 90% of the maps above the 28th parallel are of this pattern and aerial photographs, which are not very plentiful here, should be on a priority list".[5] These official maps were so poor that, throughout the war, they had to be augmented with hand-drawn maps and sketches.

On February 15th, the Section moved to Changhowon-Ni, and service with 27th Brigade. It did a survey of the area, and produced a trace for the company commanders. On the 19th, the troops advanced north to Chuam-ni, and up the valley beyond Hill 404 in a typical infantry advance-to-contact, where formal Intelligence was of little help. On February 26th, a deserter reported that the

Chinese *Second Army* front had withdrawn to the hill range on the north side of the valley, about five miles north of the Canadian position. He thought that all Chinese armies would remain on the defensive until the *41st* and *43rd Divisions* came down with tanks to spearhead the next offensive. Immediately opposite the Canadians was *II Battalion* of *375th Regiment*: "Chinese trapped six days ago on our front were warned that they were fighting a delaying action in order to prepare their defence line. They were told it would be between five and seven days before they were all back."[6] An Australian advance outflanked the objective, and the Canadians took it against little opposition. The Patricias went into reserve on March 3rd, 1951.

The main body of the Brigade trained at Fort Lewis until April 9th. During this time, Capt. W.H. Pope attended a left-wing rally in uniform; he had to answer several pointed questions afterwards. In an exercise to test the alertness of the R.22e.R., Exercise Control, working with Capt. Buckingham, released two "refugees" in civilian clothing and two "enemy" soldiers wearing Soviet uniforms, badges, and insignia, and carrying Soviet Army paybooks. The visitors found plenty of opportunities to steal things, even Bren guns; one managed to cut, undetected, all telephone lines leading forward from Battalion H.Q. The Diarist felt it likely that the units would control access to their lines in future.[7] The main body landed in Pusan on May 4th and, on the 6th, Capt. Buckingham went to H.Q. Eighth U.S. Army in Korea (EUSAK), and Capt. John Bowie, G.S.O.3 (Air), to Fifth U.S. Air Force H.Q., to collect the information they would need to carry out their duties.

No. 1 Canadian Field Security Section was the only Intelligence unit with the Brigade. Formed in September 1950, under Capt. M.G. (Eddie) Corbeil, Area Intelligence Officer, Western Ontario Area, London, it had two officers, 17 Intelligence Corps specialists, and 12 non-Corps other ranks. They were concentrated at Petawawa, where the summer Intelligence School reopened to train them. An advance party, under the second-in-command, Capt. H.F. Sutcliffe, went to Japan in early November; the others went to train at Fort Lewis, and at the American Counter-Intelligence School. Jim McDougall replaced J. Calouri as C.S.M.

The Section landed in Korea on May 4th, and checked at once with 904 British F.S. Detachment which, with 704 Counter-Intelligence Corps Detachment (U.S.), was responsible for Pusan. Two whole Sections would hardly have been enough; theft and breakage bordered on sabotage. On May 9th, they were allotted six interpreters, one per Detachment, and one at Section H.Q. Two had to be replaced almost immediately; one was found to have been involved in the theft of 70,000 won (about $219.00); the other was "non-cooperative". The Section covered the move of the Brigade to Kwang Ju, via Taegu and Taejun, trying to ensure that no unauthorized persons would be able to make contact with the troops. The Civil Assistance organization, however, had ruled that civilians would not be evacuated unless it was absolutely necessary to do so. This left a large, mainly transient population in which enemy agents were able to hide.[8]

On May 17th, the Brigade was assigned to I U.S. Corps, then building up for a counter-offensive to be launched on May 21st. To support the advance, it moved on the 24th, with 25th Division, to an area northeast of Uijong-bu. No. 1 Field Security Section sent an H.Q. element to Uijong-bu, and three Detachments to the forward battalions to take charge of civilian labour, to set up a refugee control post, and to do interrogations. The next day the now reinforced Brigade was ordered to pass through positions held by the Turks, and take an objective on the 38th Parallel.

On the 26th, 2 R.22e.R. picked up a handful of Chinese stragglers and line-crossers. When they were interrogated by the Intelligence staff and by F.S., they gave information on possible enemy deployments, and confirmed that enemy agents were being introduced into the refugee streams.[9] On May 21st, U.S. Intelligence had shown that *579* and *577 Regiments* of *193 Division* of *64 Chinese Communist Army* (*C.C.A.*) were roughly on the Brigade axis of advance; on the 28th, Buckingham reported that the R.22e.R. prisoners actually came from *4*, *5*, and *6 Companies* of *582 Regiment*.[10] "D" Company, 2 R.C.R., had so much trouble clearing Kakhul-Bong, a dominating hill near Chail-li, that the battalion was forced to pull back and regroup. The Official History says that the enemy's stiff resistance was intended to protect his main supply and communications areas. Whatever the reason, it made nonsense of the May 26th assessment that reported withdrawals all along the front.[11] On June 1st, the Brigade went into reserve, leaving 2 P.P.C.L.I. to cover the flank of IX Corps' crossing of the Imjin.

The three Commonwealth Brigades, 25th, 28th, and 29th, were now concentrated to be formed into a Division. 25th Brigade moved to Iibisang-ni, taking 1 F.S. into an area being handled by No. 904 (British) F.S. Section. Their C.O. told Capt. Corbeil that the local inhabitants had all been screened, but he very quickly found that the influx of refugees had been so great that the screening had to be done over again. He went to Seoul on June 5th to ask for a "white" list, so that he could contact reliable informants. He got his list, but it turned out to be useless, for most of those named in it had already left the area and he had to turn for assistance to the British detachment in Pusan.

The hordes of civilians roaming the Brigade area were not merely a security hazard, but a source of so much confusion that Brig. Rockingham obtained authority to have them removed and to impose a curfew between 1900 on the 7th and 0700 on the 8th. N.C.O.s patrolled the roads to make sure it was enforced. Eddie Corbeil had already divided his Section into an H.Q. and five detachments: one was at the Brigade H.Q., one was in reserve, and the three others were to be deployed to where they were needed. Men were sent forward to the British brigades (one Detachment was already with the 28th), and civilians who were wandering about were sent to the Cage at Section H.Q. About 450 were picked up on the 8th, checked against the various lists, fed, and evacuated in Brigade unit vehicles to the Civil Assistance Corps at Yongdung Po. Many of them had their oxen with them; they could not leave them behind because "in many cases the family ox provided a livelihood for the entire family . . . it was decided that the owners . . . would have to walk with them to Yongdung Po".

On June 9th, 500 civilians were evacuated, and, on the 10th, 200 more. It was feared that the sick and injured would need treatment, and that the Advanced Dressing Station would not be large enough to accept them. On the 11th, stragglers and line-crossers began to appear again. Capt. Corbeil wrote: ". . . civilians who have been evacuated . . . hear via the grape vine that the fighting has moved north and immediately pack up and head for their homes, whereas . . . the line has not moved north but only patrols. . . . The civilians, of course, must be re-evacuated. Quite a number of North Koreans are being picked up . . . nothing of C.I. interest as it was found that these were not line-crossers but the line had crossed over them."[12]

On June 18th, 25th Brigade came under command of First Cavalry Division, and Brig. Rockingham was ordered "to occupy positions, hold line WYOMING and patrol aggressively killing as many enemy . . . and destroying as much enemy supplies and equipment as possible." The Brigade was not impressed by the order; even 10 miles north of WYOMING, it had made no contact with the enemy for several days. So little, in fact, was known of his whereabouts that, on the 20th, the battalion commanders were ordered to "discover where and in what strength the enemy was, and to inflict as many casualties as possible". In a most unusual departure from their normal role, the three Field Security Detachments with the forward units evacuated civilians from as much as five miles *beyond* the F.D.L.s. Still there was no contact with the enemy.

Civilians were told to walk to Chorwon; if they were wounded or ill, they were moved by unit vehicle. On the 22nd, six sergeants, three interpreters, and six National Police went out with the R.22e.R., about 14 miles beyond the F.D.L.s, in order to control the movement of civilians along the patrol route as a "protection against ambush". The next day, they established a control line; its checkpoints were manned by more than 100 Korean police, and supplemented by roving patrols. On the 24th, they evacuated about 3,400 civilians, and on the 25th, between 1,200 and 1,500 more; far too many to interrogate. Patrols probing for enemy positions found "hundreds of civilians puttering around the fields and villages and showing great interest in the troops and their equipment. There is reason to believe that when the Chinese descend from the hills after dark, there are many ready informants among the villagers." They suspected also that the villages concealed Chinese agents dressed in plain clothes. S/Sgt. Bob Henderson tried to control a group of about 600 refugees by setting them up in a deserted village, with their own mayor and two counsellors, and telling them to manage their own affairs. It was a sound idea, but the arrangement soon broke down, and the group had to be evacuated.[13]

At Brigade, Capt. Buckingham was granted emergency leave to return to Canada; he was replaced by Lieut. R.L. Cochrane, R.C.R., and later by Lieut. Peter McKenzie of the Patricias. At Division, members of the British 904 F.S. Section were discovered to be dealing in the black market. The Canadian Section was ordered to take over the divisional area, with the remnants of 904.

Most reports sent down from higher formations focused only slightly on specific Brigade problems. Divisional Intelligence usually ended its review with an assessment that the enemy had withdrawn, possibly to a strong but unlocated defence line, but did not say clearly whether the dumps had gone back with him: ". . . withdrawal has not been planned. . . . He may be willing to participate in another mass offensive to recover his stores and regain control of the east/west communications centre". Intelligence knew, however, that only the still unlocated *18th Army Group* was in a position to launch a counter-offensive. Its divisions were estimated to be at full strength (9,500 men), instead of the normal 4,000 estimated for the others. Until they had located this *Army Group*, the Intelligence staffs at Eighth Army felt it was impossible to decide whether the enemy withdrawal would continue.[14]

On June 29th, one F.S. detachment was five miles in front of the F.D.L.s, screening and evacuating civilians. On the 30th, Sgt. Clarke actually led a patrol of the R.C.R. several miles beyond the F.D.L.s, to see if he could find unfriendly forces. Luckily, he found none, and Capt. Corbeil decided that this was not F.S. work and curbed such "extracurricular" activities. It was as well he did so. For on July 2nd, a three-man R.C.R. patrol was killed by an ambush party, probably of guerrillas dressed in civilian clothes, between the lines and a refugee collecting point. After this incident, strong infantry patrols swept the area in a manner similar to the clearance actions along the Rhine in late 1944. Each battalion evacuated all civilians it found to its own refugee collecting point, which F.S. then visited and cleared. The sweep resulted in a bag of 4,000–5,000; something obviously had been needed.

On July 26th, 1951, the Brigade came under command of I U.S. Corps, and was redeployed behind 28th Brigade which, with the 29th, was holding the line of the Imjin River. This was the first time the 1st (Commonwealth) Division, formed early in June, served as a united formation. Its G.S.O.2 (Int) was Capt. Eddie Blais, a recent graduate of the Canadian Army Staff College, a former desk officer in D.M.I., and an outstanding Regular officer. The Imjin was in flood, and operations were tied to the amphibious support and the bridging that was being prepared to cross it. It was an uneventful August for 25 Brigade, marked only by some low-key psychological warfare by the Chinese.

Eddie Corbeil began a blitz on the hordes of prostitutes, shoeshine boys, and minor racketeers swarming in the rear areas. The venereal disease rate was very high, theft was endemic and, what was more immediately worrying, the incidence of cut telephone lines was placing a severe strain on communications. He eventually learned that Koreans believed that anything strung across a field was no longer being used, and could be "salvaged", but that, generally speaking, they would not interfere with lines properly strung along a road.[15]

In late August, C.S.M. Jim McDougall and S/Sgt. Dave Kerr were returned to Canada for officer training. Jim was replaced by C.S.M. Bob Henderson. Sgt. R.E. Cardwell was wounded on September 9th, when a shell landed in a crowd of refugees he was loading into a truck. Six Koreans were killed, and 24 others, including the Australian driver and guard, were wounded. During his evacuation, someone stole the Detachment's portable typewriter and the issue watch Cardwell was wearing; it took a good deal of administrative bickering to exempt Cardwell, or the unit, from having to pay for them.

The Detachments were deployed to watch the checkpoints at the bridges over the Imjin. Once, when he was on an inspection visit, Capt. Bert Sutcliffe lost his footing and fell into a Korean storage tank of human fertilizer for the paddy fields; for several days the Section much preferred his room to his company! On September 18th, Brig. Rockingham asked "Is it true that 1 F.S. condones the abuse of civilians by the Korean National Police?" The canard had been started by that well-known, clever, but erratic, war correspondent, Bill Boss. Eddie Corbeil's explanation that "the Section did not condone abuse of any kind, but that it was impossible to change the normal behaviour patterns of Korean policemen", mollified Rockingham.[16]

The Intelligence Summaries of the period mainly contained items of general information only: a review of Chinese tank strengths, enemy tactics, a box mine report and evaluation by Capt. Don G. McClelland, then I.O. of 57 Canadian Independent Field Squadron, R.C.E. On September 23rd, the Brigade senior officers were briefed on Operation COMMANDO, a I Corps operation involving five divisions and an initial advance of 6,000–8,000 yards, followed by a second one of 4,000–5,000 yards. The Canadian task was to push the enemy out of his winter line.[17] The Canadian assault, the second phase of the Divisional attack, was launched at 1100, October 4th, against objectives lying about 3,000 yards in front of the start line. They were taken late in the afternoon of the next day, after stiff resistance.

F.S. established a rear control line on September 28th, to halt the return of the evacuees and the prostitutes. They soon discovered that a serious black market was now very active. On October 5th and 6th, one Detachment found soldiers of the Korean Army in a service vehicle loaded with grain, a cow, and a calf. They confiscated them, and subsequent enquiries exposed a syndicate equipped with false identity papers and other essential documents.

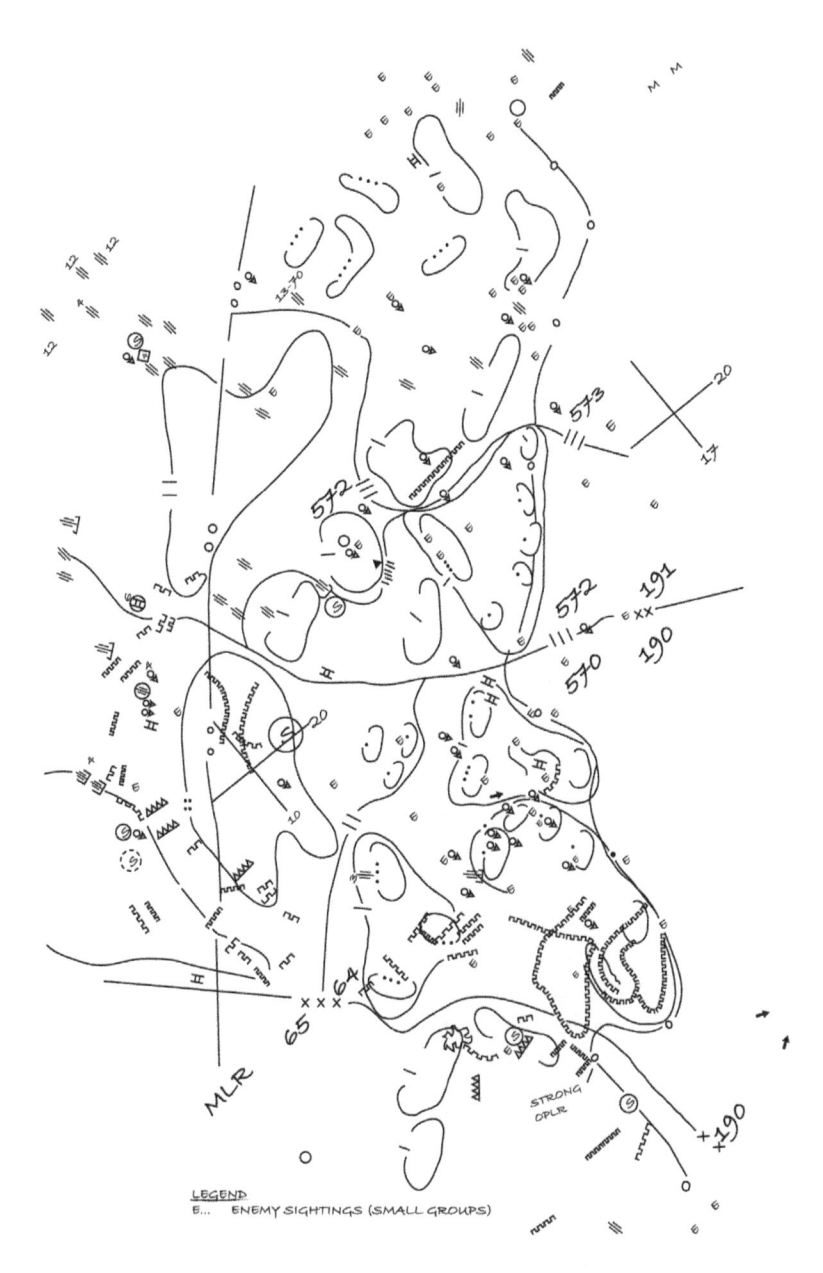

Trace of probable enemy dispositions issued by 1 Commonwealth Division, 1 October 1951. This would be inserted under a talc overlay, moved so that the co-ordinate references coincided with references drawn on the talc earlier, and transferred to the talc with grease pencil. The trace would then be removed, and deployments and map could be read together. (War Diary, 25 Canadian Infantry Brigade. This map was reproduced from a copy in the first edition of *Scarlet to Green*.)

By this time, Ottawa wished to reduce the Canadian contribution, and the War Office thought that it could get along alone. The Americans, who did not agree with either, made representations that resulted in a partial compromise. No. 1 Section was disbanded on December 15th, and its functions were absorbed by the rebuilt 904 British Section, and a small Canadian Detachment of a W.O.II and five N.C.O.s at 25 Brigade H.Q.[18] It was an unfortunate reduction, for the Commonwealth Divisional area alone had plenty of work for at least two Sections.

I(a) had managed to identify *570th Regiment, 190th Division*, located from the Sami-ch'on River to the Canadian boundary with 28th Brigade, and one battalion of the *572nd Regiment, 191st Division*, with *573rd Regiment* of *191st Division*, all of *64 Chinese Army*, located on 28 Brigade's front. During November, the Chinese launched a succession of counter-attacks against the Commonwealth Division. The first, against the R.C.R. on 2–3 November, was beaten off. On the 4th, 28 Brigade lost two hills to heavy attacks. By the end of November, the onset of winter weather brought a lull in the fighting, and only patrol activity continued.

During this period, peculiarities of reception made it possible to intercept Chinese radio traffic with normal battalion radio sets. "B" Company, 2 R.22e.R., had a Chinese-speaking operator, Pte. Morin. On November 29th, he overheard Chinese casualty returns and future patrol plans. On December 1st, the R.C.R. saw movement on Hill 227, and engaged it with mortar fire. The Chinese later reported six killed and 16 wounded, adding: "The enemy seemed very alert . . . have ammunition for at least two days and great firepower". A week later 2 R.22e.R. sent out a patrol to Hill 227. As soon as the patrol cleared the lines, at 1700, the Chinese reported: "We can see a patrol moving." The Chinese Commander reported a little later that he would be sending out a 44-man patrol. The R.22e.R. spotted it at 1745, and withdrew its own. Two other small encounters occurred later in the month. On January 1st, 1952, an enemy patrol was seen and fired on. The Chinese reports of the fall of shot helped the mortar commander to adjust until a concentration landed on the enemy patrol. Its commander was heard to say that he had suffered many casualties and had lost control of his men. Four days later a unit commander was heard discussing Canadian artillery strikes and sympathizing with his subordinate commanders: "I understand such a barrage, it is very exerting to advance in face of it."[19]

On December 13th, 2 R.C.R. captured a prisoner from the *570th Regiment*, who had been told that his Division would defend their present line for three or four months and would then launch the "Sixth Offensive". A battalion staff officer from *15th Army*, captured in October, had already provided a good deal of information on its build-up, which Commonwealth Division had tried to analyse. The most likely locale for the attack would be the area west of the

Sami-ch'on, with the Hill 227–Hill 355 sector as the next choice. Limited-objective attacks were also a possibility.[20]

On January 9th, Capt. Eddie Blais made an assessment of the enemy force to be expected, and followed it with an outline of the indicators that would signal an attack: increased resistance to Commonwealth patrols, increases in the number of enemy probes and reconnaissance patrols, air observation of known previously unoccupied assembly areas, enemy support train activity and movement forward, and forward displacement of enemy artillery and a resultant increase of harassing fire or obvious registration fire.[21]

In the next few weeks, these indicators were discussed in the context of information which Division issued in its weekly summaries of enemy capabilities. On January 13th, the Chinese intentions were "not solely defensive". On the 20th, he increased the supply dumps in the rear but not in the front. By the 31st, he was expected to "hold tenaciously any ground he now possesses or . . . gains". His order-of-battle details were not coming in quickly enough, and EUSAK ordered more aggressive patrolling. By February 12th, Capt. Blais was reporting a supply build-up and increased enemy patrolling, which he attributed to an exchange of areas between *191* and *192 Divisions*.[22]

When 25th Brigade went back into the line on March 9th, replacing 29th Brigade, the relief was not detected by the Chinese. On the 26th, the P.P.C.L.I. came under a fairly heavy attack, the preparations for which had not been detected. In fact, the Divisional assessment had read: "will continue to remain on the defensive. . . . There is reason to believe that he suspects or fears a U.N. offensive".[23] On April 15th, the First U.S. Marine Division took over the area west of the Sami-ch'on from 25th Brigade.

The rotation of the Brigade units brought new I.O.s and their staffs. Their efficiency suffered because the material needed for an Intelligence Office – clear acetate sheet, chinagraph pencils, tracing paper – was in short supply and could be obtained only with great difficulty. In the early days, maps had been scarce and poor, but an enterprising Brigade I.O. discovered that if he went down to the U.S. Engineer map unit in Seoul with a bottle or two of gin and some polite words, he could get unlimited supplies of the latest maps. Division was often short of maps. It never did discover the secret of the Brigade's success, but used it as a source, nevertheless.[24]

Brigade Intelligence kept three maps. One, at a scale of 1:50,000, covered the known or suspected enemy order-of-battle on the Divisional front and flanks. A second small-scale map showed the enemy order-of-battle across the Army front. A third showed the roads. Operations kept a 1:50,000 map, showing locations of friendly forces down to company level within the Division and the two flanking formations. The units received by scheduled despatch rider a daily summary of enemy activity opposite the Brigade front, prepared from information sent in by battalions from the Operations Log, and from relevant extracts from the reports of higher H.Q. Each battalion received its own copy of the daily Divisional Intelligence Report. Interrogation reports of P.W. taken by the Division were distributed, those from I Corps were not. By a special arrangement between Maj. Claude Searle and the S-2, reports were also exchanged with First Marine Division. The daily I U.S. Corps Periodic Intelligence Report (PIR) came to Brigade, but the daily EUSAK PIR was stopped by Division, "lest the Brigade I.O. be misled by the Intelligence jargon of so high a formation". Its excellent weather maps, however, were forwarded.

Intelligence worked very closely with Artillery. The latter's counter-bombardment reports came in daily, and H.Q.R.A. at Division sent a monthly report on enemy artillery activity that was described as "the most readable of the lot". 104 A.P.I.S., also at Division, provided Air Photo coverage. At least one sortie a week was made available to the battalions, and their reprint requests were filled speedily. 104 did not have enough staff to provide annotated photos and, although Brigade repeatedly asked for a Canadian Section, Ottawa always refused. In place of annotated photos, each company received defence overprints every three or four days; in an action that was relatively slow-moving, they were useful substitutes. The Army Security Agency provided the official Radio Intercept material.[25]

One source of valuable information was the group of Korean line-crossers known as Tactical Liaison Officers (TLOs). Their first recorded activity in the Canadian sector took place on November 11th, 1951, when five went out through the lines, to return two or three days later with information on enemy movements. In April, they observed and noted the movements of all enemy groups in defensive positions that had any relevance to Allied patrol tasks in the valley. The British Divisional F.S. N.C.O. responsible for them worked directly under the G.S.O.2 (Int), and could watch the Operational as well as the Security situation. Because they were physically located well forward, the TLOs could reconnoitre their routes, establish their links with the units through whose lines they would pass, and co-ordinate their timings with artillery and mortar activity. Their sorties required careful planning, and their successes depended "largely on the Staff-Sergeant's ability to choose his men well, keep them happy and plot their course with skill".[26]

The F.S. Detachment with 904 British Section used Canadian transport. Its W.O.II was initially located at Main Brigade H.Q. as an F.S. Liaison Officer, but since the Brigade I.O. did all the liaison that H.Q. thought necessary, he was returned to his Detachment. On May 8th, 1952, about 500 civilians who had wandered into R.22e.R. lines were concentrated near the battalion Command Post. While they were awaiting evacuation to 904, they were seen to be paying "very strict attention to the large camp sites and particularly to the new high-level bridge being built over the Imjin" – 904 was warned, and the Koreans were carefully interrogated.

Korean civilians were widely employed as labourers and houseboys, and it became increasingly clear that the enemy was infiltrating agents into the Allied units under the cover of these casuals. Canadian Brigade H.Q. had as many as 50 and, like many other H.Q., found that the various pass systems did not provide satisfactory control. On May 15th, Eighth Army ordered the numbers of casuals employed to be reduced, not because of Security considerations, but under pressure from the South Korean government, which needed them as soldiers. The Brigade was restricted to 30. Sgt. Masse and the Korean Military Police attached to the Detachment raided Main and Rear Brigade H.Q. on May 29th, and rounded them up. The 30 most essential men were given passes and sent back to work; the remainder were evacuated through 904 Section, and Brig. Bogert ordered that no others should be taken on. Food was issued only to those Koreans who could present a valid pass, and the Brigade area was frequently spot-checked. Since the I.O., Lieut. Bob Frost, had lost his own "boy", it was a waste of time to ask him to intercede for others.[27]

May and June were marked by an extensive patrolling program. I U.S. Corps directed that a prisoner was to be taken every three days. The order produced many arguments, a large number of casualties, and no very useful results. First Commonwealth Division knew what was opposite it; its troops dominated no-man's-land, and had literally to go into the heart of the enemy positions to get at potential prisoners. Brig. Bogert suspended the fighting patrols, and did just as well at lower cost. The Divisional Intelligence Summaries reported a brief flurry of enemy activity on May 30th: "Enemy vehicle sightings opposite the Brigade . . . at an all time high . . . over 200 . . . since May 19 and exact reason has not been discovered. . . . Some can be explained by the relief of *64 Chinese Communist Force Army* by . . . *40* . . . around 18 May, some by normal enemy supply moves and some by . . . stockpiling." By June 3rd, the enemy had visibly increased his communication trench network, but current assessments denied the possibility of attacks above battalion size. The report of a forthcoming offensive was considered to have been originated by an agent who was retailing the rumours current in his own somewhat restricted circle.[28]

The Canadians went into reserve on June 30th, and returned to the line on August 10th. In August, the Commonwealth Division decided to avoid duplication by combining its Operations and Intelligence Summaries. The first one that had any real importance was dated September 13th. It reviewed the summer activity: "No sooner had *40 CCF Army* replaced *64* than the enemy, confident the U.N. would not attack through the rainy season, withdrew his troops." *116 Division* of *39th Army* and *119 Division* of *40th* were in front of the Commonwealth Division. I Corps was predicting the introduction of *47th Army*, which would permit a further redeployment. The enemy had instituted a more aggressive patrolling policy which spread to the Commonwealth front as September approached and cost the Allies many prisoners. The new G.S.O.2

(Int), Maj. King McShane, predicted that this would increase with the dry weather, and commented on improvements in enemy patrol discipline. The first enemy prisoner since the return to the line was picked up by the R.C.R. on September 24th.[29]

A heavy artillery concentration in October damaged the 1 R.C.R. positions on Hill 355, and an attack on October 3rd was beaten off with difficulty. A Korean interpreter in the R.C.R. Command Post, monitoring the Chinese radio net, heard the Chinese commander report: "I am boxed in by artillery fire. I can't get reinforcements forward".[30] 25 Brigade went into reserve on November 2nd, during the rotation.

On November 18–19, 3 P.P.C.L.I. fought, in support of the Black Watch, the famous action of "The Hook", a massive Chinese attack that was beaten off at great cost. On November 29th, the Brigade went back into the line with the P.P.C.L.I. on the "Hook" itself. The left flank was in close contact with the enemy while, on the right, the lines were separated by the Sami-ch'on valley. December was quiet. Patrols were active, but contacts were few and the results minor. The Canadians again went into reserve on January 30th, 1953, to spend February in training. Courses and refreshers were arranged for the battalion Sections and the I.O.s on basic photo interpretation, observation post (O.P.) duties and techniques, and Security; lectures were given on Escape and Evasion. The Brigade went back into the line on April 8th.

The Chinese knew at once that the Brigade was back and, two days later, welcomed it in the first of many broadcasts, some of which were made by a woman announcer. These ranged from blandishment to outright threats of "We are going to attack you, you aren't going to live very long." They did not attack as expected on May 1st, but continued their vigorous patrolling, often to check the R.C.R. wire, and increased their artillery registration fire on the R.C.R. positions. One fighting patrol ran into the enemy while he was forming up to attack, and called for supporting fire. Unfortunately, their appeal could not be followed up, and the enemy penetrated an R.C.R. company area, destroying a platoon position and inflicting serious casualties. Many reports suggest that this particular attack was expected; the unfortunate platoon, however, had not been warned in advance.[31] Brig. Allard looked on it as a defeat, and the Brigade spent many weeks of rigorous study and training to prevent its repetition. They sited two-man O.P.s to observe and report enemy movement; the Brigade Intelligence Section plotted all the enemy positions on the forward slope of the hills across the valley that could overlook the Canadians; each tank crew of "A" Squadron, Lord Strathcona's Horse, was given an oblique air photograph and ordered to hit every target that was pinpointed on it. After the troops engaged, every heavy weapon that could be spared was fired at every sign of Chinese movement. The program, and the continuous and aggressive patrolling, kept the Chinese at arm's length for the rest of the period of hostilities.

On July 27th, an Armistice was signed. Next morning, as far as the eye could see in breadth and in depth, from the Canadian positions, the hills on the Chinese side were covered with Chinese and Korean soldiers, just standing. The impact of this human sea was excellent psychological warfare.[32] The Brigade withdrew to positions laid down in the agreement. The Divisional Ops/Int Summary was reduced to a weekly issue on August 28th. The Brigade I.O., Lieut. W.J. (Bill) Beaman, was ordered to interview returning P.W. to find out how Canadian prisoners had behaved, and to collect material for further study. Bill was not only totally inexperienced at this, but also he was given only a general outline of what he had to look for.[33]

The definitive assessment of the Korean War, from an Intelligence point of view, is contained in the Divisional Summary of September 12th, rewritten from EUSAK. It reviews the entire campaign in detail; for our purposes, only the conclusions are relevant:

A. The influence of politics on enemy strategy was clearly indicated by his actions preceding the truce negotiations. With utter disregard for human life he committed extravagant numbers of troops in limited objective attacks.... Apparently the enemy felt that he must give the impression that the U.N. accepted the truce under pressure and, at the same time, excused his heavy losses by propagandizing that the U.N. was attacking him.

B. As indicated ... the enemy ... is capable of resuming hostilities at any time. In addition he may take advantage of the truce by any or all of the following methods:
 - improvement of military capabilities such as: the rebuilding of airfields, increased stockpiling of critical items, training of replacements and a program of equipment standardization;
 - large-scale infiltration of South Korea leading to sabotage of friendly efforts to rebuild the Korean economy;
 - attempts at subversion of South Korean leaders and encouragement of insurgency.[34]

The Canadian Intelligence contribution to the Korean War is a story of small incidents only. From them, however, we can draw important conclusions. The staffing problem was not well handled. The first senior I.O., Capt. (Bucky) Buckingham, was not a career Intelligence officer. When he returned to Canada, no trained officer, Corps or otherwise, replaced him until Capt. Claude Searle arrived in the second contingent. At slight cost, a trained replacement could have been immediately available. Capts. Corbeil and Sutcliffe, who took the F.S. Section to Korea, were among the most experienced Intelligence officers in Canada; obviously the Counter-Intelligence task took priority. However, even an experienced Brigade I.O. was handicapped by not being given one of the most important tools of I(a), Photo Intelligence; even a small air photo detachment would have made the work very much easier.

Secondly, Ottawa never seemed to appreciate that the war was going to continue, and that it would have to arrange to replace and reinforce its Intelligence element. The whole time the Canadians remained in Korea, hordes of civilians, amongst whom line-crossers and infiltrators could easily conceal themselves, were able to wander more or less at will across the lines and through the unit rear areas. They had to be controlled, but the machinery to deal with them was weaker than it had been in the much less crowded and, from the espionage point of view, much less dangerous conditions of Europe.

Thirdly, H.Q. had not realized the extent to which skills could be lost in the five years that had elapsed since the end of the Second World War. Some training was given at the reopened summer school in Petawawa. But in Korea, Canadians were working with Americans, and the American system of Counter-Intelligence differed from the British pattern which Canadians had been following. Fortunately, there had been time to train them at the American School before the Section left. 2 F.S. (in Germany) were also given this training.

On the other hand, there were many useful lessons to be learned. All of them have great importance at the tactical level of Intelligence, and are relevant to the concept of a nuclear warfare that could involve smaller, more widely dispersed task forces designed to fight on their own. We have given examples of the essential requirement to control civilians. A simple method of monitoring enemy radio chatter was used. In the past, Intelligence had ignored this as being too difficult and time-consuming to be practical. Lt.-Col. Dextraze's R.22e.R. proved it could be done with great profit. Unfortunately, the technique was not adequately explored or expanded subsequently. Intelligence in Korea provided all the support it could, but it was not selected, trained, equipped, and supplied sufficiently well to do all the things it might have done.

CYPRUS

The immediate situation which brought about the U.N. involvement in Cyprus stemmed from an outburst of violence following a constitutional crisis in December 1963. As an interim measure, and with the agreement of the Turkish and Greek governments, Britain assumed responsibility for law and order. On March 4th, 1964, the United Nations Security Council approved the formation of an international peace-keeping force; Canada, Denmark, Finland, Sweden, and Ireland contributed troops to it.

The staff planning for the contingent occupied N.D.H.Q. for most of the early part of March. In D.M.I., Intelligence coverage of the country within the context of the Middle East had been adequate; in fact, it had been emphasized from late 1963. A good deal of information had been summarized, and issued not only to Planning staffs, but also, in simplified form, for the use of a field

23. Cyprus

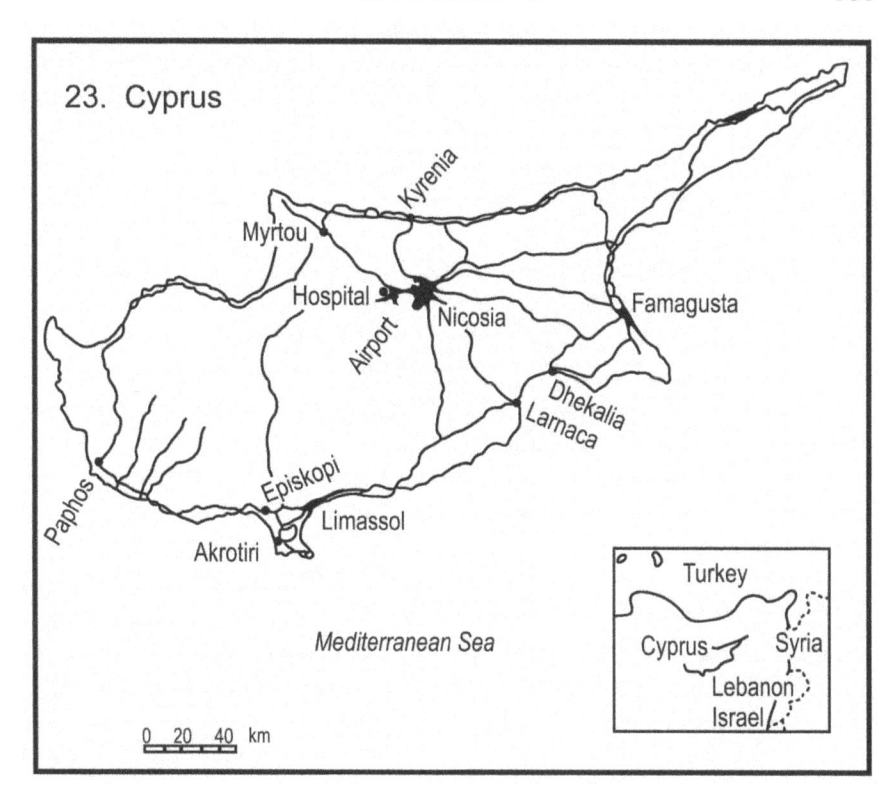

[Map of Cyprus showing: Kyrenia, Myrtou, Hospital, Airport, Nicosia, Famagusta, Dhekalia, Larnaca, Episkopi, Paphos, Akrotiri, Limassol, Mediterranean Sea. Inset map showing Turkey, Cyprus, Syria, Lebanon, Israel. Scale: 0–40 km.]

force. The approval for the Canadian Contingent was not granted until March 16th, but the advance party was already in the air en route for Cyprus before it was officially announced.[35] Canada provided a Headquarters, the 1st Battalion, R.22e.R. (the stand-by battalion for emergency duty at the time), and the Reconnaissance Squadron of the Royal Canadian Dragoons. The Contingent Commander was Col. E.A.C. Amy, D.S.O., O.B.E., M.C., C.D.

The island was divided into three Zones. The Canadians, with the Danes, and the Finns, each a battalion strong, were given responsibility for Nicosia Zone, under Brig. A. James Tedlie, D.S.O., C.D. He had a small Intelligence staff, a captain G.S.O.3 as Operations (B) Officer, and an Intelligence Platoon with its commander and one staff sergeant, two sergeants, and five corporals. Zone H.Q. was subordinate to United Nations Forces in Cyprus (UNFICYP). H.Q. UNFICYP produced a periodic Information Summary which described conditions on the island and drew appropriate conclusions from them. The Zone staff focused its attention on specific matters relating to its own tasks. Other items of information reported by observers in the Zone, were circulated within the Contingent and passed to H.Q. UNFICYP.

The Security Council Resolution was rewritten in an Operational Directive which described the Contingent's functions: "It is in the best interests of preserving international peace and security to use its best efforts to prevent a recurrence of fighting and, as necessary, to contribute to the maintenance and restoration of law and order and a return to normal conditions." The troops were clearly told that they had no power to search, arrest, detain, or interrogate any Cypriot; they were to act as mediators only, and to work through the Cypriot officials on the spot.[36]

They had to keep the two communities from physical contact, thus limiting the opportunities for violence, and creating a climate in which new disturbances would be unlikely to arise or, at least, in which they could be confined. In his role as Operations (B) Officer Capt. J.G.H. Ferguson asked the units for information on everything relevant to the forces of both sides, including the names, addresses, telephone numbers, and locations of all the leaders, including the Mukhtars (appointed village chiefs). He hoped that he would receive early warning of impending trouble so that steps could be taken to counter it.

The Platoon went through four rotations, each involving a reduction in size. The G.S.O.3 gave information to senior U.N. staffs, commanders, and distinguished visitors. The Platoon Commander understudied him, and dealt with the detailed activities of the platoon: maintenance of Operations maps and their supporting collation systems, drafting, photo reconnaissance tasks and reports, order-of-battle, and patrols. The successive G.S.O.3s had one thing in common. Not one had ever been a career Intelligence officer: few had any Intelligence training; most, however, had the wit to lean heavily on the Intelligence officers and N.C.O.s assigned to the Contingent.[37]

Lieut. Phil Bachand's group took over from a British Parachute Regiment, whose small Intelligence Section had amassed a great deal of information on both sides in the four months it had been there. All of it, however, had to be brought up to date in the light of the strengthening of the Greek-Cypriot force by an influx of mainland Greek officers disguised as students. The Section had to acquire a feel for the nature and extent of this build-up. It had to take to the air to discover the deployments and the concentrations. Phil's greatest administrative coup was his successful fight to get flying pay for his people for the hours they spent as observers; but he was also highly regarded professionally for the high standard of credibility he established in the eyes of his Commander and of H.Q. UNFICYP, through his application of sound Intelligence practices.

Lieut. Ken Edmond's Section took over from Phil Bachand. Ken's death of a heart attack on Christmas Day 1964 was a great loss. S/Sgt. Ken Young commanded the Section until Lieut. Roy Girling arrived in February 1965. In the meantime, 1 Canadian Guards had replaced the R.22e.R. This battalion took a long time to learn that a speedy flow of information was as vital in peace-keeping as in war. In one incident, Ken Young and a Canadian Artillery officer on staff went to Myrtou Monastery, where a regiment of Greek-Cypriot 25-pounder artillery pieces had been reported. With the Guards Company Commander

Operations (B) Platoon, Nicosia Zone, Cyprus, April 1965; standing, from left: Cpl. R.L. Holding, Sgt. R.N. Helm, Lieut. R.E. Girling, Capt. D.P. Ludlow, Sgt. D.P. Mattocks, Cpl. E.R. Smith; kneeling, front: S/Sgt. J.J. Dinius, Cpl. S.E. Auld, Cpl. J.J.M.P. Charbonneau, Cpl. I.W. Arnold. (K.G. Young collection/Canadian Forces School of Military Intelligence, Kingston/Canada. Dept. of National Defence)

responsible for the area, they paid an unsuccessful visit to the Greek Regimental Commander. On their return, they visited the Company Command Post, where they were shown a large folder of information on the local situation. Much of the detail it contained was invaluable, but it had never been passed to Battalion H.Q. for collation. Fortunately for Nicosia Zone, the Battalion Reconnaissance Platoon's commander, 2/Lieut. Sam Mechback, actively pursued his role, and was a good, though not a complete, source of information.

The Section used light aircraft very extensively, spending up to two hours a day, seven days a week, checking new positions and improvements to old ones. These had an important relation to the convoys on the Nicosia–Kyrenia road, which ran through the heaviest concentrations of the island's Turkish-Cypriot population. To enable the service to operate on a once-a-day-each-way schedule, the Contingent had to obtain daily information on all Turkish positions, no matter how small or insignificant they seemed. Once identified and recorded

Lieut. K.E. Edmonds beside Whirlwind helicopter, Kokkina, Cyprus, 6 October, 1964. Below air reconnaissance photo taken over the Nicosia Zone by Operations (B) on 20 September, 1964. (K.G. Young collection/Canadian Forces School of Military Intelligence, Kingston/Canada. Dept. of National Defence)

on a map, each new site had to be negotiated before the convoy could depart. The system operated for years, and although there were incidents, there were no serious clashes.

The Section tried hard to locate the equipment that the Greek-Cypriots were importing. Sgt. Don Mattocks, following a group of medium tanks from Famagusta to Nicosia in his jeep, had one train its main armament on him. He kept waiting for the bang; fortunately for him, the action was only a gesture. He later learned that their ammunition had not then been delivered. He was not nearly as worried, however, as was the Commander of the Austrian Field Hospital, who found his compound surrounded by laagering tanks and armoured personnel carriers. Capt. Don Ludlow, Operations (B), and S/Sgt. Ken Young were fired on when they were flying over an area in a light aircraft looking for surface-to-air missiles that had been reported. No hits were scored, but the British sergeant pilot loudly declared that this was not what he had joined up for, and took them home at speed. The last Detachment, under Lieut. Doug Whitley, was withdrawn in August 1965.[38]

H.Q. Nicosia Zone was also closed in August 1965. Since then, Intelligence in the Canadian Contingent has been handled by the I.O.s of the serving battalions, much as the function was performed in the static conditions of the First World War.* Information on what is happening around the island is passed down by H.Q. UNFICYP, and is handled directly by the Operations staff in the small Contingent H.Q. Selected items are briefed at the Commander's Conferences and by direct liaison. I.O.s are required to know their area as well as, if not better than, the natives themselves. For, as in all Internal Security operations, emergencies seldom appeared unannounced; events take considerable time to develop. An alert I.O., who encourages not only his own staff but also the men on the ground to watch all developments, will usually be able to pinpoint impending trouble.

The significance of Intelligence in peace-keeping operations was outlined by Gen. Tedlie in an address to the Air Command and Staff College in May 1970:

> When one has no real enemies, and that must be the aim of all peace-keeping forces, it may seem strange to talk of the necessity for a complex Intelligence organization organic to the Force. But without one, the troops' hands are tied and they cannot carry out effective work. Unless a United Nations Commander has accurate and timely information about the various armed bands involved in the war he is striving to prevent, he cannot position his forces in the most effective manner. What is true of the military situation is equally true of the political situation and the commander must also have access to up to date information on political moves by either side which will have a bearing on future military action. As in a fighting war, so it is in a peace-keeping operation; you must

---

* Second edition note: Canada withdrew its battalion-sized contingent from UNFICYP in 1993.

have an intimate knowledge of the commanders on both sides. You must study their tactical methods, their personality and what is motivating their actions.

Air reconnaissance is a must if one is to keep abreast of the tactical situation; the movement of large bodies of troops from one area to another must be known to the United Nations Commander if his interposition is to be effective in preventing an armed clash. But air reconnaissance is not enough and must be supplemented by ground reconnaissance carried out with boldness and efficiency.

All United Nations personnel must be part of the information gathering team. We found that our officers on harvesting patrols and economic projects often brought us information which allowed us to intervene. . . .

. . . the Mukhtars . . . of the various villages were excellent sources of Intelligence on which to base our work. Using these means we frequently found it possible to restore . . . conditions by putting small standing patrols in a village, thus allaying the fear of attack.

In addition to these means of gathering Intelligence, there is a requirement for a well-trained staff charged with collation and dissemination of . . . information. The staff must contain skilled photo-interpreters and be equipped with a speedy, secure means of getting the information to those who must take action on it.[39]

In U.N. operations, the contingents and their composition are all very much under the control of U.N. Headquarters in New York. The present practice is to send Canadians where their technical skills can fill the greatest need and to put less technically-skilled troops on the Cease-Fire Lines. This means that Canadian troops are less likely to find themselves in the middle of a confrontation. But the possibility that they will have to face fire cannot be ignored. The Commander of the Canadian Force bears a great responsibility, regardless of the role his troops are given. With no Intelligence capability under his control, he could be seriously handicapped in his decision-making. The Intelligence organization at National Defence H.Q. should therefore maintain a most careful watch on any situation requiring a Canadian presence abroad. If a Canadian force is ever again to play a direct part in separating opposing sides, it would be wise to ensure that it is provided with an Intelligence support that is both skilled and adequately equipped to obtain and to process the information it will need.

21.
THE RESERVES

The original plan for the Militia Intelligence that Col. Murray envisaged was not carried out. Instead, Militia Companies were formed across Canada. No. 1 in Montreal and No. 2 in Toronto started serious recruiting in 1948; No. 3 in Halifax and No. 4 in Vancouver were formed as a result of representations made by C.M.I.A. in 1950; No. 5 was formed in Winnipeg in 1951. No. 6 Company in Edmonton started as a detachment of No. 4 Company (which had another detachment in Victoria) and became a full Company in 1961. A burden common to all was a system of administration which was geared to the full-time activities of Regular units. This posed a serious burden on part-time staffs which rarely had the experience or training needed. The lucky ones found an ex-Regular, and arrangements were eventually made to have these individuals work full-time during the day, as well as during training nights. Good and loyal service made them valued members of the unit and a vast debt of gratitude is owed them. Wise Company Commanders spent time at the local Regular Headquarters, making friends with the Intelligence staff, to solve knotty problems of administration as well as training. By and large the Companies were among the most efficient of the Militia units.

Their training program consisted initially of a summer concentration with the Regulars. Policy was decided in consultation between D.M.I. (O&T) and the Director of Military Training. Winter training was given by Command and Area Instructional Cadres and Staffs. Training was basic and practical, with a good deal of reliance on the procedures of the past. Although Capt. Alphee Bake was appointed Intelligence Doctrine Officer at the Canadian School of Military Intelligence in 1956, and there were occasional attempts in other quarters to formulate Canadian Intelligence doctrine, these efforts were never sufficiently imaginative, practical, or significant. Consequently, there was little real change in the procedures.

Nevertheless, imagination and enthusiasm led to interesting unit exercises. On one occasion, No. 1 Company managed a very creditable counter-sabotage exercise in a new railroad yard in Montreal. No. 2 Company specialized in Escape and Evasion exercises with the R.C.A.F. Auxiliary. All Companies taught the Intelligence specialties, Combat Intelligence, Photo-Reading, Field Security, and language training. All participated in local Militia exercises and many took part in local Militia activities outside their units. Many went to the annual Militia Summer Camps, and as many as possible came to Camp Borden for the summer concentrations at the C.S. of M.I.

Militia Summer Concentration parade, 25 June 1967. Recalling historical ties with the Corps of Guides, the C.Int.C. flag was carried onto the parade square at Canadian School of Military Intelligence in Camp Borden by Lieut. E.J. Constantinedes, who was dressed in appropriate Corps of Guides uniform. (Photo collection Canadian Forces School of Military Intelligence, Kingston/Canada. Dept. of National Defence)

A simple trades structure permitted the Militia N.C.O. to qualify for extra pay. Each progression was divided into "Blocks" which required a year's training. Completion of a "Block" gave a small financial reward, while completion of sufficient "Blocks" to qualify as a tradesman gave the man the Regular pay level. Common-to-all-arms courses provided the required general qualifications. In 1959 and 1960, the emphasis turned to training for National Survival (Civil Defence) and, although there was tacit understanding that there was an Intelligence role, no doctrine was produced which clearly defined it. In consequence, there was little real use made of the skills available.

The amalgamation of the Regular Intelligence component with the Provost led inevitably to the amalgamation of their Militia components as well. Although there was a good deal of administrative confusion surrounding the arrangements, which led to an adverse impact on morale and hence unit strengths, most of the units had joined the local Service Battalions by the end of 1969. Much was made of the fact that Intelligence managed to keep a larger proportion of pre-amalgamation strength than many units. What was ignored was the fact that its strength had already been cut from an establishment total of about 680 (the actual strength was slightly better than half that) to a figure less than two-thirds of that enrolment.[1]

THE CANADIAN MILITARY INTELLIGENCE ASSOCIATION (C.M.I.A.)

The C.M.I.A. was open to former officers of the Canadian Armed Services and the armed forces of the Commonwealth who had experience in Intelligence or an interest in its activities. Its aim was to further the interests and to promote the efficiency of Military Intelligence. This was achieved through its representation at the annual meetings of the Conference of Defence Associations, and through direct assistance to the Militia, the Regular Force training establishments and, on occasion and under strict control, to individuals. It had no connection with the Corps of Guides Association, which had disappeared in 1926.

The C.M.I.A. began with informal meetings held in Montreal and Toronto. On February 16th, 1946, a dinner meeting for 32, held at the Queen's Hotel in Montreal, decided to form a permanent organization called the "Canadian Intelligence Corps Association, Montreal Branch". Membership was open to all who had served with Intelligence at home or abroad. Noel G. Ashby was installed as President, J.L. Tarte as Secretary, P. Weisman as Treasurer, and E.G. "Paddy" Doak and M. Dubuc as Executive Members. Maj. G. Grenier, G.S.O.2 (Int) M.D. 4, was appointed Military Liaison Officer between the Association and N.D.H.Q. On February 25th, Noel Ashby told Col. W.A.B. Anderson what had been done, and that future contacts were planned between Montreal and former C.Int.C. members in other cities.[2]

Col. Anderson first advised that they wait until the postwar Army structure was decided upon, and, later, that official recognition could not be granted until a parent Regular Corps had been formed. In July, Basil Foreman, who had replaced Tarte as Secretary, told the D.M.I. that the members (now calling themselves the "Provisional Canadian Intelligence Association") were prepared to form an unofficial association if necessary. Col. Anderson replied that there was no reason why an informal group should not be formed. He also offered to seek formal authority if they wished it.[3]

In Toronto, there were unofficial discussions between John M. Gray, George MacGillivray, Capt. Benny Greene, Tom L. Savage, and Jack M. Morehouse. The first general meeting was held on November 1st, 1946, with 70 present. Lt.-Col. G.M.C. "Spike" Sprung attended as the D.M.I. representative, and Noel Ashby represented Montreal. Voluntary contributions of $35.86 provided a small working capital, and a temporary executive of J.E. Hopkins, George MacGillivray, J.E. McEachern, Bert Sutcliffe, and G.M. Paulin was elected, with Benny Greene and Ward Binkley made honorary members.

Funds were obtained from D.M.I., and Maj. K. Reed, then responsible for administration, advised that the group had to get a charter from the Secretary of State and to make a formal request through Army Headquarters to the Conference of Defence Associations (C.D.A.). If that body approved, funds would be included in the D.N.D. Annual Estimates. Col. Peter Wright was asked to prepare the application. The official founders were: W.H. Broughall, F.K. Doody, T.C. Fairley, J.M. Gray, J.W.G. Macdougall, C.D. Kingsmill, G.B. MacGillivray, D.R. Morrice, J.K. Motzfeldt, W.W. Murray, G.M. Paulin, E.H. Smith, and G.F. Rogers.

The executive then discovered that the Association could no longer be an all ranks group if it were to be a member of the C.D.A. Reluctantly, the break was made. On December 10th, Col. Wright asked for approval of the name "Canadian Military Intelligence Association"; it was granted on January 8th, 1948. The Letters Patent were approved on June 14th and, after a number of exchanges, the C.M.I.A. was "a Body Corporate and Politic without share capital for the purpose of carrying on in more than one province of Canada . . . to further the interests and promote the efficiency of Military Intelligence in the Canadian Army".[4]

The first official general meeting was held in Toronto on November 20th, 1948. It confirmed Col. Wright as President and Col. Murray as Vice-President, and added Eric Acland as Honorary Secretary-Treasurer, W.H. Broughall as his Assistant, and 10 Directors. C.D. Kingsmill chaired a Competition Committee to recommend prizes for the Reserve Force. An advisory committee under W.H. Broughall, with J.W.G. Macdougall and G.F. Rogers, investigated the possibility of increasing the number of Intelligence units and ensuring that all aspects of Intelligence were covered in the training programs. A similar committee for the Regular Force comprised Col. Murray, J.W.G. Macdougall, and Alex Wygard. The by-laws were amended to permit members of the Active Force, the R.C.N., the R.C.A.F., and the Commonwealth countries to become Associate members on payment of a nominal $1.00 annual fee.[5]

The C.M.I.A. was accepted into the Conference of Defence Associations at its twelfth Annual Meeting, December 2–4, 1948. Intelligence Delegates were Col. Jock Murray, Peter Wright, Eric Acland, and George MacGillivray, who served on four different Resolution Committees. The C.M.I.A. has since submitted a number of resolutions, including those which, as we have seen, resulted in the formation of Militia Intelligence Companies. Russian Language training for the Militia, originally instituted as a result of the 1950 C.M.I.A. Annual Meeting, was dropped in 1959 for economy reasons. A 1961 C.M.I.A.-sponsored resolution assisted in getting it reinstated.

The details of the trophies and prizes offered by the C.M.I.A. appear in Annex 8. Competition for them was keen, and the members of all the Companies concerned, as well as individuals who competed for the more personal items, worked hard to win the distinction they represent. After Unification and the disappearance of the Militia Companies as separate entities, only those prizes which were appropriate were still awarded.

No. 4 Intelligence Training Company with trophies won during Summer Camp 1958. The Crerar Trophy (centre) was awarded annually to the Intelligence Training Company which achieved the highest efficiency rating in the training year. (Photo collection Canadian Forces School of Military Intelligence, Kingston/Canada. Dept. of National Defence)

No. 5 Intelligence Training Company, Winnipeg, with trophies won during Summer Camp 1967. The Insinger Trophy (left), named in honour of Capt. Ted Insinger, killed at Dieppe, 19 August 1942, was awarded annually to the Intelligence Training Company which achieved the greatest progress in the training year in comparison with the standard achieved in the previous year. Also shown are members of the Canadian Women's Army Corps, who performed intelligence training and work as integral members of these Reserve units. (Photo collection Canadian Forces School of Military Intelligence, Kingston/Canada. Dept. of National Defence)

In addition to the morale and political support provided by the C.M.I.A. through the C.D.A., the suggestions passed to A.H.Q., to the Companies, and to individuals through personal contact, and the incentives to competition provided through prizes, the Association gives tangible assistance. Both No. 1 and No. 2 Companies received grants to help them get established. No. 5 Company received a substantial grant to help it rebuild after the Minto Armouries fire in 1956. Lesser sums have been given to the Companies and to the C.S. of M.I.

General H.D.G. Crerar was the first Honorary Colonel Commandant, his appointment taking effect February 3rd, 1949. His advice and assistance during the early years was invaluable. His appointment was renewed in 1954, and again in 1959. In late 1962, new regulations changed his title to Colonel Commandant. Ill health prevented him from taking a very active part in C.M.I.A. affairs during the latter part of his appointment, and Intelligence said a reluctant good-bye to him in February 1964. He was replaced by Col. Peter Wright.

Gen. H.D.G. "Harry" Crerar,
C.H., C.B., D.S.O., C.D.,
P.C., Honorary Colonel
Commandant of the C.Int.C.,
1949–1964. (Photo collection
Canadian Forces School
of Military Intelligence,
Kingston/Canada. Dept. of
National Defence)

MESSAGE FROM
THE COLONEL COMMANDANT

20 Aug 1963

To All Members—The Canadian Intelligence Corps

The formation of the Canadian Intelligence Corps took place some twenty-one years ago. It has thus now formally "come of age". Its vital activities, however, date from the beginning of recorded military history.

No Commander can successfully fight a battle by his troops without accurate, timely information about the enemy and of the terrain over which his troops must fight. In such matters, I was never "let down" by the members of what is now The Canadian Intelligence Corps in the battles by the formations and units of the Canadian Army in 1944-45.

HDG CRERAR
General
Colonel Commandant
The Canadian Intelligence Corps

During Gen. Crerar's second term, he arranged for affiliation with the British Intelligence Corps. Maj.-Gen. F.H.N. Davidson, C.B., D.S.O., M.C., Col. Commandant of the British Corps, had contacted the Canadian Army Liaison Establishment in London asking about the possibilities of such affiliation. The administrative details were completed by February 21st, 1955, effective from the previous January 25th. Gen. Davidson offered a shield with the British Corps crest as a memento. Gen. Crerar suggested that he could best maintain the link with Gen. Davidson, while the C.M.I.A. worked with the Intelligence Corps Old Comrades Association. The British later sent a gift of a silver replica of their own centrepiece. The Canadian response was a Corps Flag. Both are now housed at the respective Training Centres. Gen. Davidson visited Canada in September 1956, and was entertained by the D.M.I., the School, and No. 2 and No. 4 companies. In 1963, to mark the 21st anniversary of the creation of the C.Int.C., the British Corps also sent a silver cup. It is regrettable that the Canadian Corps was never gracious enough to ascertain what dates or occasions were important to the British, and to acknowledge these occasions with some significant memento.

In March 1962, badges were exchanged with the Australian Army Intelligence Corps. Actually, the links with Australian Intelligence are very old. A senior Australian officer, Gen. Bridges, C.B., visiting Canada before the First World War, was impressed with the Corps of Guides, and took back to Australia with him much of the detail of its founding and activities. Using this as a pattern, he was instrumental in the establishment of the Australian Army Intelligence Corps on December 6th, 1907.

From the beginning of his tenure, Col. Wright took an active and personal interest in the Association. He set up the Col. Commandant's Advisory Council and the Col. Commandant's Fund. The latter was used for such Corps projects as expanding and improving the *C.Int.C. Quarterly*, subsidizing the purchase of Corps regalia for the C.S. of M.I. Kit Shop, and the inauguration of a series of annual "Crerar" dinners. Named in honour of the first Col. Commandant, these dinners were prestige occasions with guest lists which included distinguished Canadian and foreign government and military personalities. Four dinners were held: in 1965, in Toronto; in 1966, in Ottawa; in 1967, in Winnipeg; and in 1968, in Montreal. Col. Wright also instituted the Colonel Commandant's Award; this was given at infrequent intervals to individuals who, in the Colonel Commandant's opinion, had made a significant contribution to Intelligence.

Regrettably, in 1965 the C.M.I.A.'s close liaison with the Regular Force was disrupted by the onset of Integration. The first blow was the disappearance of D.M.I. (Organization and Training), which had always provided the channel for communication with the D.M.I. The next occurred in 1967, when the Regular Force C.Pro.C., the C.Int.C., and Air Force Security elements were combined under the newly-created Security Branch. This was followed in 1969 by the absorption of the C.Int.C. Militia Companies by the Security Platoon of the Service Battalions.

These changes gradually transformed Intelligence, in whose interest C.M.I.A. had originally been established, into a new organization with somewhat different aims and approaches to Intelligence problems. In particular, these changes placed the Colonel Commandant in a somewhat anomalous position as the head of a Corps which had, in effect, ceased to exist. When the matter was first raised, the Advisory Council of the C.M.I.A. met, and Col. Wright sent constructive submissions to the C.G.S. with regard to the effect of Integration. He offered then, and on a number of later occasions, to discuss the matter in Ottawa. It subsequently appeared that the submissions could not be found in Ottawa, and no invitation to discuss the future of the Corps was made before that future had already been decided. It happened that the end of the Colonel Commandant's extended term coincided with his complete frustration. As soon as he was no longer Colonel Commandant, he wrote the Minister in the strongest terms. The Minister supported his officers and the matter ended.

In view of the record of the C.M.I.A., a letter from Col. Jock Murray to Col. Felix Walter in November 1945 is particularly prophetic. In it Col. Murray said:

> I am rather keen that when we all get back to the bowler that we should have a continuous civilian association for Intelligence Corps personnel and non-Corps personnel who are engaged in Intelligence work. I envisage something along the lines of the old Defence Associations . . . an Intelligence Association. . . . It seems to me that with the whittling down of Army appropriations which must inevitably come in the years of peace, Intelligence will once again get the cold shoulder as it did in the pre-war years. A defence Association devoted to Intelligence would prevent the utter annihilation which might well threaten this a few years from now.[6]

Through its example, interest, and support, the C.M.I.A. clearly filled the role envisioned by Col. Murray. Integration forced a review of its status. A Security Services Officers Association, composed of Regular officers who were mostly Military Police, expressed a desire to amalgamate with the C.M.I.A. This was impossible under the C.D.A. regulations. The C.Int.C. Regular Officers found themselves under pressure to support the new Association. The C.M.I.A. agreed to meet the Association in a compromise that would change its name to the Canadian Intelligence and Security Association (C.I.S.A.) without changing its purpose, which would reflect the new Security entity, and which would provide ex-Provost officers with access to the C.D.A. It did so in 1972, despite the fact that its constitution, reinforced by a specific amendment in 1971, had already and specifically opened its doors to any "who profess an interest in Intelligence", which of course included Security.

At the time of writing, there have been only a few attempts by ex-Provost to join the C.I.S.A. There has indeed been a marked falling away of former supporters of the C.M.I.A., who do not approve the change and do not feel they can support what, to them, has been C.M.I.A.'s acquiescence in its own demise. But the C.M.I.A./C.I.S.A. has continued to play a part, though muted, in helping to support Intelligence. Without it the Intelligence world would have been a much more difficult and lonely place in which to work. Without it this History would not have been published.*

---

* Second edition note: In the wake of the establishment of a tri-Service Intelligence Branch in 1982, a Canadian Forces Intelligence Branch Association (CFIBA) was formed in 1985 in parallel with CISA. CISA eventually changed its name to Canadian Intelligence and Military Police Association (CIMPA); however, this organization legally dissolved in 2011. In 2013, the CFIBA changed its name to the Canadian Military Intelligence Association, officially inheriting the proud legacy of this Association, which has played a significant advocacy role in the development and professionalization of the Intelligence function in the Canadian Forces.

L'ENVOI

In the sixty years between 1903 and 1963, warfare became increasingly sophisticated. Its pace moved from that of the horse and the marching man to that of the supersonic aircraft and missile. The soldier of a modern army uses weapons capable of delivering destruction undreamed of by his grandfather. The vehicles that carry him to battle, most of them armoured to protect him against enemy fire, are capable of movement across rough ground at speeds that would have been considered good on paved roads even thirty years ago. The potential destructive force of nuclear weapons has forced on each senior commander a cruel dilemma. To escape this threat, he must deploy his force in small battle groups, which do not stay in one place long enough for the enemy to deliver a nuclear strike on them. Yet this deployment is vulnerable; these isolated units can be defeated, one by one, by superior forces.

Command and control of troops in the field has had to change to keep abreast of these new tactical requirements. Unlike the narrow battlefield of history on which orders and reports were slowly passed by hand, flag, or lamp, information and orders must now be transmitted instantaneously over enormous distances. Obviously, Intelligence, as part of the command and control system, has the same problems. But the basic division of the function into Intelligence (a) and (b) – the need to learn about an enemy, and the equal importance of protecting one's secrets from him – remains unaltered. In fact, given the nature of war, the gap in relative importance between each branch has probably narrowed.

Because of security restrictions this history has not dealt with techniques in detail. I have, however, tried to describe Intelligence (a) in sufficient detail within the limits of those restrictions to convey the fact that it has reflected the nature of the operations it was intended to support. Before the First World War, Intelligence support was geared to the open, horse-drawn warfare of the North-West Rebellion and the South African War – the location and identification of the enemy, the nature of the terrain between the two forces, and the availability of foodstuffs and water. Maps were poor, or non-existent, local guides were scarce and unreliable, and geographical information was as important as information on the enemy.

The First World War saw the decline in importance of geographical data, except in the peripheral campaigns. The pace of war became slower, and areas of Intelligence responsibility – the tactical responsibility of the commander – became narrower and shallower but, at the same time, more detailed. Because tactical changes evolved slowly and in fairly predictable form, it was necessary for Intelligence staffs to organize their data-handling so that comparisons could be made through the period of those developments. It was important to identify and to locate new enemy formations; the casualty rate among units in the line was such that new, fresh units could materially affect planning.

During the Second World War the requirement to study enemy defences in detail was important during the initial stages of a campaign and in situations where the enemy had been given time to establish a fixed position. And the German Army was very proficient at developing defences. The actual combat was more mobile than it had been twenty-five years previously. Early and accurate reporting of enemy units and, particularly, their support weapons was essential. The Korean War initially was a mobile conflict, and reporting followed the Second World War methods, but it gradually became a semi-siege campaign and techniques reverted to those of 1918. The peacekeeping missions in which the Canadian Army has played such a large part since 1955 have also required the 1918 techniques. There are many similarities between the Trench Logs of pre-1918 and the Post Reports of the present day.

The extension of the battlefield and the acceleration of movement upon it, envisaged in all concepts of full-scale war, has forced Intelligence (a) to develop new techniques for collecting, storing, evaluating, and disseminating information. There is more to watch, enemy forces can change location more quickly, and the capability of thwarting mechanical methods of gaining information is greater. At the same time, the penalty for mistakes, implicit in the nuclear threat, is infinitely greater than at any time in the past. Command decisions must be made, and implemented, quickly. More than ever before, accurate, complete and timely Intelligence is essential to effective decision-making.

Computers are assuming the laborious task of recording data on cards, of retrieving information from them, and of making traces and overlays to record changes in enemy activities. Electronic technology can provide devices which relay infrared radar, or optical images of enemy activity, while it is taking place, to command posts located considerable distances from the event. Computer records of the reports can be made and compared instantaneously with previous data, and action can be taken on them as soon as a decision is made. These devices are expensive, both in their initial costs and in their costs of operation. They require skilled manpower to operate and maintain them. They are invaluable tools, but they are vulnerable to counter-measures. And they do not replace the human intellect, sharpened by experience and training, in reading an enemy's intentions in the light of his known capabilities and tactical doctrines.

The competition between threat and defence in the field of Counter-Intelligence has also seen sophisticated developments, both in aids to espionage and in methods to combat them. It is often argued that, with the development of sophisticated radio techniques and satellite surveillance, the requirement for the spy inside an enemy country is dwindling. However, technical methods are not infallible. Each has quite significant technical handicaps which can limit its usefulness at critical times. More important, neither can obtain information on what is being considered, or planned, or set in motion. Such vital information as this can only be obtained from people. There is still plenty of scope for the spy.

Sophistication in the Counter-Intelligence field is not limited to equipment. The appeal of propaganda, and its dissemination, has been more carefully orchestrated than ever before, thanks in large measure to the raising of educational standards and to developments in mass international communication. The radical threat posed by the Communist, Fascist, and Nazi Parties of the 1920s and 1930s was perhaps less than was believed in some quarters. However, it did exist, with the respective national leaders demonstrably and cynically using their followers as tools to further the aims of their foreign masters. Their appeals were crude by today's standards and fairly readily identifiable. Those of the present time are much more subtle and plausible, appealing more directly to normal human aspirations. In the West, there is particular appeal to the idealistic intellectual who, because he is usually articulate, can serve, often totally innocently, as a mouthpiece for subversion.

Subversion has served as a vehicle for both espionage and sabotage, and undoubtedly will do so again. A disaffected official can, either directly or indirectly, facilitate the efforts of the spy and saboteur. If the fundamental aim of any hostile power is to reduce an opponent's will to fight to the point where no resistance will be offered, what more inexpensive and rewarding way is there than by manipulating his officials' intellectual fibre? Within the Canadian Army, that threat has long been recognized. For obvious reasons, the success of the measures designed to protect the troops against it cannot be accurately determined, much less described. But we have every reason to believe that, since the war, the Canadian Army has been relatively free from subversive influence in those areas where it could cause damage. However, human weaknesses, which can be exploited, remain, and evidence of them must be scrutinized.

The developments outlined in the foregoing paragraphs suggest that, in order to deal with the highly sophisticated and modern technologies of Intelligence, a highly skilled, trained, and professional Intelligence group must exist. The history of the Canadian Army does not engender confidence that this is so. Though there was a force committed to the role prior to 1914, and despite the fact that many of its members served, some of them with distinction, in the function, postwar reorganization removed the dedicated Intelligence capability. That separation of unit and function persisted until the outbreak of hostilities in the Second World War. Lack of knowledge, of understanding, and of experience, though not confined to the Canadian Forces, cost Canada dearly. By good fortune, and due to the efforts of many inspired, dedicated, and hardworking officers and men, the gap was filled before First Canadian Army met its severest tests. But it was a near thing, which quite easily could have gone wrong under the strain of reverses. In 1945, it looked as if the lessons learned so painfully were again to be forgotten. Fortunately, the foresight of Col. W.W. Murray and

Lt.-Col. Eric Acland salvaged the framework of an Intelligence system. That it was simply the framework became only too apparent five years later.

The experiences of the Canadian Army Intelligence community in the 20 years after 1945 underline a less obvious lesson – that unless a military entity is staffed by people who are intellectually and emotionally committed to it, it will not survive. Col. Murray won only part of the battle, and perhaps not the most important part. The fact that Intelligence was considered to be a Staff Directorate, and hence open to all comers, unlike the Arms Directorates – Armour, Artillery, and Infantry – meant that its few senior vacancies were often filled by officers with little or no real interest in the development and preservation of a separate body to handle Intelligence. Similarly, the high incidence of non-professionals diluted the expertise of the few. This, in turn, adversely affected the Intelligence product and hence the Directorate's international reputation. Fortunately, there were occasions when individuals, or combinations of individuals, reversed the trend. But our record could so easily have been better and more consistent.

This book deliberately has not attempted to describe the history of the post-Integration Intelligence scene. It is the author's personal belief, based on first-hand knowledge, that the training and temperament required to make a good Military Policeman are not the same as the training and temperament that make a good Intelligence, or Security, Officer. In this regard Canada is the only country in NATO which has attempted to combine the two. Perhaps a more efficient system would have been to revert to the Corps of Guides and make one of the Armoured Regiments into a combined Intelligence and Reconnaissance arm.

But this is retrospection. The political considerations of the early 1960s dictated the existing situation. As usual in the Canadian Defence Department, the need to balance a tight budget against ever-increasing demands dictates organization. It may well be that the survival of the three functions, Police, Security, and Intelligence could only be attained through combination. As time goes on, the realities of domestic and world situations will force the development of the necessary specialist expertise. Amateurs can do the work, but professionals do it better and, in the long haul, more cheaply – and the lives of Canadians could depend upon the results of that work.

It is unlikely that Canada will ever go to war on its own; we all hope that she will never have to go to war again, even at the side of an ally. Unfortunately, not all the world is in such a happy position, and the risk of war that could involve Canadians is always present. To make decisions that are wise, our government must understand not only the political but also the military aspects of international tensions. It cannot rely on the open but discontinuous source of the daily press, or on occasional papers prepared by learned institutions, or indeed by government agencies with no military knowledge. Military Intelligence, as much in the (b) as in the (a) field, must be continuous, it must be timely, and it must be as accurate as the source that provided the information can be. We cannot rely only on our allies, partly because their interests do not necessarily coincide with our own, but chiefly because we have to be prepared to contribute as an exchange for what we do get. The evaluation of material that comes into our hands can best be done by officers whose training and developed skills have given them background and experience. To develop such men Canada needs an organization and a career structure that can attract, recruit, train, and keep the best men available.*

---

* Second edition note: These comments reflect the limited integration and roles of women in the Canadian Forces at the time in which *Scarlet to Green* was written (1963-1978) and finally published in 1981. Since 1989 women have been fully integrated into all military occupations and roles with exception of the submarine service, which opened in 2000.

AFTERWORD

By Dr. David A. Charters
Professor of Military History (retd) and Senior Fellow, The Gregg Centre for the Study of War and Society, University of New Brunswick, Fredericton

Of course, the story of Canadian military intelligence does not end here. Over the next fifty plus years change was the order of the day. The forces driving this included: increasing operational commitments, personnel shortages, budgetary constraints, and rapid technological change. These tended to pull the Intelligence Branch in many directions at the same time, straining its ability to force-generate sufficient personnel to fulfill assigned tasks. Still, the Branch met this challenge.

Major structural change began in 1982, when the 'shotgun marriage' of intelligence and military police described in this book ended in divorce. The creation of the separate tri-Service Canadian Forces (CF) Intelligence Branch allowed it to begin to develop its roles, training, and doctrine with a focus on tactical and strategic intelligence support to the CF. The Reserve Intelligence Companies, which had been disbanded in 1968, were reactivated in the 1990s when the high tempo of CF operations imposed increasing demands for intelligence support. Those decisions aside, the Branch remained small in relation to the Forces as a whole. On the eve of the Afghan war it numbered less than 600 personnel (Regular and Reservist combined), barely one per cent of the total strength of the CF.

While the Canadian Forces' two longest commitments – to NATO in Germany, and to UN peacekeeping in Cyprus – both came to an end in 1993, the expected post-Cold War 'peace dividend' of fewer operations never materialized. Starting with the Oka Crisis in the summer of 1990, the CF and the Branch were challenged by continuous and overlapping new commitments: the 1991 Gulf War (air and naval); peacekeeping operations in former Yugoslavia, Somalia, Haiti, East Timor, and Eritrea; an air campaign against Serbia; the war in Afghanistan; an air campaign in Libya; naval anti-piracy and counter-terrorism operations; and an air campaign and special forces training/advisory mission in Iraq. Every one of these operations required intelligence support, with the scale and form varying according to the size and needs of the mission. The Afghan war, for example, during which the CF eventually deployed a brigade-size force, including an air wing, saw the deployment of more than 100 intelligence personnel at one time – the largest overseas commitment of Canadian intelligence resources since the Second World War. Branch personnel also served in multi-national coalition intelligence staffs on many of these missions. Consequently, the Branch increased in size significantly during the Afghan war.

The demands of these operations, many of which involved 'asymmetric' threats and counter-measures, forced the Branch to adapt structures and methods designed for conventional war to new forms of conflict and new technologies focused on a de facto counter-insurgency operation. At the tactical level the Intelligence Collection and Analysis Centre, first formed in 1985, pioneered the Branch's all-source collection efforts. This, and the Canadian National Intelligence Centre formed in Bosnia in the 1990s, paved the way for two innovations which came to fruition during the Afghan war: the Intelligence, Surveillance, Target Acquisition and Reconnaissance Company, and the All Source Intelligence Centre. Branch personnel were assigned to human source collection, to countering IED networks, and to analyze data gathered from aerial drones, which had not been in the inventory before the war. The Branch also staffed smaller Special Operations Intelligence Centres to support Canadian SOF operations. Not since the Second World War had there been so much rapid change in Canadian military intelligence as in the first decade of the new millennium. While the whole story is not yet known, preliminary assessments, as well as the number of honours and awards conferred on Branch Officers and NCOs, indicate that the Branch adapted well and performed effectively, especially at the tactical level.

Even as the CF and the Branch fought their longest war the Branch was undergoing change on the home front. The CF School of Military Intelligence moved from Base Borden to Base Kingston in 2000, and in 2015 the latter became the official 'home station' of the Branch. As the result of a major Defence Intelligence Review the position of Director General Intelligence was upgraded to that of Chief of Defence Intelligence, who now heads CF Intelligence Command. Created in 2013, the Command brings together all major CF intelligence units at NDHQ to provide direct mission-related intelligence support to CF commanders and their operations.

Perhaps the most dramatic change has been one of attitudes toward intelligence throughout the CF. Where military intelligence was often marginalized in the more distant past, the creation of CF Intelligence Command, the Canadian Army Intelligence Regiment, the Canadian Joint Operations Command and Canadian Special Operations Forces Command (with their respective Command Intelligence enterprises) represent the recognition that intelligence is central to operations. And if operations are about projecting military power then the relevance of the Canadian Intelligence Corps motto – ACTION FROM KNOWLEDGE – needs no further elaboration.

ANNEXES:
PERSONNEL AND ORGANIZATION

ANNEX 1:
SENIOR INTELLIGENCE APPOINTMENT, ARMY HEADQUARTERS 1903–1964

Lt.-Col. V.B. Rivers, R.C.A. Acting Director until 22 Apr 03	6 Feb 01–1 Apr 03
Lt.-Col. W.A.C. Denny, (Bvt. Maj., A.S.C.)	22 Apr 03–15 Jan 05
Maj. A.C.C. Caldwell, Corps of Guides	1 May 06–1 May 10
Capt. Charles J. Bruce Hay, (Queen's Own Corps of Guides) (Lumsden's) (Indian Army)	1 May 10–1 Sep 10
Capt. L.H. Sitwell	1 Sep 10–1 Sep 15
Capt. F.E. Davis (Bvt. Maj.)	21 Jul 15–31 Dec 20
Maj. (Bvt.& T.Col.) J. Sutherland Brown, C.M.G., D.S.O., R.C.R., D.M.O.&I.	1 Jan 21–1 Apr 21
Maj. (Bvt.& T. Lt.-Col.) H.H. Matthews C.M.G., D.S.O., R.C.M.G.B.	1 Apr 21–31 Dec 27
Maj. F.R. Henshaw, M.C., R.C.E.	1 Jan 28–30 Sep 29
Maj. K. Stuart, D.S.O., M.C., R.C.E.	1 Oct 29–31 Dec 33
Open	1 Jan 34–10 Jun 35
S/L. K.M. Guthrie, R.C.A.F.	11 Jun 35–21 Nov 38
S/L. C.J. Duncan, R.C.A.F. (Acting)	21 Nov 38–1 Jan 39
Maj. J.F. Preston, M.C., R.C.A.	1 Jan 39–14 Dec 39
Maj. H.G. Scott	15 Dec 39–17 Oct 40
Lt.-Col. W.W. Murray, M.C. (G.S.O.1) Colonel (D.M.I.)	17 Oct 40–4 Jul 42 4 Jul 42–16 Feb 46
Col. W.A.B. Anderson, O.B.E.	17 Feb 46–2 Oct 49
Lt.-Col. T.R. McCoy (Acting)	3 Oct 49–31 Dec 49
Col. A.F.B. Knight, O.B.E.	1 Jan 50–31 Jul 51
Lt.-Col. W.A. Todd (Acting)	1 Aug 51–30 Nov 51

Col. N.S. Cuthbert, E.D.	1 Dec 51–31 May 53
Col. E.S. Tate, C.D.	15 Jun 53–31 Aug 59
Col. R.E. Hogarth, C.D.	1 Sep 59–5 Aug 62
Col. H.T. Fosbery, C.D.	6 Aug 62–30 Nov 64

Position abolished and became Director General of Intelligence, later and variously Director General Intelligence and Security, Deputy Chief, Intelligence and Security. The first D.G.I. was Brig. L.E. Kenyon, C.D.

ANNEX 2:
CENSORSHIP ORGANIZATION, 1939

This chart shows the operative branches of Censorship and the relationship between them and the Information Section, D.N.D. This organization, which was proposed by Lt.-Col. M.A. Pope in 1938, was, with minor change, brought into effect on the outbreak of war in 1939.

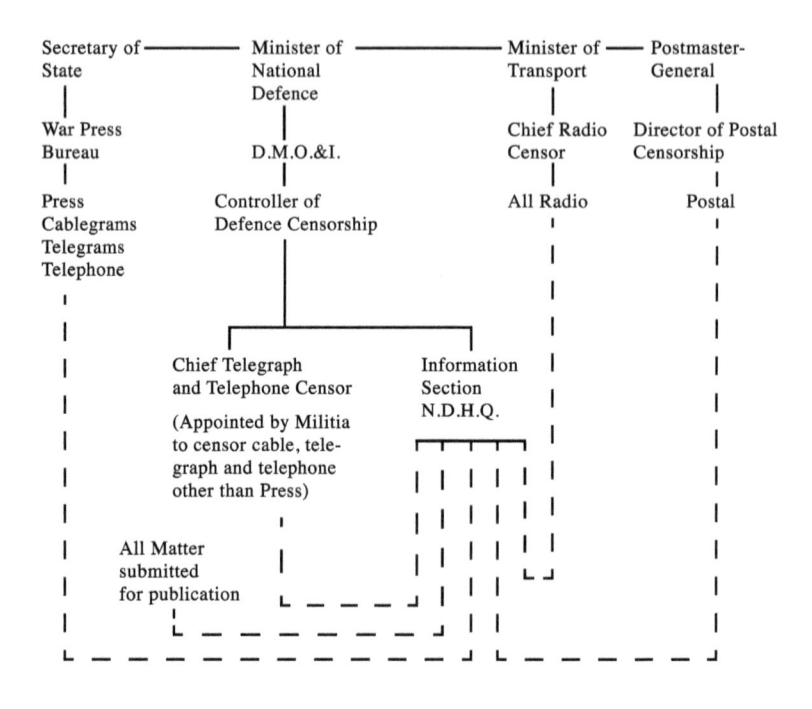

```
Secretary of ——— Minister of ——————— Minister of ——— Postmaster-
State              National                Transport      General
  |                Defence                     |             |
War Press            |                    Chief Radio   Director of Postal
Bureau             D.M.O.&I.              Censor        Censorship
  |                  |                        |             |
Press              Controller of          All Radio      Postal
Cablegrams         Defence Censorship
Telegrams
Telephone
                   ┌─────────┴─────────┐
                   Chief Telegraph      Information
                   and Telephone Censor Section
                                        N.D.H.Q.
                   (Appointed by Militia
                   to censor cable, tele-
                   graph and telephone
                   other than Press)

                   All Matter
                   submitted
                   for publication
```

───────── = Direct control

― ― ― ― = Information and guidance only

ANNEX 3:
INTELLIGENCE ORGANIZATION, CANADIAN MILITARY HEADQUARTERS, 1940–1946.

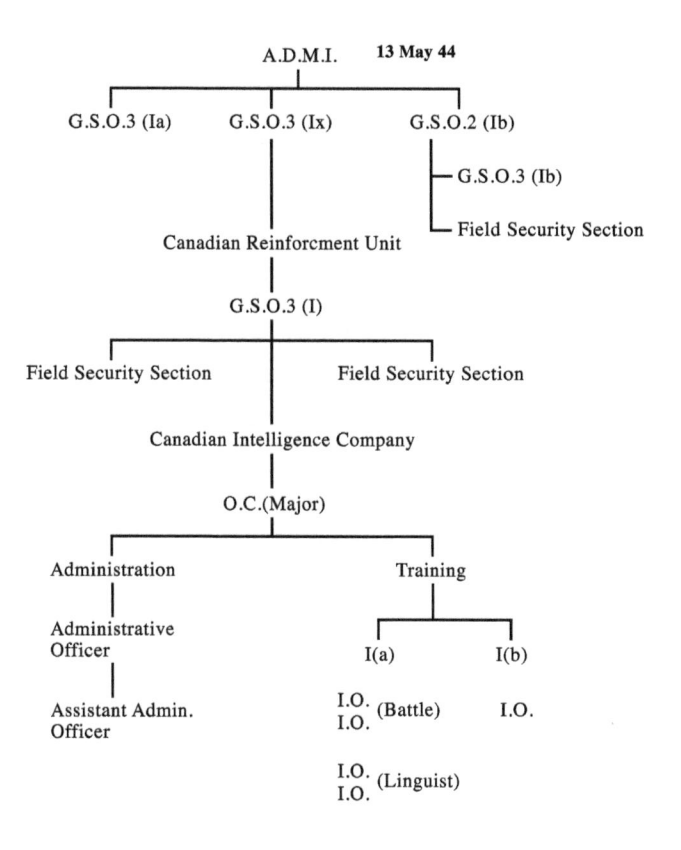

```
                          A.D.M.I.        13 May 44
              ┌──────────────┼──────────────┐
         G.S.O.3 (Ia)    G.S.O.3 (Ix)    G.S.O.2 (Ib)
                             │              ├── G.S.O.3 (Ib)
                             │              └── Field Security Section
                  Canadian Reinforcment Unit
                             │
                         G.S.O.3 (I)
              ┌──────────────┼──────────────┐
     Field Security Section              Field Security Section
                             │
                 Canadian Intelligence Company
                             │
                         O.C.(Major)
              ┌──────────────┴──────────────┐
          Administration                 Training
              │                       ┌──────┴──────┐
      Administrative               I(a)           I(b)
         Officer
              │                   I.O. (Battle)    I.O.
      Assistant Admin.            I.O.
         Officer
                                  I.O. (Linguist)
                                  I.O.
```

ANNEX 4:
ORGANIZATION OF INTELLIGENCE, CANADIAN ARMY OVERSEAS

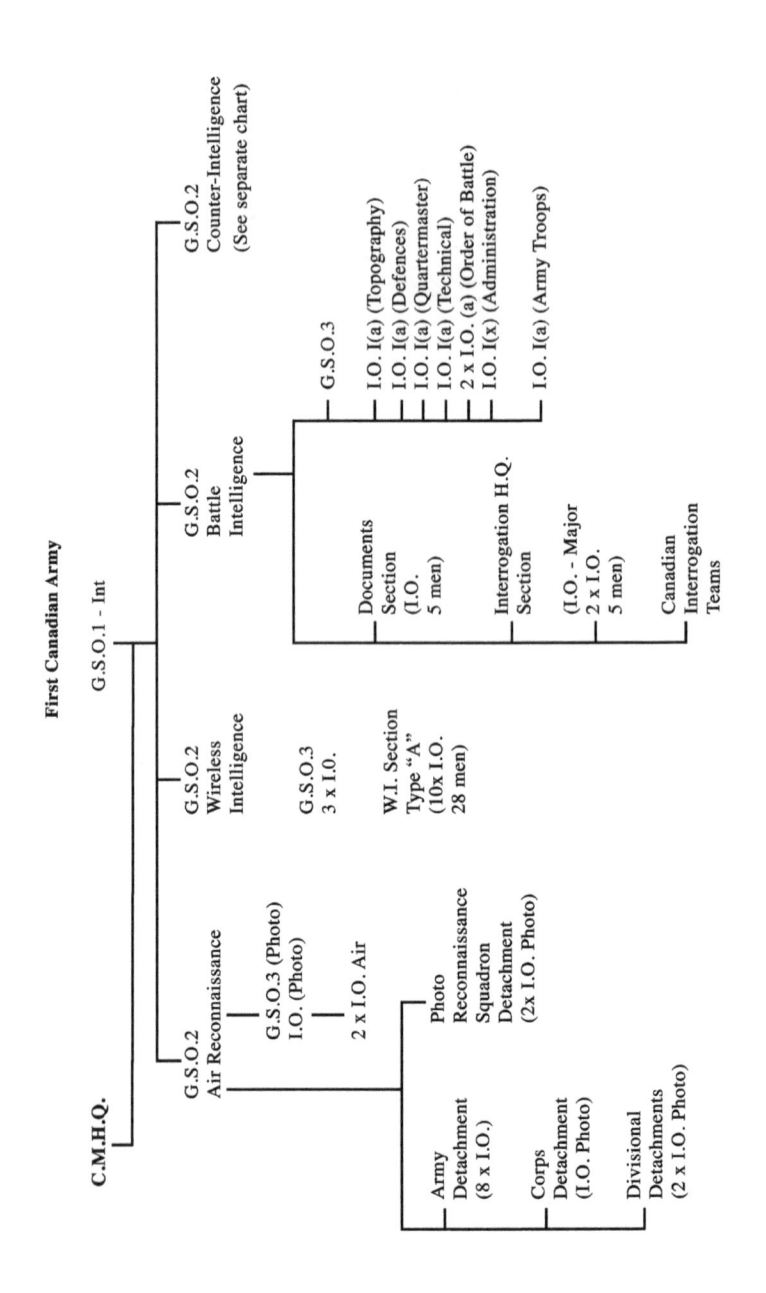

C.M.H.Q.

First Canadian Army
G.S.O.1 - Int

G.S.O.2 Air Reconnaissance
- G.S.O.3 (Photo) I.O. (Photo)
- 2 x I.O. Air
- Photo Reconnaissance Squadron Detachment (2x I.O. Photo)
  - Army Detachment (8 x I.O.)
  - Corps Detachment (I.O. Photo)
  - Divisional Detachments (2 x I.O. Photo)

G.S.O.2 Wireless Intelligence
- G.S.O.3 3 x I.O.
- W.I. Section Type "A" (10x I.O. 28 men)

G.S.O.2 Battle Intelligence
- G.S.O.3
  - I.O. I(a) (Topography)
  - I.O. I(a) (Defences)
  - I.O. I(a) (Quartermaster)
  - I.O. I(a) (Technical)
  - 2 x I.O. (a) (Order of Battle)
  - I.O. I(x) (Administration)
  - I.O. I(a) (Army Troops)
- Documents Section (I.O. 5 men)
- Interrogation H.Q. Section (I.O. - Major 2 x I.O. 5 men)
- Canadian Interrogation Teams

G.S.O.2 Counter-Intelligence
(See separate chart)

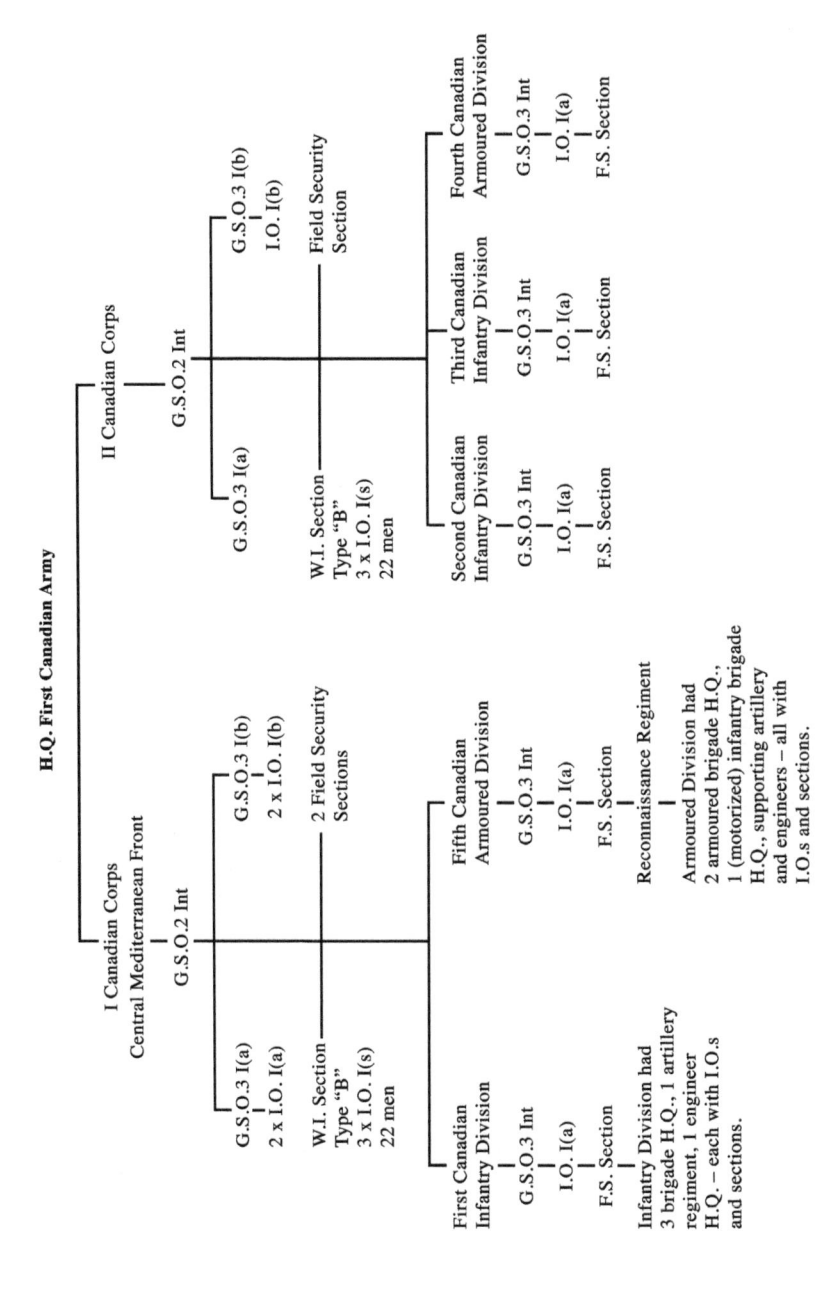

H.Q. First Canadian Army

I Canadian Corps
Central Mediterranean Front
G.S.O.2 Int

- G.S.O.3 I(a)
- 2 x I.O. I(a)
- W.I. Section Type "B"
  3 x I.O. I(s)
  22 men

First Canadian Infantry Division
- G.S.O.3 Int
- I.O. I(a)
- F.S. Section

Infantry Division had 3 brigade H.Q., 1 artillery regiment, 1 engineer H.Q. – each with I.O.s and sections.

Fifth Canadian Armoured Division
- G.S.O.3 Int
- I.O. I(a)
- F.S. Section

Reconnaissance Regiment

Armoured Division had 2 armoured brigade H.Q., 1 (motorized) infantry brigade H.Q., supporting artillery and engineers – all with I.O.s and sections.

- G.S.O.3 I(b)
- 2 x I.O. I(b)
- 2 Field Security Sections

II Canadian Corps
G.S.O.2 Int

- G.S.O.3 I(a)
- W.I. Section Type "B"
  3 x I.O. I(s)
  22 men

Second Canadian Infantry Division
- G.S.O.3 Int
- I.O. I(a)
- F.S. Section

Third Canadian Infantry Division
- G.S.O.3 Int
- I.O. I(a)
- F.S. Section

- G.S.O.3 I(b)
- I.O. I(b)
- Field Security Section

Fourth Canadian Armoured Division
- G.S.O.3 Int
- I.O. I(b)
- F.S. Section

ORGANIZATION OF INTELLIGENCE (CONTINUED)

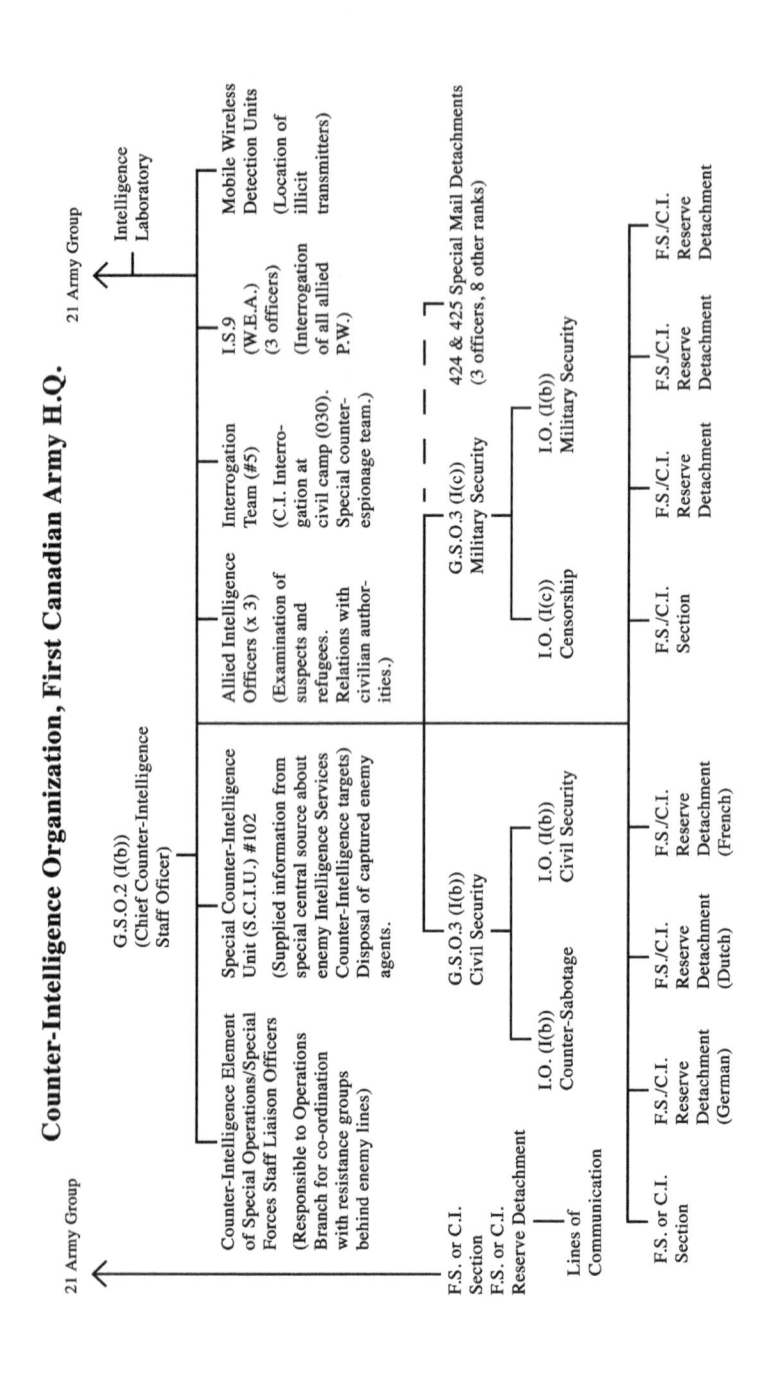

Counter-Intelligence Organization, First Canadian Army H.Q.

21 Army Group

- **G.S.O.2 (I(b))** (Chief Counter-Intelligence Staff Oficer)
  - Counter-Intelligence Element of Special Operations/Special Forces Staff Liaison Officers (Responsible to Operations Branch for co-ordination with resistance groups behind enemy lines)
  - Special Counter-Intelligence Unit (S.C.I.U.) #102 (Supplied information from special central source about enemy Intelligence Services Counter-Intelligence targets. Disposal of captured enemy agents.)
  - Allied Intelligence Officers (x 3) (Examination of suspects and refugees. Relations with civilian authorities.)
  - Interrogation Team (#5) (C.I. Interrogation at civil camp (030). Special counter-espionage team.)
  - I.S.9 (W.E.A.) (3 officers) (Interrogation of all allied P.W.)
  - 424 & 425 Special Mail Detachments (3 officers, 8 other ranks)
  - Intelligence Laboratory → 21 Army Group
  - Mobile Wireless Detection Units (Location of illicit transmitters)

- **G.S.O.3 (I(b))** Civil Security
  - I.O. (I(b)) Counter-Sabotage
  - I.O. (I(b)) Civil Security

- **G.S.O.3 (I(c))** Military Security
  - I.O. (I(c)) Censorship
  - I.O. (I(b)) Military Security

Lines of Communication → 21 Army Group

- F.S. or C.I. Section
- F.S. or C.I. Reserve Detachment
- F.S. or C.I. Section
- F.S./C.I. Reserve Detachment (German)
- F.S./C.I. Reserve Detachment (Dutch)
- F.S./C.I. Reserve Detachment (French)
- F.S./C.I. Section
- F.S./C.I. Reserve Detachment
- F.S./C.I. Reserve Detachment
- F.S./C.I. Reserve Detachment

Counter-Intelligence Organization, II Canadian Corps H.Q.

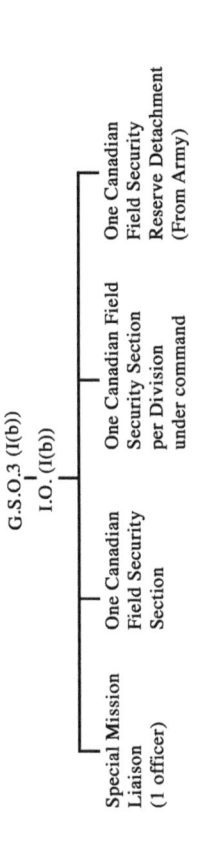

G.S.O.3 (I(b))
I.O. (I(b))

- Special Mission Liaison (1 officer)
- One Canadian Field Security Section
- One Canadian Field Security Section per Division under command
- One Canadian Field Security Reserve Detachment (From Army)

ANNEX 5:
A.H.Q. INTELLIGENCE ORGANIZATION, 1939–1946

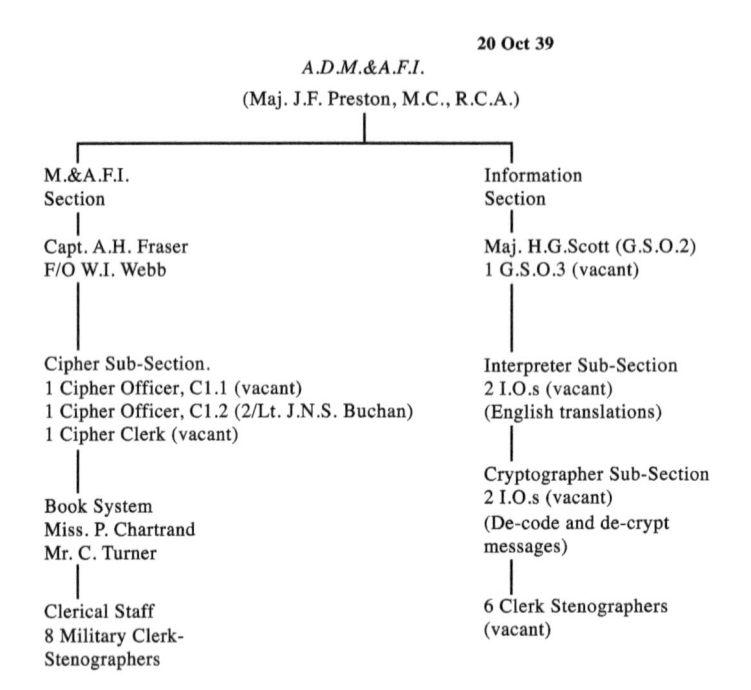

20 Oct 39
A.D.M.&A.F.I.
(Maj. J.F. Preston, M.C., R.C.A.)

M.&A.F.I.
Section

Capt. A.H. Fraser
F/O W.I. Webb

Cipher Sub-Section.
1 Cipher Officer, C1.1 (vacant)
1 Cipher Officer, C1.2 (2/Lt. J.N.S. Buchan)
1 Cipher Clerk (vacant)

Book System
Miss. P. Chartrand
Mr. C. Turner

Clerical Staff
8 Military Clerk-Stenographers

Information
Section

Maj. H.G.Scott (G.S.O.2)
1 G.S.O.3 (vacant)

Interpreter Sub-Section
2 I.O.s (vacant)
(English translations)

Cryptographer Sub-Section
2 I.O.s (vacant)
(De-code and de-crypt messages)

6 Clerk Stenographers
(vacant)

General Staff, Intelligence 3 Feb 42

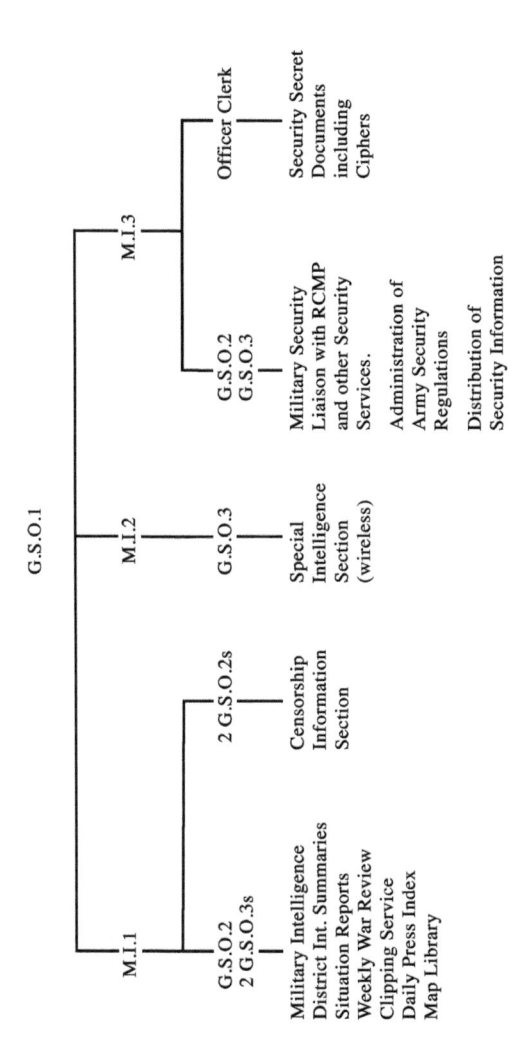

```
                                    G.S.O.1
         ┌──────────────┬──────────────┬──────────────┐
        M.I.1        2 G.S.O.2s       M.I.2          M.I.3
         │              │              │          ┌────┴────┐
      G.S.O.2       Censorship      G.S.O.3    Officer    Security Secret
      2 G.S.O.3s    Information     Special    Clerk      Documents
                    Section         Intelligence          including
                                    Section               Ciphers
      Military Intelligence         (wireless)
      District Int. Summaries                      G.S.O.2
      Situation Reports                            G.S.O.3
      Weekly War Review
      Clipping Service                             Military Security
      Daily Press Index                            Liaison with RCMP
      Map Library                                  and other Security
                                                   Services.

                                                   Administration of
                                                   Army Security
                                                   Regulations

                                                   Distribution of
                                                   Security Information
```

ANNEX 6:
HONOURS AND AWARDS INTELLIGENCE-EMPLOYED OFFICERS AND MEN, 1939–1945

Officer of the Order of the British Empire

Lt.-Col. E Acland, E.D.	A/Lt.-Col. J.W.G Macdougall	Maj. J.M. Robinson
Lt.-Col. A.P. Chambers		A/Col. F.H. Walter
Maj. C.D. Kingsmill	Col. W.W. Murray, M.C.	A/Col. P.E.R. Wright

Member of the Order of the British Empire

Maj. J.H.A. Benoit	Capt. J.M. Gray	Capt. R.T. Robinson
Maj. G.D.A. Biéler	Capt. G.B. Greene	Capt. M.W. Robinson
Maj. H.C. Bray	Capt. D.McN. Healy	Capt. E. Sirluck
Maj. W.H. Broughall	Maj. C.G. Jones	Capt. A.L.J. Sirois
Capt. I.T. Burr	Maj. E.C. Lamothe	W.O.I. H.F. Sutcliffe
Capt. H.J. Byrnes	Capt. F.A. Lypchuk	Capt. K.G. Surbeck
Capt. R.M. Caza	C.S.M. N.L. Mclean	Capt. C.M. Tetrault
Capt. W.A.C. Cooper	Maj. E.D. Magnus	W.O.II C.H. Trappit
Maj. C.M. Devaney	Maj. J.K. Motzfeldt	Lt. C. Thomas
W.O.II T.J.A. Dubois	Capt. R.H. Noble	Lt. M. Veilleus
Lt. J.H.N. Dehler	Capt. W.C. Reihle	Capt. R.F. Wodehouse
Capt. C.R.R. Douthwaite	Maj. R.L. Raymont	Capt. L.B. Yule
Capt. B.G. Foreman	Capt. W.L. Robinson	

Distinguished Service Order

Maj. G.D.A. Biéler	Capt. L.G. D'Artois	Lt.-Col. A.P. Chambers

Military Cross

Capt. J.P. Archambeault	Lt. R.J. Labrosse	Capt. L.J. Taschereau
Capt. L.M. Dumais	Maj. P. Lieven (bar)	Capt. M.P. Thomas
Lt. L. Heaps	Maj. S.E. Lipin	
Maj. P.E. Labelle	Maj. G.M.C. Sprung	

Distinguished Conduct Medal

Lt. C. Lafleur	Sgt. L.K. Pals

Military Medal

S.T. Chan	L. King	E.K. Shippon
J.H.M. Dehler	C. Lafleur	R. Vanier (bar)
L.M. Dumais	N.M. Low	
C. Joly	J. Shiu	

British Empire Medal

Sgt. P.J. Baldwin	Sgt. L.A. Plewman	
Sgt. F.J. Lockhart	W.O.II W.R. Belyea	

Mentioned in Despatches

Maj. W.E. Austin	Cpl. P.A.E. Johnston	Capt. G.F. Rogers
Lt. A. Beauregard	Capt. A.C. Kinnear	W.O.II J.A. Rahn
Maj. G.G. Black	Sgt. L. Lighter	Cpl. W. Rempel
Capt. H.E. Bowes	W.O.II W.B. Lefebvre	Maj. J.G. Ross
Capt. W. Blane	Sgt. W. Lutz	Cpl. E.O. Rohac
Capt. J.C. de Beaujeu	Capt. D.J.A. McQueen	Lt. J.G.R. Sabourin
Maj. P.E. Chassé	W.O.II W.J. McVea	Capt. M. Shulman
Capt. P.N. Cotton	Lt. J.E. McEachern	Cpl. B.M. Smith
W.O.II E.H. Denzler	Lt.-Col. C.B. McFarlane	Sgt. B.V. Smith
Lt. L.J. Durocher	Capt. J.K. Motzfeldt	Capt. P. Stratton
Capt. B.G. Foreman	Maj. E.D. Magnus	W.O.II J.P. Sullivan
Lt. J.E. Fournier	Cpl. J.S. Myyra	Sgt. B.M. Svenson
Capt. J.M. Gray	Capt. J.E.R. Montpetit	Lt. D.W. Taylor
Capt. J.A. Gray	Capt. D.G.E. Molnar	Maj. L.W. Taylor
Capt. H.P. Grauer	Tpr. J. Neuspiel	Capt. R.R. Taylor
Capt. P.A. Gallagher	Capt. R.H. Noble	Capt. P.E. Thibeault
Sgt. A.L. Gracie	Lt. F.H.D Pickersgill	Maj. J.A. Willoughby
Capt. H.A. Hunter	Sgt. J.O. Poissant	Capt. C.J. Webster
Capt. R.S.M. Hannesson	Capt. J.R. Prefontaine	Pte. M.H. Wallace
Lt. R. Hawkins	Lt. J.A. Robitaille	

Knight First Class in the House Order of Orange (Netherlands)

Lt. A.M.M. Dubois	Sgt. M. Heufe	Capt. P. Stratton
Capt. M.M. Dixon	Sgt. E.J. Leblanc	Sgt. W. Vandekamp
Capt. J.J.L.A. Gaumond	Capt. D.G.E. Molnar	
Sgt. J.C. Hadden	Maj. C. Nyenhuis	

Commander, Order of Orange Nassau (with Swords)

Col. P.E.R. Wright

Officer, Order of Orange Nassau (with Swords)

| Maj. C.M. Devaney | Maj. C.R.R. Douthwaite |

King Christian X Liberty Medal (Denmark)

G.C. Christiansen

Officer of the Order of Leopold II (Belgium)

Maj. E.C. Lamothe

Chevalier of the Order of Leopold II with Palm

| Capt. N.G. Ashby | Maj. D.F. Morris | Capt. R.J.P. Pootmans |

Croix de Guerre 1940, with Palm (France)

Capt. N.G. Ashby	Maj. P.E. Labelle	Capt. R.J.P. Pootmans
Capt. J.G.C. Chartrand	Lt. C. Lafleur	
Capt. L.G. D'Artois	Maj. D.F. Morris	

Croix de Guerre avec Etoile d'Argent

Maj. G.V. Beaudry

Croix de Guerre avec Etoile de Bronze

| Maj. C.R.R. Douthwaite | Lt. R.J. Labrosse |
| Lt. J.H.M. Dehler | Lt. P. Vanier |

Medaille de la Reconnaissance Française

| Capt. C.R.R. Douthwaite | Capt. R.H. Noble |

Legion of Merit (Degree of Officer) (United States)

Lt.-Col. E.M. Drake

Legion of Merit (Degree of Legionnaire)

Capt. L.B. Graham

Medal of Freedom, Silver Palm

Lt. R.J. Labrosse

Meritorious Conduct Cross

Sgt. J.C. Hadden

Bronze Cross

Sgt. E.J. Leblanc

Order of the Nichan-Iftikhar, 3rd class (Tunis)

Maj. G.V. Beaudry

ANNEX 7:
CASUALTIES, 1939-1945*

Killed in Action

W. Corson	T.M. Insinger	G.A. Osipoff
F. Dummer	J.S. Milne	A.D. Yaritch
J. Holt	F. Morgan	

Killed while P.W.

A. Beauregard	F.A. Deniset	R. Sabourin
G.D.A. Biéler	J.K. Macallister	
R. Byerly	F.H.D. Pickersgill	

Died

J.P. Archambeault	P.V. Halley	G. Rodrigues (while P.W.)
W.M. Clark	H.L. Hornberger	H. Rohloff
C.H. Frazier	J.W. Place	
R.O.H. Fuller	A. Pokkimakki	

Wounded

W. Blane	H.H. Hennie	W.A. McCarthy
B.H.F. Croll	J.A. Kazakoff	J.T. Moore
E.C. Direnfeld	W.B. Lefebvre	A. Weiss
J.J. Fitzsimmons	P. Lieven	

Prisoners of War

J.H. Bishop (wounded)	R.F. Hedges
L. Chauvin	L.K. Pals

Injured

R. Bozanic	R.J. Levesque
W.D. Coxon	H. Rempel

* The following casualties were not listed in the first edition but are recorded in the official "Books of Remembrance"; G.O. Curphey, W.F. Heller, O.M. Hertzberg, J.R. Holme, W.A. McCarthy, A.R. Morin, P.L. Moss, and L.S. Wald. Source: Canadian Intelligence Corps 1942-2017, 75th Anniversary Commemorative Booklet, pp. 61-65.

ANNEX 8:
CANADIAN INTELLIGENCE CORPS TROPHIES AND PRIZES

The Crerar Trophy
Awarded annually to the Intelligence Training Company which achieved the highest efficiency rating in the training year.

The Insinger Trophy
Awarded annually to the Intelligence Training Company which achieves the greatest progress in the training year in comparison with the standard achieved in the previous year. Named after Capt. Ted Insinger, killed at Dieppe, 19 August 1942.

The George MacGillivray Trophy (The 3-D Trophy)
Awarded annually to the Intelligence Training Company which sets the highest standard of Dress, Drill and Deportment during the training year. The trophy was presented by Maj. George B. MacGillivray, President, C.M.I.A., 1952–1954.

The Van der Vliet Trophy
Awarded annually to the Intelligence Training Company which achieved the highest standard in Russian Language Training during the training year. Donated by Maj. Nicholas Van der Vliet, July, 1954. Retired in 1960.

The A.P.I.S. Trophy
Awarded to the C.Int.C. Militia tradesman who achieved the highest standard of proficiency in imagery interpretation during the period of attachment to the Canadian School of Military Intelligence. Donated by Capt. Leo Durocher, Officer-in-Charge of Air Photo Interpretation training, C.S. of M.I., 1956. The Trophy was dependent upon the nature of the summer training and was suspended in 1967.

The C.M.I.A. Imagery Interpretation Trophy
Awarded annually to the Intelligence Training Company which achieved the highest standard of proficiency in an imagery interpretation exercise. Donated by Capt. A.C. Kinnear, President C.M.I.A., 1958–1960, formerly chief interpreter, First Canadian Army A.P.I.S.

The H.H. Hennie Trophy
Awarded annually to the Intelligence Training Company setting the highest standard of proficiency in the collection, collation, interpretation, and presentation of

Intelligence on a selected foreign country, with emphasis on that country's armed forces and war potential. Donated by No. 6 Intelligence Training Company to honour the services of Maj. H.H. Hennie to the Canadian Intelligence Corps.

The Wygard Prize Award
Donated by Lt.-Col. Alex Wygard to encourage the study of geography, economics, psychology and languages of the peoples of Eastern Europe by any Canadian officer, Regular or Reserve. The name was changed in 1963. A committee of the C.M.I.A. awarded first $50 and, in 1962, $100 as annual prizes. In 1969 it was awarded to the individual having most to do with the successful submission for the Hennie Trophy.

The Dixon Trophy
Donated by Maj. R.R. Dixon in 1963, this trophy was originally awarded to the top student on the Battle Intelligence (Other Ranks) Course. It consists of a carved wooden figure of the classic spy of fiction, large hat, cloak and dagger, mounted on a base. Nick named "Sinister Sam", replicas carved by A.J. Gabinet of the school staff were given to recipients while the original, with suitably engraved plate, was held at the school. In 1970 it became the prize for the Pay Level 5 Course.

The Colonel Commandant's Award
Donated by Col. P.E.R. Wright to honour the individual who, in the Colonel Commandant's personal opinion, had done most to advance Intelligence in the previous 12 months.

The Jock Murray Memorial Shield
Awarded to the Intelligence Training Company which wins the annual Summer Camp Softball Tournament. Donated by Lt.-Col. R.H. Noble as a memorial to Col. W.W. Murray.

The C.M.I.A. Golf Trophy
Originally awarded to the Intelligence Training Company fielding the best four-man team in competition on the Camp Borden Golf Course during Summer Camp, it has since been reduced to the best twosome. In 1962 it was replaced by a cash prize from Maj. H.D. Conover, C.D.

ANNEX 9:
LIST OF FIRST EDITION PERSONNEL ANNEXES

The first edition of *Scarlet to Green* included a series of annexes (over 130 pages) that listed the names of personnel who were appointed or worked in various Intelligence units and staffs between 1903 and 1963. These annexes have not been included in this second edition but their titles are listed in this annex as a testimony to the detailed work of Maj. S.R. Elliot and for readers who may wish to consult the first edition of *Scarlet to Green* for further information:

Senior Intelligence Officers – Districts, Areas and Commands, 1903–1966

Officers, Corps of Guides, 1903–1929

Intelligence Staff Appointments, Canadian Expeditionary Force

Canadian Intelligence Corps Section, France

Corps of Guides Competitions

Intelligence Staff, Canadian Military Headquarters, 1940–1946

Intelligence Appointments, First Canadian Army

Intelligence Field Unit Personnel, 1939–1946

Canadians Employed on Special Duties Overseas, 1939–1946

Intelligence Staff, 1 Sep 1939–1 Oct 1946

Intelligence Units, Canada, 1939–1945

Senior Staff and Officers, D.M.I., 1 Oct 1946–1 Dec 1964

Intelligence Units, 1946–1964

Canadian Intelligence Corps, Other Ranks, 1946–1966

Intelligence Details – Peacekeeping

Officers Commanding Canadian Army (Militia) Intelligence Units, 1948–1970

Officers and Executive, The Canadian Military Intelligence Association (from Sep 1972, The Canadian Intelligence and Security Association)

NOTES

Note: Commencing with notes to Chapter 4, the following abbreviaions are used:
Cf (for C.M.H.Q. file)
Nf (for N.D.H.Q. file)
WD (for war diary)

CHAPTER 1
1. *The Despatches of Field Marshal the Duke of Wellington,* ed. Lt.-Col. Gurwood (London, John Murray, 1837), vol. IV, p. 140, to Sir Hew Dalrymple, Commander, British Forces.
2. Ibid., p. 383, W. to Beresford.
3. Ibid., vol. V, p. 571, Mar 1810.
4. *History of the Guides* (Aldershot, Gale and Polden, 1938, 1950), vol. I, 1846–1922, regimental committee; vol. II, 1922–47, Lt.-Gen. Sir George MacMunn.
5. Militia General Orders (M.G.O.), 7 Feb 1862, para 1.
6. M.G.O., 27 Aug 1862, para 1; Apr 1863, para 1.
7. Lt.-Col. G.N. Denison, *Soldiering in Canada* (Toronto, Morang, 1900) p. 86; M.G.O.17 Apr 1866, para 4; C.E. Dornbusch, *The Canadian Army, 1865–1958* (Hope Farm Press, Cornwallville, N.Y., 1966), p. 130.
8. M.G.O., 8 Mar 1866, para 1; 26 Mar 1866.
9. Capt. Ernest J. Chambers, Corps of Guides, *History of the Canadian Militia* (Montreal, I.M. Fresco, 1907); Francis Wayland Campbell, *The Fenian Invasions of Canada, 1866–70,* the operations of the Montreal Militia Brigade in connection therewith (John Lovell, Montreal, 1904), pp. 25, 26.
10. Report of the State of the Militia (S.M.R.), 1866, p. 57. Second edition note: the order of endnotes 10 thru 12 has been altered.
11. M.G.O., 22 Feb 1867, para 3; S.M.R., 1868, p. 50; M.G.O. 29 May 1868, 31 Jul 1868.
12. M.G.O., 14 Apr 1866, paras 1, 2.
13. Maj.-Gen. Sir Frederick Middleton, Report (F.M.R.).
14. M.G.O. 8 (3), 19 Apr 1885.
15. Maj. C.A. Boulton, *Reminiscences of the Northwest Rebellions* (Toronto, Grip, 1886), pp. 202–5.
16. F.M.R., 30 Dec 1885.
17. J.P. Turner, *The Northwest Mounted Police, 1873–93* (Ottawa, King's Printer, 1950), vol. II, p. 16.
18. F.M.R., Fish Creek, 7 May 1885.
19. F.M.R., Batoche, 31 May 1885.
20. *The Penny Illustrated Paper,* no. 1249, vol. 48, 23 May 1885, p. 330.
21. Boulton, op. cit., p. 298.
22. F.M.R., (Lt.-Col. Otter), Appendix B, 5 May 1885.
23. F.M.R., (Maj.-Gen. Strange), Appendix D, 26 May 1885.
24. Turner, op. cit., p. 206.
25. Ibid., p. 209.
26. W. Sanford Evans, *The Canadian Contingent* (London, Fisher Unwin, 1901), p. 144.
27. *Hart's Army List,* 1875, 1902, 1903.
28. Report of the General Officer Commanding Canadian Militia (R(GOC)), 31 Dec 1900, p. 20.

29 Militia List, 1 Jul 03; General Order (G.O.) 100, 13 Jun 03; File H.Q.C. 3403-1 (26-1); G.O. 192, 1 Dec 03.
30 Militia Order (M.O.) 193 (1), 22 Aug 03.
31 M.G.O. 66, 19 Mar 04; G.O. 41, 1 Apr 11.
32 G.O. 41, 1 Apr 11; G.O. 246, 1 Dec 05.
33 G.O. 60, 2 May 04.
34 G.O. 163, 1 Dec 06; G.O. 63, 1 May 05; G.O. 3, 3 Jan 10; G.O. 10, 1 Feb 17; *Hart's Army List*, 1903, p. 517; G.O. 10, 1 Feb 17.
35 *Instructions for Camps*, 1904; M.G.O. 126 (1), 2 Jun 04, para 2; R(GOC), 31 Dec 04, p. 83, p. 21.
36 *Minutes of the Militia Council* (M.M.C.), para 5, 28 Nov 04.
37 M.M.C. 69, 29 Nov 04.
38 M.M.C. 830-1, 8 May 06; G.O. 84, 15 May 06; G.O. 89, 1 May 06; G.O. 165, 18 Jul 05.
39 R(GOC), 31 Dec 02, para 9; 31 Dec 1900.
40 *Annual Report of the Militia Council* (R(MC)), 31 Dec 04; 31 Dec 05; 31 Dec 07; M.M.C., para 1404, 20 Nov 07.
41 *Report of the Director of Intelligence*, 5 Jan 05, attached to R(GOC), 04; R(MC), 31 Dec 06; R(MC), 31 Mar 08; M.M.C., para 65, 19 Jan 10; M.O. 161, 30 Apr 10.
42 G.O. 67, 1 Apr 08; G.O. 41(3), 1 Apr 10; G.O. 59, 1 Apr 12; G.O. 87, 15 May 13; G.O. 41, 1 Apr 11.
43 G.O. 24, 1 Feb 12; R(GOC) in R(MC), 31 Mar 13.
44 G.O. 23, 1 Feb 12.
45 G.O. 75, 5 May 11; M.O. 192, 6 Apr 12.
46 R(MC), 31 Mar 13.
47 G.O. 43, 1 Apr 11, para 29; G.O. 106, 15 Nov 16.
48 Margaret A. Ormsby, *British Columbia, a History* (Toronto, Macmillan of Canada, 1958), pp. 365, 366.
49 Maj. T.V. Scudamore, "Aid to the Civil Power", *The Canadian Defence Quarterly*, IX, 2, pp. 257, 260.
50 Duguid, *History of the Canadian Forces, 1914–18*, Appendix 23, p. 19.
51 Ibid., pp. 5, 25–32; Appendices 82, p. 48; 84, p. 52.
52 G.O. 130, 22 Aug 1914; Duguid, op. cit., Appendix 34, p. 32; Lt.-Col. G.W.L. Nicholson, *The Canadian Expeditionary Force, 1914–1919*, (Ottawa, Queen's Printer, 1962), p. 12; Duguid, op. cit., p. 67.
53 No endnote reference in the first edition of *Scarlet to Green*.

CHAPTER 2

1 Col. A. Fortescue Duguid, *The Official History of the Canadian Forces in the Great War, 1914–19* (Ottawa, King's Printer, 1938); vol. 1, pp. 100, 101, 107, and Appendices 138–42, 153; Col. G.W.L. Nicholson, *The Canadian Expeditionary Force, 1914–19* (Ottawa, Queen's Printer, 1962), p. 31; Winston S. Churchill, *The World Crisis, 1911–18*, vol. I, p. 258.
2 Sir Arthur W. Currie, introduction to Maj. J.E. Hahn, *The Intelligence Service, 1914–1918* (Toronto, Macmillan of Canada, 1930), pp. x, xiv–xv, 12; Duguid, op. cit., p. 147.
3 *Die Deutsche Kriegführung und das Völkerrecht*, quoted in Nicholson, op. cit., p. 59, from *British Official History of the First World War* (B.O.H.).
4 Extract from V Corps Intelligence War Diary, quoted in Duguid, op. cit., Appendix 320.
5 Duguid, op. cit., p. 414.
6 Ibid., p. 463.
7 Capt. Harwood Steele, *The Canadians in France, 1915–1918* (New York, Dutton, n.d.), p. 37.
8 B.O.H., 1916, pp. 185, 192; *History of 213 Reserve Regiment*, p. 366; quoted in Nicholson, op. cit., p. 139.
9 Capt. E.N. Jungbluth; unpublished manuscript, 1941.

10 Hahn, op. cit., p. 209.
11 Letter 1.G. 498, 16 Nov 17.
12 Nicholson, op. cit., p. 389.
13 Ibid., p. 390.
14 Hahn, op. cit., pp. 200, 223–5.
15 C.R.M.J. Cruttwell, *History of the Great War, 1914–18* (Oxford, Clarendon Press, 1934), pp. 157, 437.
16 *National Encyclopaedia of Canadian Biography* (Toronto, Dominion, 1935), pp. 303 ff.
17 Hahn, op. cit., pp. 69 ff.
18 Ibid., pp. 157 ff., 235.
19 Ibid., pp. 86 ff.
20 Ibid., pp. 100 ff.
21 Jungbluth, op. cit.
22 Ibid., Hahn, op. cit., pp. 42–3, 254.
23 J.M. Bruce, "The British Aces", in *Air Aces of the 1914–18 War* (Tetchworth, Harleyford, 1959), p. 42. Maj. R. Frankland Pemberton, "The Development of British Service Aviation", in *The Army Quarterly*, LXXXVII, 2, p. 252 ff.
24 Hahn, op. cit., p. 254.
25 J.S. Moir, ed., *History of the Royal Canadian Corps of Signals, 1903–61* (Ottawa, 1962), p. 21.
26 *Report of the Ministry, Overseas Military Forces of Canada* (O.M.F.C., London), p. 265.
27 Ibid., pp. 122, 274.
28 Charteris, op. cit., p. 40.
29 Jungbluth, op. cit.; letter, 2nd Army I.G. 479 (27/5), CR 1-B- l F.34, 4 Sep 15 to II Corps, signed by H.B. Williams, Maj.-Gen.
30 O.M.F.C., p. 287.
31 Jungbluth, op. cit.
32 Duguid, op. cit., Appendices 2, 3, 13.
33 Ibid., Appendices 14, 15; p. 6, pp. 500, 549.
34 C.E.F. R.O. 781, 9 Jul 18.
35 Lt.-Col. C. Hanbury Williams, "Censorship", in *Canada in the Great World War* (Toronto, United Publ.) vol II.
36 Callwell, op. cit., p. 14; Duguid, op. cit., Appendix 235.
37 Captain Franz von Rintelen, *The Dark Invader*, Penguin Books, Harmondsworth, Middlesex, 1938.
38 Duguid, ibid., p. 19, Appendix 36; *Encyclopaedia Britannica* (ed. 1962), vol. 20, p. 263; vol. 12, p. 461.
39 Duguid, op. cit., Appendix 36.
40 Duguid, ibid.
41 Nicholson, op. cit., p. 517; Nf 2623, H.Q.C. 2698, 2758, 2763.
42 *Memoranda Respecting Work of the Department of Militia and Defence* (M.D.A.), No. 3 (1916), p. 9, paras 37–42; G.O. 84 d., 1 Sep 16; M.D.A. Nos. 5, 6, 1 Jan–31 Dec 18.
43 Nf H.Q.C. 1517.
44 Nf H.Q.C. 1635.
45 M.M.C., 30 May 17.
46 M.M.C. 496, 28 Apr 20; File 11-1-21.
47 M.D.A. No. 3 (1916), p. 9, paras 37–42; No. 4, (1 Jan–31 Dec 17); No. 5, (1 Jan–31 Dec 18); Ernest J. Martin, "Cyclists", in *Journal of the Society for Army Historical Research*, vol. 22 (1943–4), p. 277.
48 Duguid, op. cit., p. 67; M.O. 392, 26 Aug 14; R.M.C., 31 Mar 13, Appendix: G.
49 Nf H.Q.C. 3430, D.M.O.&I. to G.O.C. M.D. 11, 14 Feb 21.
50 Nf H.Q.C. 3403-1, D.M.O.&I. (War Office) to D.M.O.&I., 21 Jul 21; D.M.O.&I. to M.D. 5, 21 Jun 22.
51 Intelligence Circular Letter 163, 3 Oct 24.
52 Report of the Department of National Defence, 31 Mar 25.

53 Ibid., 31 Mar 26.
54 G.O. 4, 1 Feb 26; G.O. 5, 1 Jan 27; G.O. 122, 15 Aug 23; G.O. 36, 15 Mar 24.
55 Statement of Brig. C.S. McKee, C.B.E., E.D., D.S.O, to author, 26 Jan 65.
56 Letters, Royal Military College to D.M.I., file 3245-4, 7 Dec 62; file 4545-4 (Regr), 22 Oct 71.

CHAPTER 3

1 Gen. A.G.L. McNaughton, memorandum for the Minister, 18 Jan 29. McNaughton Papers (C.G.S. folder 17) quoted in James Eayrs, *In Defence of Canada*, University of Toronto Press, 1964, p. 92.
2 N.D.H.Q. files, H.Q.S. 5200, 5255, 5269. The responsibility for links with them had been given to the C.G.S. in Appendix VI to *Regulations and Orders for the Canadian Militia* in 1926. But the records of actual changes are incomplete.
3 A.V.M. K. Guthrie, interview with author, 8 Jun 70.
4 H.Q.S. 5200, 5255, 5269, Guthrie interview, *supra*.
5 H.Q.S. 6403, G.S. memorandum, 9 Dec 35.
6 Eayrs, op. cit., pp. 77, 91, 93; H.Q.S. 3496, vol. II, Col. H.H. Matthews to Officers Commanding Military Districts, 28 May 31; Guthrie interview, *supra*.
7 *History of Directorate of Military Operations and Planning, 1905–45*, B.D.F. M.O. 171, 4 Dec 45, memorandum D.M.O.&I. to C.G.S., 11 Mar 29, file H.W.C. 3067.
8 H.Q.S. 4720, Col. Parsons' letter, unreferenced, 21 Jan 28.
9 H.Q.C. 3430, vol. 4, 29 Apr 31; H.Q.S. 4720.
10 H.Q.S. 650-7-1: D.M.O.&I. to A.D.M.I., 4 Apr 32; A.D.M.I. to D.M.O.&I., 6 Apr 32; H.H. Matthews to G/C J.L. Gordon, 8 Apr 32; Gordon to C.G.S., 13 Apr 32; C.G.S. to M.N.D., 21 Apr 32; M.N.D., 22 Apr 32; Gordon to C.G.S., 9 May 32.
11 Guthrie interview, *supra*.
12 B.D.F. G.S. 31, 4 Feb 35, quoted in *History of D.M.O.&P.*, op cit. Guthrie, *supra*; H.Q.S. 35/6, 31 Oct, 1, 9 Nov 38.
13 H.Q.S. 35/6, 31 Jan, 3 Aug, 20, 23, 27 Oct 38; H.Q.S. 3516, 16, 20, 22, 23, 27, 29 Nov, 5, 8 Dec 39; 8, 17 Jan 40, C.A.S.F. R.O. 266, 17 Jan 40.
14 H.Q.C. 3822, D.O.C. M.D. 4 to D.N.D., 9 Jul 30.
15 H.Q.C. 5743, C.G.S. to M.D. 1, M.D. 2 22, 30 Aug 32.
16 Eayrs, op. cit., p. 67.
17 H.Q.S. 6360; H.Q.S. 6361, D.O.C. M.D. 11 to C.G.S.; H.Q.S. 6467, C.G.S. to all D.O.C.s, 7 Feb 36 *et seq*.
18 H.Q.C. 5732; C.G.S. to M.D. 11, 13 Jul 31; M.D. 11 to A.D.M.I., 16 Apr 32; H.Q. M.D.12 to C.G.S., 3 May; C.G.S. to M.D. 12, 9 May; M.D. 12 to C.G.S., 16 May 32.
19 Eayrs, op. cit., p. 140.
20 P.C. 2248, dated 8 Oct 32, quoted Eayrs, op. cit., pp. 124, 125.
21 *History of D.M.O.&P.*, op. cit., Appendix 12; H.Q.S. 4720.
22 H.Q.S. 6364.
23 Material on this period held on files H.Q.S. 6761, 6367, 6467, and 6363.
24 H.Q.C. 5688: Commr. R.C.M.P. to D.N.D., 24 Mar 31; minute, C.G.S. to A.G., 25 Mar 31; letter A.G. to all D.O.C.s, 26 Mar 31; internal minute, 14 May 31.
25 H.Q.C. 5688, 1, 14 Jul 31; H.Q.S. 5603, 6365, Jul 34.
26 H.Q.S. 6467, D.O.C. M.D. 4 to D.N.D., 16, 23 Oct, 6 Nov 36; H.Q.S. 6761, D.O.C. M.D. 11 to D.N.D., 13 Jun 38; H.Q.S. 6467 memorandum, 8 Nov 38.
27 H.Q.S. 11-1; H.Q.S. 965; cases cannot be quoted but this file has numerous reports and correspondence between D.M.O.&I. and Brig. Wood, R.C.M.P.; this item is from F.D. 33, dated 18 Jun 38; the report was brought to the attention of the Aliens Sub-Committee; H.Q.S. 5603, 6365.
28 H.Q.S. 6367, Capt. R.E.A. Morton, D.I.O. M.D. 13, quoting *Calgary Albertan*; H.Q.S. 6363, M.D. 7 to D.N.D., 13 May 39.
29 H.Q.S. 7523, Mar 38–Dec 39. Guthrie interview, *supra*.

30	H.Q.S. 828, 28 Dec 37; vol. 2, C.G.S. to D.O.C., M.D. 11, 28 Jan 38; M.D. 11 S4-2-1, D.O.C. to D.N.D., 2 Feb 38; R.C.A.F. S44, G/C G.O. Johnson, O.C. Western Air Command, Vancouver, to Secretary, D.N.D., 4 Mar 39.
31	Col. C.P. Stacey, *Six Years of War*, Ottawa, Queen's Printer, 1955, pp. 19, 30, 31, H.Q.S. 5718.
32	H.Q.S. 5199: a. Defence Scheme No. 1 Prepared April 1921, updated to 1926, never completed, abandoned 1931; defence of Canada against an attack by the U.S. "increasingly susceptible to political solution but quite incapable of being satisfactorily answered by Empire Military Action", McNaughton, H.Q.S. 5902; Stacey, op. cit., vol. I, p. 30. b. Defence Scheme No. 2 Work 1919–20, 1932, 11 Apr 38; neutrality in case of war between U.S. and Japan, H.Q.S. 3497, Stacey, ibid. c. Defence Scheme No. 3 Draft to D.O.C.s, approved Jan 32; revised 1937, approved; revised 17 Mar 37, Stacey, ibid., pp. 9, 30, 31.
33	H.Q.S. 6615-4: notes, M.A. Pope to Under-Secretary of State, 25 Apr 38; Pope, memo 2, 16 Sep 38; H.Q.S. 7236, L.R. Laflèche, Deputy Minister D.N.D. to Dr. E.H. Coleman, Under-Secretary of State, 17 Apr 39; D.O.C. M.D. 11 to Security, file VS 38-I-I, 25 Aug 39.
34	H.Q.S. 3493, extract from report of proceedings, Defence Committee 10th meeting, 21 Dec 21; report on censorship by Mr. Fulgence Charpentier, Director of Censorship, 31 Jan 46; H.Q.S. 6615-1, note on present position, D.M.O.&I., 25 Mar 38; H.Q.S. 5917, minutes of Editing Sub-Committee meetings, No. 1, 31 Mar 33, 18 Jan 34; draft preface, Chapters 1, 2 (Duties of Chief Postal Censor), 3, 27 Jan 34; Chapter (General Instruction), 9 Oct 37; memo to Deputy Minister from C.G.S., review, tasks accomplished.
35	H.Q.S. 6615-1, 23 Mar 38, agenda, second meeting of Canadian Defence Committee on Censorship, 20 Apr 38.
36	Ibid., third meeting, 14 May 38; correspondence, 26 Sep 38, H.Q.S. 236.
37	H.Q.C. 5167, L.S. Amery to Governor General to M.N.D.
38	R.C.M.P. G 355-12 on H.Q.S. 965, Commr. R.C.M.P. to Col. Pope, 2 Dec 38; Col. R.J. Orde, J.A.G., to D.M.O.&I., 12 Dec 39 (H.Q.S. 7569); memo, G/C C.M. Croil to C.G.S., 28 Dec 38.
39	H.Q.S. 6717, Defence Scheme No. 3.
40	H.Q.S. 6717, D.M.O.&I. to all D.O.C.s, 7 Dec 37; reference to its preparation is on H.Q.S. 7569, L.R. Laflèche, D.M., to Commr. R.C.M.P., 4 Aug 38; H.Q.S. 6717, M.A. Pope, A/D.M.O.&I., to C.G.S., 30 Aug 38.
41	R.C.M.P. 355-12, Commr. Wood to D.M., D.N.D., 31 Dec 38; H.Q.S. 7569, memo and minute, 20 Feb 39; R.C.M.P. G 355, Commr. Wood to Col. Stuart, D.M.O.&I., 21 Feb 39; H.Q.S. 7569, 5126, 3532, 7363, M.D.s 10, 12, 13; other Districts received similar direction.
42	R.C.M.P. G 355, D/ND, Commr. Wood to D.M., D.N.D., 24 Apr 39; R.C.M.P. B 449, Wood to Minister of Justice, 28 Apr 39.
43	R.C.M.P. G 355, Asst. Commr., D.C.L., to all Divisions, 8 May 39; H.Q.S. 6717, 1 May 39, R.C.M.P. G 355.4, 6 May 39; G 355-12, minutes of first meeting of Sub-Committee on Civil Security and the Protection of Vulnerable Points, 10 May 39; G 355, D/ND, Commr. to D.M., D.N.D., 15 May 39; H.Q.S. 6717, R.C.M.P. G 355-9-5-9, passed by D.C.L. to Col. Stuart, 16 May 39.
44	H.Q.S. 6717, L.R. Laflèche to Commr. Wood, 13 Jul 39; R.C.M.P. G 355-12, 20 Jul 39, Wood to Lafléche; H.Q.S. 6715, 31 Oct 39.
45	H.Q.S. 5199-G, Crerar to C.G.S., C.N.S., S.A.O., 19 Mar 38; C.N.S. to Crerar, 22 Mar 38; minutes of meeting, 22 Jul 38; H.Q.S. 5199, Crerar to C.G.S., C.N.S., S.A.O., 5 Aug 38.
46	H.Q.S. 3498, C.G.S. to Districts, 6 Apr 39; G.O. 135, 1 Sep 39.

CHAPTER 4

1 C.M.H.Q. file (Cf), 1/Headquarters/1, memo C.G.S. to M.N.D., 22 Sep 39. Quoted in Stacey, *Six Years of War*, pp. 195, 196.
2 Cf 1/Non Div/1, 8, 10, 11, 14 Nov 39; N.D.H.Q. file (Nf), H.Q.S. 5199S, 22 Nov 39.
3 War Diary (WD) C.M.H.Q., 30 Nov 39, 6–14 Dec 39.
4 Cf 1/Headquarters/3/4, Page to G.S.(S.D.), M.O.&I. to B.G.S., 15 Oct 41; Cf 9/Qual IO/1.
5 Cf 1/Intsum/1, memo B.G.S. to G.S.O.1, 16 Dec 39.
6 Cf 1/Headquarters/1, CanMil to Defensor, 3 Jan 40.
7 Cf 1/Headquarters/3, C.M.H.Q. to N.D.H.Q., 19 May 40; Nf H.Q.S. 8676, vol. 1, C.G.S. to M.G.O., 8 Apr 40; C.P. Stacey, *Arms, Men and Governments*, Queen's Printer, Ottawa, 1940, p. 142; Cf 4/Sec/7, 17 Sep 40; WD C.M.H.Q., dates shown; War Office to C.M.H.Q., letter 32, film 762, 27, 30 May; Cf 5/POW/1; Cf 6/Security/1, 28 Jun 40, to distribution.
8 WD C.M.H.Q., 19 Nov 40.
9 Cf 6/FS Sec/1, Pope to B.G.S., 5, 16, 18 Dec 40; WD C.M.H.Q., 2 Dec 40.
10 Cf 6/FS Sec/1, CanMil to Defensor, 25 Jan 41; A.G. 149, ibid., 2 Feb 41; A.A.G. Org to G.S.O. Int, 4 Feb 41.
11 WD C.M.H.Q., 14 Jul, 1 Nov 41.
12 Cf 6/Cdn Int Corps/1, I Cdn Corps to C.M.H.Q., 10 Oct 41; D.A.G. to McNaughton, 28 Nov 41.
13 N.D.H.Q., A.G. 213, A.O. 117/42 wef 3, 18 Jan 42, held; Cf 6/Cdn Int Corps/1/2.
14 Cf 6/Cdn Int Corps/1/2, N.D.H.Q. to C.M.H.Q., G.S.D. 1270, 22 Jun 42; C.M.H.Q. to N.D.H.Q., 29 Jun 42; authority granted under G.O. 470, dated 3 Dec 42, promulgated 6 Mar 43; notice of approval forwarded in G.S. 2241, 31 Oct 42.
15 No date shown; WD C.M.H.Q., 20 June 42, reflects discussions concerning change; report on facilities and organization C.M.H.Q., 13 Jul 42; Cf 1/Cdn Army/1 to B.G.S., C.M.H.Q.; to N.D.H.Q., Nf H.Q.S. 8676, vol. 1.
16 Second edition editorial note: sentence removed from second edition.
17 Cf 4/Aliens/1/2, 25 Apr, 9 May 42; Montague to G.O.C., 14 May, 1 Oct 42; WD C.M.H.Q., 16 May, 16 Nov 42; progress report, Oct 42.
18 Cf 4/Aliens/1/2, G.S. First Army to C.M.H.Q., 28 Oct 42; M.O.&I. to B.G.S. First Army, 31 Oct 42.
19 Cf 4/Aliens/1/2, 25 Apr 42; figures hard to reconcile and incomplete; on 28 Apr 42, 505 cases total, 261 cleared, 214 not yet reported on, 30 under observation; on 15 May, 200 were still "outstanding", 50 were expected to be moved; 18 May, 8 returned to Canada, 237 "outstanding"; 5 Sep, 39 sent to Pioneer Company, 91 as quoted; 16 Nov, 6 returned to Canada; 14 Jun, 1 returned; no other totals given.
20 Ibid., C.M.H.Q. to N.D.H.Q., 6 Feb, 1 Mar 43; Cf 4/Aliens/1/3, H.Q.S. 27, F.D. 1, 14 Jun, 23 Jul, 30 Nov 43, 3 Mar, 1 Apr, 18 Jun, 31 Oct, 7, 9, 20 Dec 44, 3 Jan 45.
21 WD C.M.H.Q., 17, 22 Jan, 2, 15 May 41; Page on Staff Course, February to April; Cf 6/FSS/3, I Corps to C.M.H.Q., 16 Apr, C.M.H.Q. to N.D.H.Q., 18 Apr, reply 25 Apr 41; Cf 12/6/12 FS Sec/1, O.C. No 12 F.S.S. to C.M.H.Q., 13 Jun, reply 26 Jun; WD C.M.H.Q., 17 May 41.
22 O.H. vol. 1, *Six Years of War* (Ottawa, Queen's Printer, 1955), p. 260; WD G.S. H.Q. 1 Div, May 40, Appendix XCI; Cf 1/MOB/3, minutes of meeting at War Office, 13 May 40; 1/L of C/2; 1/Formations/6, 13 May 40; 3/Int Duties/1/2, D.M.T. (W.O.) to distn, 23 Apr 40; 1/Formations/4/3, Ottawa to C.M.H.Q., 1 Oct 40; 4/Interpreters/1, French Military Mission, London, to C.M.H.Q., 24 Dec 39; W.O. to C.M.H.Q., 23 Jun, 25 Jun, 7 Dec 40, 12 Jun, 17 Nov 41, 24 Jun 42 *et seq.*; WD C.M.H.Q., 22 Aug, 17 Nov, 14, 24 Dec 41, 17 Jan 42; memo M.O.&I. to Senior Officer, C.M.H.Q.; Cf 9/Qual IO/1, G.S.O.2 M.O.&I. to D.A.G., 1 Nov 41.
23 B.M.A. Chungking to W.O. to C.M.H.Q., received 1 Feb 42, WD C.M.H.Q., 1 Feb 42; D.M.O.&I. to War Cabinet, WD C.M.H.Q., 21 Feb 42; M.O.&I. to M.I.12, ibid., 24 Feb 42.

24	Cf 9/IO/1, 1, 6 Aug 42. Second edition editorial note: paragraph removed from second edition.
25	Ibid., Murray to Krug, 21 Sep 42.
26	WD C.M.H.Q., 6, 9, 11 Mar; Cf 1/MOB/1, G.S.O.1 to N.D.H.Q., 7 Mar 41; R.O. No. 95, Cf 4/Censor/3, 14 May 40 *et seq.*
27	WD C.M.H.Q., 27 Nov, 6 Dec 39; letter to Des Gras, D.C.P.C., 19 Jan 40; N.D.H.Q. to C.M.H.Q., 30 Dec 39, reply 10 Jan 40; Cf 4/Censor/3, 28 May 40; Cf 4/Censor/1, Chief Postal Censor to C.M.H.Q., 5 Jan 40; Message to External, 29 Jan 40; WD C.M.H.Q., 27 Nov–15 Dec 39, C.A.S.F. R.O. 218-20, 20 Dec 39.
28	Cf 4/Censor/1/2, 6 Jan 40.
29	Cf 4/Censor/1, summary written 29 Aug 41, note M.I.11 to C.M.H.Q., 23 Aug 40.
30	C.A.S.F. R.O. 405, 26 Oct 40.
31	Items following are based on the C.M.H.Q. War Diaries, checked against relevant correspondence.

CHAPTER 5

1	G.O. 135, issued 1 Sep 39, authorized the organization of the Canadian Active Service Force (C.A.S.F.), named certain units as Corps of the Active Militia, and placed them on Active Service. Serials in it (121, 122, 234, 1, 2, and 152) represented the senior formation and unit H.Q. (Official History, vol. I, p. 43).
2	Nf H.Q.S. 3498-4, A.G. to all D.O.C.s, 29 Oct, 1, 7 Nov 39; M.D. 10 to A.H.Q., 1 Nov; M.D. 5 to D.N.D., 29 Nov; M.D. 1 to D.N.D., 18 Nov 39; Div H.Q. Int Section W.E. was III/1931/62/5, Bde H.Q. Int Section W.E. was III/1931/62R/1.
3	WD 1 Cdn Inf Div, Jan, Feb 40.
4	Conversation, Col. A.M. Fordyce and author, 1969.
5	Cf 1/Non Div/8, Burns to Senior Ordnance Officer, 15 Feb; 1/Formations/4, 1 Cdn Div to C.M.H.Q., 25 Mar; 1/Formations/1/2, 1 May; 1/Formations/4/2, 3 May 40; minute, G.S.O.1, 1 Div, to C.M.H.Q.
6	WD 1 Cdn Inf Div, 1 C.D./G.S.6, dated 28 Apr 40, to all brigades.
7	Ibid., May 40; O.H. vol. I, pp. 265 *et seq.*
8	WD 1 C.I.B. and units, Jun 40.
9	Cf 3/Int Duties/1/2, 3 Jul 40; 1/MOB/2/2, 15 Jul 40.
10	Cf 6/1 Army Int Sec/1, N.D.H.Q. G.S.D. 520, 11 Mar 42; C.M.H.Q. Adm O 66, 4 Apr 42; W.E./1931/62D (British); 1/Formations/6/2, /8, Order of Battle, 13 Apr, 11 May 42.
11	Nf H.Q.S. 8097: G/C G.V. Walsh, A.S.O. to C.G.S., 11 Sep; D.M.T. 2 to D.M.T. and S.D., 12 Sep; C.G.S. to C.A.S., 13 Sep; C.A.S. to C.G.S., 26 Sep, 23 Oct; 1 Div to C.G.S., 30 Oct *et seq.*; D.M.T. and S.D. to C.G.S., 31 Oct, 2, 6 Nov 39.
12	Nf H.Q.S. 8097, O.C. 1 Div to C.G.S.; No. 2 A.I.L Section, WD vol. 1, Jan 40; H.Q.S. 8097, D.M.T. and S.D. to C.G.S., 18 May 40; No. 1 A.I.L. Section, vols. I, II, May, Jun 40.
13	G.H.Q. Home Forces to distn, ALO/S 9/AIR, 19 Aug 40; R.C.A.F. H.Q. to C.O., 110 Cdn (AC) Sqn, 11 Sep 40.
14	A.I.L. section activities are taken from unit war diaries, principally No. 2 Section, Feb 40–May 44; also 1 Cdn Army Air Liaison Gp, vol. I, Sep 43, No. 11 Section, Cdn Air Liaison Section, vol. II.
15	Cf 6/AL Gp/I, 13 Oct 43, to D.N.D., 16 Nov 43, to 1 Army for approval, 26 Jan 44; auth Adm O 27, 22 Feb 44.
16	Cf 1/Org Int/1 G.S.D. 602, 24 Oct 43; 30 Nov 43–30 May 44.
17	WD G.S. Br. First Canadian Army, Jan 43, 12 Jan 43.
18	Cf 4/Abbreve/1, G.S. 2517 to N.D.H.Q., 20 Jul 40; 1/Non Div/4, G.S. 0537, N.D.H.Q. to C.M.H.Q., 31 Jul 40; reply 5 Aug 40, Defensor to CanMil, 22 Nov 40; 5/SW Int Sec Corps/1, 10 Dec 40 (War Establishment); C.M.H.Q. to N.D.H.Q., 26 Ap, 10 Oct 41, 5 Dec 42; N.D.H.Q. to C.M.H.Q., 31 Jan 43.

19   5/SW Int Sec Corps/1, Corps Signals to C.M.H.Q., 31 Aug 42; Maj. J.D.W. Halbert to B.G.S., 8 Sep 42; C.M.H.Q. to M.O.&I., 30 Oct 42; Oct 40; 26 Apr 42; 1/Formations/4/3 W.O. to C.M.H.Q.; 32/Wireless/717 (SD 1), 26 May 43.
20   Cf 4/Int Direct/1, *First Canadian Army Intelligence Directive No. 4*, 10 Jun 43; 5/SW Int Sec/A/1, 14 May 43.
21   WD G.S. Br. First Canadian Army, May 42.
22   Col. Henderson was made available to the Planners on 8 May 42 and according to his Section War Diary was actually employed on 10 Jun with the JUBILEE Planning Staff. WD G.S. Br. First Canadian Army, 18 Aug, 25 Sep 42.
23   Cf 2/Attach/1/4, *British Forces Training Directive No. 5*, Sep 42; 20 Oct 42.
24   Cf 4/Int Direct/1, H.Q. *First Canadian Army Intelligence Directive No. 1*, 28 Dec 42.
25   Nf H.Q.S. 20-4-Q, D.S.D. to D. Org, 13 Nov 42; Cf 6/Prov Int/1, S.D. 1 to A.G. 1, C.M.H.Q., 24 Sep 43; Cdn W.E.s II/100/1 and III/5/1; order issued Adm O 138, 29 Sep 43.
26   Cf 1/Attach Ops/1, 2 Dec 42–5 May 43.
27   WD G.S. Br. First Canadian Army, Mar 43; Intelligence Report SPARTAN, 25 Mar 43.
28   WD Int Sec, 1 Cdn Army, Lt.-Col. Henderson to Army Commander, Intelligence Personnel Requirements, First Canadian Army, 25 Mar 43.
29   WD II Corps, 9 Nov 43.
30   Cf 2/Int/1, First Army to distn, 7 Nov 43; WD II Cdn Corps, Feb 44.
31   Cf 1/Wastage/3, 1/Org Int/1, 1 Jul 43–6 Jun 44; best summary is in last item: 47 officer linguists @ 100% = 47; 200 other rank linguists @ 100% = 200; 49 non-linguist officers @ 50% = 25; 209 specialist other ranks @ 50% = 105; 72 general duty other ranks @ 10% = 7; total 384; non-availability of British reinforcements cited in Cf 4/Liais NDHQ./1 (Nf H.Q.S. 20-3-26-Q), C.M.H.Q. to D.N.D., 20 Jan 44.
32   Cf 4/Photo Censor/1 [*sic*] 9 Feb 44; C.M.H.Q. to 1 C.G.R.U.
33   WD II Cdn Corps, Apr, May 44.

CHAPTER 6

1   British Int Corps Historian, H.Q.S. 8631, vol. 3, lecture, School of Military Intelligence Field Security Wing, 1943.
2   WD C.M.H.Q., Feb 40, Cf 1/Formations/1, C.M.H.Q. to D.N.D., 1 Feb 40.
3   2/FSS/1, Col. J.W. Spencer, M.I.1 to Col. Burns, 19, 22 Feb 40.
4   Cf 6/FS Sec/1.
5   Cf 1/MOB/1, 8 Mar 40; Nf 8113-2, 2 May 40, War Establishment III/1931/62R/3; cost of a unit was $46,741, $11,325 of which was non-recurring or capital cost (transport, armaments, medical, stationery, equipment, and some personnel charges).
6   War Diaries, named units.
7   C.M.H.Q. WD, May 40; Cf 6/FSP/2, 2/Int Duties/1/3, G.O. 107, 15 Jun 40.
8   Cf 6/FS Sec/1, VII Corps to C.M.H.Q., 15 Aug 40 *et seq.*
9   Cf 4/Int/4, Maj. C.C. Mann, G.S.O.2 Int VII Corps, to C.M.H.Q., 10 Sep 40.
10   Cf 6/FS Sec/1.
11   Cf 6/FS Sec/1, 6/CMP/1, 16 Dec 40 *et seq.*; C.M.H.Q. WD, 21 Dec 40.
12   War Office letter 79/HD/1345, M.I.11, 26 Jun 40; Cf 6/FS Sec/1, B.G.S. to VII Corps, 16 Dec 40.
13   C.M.H.Q. WD, Jan, Feb 41, C.M.H.Q. Progress Report 43, 18 Jan 41.
14   Investigations in this chapter are from WD of the sections and C.M.H.Q. 4/Fd Sec/2, unless otherwise identified.
15   Cf 5/FS Sec/1, Walter to Wright, 3 Sep 43; C.M.H.Q. to N.D.H.Q., 29 Sep 43.
16   Appendix "J" to C.M.H.Q. Special Instruction No. I TIMBERWOLF, 12 Oct 43; quoted in Lt.-Col. G.W.L. Nicholson, *The Canadians in Italy 1943–1945*, Official History of the Canadian Army in the Second World War, vol. II, p. 345 (Ottawa, Queen's Printer, 1956).
17   No. 15 Canadian F.S. Section, II Canadian Corps, Monthly Report, 27 Oct 43.
18   O.H.I, pp. 427–31.
19   Bernard Newman. *Spy and Counterspy*, Robert Hale, London, 1970, p. 203.

CHAPTER 7

1. Outline Plan, Operation RUTTER, quoted in both Stacey and Terrence Robertson, *The Shame and the Glory* (Toronto, McClelland and Stewart, 1962).
2. WD 2 Cdn Inf Div, op. cit., report on Exercise YUKON II.
3. Operation RUTTER, Detailed Military Plan, dated 20 Jun 42. Appendix A.
4. Ibid., Appendix C.
5. Minutes of meeting, RUTTER Force Commanders, C.O.H.Q, 11 Jul 42, held on 2 Div WD.
6. Operation JUBILEE, Detailed Military Plan, Appendix L, Intelligence Plan, dated 8 Aug 42.
7. Ibid., Appendix A, Information – Enemy, dated 10 Aug 42.
8. Operation JUBILEE, loc. cit., William Stevenson, *A Man Called Intrepid*, Harcourt, Brace, Jovanovich, N.Y., pp. 377–89.
9. Col C.P. Stacey, *Six Years of War*, op. cit., p. 357.
10. Ibid., p. 355.

CHAPTER 8

1. Lt.-Col. G.W.L. Nicholson, *The Canadians in Italy 1943–1945*, Official History of the Canadian Army in the Second World War, vol. II (Ottawa, Queen's Printer, 1956).
2. WD G.S. Br., H.Q. 1 Cdn Inf Div Planning Intsum No. 10, 3 May 43, and O.H. II, pp. 3–67.
3. O.H. II, pp. 52–58.
4. 1 Cdn Inf Div Planning Intsums: No. 10, 3 May; No. 11, 6 May; No. 12, 6 May; No. 13, 9 May; No. 15, 11 May; No. 17, 17 May; No. 19, 27 May; updated 12 Jun (O.H., p. 53).
5. WD 1 Cdn Inf Div, May 43.
6. WD 1 Cdn Inf Div, 12 Jul, 2000 hrs, 13 Jul, 0700 hrs.
7. 78 (British) Div Intsum No. 50, 30 Jul 43, in WD 3 C.I.B. Jul/Aug 43; O.H. II, p. 104; WD H.&P.E.R., Jul 43; WD 1 Cdn Inf Div, 16 Sep 43
8. 1 Cdn Inf Div Intsums: No. 5, 23 Jul; No. 6, 26 Jul; No. 7, 28 Jul; No. 8, 30 Jul 43; O.H. II, p. 122; WD 1 Cdn Inf Div, Jul 43.
9. O.H. II, p. 193.
10. O.H. II, pp. 195, 196.
11. 1 Cdn Inf Div Planning Intsum No. 1 [*sic*], 11 Aug 43, WD 1 Cdn Inf Div, Aug 43, O.H. II, pp. 188, 189.
12. 1 Cdn Inf Div Planning Intsum No. 2 [*sic*], 31 Aug 43, WD 1 Cdn Inf Div, Aug 43
13. O.H. II, pp. 55, 173, 174, various sources.
14. O.H. II, p. 192.
15. 1 Cdn Inf Div Intsum No. 12, 7 Sep 43.
16. WD 1 Cdn Inf Div, 10, 12 Sep 43.
17. 1 Cdn Inf Div Intsum No. 13, 21 Sep 43; O.H. II, p. 228.
18. WD 3 C.I.B., 21, 23, 25 Sep 43.
19. 1 Cdn Inf Div Intsum No. 16, 3 Oct 43, O.H. II, pp. 236, 240.
20. O.H. II, p. 240, 1 Cdn Inf Div Intsum No. 22, 26 Oct 43.
21. O.H. II, p. 272.
22. WD 2 Cdn Inf Bde, 11, 13, 15, 23 Nov 43.
23. 1 Cdn Inf Div Intsum No. 27, 4 Dec 43.
24. O.H. II, p. 266, quoting German sources.
25. O.H. II, p. 290.
26. V Corps Intsum, quoted O.H. II, p. 290.
27. 1 Cdn Inf Div Intsum No. 27, 4 Dec 43.
28. Personal conversation, Maj. R.F. Wodehouse and author, Jan 71.
29. O.H. II, pp. 290–303.
30. 1 Cdn Inf Div Intsum No. 28, 10 Dec 43.
31. 1 Cdn Inf Div Intsums No. 29, 16 Dec; No. 31, 27 Dec 43.

32 Cf 1/AAI Gen/1, A.A.I. to C.M.H.Q., 2 Dec 43, f 145; 1/CMF Gen/1, approval sought 7 Dec 43, Cf 168; departed convoy KMF 28, 6 Jan 44, strength 3 and 17. WD 5 Cdn Armd Div, letter 23-1/Int, H.Q. 5 Armd Div, 9 Dec 43; 22-2/Int over 10-1/Ops, 10 Jan 44.
33 WD 1 Cdn Corps, Oct, Nov 43; Cf 4/CMF Reps/1, Jan 44; WD 1 Cdn Corps, 13 Dec 43; Intsum No. 1, 12 Dec 43.
34 Deployments are quoted in O.H. II, p. 366.
35 WD 1 Cdn Inf Bde, Jan 44; also 1 Div Intsum No. 34, 15 Jan 44.
36 11 Brigade used gridded photos for patrol control (WD 1 Cdn Inf Div, 13 Jan 44); O.H. II quotes 1 Cdn Inf Div Log, on p. 371.
37 WD 1 Cdn Inf Div, Jan 44, Annex 7; O.H. II, p. 366.
38 WDs 2 Cdn Inf Bde, 25 Jan 44; G.S. Br. H.Q. 5 Cdn Armd Div, 13 Feb 44; 11 Cdn Inf Bde, Jan/Feb 44; O.H. II, p. 375, I Cdn Corps Intsum No. 9, 31 Jan; No. 10, 2 Feb 44.
39 1 Cdn Inf Div Intsum No. 36, quoting Corps and Eighth Army.
40 I Cdn Corps Intsums: No. 13, 5/6 Feb; No. 14, 6 Feb; No. 15, 7 Feb; No. 18, 10 Feb; No. 20, 14 Feb; 1 Cdn Inf Div Intsum No. 42, 17 Feb; WD 1 Cdn Inf Div, 20 Feb 44.
41 1 Cdn Inf Div Intsum 43, 20 Feb; WD 1 Cdn Inf Div, 20 Feb; 1 Cdn Inf Div Intsum No. 45, 22 Feb; I Cdn Corps Intsum No. 26, 22 Feb 44.
42 I Cdn Corps Intsums No. 31, 4 Mar 44.
43 O.H. II, p. 385, WD 1 Cdn Inf Div, May 44.
44 O.H. II, pp. 387–94.
45 Allied Force H.Q. Note No. 53, quoted in I Cdn Corps Intsum No. 42, 12 Apr 44.
46 I Cdn Corps Intsums No. 39, 2 Apr; No. 40, 6 Apr; No. 41, 9 Apr; No. 43, 16 Apr 44.
47 I Cdn Corps Intsums: No. 44, 20 Apr; No. 45, 24 Apr; No. 46, 27 Apr 44.
48 I Cdn Corps Intsum No. 47, 1 May 44, Appendix A, quoting Eighth Army Intsum 711 and A.F.H.Q. Weekly Intsums 78 and 86.
49 I Cdn Corps Intsums: No. 48 to 2 May, dated 3 May; No. 49 to 8 May, dated 9 May 44; WD 1 Cdn Inf Div, 2 May 44.
50 O.H. II, p. 399.
51 I Cdn Corps Intsum No. 52, 14 May 44.
52 1 Cdn Inf Div Intsum No. 59, 1800 hrs, 15 May 44.
53 I Cdn Corps Intsum No. 57 to 17 May, dated 19 May; No. 58 to 2359, 19 May, dated 20 May 44.
54 I Cdn Inf Div Intsum No. 60, 16 May; 5 Cdn Armd Div Intsums 1 and 2, 20 May 44.
55 I Cdn Corps Intsum No. 61, 23 May 44; 1 Cdn Inf Div Intsum No. 62, 23 May 44; WD 1 Cdn Interrogation Team, May/Jun 44.
56 O.H. II, p. 435.
57 O.H. II, p. 448; WD 2 Cdn Inf Bde, 1 Jun 44.
58 Details on the Corps Int Message are found on WD G.S. Br., H.Q. I Cdn Corps, May 44; No. 3 dated 21 May, others missing.
59 WD 5 Cdn Armd Div, 7, 20, 27 May 44; letters from Lt.-Col. C.D. Kingsmill, E.D., to author, 26 Jul, 30 Aug 76.
60 WDs I Cdn Corps, 4, 5, 7, 8, 12 Aug; 1 Cdn Inf Div, 1–13, 20 Aug; 5 Cdn Armd Div, 6, 9, 11, 19 Aug 44.
61 I Cdn Corps Intsums No. 74, 13 Jun 44; No. 78, 24 Jun 44.
62 O.H. II, pp. 494–497.
63 I Cdn Corps Intsum No. 87, 14 Aug 44.
64 I Cdn Corps Special Intsum, 18 Aug 44; Intsum No. 88, 19 Aug 44; O.H. II, pp. 503 *et seq.*
65 1 Cdn Inf Div Intsum No. 78, 19 Aug 44.
66 O.H. II, pp. 498, 499.
67 WD 1 Cdn Inf Div, 22 Aug 44; I Cdn Corps Intsums: Nos. 89, 91, 92 (20, 22, 23 Aug) and 93, 24 Aug 44, quoting Eighth Army Intsum 788.
68 1 Cdn Inf Div Intsums Nos. 81, 82, 25 Aug; I Cdn Corps Intsum No. 94, 26 Aug; 1 Cdn Inf Div Log, 27 Aug 44, quoted O.H. II, p. 507.

69	See I Cdn Corps Intsums Nos. 100–116, 1–17 Sep; 1 Cdn Inf Div Intsums No. 90, 17 Sep; No. 91, 22 Sep 44.
70	I Cdn Corps Intsums No. 117, 18 Sep; No. 118, 19 Sep 44.
71	I Cdn Corps Intsums No. 119, 20 Sep; No. 120, 21 Sep 44.
72	I Cdn Corps Intsum No. 126, 27 Sep 44.
73	I Cdn Corps Intsums: No. 130, 4 Oct; No. 133, 11 Oct; No. 136, 14 Oct; No. 138, 16 Oct; No. 139, 17 Oct; also No. 119, 20 Sep 44.
74	I Cdn Corps Intsums: No. 119, 20 Sep; No. 131, 5 Oct; No. 132, 9 Oct; No. 133, 11 Oct; No. 134, 12 Oct 44.
75	I Cdn Corps Intsums No. 137, 15 Oct; No. 138, 16 Oct 44.
76	WD I Cdn Corps, 20 Nov 44, and Special Report Ravenna, 20 Dec 44.
77	WD I Cdn Corps, 24 Nov 44.
78	O.H. II, p. 613, I Cdn Corps Intsum No. 165, 29 Nov 44.
79	I Cdn Corps Intsums No. 163, 27 Nov; No. 164, 28 Nov 44.
80	WD I Cdn Corps, 29 Nov, 19 Dec 44.
81	Special Report Ravenna, WD I Cdn Corps, 11, 20 Dec 44.
82	I Corps Intsum No. 162, 6 Dec 44.
83	O.H. II, p. 665.
84	It listed two identifications and gave a P.W. total of 25 officers, 2,505 rank and file, since 30 Nov 44.
85	Letter, Fleming to author, Sep 76.

CHAPTER 9

1	WD H.Q. 1 Cdn Inf Div, May 1943; Cf I/Plan Memo/1, 9 Jul, 18 Aug 43.
2	Operation HUSKY, Security Regulations Planning Stage, G.S.1 Cdn Div (draft by Cooper), 30 Apr 43.
3	1 Cdn Inf Div Security Instruction No. 2, 2352/G/2, 15 May 43.
4	WD 1 Cdn Inf Div., 1–30 Jun 43.
5	H.Q.S. 6265-60-4. C.M.H.Q. to N.D.H.Q., 22 Sep 44; reports A.A.I. Counter-Intelligence and Counter-Sabotage measures in North African and Italian campaigns.
6	Narrative between 12 Jul and 1 Dec 43, taken from WD No. 1 Canadian Field Security Section, except where stated.
7	Periodic Note on Security No. 15, "Field Security Work with a Division in Italy"; HF/2308/G.I.(b), n.d., copy incomplete.
8	C.I. and C.S. in North Africa, etc., op. cit.
9	Periodic Note on Security No. 15, op. cit., report by Capt. Cooper to C.M.H.Q., Oct 43, held H.Q.S. 6265-60-4/5.
10	WD 1 F.S.S., vol. 32, Aug 43.
11	Report, Cooper, op. cit.
12	C.I. and C.S. in North Africa, etc., op. cit.
13	O.H. II, p. 287.
14	WD 14 F.S.S., 6 Nov.
15	C.I. and C.S. in North Africa, etc., op. cit.
16	Ibid.
17	Report by Capt. Cooper to C.M.H.Q., 10 Jan 44, held on Cf 4/C.M.F. Reports.
18	Cf 4/C.M.F. Reports/1, week 11 Dec 43.
19	WD 14 F.S.S., vol. 21, Feb 44.
20	I Cdn Corps Intsum 41, 13 Feb 41; WD I Cdn Corps, 15 Feb 41.
21	C.I. and C.S. in North Africa, etc., op. cit.
22	Security Intelligence Report (S.I.R.) No. 9, 12 Apr 44; the S.I.R. had been started in Corps in January; they were required every two weeks and dealt with: (1) Military Security: security of information, material, personnel, morale, rumours, troops, and civilians. (2) Civil Security: black lists, political and criminal. (3) Other matters of general interest (Cf 4/CMF Reps/1).

23 Wilson (A.F.H.Q.) to War Office, F 27125, 3 Apr 44, copy on Cf 1/AAI Gen/1/2; WD I Cdn Corps, 20 Apr 44.
24 WD 1 Cdn Inf Div, 1–30 Apr 44.
25 WD 1 F.S.S., vol. 41, May 44.
26 S.I.R. No. 14, 23 May 44 (19 May).
27 S.I.R. No. 15, 30 May 44 (26 May); WD 14 F.S.S., vol. 24, May 44.
28 I Cdn Corps Intsum No. 80, Appendix A, part 1, 3 Jul 44.
29 S.I.R. No. 16, 8 Jun 44 (27 May–2 Jun).
30 WD 7 F.S.S., vol. 32, 5 Jun 44.
31 WD 11 F.S.S., Jun 44; S.I.R. No. 17, 16 Jun 44 (to 9 Jun).
32 G.S.O.3 I(b), I Cdn Corps to C.M.H.Q.; Cf 6/4 FSS Sec/I, WD 8 F.S.R.D., vol. 2, Jul 44.
33 WD I Cdn Corps, 18 Jul, 12 Aug 44; security lecture, B.G.S. I Cdn Corps to distribution, 13 Aug 44 (copy of Security instructions dated 12 Aug attached, giving detail); O.H. II, p. 482; WD 1 F.S.S., vol. 43.
34 1 F.S.S., vol. 44, Aug 44; S.I.R. No. 22, 5 Sep 44 (Aug 16–31); O.H. II, p. 502.
35 WD 10 F.S. Section [sic], vol. 5., Appendix 5, "Special Report, Incident on Road Block, Night of 15/16 Sep 44", 9 and 10 Cdn Fd Sec Res. Dets., Cdn Army, C.M.F. to 312 F.S. Sec, to J.M. James, Capt., A/O.C.
36 Ibid., p. 3. Held Cf 4/MI Gen/1, Report 9, Oct 44.
37 Security Report for period ending 15 Oct 44, area Avellino and Benevento provinces, 910/R/2, 18 Oct 44, to G.S. (I), 3 District, Capt. J.M. James, O.C., 9–10 F.S. Res. Dets., pp. 1, 2.
38 I Cdn Corps Intsum No. 136, 14 Oct 44.
39 BASFORCE Report G, Int/Op Sec Gen/2 (I Cdn Corps), 16 Dec 44.
40 WD 9 F.S.R.D., vol. 8, 11, 12 Dec 44.
41 WD 1 F.S.S., vol. 49, Jan 45.
42 O.H., vol. II, p. 660; WD 1 F.S.S., vol. 50, 13 Jan 45.
43 O.H., vol. II, p. 665.
44 WD 9 F.S.R.D., vol. 12, Jan 45.

CHAPTER 10

1 Sir Frederick Morgan, *Overture to Overlord* (London, Hodder & Stoughton, 1950); Cf 1/Attach WO/2, 13 Jan 44.
2 Col. C.P. Stacey, *The Canadians in Europe, vol. III, North West Europe 1944–5*, Official History (O.H.), pp. 34–41.
3 Ibid., pp. 49, 52, 56, 58.
4 Ibid., pp. 64–6.
5 General Staff Branch, H.Q. 3 Canadian Infantry Division (3 C.I.D.), Operation Order (O.O.) No. 1, 13 May 44; WD 3 C.I.D., May 44; First Canadian Army (I C.A.) Intelligence Report No. 1., WD 1 C.A., Jun 44.
6 3 C.I.D., Intsums 7, 8, 16 May 44; 9, 18 May 44.
7 O.H., p. 75; Chester Wilmot, *The Struggle for Europe*, pp. 202, 215–16, 233 (Reprint Society, Bungay, Suffolk, 1954).
8 First Canadian Army Air Photo Interpretation Section (1 A.P.I.S.) WD, 21 May 44.
9 WDs 2, 3, 4, and 5 Canadian Army Interrogation Teams, C.Int.C. (C.A.I.T.), May, Jun 44.
10 WD First Canadian Army Interpreter Pool; Cf 5/Inter Pool/1, 20 May 44; letter 506/Int/1, 21 Army Group to HQ First Cdn Army, held Cf 1/Org Int/1, 52/Specs C.Int.C./1.
11 O.H., vol. III, p. 124, quoting Lt.-Gen. Richter, Commander *716 Infantry Division*.
12 WD 3 C.A.I.T., Jun 44.
13 Nos. 1–13 Canadian Air Liaison Sections (C.A.L.S.); War Diaries for these units often combined during periods Sections worked together; WD 10 C.A.L.S., 7, 10 Jun; 11, 16 Jun 44.
14 3 C.I.D., Intsums: 1, 9 Jun; 2, 9 Jun; 3, 10 Jun.

15 Ibid., No. 5, 13 Jun; No. 6, 14 Jun; No. 9, 17 Jun; No. 10, 18 Jun.
16 Ibid., No. 15, 30 Jun 44.
17 O.H., vol. III, p. 151, German sources.
18 WD G.S. Int, H.Q. 1 C.A., vol. 5, 6 Jun 44.
19 1 C.A. Special Intelligence Report, Sep 45.
20 WD 1 C.A., Attachment, Jun 44.
21 WD 1 C.A., Jun 44.
22 WDs 12 C.A.L.S., 11 C.A.L.S., 26 Jun; 1 A.P.I.S., Jun 44.
23 3 C.I.D. Intsum 16, 2 Jul; O.O. No. 3, 2 Jul 44.
24 3 C.I.D. Intsum 17, 4 Jul 44.
25 O.H., vol. III, p. 163.
26 O.H., vol. III, p. 165; II Canadian Corps (II C.C.) Intsums 1, 11 Jul, 2, 12 Jul 44.
27 Second Canadian Infantry Division (2 C.I.D.) Intsum 1, 14 Jul; II C.C. Intsum 5, 15 Jul 44.
28 II C.C. Intsums 6, 16 Jul; 7, 17 Jul 44.
29 3 C.I.D. Intsum 23, 19 Jul; 2 C.I.D. Intsum 4, 19 Jul 44; O.H., vol. III, pp. 178, 179.
30 WDs 2, 3 C.A.I.T., Jul 44.
31 3 C.I.D. Intsums 24, 23 Jul; 25, 26 Jul 44.
32 II C.C. Intsum 20, 30 Jul; 2 C.I.D. Intsum 6, 31 Jul 44.
33 WD H.Q. Section, C.A.I.T., Jul 44.
34 O.H., vol. III, pp. 185, 186–96.
35 WD 1 C.A., Jul 44.
36 WDs 1, 2, 4, 6, 10, 11, 12 C.A.L.S., Jul 44.
37 WD 1 C.A., Aug 44.
38 C.I.D. Intsum 31, 6 Jul 44.
39 II C.C. Intsum 26, 6 Aug; 2 C.I.D. Intsum 8, 6 Aug; 4 Canadian Armoured Division (4 C.A.D.) Intsum 4, 7 Aug; WD 1 C.A., 7 Aug 44.
40 WD 1 A.P.I.S., Aug 44; H.Q. 1 A.P.I.S. General Interpretation Report (GIR) Nos: 48, 1 Aug; 49, 5 Aug; 51, 7 Aug; 57, 10 Aug; 58, 10 Aug; 59, 12 Aug 44.
41 II C.C. Intsum 29, 9 Aug 44, quoting *89 Infantry Division* Intsum 30, 10 Aug; 31, 11 Aug 44; 2 C.I.D. Intsum 27 and 3 C.I.D. Intsum 35, 12 Aug 44.
42 O.H., vol. III, pp. 216–31, 234–8.
43 Personal conversation, Maj. R.F. Wodehouse and author, 6 Jan 71.
44 II C.C. Intsums 32, 12 Aug; 33, 13 Aug; 4 C.A.D. Intsum 7, 13 Aug 44.
45 Maj. R.F. Wodehouse, *supra*; II C.C. Intsum 34, 15 Aug; 2 C.I.D. Intsums 32, 33: 15, 16 Aug; 3 C.I.D. Intsum 36, Aug 44.
46 2 C.I.D. Intsums 35, 35 [sic]: 17, 18 Aug; 3 C.I.D. Intsum 37, 17 Aug; 1 C.A. Intsums 49, 51, 52: 17, 19, 20 Aug 44.
47 WD 10 C.A.L.S., 3 Aug 44.
48 WDs H.Q. 4, 3 (Aug 13, 15, 31), C.A.I.T.
49 WDs 2, 3 Wireless Intelligence Section (W.I.S.), Aug. 44.
50 WD 1 A.P.I.S.; 1 A.P.I.S. file 3-4-1-7, Air Photo check on P.W. statements to H.Q. 1 Army, 4 Aug 44; general check reports 1, 2.
51 1 A.P.I.S. GIR Nos. 69–73: 20, 22, 24, 26, 27 Aug; Nos. 75, 76: 28, 29 Aug 44.
52 II C.C. Intsums 38, 20 Aug; 41, 24 Aug; 2 C.I.D. Intsums 38, 39: 23, 25 Aug; 1 C.A. Intsums 41, 58: 24, 26 Aug 44.
53 3 C.I.D. Intsums 38, 39: 27, 29 Aug 44; O.H., pp. 294, 295.
54 1 C.A. Intsums 59, 60: 27, 28 Aug 44.
55 WD 3 C.I.D., 2 Sep 44; O.H., p. 301; II C.C. Intsums 48, 49: 5, 7 Sep 44.
56 WD 3 C.I.D., Sep 44; Intsum 42, 13 Sep 44; O.H., pp. 336–43.
57 WD 2 C.I.D., 17 Sep 44.
58 4 C.A.D. Operation Instruction (Op Instr) No. 7, 5 Sep 44; WD, Sep 44.
59 WD 4 C.A.I.T., vol. 5, Sep 44.
60 WD 1 A.P.I.S., Sep 44, including log.
61 WD 1 C.A., Sep 44.

62 O.H., vol. III, p. 302; Second British Army Intelligence Summaries 94, 96: 7, 9 Sep 44, quoted in 1 C.A. Intsums 71, 73: 8, 10 Sep 44.
63 1 C.A. Intsums 75, 76, 78: 12, 13, 15 Sep 44.
64 O.H., vol. III, p. 362; 4 C.A.D. Op Instr No. 8, 13 Sep; Intsum 14, 15 Sep 44; II C.C. Intsum 54, 16 Sep, quoting 1 C.A. Intsum 78, op. cit.; 55, 18 Sep 44; 4 C.A.D. Intsum Nos. 15, 18 Sep; 16, 22 Sep.; 4 C.A.D. file 1–6, Divisional Patrol Policy, Canal Leopold, 25 Sep 44.
65 Endnote 65 omitted in first edition of *Scarlet to Green*.
66 4 C.A.D. Intsums 21, 23: 17, 23 Oct; WD Oct, Nov 44.
67 WD 1 C.A., Sep 44.
68 II C.C. Intsum No. 54, 16 Sep 44, quoted 3 C.I.D Intsum 44, 19 Sep 44.
69 3 C.I.D. Intsums 45, 46: 5, 7 Oct; 1 C.A. Intsum 126, 3 Nov 44.
70 WD 1 C.A., 6, 7 Oct 44.
71 WD 3 W.I.S., Oct 44.
72 WD 1–6 C.A.L.S., Oct 44.
73 WD H.Q. 2, 3 C.A.I.T., Oct, Nov 44.
74 II C.C. Intsum 70, 19 Oct 44.
75 WD 1 A.P.I.S., Oct 44.
76 WD 1 C.A., Oct 44.
77 Ibid., 25 Nov 44.
78 Ibid., Appendix, Nov 44; WD 4 C.A.D., Nov 44.
79 WO No. 1 Canadian Army Intelligence Officers' Pool, C.Int.C., Nov 44–Nov 45.
80 II C.C. Intsum 80, 10 Nov 44.
81 WO 1 C.A., Dec 44.
82 1 C.A. Intsums 154, 155: 1, 2 Dec 44.
83 Ibid., 163, 10 Dec; 169, 16 Dec 44.
84 Ibid., 170, 171, 173: 17, 18, 20 Dec 44.
85 Ibid., 174, 21 Dec 44.
86 WD 1 C.A., Dec 44.
87 1 C.A., Intsum 176, 178: 23, 25 Dec 44; WD 1 C.A., 23 Dec 44; WD 1 A.P.I.S., Dec 44.
88 WD 1 C.A., Intsum 179, 26 Dec 44; letter, Col. P.E.R. Wright to author, 23 Dec 76.
89 WD 1 A.P.I.S., 27 Dec 44; 1 C.A. Intsum 180, 27 Dec 44.
90 WD 1 C.A., Intsums 181, 183, 184: 28, 30, 31 Dec 44, 1 Jan 45.
91 O.H., pp. 444–9.
92 WD 1 C.A., Dec 44; letter 59-1-10/Int, H.Q., 1 C.A., 18 Dec 44.
93 WD 1 C.A., 30, 30 Dec 44; 1 C.A. Intsums 192, 198, 201, 204: 8, 14, 17, 20 Jan 45.
94 1 C.A. Intsum 210, 26 Jan 45.
95 Ibid., 212, 214: 28, 30 Jan 45.
96 Ibid., 217, 218, 219, 220, 221: 2, 3, 4, 5, 6 Feb 45.
97 II C.C. Intsum 124, 5 Feb 45; WD 1 C.A., 12 Jan 45.
98 WD 1 A.P.I.S., Jan 45.
99 O.H., vol. III, p. 469.
100 1 C.A. Intsum 223, 8 Feb 45.
101 1 C.A. Intsum 224, 9 Feb 45 (confirmation referred to Intsum 218).
102 O.H., vol. III, p. 475.
103 II C.C. Intsum 128, 13 Feb 45.
104 O.H., vol. III, p. 484.
105 1 C.A. Intsums 231, 232, 233, 234, 235: 16, 17, 18 Feb 45.
106 1 C.A. Intsum 236, 21 Feb 45.
107 Ibid., 237, 22 Feb 45.
108 1 C.A. Intsum 238, 23 Feb; II C.C. Intsum 132, 23 Feb; WD 1 A.P.I.S., Feb 45; 2 C.I.D. Intsum 56, 24 Feb 45.
109 1 C.A. Intsums 244, 246, 248: 1, 3, 5 Mar; 11 C.C. Intsum 136, 2 Mar 45.
110 1 C.A. Intsum 250, 7 Mar 45.
111 II C.C. Intsum 135, 28 Feb 45.

112	WD 1 C.A., Feb 45.
113	WD 3 C.I.D., 2 C.I.D., Mar 45.
114	1 C.A. Intsums 259, 16 Mar; 261, 18 Mar; 274, 31 Mar; II C.C. Intsum 145, 20 Mar; WD 2 C.I.D., Mar 75.
115	1 C.A. Intsums, 275, 276, 278, 279, 280: 1, 2, 3, 5, 6, 8 Apr; II C.C. Intsum 151, 1 Apr 45.
116	1 C.A. Intsum 281, 7 Apr 45, quoting Second British Army.
117	WDs 2 C.I.D., 4 C.A.D., Apr 45.
118	1 C.A. Intsum 292, 18 Apr; 1 C.C. Intsum 27, 19 Apr 45.
119	II C.C. Intsum 160, 20 Apr 45.
120	I Canadian Corps (I C.C.) Intsum 266, 17 Apr 45 (largely a repeat of 1 C.A. Intsum 280, op. cit.).
121	1 C.A. Intsum 292, 18 Apr 45.
122	1 C.A. Intsums 297, 298: 23, 24 Apr 45.
123	1 C.A. Intsum 300, 303, 304: 26, 29, 30 Apr 45; O.H., p. 595.
124	WD 2 C.I.D., 2, 3 May 45.
125	Intsums 1 C.A. 208, I C.C. 288, II C.C. 167, 4 May 45.
126	1 C.A. ECLIPSE Intelligence Notes 48/4A – G Int (Plans), WD, Apr 45.
127	I C.C. Intsum 289, 5 May 45.
128	I C.I.D. letter/1/G, dated 15 May, WD, May 45.
129	WD 2 C.I.D., 9 May 45.

CHAPTER 11

1	WD 3 F.S.S., vol. 36, Jun 44; security report, 3 Cdn Inf Div Area, O.C. 3 F.S.S. to G.S.O.3 I(b), I Br. Corps, 15 Jun; file 3 FS/3-3-2-6-6.
2	WD 3 F.S.S., vol. 38, 26 Aug 44.
3	WD 2 F.S.S., vol. 43, Jul 44.
4	WD 2 F.S.S., vol. 44, 8 Aug 44.
5	WD 18 F.S.S., vol. 10, 5 Aug 44.
6	WD 1 F.S.R.D., vol. 4, summary, 8 Aug 44 (H.Q. co-located with 2, 3, 5, and 6 F.S.R.D.s during month); Col. Graham Blyth to author, 3 Feb 77.
7	Cf 4/Int Rep/I, H.Q. 1 Army to C.M.H.Q., 9 Aug 44.
8	Camp 030 had a strength of two officers and 28 men and an increment (No. 5 Interrogation Team) of two and 11; it had a capacity of 250 prisoners (local civilian prisons absorbed the surplus); it had three areas: a transit area for new arrivals, a compound for those willing to talk, and an isolation area (usually a civil prison) for those refusing to talk; if interrogation revealed a prisoner to be of no interest to Intelligence, he was turned over to his national authorities; if he was of interest he was sent back to Camp 020 in England.
9	WD 15 F.S.S., vol. 16, 2 Sep 44 *et seq.*
10	WD 2 F.S.S., vol. 45, 6 Sep 44 *et seq.*
11	WD 3 F.S.S., vol. 39, 5 Sep 44 *et seq.*
12	WD 17 F.S.S., vol. 11, 30 Sep 44.
13	Items in the following paragraphs are taken from September WDs 2, 4, 18, 16, and 15 F.S.S.
14	Cf 4/CI Reports/1, No. 8, 11–27 Sep 44; No. 9, 28 Sep–11 Oct 44.
15	Cf 4/CI Reports/1, No. 10, 12–27 Oct 44.
16	WD 15 F.S.S., vol. 17, Oct 44; C.I. Reports No. 6, dated 24 Sep–8 Oct; No. 7, dated 8–24 Oct.
17	WD 2 F.S.S., vol. 46, Oct 44; the White Brigade lost four men on 10 Oct 44.
18	WD 15 F.S.S., vol. 17, Oct 44.
19	Cf 4/CI Reports/1, No. 11, 26 Oct–10 Nov 44; "C.I. Plan 5".
20	Cf 4/CI Reports/1, No. 12, 11–25 Nov; No. 13, 25 Nov–10 Dec; No. 14, 11–26 Dec 44.
21	Cf 4/CI Reports/1, No. 2, Aug–Nov 44, dated Dec 44.

22 WD 15 F.S.S., vol. 15, 1 Dec 44; C.I. Reports No. 10, O.C. 15 F.S.S. to II Corps, 5 Dec 44; No. 11, O.C. 15 F.S.S. to II Corps, 21 Dec. 44.
23 WD 2 F.S.S., vol. 48, comment, Dec. 44.
24 C.I. Reports No. 15, 27 Dec 44–10 Jan 45; No. 16, 14 Dec 44–27 Jan 45 [sic].
25 WD 17 F.S.S., vol. 15, Jan 45.
26 C.I. Report No. 18, 12–26 Feb 45.
27 Correspondence First Army–C.M.H.Q., 1 C.A. 71-24-21 S.D., 19 Feb, 12, 15 Mar 45.
28 C.I. Report No. 17, 28 Jan–11 Feb 45; O.H., vol. III, pp. 466 *et seq.*
29 C.I. Report No. 18, op. cit.; WD 16 F.S.S., vol. 17, Feb 45.
30 C.I. Report No. 18, op. cit.
31 C.I. Report No. 19, 27 Feb–25 Mar 45.
32 WD 16 F.S.S., vol. 18, Mar 45.
33 No. 20 F.S.S., C.I. Report No. 1, 18 Mar 45.
34 WDs 15 F.S.S., vol. 22, 4 F.S.S., vol. 31, Mar 45.
35 WD 17 F.S.S., vol. 19, 2 May 45.
36 C.I. Report No. 21, 25 Apr–25 May 45, dated 26 May 45; Lt.-Col. J.W.G. Macdougall to author, 24 Jan 77; lecture, 18 Jul 46.
37 WDs 17 F.S.S., vol. 19; 7 F.S.R.D., May 45.
38 WD 17 F.S.S., 12 May 45.
39 WD 14 F.S.S., vol. 36, 11 May 45 *et seq.*
40 WD 14 F.S.S., vol. 37, Jun 45; Col. G. Blyth, *supra.*
41 WD 16 F.S.S., vol. 21, 23 Jun 45.
42 C.I. Reports No. 3 and No. 4, May, Jun 45, held WD 20 F.S.S.
43 Cf 4/Liais CFN/1, C.M.H.Q. to G.S.O. Int(b), H.Q. C.F.N., 26 Sep 45; Wright to C.M.H.Q., 25 Sep 45.
44 Ibid., Wright to Walter, 4 Oct; Raymont (for Walter) to Wright, 9 Oct; Wright to Walter, 16 Oct 45.
45 Ibid., Int SitRep, 29 Oct 45.
46 WD 1 C.A.P.P.U., vols. 1–5: 9, 12 Sep–31 Oct 44, Feb, Nov 45; they bought much of their material locally; one basic tool they lacked was a print trimmer.
47 WD 1 A.R.I.T., vols. 1–5, Mar–Jul 45.
48 WDs, Sections as shown.
49 Nf H.Q.S. 9128, 27 Dec 44; Cf 1/Org CAOF/1, G.S. 798 to G.O.C. 1 Army from C.M.H.Q., 5 Jan 45.
50 C.I. News Sheet No. 5, H.Q. First Army, "Provisional C.I. Policy Memorandum for the Advance through France, Holland and Belgium, and the Occupation of Germany, 19 Oct 44", on Nf H.Q.S. 6265-60-1.
51 Cf 1/Occup Gp/1, 21 A.G./Int 2025/6, B.G.S. 1 to Cdn Sec, 1 Ech, 21 A.G., 26 Jan 45; weeks' minute, 25 Feb 45; Defensor to CanMil, 16 Feb 45; (G.S. 88, G.S.O.2 S.D.1 to S.D.O., 10 Mar 45); O.M.H.Q. to 1 Ech, 21 A.G.
52 WD 3 Canadian Area Security Office, vol. 2, 28 Aug 45.
53 C.I. SitRep No. 1, 28 Sep; WD 3 A.S.O., 27 Sep, 4 Oct 45; monthly C.I. Report No. 2, 29 Oct 45; C.I. SitRep No. 4, 19–31 Oct; Cf 4/Summ/14 (M), Wright to D.C.G.S., 17 Oct 45, approved 18 Oct 45; Major Noble's Distribution List shows the organization of the period: G.S.I.(b), XXX Corps; G.S.O.3 I(b), 3 Cdn Inf Div, C.A.O.F.; G.S.O.3 Int, 1 Polish Armoured Div; A.S.O.s Aurich, Detmold, Hannover, Munster, Oldenburg; Nos. 30, 40, 50 Sub-Area C.I. Offices, Zones A-G, 40 F.S.S., 331 F.S.S.; file and three spares (WD 3 A.S.O.).
54 C.I. SitReps No. 15, 1–15 Nov, 3 A.S.O., 14 Nov 45; No. 19, 22 Jan 46; verbal comment, Lt.-Col. R.H. Noble to author, 23 Aug 76.
55 WD 1 A.S.O., vol. 8, Feb 46.
56 WD 2 A.S.O., vol. 8, Feb 46.
57 3 A.S.O., C.I. SitRep No. 23, 6–19 Mar 46, 18 Mar 46.
58 F.M. B.L. Montgomery, *Memories* (London, Collins, 1958) pp. 389 *et seq.*, 412.

CHAPTER 12

1. G.S. 1661, dated 14 Jul 43, C.M.H.Q. to D.N.D.
2. Cf 4/Censor Press/1, D.N.D. to C.M.H.Q., D.P.R. 252, 26 Mar; 1 Army to C.M.H.Q., 7 Apr; Rodger to M.O.&I., B.G.S., 12 Apr; C.M.H.Q. to D.N.D., 20 Apr, and to A.F.H.Q., 4 Sep 43.
3. Cf 4/CMF Reps/1, Lieut. W.R. Austin, 15 Sep 43.
4. Cf 1/Censor/1/3, Nf H.Q.S. 6265-57, D.N.D. to C.M.H.Q., 17, 20 Dec 43; C.M.H.Q. to D.M.I., 4 Jan 44; R.S. Malone, D.D.P.R., C.M.F., to C.M.H.Q., 21 Feb 44, to D.N.D.
5. WD 4 Special Press Censor Section, C.Int.C., report signed Curren for Robbins, 30 Nov 44–1 Mar 45.
6. Cf 1/AAI Gen/1, AFHQ Algiers, signed Eisenhower, 1 CanMil, 7 Nov 43; folio 28 to Col. G.S., 9 Nov 43; CanMil to A.F.H.Q., 4 Dec 43.
7. Cf 1/Org Int/1, 1/AA1 Gen/1/2, correspondence, 25 Mar 44 on.
8. Cf 4/Censor Press/1, correspondence, 3–13 May 44.
9. WD C.M.H.Q., R.O.s 4537, 4538, 4539, 5 May 44; C.M.H.Q. to N.D.H.Q., 10 May 44, 25 May 44.
10. Cf 4/Censor Press/1/2, correspondence, 17 Jul–21 Sep 44; 23, 25 Nov 44; 24, 29 Jan 45; 8 Mar 45; report Maj. L.W. Taylor, vol. III, p. 80; 16 Jan, 14 Feb, 3 May, 1–8 Jun, approved 26 Jun 45.
11. WDs 1, 2 Canadian Censor Sections, vol. I, 14 Apr–1 May 44; summary of Canadian censorship prior to establishment of 1 and 2 Canadian Censor Sections, n.d.; R. Bell, Capt.; 2 captains, 3 clerks, 1 batman.
12. WD 4 Special Press Censor Section, C.Int.C., report 30 Nov 44–1 Mar 45.

CHAPTER 13

1. WD "X" Force, Mar, Apr, 40.
2. O.H. I, p. 78; WD "Z" Force, May, Jun 40; WD Royal Regiment of Canada, Jun 40; WD "Z" Force, Jul–Oct 40.
3. WD C.M.H.Q., 1–3 Aug 41; Cf s/3/Cdn Corps/3 (SD), 26 Jul 41; O.H. I, pp. 302, 304; WD 2 Cdn Inf Bde, Force 111, 26 Jul 41–8 Sep 41.
4. O.H. I, pp. 306, 307.
5. O.H. I, p. 438.
6. Maj.-Gen. S. Woodburn Kirby, *History of the Second World War, The War Against Japan* (H.M.S.O. 1957), vol. 1, pp. 59–63.
7. Rt. Hon. Lyman P. Duff, *Report on the Canadian Expeditionary Force to the Crown Colony of Hong Kong* (Ottawa, King's Printer, 1942) P.C. 1160, pp. 13, 14.
8. Kirby, op. cit., pp. 80, 81; file H.Q.S. 8641-6-1, 28 Feb, 7 Mar, 21 May, 30 Jun, 1 Aug 41; Duff, op. cit., p. 13; O.H. I, p. 441.
9. H.Q.S. 8608. Eden to External, No. 84; 11 May 40; D.M.O.&I. to D.N.I., A.D.M.I. to D.M.O.&I., 14 Jun 40; G.O.C. Pacific Command to C.G.S., 25 Nov 40.
10. File 8641-6-1, Mil Int Sec; O.H. I, p. 441; Duff, op. cit., p. 6, quoting Gen. H.D.G. Crerar; CanMil to Defensor, G.S. 2332, 26 Oct 41.
11. H.Q.S. 8613/11-1, 1 Sep *et seq.*; H.Q.S. 8641-6, 21 Oct 41.
12. Duff, op. cit., p. 16; quoting Brig. J.K. Lawson, p. 46; Kirby, op. cit., p. 166.
13. Kirby, p. 113; H.Q.S. 8641-6-1, 9 Sep 41 *et seq.*
14. Kirby, pp. 116, 117.
15. H.Q.S. 8641-6-1, Station JZJ, 1930, 30 Nov, 3 Dec; Kirby, p. 118.
16. Kirby, p. 119; John Molun Carew, pseud. Carews, *Fall of Hong Kong* (Anthony Blond, London, 1960), p. 43; five bandsmen had been sent to Brig. Lawson's H.Q. for Intelligence duties; O.H. I, p. 464; H.Q.S. 8641-6-1, 14 Dec 41.
17. Kirby, pp. 120, 126, 127; H.Q.S. 8641-6-1, JZJ, 14 Dec 41.
18. Kirby, pp. 146, 110, 111.
19. WD H.Q. "W" Force, various dates.
20. O.H. I, p. 496.
21. H.Q.S. 9055, O.H. I, dates and correspondence shown.

22 H.Q.S. 9055, 12 Jun 43, D.M.I. to G.O.C. Pacific Command, G.S.I. 472; C.G.S. to G.O.C. Pacific Command, C.G.S. 635.
23 H.Q.S. 9055-2, 15 Jun 43, Japanese Information Extract No. 25 M.I.1.; P.C.S. 508-1-1-16 (G.I.O.), May 43; H.Q.S. 9055-2, WD GREEN LIGHT; material appears to have been sent to Adak but there is no report of its receipt; however, they were then working directly with their parent U.S. formations and should have been given everything they needed.
24 P.C.S. 504-1-10-2, G.S.I., 27 Jun 43; WD H.Q. 13 Canadian Infantry Brigade.
25 H.Q.S. 9058-2, WD 13 C.I.B.
26 Intsums, held WDs 6, 13 C.I.B., H.Q. Pacific Command.
27 O.H. I, pp. 503, 504.
28 O.H. I, pp. 510, 511; H.Q.S. 9131, Jan 44; C.M.H.Q. 1/ FE/1, W.O. to S.E.A.C., 6 Jul 44; W.O. to D.N.D., 24 Jul 44.
29 H.Q.S. 9131, dates shown.
30 H.Q.S. 9131-3-Q, 13, 20, 29 Jun 45; Cook to D.M.I.
31 C.M.H.Q. 1/FE/1 C.M.H.Q. to D.M.I., 10 Jul 45; G.O. 241, 20 Jul 45.
32 H.Q.S. 9131-3-Q, D.M.I. to 6 Div, 25 Jul 45.

CHAPTER 14

1 C.P. Stacey, *The Victory Campaign*, O.H. III, p. 635.
2 Col. F.H. Walter, O.B.E., *Special Report: Cloak and Dagger*, 760.013 (D.1), 1946; this report, though not quoted in specific detail, has been used as a basis for most of this portion of the chapter.
3 Cf 1/Guerrilla/1, 12 Mar 40 *et seq.*
4 (a) B. Sweet-Escott, *Baker Street Irregular* (London, Methuen, 1965) (b) H.M. Hyde, *The Quiet Canadian* (London, Hamish Hamilton, 1962).
5 M.R.D. Foot, *S.O.E. in France* (London, H.M.S.O., 1966); E.H. Cookridge, *Inside S.O.E.* (London, Barker); Walter, op. cit.
6 General report, M.I. Section (C.M.H.Q.), p. 88, 27 Dec 45.
7 B.S.C. asked for 25 Canadian Chinese on 5 Sep 44; on 16 Nov he asked for an additional 125 for Force 136; the Canadians agreed and also accepted the costs; by 5 Jan 45, 31 had been chosen and the total was oversubscribed by 20 Feb; 135 went to the U.K. in Feb, 121 to India in Mar; B.D.F. S.D. 10-1-35 Temp 2, 17 Jul 45; H.Q.S. 3488-3, vol. 4; for evaluation of the size and value of S.O.E., see Maurice J. Buckmaster, *Specially Employed* (London, Batchworth, 1952); F.M. Sir William Slim, *Defeat into Victory*, reprint Soc. Ed., 1957 pp. 530, 531; interview, Maj. H.J. Legge, S.O.E., with Maj., J.H.V. Wilson, M.C., 28–9 May 75, courtesy Maj. Wilson and Okanagan Historical Society.
8 Airey Neave, *Saturday at M.I.9* (London, Hodder & Stoughton, 1969), with additions from Walter, op. cit., and personal conversations between Lt.-Col. Labrosse and author.
9 Sam Derry, *The Rome Escape Line* (London, Harrap, 1960); conversations, H.J. Byrnes and author.
10 C.M.H.Q. file 4/M.I.9/1, liaison with M.I.9; report, Byrnes to Walter, 1 May 45.
11 Col. F.H. Walter, O.B.E., *Special Report: Cloak and Dagger*, op. cit.
12 Lt.-Gen. Sir Frederick Morgan, K.C.B., *Overture to Overlord* (London, Hodder and Stoughton, 1950) p. 228.
13 Cf 4/PW Op Old/1, 26 Feb 44 *et seq.*
14 Ibid., 20 Mar 44.
15 Appendix 30, "Intelligence" to I.C.A., WD, Intsum 97, 5 Oct 44; report, *Intelligence First Canadian Army*, vol. III, basis of much of this part.
16 Details in succeeding paragraphs from WD 3 P.R. Group, Jul 44 *et seq.*; report, vol. III, p. 72.
17 First Canadian Army Intsum 77, 14 Sep 44, quoted report, p. 74.
18 WD 3 P.R. Group, 23, 27 Sep 44.
19 James M Erdmann, *Leaflet Operations in the Second World War*, Denver, Instant Printing, 1969, pp. 337–44.

20   First Canadian Army War Diary, Appendix 30, Part II, p. 2, Intsum 97, 5 Oct 44.
21   WD 3 P.R. Group, Oct, Nov 44.
22   Report, p. 77.
23   WD 3 P.R. Group, Jan–May 45.

CHAPTER 15

1   WD N.D.H.Q., D.M.O.&I. (Ops), 25 Aug 39; 1230 hrs, 26 Aug; 1235 hrs, 27 Aug, C.G.S. to all Districts; 1330 hrs, 27 Aug, M.D. 1 to D.N.D.
2   Nf H.Q.S. 8139-1, 29 Aug 39; 14 Oct 40; H.Q.S. 6403, H.Q.S. 8139, 18 Jan 41.
3   Nf H.Q.S. 8644, F.D. 27.
4   Nf H.Q.S. 8631-1, Odium to M.N.D., 2 Jul 41.
5   Lt.-Col. K.C. Burness, Report on First Intelligence Course, G.S.O. to Commandant, R.M.C., 20 Dec 40.
6   Nf H.Q.S. 8631, vol. 1, D.M.O.&I. to D.M.T., 28 Jun 41.
7   R.M.C. C-1-5, Hertzberg to Secy, D.N.D., 28 Aug, 3 Oct 41; Nf H.Q.S. 8631, vol. 1, D.M.I. to C.M.H.Q., 10 Feb 41; D.M.O.&I. to D.M.T., 28 Feb; vol. 2, G.S.O. Int to D.M.O.&I., 9 Sep 41.
8   Nf H.Q.S. 8631, F.D. 16: 2, 12, 14 Jan 42.
9   Nf H.Q.S. 8631, F.D. 21: 21, 31 Mar, 1, 18, 23, 28 Apr, 1 May 42; R.M.C. 5-10-1, Hertzberg to Secy, D.N.D., 4 May 42; Nf H.Q.S. 8631, F.D. 21, D.M.O. to C.G.S., 21, 22, 28 May 42.
10 Nf H.Q.S. 8631-2, G.S.O. Int to D.M.T., 2 Jul 42; H.Q. B.D.F. S.D. 3-3-1, 28 Apr 42.
11 Nf H.Q.S. 741-11-16-1; 3488-3; 20-4-Q, 7 Jan, 28 Feb, 8, 26 Apr, 4, 6, 15, 26 May 43; 20-1-Q, 20 Feb 43.
12 Nf H.Q.S. 20-1-Q, 30 Apr, 11, 20 May 43; Lt.-Col. E. Acland, O.B.E., E.D., to author, 5 Oct 76.
13 Nf B.D.F. S.D. 3-3-1, 28 Apr 42; H.Q.S. 8889-1, F.D. 1 (M.I.1); Cf 9/Qual IO/1, 6 Jan 43; H.Q.S. 8631, vol. 3, D.M.I. to C.G.S., 4 Jan 43; vol. 5, 16, 18, 27 Mar 43.
14 File H.Q. 1 Canadian Army S-3-5-1 (Int), 22 Apr; to C.M.H.Q.; to D.N.D., 23 Apr 43.
15 Basso to Chief Instructor (Col. J.J. Hurley), 30 Aug 43.
16 Nf H.Q.S. 8631, vol. 6, D.M.I. to D.C.G.S.(a), 5 Oct 43; 3430-1, 11 Sep 43 *et seq.*
17 Nf H.Q.S. 3606, D.M.O.&I. to C.G.S., 6 Jul; C.G.S. to Maj.-Gen. J.S. Ross, 9 Sep 21; Ross to Defence Committee; H.Q.S. 3506.
18 Nf H.Q.S. 8631-2 (Int), Murray to Cook, 14 Jul 42; 8889-4, Int to Canadian Army Staff, Washington (C.A.S.W.), 17 Feb 43.
19 Nf H.Q.S. 8889-3, Pearkes to C.G.S., 17 May 43; 24, 28 May, 2 Jun 43.
20 Nf H.Q.S. 8889-3, vol. 2, D.M.I. to C.G.S., 17 Oct 43.
21 Ibid., Pacific Command to D.N.D., 13, 17 Nov 43.
22 Canadian Army Training Manual, Dec 45; Nf H.Q.S. 8889-3, 18 Apr 44; Pacific Command P.C. 173/1093, 15 Sep 44; G.O. 446; P.C.S. 504-22 J.L.S. (G.I.O.), 14 Nov 45.
23 Nf H.Q.S. 8889-3 Lt.-Col. P.W. Cook, C.A.S.W., to D.M.T., 17 Aug 45; D.M.I. memo.
24 P.C.S. 504-21 J.L.S. (G.I.O.), 31 Aug 43, 9 Oct 45 *et seq.*
25 Nf H.Q.S. 8889-3, WD C.M.H.Q., Cf 1/Liais WO/1, 15 Jul 42; 1/Att WO/1, misc. entries.
26 Nf H.Q.S. 741-102-16-1, 26 Apr, 20, 23 May, 8 Jun 44.
27 Nf H.Q.S. 3488-3, D.M.I. to Districts, 23 Jun 44; H.Q.S. 741-114-16-1, 28 Jan 44 *et seq.*
28 Nf H.Q.S. 3488-3, H.Q.S. 20-4-12-11-D (RC Sigs); H.Q.S. 7428-11, 13 Dec 43, Apr 44, 6 Feb, 5 May 45.

CHAPTER 16

1. Nf H.Q.S. 3626; vol. 10, 8641-6 F.D.11; 6403; 4720; personal memoir, Miss P.E. Chartrand.
2. Nf H.Q.S./C. 4720, 23 Nov 40–23 Nov 44; H.Q.S. 8641-6.
3. C.M.H.Q. Progress Report, Feb 41.
4. Nf H.Q.S. 5858; 5588; 5742; 5957; 15 Feb 41 *et seq.;* H.Q.S. 8641-6 (Int).
5. M.A. Washington to D.M.O.&I., 3, 7 Jan 42; letter, C. Chauveau to author, 25 Nov 63; Nf H.Q.S. 1450-1.
6. Nf H.Q.S. 3499-33, 14 Dec 42–2 Mar 43.
7. Nf H.Q.S. 8756, D.E.S. to Q.M.G., 3 May 41, M.A. 36-0, M.A. Washington to D.M.O.&I. H.Q.S. 8641-6, F.D. 30, 2, 18 Oct 41.
8. Nf H.Q.C. 3507-2, 11, 19 Feb, 9 Mar, 6 Apr 43; H.Q.S. 8723-3, Nov 43–20 Mar 47.
9. Washington File C.J.S. 2-4-4, Cook to Murray, 1 May 43.
10. Nf H.Q. 70-44-55 (Int), 8 Dec 42; H.Q.S. 8930-7; C.A.S.W. 2-4-7, 8 Apr 43.
11. Nf H.Q.S. 3499-5, Memo M.I.1 to D.M.I., 17 Sep 43.
12. Nf H.Q.S. 8813-4 (Tech 11,000), A.T.D.B. to M.G.O., Jan 44.
13. Nf H.Q.S. 3499-5, Memo M.I.1 to D.M.I., 17 Sep 43; H.Q.S. 2-4-23 on H.Q.S. 8813-3-1, 1 Apr 43; H.Q.S. 88-3-1 (Tech 11,000), 5 Feb 44; P.C.S. 504-22-J.L.S. (G.I.O.), 1 Nov 44; H.Q.C. 8813-3, D.V.S.A. to D.M.T., 7 Dec 44.
14. Cf 1/Enemy Equipment/1/2/SD3 to D.N.D., 8 Jan 45; Nf H.Q.S. 8813-3, minutes, 16 Apr 45.
15. C.P. 3-F-85, 27 Apr 45; O.H.I.
16. Cf 4/Liais NDHQ/1, 12 Jun–6 Jul 44
17. Nf H.Q.S. 8809, vol. 2, minutes M.N.D. working committee, 27 Dec 44.
18. R.S. 4-7-16 (G Int), M.D. 13 to D.N.D., 17 Jan 45; Nf H.Q.S. 8872-2, D.M.I. to D.M.O.&P., 18 Jan 45; personal conversation, Morgan to author, 13 May 71; O.H., vol. I., p. 178.
19. O.H., vol. 1, pp. 177–178; Brig.-Gen. W.H. Wilbur (Former Chief of Staff, U.S. Western Defence Command) in *Reprint,* Feb. 46, pp. 459–64; Nf H.Q.S. 4354-3322, vol. 22, "Inter-Service Balloon Committee Disbanded", 8 Feb 46; H.Q.S. 3367-15-22, vol. 3, F.D. 65, D.S.D.(W) to D.M.I.
20. Nf H.Q.S. 3636, vol. 10, M.D. 5 to D.M.O.&I., 28 Mar, 18–24 May; A.C.G.S. to C.G.S., 28 Jun 41.
21. Nf H.Q.S. 6499-7, 8 Nov 43; D.M.T. Circular No. 1407, 1 Sep 44; No. 1492, 19 Feb 45.
22. WDs 6, 7, 8 Intelligence Sections, 7 C.A.L.S.
23. Nf H.Q.S. 3493, C.G.S. to C.N.S., 21 May 30; D.M.O.&I. to D. Sigs., 18 Jun 32; H.Q.S. 24-4, W.H.S. Macklin, D.C.G.S., C.M.H.Q., "Comments on paper by Chief Signals Officer II Canadian Corps", 7 May 45.
24. WD D.M.O.&I., 6 Dec 39; Nf H.Q.S. 7428, F.D. 8; H.Q.S. 7428-1, 14 Sep 39; WD D.M.O.&I., Jun 40.
25. Nf H.Q.S. 8641-6, F.D.3, 26 Aug 41; M.A. 6-2, M.A. Washington to D.M.O.&I., 20 Sep 41; Lt.-Col. E. Acland to author, *supra,* 5 Oct 76.
26. C.M.A; 62, C.A.S.W., 7, 8 Oct 41; Nf H.Q.S. 8641-3, 20 Oct 41; M.A. 24-l, 22 Oct 41; H.Q.S. 7428-4, 7 Nov 41.
27. Nf H.Q.S. 7428-4, 28 Aug–30 Sep 40, 26 Dec 40.
28. Nf H.Q.S. 8621; H.Q.S. 7428-4, 3 Feb 41; H.Q.S. 8641-6-1, 28 Mar 41, 27 May 41.
29. Nf H.Q.S. 7428-9, vol. I, 23 Oct, 6, 11 Nov 41.
30. Nf H.Q.S. 7428-9, vol. I, 31 Dec 41, 11 Jan 42; W.E. Cdn V/1940/340K/1.
31. Nf H.Q.S. 8706, 26 Jul, 2, 5, Aug, 27 Sep 41; A.C.S. 3-10-2-Q, 2 Sep 41; A.C.S. 1-4(W), 12 Sep 41.
32. Nf H.Q.S. 8621, C.B.C. to A.D.M.&A.I. [*sic*], 28 Jun 40.
33. Nf H.Q.S. 8641-6-1, 22 Dec 40–22 Aug 41; H.Q.S. 8706 (Int), 22 Aug 41, 30 Mar 42; H.Q.S. 7042-2, F.D. 2, C.A.R.O. 2871 6 Feb 43, and 2947 (amendments).
34. No file, External to D.M.I., 5 Nov 43; Nf H.Q.S. 8641-6-1, D.M.I. to X.A., 15 Nov 43.
35. Nf H.Q.S. 8889-3, Aug 44; H.Q.S. 7428-4, 10, 22 Nov 44; 13 Feb, 21 May 45.

CHAPTER 17

1. Nf H.Q.C. 171, vol. 2, 1 Nov 39: H.O.C. 133, F.D. 3, 1 Nov 39; C.G.S. to distribution; H.Q.S. 665-4-A, 9 Nov 39.
2. H.Q.S. 1233, F.D. 5; WD D.M.O.&I.; H.Q.S. 1725, F.D. 643.
3. H.Q.S. 8619, 8 Jun 40; M.N.D. to Minister of Justice, 11 Jun 40; minutes, 14 Jun 40; R.C.M.P paper, 3 Jul 40; Maj. Scott to sub-committee, 1 Aug 40; minutes second meeting, 7 Aug 40.
4. H.Q.S. 6403, 73 ff.; H.Q.S. 6467, M.D. 5 to Secy, D.N.D.; H.Q.S. 6265-14, 28 Apr, 9 Jun, 29 Jul, 2 Aug; G.S.O.3 M.I.3(a) became G.S.O.2, three staff learners, Acland to Lt.-Col., 17 Jun 42; memo M.I.3 to D.M.O.&I.; H.Q.S. 6265-3-34, 2 Mar, 17 Apr 42; H.Q.S. 6265-36, 5 May 42; WD Pacific Command; Bray to Acland, 19 May 42; P.C.S. 508-1-1-1, 5 Apr 42; copy held H.Q.S. 8704-12.
5. WDs 5, 6, and 8 Field Security Sections, 42-43.
6. P.C. 47/6 567, 18 Aug 43.
7. Information in following paragraphs taken in part from Historical Record of Counter-Intelligence and Security Section (Canada), prepared early 46. (C.I. report); Security bulletins and verbal comment to author by Lt.-Col. Acland, Sep 72, Oct 76.
8. Nf H.Q.S. 5688, F.D. 21, A.G. to all D.O.C.s, 20 Nov 39; H.Q.S. 6467, C.G.S. to M.N.D., 27 Oct 39, approved.
9. Commissioner C.W. Harvison, *The Horsemen*, Macmillan & Co., London, 1967.
10. Commissioner S.T. Wood to Col. H. Desrosiers Deputy Minister of National Defence, 23 Jul 42; C.I. report, op. cit.
11. H.Q.S. 6615-4-A, F.D. 25 (A.G.I.), 22 Jan 42; report, op cit; H.Q.S. 6615-4-A, vol. 3 (AM).
12. C.M.H.Q. to D.N.D., G.S. 3944, 23 Nov 42.
13. H.Q.S. 23 F.D. 3, A.D. 3, 14 Jun 43 (Adm 1 (2)), 23 Jul 43, 30 Mar 44; H.Q.S. 6615-4-A, vol. 5, (Adm 1 (a)(i)), 12 Jul 43, 30 Mar 44; D.C. 9440, 10 Dec 43; S.C., 5 Jul, 24 Jul, 30 Sep 44; H.Q.S. 23, F.D. 34 Admin, 20 Jan, 22 May, 12 Jul 45; H.Q.S. 23, 26 Dec 42, 6 Jan, 30 Nov 44, 19 Mar, 13 Nov 45; P.C. 4309, 44. C.I. report, op. cit.
14. H.Q.S. 223 series, S-223-5-4, 17 Nov 45.
15. H.Q.S. 236, vol. 10, G.S. 152, C.G.S. to M.D.s 2, 4, 6, 11, P.C. 2513, 3 Sep 39.
16. H.Q.S. 5346, vol. 10, 4 Sep 39; H.Q.S. 236, Msg 156 to Deputy Chief Cable Censor, Montreal.
17. WD D.M.O.&I., 19 Oct 39.
18. H.Q.S. 1027-C-46, F.D. 567, 24 Oct 39; D.M.O.&I. to C.G.S., 7 Nov 39; H.Q.S. 8118-54-27-0-63, -59, -61.
19. H.Q.S. 8139, D.M.O.&I. to C.G.S., 30 Nov 39; Lt.-Gen. M.A. Pope, C.B., M.C., *Soldiers and Politicians*, University of Toronto Press, 1962; P.C. 4012, 13 May 42.
20. H.Q.S. 5199-S, F.D. 209, McNaughton to M.N.D., 1 Feb 40.
21. H.Q.S. 5199-S, F.D. 1, 1 Jul 40; H.Q.C. 1233; H.Q.S. 8696, 12 Nov 40; WD D.M.O.&I., 20 Jan, 31 May 41; H.Q.S. 8751, 11 Mar 41; H.Q.S. 8696-2, 16 Jun 41; H.Q.S. 3488, F.D. 123, 26 Nov 41.
22. H.Q.S. 3499-3-8, 19 Jun 42; *Report on Censorship*, Fulgence A. Charpentier, 31 Jan 46 (Report, Censorship).
23. H.Q.S. 171-1, 10 Mar, 9 May, 2, 11 Jun 42.
24. C.I. report, op. cit.
25. H.Q.S. 6265-8, 28 Jul 42; ibid.; H.Q.S. 6265-57, Atlantic Command to M.I.3, 28 Aug 42.
26. H.Q.S. 6265-61, 24 Jul 43; Cf 4/Liais NDHQ/1, 11 Jan 44.
27. H.Q.S. 6265-57-26, 9 Nov, 30 Dec 43, 28, 29 Feb, 1, 8, 10, 11 Mar 44.
28. H.Q.S. 8809, vol. 9; O.H., vol. I, p. 666.
29. Report, Censorship, op. cit.
30. H.Q.S. 5199-S, vol. 2, G.S. 83, approved by C.G.S., 28 Dec 39; report, Censorship, op. cit.
31. H.Q.S. 3320, 23 Mar 40–13 Aug 42.

32   H.Q.S. 7236-9, 39, 15, 22, 23 Jan 41.
33   H.Q.S. 7410-17, 5, 6–31 Aug 41; report, Chief Censor, Newfoundland.
34   Cf 4/Int/3, 14 Jul 40.
35   H.Q.S. 6265-57, 22 Apr 43, D.N.I. to D.M.I.; Cf 1/Aliens/1/2, 24 May, 1, 26, 28 Jun 43; C.M.H.Q. to Defensor, G.S. 1515.
36   H.Q.S. 70-5-305-6, 6 Jan 44–15 Feb 45; H.Q.S. 6265-44.
37   Report, Censorship, op. cit.
38   H.Q.S. 6359; R.C.M.P. 39-D-704-Q-1, Wood to D.M.N.D., 2 Oct 39; M.D. 3 K-6-36-A, 8, 10 Nov 39.
39   H.Q.S. 6467, vol. 3, 23 Oct 39; 23 May 40.
40   H.Q.S. 11, F.D. 2, 19 Mar 41; H.Q.S. 6467, vol. 3, 12 Apr 41; H.Q.S. 6265, vol. 6, 27 May 41.
41   H.Q.S. 7569, F.D. 17, M.D. 10 to D.M.O.&I., 16 Mar 40; R.C.M.P. to Pope, 23 Mar 40; Internment Operations (Col. H. Stetham) to R.C.M.P.
42   H.Q.S. 6265-71, 20 Jan, 1 Oct 43; H.Q.S. 3320; H.Q.S. 6265-14, 18 Mar 43.
43   WD H.Q. Atlantic Command, Atlantic Command S.I.S.; H.Q.S. 6265-30, M.I.3 to D.M.I., 24 Aug 42.
44   Personal comment, Lt.-Col. E. Acland to author, Sep 72, Oct 76.
45   Duff Cooper to Malcolm MacDonald, British High Commissioner to Canada, 22 Dec 42; H.Q.S. 6265-63, B.S.C. to D.M.I., 2 Apr 43; H.Q.S. 223-S-2, C.M.H.Q. to D.M.I., 13 Apr 43.
46   D-6-3 A.A.F. 586 to A.C. of S., A-2 Eighth Air Force; M.A. 46-0-3, C.A.S.W. to Secy, D.N.D., 20 May 43.
47   H.Q.S. 6265-86, vol. 1, F.S. Eld to D.M.I.
48   H.Q.S. 8251-2, 1 Jun 43; H.Q.S. 8251, M.N.D. to Minister of Justice, 23 Jun 43; M.A. 46-0-3, Lt.-Col. W.B. Wedd, Legation Washington to Secy, D.N.D., attention D.N.I.; R.C.M.P. 40-H-1282-3-40 over C11-10-10, 13 Jul 43; "H" Division to Commissioner, under covering letter n.d., n.f., Min. of Justice and M.N.D. (A).
49   Morale reports, to Feb 44.
50   H.Q.S. 6265-13, 14 Dec 42; C/CG IX-2, M.D. 13 to Secy. D.N.D., 21 Dec 42.
51   R.S. 4-7-16-133, Capt. Clear to G.S.O.1, M.I.3, 29 Dec 42.
52   H.Q.S. 8655, R.C.M.P. Det. Halifax to Ottawa to D.N.D., 4 Nov 40; to C.G.S., 8 Nov 40.
53   H.Q.S. 6265-30, M.D. 7 J/S 3-13-6, Nov 42; Harvison, op. cit., pp. 115, 116.
54   Ibid., pp. 118–120.
55   H.Q.S. 5731, M.D. 1 to D.C.G.S., 6, 11 Jun 43, 20 Apr, 2, 13 May 44.
56   WD G.S. Branch, Pacific Command, P.C.S. 504-8-6-2 (G.O.), P.C.S. 508-1-1-12 G.I.S. over F.D. 1520, 7 Dec 45; Bray to M.I.3, held on H.Q.S. 6265-85.
57   T.S. 20-5-1-N, 3 Jan 44 [sic]; H.Q.S. 6265-34 W.W.M. to C.G.S. through V.C.G.S.

CHAPTER 18

1   Nf H.Q.S. 3488-1, Col. F.W. Clarke, S.A.A.G. to External, 11 Aug 42; verbal comment, Lt.-Col. E. Acland to author, Oct 76.
2   H.Q.S. 3488, 11, 15 Aug 42; W.A. 2184, 20 Aug 42; Ex 1184, 21 Aug 42; report, Lt.-Col. O. Eadie to D.M.I., 31 Aug 42; W.A. 2368 Washington to External, 3 Sep 42.
3   H.Q.S. 3488-1, 18, 19 Oct 43.
4   H.Q.S. 9050-14-1-1, M.I.1 to Districts, 6 Dec 43; *History of S.A.A.G. Office and Directorate of Repatriation, 1942–7.*
5   Cf 34/Repat Pris War/1, C.M.H.Q. to D. Records, 9 May 44; Nf H.Q.S. 9050-14-1-1, British Army Staff, Washington to D.M.I., 9, 30 May, 28 Jun 44; ibid., Wygard to C.M.H.Q., 25 May 44; held Cf 4/MI 9/1; the officers were Maj. A.G. Wygard (M.I.4), Capts. R.J.P. Pootmans (M.I.1), C.E. Meadley (M.I.3).
6   Cf 4/Liais NDHQ/1, 10 Nov 44; held Nf H.Q.S. 9139-4.
7   H.Q.S. 9050-14-1-1, War Crimes Advisory Committee to D. Repat, Mar 45 *et seq.*

8	Cf 4/Liais NDHQ/1, M.I.9 to C.M.H.Q., 20 Aug 45; Nf H.Q.S. 3488-1, F.D. 3, D.M.I. to C.G.S., 23 Aug 45.
9	High Commissioner, Canberra, No. 412 to External, 21 Aug 45; 195/25/42, Malone to C.G.S., undated; Nf H.Q.S. 3488-1, D.M.I. to C.A.S.W., 29 Aug 45.
10	H.Q.S. 9050-14-15, 18 Sep (Repat 1), 4 Oct 45 (D.D.M.I.(S)); CANPAT 1-0-0, Cdn Repat Gp to D.M.I., 20 Sep 45; P.C.S. 508-1-1-12 G.I.S., F.D. 1549, 3 Oct 45.
11	H.Q.S. 20-1-31-Q, 4 Jan, 27 Feb. 46. Second edition note: endnote 11 missing in first edition; it has been attributed to this quoted paragraph in this edition.
12	W.I.S. 32, Capt. Howard, M.D. 10 to D.M.I. (M.I.3), 13 Sep 43; H.Q.S. 8118-32, F.D. 10, C.M.(3), 18, 21 Sep 43.
13	Wygard to D.I.O.s and Internment Camp Officers, lecture, 28 Jun 44.
14	O.H., vol. 1, p. 151.
15	H.Q.S. 6403, M.D. 2 to Secy D.N.D., A.G. to M.D. 2, 23, 27 Nov 40; H.Q.S. 7236-46, M.O.2 to D.N.D., 22 Apr, D.M.O.&I., to all D.O.C.s, 13 Jun 41; Cf 4/POW/1, 22 Feb 41.
16	P.C. 4568, 25 Jun 41; P.C. 36/500, 20 Jan 43; H.Q.S. 4660-0-1, 10 Jan 43; H.Q.S. 8658-1, vol. 1, 17 Sep 42.
17	H.Q.S. 3499-5, T.A. Stone, External to C.G.S., 22 Jul 43; H.Q.S. 7236-40, F.D. 3, 9, 14 Sep 43.
18	H.Q.S. 7236-40, minutes, 2 Sep 43.
19	Ibid., D.P.O.W. to D.M.I., 8 Oct 43
20	Ibid., correspondence, 15 Nov 43, 25 Feb, 4, 23 Mar, 9 May 44; C.S.C. 44-5, 28 Mar 44.
21	H.Q.S. 7236-40, 13 May 44; H.Q.S. 7236-25-1 (D.P.O.W.) (B), 1 Sep 44.
22	H.Q.S. 7236-40, F.D. 5, 16, 19 May 44; H.Q.S. 31-15, 31 May 44.
23	H.Q.S. 70-5-305, 9 Jun 44; H.Q.S. 7236-40, F.D. 7, 6 Jul 44.
24	H.Q.S. 7236-40; C.I. report.
25	Lt.-Col. Wygard's report, H.Q.S. 9139-7, M.I.7, 28 Feb 47; Censorship and Camp Reports.
26	H.Q.S. 9050-52-1, 22 Mar 44; Advisory Committee on Censorship, paper, 16th meeting, 2 Apr 44; special meeting, 5 Apr; C.I. report, op. cit., Lt.-Col. E. Acland, Oct 76.
27	Second edition note: first edition attributed endnote 26 to this para as well as previous para.
28	Advisory Committee on Censorship, 18th meeting, 20 Sep 44.
29	H.Q.S. 9139-4, 25 Nov 44, 28 Jan 45.
30	H.Q.S. 7236-46-PW(3), 23 Jan 45; H.Q.S. 31, 15 Jan, 14 Mar 45.
31	H.Q.S. 31, 7 May 45.
32	H.Q.S. 9139-4, 30 May 45.
33	H.Q.S. 9139-2-10-133, Lethbridge to M.D. 13, 10 May 45.
34	Cf 4/P and PW/1/2(MI), W.A. Cooper to D.M.I., 25 Nov 45; C.C.S. 914, Murchie to Foulkes and Maj.-Gen. Walford (A.G.), 22 Nov 45; CanMil to D.M.I., G.S.I. 758, 22 Dec 45; Cf 4/P and PW/1/3, Massey to External, 3 Jan 46.
35	H.Q.S. 9139-7, report, M.I.7, 28 Feb 47.
36	H.Q.S. 7236-1-2, 15 May 47.

CHAPTER 19

1	Lt.-Col. H.F. Wood, *Strange Battleground*, Queen's Printer, Ottawa, 1966; Official History of the Canadian Army in Korea (O.H.K.).
2	Of necessity impressionistic, these opinions were advanced during a number of conversations between staff officers who had been employed at N.D.H.Q. during this period, and the author.
3	Nf H.Q.S. 65-4, F.D. 18, 13 Oct 45; H.Q.S. 20-1-Q, F.D. 9, D.D.M.I. (S), 6 Sep 45 *et seq*.
4	H.Q.S. 6403, F.D. 29, Murray to C.G.S., 19 Nov 45.
5	H.Q.S. 6403-8, 3 Dec 45–17 Oct 46.
6	H.Q.C. 8664, F.D. 88, 4 Apr 46; H.Q.S. 20-1-Q, D.M.I. to D.C.G.S. (A), 5 Sep 46.
7	P.C.S. 401-8-16-1, Pacific Command to N.D.H.Q., 10 Sep 45; H.Q.S. 20-1-Q, C.G.S. to R.M.C. 13 Oct 45–13 Sep 46.

CHAPTER 20

1. O.H.K., pp. 6, 7.
2. Ibid., pp. 10, 33; war diaries, units cited.
3. Personal statement to author.
4. WD 2 P.P.C.L.I., 22 Dec 50.
5. Ibid., 12 Jan 51.
6. Ibid., 26 Feb 51.
7. WD H.Q. 25 Cdn Inf Bde, 19 Feb 51.
8. WD 1 Cdn F.S. Section, Sep 50–Mar 51; section file F.S. 1/1, 28 May 51; report to Lt.-Col. W.A. Todd from Corbeil.
9. WDs 25 Bde and 1 F.S., May 51.
10. 25 Bde Intsum No. 21, 28 May 51.
11. 25 Bde Intrep No. 2, 26 May 51; O.H.K., p. 105.
12. WD 1 F.S., 8, 16 Jun 51.
13. WD H.Q. 25 Bde, 1 F.S. Section, Jun 51.
14. HQ 25 Bde, Int Review, 14 Jun 51, *et seq.*
15. C.I. summary No. 82, 30 Aug 51.
16. WD 1 F.S.S., Sep 51.
17. WD H.Q. 25 Bde, Sep 51.
18. Personal comment, Corbeil to author, 7 Jun 71; 1 F.S.S. file F.S.S./1-3-1.
19. WD H.Q. 25 Bde, 13, 29 Nov, 1, 9, 14, 27 Dec 51, 1, 5 Jan 52; WD 2 R.22e.R., Nov, Dec 51, Jan 52.
20. Eighth U.S. Army in Korea, Periodic Intelligence Report (PIR) No. 537, 31 Dec 51; First Commonwealth Division Intrep No. 160, 2 Jan 52.
21. First Commonwealth Division Intrep No. 167, 9 Jan 52.
22. Ibid., No. 201, 12 Feb 52.
23. Ibid., No. 243, 25 Mar 52.
24. WD H.Q. 25 Bde, 6 Apr, 28 May 52.
25. Ibid., 24, 28 May, 12 May, respectively.
26. Ibid., 20 Apr 52.
27. Ibid., 30 May 52.
28. H.Q. 25 Bde Intsum, 30 May 52; Div Int Summaries 281, 2 May; 313, 3 Jun; 334, 24 Jun 52.
29. First Commonwealth Division Ops/Int Summary No. 52, 13 Sep 52; O.H.K., p. 20.
30. Maj. D.E. Holmes, quoted in O.H.K., p. 206.
31. Lt.-Col. E.H. Hollyer, M.C., C.D., to author, 7 Jun 71.
32. Maj. C.A.H. Kemsley, C.D., to author, 3 Jun 71.
33. Maj. W.J. Beaman, C.D., to author, 3 Jun 71.
34. First Commonwealth Division Intelligence Summary 339, 12 Sep 52; on WD H.Q. 25 Bde.
35. S.D. 1 letter 64/67, H.Q.S. 2000-9/80, 16 Mar 64.
36. Article 5 of Security Council Resolution S/5575, 4 Mar 64; Operation Directive No. 1, H.Q. 35/112, 26 Mar 64; WD H.Q. Canadian Contingent to Cyprus.
37. Capt. P.E. Bachand to author, 17 Jun 71; personal observation by author.
38. Personal narratives: Capt. R.E. Girling, S/Sgt. Don Mattocks, Lt. K. Young to author, 17 Jun 71; contemporary press reports on the delivery of these arms may be found in *Keesings Contemporary Archives*, Oct 2–9, 1965, p. 20991 *et seq.*
39. Address by Maj.-Gen. A. James Tedlie, D.S.O., C.D., to Air Command and Staff College, Maxwell Air Force Base, 26 May 70; reproduced by kind permission of Gen. Tedlie.

CHAPTER 21

1. Data on the Militia taken from Company files, personal narratives, conversations with the author.
2. Minutes of the first reunion dinner of former members of overseas F.S.C.I., Queen's Hotel, Montreal, 16 Feb 46; M.C. 51-S-49, Maj. Grenier to D.M.I., 25 Feb 46.
3. H.Q. 36-9-29 (D.M.I.), D.M.I. to Ashby, 28 Feb; Foreman to D.M.I., 5 Jul; D.M.I. to Foreman, 17 Jul 46.
4. H.Q. 36-9-29(AdmB), D. Adm to D.M.I., 6 Oct 47; Col. Wright to A.G., 10 Dec 47; H.Q. 36-9 29(JAG/A), J.A.G. to A.G., 24 Dec 47; H.Q. 168-7-7 (Trg Fin), D.M. to Col. Wright, 24 Feb 48; extract from letters patent incorporating (without share capital) Canadian Military Intelligence Association, 14 Jun 48.
5. Minutes of the First Annual General Meeting of the C.M.I.A., 20 Nov 48, 27 Dec 48.
6. H.Q.S. 6403, F.D. 29, Murray to Walter, 8 Nov 45; on Cf 4/Liais NDHQ/3; attached was memo to C.G.S.

INDEX

In this Index, Part I lists inter-Service and international organizations, persons, places, staff organizations and general activites; Part II lists Canadian Intelligence and Intelligence-associated units; Part III lists Canadian military units; Part IV lists British Commonwealth, United States and other Allied military units, including Intelligence; Part V lists enemy military and Intelligence units and organizations.

PART I:
GENERAL INDEX

A

Aachen 277, 285
Abbeville 163, 164, 263
Abel 86, 100
Abruzzi 180
Abwehr (German Military Intelligence). *See* Index Part V
Accra Mission 392
Aci Castello 213
Aci Trezza 213
Acland, Lt.-Col. Eric, O.B.E., E.D. 92, 414, 419, 428, 451, 454, 461, 464, 471, 472, 482, 500, 504, 542, 552, 566
Acquasparta 231
Acuto 226
Adak 365
Adams, Maj. J.F. 44
Adamson, Maj. H.D. 417
Adige 202
Adjutant-General's Branch 457, 458, 459, 475, 479, 483, 484
Adrano 173
Adriatic 193, 196, 203, 219, 229, 387
Advisory Committee on Intelligence and Security 463
Agents (Allied) 38, 178, 240, 305, 313, 377, 379, 386
  Tactical Liaison Officers 528
Agents (enemy)
  Britain 135, 139
  Canada 48, 49, 75, 96, 444, 476, 489
  Dieppe 169
  First World War 42, 43, 48, 49

Hong Kong 361
Korea 521, 522, 529
N.W. Europe 244, 246, 279, 301, 302, 303, 304, 307, 308, 309, 310, 311, 312, 315, 317, 319, 320, 321, 325, 326, 327, 330, 343
Sicily/Italy 189, 210, 211, 212, 216, 219, 222, 230, 234, 235, 236, 238
Agira 180, 212
Aid to the Civil Power 20, 52, 55, 64, 67
Air Ministry (British) 63, 82, 102
Air Observation Post (A.O.P) 40, 252
Air Photo Intelligence
  Dieppe 155, 165
  First World War 27, 31, 32, 34, 35, 37, 38, 40, 41
  Italy 170, 172, 177, 180, 186, 187, 190, 191, 196, 198
  Korea 528, 530, 531
  N.W. Europe 243, 269, 289, 362, 365
  Postwar 503, 514
Air Reconnaissance (Organization) 29, 40, 118, 124, 128, 243, 266, 285, 328, 365, 519, 538
Air Support 173, 181, 201, 247, 249
Aisne R. 259
Aksim, Maj. R. 266, 273, 331
Alaska 363, 364, 365, 471
Albert Canal 263, 268
Alcorn, J.F. 301, 332
Aldershot (Canada) 14
Aldershot (U.K.) 92, 110, 126, 130, 131, 134
Alderson, Lt.-Gen., Sir E.A.H. 25, 26, 27
Alem, Isle of 278
Aleutians 366, 442
Algiers 176, 184, 219, 347, 349, 378, 392

Algonquin, H.M.C.S. 249
Aliens
　1914 42, 47, 48, 52
　Canada 451, 454, 457, 458, 459, 470
　control planning 73, 75, 76
　in the Army 90, 92
　U.K. 95, 135
Alkmaar 326
Allard, Brig. J.V. 406, 530
Allen, Pte. 6
Allied Armies, Italy (A.A.I.) 189, 228
Allied Control Commission 223, 343, 351, 488, 496
Allied Forces H.Q. (Algiers) 219, 224, 347, 348, 378
Allied Military Government, Occupied Territories (Sicily/Italy) 211, 212, 213, 214, 217, 218, 219, 220, 221, 222, 223, 225, 226, 227, 228, 230, 231, 235, 239
Almelo 292, 320
Altamura 178, 183, 219
Altenwalde 335
Altherr, A.E. 391, 392
Amateur Radio Operators 362, 444
Amblie 249, 301
Amiens 32, 43, 54, 163
Ammerland 339
Amoore, 2/Lieut., J.P.S. 172
Amplifier Units 124, 394
Amsterdam 297, 322, 324, 325, 326, 327
Amy, Col. E.A.C., D.S.O., C.B.E., M.C., C.D. 533
Anagni 226
Anderson, Col. W.A.B. 505, 541
Anderson, Maj.-Gen. T.V. 408
Anderson, W.B. 13, 17
Andrews, K.E. 130
ANGER (Operations) 292
Ann Arbor, Michigan 423
Anse Cochat 385
Antwerp 263, 266, 268, 269, 271, 273, 277, 278, 281, 291, 307, 308, 309, 310, 312, 329
Antzonberger, Capt. 304
ANVIL (Operation) 200, 378
Anzio 184
Apeldoorn 292, 294, 318, 319, 322, 326, 406
Apennines 174, 179, 189, 200
Appreciation, Intelligence (C.M.H.Q.) 83, 84, 86
Aquila 228
Archambault, J.P. 376, 380
Archbold, R. 265
Archibald, R.L. 422, 435, 480
Ardennes 276, 277, 278, 279, 281, 311, 405
Ardres 307
Area Intelligence Officers 56

Argentan 248, 377
Ariano 224, 231
Arielli R. 184, 186, 187
Aris, Maj, J.A. 286, 288
Armentières 25
Armstrong, R. 6
Army Technical Development Board (A.T.D.B.) 435, 436
Arnhem 276, 292, 294, 295, 318, 326, 342, 388, 405, 407
Arpino 227
Arques-la-Bataille 153, 155, 161, 167
Arras 305, 372
Arsoli 227
Arvida District 414
Asbestos 51
Ashby, N.G. 541
Ashton, Maj.-Gen. E.C. 53, 69, 73
Assen 322
Assistant Director of Military Intelligence (position) 17, 18, 23, 47, 50, 51, 55
Attachés 17, 61, 446
Augusta 217
Aurelle R. 33
Aurich 323, 332, 334, 336, 337, 339, 343
Austin, W.E. 122, 346
Australia 31, 63, 367, 368, 369, 371, 383, 393, 421, 427, 428, 429, 447, 481, 546
Authie 247, 248
Avegoor Camp (Arnhem) 326
Avellino 223, 224, 231, 232, 233
Avezzano 180, 191, 227, 229
AV Putty 491, 492. *See* also Secret Writing
AXEHEAD (Operation) 128

B

Baardwijk 314, 317
Bachand, P.E. xvi, 510, 534
Bacqueville 155, 163
Badges
　British 129
　Corps 417
　Corps of Guides 14
　First World War 42
　Second World War 85, 87, 92, 105
Bad Zwischenahn 295, 323, 331, 406
Bagnacavallo 235, 236
Baillie-Grohman, V.-Adm., H.T. 160
Bake, A.S.J. 149, 539
Baker, J.C. 362
Baker, O.W. 301
Baker, Tpr. D'Arcy 6
Baldwin, R.M. 422

INDEX

Balloons, Japanese 438
Bapaume 29
Baraniecki, M.J. 149
Bari 174, 178, 183, 217, 219, 221, 349, 379
Barneveld 318
Barrett, C.D. 369
Barriefield 470
BASFORCE (Operation) 234, 235
Basse 303
Basso, H.J. 421
Batenburg 310
Batoche, Battle of 6, 10
Battleford 6, 7
Bavin, Supt. E.W. 457
Baxter, F.G. 323
Bayeux 248, 301, 303, 350, 387, 397
BAYTOWN (Operations) 174, 177, 213
Bazenville 250
B.B.C. 83, 86, 97, 226, 385, 391
Beaman, W.J. 531
Beament, Brig. G.E. 88, 126
Beaudry, C.V. 391
Beaugency 375
Beauregard, A. 375, 376
BEAVER (Exercise) 143
Becker, Insp. (Gestapo) 324
Bedburg 289, 316, 319, 406
Bee, David 424
Beekman, Yolande 374
Belgian Forces of the Interior 307
Belisle, J.M.R. 391
Bella Coola 438
Belleau, Capt. J. 113
Bellevue Spur 31
Bell, Lieut. R.M. 349
Belvedere Fogliense 199
Bendell, P.C. 149
Bennet, Lt.-Col. P.W. 295
Bennett, Gnr. R.H. 210
Benoît, B.C.J. 400, 401, 402, 404, 405, 407
Benoit, J.H.A. 376, 377, 380, 382, 566
Beny-sur-Mer 247, 250, 259
Bereau, Lieut. J.C. 115
Beresford, F.M. W.C., Viscount 1
Bergen-op-Zoom 269, 311, 323, 404
Berlin 110, 186, 242, 258, 290, 295, 332, 333, 335, 351, 377, 461, 484
 No. 1 F.S. Sec 322
Bernay 262
Bernhard Line 179, 180, 181, 182
Bernhardt, H.R.H. Prince of Netherlands 312
Bernières 243, 244
Beveland (South and North Beveland) 266, 268, 269, 271, 308, 309, 312, 323, 404
Bevin, Rt. Hon. Ernest 333

Bias Bay 355
Biéler, Maj. G.D.A. 372
Biesbosch 278, 389
Big Bear, Chief 7
BIGOT (Security Codeword) 103
Binkley, W.I. 106, 541
Birkett, Capt. T.G. 82
Bishop, J.H. 151, 165
Black, Capt. G.G. 248, 263, 264, 297
Black, J.L. 365
Black List 211, 212, 230, 236, 305, 308, 311, 318, 319, 324, 325, 332, 339
Black Market
 Germany 342, 405
 Italy 212, 218, 220, 223, 231, 232
 Korea 523, 524
 U.K. 139
Blais, Maj. E.A. 523, 527
Blane, W. 303, 339, 516, 567, 569
Blaskowitz, Col.-Gen. Johannes 295, 320
Bligh, R.N. (Paddy) 148, 314, 322
BLOCKBUSTER (Operation) 289
Blosseville 155, 163
Blyth, Graham xvi, 134, 303, 307, 310, 325
Boddington, Maj. Horatio (Con) 208
Bodwell, H.L. 13
Bogart, Capt. J.L.H. 17
Bogert, Brig. M.P. 178, 529
Boldrini, Lieut. Arrigo (Maj. Bülow) 203, 205, 235
Bolingbroke, W.O.II George 408
Bong, J.K.O. 481
Bonin, Col. Bogislaw von 170
Bonnell, Capt. R.T. 352, 353
Book System (Collation) 62, 63, 65, 432, 500
Bordewick, G.R. 301
Bordon, Camp (U.K) 130, 131, 138
Bornebrock 320
Bosca, M.V. 333
Boss, W. 524
Bosworth, Capt. A.F. 114, 115
Boulogne 110, 163, 164, 263, 264, 265, 266, 269, 305, 306, 401
Boulton, Maj. C.A. (Scouts) 4
Bourassa, J.L. 328
Bourlon Wood 33
Bourne, T.H.H. 369
Bowers, Maj. V.R. 121, 122
Bowie, Capt. John 520
Bowser, A/Premier, W.J. 20
Boxer, Maj. Charles (Br.) 360
Boxhill 149, 150
Boxmeer 316
Boxtel 285
Boyd, W.M. 146

Boy-Ed, Capt. Karl 48
Bozanic (Bozanich), R. 387
Braakman Inlet 266, 269
Bracigliano 222
Bradbrooke, Lieut. G.A. (C. of G.) 54
Bradley, Capt. J.P.D. 122
Brandon 471
Bras 260
Brattisany, Sgt. (Interpreter) 214
Braun, W.E. 481, 506, 519
Bray, Maj. H.C. 427, 477, 482, 566
Breda 266, 323, 404, 405
Breskens 269, 270, 404
Brest 114, 134
Brett, C.C. 393
Bretteville-sur-Laize 244, 253, 254, 256, 257, 260
Brienne 388
Brigade Blanche (White Brigade) 268, 308, 309, 312
Brindisi 183, 219
British Empire 4, 11, 23, 47, 358, 458
British Overseas Defence Committee 45
British Security Co-ordinator (B.S.C.) 370, 378, 383, 410, 427, 428, 443, 444, 457, 477, 489
Brittlebank, Lieut. 6
Brooke, Gen. Sir Alan 134
Brookhouse, H.G. 323, 334
Broughall, W.H. 127, 128, 291, 297, 400, 542, 566
Brown, Capt. E.L. 6
Browne, J.F. 479
Browne, Maj. J.E. (C. of G.) 54
Brown, L.C. 95, 235
Bruce, Tpr. V. 6
Bruges 263, 265, 267, 305, 307, 312, 404
Brussels 278, 306, 317, 327, 350, 403
Brutinel, Brig.-Gen. R. 54
Bryan, Maj. T.W.G. (C. of G.) 86
Buchenwald 375
Buckibaum, Sgt. (Interpreter) 223
Buckingham, N.A. 518, 520, 521, 523, 531
Buck, Tim 69
Buitenhoff 322
Bülow, Maj. 203, 205, 235
BUMPER (Exercise) 142
Buren 324
Burgundy (Escape Line) 385
Burma 108, 366, 380, 381, 382, 393, 434
　Burma Road 355
　Burma-Siam Railway 393
Burness, Lt.-Col. K.C. 411, 413
Burnett, R.V. 211
Burns, A.C. 368, 369, 481, 482
Burns, Lt.-Col. G.E. 51, 52
Burns, Maj.-Gen. E.L.M., C.C., D.S.O., O.B.E.,
　M.C. 81, 86, 87, 91, 99, 129, 196, 200, 431
Burns, Sgt. I.S.9 W.E.A. 388
Burrell, F.A. 127
Burr, I.T. 158, 188, 194, 196, 566
Busch, Field Marshal 335
Bussum 327
Byerley, R. 375, 376
Byrnes, Capt. H.J., M.B.E. 387, 390, 566

C

Caele R. 266
Caen 248, 250, 251, 252, 254, 255, 256, 258, 260, 277, 301, 302, 303, 304, 388, 397
Cairo 392
Cairon 252, 301, 303, 377
Calabria 213, 215
Calais 110, 114, 144, 168, 263, 265, 266, 269, 305, 306, 307, 308, 401, 402, 403
Calcar 282, 288, 289, 290
Calder, J.F.A. 346
Caldwell, Capt. (Br.) 322
Caldwell, Col. A. Clyde 9, 13, 17, 18, 556
Calgary 7, 53, 160
Calouri, J. 520
Calpe, H.M.S. 164
Cambrai 33
Cambridge (U.K.) 103, 106, 275
Cameron, D.F. 367
Camilly 249
Camp 030, Civilian Interrogation Camp 305, 308, 311, 312, 316, 317, 318, 319, 323, 324, 326, 330
Campbell, Capt. C.H. 115, 143
Camp Borden 80, 116, 453, 500, 511, 539, 571
Camp Debert 440, 442, 453
Campiano 236
Campobasso 216, 217, 223
Campoli Apennino 229
Camp Ipperwash 477
Camp Petawawa 19, 418, 453, 471, 500, 511, 520, 532
Camp Ritchie (U.S.A.) 367
Camp Savage (U.S.A.) 416, 423, 424, 425, 427
Camp Valcartier 22, 23, 25, 453
Camp Wainwright 442, 453
Canadian Army Journal 58
Canadian Army Staff, Washington 422, 423
Canadian Broadcasting Corporation 346, 447
Canadian Defence Quarterly 58
Canadian Military Intelligence Association 511, 541
Canadian Military Mission (Berlin) 110
Canadian Press 346, 460

Canadian Signals Experimental Establishment 447
Canadian War Intelligence Course 107, 275, 418, 419, 422, 487
Canadian War Museum 328
Canal de la Dérivation de la Lys 267, 268
Canal du Nord 33, 43
Canton 355, 358, 359, 360
Cap Badges
   C.Int.C. 419
   C. of G. 14, 419
Capellen 309
Cape Town 9, 479
Captured documents (*See* also Index Part II) 37, 166, 184, 264, 276
Carabinieri (CC.RR.) 212, 214, 218, 219, 221, 223, 226, 234, 235
Carden-Lloyd Armoured Car 68
Cardwell, R.E. 524
Carentan 397
Caron, Hon. A.I.P. 4
Carpiquet 250, 301, 302
Carrier pigeons 43, 313, 315, 444
Cassino 181, 184, 189, 190, 191, 193
Castelbordino 218
Castelnuovo 227
Castiglione di Laso 227
Catania 171
Catanzaro 174, 177, 215
Catto, Capt. J.M. 88
Caude-Coté 161, 163
Caumont 303
Caza, R.M. 375, 376, 380, 382, 566
Censorship (I(c)) xx. *See* also Military Intelligence, Directorate of (Br.), M.I.12; *See* also Chief Telegraph Censor;
   Ad Hoc Committee on Stops and Releases 463
   Advisory Committee on Censorable Communications of Military Interest 461
   Advisory Committee on Publication of Military Information 461
   Aims 47, 75
   Canada 47, 460, 483
   Canada - Press 462
   Censor Units 347, 350
   C.M.H.Q. 85, 90, 99, 100, 106, 108, 133
   Co-ordination Committee 460
   Deputy Chief 21, 46, 47
   Dieppe 159, 166
   Director of Cable 47
   Editing Committee 74, 75
   Enemy 480
   Europe 346
   Interdepartmental Committee on Censorship 74
   Italy 209, 347
   Kiska 364
   Newfoundland 362
   Planning 74
   Postal 101, 362
   Press 9, 21, 46
   Press and Radio 409, 462, 463
   Radio and Cable 45, 51, 74, 75
   relationship with Public Relations 100
   relationship with the British War Office 92, 99
   Section, D.M.O.&I. 461
   Stamps 96, 101, 102, 148, 162, 209
   Unit 105, 128
Central Mediterranean Forces, H.Q. Algiers 184
Cervia 235
Cesenatico 235, 236
Chamberlain, E.A. 114, 130, 133, 134
Chambers, A. 172, 173, 176, 401, 566
Chambers, Col. E.J. (C. of G.) 47
Champendale, Sgt. (Interpreter) 214
Changhowon-Ni 519
Channel Islands 141, 243, 401
Chan, R. 383
Chartrand, Capt. J.C.G. 350, 374, 568
Chartrand, Miss Paule 408
Chartres 376
Chassé, P.E. 378, 380, 383, 567
Chateau Cairon 303
Chateau Maulny 311
Chater, Lt.-Col. Leslie 256, 258, 284, 285, 295, 328
Chauveau, C. 433, 434
Chauvin, L. 143, 151, 569
Chemainus 365
Cheng, R. 383
Cherbourg 243, 248, 401
Chetniks 379
Cheyne, D.B. 228, 235
Chiang Kai-shek, Generalissimo 357
Chief Cable Censor 460, 461
Chief of Staff to the Supreme Allied Commander (C.O.S.S.A.C.) 240
Chiefs of Staff (Canadian) 153, 366, 437, 504
Chief Telegraph Censor 444, 448
Child, Maj. C.C. (C. of G.) 54
Chinese
   Canadian 382, 429
   Nationalist 355, 359
   People's Republic 519
Chinn, B.L. 382
Chown, J.H. 147, 325
Chung, C. 382
Chungking 97, 355, 361, 383
Churchill, Rt. Hon. Winston 75, 99, 168, 333, 342, 357

Cigona, C.P. 196
Cinti, Gen. Agostino (It.) 170
Cipher 64, 114, 115, 123, 142, 447, 457
   A.D.M.&A.F.I. 113
   C.M.H.Q. 81, 85
   D.M.O.&I. 408, 443
Cittanova 174, 176, 179
Civil Affairs. *See* also Allied Military Government, Occupied Territories (Sicily/Italy)
   Italy 208, 211
   N.W. Europe 301, 309, 312, 324, 325, 396, 397, 400, 404, 405
Civil Assistance Corps, Korea 522
Civitavecchia 189, 232, 233
CL 89 Drone 507
Clark, Capt. S.F. 443
Clark, Col. (D.P.R.) 394
Clarke, Col. F.W. 480
Clarke, G.F. 523
Clarke's Crossing 6
Clarkson, J.M.E. (Johnnie), M.C. 196, 198
Clear, G.F. 475
Cleve 274, 284, 285, 286, 288, 290, 316, 318, 320
Clifford, F. LeP. T. 115
Cloppenburg 330, 334, 335, 339
Cobalt 52
Cochrane, Capt. R.L. 523
Cockin, Lieut. M.H.B. 173
Codes and Cipher 64, 408, 443, 447
Cole, Pat D.H. 223, 233, 322, 326
Collaborators 227, 305, 308, 312, 314, 318, 319, 324, 377, 479, 481
Collation (of Int.) 35
   Book System 57, 62
Cologne 277, 373
Colombelles 251, 252
Colonel Commandant, Canadian Intelligence Corps
   Col. P.E.R. Wright 546, 547
   Gen. H.D.G. Crerar 544
Colonel Commandant's Advisory Council 546
Colonel Commandant's Award 511, 546
Colonel Commandant's Fund 546
Combined Operations Headquarters 153, 155, 157, 159, 160, 163, 165
Combined Services Detailed Interrogation Centre 183, 216, 225
Combined Services Photographic Library 434
Comitato di Liberazione Nazionale 226, 232
COMMANDO (Operation) 524
Commands, Canada. *See* Index Part III, Atlantic, Pacific
   postwar 505
   wartime 409

Communists 136, 137
   Canada 69, 70, 453, 455, 470, 471, 477
   Far East 382
   Italy 226, 227, 229, 231, 233, 238
   N.W. Europe 326, 334
Comox 365
Conca R. 201
Conference of Defence Associations 541, 542
Constantine, Maj.-Gen. C.F. 60, 470
Control Line
   Ems-Jade 334
   Grebbe 325
   Ijssel 318, 320
   Italy 219, 222, 225, 227, 228, 229, 232, 237
   Korea 524
   Maas 311, 314, 316, 323
   Scheldt 309
Controls, general
   Germany 343
   N.W. Europe 304, 310, 313, 318, 325, 334, 338
   Sicily/Italy 219, 236, 238
Cook, G.C. 367
Cook, Pte. 6
Cook, P.W. 367, 434
Cooper, W.A.C. (Bill) xvi, 139, 208, 209, 210, 211, 213, 214, 215, 218, 221, 566
Corbeil, M.G. (Eddie) xvi, 319, 322, 323, 334, 520, 521, 522, 523, 524, 531
Cornwall 49
Corps of Guides. *See* Index Part II, Guides, Corps of
Corsica (Cover Plan) 209
Corson, W. 143, 151, 164, 165, 569
Coryell, Lieut. 4
Côté, M. 519
Cotentin Peninsula 243
Cotignola 203
Cottam, K.A. 181, 188
Coulter, H.S. 121
Counter-Espionage 43, 44, 75, 76, 134, 139, 144, 210, 216, 305, 377. *See* Counter-Intelligence I(b), Operations and Plans, Security of;
   Canada, Ch. 17 451
Counter-Intelligence (I(b)) 86, 108, 129, 149, 208, 219, 272, 304
   C.A.O.F. 337
   C.A.P.F. 367
   Courcellette 29
   duties 314, 327
   First World War 41
   H.Q. 299, 314, 319, 334
   organization 321
   Plan No. 5 310
   review 343, 501

INDEX

Counter-Sabotage 75, 90, 135, 138, 144, 314, 322, 331, 332, 344, 453, 539. *See* Materiel, Security of; Vulnerable Points
Canada 452
Courcellette 29
Courseulles-sur-Mer 243, 244, 247, 249, 350
Courtenay 364, 365, 477
Courtrai 308, 312
Cowan, Maj. R.W.T (Austral.) 421
Cowie, M.A. 400
Coxson, W.D. 260
Crerar Collection/Library 110, 501
Crerar, Gen. H.D.G. 62, 72, 79, 81, 83, 84, 110, 123, 126, 148, 183, 266, 279, 303, 351, 356, 546, 570
 Colonel Commandant 544
Croll, B.H.F. 149, 305, 569
Crow's Nest Pass 52
Croydon 117, 136, 137
Cumberland (B.C.) 20
Cunningham, William 4
Curran, J.B. 347
Currie, Sir Arthur 25, 54
Currigall, D.M. 116
Curry, T.E. 329
Cuthill, G.K. 305
Cut Knife Hill, Battle of 6, 7
Cuxhaven 335
Cyclists 54, 59
 British 54
 duties 60
 organization 54
Cyprus 508, 514, 517, 532

D

Dachau 374
Daily Press Service 432
Dalum 330
D'Artois, L.G. 376
Darwin 369
DAVID (Exercise) 141
Davidson, C.L. 307
Davidson, Lieut. Thomas 4
Davidson, Maj.-Gen. F.H.N. (Br.) 546
Davies, D.M. 393
Davis, Bvt.-Maj. F.E. 50, 51, 556
de Beaujeu, J.C. 106, 291, 567
Deception
 France 246
 Italy 189
Defence of Canada Regulations (D.O.C.R.) 448, 454, 455, 460, 474, 504
Defence Schemes
 No. 1 57, 58, 63, 64
 No. 2 63
 No. 3 72, 76
de Freitas, Geo (Br.) 213
Dehler, J.H.M. 378
Delfzijl 294, 295
Delianuova 215
Delmenhorst 110, 296, 332, 339, 343
Demery, W.R. 116
de Mille, R.J. 349
Demobilization 106
Demuin 41
Denain 44
Den Heuvel 286
Deniset, F.A. 375, 376, 569
Dennis, Capt. J.S. 4
Dennis, Lt.-Col. J.S. 4
Dennison, Capt. 247
Denny, Lt.-Col. William A.C. 12, 17
Denzler, E.H. 260, 567
Depew, J.H.H. 127
Desvres 306
Devaney, C.M. 273, 566, 568
Deventer 292, 318, 319, 320, 406, 459
Dewar, W.S. 180, 196
De Witt, Lt.-Gen. J.L. (U.S.A.) 363, 364
Dextraze, Lt.-Col. J.A., D.S.O., O.B.E. 532
Diehl, William 6
Dieppe 98, 117, 121, 122, 125, 143, 144, 151, 210, 244, 252, 263, 305, 343, 384, 385, 390, 570. *See* also JUBILEE
 defences 153, 156, 163
 German comment 167
 Intelligence Plan 157, 161
 Intelligence recommendations 166
 planning 153, 155, 159
 security 153, 155, 160, 161, 166, 167
 training 155
Diest 272
Dietze 332
Dignam, Mary 383
Directorate of Military Intelligence. *See* Military Intelligence, Directorate of
Director of Military Intelligence (position) 9, 17, 23, 410, 509. *See* also Military Intelligence, Directorate of
Director of Military Training. *See* Military Training, Director of
Direnfeld, E.C. 210, 211, 225, 318, 569
Discrimination Unit, No. 1. *See* Index Part II
Displaced Persons (Executive) 316, 318, 336. *See* also Refugees
District (Military) Intelligence Officer 10, 11, 12, 15, 17, 18, 55, 57, 63, 72, 409
 duties 459, 470, 477, 480, 482, 488
 First World War 51

name change (1929) 64
postwar 502
Dives R. 242, 256
Dixmude 307, 308
Doak, E.S. 313, 541
Dodecanese Islands 378, 392
Doerksen, C.J. 296, 298
Doetinchem 291, 326
Dolly, C.C. 380, 381
Dominion Land Survey. *See* D.L.S. Scouts, Index Part II)
Dominion Police 45, 48, 49, 50, 52
Dönitz, Adm. 295, 335
Donovan, R.M. 328
Doody, F.K. 542
Dordrecht 322, 326
Dostler, Gen. Anton (Ger.) 205
Doukhobors 68
Douthwaite, C.R.R. (Rafe) 122, 146, 147, 301, 316, 322, 566, 568
   C.A.O.F. 339
Dover 148, 149
Doyle, G.A. 301
Dozule 257
Drake, E. 444, 446, 450, 568
Dress Regulations
   C. of G. 14
Drocourt-Quéant Line 33
Drury, D.K. 147
Drysdale, G.J. 319
Dubois, A.M.M. 307, 323, 567
Dubois, T.J.A. 566
Dubuc, M. 541
Duckett, W.A. 350
Duck Lake 4
Duguid, Col. A.F. 418
Dumais, L.A. 385, 386, 566, 567
Dummer, F. 302, 569
Duncan, S/L C.J. 66
Dundurn 69
Dunkirk 114, 168, 263, 265, 266, 296, 305, 307, 308, 401, 402, 403
Dunn, Sgt. 4
Durham, Sgt. (Br.) 231, 232
Durocher, L.J. 378, 567, 570
Durovecz, A. 379
Düsseldorf 317
Dyck, L.H. 403

E

Eadie, O. 275, 413, 414, 436, 437, 479, 480
Earle, Capt. W.E. 14
Eaton, W. 116

Eayrs, James 63
Eberding, Maj.-Gen. Kurt (Ger.) 270
ECLIPSE (Operation) 275, 297
Economic Warfare 47, 52, 461
   Ministry of 158, 161, 370
Ede 322, 325
Eden, Hon. Anthony 357
Edmond, K.E. 534
Edmonton 7, 53, 213, 503, 505, 539
Edwards, W.E. 183
Eecloo 307
Eggleston, Wilfred, Chief Press Censor 461
Eindhoven 311, 404
Eire 136
Eisenhower, Gen. D.D. (U.S.A) 176
Elbe R. 289
Elbeuf 262, 263
Eld, F.S. 473
Elliot, S.R. 393, 510
Elliott, R.C. 387
Elliott-Smith, D.D. 347
Emden 294, 295, 320, 323, 334
Emmerich 285, 288, 291, 317, 318, 319, 389
Ems R. 292, 294
ENDOR (I.S.9 operation) 389
Engineer Intelligence 205
Enna 211
Epe 323
Epernay 377
EPSOM (Operation) 250
Equipment, enemy 432, 436. *See* also Technical Int.
Escape and Evasion 103, 106, 110, 122, 208, 255, 316, 351, 382, 384, 480, 530, 539. *See* also I.S.9, M.I.9 (Br.)
Espionage 45, 71, 73, 93, 550. *See* also Agents
   Canada 451, 489
   First World War 48
Esquelbecq 308
Esquimalt 440
Establishments
   C. of G. 17
   First World War 80
   postwar 127, 499
   Second World War 81, 88, 113, 115, 404, 420
Esterwegen (Internment Camp) 298, 323, 332, 334, 339
Eteauville 303
Eu 163
Evans, S.O.F. 331, 506
Everall, Capt. W.W. 54
Ewijk 318
Ewing, R.M. 369
Exeter 134
External Affairs, Dept. of 45, 46, 61, 62, 74, 86,

357, 370, 394, 428, 448, 452, 463, 479,
480, 481, 486, 488
Political Warfare Committee 435, 496
Psychological Warfare 370, 394, 428

F

FABIUS (Exercise) 147
Faenza 204, 236
Fairley, T.C. 127, 542
Falaise 240, 248, 251, 252, 254, 255, 256, 257, 258, 260, 398
Falkland Islands 97
Falmouth 134
Farnborough 92, 146, 149
Farnham (Quebec) 20, 495
Fascists in Canada 71, 455, 470, 476, 551
Fast, A.H. 331
Faust, P. 331
Fawcett, C.R. 319
Fawdry, K.L. 249, 291
Federal Bureau of Investigation (F.B.I.) 371, 438, 444, 479
Federal Communications Commission (U.S.) 444
Feeny, P.J. 143
Feilman, Lt.-Cdr. G.A. 488
Fenian Raids 3, 11, 49
Ferguson, J.G.H. 534
Fernie 52
Fernie, H.M.S. 158, 164
Festubert 27
Fiebig, Maj.-Gen. Heinz (Ger.) 289
Field Security 9, 87, 88, 89, 92, 95, 103, 105, 109, 110, 114, 125, 159. *See* also Index Part II, Field Security Sections
  Canada 453
  Canada - M.I.3 409
  C.A.P.F. 367
  Ch. 6 129
  Ch. 9 208, 301
  Dieppe 155, 159, 161, 162
  establishment (1944) 127
  Italy 178, 205, 219, 224, 238
  Korea 520, 528
  N.W. Europe 251, 301, 304, 343, 348
  postwar 509, 511, 539
  postwar Europe 516
  responisbilities 135
  training 413, 422
Field, W. 331
First Canadian Contingent (1914) 42
Fish Creek, Battle of 6, 10
Fisk, Scout 7
Fitzsimmons, J.J. 225, 318, 569

Fiuggi 226, 229
Fiume Marecchia 238
Fiumicino 202
Fleming, A.S. 223, 227, 228, 230, 236, 322, 333
Fleming, B.H. 367
Fleming, Ian N. 206
Fleury-sur-Orne 251, 303, 397
FLIT (Exercise) 148
Flossenbürg 374
Flushing 263, 266, 271, 272, 311
Flynn, J.F. 196
Foch, Marshal. Ferdinand (Fr.) 32
Foggia 217, 392
Foglia R. 196, 198, 199, 200
Foligno 229
Folkestone 149
Fontaine Henry 247, 301, 305, 388
Fontenay-le-Marmion 253, 256
Forbes, R.S. 245, 247
Fordyce, A.M. 92, 113
Foreign Intelligence 12, 23, 409, 497, 500
  M.I. (Int) 517
  Section 506, 532
  sources 500
Foreign Office (Br.) 61, 62, 96, 355, 361, 370, 391, 435
Foreman, B.G. 92, 183, 217, 224, 228, 230, 234, 236, 322, 541, 566, 567
Forest Row 149
Forêt de Cinglais 244, 257
Forêt de Freteval 386
Forêt de Soulaines 377
Forli 200, 347
Formia 190
Foro R. 184, 188
Fort Cataraqui, S.S. 271
Fort Fredrik Hendrik 270
Fort Frontenac 416
Fort Henry 470, 483
Fort Lewis (U.S.A.) 519, 520
Fort Macleod 4
Fort Montluc (Fr.) 376
Fort Pitt 7
Fort Qu'Appelle 6
Fort Saskatchewan 7
Fort William 49
Fosbery, Col. T.H. 507, 508, 509, 511, 557
Fossacesia 218
Foster, Brig. H.W. 363
Foulkes, Gen. C. 126, 206, 320, 506
Fournier, J.E. 378, 380, 567
Fowler, R.W. 210, 226
Foyer, S.H. 183
Francofonte 213
Franeker 330

Frankenberg, Capt. (Br.) 213
FRANK (Exercise) 147
Fraser, A.H. 408
Free French 105, 136, 225, 363
Freeman, A.F.P. 365
French, Capt. John, French's Scouts 4
French Forces of the Interior (F.F.I.) 302, 305, 306, 377, 378, 400, 403. *See* also Resistance, French; *See* also Special Operations Executive (S.O.E.)
   Gen. Koenig 370
Frenchman's Butte 7
French's Scouts 6
Fresnes 374
Freypons, R.W. 210, 301
Friesland 144, 339
Frisa 223
Froggett, C.C. 332
Frog Lake 7
Frosinone 193, 194, 226
Frost, Lieut. R.J. 529
Führer Freiheitsbewegung Deutschlands 342
Fuller, R.O.H. 151, 569
Funds, Intelligence 64, 507, 541
Fung, H.W. 382
Fury, Sgt.-Maj. W. (N.W.M.P.) 7

G

Gallagher, P.A. 350, 567
Gallina 215
Galluzzo 230
Gardiner, Capt. Meopham 4, 6
Garigliano R. 180, 181, 189, 190
Gari R. 189, 190
Garvey, Sgt. 401
Gas (chemical warfare) 26
Gaspé 476
Gatchell, Tpr. H.G. 247
Gayfer, Capt. John 507
Gazelle 259
Geertruidenberg 279
Geisler, R. 260, 272, 331
Gelleny, J.J. 379
Genazzano 226
General Staff (A.H.Q.) 15, 17, 59, 61
Gennep 288
George, G.E. 307
Georgescu, George 379
George VI, H.M. King 229, 309
Gerloch, Col. Bruno (Ger.) 259
German Refresher Course, R.M.C. 420
Gertrude Cove, Kiska 364
Ghent 265, 267, 268, 307, 308, 404

Gibbs, Lt.-Col. Eric, A.D.P.R. C.M.H.Q. 394
Gilze Rijen 273
Girling, R.E. 534
Givenchy 27
Gladwin, E.S. 365
Glasgow 148
Goch 274, 284, 285, 286, 288, 289
Godfrey, Lieut., R.N.V.R. 269
Goes 404
GOLDFLAKE (Operation) 237
Goldie, S/Sgt. Bert 408
GOODWOOD (Operation) 255
Gordon, Lieut. J.F. 6
Gorinchem 280, 294, 317, 326
Gothic Line 191, 196, 198, 199, 200, 201, 229, 230
Gouda 322
Gough, N.R. 329
Gouzenko, Igor 342
Governor General, H.E. the 23, 61
Gow, Lt.-Cdr. H. 75
Gracie, A.L. 323, 329, 567
Grant, W.E. 249, 260
Grasett, Maj.-Gen. A.E. (Br.) 355, 356
Grauer, H. Peter 365, 567
Gravensbergen 320
Grave R. 286
Graye-sur-Mer 243, 301
Gray, G.B. (Bud) 408
Gray, J.A. 286, 388, 389, 541, 542, 567
Gray, J.M. 92, 128, 269, 322, 328, 566, 567
Great War Veterans Association 53
Grebbe Line 294, 322
Greenberg, L. 326
Greene, G.B. 541
Green, J. 92, 130
Greenland ("X" Force) 352
GREENLIGHT (Operation) 363
Green Police 324
Grenier, G. 541
Grenswacht (Dutch) 316
Grew, Richard 98
Griesbach, Inspector A.H. (N.W.M.P.) 7
Griffin, G. R.C.A.F. 408
Griffith, E. (and T.) 424
Gripsholm, S.S. 479, 480, 481
Groenlo 320
Groesbeek 286, 316
Groningen 294, 322, 325, 330
Grumo 220
Grunberg, A.P. 233
Guardia di Finanza 219
Guardia Nazionale Republicana (G.N.R.) 227, 228
Guardia Stradale 218, 221

Guelph 52
Guernsey (Island) 401
Guides, Corps of. *See* Index Part II, Guides, Corps of
Guînes 307
Gustav Line 189, 190, 193
Guthrie, Kenneth M. R.C.A.F. xvi, 62, 65, 66, 71, 75, 79, 80

H

Haarlem 322, 324
Hadden, J.C. 211, 230, 236, 318, 567, 568
Hadfield, D.A. 322
Hague, The (Den Haag) 19, 111, 297, 298, 308, 322, 326, 407
Haig-Smith, Maj. J. (Newfoundland) 362
Halbert, J.D. 83, 91, 92, 95, 98, 123
Halifax 45, 49, 51, 57, 92, 115, 392, 418, 461, 473, 474, 494, 503, 505, 539
 Security weaknesses 471, 472
Halley, Paul V. 392, 424, 569
Hall, T/Capt. (Bill) 182
Haltwhistle 110
Haly, Maj.-Gen. R.H. O'Grady 9
Hamburg 51, 407, 443, 444, 483
Hamer, I.A. 204
Hamilton, C.F. 21, 46
Hampton, R.W. (Dick) 111
Hancock, R.L. 196
Hanel, H.R. 294
Hanna, J.E. 382
Hanover 336, 483
Han R. 517
Harder, G. 332
Harding, J.J. 392
Harding, L.A.A. 233
HARLEQUIN (Exercise) 145
Hartwell, O.K. 369
Harvison, Inspector, R.C.M.P. 476
Haskins, R.H. 362
Hata, Gen. (Jap.) 360
Hatert 319
Hatton, Maj. 4
Hautmesnil 256, 260
Hawkins, R. 143, 161, 567
Hay, Capt. C.J.B. 18
Hayes, C.M. 248
Haynes, Lt.-Col. C.P. (Ced) 506, 508
Hay, Pte. 6
Headley Court 114, 127, 130
Healy, D.M. 183, 203, 235, 566
Heaps, Leo M.C. 566
Hébert, L. 479

Hedges, R.F. 130, 143, 151, 569
Hees 319
Heide-Brasschaet 312
Heidrich, Gen. Richard (Ger.) 179
Heilmann, Lt.-Gen. Ludwig (Ger.) 179
Heim, Lt.-Gen. Ferdinand (Ger.) 110, 265
Helmond 314, 315
Henderson, Lt.-Col. G.P. 121, 123, 124, 125, 161, 164, 167, 344, 420
Henderson, R. 522, 524
Henley, J.W. 268
Hennie, H.H. 318, 322, 341, 569, 570, 571
Herchmer, Lt.-Col. (N.W.M.P.) 6
Heyst 269, 404
Hickerson, J.D. 363
Hill *70* 31
Hill *227* 526, 527
Hill *335* 527, 530
Hill, Lt.-Col. C.H., D.P.M. 132
Hilversum 276, 280, 322, 324, 406
Hindenburg Line 54
Historical Branch 59
 C.M.H.Q. 84, 108, 110
Hitler, Adolf 144, 179, 242, 253, 263, 295, 332, 335, 341, 493, 495
Hitler Line *(Führer/ Senger Riegel)* 189, 190, 191, 193, 195, 224
Hitler Youth *(Hitler Jugend)* 251, 253, 327, 337, 339, 340
Hobbs, A.N.K. 457, 459
Hochwald Layback (Schlieffen Line) 284, 286, 288, 289
Ho, F.C. 382
Hoffmeister, Brig.-Gen. B.M. 180
Holland, E.H. 301
Hong Kong 62, 63, 79, 355, 393, 433, 448, 479, 481, 482
Hook, Battle of the (Korea) 530
Hook of Holland 324
Hope, K.J. 506
Hopkins, J.E. 541
Hornberger, H.L. 151, 569
Horn, Werner 49
Horrocks, Gen. Sir Brian (Br.) 336
Hourie, Tom 6
Hoven 318
Howarth, J.F.E. 130
Hubbel, C.R. 210, 314
Hucqueliers 307
Hughes-Hallett, Capt. John, R.N. 160
Hughes, S.H.S. 90
Hughes, Sir Sam 22, 25, 46
Hungarians, Canada 507
Hungary 379
HUSKY (Operation) 209

Hutchison, A. 130
HYDRA (Special Operations School) 371. *See also* S.T.S. 103

I

Iceland 342, 352, 462
"Z" Force 131, 352
Ignatieff, Maj. N. 106
Ijmuden 326
Ijssel 320
Ijsselmeer (Zuider Zee) 294
Ijssel R. (Line) 292, 318, 326
I Mess 249
Imjin R. 519, 521, 523, 524, 528
Independent Front (O.F.I.) 312
India 1, 63, 368, 371, 393, 428, 436, 447
Indian National Army 381
Indo-China 355, 360, 380, 382, 393, 434
Industrial Workers of the World 52
I Net (enemy agents) 308
INFATUATE (Operation) 269, 308
Information Branch 11, 23
Information, Control of. *See* also Psychological Warfare; *See* also Censorship
 1914 23, 25, 45
Innes, W.C. 83
Insinger, T.H. 158, 164, 569, 570
Integration 505, 508, 510, 511, 546, 547, 552
Intelligence (a) xviii
 1914 23, 25, 27, 31, 36
 1914-18 29
 1918-39 58
 1945-63 502, 549, 553
 Ch. 5 113
 Ch. 8 170
 Ch. 10 240
 Dieppe 166
 Korea 517, 518, 519, 521, 523, 526, 527, 528
Intelligence (b) xviii, 268, 390, 511, 549, 553
 1914-18 29, 41
 1918-39 70
 1939 British organization 129
 Canadian organization 130
 Ch. 6 129
 Ch. 9 208
 Ch. 11 301
 Ch. 17 451
 duties 131
 Korea 519
Intelligence duties 11, 12, 27, 31, 33, 34
 A.D.M.I. 50, 55
 Districts 50, 54
 First Canadian Army 123

postwar 56, 58
strategic 62
with Air 65, 68
Intelligence organization 1
 1921 56
 Army H.Q., Ottawa 10, 505, 508
 Battalion 25, 35, 56, 113, 122
 Brigade 25, 35
 British 9
 Canada 9, 17, 18, 20, 409, 503
 Corps 27, 33, 113, 115
 Division 25, 36, 113, 170
 Field Army 115
 post-1945 mobilization 503
 U.S. pattern 367
Intelligence Planning Committee 508
Intelligence Plans 275, 297, 500
Intelligence Police 42, 43, 44
Intelligence Process xvii, xviii
Intelligence Report No. 1 (First Canadian Army) 243, 501, 502
Intelligence Staff Officer (position) vi, 10, 11
Intelligence Summaries 25, 27, 31, 34
 A.H.Q. 57, 62
 Army 108, 170, 249, 276
 C.M.H.Q. 432
 I Corps 184, 206, 292
 II Corps 251
 II Division 251
 III Division 243
Intelligence Units. *See* Index Part II
Intelligence (x) xxi
 C.M.H.Q. 87, 88, 90, 91, 116
Interdepartmental Committee (on Information Control) 45
Internal Security Sub-Committee 73
International Control Commission 517
Internees xix, 73, 74, 311, 471, 483, 484
Internment Camps 73, 336, 341, 483
Internment Operations, Directorate of 483, 488
Interpreters xix, 33, 40, 42, 51, 97, 105, 111, 172, 173, 205, 206, 210, 212, 214, 223, 252, 260, 279, 304, 307, 353, 379, 382, 406, 416, 421, 425, 519, 520, 522, 538
Interrogation xx
 1914-18 32, 38
 Britain 139, 148
 C.M.H.Q. 106, 110, 121
 Dieppe 158, 159, 166
 Italy 170, 173, 174, 178, 181, 182, 183, 186, 187, 194, 196, 200, 213, 216, 217, 218, 222, 226, 230, 231, 234, 236, 237
 Korea 522, 528
 N.W. Europe 246, 247, 248, 249, 252, 253, 254, 255, 259, 263, 265, 269, 272,

273, 278, 289, 297, 304, 305, 307, 309, 312, 316, 317, 318, 320, 321, 323, 324, 325, 326, 328, 329, 330, 331, 337, 387, 388, 389, 392, 395, 398, 405, 406
Inter-Service Security Board 208
Inter-Services Topographical Section 502
I.S.9. *See* Index Part IV, Intelligence Units, I.S.9
Isabella Polder 269
Isernia 179
Isola di Liri 227
Isolani, 2/Lieut. C.T. 172
Ispica 211
Italy 33, 63, 71, 103, 107, 109, 114, 134, 141, 149, 246, 299, 304, 314, 347, 350, 371, 378, 379, 387, 390, 392, 437, 444
   Ch. 8 170
   Ch. 9 208

J

Jade 334, 336
James, J.M. 231, 233, 319, 322, 325, 383, 533
Janisse, C.B. 400, 404
Janssen, A. 303
Japanese-Canadians 416, 424, 427, 428, 429
Japan (Japanese) 62, 72, 97, 109, 358, 359, 367, 421, 425, 433, 440, 482
   equipment 438
   Hong Kong 355
   Kiska 363, 364, 365
   Korea 517
   language 414, 416
   radio (JZI, J2J) 357, 360, 446
Jean, J.R. 130
Jennings, P.J., O.B.E. 57
Jezewski, Cpl. 143
Jezewski, Lieut. J. 305
John Inglis Co 77
John, Lieut., M. 352
Johnson, Capt. J.A. 4
Johnson, S/Sgt. H.D.G. 13, 18
Johnston, P.A.E. 210, 215, 230, 567
Johnston, W.S. 274
Joint Intelligence Bureau 508
Joint Intelligence-Combined Service Bureau Committee 79
   Atlantic Command 362, 442, 472
   Ottawa 504, 506, 518
   Pacific Command 442, 453
Joint Intelligence Committee, British 98
Joint Intelligence Staff 506
Joint Photographic Interpretation Centre 514
Joint Security Committee 505
Joint Security Staff 505

Joint Services Security Bureau 504
Joint Staff Committee 73, 79, 440
Joliffe, F.E., Chief Postal Censor 461
Joly, C. 384, 567
Jones, C.G. 464, 479, 566
Jones, D.H. 260, 272, 330
Jordan, H. 143
Joyce, William (Lord Haw-Haw) 332, 407
JUBILEE (Exercise) 121, 143, 161. *See* also Dieppe
JUDEX (Codename) 378. *See* also S.O.E.
Jukes, Maj. A.E. 53
Jungbluth, Capt. E.N. 29
Justice, Department of 48, 78, 472
Justice, Minister of 46, 68, 472, 474

K

Kamloops Kid (Kanao, Inouye) 482
Kapala, W.A. 138
Kates, E.H. 122, 128
Kato, A.S. (Tony) 392, 393
Katwijk 316
Kazakoff. J.A. 138, 303, 569
Keller, Maj.-Gen. R.F.L., C.B.E. 149, 240
Kelman, J. 95
Kemmel 32
Kent, G.L. 115
Kentville (N.S.) 18
Kenyon, Brig.-Gen. L.E., C.D. 511
Kerr, D.G. 524
Kesselring, F.M. Albert (Ger.) 174, 180, 188, 193, 196, 201
KING (ammunition dump) 308
King, Asst. Cmmr., R.C.M.P. 75
King, L. 383
King, Rt. Hon. W.L. Mackenzie 62, 63, 351, 357, 365, 429, 437
Kingsmill, C.D. xvi, 183, 187, 188, 192, 196, 200, 201, 202, 203, 229, 297, 542, 566
Kingston (Ont.) 19, 69, 98, 275, 413. *See* Index PART III Military Districts
King, Tpr. Charles 6
Kinnear, A.C. 122, 567, 570
Kippen, Lieut. E.A.W. 6
Kirke, Gen. Sir W.M. St.G. (Br.) 42
Kirk, F.M. 138
Kiska 363, 454
Kitching, Brig. G. 211
KLONDIKE (Exercise) 143
Kluge, F.M. Günther von 265
Knight, Lieut. J. (Br.) 322
Knocke-sur-Mer 269, 404
Knoop, Leo 506
Koenig, Gen. M.P. (Fr.) 370, 376

Kombol, Nicola 379
Korea 514, 516, 517
   Democratic People's Republic 517, 519
   Republic of 517
Krug, C. 98, 422
Kuhlbach, E.G. 122, 260, 331
Kurile Islands 363
Küsten Canal 294
Kyrenia 535

L

Laban, J.H.F. 298, 331, 379
Labelle, P.E. 378, 380, 566, 568
Labrador 440
Labrosse, R.J. xvi, 385, 386, 566, 568
Ladner, G. 487
Lady Nelson, S.S. 480
Lafleur, C. 384, 385, 566, 567, 568
Lafontaine, Baptiste 7
Lage Zwalume 317
La Hogue 253, 256
Laing, B.E. 228
Laison R. 257, 258
Lake, R.H. 149
Lamb, 2/Lieut. O.M. 172
Lamone R. 204, 205, 237
Lamothe, E.C. 347, 350, 566, 568
Lancaster, R.G. 349
Lanciano 221, 222, 223
Landry, R.P. 460
Langemarck 26
Langford, Tpr. J. 6
Langley, J.W.G. 322
Langley, Lt.-Col. J.M. (Br.) 387
Laperrière, M.L. 308
Lapointe, F.J. 378
Larino 223
La Rivière 249
Larkin, M. 368
Larouche, J.R. 301
Larsen, J. 322
Latin America 432, 444
Lauder, Sgt. 4
Laver, A.B. 183
Laviola, J. 307
Lawson, Brig. J.K. 359
Lawton, G.M. 318
League of Nations 59, 62, 64, 73
Leatherhead 114, 130
Lee, B.C. 382
Lee, B.K. 382
Leer 295, 323, 332, 334, 341
Leese, Lt.-Gen. Sir. O.W.H. 184

Leeuwarden 322, 325, 330
Lefebvre, W.B. 211, 213, 303, 567
Le Havre 25, 128, 240, 263, 265, 308, 374, 400
Lehman, W. 196, 328
Leiden 322, 324, 326
Leigh Mallory, A.V.M., T.L. 159
Le Mans 311
Le Mesnil-Patry 248
Lens 31
Leonforte 211, 212
Leopold Canal 265, 266, 267, 268, 269, 270
Lethbridge 4, 487, 489, 490, 493, 495, 500
Letoiani 218
Le Tréport 163
Leur 319
Lévesque, G.E. 388
Levesque, R.J. 569
Lew, R.W. 382
Leys, J.F. 517
L'Hereault, G. 130, 136
Liane R. 265
Library, D.N.D. 58
Lieven, Maj. P.M.C. 106, 391, 392, 407, 566, 569
Liewer, Philippe 374
Lightstone, Capt. (Br.) 192
Line-Crossers 180, 200, 255, 286, 302, 303, 311, 315, 316, 318, 320, 325, 522
   Korea 521, 522, 528, 532
Lines, T.H. 130, 131, 247
Linguists xix, 89, 96, 97, 108, 119, 121, 122, 127, 147, 272, 318, 344, 396, 416, 419, 423, 424, 483, 492
   Chinese 426
   G. Hansen, A Johannson 97
   Japanese 97, 365, 367, 393, 416, 423, 426
   postwar 503, 514
   S.E.A.C. 393, 427, 428
Liri R. 180, 188, 189, 190, 191, 193, 194, 195, 225
Lisieux 260, 262, 302
Little Kiska 364, 365
Littner, M. 130
Lochem 318, 406
Locri 215
Loire 375
Lombardy Plain 201
London District Transit Camp 106, 388
London (Ont.) 14, 18, 52. *See* also Index Part III, M.D.1
London (U.K.) 19, 51, 136, 142, 145, 146, 148, 149, 328
Long, G.R. 319
Long Lake (Sask.) 6
Loon Lake (Sask.) 7

INDEX

Lord Haw-Haw 332, 407
Louie, K. 382
Louie, V.J. 382
Louis Pasteur, S.S. 473, 474
Lowe, R.Y. 383, 481
Low, N.M. 383
Ludlow, Capt. Don 537
Lugo 203, 204
Lustringen 340
Lyons 376, 377

M

Maas R. 268, 269, 272, 275, 276, 278, 279, 281, 282, 284, 285, 288, 289, 290, 309, 310, 311, 314, 316, 317, 319, 323, 325, 389
Maastricht 263, 276
Macallister, J.K. 375, 569
MacAuley, D.M. 210
Macdonald, Maj. A.F. 117
Macdougall, J.W.G. xvi, 125, 127, 149, 150, 249, 272, 313, 320, 328, 344, 542, 566
MacDougall, Maj. Donald Lorne 2, 3
Macerata 237
MacFarlane, R.O. 422
MacGillivray, G.B. 125, 128, 541, 542, 570
Macintosh, H.K. 172
MacKenzie, A.H. 272
Mackenzie, District of 440
MacKenzie, Hon. Ian 408
Mackenzie-Papineau Battalion 71, 454
Macklin, Maj.-Gen. W.H.S., C.B.E. 365, 443
MacLean, Victor 461
MacMillan, H. 143
MacPherson, R.S. 149
Magnus, E.D. 114, 158, 566, 567
Malaya 356, 357, 359, 366, 382
  Malayan People's Anti-Japanese Army 382
Malone, Lt.-Col. R.S., D.P.R. 347, 350, 394, 481
Maltby, Maj.-Gen. C.M. (Br.) 356, 360, 361
Malton 115
Manchuria 358, 519
Mang, L.H. 330
Manila 369, 481
Mann, Maj.-Gen. C.C. 114, 126, 127, 130, 131, 155
Maple Leaf, The 229, 237, 329, 333
Mapping Branch (D.M.I.) 11, 12, 13
  Directorate of Survey 17
Maps, military 17, 549
  1915 27
  Army 115
  Brigade 35
  Corps 32, 37, 41

C.S.E.F. 44
Division 34
First World War 31
historical 59
Invasion 103, 105
Italy 186, 192, 198
Korea 519, 527
Maqui 311, 377, 386
Marchand, E. 347
March, C.Int.C. Regimental 507
Marcotte, J.M. 391, 392
Marks, R. 249
Marne R. 32, 259, 376
Martin, H. 130
Mary of Arnhem 407
Masinda, F. 231
Masse, Sgt. L.A.L. 529
Massey, Rt. Hon. Vincent 101
Massy, D.H. 320
Mastronardi, Lieut. E.J. 519
Matera 216
Materborn 286, 288
Materiel, Security of 135, 137, 138. *See* Counter-Sabotage
Matlock 98, 275, 413, 414
Matsuyama, E. 426
Matthews, T/Lt.-Col. H.H., C.M.G., D.S.O. 55, 59, 63, 64, 556
Mattocks, D.P. 537
Maynard, Mr. (External Affairs) 86
Maystorovich, J. 387
McAllister, C.C. 116
McCarthy, W.A. 303, 569
McClelland, D.G. 524
McCordick, J.A. 121
McDougall, J.J. 367, 520, 524
McEachern, J.E. 265, 328, 541, 567
McGuire, W.D. 301
McIntyre, H.T. 322
McKay, R.B. 326
McKenzie, A.P.M.C. 424, 425
McKenzie, A.P.P. 519, 523
McLaughlan, Lt.-Col. G.M. 274
McLean, N.L. 389
McMurrich, A.R. 268
McNamee, J.O. 442
McNaughton, Gen. Hon. A.G.L., P.C., C.H., C.N., C.M.G., D.S.O. 61, 68, 70, 88, 89, 101, 114, 123, 126, 150, 153, 370, 437, 477
McRae, Pte. J., (N.W.M.P.) 7
McShane, K.G. 150, 508, 509, 530
McVea, W.J. 303, 567
Mechback, 2/Lieut. S 535
Medical Intelligence 104, 106

Medical Services, Director General of 434
Medmenham (Danesfield Hall) 155
Megill, M.T. 443
Melfa R. 194, 223
Melfi 178
Mendel, G.A. 247, 330
Menin 308
Menny, Lt.-Gen. Erwin (Ger.) 259
Menzies, A.R. (External Affairs) 435
Meppen 292, 320, 322, 330, 331, 334, 340, 406
Meredith, Bryan 86
Mericourt 31
Merritt, Maj. W. H. 9
Merxem 268, 308
Messina, Straits of 173
Metauro R. 198, 199, 200
Meunier, F.C. 380
Meunier, P.C.M. 376, 380
Meuse R. 278, 291
Meyer, S.S. Maj.-Gen. Kurt (Ger.) 247, 328, 351
MGB 503 386
M.I.5 (British Security Service) 85, 109, 132, 133, 137, 144, 147, 208, 285, 344, 488
M.I.6 (British Secret Intelligence Service) 377, 488
Middleburg 311
Middleton, Maj.-Gen. Sir Frederick 4, 6, 7
Middle Wallop 248
Mignano 180, 225
Mihajlovic, Gen. (Yugoslav) 379
Military Attachés 48, 97, 106, 358, 437, 473, 503, 506
Military Districts. *See* Index Part II
Military Intelligence xvii
Military Intelligence, Assistant Director of 23, 47, 55, 57, 58, 59, 61, 62, 63, 64, 65, 66, 70, 105, 106, 107, 108
  A.C. Caldwell 17
  B.H. Hay 18
  combined with Air Int. 65
  F.E. Davis 51, 55
  H.H. Matthews 55, 59
  L.H. Sitwell 18
  seperated from Air Int. 408
  Sutherland-Brown 55, 59
Military Intelligence, Directorate of 409, 410, 422, 427, 436, 444, 451, 496, 497, 500, 507, 509, 532, 546. *See* also Directorate of Military Intelligence (position)
  Ch. 15 408
  Ch. 16 431
  Ch. 17 451
  duties 11, 56
  established 1903 11
  funds 64

Information Branch (censorship) 74, 409
Information Branch (foreign) 11, 23, 62
Information Room 437
Library 435
Mapping Branch 11
M.I.1 357, 364, 409, 432, 434, 437, 438, 439, 440
M.I.2 85, 409, 443, 479, 498
M.I.3 95, 377, 409, 438, 439, 444, 454, 455, 456, 473, 479, 489, 498
M.I.3(a) 454, 483
M.I.3(b) 454, 460
M.I.3(d) 488, 489
M.I.4 483
M.I.4(a), M.I.4(b), M.I.4(c) to M.I.7 483
M.I.5(M.I.7) 487
M.I.7 483, 488, 489, 490, 495, 496
  sources 431, 437
  to Directorate of Survey 17
Military Intelligence, Directorate of (Br.). *See* also Escape and Evasion, I.S.9
  Leo Heaps 99
  M.I.9 208, 370, 384, 481
  M.I.12 98, 102, 209, 349
Military Intelligence, Director General of 12
  duties 11, 23
Military Operations and Intelligence, Directorate of 55, 61, 63, 73, 76, 79, 414, 423, 439, 443, 446, 447, 471
  censorship 462, 463, 464
  Gen. M.A. Pope 461
  Hong Kong 357, 362
Military Operations and Plans, Director of 463
Military Training, Director of 275, 413, 414, 416, 421, 425, 436, 439, 472, 474, 539
Militia Intelligence Training Companies. *See* Index Part II
Militia (Reserve Army) 9, 11
  1885 4, 7
  aliens 48
  censorship 45
  Council 15, 53
  Nanaimo 20
  post-1945 499, 502, 503, 509, 511, 514, 539
Miller, O.J. 326
Miller, P.B. 131
Millingen 316
Mills, J. 365
Milne, J.S. 143, 151, 164, 569
Ministry of Overseas Military Forces of Canada (London, U.K.) 81
Minley Manor 113, 384
Minton (Sask.) 438
Mitchell, Brig.-Gen. Charles Hamilton 13, 33, 461

Mobilization
　1914 22, 25
　post-1945 501
　pre-1939 54, 56, 64, 72, 74, 408
Models (tactical)
　1 Canadian Army Modelling Team 127, 266, 285
　1914 31
　Reichswald 285
Modica 171, 172, 210, 211
Moldovan, V. 379
Molnar, D.G. 183, 196, 224, 567
Molson, Cornet W. Markland 2
Mombaroccio 230
Mons 33
Montague, Lt.-Gen. Hon., P.J., C.B., C.M.G., D.S.O., M.V., V.D. 81
Monteray, U.S.A.T. 368
Monterey (California) 514
Monterey, S.S. 217
Montgomery, F.M. the Viscount 141, 147, 153, 178, 180, 255, 263, 279, 333, 335, 343, 396
Montone 204, 237
Montreal (P.Q.) 2, 49, 51, 68, 70, 98, 433, 460, 461, 476, 477, 480, 505, 539, 541
Montreuil 305
Mook 286, 316
Moore, H.F.W. 326
Moore, J.T. 231, 569
Moose Mountain Scouts. *See* Index Part II
Morale 108, 109, 136, 150, 166, 232
　Army 327
　Belgian civil 309
　Canada 439, 455, 476
Morconi 225
Morehouse, J.H. 488, 541
Morgan, F. 158, 164
Morgan, J.R. 438
Morgan, Lieut. R. (Interpreter) 214, 215
Morgan, Sir. F.E., K.C.B. 370, 394
Mori, H. 393
Moro R. 181, 182
Morrice, D.R. 249, 273, 542
Morris, D.F. 314, 322, 339, 568
Motta Montecorvino 178, 179
Mottos, Official
　C.Int.C. 419
　C. of G. 14
Motzfeldt, J.K. 252, 260, 542, 566, 567
Mountbatten, Admiral Lord Louis 165, 427
Mount Sorrel 29
Movement Control 162, 219, 235, 236, 305. *See also* Controls, Control Lines
Mowat, F.M. 328

Moyland Wood 288
Mueller, Maj. Kurt (Ger.) 489, 491
Mullaly, Lt.-Col. B.R. 358, 365, 424, 430, 446
Mulvihill, T.C. 130
Munro, C.D. 382
Murchie, Lt.-Gen. J.C., C.B., C.B.E. 437
Murphy, Sgt. (I.S.9) 388, 389
Murray, Col. W.W. 111, 364, 365, 414, 416, 471, 542, 547
　D.M.I. 344, 416, 419, 421, 424, 427, 430, 448, 460, 461, 474, 481, 486, 499, 500, 501, 502, 504, 505, 508, 511, 539, 542, 547, 551, 552, 556, 566, 571
　G.S.O.1 357, 410
　Kiska 364
Mussolini, Benito 174
Mustard, P.P. 249
Mutiny, Pacific Command 477
Mymka, J. 143
Myrtou Monastery 534
Mytchett 129

N

Nam Tau 359, 360
Nanaimo (B.C.) 20, 365, 477
Napier, Ross R. 20, 21
Naples 174, 183, 217, 227, 349
National Defence H.Q./Army H.Q. 81, 82, 83, 86, 87, 90, 92, 95, 98, 105, 113. *See also* Military Intelligence, Directorate of
　censorship 99, 101
　F.S. 130
　Kiska 364, 436
　P.W. 106, 109
National Defence, Minister of
　1885 4
　1900 9
　1914-18 46, 65
　Gen., the Hon. A.G.L. McNaughton (November 1944-August 1945) 437, 477
　Hon. Ian MacKenzie (1935-39) 408
　Hon. J.L. Ralston (1940-44) 456, 477
　Hon. Norman Rogers (1939-40) 451, 462
　Sam Hughes 22, 25
National Film Board 407
Nationalsozialistische Deutsche Arbeit Partei (N.S.D.A.P.) 319, 320, 337
National War Services, Department of 461
Nazi (Nazism)
　Austria 495
　Camps 484, 489, 490, 493, 495
　Canada 71, 453, 454, 470, 476, 551
　Germany 331, 332, 333, 335, 336,

337, 338, 339, 340, 341, 432
Iceland 352
N.W. Europe 247, 254, 297, 298, 319, 320
Nederlandsche Binnenlandsche Strijdkrachten (N.B.S.) 312
Neder Rijn R. 278, 292, 294, 295
Needham, F.W.W. 115
Neelands, D.E. 481, 482
Nestlerode 319
Neufeld, P.H 404
Neuve Chapelle 25
Neuville 156, 162
Newark-on-Trent 149
New Brunswick 18, 46, 55, 71, 454, 477, 507
New Carlisle (N.B.) 476
Newcastle (N.B.) 46
Newfoundland 362, 471, 473, 474
  Atlantic Command 440
New Water Line 294
New York 48, 51, 52, 71, 72, 370, 378, 410, 432, 447, 457, 461, 479, 480, 538
Niagara-on-the-Lake (Ont.) 14, 15, 18
Nichols, S., R.H.C. 389
Nicosia 533, 535, 537
Niers R. 282, 288
Nijmegen 275, 276, 282, 284, 285, 286, 291, 304, 310, 311, 312, 315, 316, 318, 319, 342, 388, 459
Nispen 310
Nissenthal, Flt. Sgt J., R.A.F. 161
Nissoria 212
Noble, A.A.B. 130
Noble, Lt.-Col. R.H., M.B.E., C.D. 296, 302, 303, 305, 323, 339, 340, 507, 511, 566, 567, 568, 571
Non-Permanent Active Militia (N.P.A.M.) 68
Noord Brabant (Prov.) 312
Noordsingel 323
Norderney 342
Norfolk House 208
Norman-Crosse, E.G. 130
Normandy 138, 149, 240, 259, 386
North Saskatchewan R. 7
North Sea Canal 326
North West Mounted Police (N.W.M.P.). *See* Royal Canadian Mounted Police
North West Rebellion, 1885 4, 549
Nuremberg Trials 341
NURSERY (German Underground Organization) 342

O

Oaktree (Escape Line) 385
Oakville (Ont.) 505
Occupation of Germany 275. *See also* Index Part III C.A.O.F.
  C.I. planning 108, 323
  operations 331, 483, 496
Odiham 248, 256
Odlum, Maj.-Gen. V.W., C.B., C.M.G., D.S.O., V.D. 410, 411
Odon R. 248
Ofenheim, E. 330
Oisterwijk 314, 317, 318
Oldenburg 294, 295, 296, 320, 323, 330, 331, 334, 336, 337, 339, 343, 483
O'Leary, Pat (Escape Line) 384
Olmstead, L.D. 369
One Big Union 53
OOSTACKER (aummunition dump) 308
Orde Dienst (O.D.) 312, 318, 320
Orders in Council (text references only)
  P.C. 531, 14 May 38 73
  P.C. 1836, 20 May 14 45
  P.C. 2029, 2 Aug 14 45
  P.C. 2358, 19 Sep 14 23
  P.C. 2409, 20 Sep 14 46
  P.C. 2481, 1 Sep 39 460
  P.C. 2499, 1 Sep 39 460
  P.C. 2506, 1 Sep 39 460
  P.C. 2821, 6 Nov 14 46
  P.C. 5842, 9 Jul 42 458
Organization & Training, D.M.I. (O&T) 507, 510, 514, 539, 546
Orne R. 242, 251, 252, 253, 254, 256, 302, 304
Ortona 174, 179, 181, 182, 183, 184, 186, 195, 221
Orvieto 227
Oshawa (Ont.) 69, 371, 410, 489. *See also* Hydra, STS 103
Osipoff, G.A. 149, 302, 569
Oslee, F.L. 4
Osnabrück 337, 339, 340, 342, 343
O.S.S. (Office of Strategic Services) 371, 380
Ostend 305, 312
Oswald, Capt. 4
Ottawa (Ont.) 23, 81, 115, 119, 176, 328, 340, 352, 443, 477, 546. *See* National Defence H.Q./ Army H.Q.
Otterbourne 147
Otterloo 294, 298, 318, 325, 326
Otter, Maj.-Gen. W.D., C.V.O., C.B. 6, 7, 19, 45, 48, 72
Overflakkee 272, 280, 281

OVERLORD (Operation) 149, 240
O.V.R.A. (Fascist Secret Police) 214, 215
O.W.I. (Office of Wartime Information) 371

P

Pachino 171, 210
Paduani, Gen. Egio (It.) 226
Page, Brig. L.F. 352
Page, Col. D.R. (U.S.) 396
Page, John xvi, 87, 88, 89, 90, 91, 92, 96, 97, 98, 102, 109, 127, 132, 133, 384
Pals, L.K., D.C.M. 143, 151, 390, 566, 569
Panet, Lt.-Col. H.A., D.S.O. 20
Papen, Franz von (Ger.) 48, 49
Paris 157, 240, 303, 350, 372, 374, 375, 378, 384, 385, 386
Parry, G.R. 391, 392, 507
Parsons, Col. J.L.R. 31, 33, 64
Partisans 203, 204, 205, 226, 227, 228, 229, 230, 234, 235, 236
   Gothic Line 200
   Yugoslavia 379
Pas de Calais 246, 263
Passchendaele 31, 35
Passive Air Defence
   C.M.H.Q. 86
   Newfoundland 362
Paterson, G. 379
Paulin, M. 127, 344, 541, 542
Pay and Allowances 57, 66, 83, 92, 108, 120, 122, 130, 232, 275, 344, 349, 371, 423, 425, 427, 454, 471, 510, 534, 540
   C. of G. 13, 14, 15, 18
   Royal Guides 3
Pearkes, Maj.-Gen. G.R., V.C., C.B., D.S.O., M.C. 363, 364, 365, 366
Pearson, Rt. Hon. Lester B. 82, 86
Pembroke (Ont.) 471
Pender, R.H. 487, 488
Peniakoff, Lt.-Col. Vladimir ("Popski") (Br.) 179
PENKNIFE (Exercise) 237
Penner, Lieut. John 3
Penny, C.T. 367
Perceval, Lt.-Col. R.R.M. (Br.) 87
Permanent Joint Board of Defence 363
Perrault, M.M.K. 422, 479
Perrin, Tpr. H. 6
Perugia 229
Pescara R. 181, 188, 223, 229
Petainism 455
Petawawa (Ont.) 19. *See* also Camp Petawawa
Petersson, H.J.L. 323, 331, 334
PHERUDA Report 493

Philip, D.G. 183
Philip, J.A. 183
Photographic Interpretation Course 420
Pickersgill, F.H.D. 375, 567, 569
Pickford, H.N. 131
Pickup, T. 144, 272
Pierre Artus 247
Pignotta, Michele 217
Pine-Coffin, 2/Lieut. R.S. (Br.) 172
PIRATE (Exercise) 145
Pisa-Rimini Line 191, 196. *See* also Gothic Line Harrods 237
Place, J.W. 151, 569
Playfair, G.C.P. 308
Plewman, J.A. 301, 567
Plouha 385, 386
Plumer, Lt.-Gen. Sir H.C.O. (Br.) 33
PLUNDER (Operation) 291, 316
Plymouth 134
Pofi 226
Police (German) 147, 339
   Geheimfeldpolizei 337
   Geheimstaatspolizei 337. *See* also Index Part V Gestapo
   Kriminalpolizei 337
   Staatspolizei (Sipo) 319, 325, 337
Political Intelligence Department/ Directorate 103, 104, 370, 391, 392
   P.W. 496
Political Intelligence Report/Summary 110, 340, 432
Political Warfare Committee 435, 486
Pollak, F.A. 252
Pootmans, P 256
Pootmans, R.J. 128, 568
Pope, F.N. 172, 180
Pope, Lt.-Gen. M.A., C.B., M.C. 74, 75, 77, 110, 132, 134, 135, 363, 439, 447, 460, 461
Pope, W.H. 520
Po R. 196, 202, 522
Port Arthur (Ont.) 49
Porter, J.A. 211, 215
Porto Corsini 203, 205
Port Security 144, 145, 148, 218, 230, 234, 310, 322, 323, 326, 473, 474
Portsmouth 145, 155, 160, 167
Potenza 174, 178
Potigny 256, 257, 258
Potsdam Conference (1945) 333, 339
Potter, A. 408
Potter, S. 408
Potts, Brig. A.E. 353
Poundmaker, Chief 7
Pourville 155, 161, 164
Powers, Col. T.E. 461

Prato-Preride, L.I. (Interpreter) 196
Preston, Maj. J.F., M.C. 66, 408, 454, 556
Prette, B. 408
Prime Minister, the 25, 61, 62, 63, 105, 357, 365, 429
Prince Albert (Sask.) 4
Prince George (B.C.) 421, 440, 453, 454, 477
Prince, R.D. 172, 187, 188, 194
Prince Rupert (B.C.) 440, 477
Prince Rupert, S.S. 481
Prisoners of War. *See* also Interrogation
   1914-18 31, 32, 35, 37
   Dieppe 106, 165, 166
   Korea 531
   N.W. Europe 252, 258, 259, 262, 265, 273, 284, 289, 297, 318, 320, 337, 400
   postal censorship 479
   Sicily/Italy 172, 174, 178, 186, 187, 193, 194, 200, 201, 211
Prisoners of War, Directorate of (D.P.O.W.) 484, 486, 488, 490, 493
Prisoners of War Intelligence, Directorate of 488
Prisoners of War, Re-education of 486, 495
Proctor, R.L. 353, 354
Pronger, L.J. 196
Propaganda, Enemy 49, 196, 444
   1941 357, 358, 360, 450
   1943 319, 480
   Daily Digest of World Wireless Propaganda 432
   Dieppe 144, 167
   Japanese (1937) 72
   Korea 531
Prowse, D.F. 341
Psychological Warfare xxi, 186, 204, 221, 222, 391
   Indian Field Broadcasting Units (Force 136) 393
   Information Control Units 107
   M.I.1 432, 435, 480
   No. 2/ No. 3 Public Relations Group 394
   N.W. Europe 265, 268, 296
   Overt Psy. War. 394
   P.W. 486, 487
Public Information, Director of 357, 461, 462
Public Relations 86, 100
   censorship 346, 349
   Control of Psychological Warfare 394, 398
   Lt.-Col. Henderson 123
   Press Censorship, Canada 364
Puits (Puys) 161, 162, 163, 164, 397
Pusan 517, 519, 520, 521
P.W. Camps (Canada) 420, 483, 484, 488, 489, 490, 492, 494, 495
   30 (Bowmanville) 489, 494
   40 (Farnham) 495
   42 (Sherbrooke) 491
   44 (Grande Ligne) 489, 493
   45 (Sorel) 495
   100 (Neys) 476, 493, 494
   130 (Seebe) 493
   132 (Medicine Hat) 487, 489, 490, 491, 493, 500
   133 (Lethbridge) 487, 489, 495, 500
   "C" (20, Calydor) 483
   "E" (Espanola) 483
   "F" (Fort Henry) 483
   20 (Gravenhurst) 489
   Lethbridge 490, 493
   "Q" (Monteith) 483
   "R" (Red Rock) 483

Q

Q List 240
Qu'Appelle (Sask.) 4
Quebec City 454
QUEEN (ammunition dump) 308
Queen Elizabeth, S.S. 472, 473, 474
Quesnay 257, 258
Questura 214, 215, 235
Quinn, F.G. 130

R

Rabinovitch 375
Ragusa 172, 211
Rahn, J.A. 301, 567
Ralston, Col., the Hon. J.L. 100, 150, 437, 456, 472, 473, 474, 477
Ramsay, Lieut. William M. 3, 4
Rapido R. 190, 193, 225
Ratlines 388
Ravenna 203, 204, 205, 235, 236, 237
   BASFORCE (F.S.) 234
Raymont, Col. R.L., M.B.E. xvi, 92, 110, 111, 126, 566
Reading 140
Reconnaissance xviii, 1, 7, 8, 11, 14, 15, 19, 31, 32, 33, 38, 40, 54, 55, 56, 60, 116, 117, 122, 124, 168, 178, 179, 188, 205, 213, 214, 233, 240, 246, 248, 249, 253, 254, 279, 294, 311, 315, 353, 354, 361, 365, 411, 527, 534, 538
Reed, K. 541
Rees 284, 285
Reese Camp 316
Rees, F/O J. 203
Reesor, F.K. 204

INDEX

Refugee Interrogation Posts 216, 219, 223, 225, 227
Refugees (Displaced Persons) xix, 29, 211, 216, 217, 218, 219, 221, 224, 225, 227, 230, 240, 301, 303, 311, 313, 316, 325, 330, 337, 340, 397, 403
   Korea 521, 522, 524
Regalbuto 174, 212
Reggio di Calabria 174, 176, 177, 213, 214, 215
Regina 162, 438, 476. *See* also Index Part III Military Districts
Reichswald 274, 276, 277, 278, 280, 281, 292, 316
   defences 284, 285, 286, 316, 405
Rejang R. 383
Relief Camps 69
Rempel, H. 314, 320, 569
Rempel, W. 301, 567
Replacement Rates 127
Resistance 310, 314, 318
   Belgian 307, 308, 310, 312, 404. *See* also B.F.I., Brigade Blanche/ White Brigade, Independent Front
   Dutch 310, 312, 324
   French 302, 303, 304, 305, 311, 377, 386. *See* also F.F.I
   Malaysian 382
Reykjavik 352
Rheinberg 290
Rhine R. 44, 276, 277, 281, 282, 284, 285, 286, 288, 289, 290, 291, 292, 294, 316, 317, 325, 389, 523
Rhône R. 378
Ribolla, Sgt. (Interpreter) 214
Richardson, T.J. 307, 308
Ridderkerk 324, 326
Riehle, W.C. 255
Riel, Louis David 4, 6, 7
Riel Rebellion, 1869 4
Rijessen 314, 322
Rimini 191, 201, 202, 237
Rimini Line 201
Rintelen, Capt. Franz von (Ger.) 48
Ripley, E.J. 393
Rivers, Lt.-Col. Victor Brereton 10, 13, 17
Robbins, D.A. 346, 347
Robertsbridge 145
Roberts, Maj.-Gen. J.H., C.B., D.S.O., M.C. 153, 159
Roberts, O.M. 172
Robertson, Capt. J.M. 249, 269, 296, 298
Robertson, Cornet Duncan 2, 4
Robertson, D.K. 88, 127
Robertson, Terrance 157
Robinson, H.B.O. 128

Robinson, Maj. Jack, R.C.E. 172, 180, 182, 186
Robinson, Maj. J.M. 566
Robinson, Mark W. 258, 514, 566
Robinson, N. 116
Robinson, R.T. 566
Robinson, W.L. 130, 322, 566
Robitaille, Lt.-Col. G., M.C., C.D. 567
Rockcliffe (Ottawa) 443, 444, 514
Rockingham, Brig. J.M., C.B., C.B.E., D.S.O., E.D. 265, 521, 522, 524
Rodger, Maj.-Gen. N.E., C.B.E. 82, 84, 85, 86, 87, 99, 128
Rodrigues, G. 386, 387, 569
Roer R. 277, 288
Rogers, D.M. 369
Rogers, G.F. 328, 542
Rogers, T.C. 128
Rome 98, 174, 180, 183, 184, 186, 196, 203, 225, 226, 227, 228, 233, 237, 238, 347, 387, 390, 461
Rommel, F.M. Edwin (Ger.) 176, 180, 242, 244, 247
Roosendaal 404
Rosen, R.H. 308
Rosolini 172
Rossano 215
Ross, Charlie (N.W.M.P.) 6, 9
Ross, D.E. 349
Ross, Maj.-Gen. J.S. 423
Rotterdam 51, 297, 298, 322, 323, 326, 327
Rouen 128, 157, 240, 262, 263, 305, 307, 374
Rouvres Defence Line 257
Rowe, Capt. Norman 203, 204
Royal Automobile Club of Italy (R.A.C.I.) 214
Royal Canadian Legion 78, 79
Royal Canadian Military Institute 418
Royal Canadian Mounted Police (R.C.M.P.) xx, 52, 55, 61, 62, 66, 68, 70, 75, 423, 428, 438, 444, 451, 452, 453, 454, 455, 456, 457, 470, 471, 472, 490, 494, 500, 507
   Kiska 365
   N.W.M.P.
      1885 4, 6, 7
   R.N.W.M.P.
      1914 48, 50, 51
   Special Security Service Sections 454
Royal Military College of Canada (R.M.C.) 17, 98, 110, 411, 413, 414, 416, 417, 419, 420, 421, 422, 501
Roy, A.R. 116
Rumours 134, 139, 140, 145, 471, 476
   Germany 334, 340, 341, 342
   Kiska 365
Rundstedt, F.M. Gerd von (Ger.) 240, 276, 277, 289

Russi 204, 235
Russia (Russians) 50, 106, 243, 260, 273, 296, 303, 333, 340, 342, 386, 387
  language training 542
RUTTER (Operation) 153, 155, 159, 161
Ruurlo 320
Ruysbroek 273
Ryckevorsel-Beersee 273

S

S-20 (Japanese Language School) 368, 392, 393, 425, 426, 427, 428, 429, 448, 514
Saar Valley 277
Sabotage
  1914-15 49
  Canada 452, 470
  devices 227
Sabourin, R. 375, 567, 569
Sacco R. 180
Saher 306
Saint John (N.B.) 49, 71, 115, 454, 507
Sakai, Gen. (Jap.) 361
Salerno 174, 177, 178, 189, 216
Salois 7
Sami-ch'on R. 526, 527, 530
San Arcangelo 238
San Bartolommeo 179
Sandhorst 334
San Diego (U.S.A.) 364
Sandys, Hon. Duncan (Br.) 273
San Fortunato Ridge 201
Sangro R. 180, 181, 199, 218, 222
San Marino 201, 238
Sansom, Lt.-Gen. E.W., C.B., D.S.O. 123
San Stefano 173
Santa Elena, S.S. 217
Sant' Angelo 225
Santerno R. 204
San Vito Chietino 218
Saran, D.R. 402
Sarantos, Lt.-Col. L.E. 506
Sardinia 171, 174, 219
Saritch, G.M. 391
Saskatoon 69
Sasson, Wim 325
Savage, T.L. 541
Savignano 202
Savio R. 232, 236, 237
Savojaards Plaat 266, 269, 270
SAVVY (Exercise) 147
Scarpe 33
Schasny, M.S. 301
Scheldt 266, 269, 271, 272, 273, 305, 309, 459

Scheveningen 324
Schiedam 324
Schiermonnikog 325
Schilde 307
Schlemm, Gen. Alfred (Ger.) 291
Schlesinger, Sgt. (Br.) 223
Schmettow, Gen. von (Ger.) 401
Schmitt, Lt.-Gen. A. (Ger.) 489
Schoengarth, SS Brig. Dr. 327
Schooten 268
Schouen, Island of 272, 280, 281
Scientific Intelligence, Directorate of 508
Scie R. 156
Scott, Maj. H.G. 408, 444, 446, 447, 448, 451, 452, 556
Scrogg, Det. Sgt. T. R.C.M.P. 473
Scudamore, Maj. V.D. 20
Searle, Claude 528, 531
Seattle (Wash.) 368
Secret List 98, 442, 464
Secret Writing 488, 489, 491
Security Branch 546
Security Control Organization (Br.) 150
Security of Information 108, 109, 408, 451, 454, 506
  M.I.3(b) 460
Security of Materiel 98, 100, 135, 137, 138. See also Counter-Sabotage
Security of Operations
  1940 100, 135, 139
  Canada 472
  C.E.F. 23, 25, 32
  Dieppe 160, 167
  Italy 146, 189, 208
  N.W. Europe 303
Security of Personnel 76, 85, 90, 93, 95, 103, 106, 110, 135, 138, 509
  Canada 452, 454
  M.I.3 454
  postwar 500, 501, 506
Security Platoons 509
Security Services Officers Association 547
Sehull, F.C. 367
Seine R. 163, 258, 260, 262, 398
Senio R. 203, 206, 235
Sertorius (German propagandist) 285
Service de Sécurité Militaire (S.M.) 305
Services Reconnaissance Detachment (S.O.E.) 481
Sewell (Man.) 20
Seyss-Inquart, Reichskommissar A. (Ger.) 334
Sham Chun R. 359, 360
Shawnee, U.S.A.T. 368
Shelburne (Escape Line) 385, 386
Shelley, Ray 134, 296, 303, 317, 322

s'Hertogenbosch 309, 311, 315, 326
Sherwood, Commissioner Percy, R.C.M.P. 49
Shiu, J. 383, 567
Shook, A.L. 138, 236
Shulman, Milton 110, 111, 256, 328, 567
Shultis, P.A. 274
Siberia. *See* Index III C.S.E.F.
Sicilia Libra 211
Sicily (Sicilians) 170, 174, 176, 210, 212, 217, 219
Siddons, J.D. 391
Siebengewald 316
Siegfried Line 284, 288, 289
Sifton, C. 19
Sifton, J.W. 19, 54
Sifton, V. 463
Sifton, W.B. 19
Signals, Director of 444
Signals Intelligence xix, 114, 124, 368, 443, 500, 503. *See also* Military Intelligence, Directorate of, M.I.2, and Wireless Intelligence
dispute over control 119, 443
personnel 368
Signals Sub-Committee 74, 443
Sillanpaa, P. 235
Silver & Green (C.Int.C. march) 507
Silzer, M.C. 253
S.I.M./C.S. 216, 219, 234, 235
Simmons, R.J. 332
Simonds, Lt.-Gen. G.G., C.B., C.B.E., D.S.O., C.D. 89, 176, 211, 249, 257, 271, 298, 406
Singapore 62, 63, 355, 357, 382, 393, 433, 434
Singer, F. 308
Sipo 319, 325, 339. *See also* Police, German
Si R. 355
Sirois, L.P.J. 375, 376, 566
Sitwell, Capt. L.H. 556
Skelton, Dr. O.D. (External Affairs) 61
Skilbeck, G. 489
Skippon, E.K., M.M. 143, 144, 150
Skutezky, E. 260, 265, 272, 298
Smart, Sgt. (N.W.M.P.) 7
Smith, B.M. 567
Smith, Brig. A.A. 114
Smith, B.V. 567
Smith, E.H. 269, 542
Smith, J.R. 210, 236, 318
Smith, R.L. 324, 333
Social Credit Party 70
Solomon M. 308
Somme R. 163
Sommervieu 255
Sonsbeck 290, 406
Sorby, Lieut. 142

Souter, J.S. 116
South African (Boer) War 9, 12, 549
Southampton 145
South East Asia Command (S.E.A.C.) 383, 392, 393, 427, 428, 429
South East Asia Translators and Interpreters Corps (S.E.A.T.I.C.) 393, 427
South Saskatchewan R. 6
Spanish Civil War 70, 378
Sparling, Maj.-Gen. H.A., C.B.E., D.S.O. 414
SPARTAN (Exercise) 120, 122, 144, 421
Spears, Lieut. J.W. 6
Special Advisor to the Adjutant General (S.A.A.G.) (Lt.-Col. F.W. Clarke) 479, 480
Special Operations Executive (S.O.E.) 110, 159 Ch. 14 370
Dieppe 158, 159, 161, 162, 165
Special Training School (Hydra) 410
Special Security Service Sections (R.C.M.P.) 454
Special Service Companies 68
Special Wireless Sections *See also* Index Part II
No. 1 127, 348
No. 2 127, 252
Speelberg 319
Spitzbergen 141
Sproule, W.D. 331
Sprung, G.M.C. (Spike), M.C. 122, 172, 173, 174, 176, 177, 187, 274, 275, 297, 402, 541, 566
Spry, Maj.-Gen. D.C., C.B.E., D.S.O. 265
Squillace 174, 176
Stacey, Col. C.P. 358
Staff Duties, Directorate of 83, 88, 370, 371, 409, 410
St. Aignan-de-Cramesnil 257
Stalin, Josef 168, 333
St. Andre-sur-Orne 251
St. Armand (Que.) 3
Station JZJ (Japan) 361
St. Aubin-sur-Mer 161, 243
St. Catharines (Ont.) 69
St. Clair Tunnel 50
St. Croix-sur-Mer 250
Steele, Maj. (Inspector) 4, 9
Steen, J.D. (Jake) 128, 322, 332, 506
Stein, Brig. C.R.S. 95
St. Eloi 29, 37
Ste. Marie, R.E.L. 432
Stephen, Hugh R. 392
Stephens, L.A.D. 252, 260
Stephenson, W.E. 13
St. Etienne 265
Stewart, Lt.-Col. Arthur R. 382
Stewart, Maj. 4
Stewart, Sgt. Alex 6

St. Germain-en-Laye 240, 251
Stickland, D.A. 398
St. Jean (Que.) 3
St. John's (Nfld.) 473
St. Lambert 265
St. Laurent, Rt. Hon. Louis 472, 473
St. Lô 396
St. Nicholas 308
St. Omer 305, 403
Stonborough, J.J. 252, 273
St. Pierre and Miquelon 363
St. Quentin 373, 374
Strange, Maj.-Gen. T.B. 7
Strategic Intelligence xvii, xviii, 62, 431, 440. *See* also Foreign Intelligence and Military Intelligence, Directorate of, M.I.1
    Japanese 361
Stratford (Ont.) 69
Strathcona, Lord 9
Straube, Gen. Erich (Ger.) 298, 406
Strojich, W.S. 274, 276, 282, 285
Strooibrug 265, 270
S.T.S. 103 (HYDRA) 371
St. Sylvain 254, 256
Stuart, Lt.-Gen. K., C.B., D.S.O., M.C. xiii, 62, 65, 556
Student, Col.-Gen. Kurt (Ger.) 276, 283
Studland Bay 138, 145
St. Valery-en-Caux 163
St. Valery-sur-Somme 155, 163
Subversion 42, 70, 137, 146. *See* also Security of Personnel
    1940 85, 132, 135, 136
    C.S.E.F. 50, 52
    peacetime 61
Suessman, E. 396, 404
Sulmona 180, 181
Supreme H.Q., Allied Expeditionary Force (S.H.A.E.F.) 105, 109, 320, 335, 336, 350, 387, 407, 483
    censorship 347
    Psychological Warfare 394, 401
Surbeck, K.G. 106, 388, 389, 566
Sûreté (Fr.) 308, 312
Surveillance du Territoire (S.T.) 305
Sussex (N.B.) 14, 18
Sutcliffe, H.F. 173, 305, 313, 520, 524, 531, 541, 566
Sutherland-Brown, J. 55, 56, 57
Sutherland, J.D. 367
Sutton, E.A.R. 367
Suwon 519
Suzuki, G.D. 393
Swift Current (Sask.) 6
SWITCHBACK (Operation) 269, 404

Sydney (N.S.) 51, 454
Symes, W.A. 130
Syracuse (Sicily) 170
Szun, A. 303

T

Tactical Liaison Officers 528
Tactical Reconnaissance (Tac R). *See* also Air Photo Intelligence
    1915 27, 29
    1940 124
    Italy 190, 193, 200, 203
    N.W. Europe 243, 248, 253, 258, 272, 278, 285, 286, 292
Taggart, Charles I. 128, 514
Taormina 218
Taranto 178, 183
Target (T) Force 275
Tarte, J.L.O. 322, 326, 329, 541
Taschereau, J.C.C. 350
Taschereau, L.J. 376, 377, 380, 566
Taschereau, L.M. 130
Taylor, D.W. 127, 567
Taylor, L.W. 346, 347, 351, 567
Taylor, R.R. 301, 323, 567
Technical Intelligence xix, 104, 255, 266, 331, 436
Technocracy Inc. 455
Tedlie, Brig. A.J., D.S.O., C.D. 533, 537
Teora 233
Teramo 221
Termoli 179, 223
Terneuzen 265, 266, 268, 269, 271
Terni 228, 231
Tetrault, C.M. 256, 328, 566
Thaon 301
Theatre Intelligence Section 240, 246
Thibeault, P.E. 376, 567
Thiel Detective Service Company 51
Thomas, C. 427, 481, 566
Thomas, M.P. 398, 566
Thompson, Tpr. F.H. 6
Thompson, Walter S. 460, 461
Thornton, Maj. 386
Thrupp, Capt. C.C.G. 172
Ticchiena (convent) 194
Tiel 326
TIGER (Exercise) 121
Tilburg 276, 279, 281, 311, 317, 319
Timmerman, J. 92, 249
Tirpitz, Grand Admiral von (Ger.) 25
Tito, Marshal (Yugoslav) 379
Tivoli 227, 228, 229

INDEX   623

Tojo, Gen. (Jap.) 358
Tokyo 359, 360, 363, 368, 446, 517
Tomita, G. 428
Tomiyama, N 393
Tonningen, Rost von 325, 327
Topographical Sections 41, 502
TORCH (Operation) 392
Torella 179
Tormentor II, H.M.S. 155
Toronto 51, 60, 71, 440, 460, 461, 476, 478, 503, 539, 541, 542, 546
Toronto Star 68, 377, 460
Toronto Telegram 461
Torre Annunciata 225
Toseland, N. 354
TOTALIZE (Operation) 255, 256, 257, 303
Touchwood Trial 6
Tournebu 254
TRACTABLE (Operation) 257
Trade and Commerce, Department of 61
Trade Structure, Intelligence (post-1945) 502
Training
    1 C.G.R.U. 89, 92, 93, 108
    1914 19, 25
    C.W.I.C. 419, 422. *See* also Canadian War Intelligence Course
    First Army 274
    F.S. 129, 147
    general 98, 103, 105, 107, 121, 126, 188, 410, 411
    Guides 17
    post-1918 59
    post-1945 511, 539
    Psychological Warfare 107
Training and Intelligence, Director of 17, 50
Transport, Department of 77, 357, 446, 460, 488
Trasenko, A. 247
Tremaine, Capt. H.S. 14
Trench Logs 34
Tresidder, H.O. 116
Trident Conference 174, 363
Troarn 256, 257
Trois-Rivières (Que.) 14, 454
Trotobas 372
Trueman, W.J. 211, 213, 215
Truro (N.S.) 474
Tsubota, U. 426
Turk, M. 379
Turner, C. 408
Turnhout 279, 281, 311, 313
Tweedsmuir, Lt.-Col., The Lord 92, 113, 114, 115, 132, 173

U

Ubbergen 316
Üdem 289, 290, 291, 406
Uieil-Perara, Capt. U. 196
Uitwaterings Canal 270
U.N. Forces in Cyprus (UNFICYP) 532
United Nations 339, 517, 532, 533, 537, 538
United States 4, 18, 46, 47, 48, 50, 51, 52, 55, 57, 58, 61, 62, 64, 72, 74, 96, 168, 335, 355, 358, 364, 379, 416, 423, 454, 458, 461, 462, 484, 499, 501, 517, 568
Uniti R. 234
Unwin, R.C. 164
Ursaki, V.G. 128
Utrecht 294, 295, 297, 321, 322, 323, 325, 326, 389
Uxbridge 249
Uzawa, G.T. 393

V

Valcartier. *See* Camp Valcartier
Valenciennes 33, 44, 372
Valguarnera 173, 211
Valmontone-Avezzano Line 191
Vancouver (B.C.) 20, 50, 51, 52, 53, 364, 366, 368, 392, 440, 442, 446, 453, 460, 461, 462, 477, 482, 503, 539
Van Ert, L.P. 369
Vanier, R. 384, 385, 567, 568
Vannier, B. 322, 325
Van Nostrand, Lt.-Col. A.J. 19
Van Tuyl, L.C. 13
Varel 339
Varengeville 156, 163
Vaucelles 251, 252, 302
Vaucher Commission 107
Veale, W.S. 369
Vechta 335, 339
V.E. Day 330, 483
Veilleux, M. 376
Venlo 285, 290
Veregin, Peter 69
VERITABLE (Operation) 281, 285, 289, 314, 316
Vernon (B.C.) 477
Verrières 251, 252, 253
Vestmann Islands 352
Vetere, R. 379
Vichy (Government) 355, 376, 400, 455
Victoria (B.C.) 20, 45, 368, 421, 423, 440, 446, 539
Vietinghoff, Col.-Gen. Heinrich von (Ger.) 178,

186
Viet-Minh 380
Vietnam 517
Vimy Ridge 31
VITALITY (Operation) 271
Vokes, Maj.-Gen. C., C.B., C.B.E., D.S.O. 75, 231, 336, 343, 451
Volpel, G. 326
Voorst 318
Voorthuizen 318
Vught 311, 404
Vulnerable Points 73, 75, 408, 440, 470
V-weapons (Vergeltungswaffen)
  V-1 149, 310, 377
  V-2 273, 278, 310

W

Waal R. 276, 278, 292, 309, 311, 319, 388, 405
Waalwijk 312, 317, 319
Waite, K.C. 274
Walcheren 266, 269, 271, 272, 310, 311, 312, 323, 351, 404
Waldie, V.E.K. 487
Walker, F/L C.C. 65, 452
Walkerville (Ont.) 50
Wallace, M.H. 567
Wallace, M.P.S. 301
Walsh, G/C. G.V. 84
Walter, Col. Felix H. 92, 103, 107, 111, 126, 209, 214, 275, 349, 350, 367, 460, 547, 566
Waluch, Capt. (Br.) 404
War Book
  pre-1914 45
  pre-1939 64
War Crimes 109, 111, 222, 298, 328, 329, 383, 480
W.C. Advisory Committee 481
War Graves 326
War Office (Br.) 25, 41, 42, 46, 48, 50, 57, 61, 62, 87, 96, 97, 98, 99, 104, 208, 224, 353, 370, 427, 428
  Daily Chief of the Imperial Staff Summary 437
  P.W. 106
  Weekly Intelligence Commentary 83
Washington (D.C.) 46, 62, 111, 174, 352, 363, 365, 367, 383, 421, 422, 423, 426, 428, 434, 435, 444, 446, 447, 473, 474, 479, 509, 517
WATCHDOG (agent) 476
Watling, C.R. 217, 324
Watson, A.W. 113
Watson, C.R. 400

Watson, D.A. 301
Webb, F/O. W.I. 408
Webster, C.J. 110, 260, 265, 331, 567
Weekly War Review 432
Weeks, R.J.G. 339
Weibe, V.J. 301
Weins, J.C. 314
Weiss, A. 307, 569
Weissman, P. 149
Welland Canal 50, 77
Wellington, Arthur Wellesley, Duke of 1
Wemyss, R.-Adm., Sir R.E. 25
Werewolves 324, 325, 326, 332, 334
Wesel 282, 290
Weser R. 318
Westaway, D.C. 329
West, Scout William R. 7
Wheeler, Pte. 6
White, Capt. George W.R. 4
Whitehead, H.S. 180
Whitley, W.D. 537
Wickey, Maj. John H. 376, 377
Wiens, D. xvi, 249, 269
Wiens, J.C. 225
Wight, Isle of 143, 145, 153, 155, 160
Wilhelmshaven 294, 295, 298, 320, 323, 330, 332, 334, 335, 339
Wilkin, Capt. F.A. 54
Williams, Brig. E.T. (Br.) 127, 128, 279
Williams, C.E. 130
Williams, E.F. (Br.) 260
Williams, E.L. 463
Williams, Val (Br.) 384, 385, 386
Willoughby, Maj. J.A. 350, 567
Wilson, President W.W. 49
Wilson, W.J.R. 249
Winnipeg (Man.) 4, 49, 52, 59, 65, 66, 70, 72, 505, 539, 546
Wireless Intelligence (Signals Int.) xix, 89. *See* also Signals Intelligence; *See* also Index Part II, Special Wireless Sections
  1916 32, 40
  1939-45 85, 98, 119, 124
  Canada 357, 409, 416, 443
  establishment 127
  Italy (Br.) 170, 177, 180
  Korea 526, 528, 530
  N.W. Europe 240, 243, 249, 252, 254, 272, 278, 289, 294, 309, 344
  postwar 500, 503, 514
Wittmund 298
Wodehouse, R.F. xvi, 122, 127, 258, 266, 566
Wolpe, Hans 459
Women's Voluntary Services 140
Wong, O. 382

Wong, W.D. 481
Wood, Cmmr. S.T., R.C.M.P. 75, 78, 456, 470, 473
Woodhouse, A.W. 255
Wood, J.E.R. 110
Woodsworth, K.C. 369, 481, 482
Worsdall, G.L. 301
Worthington, Maj.-Gen. C.B., M.C., M.M. 66
Wright, Col. P.E.R. C.B., M.C., M.M. xvi, 125, 566, 568, 571
  Col. Cmdt. 544, 546, 547
  Dieppe 164
  N.W. Europe 249, 256, 258, 271, 275, 277, 278, 279, 281, 300, 328, 329, 340, 344, 502, 542
Wright, J.M. 301
Wygard, Lt.-Col. Alex 483, 495, 542, 571
Wyler (Meer) 286, 316
Wyman, Brig. A.A. 149

X

Xanten 282, 285, 288, 290, 291
X Force 352

Y

Yalta Conference 335
Yalu R. 519
Yamamoto, F. 426
Yamauchi, S.P. 426, 427
Yaritch, A.D. 387, 569
Yatabe, E. 428
Yorkton (Sask.) 69
Young, K.G. xvi, 534
Young, Maj.-Gen. H.A., C.B., C.B.E., D.S.O. 83
Ypres 25, 26, 32, 37, 305, 307, 312
Yuill, H. 461
Yukon Territory 440, 453

Z

Zaltbommel 291, 323
Zeebrugge 265, 266, 269
Z Force 352
Zunti, E.M. 210
Zutphen 291, 292, 319, 320, 326, 406

PART II:
CANADIAN INTELLIGENCE AND INTELLIGENCE-ASSOCIATED UNITS

Air Intelligence Liaison 40, 80, 113, 115, 118
Air Intelligence Liaison Sections
  disbanded 299
  general, training 116, 246
  No. 1 80, 113, 115, 249, 255, 272
  No. 2 113, 115, 116, 249, 255
    redesignated 117
  No. 3 113, 249, 255
  No. 4 249, 255, 272
  No. 5 249, 272
  No. 6 249, 255, 272
  No. 7 (Canada) 442
  No. 8 247, 250, 255
  No. 9 247, 250, 298
  No. 10 247, 255
  No. 11 247, 249, 255
  No. 12 249, 250, 255
  No. 13 247, 250, 255
  Normandy 247, 249, 259
  reorganization 255
Air Liaison Group, No. 1 Canadian Army 118
Air (Survey) Liaison Section, No. 30 Canadian (R.C.E.) 104, 273
Alberta Mounted Rifles (Scout Cavalry) 4, 7
Amplifier Units (Psychological Warfare) 394
  No. 1 396, 397, 398, 400, 403, 404, 405, 406
  No. 2 396, 397, 398, 400, 401, 403, 404, 405, 406
  No. 3 396, 397, 398, 400, 401, 403, 404, 405, 406
Area Security Offices (N.W. Europe) 321
  C.A.O.F. 338
  N. Holland 322
  No. 1 339, 342, 343
  No. 2 339, 342
  No. 3 339, 340, 343
  S. Holland 322
  Utrecht 322
Army Photographic Interpretation Section, No. 1 Canadian 124, 128
  formed 118
  Italy (I Cdn. Corps Mobile Unit) 203, 205, 206
  N.W. Europe 246, 249, 253, 258, 278, 329, 330
  postwar 299, 328, 367, 514
  Reichswald 285, 290
  Scheldt 266, 271, 273
  TOTALIZE 256, 257, 260
Army Processing Centre (Photographic censorship) 329
Boulton's Scouts (Boulton's Mounted Infantry, The Mounted Corps, Fort Garry Horse) 4, 6, 8
Branch Intelligence Sections 40
Brittlebank's Scouts (French's) 7
Canadian Intelligence Corps 87, 416, 420, 502
  Quarterly 546
Canadian Repat. Liaison Group 482
Canadian School of Military Intelligence 413, 511, 539, 540, 544
C.F.S.I.S. 511
Captured Document Teams 255, 331
Censor Sections 348, 488
  No. 1 Field Press Censor Section 348, 350, 351
  No. 2 348, 350, 351
  No. 3 348, 350, 351
  No. 4 Special Press Censor Section 347, 348
Counter-Intelligence, H.Q. 299, 314, 319, 329, 335, 344
Cyclists 54, 59
Defence Photographic Interpretation Unit 514
Discrimination Unit, No. 1 368, 418, 447, 450
Document Control Teams/Units 337
Dominion Land Surveyor's Intelligence Corps (Dennis's Scouts, Dominion Land Surveyor's Scouts, The Intelligence Corps, Intelligence Mounted Corps, Land Surveyor's Scouts, Surveyor's Scouts) 4, 6, 7
Field Security Reserve Detachments 321, 344, 388
  deployed as of July 1944 149
  H.Q. F.S.R.D. 303, 304, 305, 310, 314, 317
  No. 1 134, 319, 323, 324, 327
  No. 2 134, 309, 322
  No. 3 134, 307, 309, 318, 322, 325, 327
  No. 4 134, 149, 301, 302, 305, 323, 335, 339
  No. 5 134, 309, 314, 318, 322, 325
  No. 6 134, 303, 309, 322, 325, 333, 335
  No. 7 134, 150, 227, 303, 305, 322, 324, 326
  No. 8 134, 224, 227, 230, 231, 235, 319, 322
  No. 9 134, 230, 231, 234, 238, 323, 325, 329
  No. 10 134, 230, 231, 234, 237, 319, 322, 324, 326
  No. 11 134, 224, 227, 231, 233, 319, 320, 322, 324
  No. 12 134
Field Security Sections
  deployed as of July 1944 149
  Deployment of Sections, May 1945 321
  No. 1 89, 130, 141, 142, 144, 151
    Britain 136
    France 134

INDEX

Germany 333, 343
Italy 213, 215, 218, 221, 223, 224,
   226, 227, 229, 230, 236, 238
Korea 520, 524
N.W. Europe 303, 318
postwar 516
Sicily 208, 210
No. 2 89, 136, 138, 140, 143, 148, 149, 151
C.A.O.F. 339
Dieppe 159
Germany 331, 343
N.W. Europe 302, 303, 305, 306,
   309, 313, 316, 318, 319
postwar 516
No. 3 89, 138, 145, 147, 149, 319
Germany 332, 333, 334
N.W. Europe 301, 302, 303, 305,
   306, 316, 319, 320, 330
No. 4 149
Germany 331, 333, 334
N.W. Europe 307, 309, 311, 318, 319, 320
No. 5 (Canada) 453
N.W. Europe 303
No. 6 (Canada) 365, 453
No. 7 89, 145
Italy 217, 218, 222, 225, 226,
   228, 230, 231, 234
N.W. Europe 318, 325, 329
No. 11 89, 131, 138, 142, 144, 146, 151
Italy 217, 218, 219, 220, 222, 223,
   226, 230, 232, 234, 236
N.W. Europe 318, 324, 325, 327
No. 12 89, 131, 136, 138, 146, 150
N.W. Europe 307
No. 13 145, 150, 365
No. 14 137, 143, 145, 146
Italy 217, 220, 222, 223, 225, 233
N.W. Europe 318, 319, 324
No. 15 141, 146, 148, 149, 150
N.W. Europe 303, 305, 308, 309,
   310, 313, 317, 319, 324
No. 16 146, 147, 148, 149, 150
N.W. Europe 305, 307, 308, 309,
   312, 314, 319, 325, 329
No. 17 138, 148
N.W. Europe 303, 305, 306, 308, 310,
   314, 318, 319, 323, 326, 327
No. 18 148, 150, 305
Germany 332, 333, 334
N.W. Europe 303, 307, 310, 312, 319, 320
No. 20 150, 319
C.A.O.F. 339
Germany 332, 334
N.W. Europe 314, 317, 319
Forward Interrogation Centre (Corps) 183, 304,
   312, 316, 324
French's Scouts 4
Guides, Corps of 10, 11, 56
   Association 541
   Challenge Cup 19
   companies 19
   disbanded 60
   duties 12
   mobilized 22, 50
   Nanaimo 20
   No. 11 detachment 22
   reorganized (1920) 54, 55, 56, 59
   Reserve of Officers 20
Information Control Unit, No. 4 392, 407
Intelligence and Field Security (Reinforcement)
   Pool 89
   becomes Intelligence Company 92
Intelligence Control Section, No. 1 321, 323
Intelligence Observation Sections (artillery) 41
Intelligence Officers Pool, No. 1 Cdn. Army 275,
   298, 330
Intelligence Platoon (Cyprus) 533
Intelligence Pool, No. 3 Cdn. Army 110, 314,
   328, 331, 337
Intelligence School, First Cdn. Army 275
Interpreter Pool, First Cdn. Army 105, 246, 298
Interrogation Pool, No. 1 Cdn. Army 273, 330
Interrogation Sections/Teams
   H.Q. 246, 259, 265, 272, 297
   No. 1 (I Corps) 196, 321
   No. 2 246, 252, 265, 272
   No. 3 246, 253, 260, 265
   No. 4 246, 252, 259, 265, 272
   No. 5 246, 305
I.S.9 (W.E.A.), Canadian Field Section 388
Joint Service Air Photo Interpretation School 514
Joint Service (Tri-Service) Language School 514
Leaflet Units (Psychological Warfare) 395, 397
Militia Intelligence Training Companies
   No. 1, Montreal; *No. 2*, Toronto; *No. 3*, Halifax;
   No. 4, Vancouver, Edmonton, Victoria; *No.
   5*, Winnipeg; *No. 6*, Edmonton 539, 544
Mobile Field Processing Section 118, 119, 128,
   246, 279
   No. 5 256
Mobile Field Processing Unit 118
Modelling Team, *No. 1* Cdn 127, 266, 285
Moose Mountain Scouts (White's North Saskatch-
   ewan Regt.) 4, 8
Order-of-Battle Team, 6th Div. 367
Pacific Command Militia Rangers, The 453
Photographic Processing Unit, No. 1 Cdn. Army
   329
Photo Interpreter Team, 6th., C.A.P.F. 367
Recovery Team, Canadian (Manila) 369, 481

Refugee Interrogation Team, No. 1 Cdn. Army 329, 330
Rocky Mountain Rangers 4
Royal Guides, The (4th Troop of Volunteer Cavalry of Montreal, Governor General's Body Guard) 2
S-20 Japanese Language School 368, 392
Security Intelligence Section(s)
   Atlantic Command 362, 418, 453, 471
   Pacific Command 365, 418, 453
   postwar 499, 500, 502, 505, 506, 509
Special Wireless Group (Australia), No. 1 Intelligence Section 369, 426, 428
Special Wireless Sections 89, 119, 420. *See* also Index Part I, Wireless Intelligence and Signals Intelligence
   No. 1 119, 184, 196
   No. 2 255, 260
   No. 3 255, 260
Special Wireless Stations
   Amherst, N.S. 447
   Grande Prairie, Alta 447
   Ottawa 443, 447
   Point Grey, Vancouver 446, 448
   Riske Creek, B.C. 447, 450
   Victoria 447
Steele's Scouts 4, 7
War Crimes Investigation Unit, *No. 1* Cdn. 328, 329
White's Scouts 4

PART III:
CANADIAN FORMATIONS, UNITS AND CORPS

Alberta Field Force 7
Army, First Canadian 90, 93, 95, 105, 107, 108,
    110, 115, 118, 119, 122, 127, 134, 146,
    148, 166, 246, 248, 256, 266, 269, 275,
    276, 277, 279, 291, 296, 298, 299, 312,
    322, 324, 329, 346, 347, 350, 351, 367,
    387, 388, 402, 405, 420, 437, 459, 501,
    551
    Channel Ports 262, 263, 266
    Dieppe 121, 165
    F.S. 141
    Holland 274, 291, 295
    Intelligence Report 502
    Int. Section vii, 115, 121, 280
    Italy 208, 209
    N.W. Europe 240, 243, 246, 248, 249, 254, 299
    Psychological Warfare 396, 398
    P.W. Cage 259, 265, 273
    Reichswald 274, 276, 284, 285, 288, 290, 291
    SPARTAN 120, 123
    TIGER 121
Atlantic Command 362, 409, 414, 418, 442,
    453, 464, 471, 472
BASRA Unit, First Canadian 237
Brigades, Armoured
    1st (Army Tank) 172, 188, 209, 210, 346
    2nd 147, 149
    4th 292
    5th 189, 194
    Automobile Machine Gun, No. 1 54
Brigades, Infantry
    1st 114, 172, 204, 210
    2nd 97, 172, 180, 181, 182, 210, 213, 218, 353
    3rd 113, 172, 173, 176, 178, 184, 211
    4th 162, 296
    6th 159, 161, 162, 296, 406
    7th 247, 270
    8th 252, 270
    9th 270, 401
    10th 265
    11th 184, 186, 196, 217, 223
    12th 196
    13th (GREENLIGHT) 363, 365
    16th 44, 50
    19th 442
    25th (Korea) 519, 521, 522, 523, 526, 527, 530
    27th (postwar Germany) 519
Canadian Army Occupation Force (C.A.O.F.)
    109, 110, 328, 332, 334, 336
Canadian Army Pacific Force (C.A.P.F.) 298, 366
Canadian Army Special Force 518

Canadian Expeditionary Force (C.E.F.) 22, 23
    2nd 27, 29
    3rd 31
    Divisional Cyclist Coy. 54
    Divisions, 1st 25
    Intelligence 25, 27
Canadian Forces Netherlands, H.Q. 326, 328
Canadian Mediterranean Forces 347
Canadian Military Headquarters (C.M.H.Q.)
    119, 120, 121, 126, 147, 208, 240, 328,
    358, 370, 416, 435
    Censorship 99, 209, 346
    Ch. 4 81
    Cipher 82, 85, 88, 115
    duties 81, 83, 88, 90, 92, 96, 103,
    110, 115, 324, 431, 437, 458
    Formation 81
    I(b) 130, 132, 135
    Information Room 103
    Intelligence Corps, role in 88, 89, 92
    Psychological Warfare 394, 404
    P.W. 389, 480, 483
    security 85
    sources 83, 426, 437
Canadian Military Intelligence Association 511,
    539, 541
Canadian Siberian Expeditionary Force 44, 50, 53
Canadian Women's Army Corps 383, 426, 457,
    471, 475, 476
Corps
    Canadian (1915)
        Amiens 32
        C.I. 43
        Cyclist Battalion 54
        Intelligence 27, 33
        Passchendaele 31
        Survey Section 41
        Topographical Section 41
        Wireless Int. 40
    I
        GOLDFLAKE 237
        Intelligence 88, 89, 96, 108, 114,
        115, 142, 145, 207
        Italy 183, 188
        F.S. 217, 219, 223, 226, 229, 232, 235, 237
        Gothic Line 200, 229
        Hitler Line 189, 191, 193, 194, 195, 202
        N.W. Europe
            I(a) 292, 294, 297, 299
            I(b) 318, 321, 324, 384, 389, 392
        SPARTAN 122

TIGER 121, 143
TIMBERWOLF 146
II 93, 148
  F.S. 313, 314, 316, 317, 389
  Germany 330
  N.W. Europe 249, 251, 252, 254, 276, 289, 290, 291, 292, 294, 297, 298
  Psychological Warfare 396, 398, 400
  Scheldt 262, 266, 269
  SPARTAN 123
  TOTALIZE 256
VII 87, 114
Divisions, Armoured
  1st (became 4th) 117, 246, 413
  4th 122, 145, 246, 253, 256, 258, 263, 265, 267, 268, 291, 292, 294
  5th 89, 115, 122, 146, 184, 196, 205, 206, 226, 230, 237, 292, 379
  Italy 246
Divisions, Infantry
  1st
    1914-18 25, 27, 33, 54
    1939-45 82, 83, 85, 89, 97, 99, 101, 103, 114, 115, 116, 122
    France, 1940 114, 115
    F.S. 129, 208, 462
    Italy 171, 172, 177, 181, 183, 186, 187, 188, 192, 193, 194, 198, 199, 200, 209, 218, 224, 229, 230, 237, 246
    N.W. Europe 318, 378, 408
    training 125, 130, 143, 145
  2nd 252
    1914-19 27
    1939-45 85, 89, 100, 115, 122, 123
    Dieppe 153, 155, 157, 160, 166
    F.S. 130, 141, 143, 151, 336, 390
    Italy 209
    N.W. Europe 246, 249, 251, 252, 253, 256, 257, 258, 259, 262, 263, 265, 266, 268, 270, 271, 276, 285, 286, 289, 291, 292, 295, 298, 384
  3rd
    1939-45 89, 115, 122, 123
    C.A.O.F. 328, 336
    F.S. 134, 143, 147, 148, 301, 305, 320, 440
    N.W. Europe 31, 240, 243, 246, 247, 248, 250, 251, 252, 253, 256, 257, 258, 263, 264, 265, 266, 269, 270, 276, 285, 286, 288, 289, 291, 295, 297, 401, 413
    Passchendaele 31
  6th (Canada) 246, 364, 367, 418, 442, 453
  7th (Canada) 246, 418, 442, 453
  8th (Canada) 246, 418, 442, 453
Military Districts 482
  1903 10, 13

1921 establishment 56
aliens 48
changes 17, 18
Divisional Areas 19
duties, 1935 62
funds 64
internal security 52
M.D.1 (London) 56, 413, 471, 476
  Western Ontario Area 408, 446, 477
M.D.2 (Toronto), Central Ontario Area 64, 75, 418, 446, 453, 502
M.D.3 (Kingston), Eastern Ontario Area 56, 418, 446, 453, 470
M.D.4 (Ottawa, Montreal) 51, 57, 75, 413, 479, 502, 541
M.D.5 (Quebec City), Eastern Quebec Area 56, 57, 409, 439
M.D.6 (St. Johns), Nova Scotia/P.E.I. Area 57, 75, 409, 413
M.D.7 (Quebec City, Saint John, Fredericton), New Brunswick Area 56, 57, 71, 409, 413, 476
M.D.10 (Winnipeg), Manitoba Area 58, 446
M.D.11 (Victoria, Vancouver), British Columbia Area 53, 56, 57, 69, 72, 75, 409, 413, 423, 440, 446, 502
1914 22
M.D.12 (Regina), Saskatchewan Area 56, 69, 475
M.D.13 (Calgary, Edmonton), Alberta Area 409, 438, 440, 446, 475, 500
mobilization, 1939 408
morale 439
security 49
staff 51, 55
Vulnerable Points 75
Military Police (Canadian Provost Corps) 42, 122, 129, 132, 137, 144, 214, 219, 228, 303, 305, 333, 339, 471, 509, 529, 547, 552
Militia 509, 547
No. 1 Provost Company 130, 131
Pacific Command 357, 358, 363, 369, 409, 414, 424, 427, 428, 436, 440, 446, 447, 453, 477, 478, 482, 489
Intelligence, S.I.S. 364, 365, 490
Japanese language training 416, 425
Kiska 364, 366
photo interpretation training 421
Public Relations Group
  No. 2/3 394
P.W. Cage, First Canadian Army 305
P.W. Transit Cage, No. 1 Cdn. 298
Reinforcement Units
  Int. Coy 92, 93, 107, 108, 110, 126

INDEX 631

No. 1 Canadian General Reinforcement 89
No. 2 Canadian Base Reinforcement Group 146, 150
Repatriation Depot, No. 4 (Witley) 343
Royal Canadian Air Force, The 62, 65, 66, 84, 101, 115, 116, 118, 250, 255, 363, 408, 416, 426, 442, 475, 479, 494, 503, 504, 509, 510, 539, 542
Royal Canadian Artillery 66, 375
   1 Field Regt., R.C.H.A. 96, 139
Royal Canadian Corps of Signals 19, 147, 375, 443, 446, 514
Royal Canadian Engineers 18, 77
   30 Canadian Air Survey Liaison Section 104
   57 Canadian Independent Field Squadron (Korea) 524
Royal Canadian Navy 62, 64, 79, 357, 416, 426, 434, 444, 461, 472, 473, 479, 504, 509, 510, 542
Service Battalions (Militia) 509, 540, 547
Units, Armoured
   4th Princess Louise Dragoon Guards (4th Recce. Regt.) 211, 215
   14th Canadian Hussars (8th Recce Regt.) 161
   Calgary Regiment, The (14th Armd. Regt.) 100, 160
   Canadian Light Horse 54
   Governor General's Horse Guards (Governor General's Body Guard) 2
   Lord Strathcona's Horse (Royal Canadians) 9, 530
   Royal Canadian Dragoons, The (1st Armd. Car Regt.) 533
Units, Infantry
   21st Battalion 31
   27th Battalion 32
   Canadian Guards, 1st 491
   Canadian Mounted Rifles 32
   Canadian Scottish Regt. 26, 248
   Essex Scottish Regt. 109, 159
   Fusiliers, Mont-Royal, Les 159, 376
   Hastings & Prince Edward Regt., The 172, 173
   Highland Light Infantry of Canada, The 401
   Kent Regiment, The 413
   Loyal Edmonton Regt., The 195
   North Nova Scotia Highlanders, The 404
   Pacific Command Militia Rangers, The 453
   Princess Patricia's Canadian Light Infantry 70, 172, 180, 408, 519, 521, 527, 530
   Queen's Own Cameron Highlanders of Ottawa, The 158, 159, 161
   Régiment de Hull, Le 365, 436
   Régiment de la Chaudière, Le 376, 377, 406
   Régiment de Maisonneuve, Le 372, 374
   Royal 22e Régiment 100, 378, 519, 520, 521, 522, 526, 528, 532, 533, 534
   Royal Canadian Regiment 116, 172, 519, 521, 523, 526, 530
   Royal Hamilton Light Infantry, The 159, 296
   Royal Regiment of Canada, The 140, 159, 161, 352
   Royal Rifles of Canada, The 357
   Royal Winnipeg Rifles, The 144, 459
   School Corps 6
   Seaforth Highlanders of Canada, The 136, 172, 187, 196, 236
   South Saskatchewan Regiment, The 159, 161, 164, 296
   Veterans Guard of Canada, The 414, 484, 488
   Winnipeg Grenadiers, The 357, 448, 482

PART IV:
BRITISH COMMONWEALTH, UNITED STATES AND OTHER ALLIED FORCES

British Commonwealth

Air
 Royal Air Force 40, 66, 90, 117, 118, 123, 158, 205, 206, 250, 254, 255, 271, 294, 307, 333, 384, 386. *See also* Index Part I, Air Ministry (Br.)
  84 Group H.Q. 148
  140 Sqn. 124
  Desert Air Force 173
  No. 16 Sqn. 266
 Royal Flying Corps 27, 40
Armies
 First 33
 Second 25
  1914 31, 33, 42
  1939-45 247, 251, 254, 266, 272, 291, 292, 388, 404
 Third 31, 32
 Fourth 32
 Fifth 29
 Eighth 124, 170, 178, 181, 183, 184, 188, 190, 193, 194, 195, 196, 200, 201, 203, 204, 206, 207, 213, 215, 216, 221, 222, 223, 225, 227, 229, 235, 236, 238, 347
 Army Group, 21st 103, 105, 106, 107, 108, 118, 127, 150, 249, 266, 275, 277, 278, 279, 296, 310, 311, 314, 321, 349, 350, 351, 394, 395, 398, 400, 401, 404, 405, 407, 437
Bethune's Mounted Infantry 9
Brabant's Horse 9
Brigades
 25th Tank 188
 27th Infantry (Korea) 519
 28th Infantry (Korea) 521, 523, 526
 29th Infantry (Korea) 521, 523, 527
 157th Infantry 271
 231st (Malta) 213
 307th Infantry 335
Burmese National Army 380, 381
Central Mediterranean Forces, H.Q. (Algiers) 184
Corps
 I 147, 208, 240, 248, 259, 262, 263, 265, 272, 275, 276, 313, 400, 404
 II 42
 II Anzac 31
 V 26, 42, 181, 184, 204, 218, 223, 230
 XII 123
 XIII 174, 183, 188, 213, 216
 XXX 211, 279, 286, 298, 311, 339, 342
Counter-Intelligence Centre (Brussels) 317
Divisions, Armoured
 1st 114
 2nd (New Zealand) 218
 6th (South African) 225
 Guards 123, 279, 285
Divisions, Infantry
 1st Commonwealth (Korea) 523, 526, 529
 1st New Zealand (1917) 31
 3rd 121
 4th 193
 5th 177
 8th 193
 9th (Australian) 383
 15th 285, 289
 38th 141
 43rd (Wessex) 123, 285
 46th 202
 49th (West Riding) 292, 294, 318, 400, 405
 51st (Highland) 265, 285, 286, 288, 308, 396
 52nd (Lowland) 271, 286
 53rd (Welsh) 123, 268, 286, 289
 78th 181
 82nd (Northumbrian) 276
Far Eastern Combined Intelligence Bureau 357
Force 136 380, 382, 392, 393
 Jungle Warfare School 380
Forward Counter-Intelligence H.Q. 219
Guides, The 1
Howard's Scouts 9
Intelligence Units, Intelligence Corps 546
 2/5 Air Suport Control Unit 173
 12 Amplifier Unit 397, 398, 404
 Air Photo
  104 A.P.I.S. (Korea) 528
  R Section, MIAU 206
 Counter-Sabotage Section 331
 Field Security Reserve Detachments
  1003 316
  1004 343
  1016 323
 Field Security Sections 132, 213
  8 303
  13 308, 343
  23 323
  29 316

33 302
34 326
40 317, 319
60 318, 319, 322
68 222
74 343
78 146
88 218
273 303
310 217, 218
312 231
318 319
322 310
325 323, 339
327 323
330 322, 324
336 322
340 322
341 322
412 222
904 520, 521, 523, 526, 528
Naval 298
Interrogations Centre, Cannons Park (Wormword Scrubs) 246
I.S.9 110, 217, 222, 226, 255, 307, 384
  Interrogation Sections 388
  No. 15 Adm. Group 388
  "The Water Group" 389
  W.E.A 388
  No. 7 Base Censor Unit 349
  Port Security Sections 144, 234, 235, 310
  Security Control Unit, No. 8 255
  Wireless Intelligence Section, No. 108 260
Kitchener's Horse 9
Long Range Demolition Squadron, No. 1 (Popski's Private Army) 178
P.W. Cages 183, 196, 217, 228
Rimington's Guides 9
Robert's Light Horse 9
Royal Marines 332
Royal Navy 25, 79, 106, 189, 232

United States Forces

American Ordnance Intelligence Unit 436
Armies
  First 254, 396, 397
  Third 377
  Fifth 174, 186, 216
  Seventh 376, 378
  Eighth 519, 520, 523, 529
  Ninth 278, 288
Brigade
  No. 4 Special Service 265
Corps
  I 521, 523, 524, 528, 529
  IX 521
  VIII 397
  XVI 290
Division, Airborne
  101 276
Divisions, Armoured
  1 Cavalry 522
  4th 398
Divisions, Infantry
  7th 363
  25th 521
  35th 396
  36th 189
  83rd 397
  104th 403
Headquarters
  E.T.O.U.S.A 105, 107
  E.U.S.A.K. 520, 527, 528, 531
Intelligence 434, 457, 480, 521
  704 Detachment 520
  Counter-Intelligence Corps 105, 219, 227, 237
  P.A.C.M.I.R.S. 426, 429
Marine Division, First 527
U.S. Air Force
  Fifth U.S.A.F. H.Q. 520
  reconnaissance 519
U.S. Army 127, 362, 436, 473
U.S. Navy 473

Other Allied Forces

Belgian Army 26, 310
Czechoslovakian Forces
  No. 1 Independent Armoured Brigade 403
French Forces
  No. 10 Inter-Allied Commando 161
  XX Corps 27
Greek Forces
  No. 3 Mountain Brigade 201
Polish Forces
  1st Armoured Division 266, 269, 276, 340
  10th Armoured Brigade 294, 334
  II Polish Corps 198, 204, 229, 230
  No. 1 Polish Field Security Section 223, 230, 323, 339

PART V:
FORMER ENEMY FORCES

Chinese People's Republic

Armies
  Second 520
  Fifteenth 526
  Thirty-Ninth 529
  Fortieth 529
  Forty-Seventh 529
  Sixty-Fourth 521, 526, 529
Army Group, 18th 523
Divisions
  41st 520
  43rd 520
  116th 529
  119th 529
  190th 526
  191st 526, 527
  192nd 527
  193rd 521
Regiments
  375th 520
  570th 526
  572nd 526
  573rd 526
  577th 521
  579th 521
  582nd 521

Germany

Abwehr (German Military Intelligence, G.I.S.) 210
  Canada 489, 491
  Frontaufklärungstruppe 327
  Germany 337, 338, 343
  Italy 212, 216, 222, 230, 233, 238
  N.W. Europe 246, 302, 304, 305, 306, 308, 310, 311, 320, 321, 324, 325, 326, 327, 491
Armee Abteilung Straube 320, 334
Armies
  Ersatz 297
  First Parachute Army 283, 285, 291
  Fourth (1914) 26
  Sixth Panzer 277
  Seventh 242
  Tenth 174, 178, 179, 180, 183, 184, 186
  Fourteenth 180, 226, 380
  Fifteenth 242, 266, 268, 276, 381
  Twenty-Fourth 285
  Twenty-Fifth 281, 285, 294, 295, 320
Army Groups
  B 174, 180, 242
  C 180
  D 240
  H 276, 283, 285, 288, 294, 295
Battalions
  Anti-tank
    95 193
    525 198
  Infantry Fusilier
    64 270
    278 198
    346 288
  Infantry (not Fusilier)
    858 295
    992, 993, 994 198
  Reconnaissance
    95 193
  Tank, Heavy
    102 251
Battle Groups
  Blocking Group Bode 193
  Gericke 294
  Heilmann 179
  Krauss 258
  Schultz 193
Brigades
  Assault Gun
    242 198
    914 198
  Mobile 30 248
Corps
  Flak 258
  II Parachute 283, 285
  I S.S. Panzer 254
  LXVII 266
  LXXIII 204, 205
  LXXVI Panzer 174, 179, 184, 186, 204
  LXXXIV 242
  LXXXIX 266
  LXXXVI 266, 278, 283, 285
  LXXXVIII 280, 281, 285, 295
  XIV Panzer 174
  XLVII Panzer 254
  XXX 285, 295
Dienststelle Hans 227
Division, Coastal
  989 248
Divisions, Infantry

INDEX

64th 263, 270, 271
65th 181
70th 269, 270
71st 198, 200
84th 259, 276, 283, 284, 286, 288, 289, 291
85th 198, 258
89th 256, 257, 258
98th 201, 205
110th 161, 163, 165
149th 298
162nd (Turkoman) 203
180th 284, 286, 288, 291
190th 276, 283, 284
226th 264
243rd 243
271st 252, 257, 258, 263
272nd 252, 253, 254, 256, 257, 258
278th 198, 199, 200, 203, 205
302nd 155, 163, 165
305th 181, 186, 188, 193
321st 163
332nd 163
334th 184
346th 252, 278, 280, 288, 289, 291, 295
352nd 243, 248
356th 204, 205
361st 295
708th 259
709th 243
711th 256, 263, 278, 280, 281
712th 270, 280
716th 243, 244, 247, 248
Divisions, Miscellaneous
  Jäger
    114th 190, 193, 203, 204, 205
  Luftwaffe 242, 252, 264, 278, 324, 392, 487
    16th "Field" 250, 251, 252
  Marine 162, 264, 269, 324, 330
  Mountain, 5th 193, 198, 200
Divisions, Panzer
  1 S.S. (Adolf Hitler) 248, 252, 254
  2nd 254, 398
  3rd 181
  9 S.S. (Hohenstaufen) 253, 254, 256
  10 S.S. (Frundsberg) 254, 256, 259
  10th 163, 164
  12 S.S. (Hitler Jugend) 242, 247, 250, 251, 258, 262
  15th 193
  16th 181, 182
  21st 243, 244, 250, 252
  26th 174, 179, 184, 193, 201, 203
  116th 248, 254, 288, 289, 291
  179th (Training) 244
  Hermann Göring 171, 174, 177, 181
  Lehr 242, 289, 290
Divisions, Panzer Grenadier
  3rd 174
  15th 170, 171, 174, 176, 190, 192, 200, 288
  17th S.S. 242
  29th 174, 177, 179, 181, 201
  90th 171, 174, 181, 182, 184, 193, 200, 203, 205
Divisions, Parachute
  1st 174, 178, 179, 180, 181, 184, 186, 193, 194, 199, 201
  2nd 174, 176
  6th 278, 280, 288, 291, 292
  7th 285, 286, 288, 289, 291, 294
  8th 291, 295
  61st 291
  Training 292
Fortress (Festung) Holland 295
Gestapo 307, 311, 316, 321, 324, 325, 326, 327, 332, 337, 371, 374, 376, 377, 444
P.W. Camps 489, 490, 491, 492, 493
Grenzpolizei 337
Miscellaneous
  Feld Gendarmerie 311
Oberkommando der Wehrmacht 242
Organization Todt 246, 306, 459
Regiments
  Infantry
    145 181
    146 181
    171 198
    191 198
    194 198
    211 198
    252 163
    254 163
    255 163
    356 204
    721 194
    726 243
    736 243
    992 198
    994 198
    1037 270
    1038 270
    1039 270
    1053 257
    1054 257
    1222 286
  Luftwaffe
    39 202
    40 203
    46 250
  Marine *162* 292
  Mountain

100 198
Panzer
  26 182
Panzer Grenadier
  1 173
  1 S.S. 251, 253
  3 200
  15 176, 177
  20 253
  25 251
  60 288
  71 179
  79 181
  90 186
  104 170, 193
  115 170, 193
  129 170
  134 194
  146 188
  192 252
  200 182, 184
  361 182
  576 193
  578 187
  902 Lehr 248
  980 252
  982 252
  994 199
Parachute
  1 179, 181, 186, 187, 193, 200, 201
  3 178, 179, 181, 182, 187, 193, 201
  3 Training 292
  4 181, 187, 193, 200
  16 288, 289, 290
  18 290
  19 289
  21 289
  23 405
Schutzstaffel (S.S., Waffen S.S., 22 divisions) 174, 242, 252, 253, 297, 298, 317, 319, 326, 331, 337, 374, 388
  34 S.S. Netherlands Division 295, 297, 298, 324, 326
  84 Regt. 405
  Flemish Brigade 307, 310
Sicherheitsdienst (S.D. - information-gathering branch of the Gestapo) 216, 307, 311, 318, 321, 323, 324, 325, 326, 337
Volks Artillery Corps, 766th 289
X Flotilla 235

Italy

Airfield Defence Unit, 517th 171
Armies
  Sixth 170
  Seventh 174
Battalions
  55th Bersaglieri 177
  78th Field Artillery 177
  160th 172
  173rd Blackshirt 172
  243rd 172
Blackshirt Militia 172, 174
Corps
  IX 174
  VI 170
  XIX 174
  XXXI 174
Divisions
  4th (Livorno) 170
  54th (Napoli) 170
  104th (Mantova) 174, 177
  Coastal
    206 170, 171
    211 174, 176, 177
    212 174, 177
    213 170
    214 174
    227 174
  Parachute, 184th (Nembo) 174, 225
Naval Coastguard 219

Japan

45th Air Regiment 360
Armies
  Fifteenth 381
  National Peace and Regeneration Army (Chinese, Japanese controlled) 355
  Twenty-Third 360, 361
Divisions, Infantry
  4th 381
  18th 360
  38th 360
  41st 381
  48th, 51st, 104th 360
Fifth Air Division 360
Indian National Army 381
Regiments, Infantry
  66th, 228th, 229th, 230th 360
  Mountain Artillery 360

ABBREVIATIONS

A Branch	Staff branch for personnel administration
A/	Acting (with rank)
A.A.	Anti-aircraft
A.A.&Q.M.G.	Assistant Adjutant and Quartermaster General (personnel and logistics staff officer)
A.A.G.	Assistant Adjutant General (personnel staff officer)
A.A.I.	Allied Armies in Italy
A.C.G.S.	Assistant Chief of the General Staff
A.D.M.&A.F.I.	Assistant Director of Military and Air Force Intelligence (1932–39)
A.D.M.I.	Assistant Director of Military Intelligence
A.D.P.R.	Assistant Director of Public Relations
A.F.H.Q.	Allied Force Headquarters (Mediterranean)
A.G.	Adjutant General (senior staff officer, personnel)
A.I.L.	Air Intelligence Liaison (cf. A.L.O.)
A.I.L.O.	Air Intelligence Liaison Officer
A.L.O.	Air Liaison Officer
A.M.G.	Allied Military Government
A.O.P.	Air Observation Post = light aircraft
A.P.I.S.	Air Photograph Interpretation Section
A.S.C.	Army Service Corps (British)
A.S.O.	(1) Area Staff Officer, (2) Area Security Office (C.A.O.F.), (3) Area Security Officer (C.A.O.F.)
A.T.D.B.	Army Technical Development Board (N.D.H.Q.)
B.F.I.	Belgian Forces of the Interior (partisans)
B.G.S.	Brigadier, General Staff (senior Operations staff officer)
B.M.	Brigade Major (senior Brigade operations staff officer)
B.N.V.	Binnenlandsche Nederlandsch Veiligsheidsdienst (Dutch counter-intelligence agency)
Bvt.	Brevet (with rank) = unpaid rank
B.S.C.	British Security Co-ordinator
C.A.C.	Canadian Armoured Corps
CANAWASH	Telegraphic address for Canadian Army Liaison Office, Washington, D.C.
CANMILITARY	Telegraphic address for C.M.H.Q., London, England
C.A.O.F.	Canadian Army Occupation Force (1945–46)
C.A.P.F.	Canadian Army Pacific Force
C.A.S.F.	Canadian Active Service Force
C.A.S.(W)	Canadian Army Staff (Washington)
C.B.	Companion of the Order of the Bath
C.B.E.	Commander of the Order of the British Empire
C.C.	Companion of the Order of Canada
CC. RR.	Carabinieri Reali (Italian, Carabiniere)
C.D.	Canadian Forces Decoration
C.D.A.	Conference of Defence Associations
C.F.A.	Canadian Field Artillery
C.E.F.	Canadian Expeditionary Force (1914–19)
C.F.N.	Canadian Forces, Netherlands

638   SCARLET TO GREEN

C.G.R.U.	Canadian General Reinforcement Unit
C.G.S.	Chief of the General Staff
C.I.	Counter-Intelligence
C.I.A.	Central Intelligence Agency (U.S.A.)
C.I.B.	Canadian Infantry Brigade (with a number)
C.I.C.	Counter-Intelligence Corps (U.S. Army)
C.-in-C.	Commander-in-Chief
C.I.S.A.	Canadian Intelligence and Security Association
C.M.G.	Companion of the Order of St. Michael and St. George
C.M.H.Q.	Canadian Military Headquarters, London
C.M.I.A.	Canadian Military Intelligence Association (1948–72)
C.M.S.C.	Corps of Military Staff Clerks
C.N.R.	Canadian National Railway
C.O.	Commanding Officer
C. of G.	Corps of Guides
C.O.H.Q.	Combined Operations Headquarters
C.O.S.S.A.C.	Chief of Staff, Supreme Allied Commander (Invasion planning, North-West Europe)
C.P.R.	Canadian Pacific Railway
C. Pro. C.	Canadian Provost Corps (Military Police)
C.Q.M.S.	Company Quartermaster Sergeant (staff sergeant)
C.S.D.I.C.	Combined Service Detailed Interrogation Centre
C.S.E.F.	Canadian Siberian Expeditionary Force (1919)
C.S. of M.I.	Canadian School of Military Intelligence
C.V.O.	Commander of the Royal Victorian Order
C.W.A.C.	Canadian Women's Army Corps
C.W.C.I.U.	Canadian War Crimes Investigation Unit
C.W.I.C.	Canadian War Intelligence Course
D.A.A.G.	Deputy Assistant Adjutant General
D.A.G.	Deputy Adjutant General
D.A.I.	Director(ate) of Air Intelligence
D.A.Q.M.G.	Deputy Adjutant and Quartermaster General
D.C.G.S.	Deputy Chief of the General Staff (brigadier); (a)/(A) –Operations, plans, staff duties, (b)/(B) – Intelligence, staff duties (weapons), signals, operations, research, history, (c)/(C) – Training (including trade training)
D.C.M.	Distinguished Conduct Medal
D.D.	Duplex drive (tanks, 1944)
D.D.M.I.	Deputy Director of Military Intelligence ((S) = Security)
D.F.	Direction-Finding – to locate source of radio emissions
D.G.M.S.	Director General of Medical Services
D. Hist.	Director(ate) of History (also D.H.S.)
D.I.O.	District Intelligence Officer
D.M.I.	Director(ate) of Military Intelligence
D.M.I.O.	District Military Intelligence Officer
D.M.O.&I.	Director(ate) of Military Operations and Intelligence
D.M.O.&P.	Director(ate) of Military Operations and Plans
D.M.T.	Director(ate) of Military Training
D.N.D.	Department of National Defence
D.N.I.	Director(ate) of Naval Intelligence
D.O.C.	District Officer Commanding
D.O.C.R.	Defence of Canada Regulations
D.O.T.	Department of Transport

ABBREVIATIONS

D.P.M.	Deputy Provost Marshal
D.P.O.W.	Director(ate) of Prisoners of War
D.P.R.	Director(ate) of Public Relations
D.S.D.	Director(ate) of Staff Duties (establishments)
D.S.O.	Distinguished Service Order
D.U.	Discrimination Unit (No. 1, Ottawa)
D.V.A.	Department of Veterans' Affairs
E.D.	Canadian Efficiency Decoration
E.T.O.U.S.A.	European Theatre of Operations, United States Army
EUSAK	Eighth United States Army in Korea
F.B.I.	Federal Bureau of Investigation (U.S.)
F.C.C.	Federal Communications Commission (U.S.)
F.D.L.s	Forward Defended Localities
F.F.I.	French Forces of the Interior
F.I.C.	Forward Interrogation Centre
F.M.R.	Les Fusiliers Mont-Royal
F.S.	Field Security
F.S./C.I.	Field Security/Counter-Intelligence
F.S.O.	Field Security Officer
F.S.P.	Field Security Police
F.S.R.D.	Field Security Reserve Detachment
F.S.S.	Field Security Section
G.H.Q.	General Headquarters
G.I.S.	German Military Intelligence Service (*Abwehr*)
G.O.C.	General Officer Commanding (-in-C. = in-chief)
G.N.R.	Guardia Nazionale Republican = Italian Fascist paramilitary force
Gr. (Gren.)	Grenadier (German infantry)
G.S. (G)	General Staff = Branch responsible for operations, plans, intelligence, staff duties, history
G.S. I(b)	General Staff, Counter-Intelligence
G.S.O.	General Staff Officer (graded 1 = Lt.-Col.; 2 = Maj.; 3 = Capt.)
G-2	Intelligence Branch, U.S. Army
H.L.I.	Highland Light Infantry (British)
H.U.P.	Heavy Utility Personnel (truck)
I., Int.	Intelligence (a) Combat, (b) Counter, (c) Censorship, (ph) Air Photo Interpretation, (s) Wireless (radio, also (e)), (x) Administration
INTSUM	Intelligence Summary – periodic review of enemy situation with appreciation of capabilities and possible intentions; also INSUM (I Corps, Italy)
I.C.	Intelligence Corps (British, 1918)
I.O.	Intelligence Officer
I.R.A.	Irish Republican Army
I.S.	Internal Security
I.S.9	Intelligence School 9, British cover term for Escape and Evasion Agency
I.S.O.	Intelligence Staff Officer
J.I.C.	Joint Intelligence Committee
K.C.B.	Knight Commander of the Bath

L.C.T.	Landing craft, tank
Ld.S.H.(R.C.)	Lord Strathcona's Horse, (Royal Canadians)
L. of C.	Lines of Communication
M.A.I.U.	Mobile Air Photo Interpretation Unit
M.B.E.	Member of the Order of the British Empire
M.C.	Military Cross
M.D. (1-13)	Military District (Canada)
M.E.W.	Ministry of Economic Warfare (British)
M.F.P.S.	Mobile Field Photographic Section (also as *Processing* = unit to develop and print air photos)
M.G.B.	Motor gun boat – light, armed, fast vessel
M.I.D.	Mentioned in Despatches
M.I.5	British Security Service
M.I.6	British Secret Intelligence Service
M.M.	Military Medal
M.N.D.	Minister of National Defence
M.T.	(1) Motor transport, (2) Military training (with number) branch of D.M.T.
M.V.O.	Member of the Royal Victorian Order
N.B.S.	Nederlandsche Binnenlandsche Strijdkrachten = Dutch Forces of the Interior (partisans)
N.C.O.	Non-commissioned Officer
N.D.H.Q.	National Defence Headquarters
N.P.A.M.	Non-Permanent Active Militia = pre-1939 Army Reserves
N.R.M.A.	National Resources Mobilization Act = conscription for service in Canada only. Men were "zombies" in the jargon of the day.
N.S.D.A.P.	Nationalsozialistische Deutsche Arbeit Partei = Nazi Workers' Party
N.V.D.	Nederlandsche Veiligsheids Dienst = Dutch Security Service
N.W.M.P.	North West Mounted Police
O.B.E.	Officer of the Order of the British Empire
O.C.	Officer Commanding (below Lt.-Col.)
O.D.	Orde Dienst = Dutch veterans' group
O.P.	Observation Post
ORBAT	Order of battle (units, commanders, equipment)
O.R.	Other ranks (i.e., not commissioned)
O.S.S.	Office of Strategic Services = U.S. clandestine force
O.V.R.A.	Organizzazione Voluntaria Repressione Antifascismo (Italian Fascist Counter Intelligence Agency)
O.W.I.	Office of Wartime Information (U.S.)
P.A.C.M.I.R.S	Pacific Military Intelligence Research Section (U.S.)
P.&P.W.	Press and Psychological Warfare
P.C.	Privy Council (with numbers = Order-in-Council)
P.C.M.R.	Pacific Coast Militia Rangers
P.F.	Permanent Force (pre-1939 Regular Army)
PHERUDA	P.W. psychological test
P.I.D.	Political Intelligence Directorate (British)
P.L.D.G.	Princess Louise Dragoon Guards, 4th (recce)
P.P.C.L.I.	Princess Patricia's Canadian Light Infantry
P.R.	Public Relations

ABBREVIATIONS

P.R.O.	Public Relations Officer
psc.	Passed Staff College
P.S.M.	Platoon Sergeant Major (W.O.III)
P.S.O.	Port Security Officer (to 1945)
Psy. War.	Psychological warfare
P.W.	Prisoner(s) of war
P.W.B.	Psychological Warfare Branch (S.H.A.E.F.)
P.W.D.	Psychological Warfare Division (S.H.A.E.F.)
Pz.	Panzer = tank (German)-armoured
Q.M.G.	Quartermaster General = logistics branch
R.A.F.	Royal Air Force
R.C.A.	Royal Canadian Artillery
R.C.A.C.	Royal Canadian Armoured Corps
R.C.A.F	Royal Canadian Air Force
R.C.A.M.C.	Royal Canadian Army Medical Corps
R.C.A.S.C.	Royal Canadian Army Service Corps
R.C.A.V.C.	Royal Canadian Army Veterinary Corps
R.C.C.S.	Royal Canadian Corps of Signals (also R.C. Sigs, R.C.C. of Sigs)
R.C.E.	Royal Canadian Engineers
R.C.H.A.	Royal Canadian Horse Artillery
R.C.I.C.	Royal Canadian Infantry Corps
R.C.M.G.B.	Royal Canadian Machine Gun Brigade
R.C.M.P(olice)	Royal Canadian Mounted Police
R.C.N.	Royal Canadian Navy (R. = Reserve)
R.C.O.C.	Royal Canadian Ordnance Corps
R.C.R.	Royal Canadian Regiment
R.de Mais.	Régiment de Maisonneuve
R.D.F.	Radio direction-finding (radar)
Recce.	Reconnaissance
Repat.	Repatriation
R.F.C.	Royal Flying Corps
R.G.A.	Royal Garrison Artillery
R.H.C.	Royal Highland Regiment of Canada (The Black Watch)
R.I.P.	Refugee Interrogation Post
R.M.C.	Royal Military College of Canada
R.M.R.	Royal Montreal Regiment
R.N.	Royal Navy (British)
R.N.W.M.P.	Royal North-West Mounted Police
R.22e.R.	Royal 22e Régiment
S.A.A.G.	Special Advisor to the Adjutant General (NDHQ)
S.C.(I.)U.	Special Control (Intelligence) Unit (agent control)
S.E.A.C.	South East Asia Command (Kandy, Ceylon)
S.D.	Sicherheitsdienst = Counter-Intelligence Service (German)
S.D.I.O.	Sub-District Intelligence Officer (C. of G.)
SECO	Security Control Organization (British)
S.I.M./C.S.	Servizio Informazioni Militari/Controspionaggio = Military Counter-Intelligence Service (Italian)
Sipo.	Staatspolizei (state police, Germany)
S.I.S.	Security Intelligence Section
S.O.E.	Special Operations Executive
S.S.	Schutzstaffel = protective unit, Nazi Party, Germany

Tac. R.	Tactical Reconnaissance = air-to-ground visual recce
U.N.	United Nations Organization
U.N.F.I.CYP.	United Nations Force in Cyprus
U.S.A.A.F.	United States Army Air Force
U.S.A.T.	United States Army Transport (ship)
U.S.C.I.C.	United States (Army) Counter Intelligence Corps
U.S.N.S.	United States Navy Ship
V.C.	Victoria Cross
V.C.G.S.	Vice-Chief of the General Staff
V.D.	Colonial Auxiliary Forces Officers' Decoration (popularly known as the Volunteer Decoration)
V.E./J.	Victory, Europe/Japan
V.G. of C.	Veterans' Guard of Canada
V.H.F.	Very High Frequency
V.P.	Vulnerable Point
W.I.	Wireless Intercept (radio intelligence)
W.O.	1) War Office (British), (2) Warrant Officer (with number I, II, or III)

ABOUT THE AUTHOR

Major Stuart Robert (Bob) Elliot was born in Alberta, Canada, in 1922. He enlisted in the Royal Canadian Artillery in 1942 before transferring to the Canadian Intelligence Corps (C.Int.C.). Following intensive Japanese language training, he deployed to the South East Asia Command and served in India, Malaya and Java (Indonesia).

After obtaining a Bachelor of Commerce degree from the University of British Columbia in 1948, he joined the Defence Research Board and then, in 1952, took a commission as an Intelligence Officer with the C.Int.C., where he spent the remaining 20 years of his military career. In 1967, he was awarded a Canadian Centennial Medal on recommendation from the Canadian Armed Forces.

Most of his subsequent career was with the London-based International Institute for Strategic Studies, where he was responsible for *The Military Balance* as the Institute's Information Officer, a position from which he retired in 1987.

Major Elliot undertook *Scarlet to Green* as a labour of love in support of the Canadian Military Intelligence Association's History Project and spent more than 15 years of intensive research and writing to see it through to completion and its first publication in 1981.

Following the death in 1981 of his first wife Helen (née Christie), with whom he had two children, he married Shirley Hubbard. He and Shirley remained in England following his retirement. He died in York in 2015 at the age of 92.

Lightning Source UK Ltd.
Milton Keynes UK
UKHW010631110820
368051UK00001B/3